DEATH

an interdisciplinary analysis

by
Warren Shibles
University of Wisconsin - Whitewater

The Language Press
Whitewater, Wisconsin

ISBN 0-912386-06-1 (Paperback)

ISBN 0-912386-05-3 (Hardcover)

Library of Congress Catalog Card Number 72-82990

By the same author:

Metaphor: An Annotated Bibliography and History Whitewater, Wisc.: The Language Press 1971.

Philosophical Pictures Dubuque, Iowa: Kendall-Hunt 1969 (revised 1972)

Wittgenstein, Language and Philosophy Kendall-Hunt 1969 (1971)

Models of Ancient Greek Philosophy London: Vision Press (New York: Humanities) 1971

An Analysis of Metaphor The Hague: Mouton (New York: Humanities) 1971

Essays On Metaphor The Language Press 1972

Emotions The Language Press 1974

Illustrations:

Bruegel *The Triumph of Death* Prado Museum, Madrid

"Even normal people tend to accept the validity of their thoughts without subjecting them to any kind of careful scrutiny."

Aaron Beck, Prof. of Psychiatry

"We insulate ourselves as much as possible and are habitually incurious."

Mary Mothersill, Prof. of Philosophy

"Believing what we don't believe
Does not exhilarate."

Emily Dickinson

Nietzsche:
A preference of strength for questions for which nobody today has the courage; the courage for the *forbidden* ... A new conscience for truths which have hitherto remained mute ...

All truths are bloody truths for me.

There are more idols than realities in the world: that is my 'evil eye' for this world.

There are eternal idols which are here touched with the hammer.

Not to question, not to tremble with the craving and the joy of questioning ... That is what I feel to be contemptible.

1012.

Preface

"What is death?" and "How can we cope with it?" are the greatest problems man has to face. How man has coped with these problems is mainly by avoidance, denial, superstitious and mystical belief. Almost entirely lacking was honest, open inquiry. Death is still a taboo topic.

It is often thought that one solves the problem of death by going to church. But contemporary theologians point out that religion does not clarify the concept of death or dying and in fact, it says almost nothing about it. These views will be presented and examined. Religion is found to have more to say about how one should live. In any case, religion involves faith and fixed beliefs and cannot serve as a means of adequate, objective inquiry. But this is just to say that the philosopher's task is not merely to present religion or science but rather to do philosophy, for example, the philosophy of religion and the philosophy of science. Philosophy is taken here to be a critical clarification of concepts and methods in any area of study for the purpose of understanding and to solve man's practical problems. Philosophy should be clear, concrete, and relevant to man's everyday problems.

The above situation led to my offering in the spring of 1972, an interdisciplinary 3-4 credit Seminar on Death at the University of Wisconsin - Whitewater. The method and sources used in the course were the same as those used in this book except that the class situation allowed for discussion, group therapy and confrontations, and term papers.

An attempt is first made to find out what people actually believe and say, both directly and in traditional literature. Quotations of both professional and non-professional people are extensively used not just to support arguments, but at times only to indicate what beliefs they hold. The survey is made adequate by being an interdisciplinary analysis. An extensive bibliography, which was not previously available, was gathered and is included in this book. A student questionnaire was devised and administered to provide actual statements and beliefs currently held.

The next step is to examine such concepts to see if they can withstand criticism and counterexample. Are they category-mistakes, naming-fallacies, misuses of language, etc.? Do the terms involved have an intelligent use in the context of everyday experience? The method specified here is very similar to that used in ordinary-language philosophy, but it is a modified and expanded version of it. One particular way it has been modified or even replaced is by the development of a "metaphorical method" of doing inquiry. This book is in part an extension and application of my previous work on metaphor. (See bibliography) The "metaphorical method" is seen at work throughout this book. But also any method is and may be used as long as it can withstand critical examination or give suggestive insight. Thus there is also an examination of methods.

So after beginning with a report of the ordinary language used an attempt is made to clarify the concepts of death and dying, as well as the existing theories and methods used. An attempt is made to provide both a broad comprehensive presentation as well as a concrete in-depth analysis. It will be seen that statements made about death and dying are often misuses of language, and that prevailing views in a number of cases must be radically revised. The study does not just leave everything as it was. This means that many will find what is said here controversial or even shocking.

In many cases much more work is needed, and this book is in part an attempt to encourage such research and to break the taboo on the discussion and study of aging, death and dying. This book is not just a survey. Some contemporary and some original research is presented here, especially in the area of philosophical psychology in examining the relationship between emotions and death. An original analysis of the concept of death is also given.

One of the arguments which seems to come out of the material presented is that inquiry into death points up the importance of inquiry itself. Some reasons for this are the following:

1. Emotions are seen to be largely assessments which guide feeling. For our emotions to be positive, to prevent fear, anxiety, shock, etc., our assessments must be clear and intelligent — thus the need for inquiry.

Inquiring into death is one of the best ways of overcoming and coping with the fear of death. The very act of discussing and communicating about death is therapeutic. This book has, as one of its goals, to help one cope with death by providing clarifications of both death and emotions. If one's assessments are clear he will be less subject to negative emotions, and merely openly discussing the subject of death will help to prevent fear, anxiety, shock, etc., when confronted with the death of a friend or the approach of one's own death. Informed open communication is crucial.

2. Facing death leads one to consider how best to live. Inquiry as a goal allows one to examine what is most important in life, and to inquire into goals themselves.

3. Inquiry is needed for one to become clear about the concept of death. The question as to the nature of death and how to cope with it offers man his greatest intellectual challenge. To avoid it, deny it, or create a myth of a magical immortality is to be less than a complete human being. To avoid the issue by busying oneself with T.V., art, church, money, sports, stamp-collecting, gardening, social activities, etc., valuable as they may be in themselves, is nevertheless an avoidance. No philosophy can be complete which does not honestly and objectively deal with the question of death. In this sense, "to philosophize is to learn how to die."

4. Research into death is needed by each discipline. Especially important is research in philosophical clarification, and research in the biology of aging so that the elderly may live a long and healthy life. We in 1973 still do not know what causes aging. This is a telling commentary on the status of present scientific knowledge.

5. Confrontation with death may sometimes make one more realistic and honest, e.g., his beliefs about an "afterlife" may

vanish when faced with the reality of death. Often there are defense-mechanisms of avoidance and denial, but when faced with the reality of death we sometimes stop playing deceptive social games with others and stop deceiving ourselves.

6. To understand death one must understand life. This leads to the need for a conceptual clarification of our language, environment, ourselves, ethical concepts, science, psychology, etc. Thus not only is "to philosophize to learn how to die," but "to learn how to die is to philosophize."

7. Inquiry is needed to avoid being captivated by a single model or metaphor and it provides diverse perspectives. It is not acceptable to present a single, fixed, exclusive, and unquestioned view of the experience and nature of death.

8. Ongoing inquiry has more reason to be universally believed in than any other method. Our present methods are often those of more primitive superstitious beliefs peculiar to the particular culture we happen to be in. If one must have ritual then he may light a candle for inquiry.

9. The realization that all men die may force one to realize that man has something like a blood pledge to make this short life the best possible for others as well as for himself. Inquiry is needed to make this possible. Threats that man is guilty from birth or that he may be punished in a hell, need reexamination.

10. Inquiry deals with suicide, what leads one to it, how a clarification of one's emotions and thinking can avoid it, and provides the motive that one should not commit suicide thereby allowing him to continue inquiring.

11. Aristotle spoke of contemplation (of sciences and knowledge) as the highest goal of man, that which makes man most perfect. By suggesting that it is the rational "soul" which is immortal he may have been covertly proposing that honest inquiry and its resulting knowledge can in every way make man most immortal. What survives is man's knowledge. "Soul" often meant simply "reason," and the soul seeks to improve its knowledge. Inquiry makes man less subject to misconceptions and poor emotions. It therefore allows him to be most free.

12. What man basically seems to desire is understanding, concern, care, friendship, and emotional warmth. He is usually prevented from having such experiences. The reason is due to his own and others' inability to cope with and understand their

emotions. Up to now there has been too little effective inquiry into the nature of emotion. Some attempt at such clarification is given here. Inquiry allows man to be the sort of emotionally fulfilled person he wishes to be. By changing his assessments one can greatly alter one's personality and emotions. What begins as a study of death ends up, to some extent, as a study of life and love.

Contents

Student Questionnaire Results

The following 55 questions were answered by 49 students at the beginning of a 3-4 credit undergraduate philosophy seminar on death in the spring of 1972 at the University of Wisconsin at Whitewater, Wisc. This was the first course of this sort taught at this university and one of the first taught anywhere. It was taught as an interdisciplinary subject by the author. Although answers are grouped by question, they sometimes have more significance if related to the individual and his other individual answers. Results stress qualitative rather than quantitative factors. The results offer a description of beliefs typically held. Such statements are analyzed and explored throughout this book. One of the procedures of ordinary-language philosophy is to first look at actual beliefs and statements and then examine them to see if they withstand criticism and counterexample. I wish to express my appreciation to those students who so openly gave their views on this questonnaire and went on to inquire into these views and the subject of death.

1. What is death?

Replies were that it is: a cessation of bodily functions, ceasing to exist, a final end, total loss, an afterlife, the beginning and end at the same time, the most important part of life, nothing we can talk about, a feeling like living, something we cannot experience, like being bored, being completely broken into elements again, the survival of the mind, a passage to a higher more intelligent form. It can only be described through metaphor.

1

2. What do you think it is like to be dead?

Several replied, "I don't know," and some that it is not "like" anything or that death is like nothing or a void. Others said it is like the following: a stopping, cessation of all but mind, end of life, opposite of life, calm and peaceful, end of communcation, dispersion of elements, rest for soul, before birth, being unconscious, permanent sleep, dreamless sleep, being dormant, stagnation, a waiting, change of dimension. Some believe in heaven and hell, others that death is different for each person. One asked in reply, "What is it like to be alive?"

3. Can you imagine your own death?

No — 50 percent. Replies were: I don't want to, I'm afraid to, we never die, no — we take both life and death for granted, it is the end of the present, there is nothing to imagine or it would be imagining nothing, no but I can imagine my funeral, or dying, or other's reactions, yes — it varies, it is like trying to imagine a hot fudge sundae if you have never seen one.

4. Is death necessary or is it a disease which man may be able to conquer?

Replies were almost equally divided. Some replied that death: can be eliminated completely, can be partly overcome by life extension, cannot be conquered, is a necessary disease, does not affect the soul; is necessary: for the soul to evolve, to define life, for life to evolve, to check population, to allow for change, to provide stages. Others replied: neither necessary nor conquerable — it just exists, it depends on the definition, it doesn't need to be conquered, and I don't know but it's worth looking into.

5. Is death a bad thing or a good thing? Why?

Replies were not quantifiable. Death is bad because: one will no longer be alive, it ends life, it gives anxiety and sadness, it is an end to satisfaction, it may come by accident. Death is good: as a limit to life, as a transition to a next life, if there is an afterlife, because it stops suffering and body deterioration, if one is not happy, because it forces one to set goals, as a release, as a population control, if one is old, because it allows new beliefs and change. Some replied that it is neither good nor bad, it has no intrinsic value, that good and bad do not exist. One replied, "It's not exactly what I'm living for."

6. Do you have a terminal illness? If so, describe.

No one had a terminal illness. Some would die if certain medication were not available. A few think of life as a terminal illness. Others suspect their individual psychological makeup might cause an early death.

7. Are you interested in any dangerous sports, e.g., racing, mountain climbing, etc? Discuss.

Nearly all replied "no." Others feel that risk and dangerous sport give life meaning, excitement, and break boredom. Several like danger only as a spectator.

8. Have you discussed death a) with your family? b) with others? Describe the main views of death given.

One-sixth had not discussed death at all. Most had discussed it in terms of heaven, hell, reincarnation, afterlife, and the religious context. It was found that the topic of death was seldom discussed and generally avoided. One replied that there is too much reverence for the dead, and another wrote, "They said that 'it' wasn't a hot fudge sundae. But upon further inquiry they couldn't tell me why."

9. Describe your personal experiences with death.

Majority had immediate personal experiences with death. Experiences involved: murder, accidents, war wound and war deaths (2 1/2 ton trucks filled with dead in Vietnam), being on critical list in hospital, one as a child killing things "to prove there was death." Three students dreamt they died, one saw his dead grandfather's "spirit" about twelve times, one likes walking through graveyards and intends to be a mortician, one hates funerals, one said funerals are fun to observe and the conversation comical.

10. Which books (and other media) most influenced your thought about death?

Three were influenced by the Bible. Others gave: Faulkner's *As I Lay Dying, Johnny Got His Gun, Death Be Not Proud, The Prophet, The Devil's Own, Third Eye, The Saffron Robe, The Hermit, Death of Ivan Ilych,* Hemingway, Hesse's *Steppenwolf, The Upanishads,* philosophy books, *Teachings of Don Juan,* T. S. Eliot's "Love Song of J. Alfred Prufrock," *Revolutionary Notes, The Trial, The Pleasures of Philosophy,* Sartre's *The Wall,* Existentialism — novels and plays [has as much influence as the Bible], The Jefferson Airplane, Tao, *Psychedelic Prayers After the Tao, The Politics of Esctasy, A Search for the Girl With the Blue Eyes,* Zen Buddhism, Edgar Cayce, TV, movies, books in general, books on reincarnation, history books, books on biology, books on death.

11. Are you especially concerned with death, funerals, dying, cemeteries, etc.? Specify.

Many say that the open-casket viewing and funerals are "barbaric," "a waste," "fake," "morbid." A number are mainly concerned with care of the dying and eliminating suffering. A few find funerals, death, and cemeteries intriguing.

12. Have you ever wanted to die? If so, why?

Yes — 28. Reasons given were: life seemed a waste, felt I didn't know my parents, hated my life, wanted to stop some experiences I was having, bored with life, death is peaceful to imagine, social and personal pressures, to release other people of the burden of me, parental problems, when I hurt my parents, when I broke up with a boyfriend, when I was in pain due to a car accident, because of the way I am, to know what comes after, to make people feel sorry for me, failure to follow man, wanted to be 6' under but never lose consciousness.

13. Have you ever or do you contemplate suicide? If yes, discuss.

Yes — 22. Reasons given were: existence seemed useless, unknown death holds less fear than pain of life, if in pain, if death seemed more desirable than despair, because I failed to help fellow man before entering the Marines, love problems, to escape from responsibility of living, because of conditions of life as they now exist, unwanted pregnancy — husband out of work and feeling personally ill, because life is absurd [existentialistic view].

14. Should one have a right to take his own life? Specify.

Yes — 32. Reasons given were: it is a basic freedom, life is the only real thing one possesses, one should have the right unless he is insane, life may be too painful or useless, one must use one's own intelligence to decide the matter for himself, it fits into nature's survival pattern, if it does not avoid responsibility or impose on others, to free oneself from life's burden.

15. Do you fear death? Describe.

Yes — 21. Reasons given were: fear sudden death only, fear pollution will kill us, fear dying not death, fear that I will miss something after I die, fear hell, at age 10 feared death and became physically ill from thinking about it, I avoid the topic because views are too stereotyped. Death is feared because: mate will be left alone, it is a change, it is nothingness, fear lack of fulfillment, it is an unknown, fear pain.

16. What is the best approach to the study of death?

Replies were: similar to approach as you would study a car, the one you believe in — what you want to believe about death, experience, looking at the best things in life — love, painfully direct, "tell it like it is," honest and personal, reading outside of class and lectures, intellectual inquiry which is honest and factual, scientific objectiveness, conversations and activities such as this seminar, open and extensive, approach that would allow me not to fear death, reading various writers, study from all aspects openly, no best way because it is personal, metaphorical approach, best approach involves those who have been there, philosophical approach, biological, theories about an afterlife, religious theories, study of forms of life, combination of intellectual and emotional approach, the non-approach.

17. Do you believe in immortality? Discuss and specify kind.

Fifteen believe in immortality or the possibility of immortality. Replies were: some are immortal after they die once, life-energy is not destroyed, we live on only in the memory of others, we continue in another environment, we go to heaven or hell, soul lives on, scientific immortality may be possible, not sure, there is always some kind of life regardless of form, mind is immortal, we are reincarnated until Nirvana. Others said that belief in immortality is illogical and outside of our experience.

18. Do you believe you have a soul?

Fifteen believe they have a soul of some kind. Some think of it as mind, intelligence, or as not the kind the Christian believes in. Sixteen believe there is no soul. The rest are not sure or believe one cannot prove or disprove that there is a soul.

19. Do you think that science can one day make man immortal or nearly so?

Yes — 18, no — 6, 12 possibly or probably. Some comments were: it is worth trying, can't imagine it, man can be nearly immortal only, if man were immortal he wouldn't be "man," we must also find a desire for man to live, it is not a good idea, we can bridge the gap between life forms, it would cause over-population, man would destroy each other anyway, only stupid people would want to remain living, I don't think it was meant to be that way, science must eliminate aging first, science is a farce.

20. What is the afterlife like, if you believe there is one?

Fourteen replied that they do not know. Others stated: everything beautiful, an angel in heaven, a fly in India, many things, place where people are happy and content, some sort of consciousness without communication, something more personal than heaven or hell, just as the Bible describes, stopping ground - soul waits, a congregation of spirits, perpetual existence, spirits roaming the earth, soul lives on, could be anything, reincarnation, state of mind, heaven or hell, another higher level of consciousness.

21. Are you religious? Specify faith and describe briefly.

Twenty-seven stated they are not religious. From the comments many were not clear what religion actually is. Seven were confused about their religion or not sure. One reported being a "participant" in the Catholic faith, two rejected their Catholicism, and two were confused about or trying to understand the Catholic beliefs. Four reported being Lutherans but three of these seldom or no longer practice the faith. One student believes in Zen Buddhism. Some of the comments were: I am looking for something to believe in, my faith is in people, I wish to find a purpose for myself and gain satisfaction, there is a higher order of being than man, Christian ideals are noble, I believe in God but am not religious, faith is in my own thoughts, I believe that all people should be loved by all other people.

22. Does your religion, if any, give you insight into the problem of death? Specify.

Twenty-two report that their religion does not give insight into the problem of death. Nine gave no reply. Eight said it does. Comments were: God rewards us, there is a better life, it gives faith to overcome fear of death, there is a heaven and hell, religion has an absurd fairy-tale view of afterlife, soul leaves the body and lives forever with God — but these are ambiguous terms, religion claims it can see the truth but I believe it is as blind as I.

23. Do you believe in reincarnation or that people live over again? Specify.

No — 19. Seventeen believe in it or think it is possible. Comments were: there is an eternal present, drugs made me feel the presence of another complete entity within myself, life energy is indestructible, mind remains, it explains one's talents and interests which are not otherwise explicable, the belief in reincarnation seems to be an attempt to wish oneself immortal.

24. Do you hope for life after death?

Yes — 16, no — 8. Comments were: I would want a conscious life but not wakefulness without change, I am immortal, an afterlife gives reason for one's existence. I wouldn't want to live over again, I don't care, not sure, it is a nice thought for people afraid of dying or not satisfied with life, it would be weird, it would not be like this life.

25. Have drugs such as LSD, etc. given you insight into death and immortality? Specify.

Thirty-two reported "no" or that they had no drug experience. Seven reported the following experiences: mescaline gives one out-of-body experiences and awareness of our mental and physical nature, a large dose of LSD [very dangerous] gave me a feeling of another complete entity within myself, my perspective on death was widened, it showed me that man is basically evil, while under drugs I am afraid to think of death, death seemed to be part of a whole system, made me appreciate life more at times — life as a joke — death as the last laugh, drugs can cause fear of death.

26. If religious, how strong is your religious belief?

Four reported a genuine belief. Fourteen did not reply. Fourteen reported that they were confused about religion or had a weak belief. [includes some who said they were not religious]

27. Have you ever had evidence of immortality such as visions, ESP, psychic, out-of-body, or other such experiences? Specify.

No — 28. Others reported the following experiences: out-of-body and awareness of physical and mental nature while under drugs, under drugs felt presence of a complete entity within myself, sometimes feel my dead mother is near, something I had done seemed a replay of a past dream, I became aware of Winston Churchill's death before the news arrived — I had been following his illness closely, I have seen my dead grandfather 12 times, with various people communication is strong, my mind can leave my body and watch me, being a twin my brother and I think many of the same thoughts, I thought I saw my grandmother after she died, at times I knew what people were going to say before they said it, I had visions of future happenings, I had feelings of spiritual presence in a dark room, dreams have materialized into actual life, I used to have premonitions of bad things that would happen.

28. Do you believe in ESP, or Astrology? Specify.

Neither — 7, ESP — 22, astrology — 2. One believes in metaphysics, ESP, and astral projection.

29. What kind of death and funeral would you prefer?

Ten prefer cremation. Others responded: it doesn't matter, I don't know, inexpensive and informal, no funeral (3), funeral feast with music, non-violent fast death, non-church funeral by friends, pine box, simple funeral, painless death, glamorous funeral, Catholic service, prefer violent death, death in sleep, closed casket, no grieving (2), no flowers, wooden casket under oak tree by my log cabin, donate body to science, Irish funeral, large church funeral, buried without casket, painful and slow death, cremation ashes scattered over water. [In a separate survey of adult students all desired a quick, simple, inexpensive, painless funeral. No one specified open-casket viewing, several opposed such viewing.]

30. Do you want to know when you will die?

No − 26, yes − 8. Some who said, "no," thought it would create too much anxiety and would cause one to neglect responsibilities. Some would want to know only shortly before death.

31. Would you want the doctor to tell you if you have a terminal illness?

Yes − 42. Five would not want to know.

32. Should a dying person be kept alive under all conditions?

No − 30. Ten said it is up to the person dying. Some believe that one should not be kept alive if he cannot function without life-saving machines, or if there is no hope that he will survive.

33. Under which conditions, if any, should one not be kept alive?

Under no circumstances − 3, up to the person − 8, all cases which are definitely terminal − 8. Comments were: weak babies should not be kept alive if they are being sustained only by drugs, a young person should be given a chance — but not the elderly, persons in permanent vegetative state should not be kept alive, cancer patients in great pain should not be kept alive, persons who are dangerous to society should not be kept alive, if there is much pain and the person asked to die he should be allowed to do so, it is impossible to determine, some suicidals say they do not want to die but commit suicide — they should be kept alive.

34. Would you a) allow your own autopsy? Yes — 39, no — 8.
b) donate your organs after death? Yes — 31, no — 7, maybe — 3.
c) allow your body to be sent to a medical school for research? Yes — 31, no — 10, maybe — 2.
d) have your dead body frozen for later possible scientifically given immortality? Yes — 10, no — 12, maybe — 1.

35. Do you believe in life insurance and a will for yourself?

Three want no life insurance, 33 wish both will and insurance, three desire neither.

36. Under what circumstances would give up your life?

Six would not give up their lives. Some others would possibly give up their lives for the following: to end painful illness, for family or loved ones, if I would soon die anyway and it would help someone by dying, for another's life, for a cause I believed in, under a great emotional experience, when I couldn't any longer accomplish a worthwhile task.

37. Do you consider yourself to be emotional?

Very emotional — 5, emotional — 22, no — 14.

38. Do you prefer emotional or intellectual approaches to inquiry?

Intellectual − 24, emotional − 2, both − 17. Some say that emotions and intellect cannot be separated. One said that emotions prove to be "better" more often than anything else.

39. Do you learn most by conversations or by reading?

Conversation − 21, reading − 13, both − 11.

40. What would you do if you knew you had to die tomorrow? next month? next year?

If knew tomorrow: spend time with best friends, wouldn't sleep − do as much as possible, would be too upset to do anything, straighten out finances and spend night with wife, seek peace of mind, start thinking, pray, see family, go to the pub, meditate, play mellow country blues and read Faust, call people and express emotions, seek pleasure, get drunk and make love with boyfriend, take LSD and have lots of sex.

Next month or next year: have fun, have boyfriend's baby, do what I'm doing now, travel, experience everything, enjoy myself, finish my book, sky-dive, do the things I was afraid to do, relax, pray, think a lot, go to live in a brothel, walk outside and talk to people I meet, convert all energy to helping others, contemplate on last moments, be alone, quit school, bum around, do what I've always wanted to do, do nothing special. One said that for a person to change radically would betray his past life and be an admission of failure to achieve life's goals.

41. Which courses would you take and which books would you read if you planned to stay in school and knew you would die at the end of the semester?

Courses: (several) art, English, psychology, (many) seminar on death, piano, biology, woodworking, flight training, (several) philosophy, (several) religion, same courses as now, etc.
Books: Camus, *The Stranger; Crime and Punishment*, poetry, books on ESP and telepathy, Bible, books on psychic phenomena, *Doors of Perception, Book of the Dead*, philosophy.

42. Answer question number 40 again assuming you could do anything in the world you wanted to.

Most answers were the same as for question number 40.

43. What are your main goals in life?

To be happy with myself and others, find out what I'm like, to love, have a good job, get out of school and live, gain knowledge, have satisfying personal relationships, experience everything, marry, have children, become famous, be fair and just, I have no goals, travel, become a teacher, make others happy, be a good person, earn enough money.

44. What are the most valuable things in your life?

Ability to reason, friends, things which no one has seen, health, ability to help others, nature, parents, music, pets, spouse or mate, education, hobby, morality, beliefs, goals, reputation, conversations, love, understanding, consideration, happiness, hard to list abstract things, security, books, hanging on to the past, eyes, my life as it exists now, privacy, peace with myself, college, children, self-esteem.

45. Do you think life is absurd? Why?

Yes − 23, no − 17. Comments: What do we ever really accomplish?, it is not absurd because there is a unity of all things, life's game is worth playing, it is ludicrous to strive hard for transitory pleasure, life is absurd if it is looked at closely, I can enjoy life's shortcomings, life is absurd because of my awareness of the certainty of death, life is sometimes absurd because it fits into the definition of "absurd," forced rituals and small talk make life absurd, life is absurd because we work to live to die, life has no importance, society is absurd, what some people do with their lives is absurd, people work to get ahead but exclude personal things, (several) I love life, everyone is waiting for tomorrow, people rarely question what it might all mean, life is not absurd — there are logical explanations for everything, life is not absurd but at times rather funny, there is never a good answer for anything, life is what you make it, people sometimes try to make life hard for themselves, life seems absurd when I am depressed, what is life compared to here?

46. Do you pray? If so, how often?

No — 20, yes — 19. Comments: when I need help from God, when I want something for someone or myself, when I feel grateful for my life, when I need something greater than myself, when I feel sorry for myself, only as a crutch, I pray when I am in deep trouble but not to God, when something good happens, not conventional prayers — merely talk, when I've done things I'm not proud of, not sure if I pray or have highly ethical hope, I pray only when things are bad.

47. Do you think you can be punished for your sins after death?

No — 29, yes — 4, not sure — 3. Comments: do not believe there is a supreme being who cares about us, if so I would be in a lot of trouble, there are no such things as sins, only reincarnation, we are punished for sins in life not after death, only in the sense that you will take longer to reach your ultimate goal, I hope so, God is forgiving, who punishes you worse than yourself?

48. Do you think most people waste their lives? Why?

Yes — 29. Comments were: by wondering when they will die, we just live till we die, many maximize problems and minimize happiness, we are too materialistic, we are too content being lazy, they do not realize they are alive, they are too concerned with themselves rather than others, sin is often the reason for living, they are ignorant of living, most people never question the basic things, all they do is wait, they are unhappy, they do not realize how short life really is, they think too much of tomorrow — not of today, they do nothing constructive, they are afraid to do what they really want to do, they are too narrow-minded, they are afraid to experience; rules, morals, and society restrict them; they value the wrong things, they are captivated by a single model and do things blindly, they spend too much time escaping from reality, they take life too seriously, they spend a lot of time doing things which are meaningless to themselves and others, they lead inauthentic lives, they waste life by creating countless forms of attachment, they do not use their full potential, they seek transitory pleasures, they are too concerned with trivia.

49. What would your last words be if you were now to die?

Good luck, good-bye, I'm sorry, fooled you, it's been nice, it was a good life, it was fun while it lasted, hope I haven't done anything to hurt anyone, hope I have helped others, I would make peace with God, I don't want to die, why me?, (curse words), I believe, I would say nothing (6), I'm afraid, Oh, well!, goodnight — gotta go, depends on the situation, sorry I did not make my boyfriend's life happier, something trivial, thanks to the people I loved who gave enough to love me back, don't tell anyone about this, death is finished, life here was insanity, Jesus — I love you, Don't resist life — join the dance, I would thank my parents for my life and fulfillment.

50. Have you been honest in the views and attitudes you have regarding death?

Yes — 42. Others were not sure.

51. Write your own eulogy (what others might honestly say about you.)

Nice guy, odd, aloof, possessive, taciturn, anti-social, unfulfilled, he tried to join society but something always held him back, did not realize his potential, a victim of his

rage, he "got things together," why did he die?, will he
return?, he got me pregnant, once again here lies Ivan Ilych
– trapped, he was sincere, she was a lovely and intelligent
girl, he was honest, sometimes she was a bitch – but if she
wasn't scared to open up she loved deeply, probably no one
would say anything honest at the funeral, he was a logical
thinker, here lies a wasted man, he has lived well, she was a
bitch – but a good person to laugh with, he left the world
better than he found it, here lies one old beyond his years,
she made many friends, nothing, she often hid her feelings,
I'm sure he was crazy, he tried to understand our faith but
his lack of belief confused him, he was half-hearted, she
was moody and unfulfilled but honest and intelligent.

52. Write your own eulogy as you would like it to be.

I have liberated my soul, he gave more than he took, he was
duly afraid of people, he wanted no part of this economic
and political system he couldn't respect – a family he
couldn't talk to – an education he didn't want, he
struggled helplessly, may he not fear death as he feared life,
she was devoted to her husband and children, she tried to
comfort people, she was loving and happy, she tried to
understand, she cared about others, she was oppressed, he
was honest, death puts an end to waiting – your turn will
come, I have tried to be free, Born 1950 – Died ––––––,
she enjoyed every experience in life, she enjoyed deep
thinking, she was compassionate, eulogies are ridiculous,
she needed strength, "Could flowers and verses have
cancelled this fate I'd have filled every field with rose petals
and rhyme," this person has not died – he has lived, she
was human, etc.

53. Complete the following sentence giving several versions as
significantly as possible: "Dying is like . . ."

A one-way ticket to another place, going to sleep without
contemplating awakening, being born again – into a world
less confining, nothing ever seen before, humiliation,
hush-hush, a play, something I've never tried before, cosmic

traveling, the ultimate trip, a final orgasm, like nothing else, falling asleep or getting knocked out, falling, entering another world, the end of a mysterious dream, a long sleep, a permanent place, nothing, being trapped in a box, fallen apple rotting in dirt, waiting for the answer, stopping and maybe starting, getting it over with, feeling yourself being the snake you killed as a little boy, letting go, making the last turn, filling the last blank, becoming the 360th degree, [no answer], going beyond, an eternal dream, beginning of the end, an infinite voyage, explosion of a super nova, being born, comma in a sentence, nightmare, ultimate in tranquil meditation, turning off a faucet, finding that the end of a tunnel is a deep dark pond, falling in a void, stone rolling and coming to a stop, bricks falling through air, a child swallowing a bottle of sleeping pills, falling asleep and never waking, leaving this life for another, driving 140 mph into a snowstorm, being in a cement-block room, looking up through a long hole, hell, a nap after eating, a sunset, finding out what it's really like, walking into a different room alone, letting go of your security blanket, leaving this world for another, not being, I don't know, coming to the end of an existence, extinguishing a match, unplugging T.V., turning off a light, passing out, stepping off the orange, cutting off the power of a trolley car, closing-night of a theatre, finale, deep sleep, ending of physical senses, nothing you could ever conceive of or experience, walking into a cave and forgetting to come out, screaming at the top of your lungs and no one hearing, dropping a pin into the ocean, finding out that people are laughing at you, jumping off the high dive, a large magnet pulling on a small magnet until all its energy has been drained, trying to advance a genetic strain and failing, death is like almost nothing, feeling embarrassed, turning off a loud radio, having a mental block, getting lost, sleeping, breaking a movie film, taking an old car out on the road not knowing what's going to happen next, waiting to go on a vacation, coming down from amphetamines, watching a blind person fall, dry heaves, listening to the static of an old-time radio and having the plug pulled out, slowing down of a record, going on to a better life, judging yourself, final masturbation, not having the cherry of a hot fudge sundae, >>>—• , making love, changing your bad habits, a curtain coming down.

54. Do you think most people are honest in their statements about death? Discuss.

Yes — 7, no — 20 plus. Comments were: everyone wants to hold onto life as long as they can despite what they say, they do not realize they are dying, they make up excuses for unpleasant situations, society influences their thoughts, most people don't like to talk about it or think about it, those who have a ready answer from the Bible are not honest, they are not honest because when faced with death their real feelings are exposed, most fear death and so distort it, most people are no more honest about death than anything else, most people are dishonest, the question is absurd, people have to distort truth to protect themselves from strong feelings, their emotions fool them, the subject is too personal to look at objectively, it is not clear what is meant by "honest," they become honest when they overcome fear of death, most cannot comprehend the concept, most do not question their beliefs enough; people react to death as they react to life — if he avoids unpleasant things he will avoid death — if he is practical he will take a practical approach, if he is emotional he will take an emotional approach.

55. Please add other remarks regarding death which you feel may be interesting, or informative.

Thirty-one gave no suggestions. Previous statements repeated.

Quotations Regarding
Questionnaire

1. What is death?

"We do not know anything about life; what can we know about death?" Confucius

"The meaning of death is never rigidly established at any given time for the society or for the individual." G. Vernon

"Mere oblivion, sans teeth, sans eyes, sans taste, sans everything." Shakespeare

"The problem of death is probably the first to deserve this name in the history of thought." Prof. Hans Jonas

"It is the same thing in us that is alive and dead, awake and asleep, young and old: the former are shifted and become the latter and the latter in turn are shifted and become the former." Heraclitus

"And I saw, and behold, a pale horse, and its rider's name was Death." *Revelation* 6:7

"The word 'death' has become a repository for pervasive logical and epistemological confusions — 'Idols of the Dead.' " Dr. Edwin Shneidman

"Life's not a paragraph
and death i think is no parenthesis." E. E. Cummings

"Death is Nature's expert advice to get plenty of life."
Goethe

"Death is frozen time. Time is molten death." Franz
Werfel

"The mystery of death is of our own making." S.
Caveeshar, Prof. of Religion

"Who knows if what's called death is not life and life not
death?" Euripides

"Animals are unaware of death because death is a symbolic
form." Jules Vuillemin

"*La vie c'est la mort.*" Claude Bernard

"Most ignorant of what he's most assured — His glassy
essence . . . " Shakespeare

"Death is a contradiction . . . comical. . . . I can see death
being really funny, in a comic sense." Thomas Shaffer

2. What do you think it is like to be dead?

"To assert 'I now die' is either an anticipation or a guess."
William Hocking

"Men who have not been awakened to the philosophic life
and their whole circumstances are described as dead."
Rudolf Bultman

"All this is foul smell and blood in a bag." Marcus Aurelius

"Altogether, the analogical argument has been misused
extensively in connection with immortality." Jacques
Choron

"We are such stuff
As Dreams are made on and our little life
Is rounded with a sleep." Shakespeare *Tempest*

3. Can you imagine your own death?

"The inquiring self becomes part of the datum for its own inquiry." William Hocking

"The reports of my death are greatly exaggerated." Mark Twain

"Neither the sun nor death can be looked at with a steady eye." La Rochefoucauld

"A man's dying is more the survivor's affair than his own." Thomas Mann *Magic Mountain*

"No analogy can hold between my death and any experienced event of my life." Prof. Mary Mothersill

"To die! The grave! I do not understand these words." Goethe

"The sweetness of life is felt even in the grass growing over the tomb." Anatole France

"You [death], while I breathe, are subject unto me,
You are merely a thought that I am thinking,
The frail toy of my anguished revery." Afansy Fet

4. Is death necessary or is it a disease which man may be to conquer? (e.g. death as caused by poisons in our food.)

"No death is wholly 'natural'; no one dies *merely* of the burden of years." Peter Medawar

"There are no reasons why aging processes will not be completely understood eventually, and methods devised for their inhibition. . . . Basic mechanisms of aging are currently at the level of hypotheses or theories." Dr. Robert Kohn

"To the question 'Can the effective human life-span be prolonged artifically?' the most probable answer . . . would appear to be 'Yes.' " Dr. Alex Comfort *Biology of Senescence*

"A little informed lobbying could now get us a longer life." Dr. Alex Comfort

"There is still no generally accepted theory to explain aging, nor is it safe to assume that aging is an inevitable consequence of living." Dr. Alex Comfort

"The feasibility of an anti-aging pill should no longer be doubted. . . . Therapy based on any one of the major aging theories can probably extend our lives." Patrick McGrady, Jr. "The Youth Pill"

"Oh, that there were a medicine curing age . . ." *Regimen of Health of Salerno* ((11th century)

"All diseases may by sure means be prevented or cured, not excepting even that of old age, and our lives lengthened at pleasure even beyond the antediluvian standard." Benjamin Franklin

"We cannot conclude once and for all that a higher organism dies inevitably and necessarily. . . . Death does not appear as an absolute or as an absolutely necessary fact." Dr. Jose Ferrater-Mora

"Death is not, as has been hitherto assumed, an inevitable phenomenon essential to the very nature of life itself." August Weismann

"But you must know, your father lost a father; that father lost, lost his. . . ." Shakespeare *Hamlet*

"Within the recent past, biochemical knowledge and medicosurgical techniques have been advanced to the point that the possibility of physical immortality for man can no longer be limited to science fiction." Dr. Claiborne Jones (Zoologist)

5. Is death a bad thing or a good thing?

"The weight of all things must be defined anew." Nietzsche

"War on the destiny of man." Dylan Thomas

"The order of the world is shaped by death." Camus

"Life does not cease to be funny when people die anymore than it ceases to be serious when people laugh." George Bernard Shaw

"Now death is the most terrible of all things; for it is the end, and nothing is thought to be any longer either good or bad for the dead." Aristotle *Ethics*

"We are quite mistaken in supposing death to be an evil." Socrates *Apology*

"A man who has really devoted his life to philosophy should be cheerful in the face of death . . ." Socrates *Phaedo*

6. Do you have a terminal illness?

"O gentlemen! The time of life is short." Shakespeare (Hotspur)

7. Are you interested in any dangerous sports, e.g., racing, mountain climbing, etc?

"Live dangerously." Nietzsche

8. Describe the main views of death.

"Death has not in recent years, attracted great attention among philosophers." Jacques Choron

"The average parent is of but little help to the child in his search for answers about death." G. Vernon

"How is it that death, the most persistent and common event in the life of man, remains the one we know least about? Why the absence of curiosity about death in the continued presence of death? . . . Scarcely questioning the fate that awaits them . . . is characteristic of the almost universal disregard for the problem of death." August Wagner

9. Describe your personal experiences with death.

"The summons of death comes to us all, and no one can die for another. Everyone must fight his own battle with death by himself alone." Luther

"While I thought I was learning how to live, I was learning how to die." Leonardo da Vinci

10. Are you especially concerned with death, funerals, dying, cemeteries, etc.?

"The conquest of death appeared to me as the fundamental problem of life." Berdyaev

"Death is the most important question of our time." Robert Lifton

"There is nothing too good for the dead." W. Hohenschuh

"Let us take our laughter to the dead." J. Niggli

"Let's talk of graves, of worms, and epitaphs
Make dust our paper and with rainy eyes
Write sorrow on the bosom of the earth." Shakespeare
Richard II

"Man is a tomb-building animal." Dr. Frank Crane

11. Have you ever or do you contemplate suicide?

"Suicide ranks tenth in leading causes of death in the United States and if properly reported might rank as high as fifth." [It ranks fifth as cause of death among 15-19 year olds.] Jeffrey Schrank

12. Should one have a right to take his own life?

"In a certain state it is indecent to live longer. To go on vegetating in cowardly dependence on physicians and machinations, after the meaning of life, the right to life, has been lost, that ought to prompt a profound contempt in society . . . To die proudly when it is no longer possible to live proudly. Death freely chosen, death at the right time, brightly and cheerfully accomplished amid children and witnesses: then a real farewell is still possible." Nietzsche

"Inhibition against committing suicide is a Christian superstition that is an anachronism in a post-Christian society." Toynee

"The Judeo-Christian tradition has made suicide a sin of much the same character as murder." Robert Morison, Prof. of Science and Society, Cornell University.

"It is in your power to live here. But if men do not permit you, then get away out of life." Marcus Aurelius

(Note: These quotations are not intended to encourage suicide. Rather the suicidal person often is in need of psychiatric care and after treatment is glad he did not commit suicide.)

13. Do you fear death? Do you usually try to avoid the topic?

"I truly think it is those dreadful faces and trappings with which we surround it, that frighten us more than death itself." Montaigne

"Down, down, down into the darkness of the grave. . . .
I know. But I do not approve. And I am not resigned."
Edna St. Vincent Millay

"Nothing in life is to be feared. It is to be understood."
Marie Curie

"Attitudes toward death have received little attention
from social scientists in this country; yet few attitudes
are more central to human motivation. . . . Behavioral
scientists must not avoid such inquiries simply because
our culture regards death so morbidly." Alan Howard
and Robert Scott, *Journal of Existentialism*

"No philosophy, religion, or overall way of life can be
judged complete or adequate unless it includes a definite
position on whether or not the human personality can
surmount the crisis called death . . ." Corliss Lamont

"And thus, in one continued strife,
'Twixt fear of death and love of life." Shakespeare

"Fear is expectation of displeasure but this is using the
word in its broadest sense. In the narrowest sense, it is
the refusal of death. Every fear is fear of death." William
Stekel *Nervous Anxiety States*

"Death is only dreadful for those who dread it." Isaac
D'Israeli

"True philosophers make dying their profession, and to
them of all men death is least alarming." Socrates
Phaedo

14. What is the best approach to the study of death?

"Scientists are just now beginning to realize the value of
death study." Jeffrey Schrank

"The study of death is an important aspect of sociology which has been somewhat neglected." Glenn Vernon

"The philosopher will get no help from those who are professionally concerned with dying." L. Boros

"In delving into the scientific part of aging you are in a field that historically and today as well is rampant with pseudo-science, quackery, and just not very good." Roy Walford (Prof. of Pathology)

"We have as yet no scientific way of accounting for the functionally relevant patterns of behavior observed in attempts to cope with the death crisis. . . . Serious as the situation now is from a mental health viewpoint, it is tending to worsen . . ." Dr. Robert Fulton and Phyllis Langton, R.N.

"There is a comparative lack of scientific writing on death." Samuel Shrut, *Mental Hygiene*

"Vain is the word of a philosopher which does not heal any suffering of man." Epicurus

"Unfortunately, biological science does not as yet know the precise nature of life." Hereward Carrington

"Death is the true inspiring genius, or the muse of philosophy." Schopenhauer

"Logic, conceived as an adequate analysis of the advance of thought is a fake." A. N. Whitehead

"When Logics die,
The secret of the soul grows through the eye,
And blood jumps in the sun." Dylan Thomas

"To understand the issue of immortality, you must look at the ways people talk of death. . . . Such issues are only made explicit to us by means of language. . . . The experience, indeed, which takes shape through such expression." D. M. MacKinnon *New Essays in Philosophical Theology*

"There have been comparatively few scientific investigations of the varying meanings and functions of death concepts and attitudes." Samuel Shrut

"Those who really apply themselves in the right way to philosophy are directly and of their own accord preparing themselves for dying and death." Socrates *Phaedo*

15. Do you believe in immortality?

"Let us confess our ignorance, but let us not resign ourselves to the belief that we can never know. If there be a beyond for conscious beings, I cannot see why we should not be able to discover the means to explore it." Henri Bergson

"We must . . . so far as we can, make ourselves immortal, and strain every nerve to live in accordance with the best thing in us." Aristotle *Ethics*

"Mortals are immortals and immortals are mortals, the one living the other's death and dying the other's life." Heraclitus

"One cannot, if one is honest, ignore the extent to which metaphysical arguments, like those concerning immortality, have gained plausibility from a refusal to attend to the logic of our language." D. M. MacKinnon *New Essays in Philosophical Theology*

16. Do you believe you have a soul?

"The existence of the soul is absolutely denied, and the whole concept is a bad invention." Fichte

17. Does your religion, if any, give you insight into the problem of death?

"Christianity has exploited the weakness of the dying for a rape of the conscience." Nietzsche

"No human eye penetrates the shadows of death and we are misled by the delusions of belief." (Hyppolytus) Aeschylus

"Let's break the tablets of the preachers of death." Nietzsche

"If persons were freed from misconceptions about death, many whose creative energies are now stymied could seek solutions to genuinely resolvable and vitally important problems of existence." Alan Howard and Robert Scott, *Journal of Existentialism*

"Religious solutions to the problems of death are only a minor consolation, if any at all. . . . I draw a negative inference . . . about the value of religious faith in coping with the anxieties caused by death." Thomas Shaffer

18. Do you hope for life after death?

"All union of the sexes is a sign of death; and we could not know love were we to live indefinitely." Anatole France

"I accept the finality of death as a necessary part of life." ("Bioethical Creed") Van R. Potter

"I would not positively assert that I shall join the company of those good men who have already departed from this life; but I cherish a good hope." Socrates

"The search for certainty and for incontrovertible proofs of survival upon death will continue, for it has proved itself to be one of the most potent remedies against the fear of death and the haunting sense of the futility of life." Jacques Choron

19. Have you ever had evidence of immortality such as visions, ESP, psychic, out-of-body or other such experiences?

"As the lover's joys grow perfect, death is swallowed up in aesthetic glory, in a realized subjective beauty." Shelley

"A thing of beauty is a joy forever:
Its loveliness increases, it will never
Pass into nothingness." Keats

20. What kind of death and funeral would you prefer?

"One should make a feast out of one's death." Nietzsche

"Undertaking or mortuary practice is a business rather than a profession." Florida District Court of Appeal, Feb. 1962

"The collective needs of the community and of the nation . . . is changing. . . . Concomitantly the role of the funeral director must be adaptive. . . . He must continue to develop his sensitivity to the various levels or degrees of loss that death creates in our present day society. . . . There are unscrupulous funeral directors." Howard Raether (National Funeral Directors Assoc.)

"When I am dead, my dearest,
Sing no sad songs for me;
Plant thou no roses at my head,
Nor shady cypress tree." Christina Rossetti

21. Do you want to know when you will die?

"Die at the right time." Nietzsche

22. Should a dying person be kept alive under all conditions?

"He is useless on top of the ground; he ought to be under it, inspiring the cabbages." Rupert Brooke

23. Do you consider yourself to be emotional?

"A large part of what we call emotion is nothing more or less than a certain kind — a biased, prejudiced, or strongly evaluative kind — of thinking. . . . Thinking and emoting . . . in certain respects are essentially the *same thing* . . ." Albert Ellis *Reason and Emotion*

24. Do you prefer emotional or intellectual approaches to inquiry?

"The emotional preoccupation of former workers with magical rejuvenation did no good to the progress of science." Dr. Alex Comfort, *Biology of Senescence*

"The existence of some unique, specific experiential content in emotion has never been demonstrated adequately." William Hunt *Psychological Bulletin*

There is no such thing as *the* emotion of fear, hate, love. The unique, unduplicated character of experienced events and situations impregnates the emotion that is evoked." John Dewey *Psychological Review*

"A dynamic solution to the problems of emotions has not been reached." David Rapaport *Emotions and Memory*

"Exactly how emotional experience arises is still a mystery." Clifford Morgan *Physiological Psychology*

"The psychology of the emotions, notwithstanding some recent advance, is still perhaps the most backward part of the science." Alexander Shand *Mind*

"Emotion is virtually impossible to define . . . except in terms of conflicting theories." H. English and A. English *Dictionary of Psychological and Psychoanalytical Terms*

"The discussion of emotion has been about as confused as that of any topic in psychology." D. O. Hebb *Organization of Behavior*

"Grief is a disease. . . . One may escape both measles and grief." Dr. George Engel *Psychosomatic Medicine*

"Those to whom contemplation more fully belongs are more truly happy." Aristotle *Ethics*

25. What would you do if you knew you had to die tomorrow? next month? next year?

"Crito, I owe a cock to Asklepios." Socrates

"Look on each day as if it were your last
And each unlooked-for hour will seem a boon." Horace

"I want death to find me planting my cabbages." Montaigne

"If the dead are not raised, let us eat and drink, for tomorrow we die." *Corinthians* 15:32

"Live now." Horace

Carpe diem ("Gather the day," "live well now")

26. What are your main goals in life?

"The continuous task of your life is to build death." Montaigne

"The goal of our career is death." Montaigne

"Perfect happiness is a contemplative activity." Aristotle *Ethics*

27. Do you think life is absurd?

"Human life is frightful and still without meaning." Nietzsche

"Man's greatest offense is that he was born." Calderon

"Life's but a walking shadow, a poor player
That struts and frets his hour upon the stage,
And then is heard no more." Shakespeare

"All the world's a stage
And all the men and women merely players."
Shakespeare

"There's nothing serious in mortality.
        All is but toys." Macbeth II, iii

28. Do you think most people waste their lives?

"The greatest part of what we say and do is
unnecessary." Marcus Aurelius

29. What would your last words be if you were now to die?

"It has all been very interesting." Lady Mary Montagu

(A man's last words are usually little different than his
others, e.g., "Did the Dodgers win the last game?")

"I don't know what I may seem to the world. But as to
myself I seem to have been only like a boy playing on
the seashore and diverting myself in now and then
finding a smoother pebble or prettier shell than ordinary,
whilst the great ocean of truth lay all undiscovered
before me." Newton

30. Complete the following sentence giving several versions
as significantly as possible:

"Dying is like . . ."

"There awaits men when they die such things as they
look not for nor dream of." Heraclitus

(. . . a game of chess where the players disappear.)

(. . . the disappearance of the word "death.")

"Nothing explains my death,
for silence is a mirror where
all the questions drown.
And in their silence there was only
an infinite yawn – and then, nothing." Octavio Paz

31. Do you think most people are honest in their statements
about death?

"Each individual imbibes the general view current in his
society." William Hocking

"Nothing is rarer among moralists and saints than
honesty." Nietzsche

"Christianity has exploited the weakness of the dying for
a rape of the conscience." Nietzsche

"The remedy of the common herd is not to think about
it. But from what brutish stupidity can come so gross a
blindness." Montaigne

"There are few happenings to which we have grown so
blind as we are to death." L. Boros

"Obscenity reveals a culture's most threatening taboo. . .
Death is becoming the new obscenity." Jeffrey Schrank

"Those of us who work in the social and medical
sciences and arts are just beginning to express a
willingness to look at the significance of death in modern
America." Richard Kalish

"Death has been a taboo topic for behavioral scientists in
general." G. Vernon

"The ways we repress death and its symbolism are
amazingly like the way the Victorians repressed sex." Dr.
Rollo May

"Our own era simply denies death . . ." Erich Fromm

"There is, in philosophy, science, and religion, a long tradition of apologism, the belief that the prolongation of life is neither possible nor desirable." Gerald Gruman

"In the vast majority of cases, people are not only disinterested, but actually opposed to its discussion." Hereward Carrington

"Believing what we don't believe
Does not exhilarate." Emily Dickinson

32. Other Remarks.

There are "unquestionably deficient social and psychological aspects of contemporary terminal care." B. Glaser and A. Strauss

Epicurus

Epicurus (352-270 B.C.) wrote:

"Death means nothing to us, because that which has been broken down into atoms has no sensation and that which has no sensation is no concern of ours." (1963)

Another statement of this sort is by Feuerbach:

"Only before death and not in death is death really death and painful; death is such a spectral being that it only is, when it is not, and is not, when it is." (Choron 1963)

In his *Letter to Menoeceus* Epicurus states:

"You should accustom yourself to believing that death means nothing to us, since every good and every evil lies in sensation; but death is the privation of sensation. Hence a correct comprehension of the fact that death means nothing to us makes the mortal aspect of life pleasurable, not by conferring on us a boundless period of time but by removing the yearning for deathlessness."

After death there is supposedly no sensation. But loss of sensation is the very thing which is dreaded. Epicurus' view that one would not experience pain or pleasure is a useful view especially against Christians who fear the torments of hell. Epicurus' statement, then, is therapy for Christians. Why do we pity the dead? We do not pity atoms.

"It is silly for a person to say that he dreads death – not because it will be painful when it arrives but because it pains him now as a future certainty; for that which makes no trouble for us when it arrives is a meaningless pain when we await it."

What is most painful about death is our apprehension of it. We also associate and confuse death with pain. They are different. When death comes, as a rule the mind and body naturally and peacefully adapt to it and even welcome it. Being fearful of death is a waste of life and puts a known, certain present evil in place of a future unrealistic possibility. It is similar to wars fought in "self-defense" far from one's own country. A known certain death of the "enemy" is put in place of a future possible death of oneself or one's fellow citizens.

"This, the most horrifying of evils, means nothing to us, then, because so long as we are existent death is not present and wherever it is present we are nonexistent."

We cannot fear the state of death because we will not be conscious after death. But we certainly can fear losing consciousness. In general Epicurus is offering us therapy against the debilitating and negative emotions experienced regarding dying and death. Rather the way to approach death and prepare for it is to live well: "Living well and dying well are one and the same discipline."

Atarxia is the worry-free state reached by conquering one's negative emotions. The pleasurable state is reached by overcoming man's greatest fear which is the fear of death. The result is a rational man freed from crippling emotions. The resulting pleasure involves comprehensive and adequate intelligent behavior rather than just sensuality. Life is good only if one learns how to live and to die.

Epicurus *The Philosophy of Epicurus* G. Strodach, ed., Northwestern University Press 1963 esp. "Letter to Menoeceus" pp. 178-195.

Jacques Choron. *Death in Western Thought* New York: Collier 1963 p. 159

Joseph Kupfer. "What's So Bad About Death: Epicurus' Catch" Paper presented at Symposium "Philosophical Aspects of Thanatology" Columbia University, College of Physicians and Surgeons, May 1973

Epictetus

The stoic Epictetus (ca. 80 A.D.) in the *Enchiridion* presents the following view of death.

"Men are disturbed not by things, but by the views which they take of things. Thus death is nothing terrible, else it would have appeared so to Socrates. But the terror consists in our notion of death, that it is terrible. When, therefore, we are hindered or disturbed, or grieved, let us never impute it to others, but to ourselves — that is, to our own views."

If death is a fact, and nothing can be done about it, then it makes no sense to have negative attitudes or emotions concerning it. Such emotions would themselves be the only things which are undesirable. The particular illusory view we have of a fact determines the sort of misconception we have of it and the sort of fear resulting from such misconception.

The above view would be more interesting if death were an absolute necessary fact. One gets here a picture of cement or concrete, a "hard" fact. This has, however, not been shown to be the case. Death may be found to be no more necessary than disease. Thus one of the difficult things about death is that it may be avoidable. But Epictetus' statement is still important, because it advises us not to incur needless negative emotions. They may be found to serve no useful or adjustive purpose and may be unintelligent sorts of behavior. Whether death is final or not, negative emotions if avoidable should be avoided.

41

"Never say of anything, 'I have lost it,' but, 'I have restored it' . . . . Has your child died? It is restored . . . . Hold it [life] as something not your own, as do travelers at an inn."

"Lost" is a euphemism for death, and "loss of life" is not like "loss of an object." "Loss" is a metaphor and one could as well speak of death as a restoration to what it was before. On the model of possessing something we do not own ourselves and so cannot lose ourselves. One cannot lose his life for he will no longer be. Perhaps someone else can lose another's life. We may also ask what being born is a loss of. In the sense that we cannot possess another person we cannot lose him either. In other respects we can lose another. The above view regards nature as the most valuable or true state for one to be in. Human life is regarded as being unnatural and destined to return to its inanimate state. Freud held a similar view in stating that the goal of life is death or the return to the inanimate state.

Also one cannot lose what one never had. We cannot lose that with which we are not familiar. It is not tragic that moles are blind or trees do not have eyes. It is more tragic to lose abilities and know it, than not to know it. To pity an insane or senile man may be no more sensible than to pity a three year old. What is there left of the insane or senile to pity? But we may wish to try to prevent one from becoming senile.

"If you wish your children and your wife and your friends to live forever, you are foolish, for you wish things to be in your power which are not so, and what belongs to others to be your own."

Epictetus' view that at the present time and before one inquires into death it is an absolute fact, is true. That is, however, only to say that the average person can often only see death as final and so he must accept his view at the time. However he could change and modify his view in the light of further inquiry. The above quotation, however, is dogmatic in stating that a man can never overcome death. Can death be "absolutely permanent" if we have *in* our experience no model of absolute permanence?

Epictetus is stating that one should do only what he is able to do. But at one time we were not able to cure fatal diseases and we now do have such power. Evidence, in fact, suggests that increasing our life span and conquering death may well be possible and within our power. However, he does provide sound therapy in suggesting that one must for his own well-being adjust to what is now within his and others' present powers.

"Let death and exile, and all other things which appear terrible, be daily before your eyes, but death chiefly; and you will never entertain an abject thought, nor too eagerly covet anything."

Recognizing that life is short one may be encouraged to spend his time in important and useful rather than trivial activities. This view may sometimes be the case. To assume that because it is sometimes true that it will always be true is to commit the same fallacy as existentialists commit when they say that dread of death is necessary to live a full life. Rather, facing death is not a necessary or sufficient condition for showing one how to live well. It does not in itself make one more intelligent, and facing death may even turn one to criminal activity or suicide. Prisoners condemned to the electric chair often commit suicide beforehand.

"These reasonings have no logical connection: 'I am richer than you, therefore I am your superior' . . . . The true logical connection is rather this: 'I am richer than you, therefore my possessions must exceed yours' . . . . But you, after all, consist neither in property nor in style . . . . The condition and characteristic of a philosopher is that he looks to himself for all help or harm . . . . Thus Socrates became perfect, improving himself by everything, following reason alone. And though you are not yet a Socrates, you ought, however, to live as one seeking to be a Socrates."

To act and live intelligently and realistically requires that one be involved in rational philosophical inquiry. This involves critical ability and accepting nothing uncritically.

Seneca in "Shortness of Life" says,

"The only people really at leisure are those who take time for philosophy. They alone really live . . . [It will] raise you to a height from which none can be cast down."

By such inquiry one prolongs mortality. It is as close as one can come to immortality. On his view, only philosophical inquiry can allow one to advance on, adapt to, and overcome the thought of death.

It was thought that if one could not rationally inquire, suicide is best. The Cynic stated that if one cannot live a full rational life suicide is best. Diogenes Laertius said similarly, that fools are better off dead. It is reason or the rope. Socrates' death seemed to be a kind of suicide. He could have avoided death and it is not clear why he did not. He was old and the law of Athens stated that the condemned should kill themselves by drinking hemlock. But perhaps Socrates' death was to proclaim freedom or to take a belief in the survival of the soul literally. But Socrates was not sure about an afterlife. His death seems at least to be a reaction to the irrationality and lack of rational inquiry on the part of the average man who condemned him by bringing him to trial for "perverting the minds of youth." Perhaps he thought it would take at least his death to point up that fact. All this is in great contrast to the Christian view of not allowing suicide except, for example, as St. Jerome says, in cases where young girls would have to kill themselves in order to preserve their virginity.

Epictetus *The Enchiridion* T. Higginson, trans., Indianapolis Indiana: Bobbs-Merrill 1948

Lucretius

According to Lucretius, men needlessly and dishonestly torment themselves in this life by the very superstitions which are supposed to resolve problems concerning death and life:

"I shall drive out neck and crop that fear of Hell which blasts the life of man from its very foundations, sullying everything with the blackness of death and leaving no pleasure pure and unalloyed. I know that men often speak of sickness or shameful life as more to be dreaded than the terrors of Hell . . . These same men, though they may be exiled from home, banished far from the sight of their fellows, soiled with some filthy crime, as prey to every torment, still cling to life. Wherever they come in their tribulation, they make propitiatory sacrifices, slaughter black cattle and despatch offerings to the Departed Spirits. The heavier their afflictions, the more devoutly they turn their minds to superstition." (97)

When faced with death or serious danger such men often reveal that they do not believe what they profess to believe. In addition he finds that desire for power is based on the fear of death and leads to crime and killing:

"Consider too the greed and blind lust of power that drive unhappy men to overstep the bounds of right and may even turn them into accomplices of crime . . . These running sores of life are fed in no small measure by the fear of death. For object ignominy and irksome poverty seem far indeed from the joy and assurance of life, and in effect loitering already at the gateway of death." (97-98)

45

Thus another dishonest escape from inquiry into or facing death is to surround oneself with wealth and expensive objects and activities. These help one forget death. Not only does it eventually fail but it may even bring about one's own death (as we find in the phenomenon of "voodoo death," recent widow deaths, "predilection to death," and psychosomatic causes of death due to a bad conscience, worry or shock):

> "Some sacrifice life itself for the sake of statues and a title. Often from fear of death mortals are gripped by such a hate of living and looking on the light that with anguished hearts they do themselves to death." (98)

Lucretius' cure is by inquiry into causes and effects and into the nature of man and nature. He stresses an honest, rational, intelligent inquiry devoid of superstition:

> "This dread and darkness . . . cannot be dispelled by the sunbeams . . . but only by an understanding of the outward form and inner workings of nature." (98)

His own view of spirit and mind is to regard them as extremely fine material and spherical atoms — a view nearly identical with that of contemporary science. He found that at death the body does not lose weight and so the atoms must be quite fine. According to the religious and mythical tradition one looked for weight loss as evidence that the soul leaves the body. The soul hypothesis did influence Lucretius' view but he held that body and spirit and mind are all mortal. They are combined so as to constitute a single substance. Our mind ages and we become senile. Only the sum total of the universe is eternal. Again, entropy notwithstanding, this view is quite contemporary.

For the following reasons Lucretius concludes, "Death is nothing to us and no concern of ours."
1. Death is not our concern because the mind is mortal and knows nothing after death.
2. When body and spirit are dissolved we become nothing and so nothing can happen to us further.

3. Nothing can happen to the soul, for the soul cannot exist alone without the body, and body without soul, feels nothing.
4. Even if after death we were to be reassembled into a new body it would not concern *us* because our old identity would be lost – so also we are not now concerned with any previous existence.
5. Nothing can harm us after death for the self will no longer exist and so cannot suffer any longer.
6. Those who think there will be punishment after death are wrong for we will not then be able to experience sensation. Such a man falsely thinks that he can witness and visualize his own funeral, that as an onlooker he can suffer after death.
7. There is no reason to mourn the dead man for he has returned to peace and sleep. Lucretius' view here abuses the notion of peace and sleep.
8. We speak erroneously and even humorously by speaking of death as if it were a state of life:

> "Men often talk . . . when they recline at a banquet, goblet in hand and brow decked with garlands: 'How all too short are these good times that come to us poor creatures! Soon they will be past and gone, and there will be no recalling them.' You would think the crowning calamity in store for them after death was to be parched and shrivelled by a tormenting thirst or oppressed by some other vain desire."

9. In sleep we do not miss ourselves or sigh for life. We could not do so in death. Lucretius regards death as having less existence than does sleep. His view that death and sleep are on a continuum would seem to be mistaken. One survives sleep to call it sleep and so we are aware of it. One is not thought to survive death in the same way, especially because, on Lucretius' view, consciousness dies.
10. If you lived well and had your fill of life you would leave life willingly as a guest leaves a party; if you have not lived happily why go on to add to your unhappiness? This view seems unsound. If one lives well it would seem that he

would especially not want to give up life. If one lives poorly he may still seek to find life worthwhile in some way.

11. Life becomes repetitious and so life should not be prolonged indefinitely. "Do you expect me to invent some new contrivance for your pleasure? I tell you, there is none." Thus death is a way to end such boredom. Again this reasoning seems unsound. If one is bored one must learn how not to be bored. One does not cure a disease by killing the patient. If, however, one is incurably bored and can in no way find life satisfactory he may choose death. That does not mean he would even then welcome it to come if he has not chosen it.

12. Death allows progress. The old give up their jobs and place to make way for the young. This is like the evolutionist's position. On this view death would seem to be a concern of ours, for it assumes we desire progress, e.g., of the race or culture. But it is hard to be consoled merely by the thought that there will be progress. One will no longer be around to enjoy such progress.

13. We were not concerned with the eternity before we were born, why should we be concerned with the eternity after we die?

    On this view one might be less afraid to return to a state one was once in. It is not clear, however, that our state before birth is the same as our state after death. One may wonder about the nature or supra-nature of both "states." Certainly one need not fear the nothingness of pre-natal existence because that stands behind him. But he may nevertheless fear the apparent nothingness of death. Eternity, in either case, would be nothing to fear.

14. Death comes to all regardless of status or occupation. This view reminds us of the medieval dance of death according to which death is seen as the great democratic leveler who takes all regardless of rank, position, or beauty.

15. The torments we think take place after death are only present ones: "As for all those torments that are said to take place in the depths of Hell, they are actually present here and now, in our own lives." This is a strong anti-religious, anti-metaphysical statement showing Lucretius' stress on reason and common sense.

It is almost incredible to believe that the majority of people still believe in the myths of an afterlife. It would seem that honesty and inquiry never were man's greatest attributes. We invent new troubles rather than attend to our present ones. Lucretius wants to reconcile us to death because it is natural and inevitable. Like contemporary psychiatrists, he seeks to help us to die willingly and easily. To do so is thought to be a proper adjustment, the pragmatic thing to do. But many of Lucretius' arguments are unsound and unconvincing. Because of this it is questionable whether Lucretius could honestly die easily. Nor is it clear that death is natural and inevitable. It happens, and we cannot now in terms of the present state of knowledge stop death from taking place. Disease is natural too, but we have managed to curb and eliminate it. Death may, then, rather be something not to take as inevitable and with soporific ease, but rather as a challenge to knowledge and inquiry, as something to overcome. Lucretius seems to hint at this when he says,

"This dread and darkness of the mind cannot be dispelled by the sunbeams, the shining shafts of day, but only by an understanding of the outward form and inner workings of nature."

Lucretius. *On the Nature of the Universe* R. Latham, trans. Baltimore, Maryland: Penguin Books, 1951 esp. Book III "Life and Mind."

Marcus Aurelius

Marcus Aurelius (121-180) in his *Meditations* presents the following views regarding death, and emotions concerning death — and life. Do not be concerned with trivial matters. (9) Be concerned with intelligent purposive action rather than with reputation. (14) Most of what men do and say is unnecessary. (39) Always ask, "Why am I doing this?" (39) One of the reasons for not being concerned with trivial things is that because man must die he should make every minute of his life meaningful. He wrote, "Do every act of your life as if it were the last." (20) Turn every situation into a positive one. (53) If life ceases to be meaningful or if it is not within your power to enjoy life you may still commit suicide:

> "It is in your power to live here. But if men do not permit you, then get away out of life . . ." (54); "Let men see, let them know a real man who lives according to nature. If they cannot endure him, let them kill him. For that is better than to live thus [as men do]." (114, 93)

The above statements are superior to those of the existentialists for the latter advise even traumatically facing death to then be able to live a more meaningful life, but give no idea of how to live such a life. Aurelius does give some guides. One way is not to be concerned about trivia, another is to prevent traumatic emotional experiences, another is to be rational and realistic, another is to see how to cope with and understand one's negative emotions. Another way involves the rejection of metaphysics and superstition (miracles, incantations to drive away demons, etc.) (9):

51

"Do you think that a false opinion has less power than the bile in the jauncided or the poison in him who is bitten by a mad dog?" (69)

One caution with the above statements about suicide is that it is often people who are deranged who commit suicide. It is certainly an option which one should be aware that he has. That if things get too bad one can commit suicide. But when would life get so bad? Isn't it always possible that by reassessing the situation, one's needs, values, outlook, that one could find ways to make life once again valuable. Unmarried pregnant youths, jilted lovers, etc. have committed suicide because they thought their problems too great to continue living. This seems not to be the case. Aurelius was not unaware of this problem for he saw that man often imagines things to be worse than they are. It may well be a rare case in which rational suicide is justifiable. The point may be merely that it is consoling to know that if things did ever get intolerably bad one has the option to die. In addition, in this case death would not be feared.

Aurelius suggests that man pursue philosophy. (9) This involves careful, ongoing inquiry, realistic acceptance of the laws of nature and being intent on what we are actually doing rather than on theoretical considerations. The view is very close to that of ordinary-language philosophy on this point. He wrote,

"What then is that which is able to conduct a man? One thing and only one, philosophy." (24) "Examine methodologically and truly every object which is presented to you in life . . ." (31) But he offers a qualification directed against superstition and metaphysics, "I did not fall into the hands of any sophist, and I did not waste my time on writers [of histories], or in the resolution of syllogisms, or occupy myself about the investigation of appearances in the heavens." (16, 85)

The ordinary-language philosophy element comes in his concern with the purpose of the present action performed or language actually spoken and his stress on that which is in front of our eyes but which we often fail to see due to our over-theorizing or over-imagining. In one important sense we know all about death. It is something like our observing a leaf falling from a tree. On this point Aurelius states,

"Use plain discourse." (90)
"Be intent only on that which you are now doing and on the instrument by which you do it." (106)
"He who has seen present things has seen all." (65)
"Everything which happens is as familiar and well known as the rose in spring and the fruit in summer; for such is disease, and death, calumny, and treachery, and whatever else delights fools or vexes them." (42)

Our notions of death then must be related to and reduced to paradigms of what we know of what is present before us in the here and now. For example, we can only know and speak of death in terms of our present use of "plain discourse." The reduction to the common and everyday is one interpretation of what is meant by Aurelius' stress on living according to nature. (15)

Perhaps Aurelius' main insight is that if we learn how to understand our emotions we will be able to live a happier life, prevent negative emotions from arising and be better able to cope with the experience of dying and death. His view of emotions seems to be close to my view that they are largely assessments or judgments which guide feelings. If our statements are rational, realistic, and well thought out we will avoid negative emotions. "Tranquillity is nothing else than the good ordering of the mind." (34) Thus if one's view of cause-effect, and the laws of nature, are clear then he can accept such facts realistically and so better assess and accept reality so as to induce realistic and positive emotions. If one does not understand how he thinks, how emotions work, he will be unhappy. (21) The stress is on promoting "good emotions and good actions." (56) By "good" emotions he means emotions such as love. He says, "To care for all men is according to man's nature." (28) This is perhaps to say that it would be irrational and self-defeating if we did not concern ourselves with and cooperate with our fellow man.

"We are made for co-operation . . . To act against one another then is contrary to nature." (19) "Love mankind." (74) "Be cheerful in all situations." (12) "Develop a sense of humor." (12)

Some "bad" emotions which he thinks it irrational to have are anger, disgust, discouragement, dissatisfaction, fear. (11, 19, 49) We should not be angry if another, even mistakenly, finds fault with us, but rather merely attempt to find the cause of the agitation and correct the cause. (11)

"No joining others in their wailing, no violent emotion." (75)

One must learn to realistically assess and so induce only positive feelings. One must learn to accept his nature as well as that which is and that which is not within his power to change. (47, 28, 105) If one does not expect unrealistically and if one is satisfied with what is, he will avoid irrational fears and negative emotions. (31)

He advises us to accept even those who do wrong, because they do wrong only out of ignorance (73, 10):

"Begin the morning by saying to yourself, I shall meet with the busybody, the ungrateful, arrogant, deceitful, envious, unsocial. All these things happen to them by reason of their ignorance of what is good and evil." (19) "He who does wrong does wrong against himself." (99)

It is self-defeating to do wrong.

His views are similar in many ways to those of the therapist, Albert Ellis (*Reason and Emotion*) for both agree to the following:

"Things do not touch the soul, for they are external and remain immovable; but our perturbations come only from the opinion which is within." (35) "It is our own opinions which disturb us." (128)

Aurelius' statements are almost direct expressions and possible sources of Ellis' "ABC Theory" according to which emotional problems are not caused by the event but by our irrational thought concerning the event. Aurelius wrote,

"If you are pained by an external thing it is not this thing that disturbs you, but your own judgment about it." (93)
"Cast out all trouble, for it was not outside, but within and in my opinions." (101)
"Take away your opinion, and then there is taken away the complaint, 'I have been harmed.' Take away the complaint 'I have been harmed,' and the harm is taken away." (36)
"You must blame nobody. For if you can, correct [that which is the cause]; but if you cannot do this, correct at least the thing itself; but if you cannot do even this, of what use is it to you to find fault? For nothing should be done without a purpose." (88)

To blame is, according to Ellis, one of the basic irrational ideas which leads to emotional problems.
Man has the power to bear and change almost anything. (52) He makes himself what he chooses to be. (123) Ellis also stresses the view that man can to a large extent alter and change his emotions. He states that one of the most irrational ideas preventing a patient from overcoming emotional disorder is the view that one's emotions cannot be changed. If, however, emotions are largely assessments one can change one's emotions by changing one's assessments.
Ellis would also agree with the following:

"A cucumber is bitter — Throw it away. — There are briars in the road — Turn aside from them. — This is enough. Do not add, And why were such things made in the world?" (94)
"Say nothing more to yourself than what the first appearances report.. Suppose that it has been reported to you that a certain person speaks ill of you. This has been reported; but that you have been injured, that has not been reported." (93)

It is only our imagination which fabricates reality and gives us baseless fears, anxieties, and dread. "Wipe out the imagination. Stop the pulling of the strings. Confine yourself to the present." (74)

Be rational at all times. (10) Constantly question and inquire regarding all important matters. (12) Accept reality as it is. (24) This is what it means to pursue philosophy.

By accepting the facts we now know concerning death we may be able to face death without much negative emotion such as fear or dread. We must supposedly accept as an absolute fact that we must die and that it is necessary to do so.

"Everything is so constituted by nature as to die." (114) It is necessary that man die. (36) We must accept the fact that man is of flesh and bone and will die. (19)

But it is not clear that it is a necessary law of the universe that man must die. Some bacteria and other living things can apparently be kept alive indefinitely. Perhaps with research man will one day be able to achieve immortality. Aurelius is certainly correct in asserting that in terms of what man now knows, man must die. Because scientific inquiry is stressed by Aurelius one would guess that he would give support to the attempt to gain immortality. At one time certain diseases seemed to be necessary and required acceptance. They are now no longer regarded as necessary or as fatal. For emotional stability, however, one must at the present time assess death as inevitable but he must also clarify what could be meant by the term "death."

Marcus Aurelius presents a number of questionable arguments as to why one should accept death:

1. Death is a natural happening and so it is neither good nor bad. (22)

But we do regard some natural happenings as bad, e.g., disease. Also it is not at all clear what is meant by "natural." One could say it is "natural" to have great fears. Perhaps, but it is not necessary to do so. To say we must accept death for the present because we cannot as yet do anything about it is, of course, a rational assessment.

2. Death is neither good nor bad, because it happens to good and bad men alike. (22)

This is to say merely that death is indifferent to good and evil. It does not follow that death itself is neither good nor bad.

3. Because man lives but a short time he should not worry, because that is not much to lose. (23) (44)

It is not much for all of time to lose but for man it is all the time there is. For man all is lost. The argument depends on an equivocation.

4. Death is merely a dissolution of elements and because no harm can be done to changing elements and it is natural for elements to change, man should not worry about death. (24)

It would rather follow that the elements should not worry about death. Man may think that because something is natural it is therefore good. But disease is natural. It is another thing to see that what is natural is inevitable. But not all that is natural is inevitable.

5. At death one will no longer be a slave to his emotions. (27)

In the first place Aurelius has already shown us ways in which to prevent having negative emotions. Secondly this argument is like that of suggesting that suicide is a way to cure a disease. One will not be around to have emotions to be or not be a slave to.

6. "Nothing will happen to me which is not conformable to the nature of the universe." (50)

Again it may be assumed that what is natural is necessary, inevitable, and good. Why should man be comforted just because something is natural. Also it is not clear what is natural. Certainly what happens, happens, but we may be able to have some rather than other "natural" things happen.

7. One may even prepare for death by experiencing small losses. (52)

This would not be the case in the sense that death is not a loss to the one who dies. But by experiencing losses one may consider what losses are involved in dying, that death will come, that nothing remains the same.

8. "He who fears death either fears the loss of sensation

or a different kind of sensation. But if you have no sensation, neither will you feel any harm; and if you acquire another kind of sensation, you will be a different kind of living being and you will not cease to live." (96)

It is not consoling to know that if one has no sensation he need fear no harm. It is the loss of sensation which is not desired.

One reason why these arguments are not emotionally satisfying is that they are not all good arguments. What is needed are more careful, realistic arguments which may then properly guide emotions toward death and dying. And to say this is to give support to Aurelius' argument that to properly adjust to death without negative emotions one must realistically inquire into death and emotions.

The views of Epicurus, Epictetus and Marcus Aurelius may be seen in the following poem by John Dryden (1631-1700):

Against the Fear of Death

What has this bugbear Death to frighten man,
If souls can die, as well as bodies can?
For, as before our birth we felt no pain,
When Punic arms infested land and main,
When heaven and earth were in confusion hurl'd
For the debated empire of the world,
Which awed with dreadful expectation lay,
Soon to be slaves, uncertain who should sway:
So, when our mortal frame shall be disjoin'd,
The lifeless lump uncoupled from the mind,
From sense of grief and pain we shall be free;
We shall not feel, because we shall not be.
Though earth in seas, and seas in heaven were lost,
We should not move, we only should be toss'd.
Nay, e'en supposed when we have suffered fate
The soul should feel in her divided state,
What's that to us? for we are only we,
While souls and bodies in our frame agree.
Nay, though our atoms should revolve by chance,
And matter leap into the former dance;

Though time our life and motion could restore,
And make our bodies what they were before,
What gain to us would all this bustle bring?
The new-made man would be another thing.
When once an interrupting pause is made,
That individual being is decay'd.
We, who are dead and gone, shall bear no part
In all the pleasures, nor shall feel the smart,
Which to that other mortal shall accrue,
Whom to our matter time shall mold anew.
For backward if you look on that long space
Of ages past, and view the changing face
Of matter, toss'd and variously combin'd
In sundry shapes, 'tis easy for the mind
From thence to infer, that seeds of things have been
In the same order as they now are seen:
Which yet our dark remembrance cannot trace,
Because a pause of life, a gaping space,
Has come betwixt, where memory lies dead,
And all the wandering motions from the sense are fled.
For whosoe'er shall in misfortunes live,
Must be, when those misfortunes shall arrive;
And since the man who is not, feels not woe,
(For death exempts him, and wards off the blow,
Which we, the living, only feel and bear,)
What is there left for us in death to fear?
When once that pause of life has come between
'Tis just the same as we had never been.

Marcus Aurelius. *The Meditations of the Emperor Marcus Aurelius Antoninus* George Long, trans., New York: Doubleday (numbers refer to pages)

Humanism

Although there is perhaps no rigid humanistic view of death the general view has been presented by Corliss Lamont. It involves the following beliefs:

1. Immortality is an illusion. Belief in immortality is a dishonest belief for which there is no evidence. Lamont agrees with John Dewey who states, "Religion is the opium of peoples." (Lamont 1965) The belief in immortality is a mere superstition arising out of man's desire to live forever. All supernaturalism, personal immortality, and conscious survival are rejected. Life after death is an impossibility.

Lamont's conclusion that life after death is an impossibility is too strong. It is enough to say that there is no evidence for an afterlife. But what is also meant is that the notion of immortality and an afterlife is unintelligible.

2. Belief in immortality or an afterlife is harmful. Christianity has made man disregard this life in favor of the next, thereby causing great suffering and inhumanity to man and nature. By accepting this life as the only one, humanists think that man will make it a better world to live in, instead of mere preparation for the next life. Lamont cited the following typical instance from *The New York Times* (Sept. 11, 1950): Monsignor William Green said as reported, "Sorrowing parents whose sons have been drafted for combat duty were told yesterday in St. Patrick's Cathedral that death in battle was part of God's plan for populating the kingdom of heaven." (Lamont 1967) Since one need no longer bother about an afterlife he can spend more time and energy making this life better. One may, for example, attempt to increase man's present lifespan. To prolong healthy life is regarded as a humane idea but, "It is best

61

not only to disbelieve in immortality, but to *believe in mortality*." (Lamont 1965)

3. Death is a natural event and is in accordance with our scientific views of it. It is a part of biological evolution, and life comes to an end. The material ingredients of the body, alone survive.

The view that death is an end or natural scientific event has been criticized in connection with Lucretius' view of death. It can be dogmatic to say that death is a natural event. Our knowledge of elementary particles is not well enough developed to allow us to state exactly what happens when the body dies. Also there are conceptual confusions involved in saying that death is an end. "End" only applies within our experience. Humanists, including John Dewey, take science too literally. One can hold the doctrines of science as tenaciously and dogmatically as any other area of knowledge. What is needed is a careful philosophical analysis of scientific concepts such as time, mass, energy, etc. The "scientific method" is well-known among philosophers of science, to be a fiction. Scientists use all kinds of methods, intuitions, metaphors and models.

In this respect philosophy and the philosophy of science examine the concepts and methods of science, they do not just assume or presuppose them. But such a distinction need not be made. Both areas may work together. As Corliss Lamont and John Dewey are both philosophers it is likely that they would agree with the above remarks.

4. Death is needed for man to evolve. We need to die for the sake of our descendants.

This may have been true for us to have reached our present state of being but it need not be true in regard to the future. There is no necessity that we die for the sake of our descendants.

5. There is social immortality. One can only survive in the sense that his deeds will have affected society. Lamont hopes that science will advance to ensure the immortality of the human race.

6. Our present funeral practices are inadequate to the extent that they are based on superstition, religious or otherwise. If there is no future life we need not be concerned about the dead, but our present practices seem more concerned about the dead than the living.

"Where the impact of death may be lessened, for many, is in a change in the accepted manner of disposing of dead bodies and in the customs of mourning. In these matters we are still to a large extent barbaric." (Lamont 1965) Besides being based on superstition he finds our burial practices are unintelligent in that they use up valuable land for cemeteries, cost too much, (especially for those who do not have enough money to live on), try to unnecessarily preserve the body for viewing, are too lavish and undignified. Thus he instead proposes a simple, dignified, inexpensive funeral, preferably cremation to burial, and not church connected unless the person is religious. He adds, "The proposal, however, to do away with funeral services entirely does not seem sound." (Lamont 1965) But funeral practices should be based on an informed and intelligent philosophy of death.

The Humanists often establish memorial societies in order to provide a low cost but dignified and intelligent funeral for its members.

7. Our emotions concerning the dead should be rational and intelligent. "We cannot rationally feel sorry for the dead person himself, since he is non-existent and can know neither sorrow nor gladness." (Lamont 1965) Any ritual performed should have a rational basis in man's relationship to other men and to nature. It should be a humane ritual rather than based on religious illusions of an afterlife, eternal punishment, hell, etc.

The Humanist is often called a rationalist. The journal, *The American Rationalist* presents the following as its program:

"The American Rationalist — (1) regards reason and the scientific method as the only tools for the solution of human problems, (2) [favors] the democratic way of life, (3) believes [in] a complete separation of church and State, (4) believes [in] free public education . . . in a secular manner and . . . "fully functioning personalities," (5) believes that civilization can be improved only if conscientious citizens are informed about and willing to combat all forms of political, religious, social and economic tyranny." The view is often presented that the church should not be tax exempt. People are encouraged to give money and make out wills to rational, intelligent institutions which will help advance mankind, rather than give to the church. The millions now given to the churches could then go toward feeding the poor, improving education and knowledge of oneself and one's environment, increasing our knowledge of death and dying, etc.

Close to the humanist position is that of the Humanistic Psychologist, Rational Psychotherapist and the extensive work of the Institute for Rational Living (New York). Their view stresses a rational approach to death and dying and attempts to promote honest, factual inquiry into these concepts. The following is presented by Albert Ellis in his article, "The Case Against Religion." Religion is seen to be a faith not founded on fact, a belief in a superhuman power to be worshipped, etc. Ellis finds religion to be "pernicious, . . . for virtually all the commonly accepted goals of emotional health are antithetical to a truly religious viewpoint." He finds that the religious person is masochistic and denies himself, is unable to be independent and self-sufficient, is intolerant due to his absolute beliefs, is usually blindly obedient, is unable to truly accept himself due to the belief that one is guilty from birth and a sinner and so deserving severe punishment, dehumanizes himself by belief in an inhuman absolute law, by damning himself and others creates emotional disorder, dishonestly imagines absolutes and perfection instead of facing the risk of imperfection and chance which daily confront us, does not allow for intellectually and emotionally necessary flexibility, inquiry and openness because of a belief in absolute truth; is thus "bigoted." The religious person by accepting an absolute moral code based on "authority" is prevented from using his intelligence to decide what in fact is right or wrong, harmful or beneficial. The religious person is unscientific. Science and religion are in significant conflict. Ellis states,

"Religious commitment tends to be (a) obsessive-compulsive, motivated by anxiety and dire need rather than joy-giving desire; (b) opposed to other beneficial commitments, such as to sex-love relations, to science or to art; (c) guilt-ridden or hostile; (d) based on falsehoods and illusions (e.g., rewards in heaven and punishments in hell) and therefore easily shatterable and prone to cause severe disillusionments; and (e) fanatical and over-compensatory, masking the individual's underlying feelings of extreme inadequacy."

He states, "True believers in just about *any* kind of orthodoxy — whether it be religious, political, social, or even artistic orthodoxy — tend to be distinctly disturbed, since they are obviously rigid, fanatic, and dependent individuals. . . . Religiosity, in my estimation, is another name for narrow - mindedness, emotional disturbance, or neurosis. Or, in some extreme cases, psychosis."

The reader will no doubt wish to discount these statements without further examination. Certainly Ellis has put his case boldly. But there is no substitute for the careful examination of each of the accusations he makes. One may, for example, compare his statements with those presented in the chapter of this book on death and religion. As to the religious person being neurotic or even psychotic one may refer to the statement made by Freedman and Kaplan:

"The ecstatic states occurring in acute schizophrenia are related to the ecstatic transports of religious mysticism. The mystical experience, whether religious or not, possesses certain distinguishing qualities:
1. *Ineffability.* The subject often insists that his experience is inexpressible and indescribable . . .
2. *Noesis.* The subject has the feeling that the mystery of the universe has been plumbed . . . Along with this may go a curious sense of authority, the conviction that one is privileged to lead and to command . . .
3. *Transiency.* The actual mystical state may last only a moment . . . Yet it is as unforgettable as it is highly treasured, and it colors all subsequent activity.
4. *Passivity.* In the mystical state there is an abeyance of the will, as if the subject were in the grip of a superior power to whose direction he is highly responsive.
5. *Unio Mystica.* There is a sense of mystic unity with an infinite power, an oceanic feeling in which opposites are reconciled, in which there are 'darknesses that dazzle' and 'voices of silence.' "

It is thus seen that there is a close and often identical relation between the neurotic or psychotic and some religious people.

Roger Callahan in *Rational Living,* a journal of the Institute for Rational Living, presents a paradigm case to show that it is not impossible to live without religious faith and concludes that it is, in fact, the rational thing to do. A woman, after careful inquiry, gave up her religious faith, became an atheist, and even in the face of death found no need to return to her religious faith. Callahan also suggests that we use rational rather than religious or irrational approaches to understanding and coping with death. He suggests that we encourage medical research to extend a healthy old age and perhaps by scientific research even death can be conquered:

"Fear of mortality can be relieved with certain rational hopes based on scientific facts, in place of the irrational, unscientific faiths in reincarnation, the disembodied soul, and similar bromides — which only serve to neurotically perpetuate further anxieties."

Paul Travis in *Rational Living* gives what he thinks to be a rational approach to death. It involves disposing of the body with a minimum of expense, donating needed organs to patients, donating one's body to medical science, leaving one's money to research or worthy causes. He details the way in which this may be done.

Roger Callahan. "Overcoming Religious Faith: A Case History" *Rational Living* 2 (1967) 16-21

John Dewey. "Introduction" *The Illusion of Immortality* Corliss Lamont, New York: F. Unger 1965 (1935)

Albert Ellis. "The Case Against Religion" *Mensa Journal* no. 138 (Sept. 1970). See also his "Humanism and Psychotherapy: A Revolutionary Approach" *The Humanist* 1972

Alfred Freedman and Harold Kaplan. *Diagnosing Mental Illness* New York: Atheneum 1972 pp. 170-171

Corliss Lamont. "The Crisis Called Death" *Humanist* 27, 1 (1967)

—————. *The Illusion of Immortality* New York: F. Unger 1965 (1935)

Paul Travis. "A Rational Approach to Death" *Rational Living* 3 no. 2 (1968) 1-8

The American Rationalist 4124 West 26th St. Chicago, Ill. 60623

Wittgenstein

I. *Tractatus*

6.431 ". . . At death the world does not alter, but comes to an end."

Thus it is difficult to imagine one's own death, . . . to imagine the world and experience coming to an end. Absolute nothingness or an absolute end .seems not to be within our experience. Of another's death we can say his world alters. We are conscious of it altering. But we cannot say of our death that it alters, because "alter" implies "alters for my consciousness," and there supposedly is no consciousness. I can alter only from the viewpoint of another. But at death my consciousness of the viewpoint of another comes to an end also. What is meant by "end" here must remain in question. The end of life is not necessarily like the end of a road or end of a trip. It may be more like the end of knowing or more carefully, an unknown sort of end. It is the end of that which determines that there are ends in the first place. It is a paradoxical ending.

6.4311 "Death is not an event in life: we do not live to experience death.

If we take eternity to mean not infinite temporal duration but timelessness, then eternal life belongs to those who live in the present.

Our life has no end in just the way in which our visual field has no limits."

*Paper presented at the May 1973 Symposium "Philosophical Aspects of Thanatology" sponsored by the Foundation of Thanatology and the College of Physicians and Surgeons, Columbia University.

That death is not an event in life and so cannot be experienced reminds us of his statements, "What we cannot speak about we must pass over in silence," (7.) and "The limits of my language mean the limits of my world." (5.6) We cannot talk about or perhaps even name it for it is not clear what we are naming. We have experienced being unconscious or asleep and we think death must be like that. We think this in our conscious life. We do not think this out of consciousness. In a sense death is only something within life, in opposition to Wittgenstein's statement that death is not an event in life.

His statement "We do not live to experience death," is circular. It reduces to "We do not experience to experience." That is, we do not experience non-experience. It would seem that the one thing we certainly cannot experience is non-experience. But then we cannot phrase this statement meaningfully because "non-experience" has no use, no meaning for us. We want to talk of absolute non-experience where we only experience qualitative and relative degrees of experience.

"Our life has no end in just the way in which our visual field has no limits," may suggest that the notion of limit or end (of life) is not perceivable. We never experience the boundary of vision or of life. One might say in this regard that concerning death there is much to draw on and little to draw on. Our paradigms or analogies for the nature of death are all models within our experience. Even to speak of "within" and "outside" our experience presupposes a picture or model which we have. This yields a paradox or puzzle. We are creating metaphors for death.

> "If we take eternity to mean not infinite temporal duration but timelessness, then eternal life belongs to those who live in the present." (6.4311)

This statement suggests that time is some thing in itself and independent of change, that if time stops or is no more we live "forever" or "always in the present." But if there is no time there is no "forever" or "always" "present." But I think Wittgenstein's statement is partly correct and furthermore that we do live in a timeless world. (Shibles "Timelessness")

We never have evidence for time as such. Time only refers to a change of objects or a relation of changes of objects. We see the movement or change of hands of a clock against the face of the clock. In "timing" a race, for example, we merely compare clock changes with the change of the runner. There is not time as such, and no time enters into the situation at all. Time and time words reduce to relations of changes. "Time" is an elliptical word referring merely to change. We thus live in a timeless world. Past, present, and future, are merely different types of changes. There is no past, present, or future as such. And so there is not even a present for Wittgenstein to refer to. We could not even ask how long the present is or ask when the future becomes the present or the past. There is no such thing as eternity or infinity. Both of these are experiences within our experience, not outside of it. We often equate obscure terms because they share obscurity or are alike in being obscure. Thus we say that death is infinite or eternal nothingness.

But this is outside of our knowledge. There is no absolute eternity or infinity, not even in mathematics. They always reduce to some concrete event or are modeled after a concrete event within experience. Even to speak of "within" or "outside of" experience here is taken from a model and gives rise to a paradox. That is, it makes no sense to talk of an "outside of" experience. To do so is to talk of there being no experience. And to speak of there being no experiences is still to speak of something within experience. "No experience" is still within experience. All negations are relative, not absolute, and so negations refer to real contexts. To report there being an absence is not to report absolute nothingness but to report an actual and real configuration of events. There must first be something for it to be absent and it must be absent from a particular situation and it must be somewhere else or in some other form. It is not absence as such. There is no absolute negation, absence, nothingness. Nothing can be only where something could be. There cannot be nothing where something could never be.

Wittgenstein concludes above, "Eternal life belongs to those who live in the present."

On the view that time is change of objects, this statement could only mean that one lives in a world of different types of change, not in a world of time. But the statement suggests that one can be "eternal" in the "present." This is wrong. The changes we know without time are the same as the changes we know with time, because there is no time. The changes are just the same. The change we mean by the present is different from the changes we mean by the future. In other words "eternal" change is not "present" change and it makes no sense to say that in a timeless world "eternal life belongs to those who live in the present."

To say this only means that there is no time, that one only lives with various experienced changes of events and objects outside of which he can say nothing. He therefore should perhaps make the most of such experiences.

> 6.4312 "Not only is there no guarantee of the temporal immortality of the human soul, that is to say of its eternal survival after death; but, in any case, this assumption completely fails to accomplish the purpose for which it has always been intended. Or is some riddle solved by my surviving for ever? Is not this eternal life itself as much a riddle as our present life? The solution of the riddle of life in space and time lies *outside* space and time. (It is certainly not the solution of any problems of natural science that is required.)"

The question about eternal life is a metaphysical and meaningless question because it is not a question that makes sense within our experience. It is not a question which can arise for us in some situation which confronts us. Our problems are not outside of our experience but within it. "Eternal survival after death" is meaningless language which has no use. Thus the question as to whether such survival is guaranteed or not makes no sense. It is not the sort of question that can have an answer. Or perhaps the answer to such a question would be, "It has no answer," "It is not a question," or even that since the question is outside our experience the answer is outside our experience also. "The solution to the riddle of life" lies outside of life. And of course we cannot know that this is the case either.

To speak of "outside our experience" has no use. What would it mean to say, "I am outside of my experience"? What kind of riddle could this be? How could one understand it, much less solve it?

To speak of it as Wittgenstein does, as a problem or riddle which "lies *outside* space and time" is misleading. Space is a metaphysical, i.e., obscure term. It does not refer to an entity in itself but can only refer to or be elliptical for things and relations of things. There is not space in a vacuum but a vacuum is removal of air and a relation between objects. There is no space as such between objects. Thus one cannot go "outside" space or stay "inside" space. Nor, if space refers to objects, can one go outside of our world of objects, for it would make no sense to "go" "there."

The fallacy of assuming that there is space as such, absolute space or absolute places was shown by Zeno's brilliant analysis of the paradoxes involved. (Shibles "Zeno") The paradoxes vanish when space is no longer regarded as an entity in itself or as absolute. Some of the paradoxes are also resolved when it is seen that time isn't a thing or entity but is relations of changes of objects.

To speak about something "outside" of time makes no sense if there is no such thing as time in itself. There is no time to be inside of or outside of. If time is merely relations of changes of objects or events, then to be outside of objects and events is no good because objects and events comprise the only world we know. There is then no "outside" of space and time such that "The solution of the riddle of life in space and time lies *outside* space and time."

The difficulty of intelligibly speaking of an outside of experience or life also suggests a difficulty of speaking of an "inside" of life. And in addition we find it difficult to really understand and account for phenomena and events which are "in" life. Thus it is not clearly the case that though we don't know what death is as "outside" our experience we do know that we die "within" our experience.

Many of our concepts seem to be confused, misleading, category - mistakes, naming fallacies, etc. If we cannot explain how perception works or what thinking is or how it relates to physiology, what subatomic particles really are, perhaps an almost total restructuring of our world is possible, new Copernican and scientific revolutions are possible. Such reconsiderations, especially by means of careful, well analyzed, conceptual clarifications, many of which are now available in contemporary philosophy, philosophical psychology and the philosophy of science, could greatly revise our notion of the nature of death. This book is a step in this direction.

Thus the question of eternal life and death raises at the same time questions about the nature of life. Wittgenstein put it in the quotation given earlier, "Is not this eternal life itself as much of a riddle as our present life?"

II. "Lectures on Religious Belief" (1966)

"An Austrian general said to someone: "I shall think of you after my death, if that should be possible? We can imagine one group who would find this ludicrous, another who wouldn't." (53)

This statement is perhaps best left uncommented on. We know what and whom it has reference to, at least generally so.

"Suppose you say: 'I have the idea of myself being a chair after death?' " (65) Why is it any less absurd to say I will survive my death? What more evidence is there for the survival of a soul than for one turning into a chair after death? One could imagine a dog-lover wanting to be a dog or a gardener wanting to be soil and its contents. Things may work out better for the gardener.

In speaking of beliefs, Wittgenstein asks how they may be compared with one another. (54) Does it involve grounds or a state of mind? He suggests that the appeal will be to various paradigms or pictures. What is offered for a belief, e.g., for an afterlife, may be what we are willing to stake on the belief, that there is "retribution," or the idea that "This will be punished." (54) Our view of an afterlife as well as of death depends on our paradigms, models, and metaphors.

"Are you clear when you'd say you had ceased to exist?" (65)

"I ceased to exist at all" has no use or intelligible meaning. We often talk about life after death as if we were talking about ourselves in the past, as if we could witness our own funeral.

"We are all here using the word 'death,' which is a public instrument, which has a whole technique [of usage]." (68-69)

When we talk of death we are not talking of an unknown or the other side of life but of techniques or uses of our language in a concrete situation of our life. The meaning of the words of death and afterlife are uses in a living language-game. Since there is no death on this view, there is no living and so this becomes simply, the meaning of a word is its use in a language-game, i.e., as determined by the structure and nature of the language and as determined by a concrete context, situation ("game"). "Death" is not a private or mental term, something I alone picture, but a term which we have learned in the context of an intersubjective situation. The use of this word is an intersubjective use.

" 'My idea of death is the separation of the soul from the body' — if we know what to do with the words." (69)

That is, these words have no use. They do not matter. They solve no problem, answer no question and do not serve as a description, nor are they usually used for such purposes as to greet people with. However, they *may* be used to greet someone with, to put him at ease. Two people may utter sentences of this sort often until they become familar sounding, and such sentences may be used to create a friendship. Two people learned to talk in a similar way. They may even envisage a "soul" in the same way, e.g., as a cloudy sort of object having wings. But "the soul separates from the body" seems like our common expression "give up the ghost." "The soul separates from the body" is not like "The cover separates from the book," or "The oil separates from the water." This sort of separation of soul from body is not the sort of thing one can learn. It is only a verbal technique or use and cannot serve as a description. It has no descriptive use or function. It may have a consoling function, however.

"If he connects  with death, and this was his idea, this might be interesting psychologically." (69)

In trying to conceive of death we make analogies to pictures or objects or things associated with what we imagine death and dying to be. To describe death we use such models or metaphors as darkness, absence, unfulfillment, abyss, etc. Our models of death are within our experience and so constitute their object rather than merely illustrate it. They say something about us, something psychological. "The whole weight may be in the picture." (72) Death may be seen as black chaos, scattered burnt-out feelings, used up thoughts, a scribble, one's electrons though scattered continuing to circle their microscopic orbs.

In presenting a Wittgensteinian analysis of death R. Liveritte points out that to be ill is not to be dying. To say someone is dying is a guess. Also a person cannot die, because it is not something he can do or not do. If it were something I could do, I could supposedly refuse to do it. I can only know that I am ill, not that I am dying. Thus I cannot experience "pangs of death." Liveritte states, "My death is not an event in my life that I can avoid or not avoid." (p. 29) We can thus become misled by confusing pictures.

> " 'The separation of soul from body' . . . If he says this,
> I won't know yet what consequences he will draw. I don't
> know what he opposes this to." (Wittgenstein p. 69)

Another way of showing that "the soul separates from the body," has no use is to see that nothing follows from such a view and that one might hold that the reverse is the case without consequence either. Some do say, "Well what else could happen then if the soul doesn't separate from the body?" It stays in it? It dies too? Some other invisible thing (non-existent existent) separates from the body? Nothing would seem to verify, falsify, or count against having a soul and the claim that the soul separates from the body. Soul as such, is valueless, makes no distinctions, serves no purpose, leads to no consequences. It does not serve well as a regulative idea or useful fiction. John Dewey stated similarly that the meaning of a word is its consequences, and so in this case if soul has no consequences, if it does nothing and clarifies nothing, it is a meaningless metaphysical term. It may, of course, have trivial uses, e.g., a use as a word in a religious book or a use to refer to pictures one might draw of the soul, or as a term elliptical for the word "life" or for a feeling one has, e.g., of warmth, or *soul may simply refer to those things about man of which we are ignorant.* Strange unintelligible questions arise such as, "Do ants have souls?," "Do only metaphysicians have souls?," "How many souls are there?," "How can a soul move or separate from the body?" Mediaeval man said the soul roots in the body like tree roots and at death the soul roots come out causing much pain.

"If you say to me — 'Do you cease to exist?' — I should be bewildered and not know what exactly this is to mean." (70)

"Suppose someone said: 'What do you believe, Wittgenstein? Are you a sceptic? Do you know whether you will survive death?' I would really, this is a fact, say 'I can't say, I don't know,' because I haven't any clear idea what I'm saying when I'm saying 'I don't cease to exist,' etc." (70)

Being and existence are vague metaphysical terms which are usually based on a naming - fallacy, category - mistake or misleading analogies. "This book is brown, therefore this book *is* or exists" (has being in general), does not follow. "Is" or "exists" is an open-context word meaning anything at all or everything. Thus the sentence could mean, "This book is brown, therefore this book is black," which is false. To follow, "is" or "exists" could only refer to what the antecedent says, namely, "This book is brown therefore this book is brown." And this is trivial. Either exists and Being are vague terms only elliptical for specific instances and meaningless as such, or they are used incorrectly as if they name something in themselves, i.e., they are naming - fallacies. Exist and Being are not proper attributes. To say "I exist," is not to describe anything. It may be elliptical for saying such things as that I am here, I am now awake, or conscious again, I am now successful, etc. "Exist," as such, has no opposite such that it would make sense to ask, as Wittgenstein points out, "Do you cease to exist?" Nothing specific is being referred to and so nothing specific can cease. In addition, the specific kinds of existence we know are "within" our experience such that I would not know what it would mean to say that they are *all* "gone," or what "gone" could mean here. "Do you cease to exist at all?" is not an intelligible use of language, or technique one can learn to use in a descriptive sense or language - game of describing, or in a metaphysical or abstract sense. What could it mean not to exist in every way, or in no particular way, but just abstractly?

What would it mean to say, "I exist abstractly," or "I exist obscurely," but not in any particular context or language - game? It cannot mean something "exactly," for "exact" does not apply. "I exist exactly," gives no help. It is not like "I calculate exactly."

> "A great writer said that, when he was a boy, his father set him a task, and he suddenly felt that nothing, not even death, could take away the responsibility [in doing this task]; this was his duty to do, and that even death couldn't stop it being his duty. He said that this was, in a way, a proof of the immortality of the soul — because if this lives on [the responsibility won't die.] The idea is given by what we call the proof. Well, if this is the idea, [all right]." (70)

This states that by "immortality of the soul" all that is meant is that one feels he has a duty to perform, a responsibility, and the duty is permanent. This is all one may mean by soul and immortality. It is the use of the words, the paradigm-case for their use. Such a use is concrete (excluding the problem of responsibility "living on"). "We associate a particular use with a picture." (71)

"Are eyebrows going to be talked of, in connection with the Eye of God?" (71)

Our models dealing with religious notions of God, death, afterlife, etc., are metaphors. To see that they are metaphors, to enliven the metaphors we expand them. "Eye of God" suggests eyebrows, far- or near-sightedness, blindness, eyelids, etc. When we see the strangeness of the expansion we want to go back to see what made us want to talk of the "Eye of God." Compare "The Eye of God," "The eye of a potato," "The eye of a button," "The eye of eternity," "The eye of St. Nick," "The eyebrow of a potato," "The eyebrow of a button." It would make sense to speak of an eyebrow of a potato or buttonhole but not in the same way as the eye, or the eyebrow of eternity, or God. Eternity or God are meaningless in abstraction or description but may have concrete uses such as when one utters "God" when he is in great trouble, just as he might utter "Help!" If no one is there to help we invent someone: God.

"Suppose someone, before going to China, when he might never see me again, said to me: 'We might see one another after death' — would I necessarily say that I don't understand him? I might say [want to say] simply, 'Yes, I *understand* him entirely.'" (70-71)

The understanding involved here is the understanding of a use, not the descriptive understanding of what life is like after death. This would not be understood. To say "We might see one another after death," is to say something like "I would like to see you again but it will be unlikely for awhile since we will be so far apart."

"All I wished to characterize was the conventions he wished to draw. If I wished to say anything more I was merely being philosophically arrogant." (72)

Death talk reduces to concrete experiences, events, uses, or techniques in specific language - games we play. Our notions of death are determined by our analogies and metaphors which cannot be taken literally or as the only possible ones. To do so would be to misunderstand the use of our language and to misuse our language as is often done in dogmatic metaphysics. To understand what death is we should look and see how and in what contexts death language is used. Its meaning will only be its use. To know what death is is to know how to speak the language. The meaning of death can only fly out of its use as the soul flies out of the body. That is, it doesn't. Only the arrogant have souls.

Rudy Liveritte. "Some Thoughts on Death and Anxiety" *ETC* 28 (1) (March 1971) 21-37

Warren Shibles. "Timelessness" *Philosophical Pictures* 2nd revised edition, Dubuque, Iowa: Kendall-Hunt 1972

—————. "Zeno: How to Become Turtled" *Rivista Critica di Storia della Filosofia* 2 (1969) 123-134. Also in *Models of Ancient Greek Philosophy* London: Vision Press (New York: Humanities) 1971 pp. 59-73

Ludwig Wittgenstein. *Lectures and Conversations on Aesthetics, Psychology and Religious Belief* C. Barrett, ed., Oxford: Blackwell 1966 pp. 53-72

—————. *Tractatus* D. F. Pears & B. F. McGuinness, trans., London: Routledge & Kegan Paul 1961

Existentialism and Death:
A Critique

Death forms a central part of the philosophy of the existentialist, Heidegger. Sartre discusses death but it is less important for him. In several significant ways both philosophies are found to be inadequate and so their views on death far from convincing. In the first place both take consciousness (the ego, or Descartes' "I think" or *cogito*) as an unquestioned or inadequately questioned starting point for philosophizing. Now although Aristotle thought the nature of man was to be rational and so defined man as a rational animal we have been puzzling over what it is to think or be rational ever since. Contemporary philosophers, especially those having done work in the area of philosophical psychology, as well as the behaviorists, have given devastating arguments against mentalism, faculties, and consciousness, or the "I think" as an entity. (See W. Shibles "The Linguo-Centric Predicament") Regardless of the position one takes about consciousness it is naive to accept it unquestioningly or take it as a starting point of philosophy. The philosophers Gilbert Ryle and Ludwig Wittgenstein have amply shown this to be the case. My own position is that language is a better starting point. We must assume it even to present a theory. We may have the word "consciousness" but what is behind the word or what it refers to remains in question. We must assume that we speak or use language but need not assume that we think.

Another reason why existentialism of the sort Heidegger and Sartre do lacks relevance to death, is because in a sense their theories are not about death or our usual experiences at all. They are metaphysical theories, theories concerned with being. Heidegger states, "What we are *seeking* is the answer to the question about the meaning of Being in general . . . " (p. 274) But what is "Being"? If it is found to be a vague, unintelligible notion then the philosophy of Heidegger and Sartre would be left as itself inauthentic, and inadequate, for the key terms in both philosophies are terms such as "being-in-itself," "being-for-itself," "Being," "Being-there" (Dasein), "Being-toward-death," "existence," etc. Walter Kaufmann put it this way,

> "In the wake of Heidegger, discussion concentrated . . . on his terms and weird locutions. Death, anxiety, conscience, and care became part of the jargon tossed about by thousands, along with Being-there, to-hand-ness, throwness, being-with, and all the rest." (p. 49)

One of the main reasons for such confusion is that such metaphysical concepts are seldom made clear or are category-mistakes. If one investigates being, as the Existentialists do, he should know what being or even existence is. But this we are never told. We are told about things like "being-in-the-world," but this neither clarifies nor helps, but only adds the further question as to what is meant in this context by "world."

Suppose one asks, "What is Being?" or "What is existence?" To say "Being exists," is merely redundant because being means to exist. This says only "Exists exists." One could add that Exists exists exists *ad infinitum*. But what does it mean to exist at all? What could be meant by these questions? Where or in what circumstances could such a problem arise? One becomes unconscious and then regains consciousness, saying "I still exist." Here by "exist" we mean only that one is alive or is now conscious. This usage is clear. But now suppose one says, "There is a stone in this room, therefore stones exist." This is no good. The statement in one sense is trivial and circular because it can only mean "If there is a stone in this room, then there is a stone in this room." In another sense the statement is false, for if there is a stone in this room it does not follow that the stone exists in some other sense. It does not exist in the next room, for example. And to say it is alive will not do. To say it exists may mean that it was made. But "made" here is odd, for everything was formed or changed somehow. We cannot intelligently say the stone or world was originally created, without abusing our language, for we do not honestly know who or what caused the world to be created or if in fact the world was ever created at all — possibly it never was. Thus to ask "Who created the world?" is to ask two questions not one. It commits the "many-questions fallacy" of informal logic.

To ask "Do I exist?" or "What is being?" is to ask unintelligible questions because no specific context is given in which "exist" and "Being" make sense. To say, "I know that I exist," is either trivial or unintelligible. We do not ordinarily have problems of this sort. To say "I exist" is merely to say I am in this room not that one, or that I am alive, or that I just regained consciousness. It does not mean I exist *as such* or have *Being* as such. It would appear that those who speak of existence and Being have made a simple category-mistake.

One says, "The chair is in this room." One may also think that therefore it may also make sense to say the equally grammatical sentence "The chair is." But what could that mean other than that it is an overgeneral and incomplete sentence? Perhaps our grammar is inadequate here for it allows too much. To "I am" or "I have Being," one must always ask, "You are what?" or "What do you mean when you speak of Being?" In addition to being a category-mistake we have here a naming-fallacy, because "Existence," and "Being" are sometimes regarded as naming entities as such.

At times "ontology" or "Being" seems to refer to "objects" somehow quite outside of the realm of language. But this view is undermined by the fact that we see reality in terms of and by means of language. We can hardly see or think of anything without language. Language seems, to a great extent, to constitute and mold reality. It does not just stand for or represent "ideas" and "objects." To get outside of language is like getting outside of one's skin. There are not, then, simply objects or entities existing entirely outside of or independent of language. To think there are would be to know how one would think without language, without ever having learned a language, or to know how insects think and what they perceive. We see in terms of our language and thought. The poor boy sees the half-dollar as larger than does the rich boy. Reality seems to be inextricably bound up with language. Thus there is no ontology separate from language. Language, not thought or "objects," is the soundest (epistemological) starting point of knowledge.

Naturally, these sorts of things are unpopular to say about "being" and "existence," for such terms have been with us too long to dismiss. But I do not wish to dismiss them. If they are used they should always be reducible to a specific concrete context and instance, but not spoken of with vague metaphysical generality. To do so is to misuse our language. One concrete instance is that one may speak of a person who got lost but was later found, as still "existing."

There is a specific context one may consider, however, which has special relevance to death. To say one exists may in some contexts imply that one is alive, not dead. If no one knows what death is, if it is not within our experience, then it makes no sense to talk of existing for it would have no opposite. One can only exist or exist, that is be alive or be alive. To exist in the sense of being alive would be the opposite of something one knows nothing about. One cannot be alive if one cannot not be alive. All we ever experience is consciousness, including consciousness of having had dreams, and even being aware of having been unconscious or having slept. This is not to say scholars or anyone else is clear about what consciousness is. But we need not deal with this question here. We sometimes say that to be' dead is no longer to be alive, no longer to be conscious. This is a clear enough meaning for the abstract word, exist, or Being, with the exception that the nature of consciousness is obscure. But in addition it is often said that death is the state of nothingness or of non-being. These two states are different. "Non-being" is just as open-context or contextless and so just as vague and meaningless as being is. One could not satisfactorily define being by means of non-being. To do so would in addition be circular since being occurs in the definition of non-being. But nothingness appears to be unlike being. Nothing is not within our experience or without it.

To say "I am," "I have Being," or "I am alive," may refer to the fact that I am not nothing, I still have consciousness and experiences. But what does it mean to say I "still" have consciousness when I have never experienced not having it. How can I apprehend something, or as Heidegger says, "anticipate" something outside of my experience such as nothingness, death, total absence of consciousness? This does not at the moment involve the observation that without a healthy body one has no consciousness. Strictly speaking we can only observe the death of others not our own death. But the point here is that a so-called absolute nothing or absolute nothingness, such as that which death is supposed to be, is not within our experience. At times Sartre and Heidegger seem to suggest this but at other times they seem to take death as a final absolute fact of some kind. If the nature of death is only determined by the way in which our imagination regards or creates it then it would be too dogmatic to say, as Sartre and Heidegger do, that death is an absolute fact.

The nature of nothingness is not something outside our experience but rather something within our experience. We never experience nothingness. We know what it is like for there to be no one or nothing in the room because we know what it is like for there to be someone or something in the room. But it makes no sense to talk of nothing where something can never be, for we do not know what it is like for there to be something there. "Nothing" can be a naming-fallacy if we use it in a contextless and absolute way. Nothing means only "no specific things," e.g., no person here, no book there, etc. It is a term relative to a known circumstance and real known things. Absolute and contextless nothingness is vague, meaningless, and outside of our experience. We cannot, then, intelligibly say that death is a state of nothingness. Nor can we intelligibly say then that being is a state opposite of nothingness. In these senses being and exist have no use. Both Being and nothingness are vague, metaphysical naming-fallacies or category-mistakes. Sartre's book is entitled *Being and Nothingness*. But it is these terms which Heidegger and Sartre employ as the central terms of their philosophies. They are not terms which should be employed uncritically or merely elaborated on or deduced from.

Perhaps a worse aspect of the above existentialist views is that these philosophers seem captivated by their own slogans and models. They take their models as representing the truth, that is, the only way of looking at reality, and in this respect are themselves exercising "bad faith" and being "inauthentic," (which they accuse others of being). There are other ways and perhaps more careful ways of viewing the world and the question of death. Heidegger, however, must be commended in seeing death as an important issue to philosophize about, for most other philosophers have never even considered the subject.

Kaufmann asserts:

"If there are a few who know his (Heidegger's) work and don't respect it, this is because most critical readers soon discover that it is not worth their while to go on reading," and "Without these quaint locutions (metaphysical terms and combinations of terms) the book [*Being and Time*] would not only be much less obscure . . . but also a fraction of its length — considerably under 100 pages instead of 438. For Heidegger does not introduce coinages to say briefly what would otherwise require lengthy repetitions. On the contrary." (41-42)

Jacques Choron (1963) also states that neither Sartre nor Heidegger give a satisfactory analysis of death. (237, 253) An example of Heidegger's metaphysical language as well as a summary of his view concerning death follows:

"Our characterization of authentic Being-towards-death as we have projected it existentially: anticipation reveals to Dasein its lostness in the they-self, and brings it face to face with the possibility of being itself, primarily unsupported by concernful solicitude, but of being itself, rather, in an impassioned *freedom towards death* — a freedom which has been released from the Illusions of the 'They,' and which is facticial, certain of itself, and anxious." (Heidegger p. 311)

All this is on a metaphysical level and as such has little to do with non-metaphysical ordinary experience. Nevertheless existentialists often write as if it does and so rephrase the theory in terms of ordinary language. Although ordinary language phrasing of the view may be illegitimate and yet another category-mistake, some of the statements made may be found useful and suggestive in themselves.

An ordinary language translation of what the above quotation by Heidegger might mean is in part this: Because we are confronted with death we realize we must make our lives richer and more worthwhile rather than merely play roles and just accept others' views and ways of acting. It is I, not another, who must face and die my death. This quote seems to be a revision of Descartes' "I think therefore I am," to "I am going to die therefore I am." To know I will die is part of what it means to be. The difficulty with Being, existence and what is meant by death or non-being, has already been mentioned. "Dasein" which appears in the above quotation refers to "being-there" and is described as being "care," and about "care" Heidegger states,

" 'care' has been expressed in the 'definition': 'ahead-of-itself-Being-already-in (the world) as Being-alongside entities which we encounter (within-the-world).' " (293)

A brief analysis of the concepts of "possible" and "meaning," should be given here. They relate to existentialist as well as other views on death.

There are various senses of "possible" each of which must be kept distinct in order to avoid error. Many have asserted, "It is possible that I have a soul," or "It is possible that there is an afterlife." "Possible" here may mean 1) I have evidence or know that I have a soul or that there is an afterlife. This requires positive knowledge. 2) I don't know that there is not a soul or afterlife, that is, I have no evidence against there being an afterlife or soul. One cannot be wrong about this. 3) I am ignorant of whether there is or is not a soul or afterlife. One cannot be wrong about this. 4) It is a genuine possibility that there is an afterlife or soul, that is, there are such things as afterlives although we may not know it yet. This sense of possible assumes positive knowledge, for one could be wrong about it. Some things are not possible. It may not be possible to walk to the moon or make water balls, etc.

Because of these various senses of possible we may unintentionally equivocate or confuse one sense with another. One may say "No one can prove there is no afterlife, therefore it is possible that there is an afterlife." But we may find that there can be no such thing. In which case we find that it was not possible. Is it possible to have a round square? One reason why it would not be a genuine possibility is that our concepts of round square or afterlife are self-contradictory, or confused or unintelligible concepts. In the above statement sense No. 4 is implied, but lacks support. If pressed, the asserter may even be driven back merely to sense No. 3, i.e., "I really don't know if there is an afterlife or not."

In one context "possible" may have a concrete and intelligible use, but be a misuse in another context. Compare

1. It is possible to tie a knot with this rope.
2. It is possible to live after death.

or

1. It is possible that he has a wife.
2. It is possible that he has a soul.

The difference between these examples is that we have evidence and criteria of a quite concrete sort for tying a knot in a rope or determining whether or not one has a wife. This is the sort of context in which possible has a definite use and meaning. We then use the word "possible" in an entirely different context to ask if it is possible that there is a soul or afterlife. This is to make a category-mistake. The new sorts of relevant evidence and criteria are of a much different sort. Having a soul is not like having a book. Living forever is not like living for a week. Life after death is not like life in a valley.

Thus the fact that one is ignorant of something or has no evidence for it is no argument that it in fact could be the case or is possible in sense No. 4. Perhaps the best procedure when confronted with one's ignorance about something is merely to admit the ignorance. "I don't know," is a statement which can often have a great deal of support and be an elevating statement as well.

As to the concept, meaning, e.g., "The meaning of death," or "In the face of death one must make one's life more meaningful," we find difficulties. What is meaning? Is it an idea, thought or a correspondence of a word to a thought? Are there meanings as such? Is "meaning" used metaphorically here? To say one makes one's life meaningful and that it has more meaning if one knows one will die, is not specific.

Does it mean one will enjoy life more, or that one will do more things, or that one will be more depressed and pensive as he becomes overconscious and preoccupied with his future death? In addition, even as it applies to a theory of language, "meaning" is thought today to be a confused and unfounded notion. What is a "meaning"? Do words just somehow stand for, contain, or represent so-called "meanings"? Although the issue or status of "meaning" need not be decided here, at least whenever the term is used it should be given a concrete exemplification. If everything we do has meaning it makes no sense to say one thing has meaning and not another — certainly at least not on the abstract level, or independent of specified contexts. Meaning often serves merely as a value statement such as, "After facing death I find my life is more meaningful," that is, my life is "better" somehow.

A number of observations concerning death and dying are made in Tolstoy's short novel, *The Death of Ivan Ilych*. Heidegger is said to have based his existentialist view of death partly on this story. Kaufmann says, "Heidegger on death is for the most part an unacknowledged commentary on *The Death of Ivan Ilych*." (47) Heidegger's and Sartre's views of death will be related to Tolstoy's story, a story frequently cited by writers on the subject of Death.

1. *The Death of Others*

The death of another person is usually taken as an objective fact like other facts one encounters and not as really relevant to oneself, to one's own impending death. Heidegger and Sartre stress the significant difference between the death of another and my death. Tolstoy writes,

"So on receiving the news of Ivan Ilych's death the first thought of each of the gentlemen in that private room was the changes and promotions it might occasion among themselves or their acquaintances." (65)

"The mere fact of the death of a near acquaintance aroused, as usual, in all who heard of it the complacent feeling, 'it is he who is dead and not I.' " (65)

"There was in that expression [on dead Ivan's face] a reproach and a warning to the living. This warning seemed to Peter Ivanovich out of place, or at least not applicable to him." (66)

"The doctor summed up . . . brilliantly, looking over his spectacles triumphantly and even gaily at the accused . . . For the doctor, and perhaps for everybody else, it was a matter of indifference." (76)

This expresses almost exactly Heidegger's view:

"The dying of others is not something which we experience in a genuine sense; at most we are always just 'there alongside,' " (H 282) and "No one can take the other's dying away from him." (H 284)

Sartre's view is similar:

"*Mortal* represents the present being which I am for the other; *dead* represents the future meaning of my actual for-itself for the other." (S 547)

One may try to make sense of this as follows. Mortal refers to the way in which others see me, not the way I see myself, in regard to my death; "dead" refers only to how others will regard me.

Nevertheless the death of a close friend may be one of the initial experiences by means of which one begins to become aware of one's own impending death.

"The thought of the sufferings of this man he had known so intimately, first as a merry little boy, then as a schoolmate, and later as a grown-up colleague, suddenly struck Peter Ivanovich with horror. . . . He saw that brow, and that nose pressing down on the lip, and felt afraid for himself." (T 68)

Sartre states that we only know of our deaths by other's deaths as a sign of ours.

2. *Death as an Unknown or Mystery*

There is much ignorance of the cause of death on the biological level. Perhaps we are all dying simply because we eat poisons in our food. Our medical knowledge leaves something to be desired in that it can only specify the cause generally and often not at all. Doctors can often tell the cause well enough for ordinary practical purposes, but not enough for philosophical ones or for understanding the nature of death. Our research into and control of biological aging is just beginning.

Dr. Robert Kohn of the School of Medicine of Case Western Reserve University in his 1971 book on aging, *Principles of Mammalian Aging,* states:

"Questions about aging have only recently begun to interest large numbers of scientists . . ." (p. 2)

"Aging has never been the major interest of the community of biologists . . ." (3)

"No textbook on aging exists." (4)

"Very few of the explanations of biological phenomena that we accept as proved could actually survive a rigorously logical criticism." (5)

"Agreement has not been the case; notions about causes of aging have generally followed the fashions of the times, and virtually every conceivable phenomenon has been proposed in the past, or is currently under consideration as a primary cause. . . . The basic mechanisms of aging are currently at the level of hypotheses or theories." (148)

Tolstoy wrote,

" 'But what really was the matter with him?' The doctors couldn't say — at least they could, but each of them said something different." (T 65) "The doctor said that so-and-so indicated that there was so-and-so inside the patient, but if the investigation of so-and-so did not confirm this, then he must assume that and that. If he assumed that and that, then . . . and so on." (T 76) "If only it would come quicker! If only *what* would come quicker? Death, darkness?" (T 85) " 'And death . . . where is it?' . . . 'Where is it? What death?' There was no fear because there was no death." (T 92) [Here death seems to be almost personified.]

Heidegger speaks not of biological death but of existential ontological aspects of death. He is not concerned with physical death. He rather stresses consciousness or the "anticipation" of death. By "being" or "existing" (ontology or the existential) he mainly seems to imply being conscious, being aware, or having consciousness. Thus we cannot know death in terms of another's death because we cannot know or have his awareness or consciousness of it. When another dies we are still around to be conscious of it. Heidegger thus states,

"Dying is not an event; it is a phenomenon to be understood existentially." (H 248) "Death in the widest sense, is a phenomenon of life." (H 290)

For Heidegger death is something we cannot experience. It is just meaningless, and annihilation. It is a mere possibility.

"Death gets passed off as always something 'actual'; its character as a possibility gets concealed . . ." (H 297)

Later we will see that he asserts that death is an absolute fact. Here he asserts that we cannot know death but only be aware of our living, conscious experience, or of death as a possibility. This seems to be a contradiction in his theory. It is not clear which senses of possible he is using. It seems to be that by possible he means that we are aware of death as being a certain sort of thing but that we have not yet and cannot ever experience it. Although his view may be self contradictory and confusing it is nevertheless an interesting point to make that we can never know death because it is not within our conscious experience. The Epicurean rendering of this was, "If death is there, you aren't; if you are there death isn't."

The existentialist Antonia Wenkart quotes Lao-Tze in this regard, "To be born is to leave the nameless, to die is to reenter the nameless."

The existentialist psychiatrist Bugenthal presents and popularizes the metaphysical language of Heidegger in the following:

"Phenomenologically, we know nothing of death. The only knowledge we have of it is physical-science information which has little utility for existential and psychotherapeutic thinking. The *anticipation* of death, on the other hand, is a crucial existential and psychotherapeutic matter. Death as the definitive non-being becomes apparently synonymous with nothingness, but it needs to be recognized that this is speculative rather than documentable. . . . Clearly one experiences the existential anxiety of finiteness not in terms of his death itself, but in terms of the anticipation of it." (294)

Bugenthal again stresses these points which appear to be Heidegger's views:

"We have no phenomenological evidence on what death means, only external observation. All our evidence is inferential. . . . Ontologically [i.e., regarding the "existence" of death] and phenomenologically we can say little or nothing about the death of one's own being but much about the anticipation of that death." (232)

It is not clear here how, if one has no idea of death, one can "anticipate" death. A misleading analogy: a) I am waiting for the train. b) I am waiting for death. If death is an unknown how can one wait for or anticipate it? This may be compared to the following brief dialogue at a railway station:
"Are you waiting for a train? There hasn't been a train go through here in ten years."
"No."
"What are you waiting for, then?"
"I don't know, I'm just waiting."
"Then you are waiting for an unknown?"
"No not for an unknown, just anticipating."
How can one anticipate nothing? One may perhaps

anticipate something vague, feel something may happen, etc., but if one does not know what death is he cannot anticipate death. He might anticipate something or other, or perhaps he might merely be apprehensive. This kind of vague anticipation may give one a feeling of meaninglessness or of absurdity, that is, a feeling of being ignorant and unable to dispel the ignorance. Sartre appears to hold a view of this sort:

"Death is "out of reach of all ontological conjectures." (S 545) "It is outside my possibilities and therefore I cannot wait for it." (S 545) "I can neither discover my death nor wait for it nor adopt an attitude toward it, for it is that which is revealed as undiscoverable . . ." (S 545)

His view is that death is absurd because our freedom, from which death is derivative only, never encounters death as a limit. One may compare this with Heidegger's view that consciousness can never experience or know death. Death is absurd because by being conscious and choosing certain concepts to explain with, we create our own notion of what death is — and that notion is nothing more than our creation. The concept of death tells me about nothing except myself. "I am not 'free to die.' " (S 547)

Sartre seems then to contradict himself when he states,

"Death haunts me at the very heart of each of my projects as their inevitable reverse side." (S 547)

If we do not have access to death how do we know it is the "reverse side" of our possibilities? The terminology is, in any case, too vague to be informative. What is a "possibility?" Sartre supposedly does not know what death is, yet he says that to die is to exist only through the Other. This imples that he does after all know what death is.

3. Dishonesty Regarding Death

We rationalize or invent myths and fictions rather than face or inquire into death. Dying and death are regarded with remote ritual, custom, confusion, habit or mechanical responses rather than with intelligence, honesty or inquiry. Tolstoy presented a number of examples of this.

"Peter Ivanovich, like everyone else on such occasions, entered feeling uncertain what he would have to do. All he knew was that at such times it is always safe to cross oneself. But he was not quite sure whether one should make obeisances while doing so. He therefore adopted a middle course. On entering the room he began crossing himself and made a slight movement resembling a bow." (T 66)

Tolstoy may have wanted to show that there is not enough religion in our life but this story does not show it. It does suggest that one should live a more loving, aware life and that Christian ritual is usually on par with any other unfounded and useless habit.

"And Peter Ivanovich knew that, just as it had been the right thing to cross himself in that room, so what he had to do here was to press her hand, sigh, and say, 'Believe me. . . .' " (T 67) " 'It's God's will. We shall all come to it someday,' said Gerasim." (T 68)

This is a traditional escape from facing death or inquiry into the nature of death. It is to suggest that inquiry would be of no use because everything is in God's hands. It is to give up one's intelligence and so one's very humanity to a myth. For a long time in the history of mankind religion forbade the use of medicine and the practice of physicians because it supposedly interfered with God's will and God's powers.

" 'What? Take communion? Why? It's unnecessary! However . . .' " (T 91)

Ivan merely agrees to take communion so he won't have to fight with his wife, and perhaps merely because of custom. As he says, "It's unnecessary!"

"The doctor put on just the same air towards him as he himself put on towards an accused person." (T 76)

There was thus no genuine experience or feeling involved. These were kept discretely hidden. The doctor and lawyer and clergy merely play roles, and play them in terms of institutionalized procedures and polices.

"His colleague Shebek would come, and instead of weeping and being petted, Ivan Ilych would assume a serious, severe, and profound air. . . . This falsity around him and within him did more than anything else to poison his last days." (T 84)

"In them (those around him) he saw himself . . . a terrible and huge deception which had hidden both life and death." (T 90)

Ivan says to himself, "All you have lived for and still live for is falsehood and deception, hiding life and death from you." (T 91)

"He had been within a hairbreath of calling out to them: 'Stop lying! You know and I know that I am dying. Then at least stop lying about it!' " (T 83)

"Those about him did not understand or would not understand it." (T 78)

"Her attitude was this: 'You know,' she would say to her friends, 'Ivan Ilych can't do as other people do, and keep to the treatment prescribed for him.' " (T 78)

"He felt that he was so surrounded and involved in a mesh of falsity that it was hard to unravel anything." (T 86)

One clings to irrelevant or medical knowledge given by doctors even while half-knowing such knowledge is false. Although the doctors did not really know the illness they gave their diagnosis and Ivan tried to console himself by pretending what the doctor said was true.

"The appendix is getting better, absorption is occurring?" (T 80)

"What tormented Ivan Ilych most was the deception, the lie, which for some reason they all accepted that he was not dying but was simply ill. . . ." (T 83)

One way to avoid thoughts of death both real and in the symbolic form of boredom is to keep busy or preoccupied. And one tends then to become involved with trivia of all sorts:

"He was so interested in it all that he often did things himself, rearranging the furniture, or rehanging the curtains. He wrote, 'I feel fifteen years younger.' " (T 74)
"When nothing was left to arrange it became rather dull." (T 74)
"Schwartz . . . wanted to arrange where they would play bridge that evening [of the funeral]." (T 66)

Even argument and unpleasant experiences are used to avoid inquiring into or becoming concerned with dying and death:

"They would not agree, and his wife would contradict him, and he would dispute and grow angry. But that was all right, for then he did not think about It [Death]. It was invisible." (T 82)

Here there is irony as well, for her insensitivity and dishonest assessments of the situation actually have a beneficial result, that of so preoccupying his mind for a moment that he could forget about death. On the other hand, to avoid thoughts of death is a dishonest lack of adjustment.

On Heidegger's view both life and death can be "authentic" or "inauthentic." He speaks of "fallenness," which is the tendency of Dasein to exist inauthentically in the they-self [to think of death only passively as the death of others?]. "Falling" is alienation, temptation, and tranquilization. He states, "As falling, everyday Being-towards-death is a constant *fleeing in the face of death.*" (H 298)

On his view the everyday perspective is inauthentic and is characterized by avoidance of the ontological question. We distract ourselves by the trivia and idle talk of daily life and so fail to ask the ontological question of what it means to *be.* (As was pointed out against Heidegger, in some senses we don't ask the ontological question because it is a confused or meaningless question.) We try to avoid death by treating it as something only happening to another person. We may equivocate with the word death treating it as if it just refers to the death of another but not our own death. It may also be treated abstractly or obscurely, thereby diminishing one's concern about it. Heidegger himself by speaking in obscure technical language, in effect, obscures the notion of death at the same time he asserts that we must face death. His own view is inauthentic in this respect. We also try to escape death by becoming overly emotional, grieving too much, being oversympathetic, brooding, etc. We seem to want always to avoid catching ourselves alone with our own thoughts and honestly facing life and death. We feel that to do so is too much of a risk, too much of a challenge.

Peter Koestenbaum translates what he thinks Heidegger is saying about dishonesty or inauthenticity:

"We are not honest with ourselves in thinking about our own death." (K, a 28)

"The distanced or *callous* and *practical* response to or meaning of death — It is the response of the professional soldier, the policeman, the nurse and the doctor." (K, a 32)

His recommendation is to face death honestly and thereby it will be seen to give a "vitality" to life.

"All this represents far more intelligent and rational behavior than the escapes of drink, busy-work, or suicide." (K a 37)

Note that he stresses rationality and intelligence, terms which Heidegger and Sartre avoid. The latter prefer to stress emotions such as dread, *Angst,* anxiety, nausea, anticipation, etc. The existentialists may themselves be avoiding inquiry into death by becoming distracted and immersed in emotions. Emotion will be discussed in section 9 and in the chapter on psychiatry.

Perhaps the average man is then a misologist, one having aversion to inquiry. This aversion may even result in neurotic behavior. Bugenthal points out:

"When many neurotic symptoms are analyzed it can often be found that they have, among other meanings, something to say of the fear of death and the sense of fate." (294)

This is not to say that the views of Heidegger or Sartre stress inquiry. Theirs is merely a statement that we should not avoid death. It is a vague and general observation but nevertheless an important one as far as it goes. Sartre calls it "bad-faith" for one to hide behind conventions and not to face what one really is. Sartre, however, appears dogmatic in holding that man really is what Sartre says that he is. Bugenthal presents his interpretation of the matter and even implies that metaphysics (thus including that of Sartre and Heidegger) may be "inauthentic" and in "bad faith":

"It is hard for us, in our culture to conceive of death as anything but an imposition and an unhappy event. We regard the Japanese tradition of hara-kiri as bizarre and the Scandinavian higher suicide rate as evidence of some strange moral degeneracy. We sugarcoat all limits and endings and especially death, dreading even to say the word and preferring euphemisms such as 'passed away,' 'crossed over,' 'gone to sleep.' Euthanasia (the painless putting to death of persons suffering from incurable diseases) is strictly punished, and medical science exerts itself to perform obscene miracles of prolonging vegetative, suffering life in burned out shells of what were once people. . . . Those who have a metaphysical conviction that the afterlife is very similar to that we know now are no exception to this generalization. They, in effect, negate the fact of death and thus demonstrate the terrible negative regard with which they hold it." (331)

4. *The Time of One's Death Is Indeterminate.*

Tolstoy writes of Ivan: " 'Why, that might suddenly, at any time happen to me,' he thought, and for a moment felt terrified." (T 68)

Ivan, who died at the relatively early age of forty-five, says " 'And death . . . where is it?' " (T92) as he waits for something to happen.

According to Sartre my death cannot be foreseen for any date and so not waited for. One cannot find the end if he does not know when it will be. Death is seen only in the perspective of my subjectivity and so not waited for. To wait for a person is determinate, but to wait for death is indeterminate. This is an attack on Heidegger's view of anticipating death. Whether one can wait for death was also discussed earlier. Though one cannot wait for death it is still regarded by Sartre as a "not yet": "Life decides its own meaning because it is always in suspense . . . a 'not-yet.' " (S 543) But 'not-yet' implies that something is 'not-yet' and seems not so distant from Heidegger's "anticipation" or "Being-towards-death" after all.

Heidegger himself says Dasein is a "not yet." (276) He also stresses the indeterminacy of the time of death:

"As soon as man comes to life, he is at once old enough to die." (H 289)
"Death is something that stands before us − something impending." (H 294)
Death is "a possibility which is certain and at the same time indefinite." (H 302)

Death is on his view, indefinite − indefinite as to its when and so reveals a terrible temporality of our existence. His book *Being and Time* rests heavily on such considerations of time. It may, however, be pointed out that he has given little insight into the notion of time but, as with being and his other metaphysical terms, has simply assumed that we are clear about their meaning and uses. Time is one of the most abused concepts in human thought both among scientists as well as among non-scientists. Time words − past, present, future, not-yet, now, etc. seem to name entities as does the word time itself. Our expressions regarding time are metaphorical, e.g., time on one's hands, march of time, speed of time, time passes, time exists, etc. Yet upon examination these expressions are found to lack support. Time does not go fast. Time does not go slow. Time is merely change and relations of change. (W. Shibles "Timelessness")

A clock does not "tell" time. Time is merely the observed change of a moving object in relation to other moving objects. The hands of a clock move relative to the face of the clock, or relative to the change of movement of a runner if a race is being "timed." Thus clocks do not "tell" time, their changes constitute or *are* time. We do not have two things: change of the hands of a clock *and* time, but only one thing, changes. What Heidegger wanted to say about "anticipation," "not-yet," etc. regarding time could have been greatly clarified had he realized that time is change and not a thing in itself. Heidegger and Sartre commit the naming-fallacy in regard to "time" as well as in regard to "being."

Nevertheless there is an insight to be gained here for we do not usually know just when our death will come. If death is indeterminate or a mystery and if I only have evidence for and know the death of others, perhaps by some unknown means I will not die. This argument may be further developed. In addition no stress is placed on the dying moment because death cannot be experienced anyway, only dying can. The last words of a dying man may be no better or worse than any of his words spoken at any other time. The Christian tradition gave special mystical emphasis to the last moment before death. It was and still is thought that at such a time one might have a vision of the next world or reveal the secret of this life while one's soul is on the way to the next life, or reveal the mystery of how the soul departs from the body or if it does. In the Ozarks there is thought to be a special death snap heard in the house a few days before a death occurs, and "bone-rattlin' " just before someone dies.

We find it hard to face death when we know it close at hand, or we give it a challenge by mountain climbing or bull fighting, but why do we not find it hard to face otherwise since we all think we will die sometime. Perhaps this is because we are able to rationalize so well, and think of our death only as the death of another.

Heidegger seems to want to say that the "not yet" element is already there in its indeterminacy. In this sense he avoids Epicurus' view that if you are death isn't, and if death is you aren't. It seems like double talk to say as Heidegger does that Dasein (Being-there) is its not-yet, that Dasein is

"Being-towards-the-end" where we know of no end. Perhaps all he means by this, if one removes the jargon, is that one can only live at the present moment. To speak of a "not-yet" is simply to abuse language and be confused by the nature of time. To live at the present moment means only to have certain experiences and be aware of certain changes. I am not a not-yet or a new, I am a process of changes.

5. *Can One Imagine His Own Death?*

> Ivan asks himself, "When I am not, what will there be? There will be nothing. Then where shall I be when I am no more?" (T 80)
> "The customary reflection at once occurred to him . . . that it should not and could not happen to him. . . . as though death was an accident natural to Ivan Ilych but certainly not to himself." (T 68)

The images Ivan has of his own death are those based on things and events within our experience:

> "I think of the appendix — but this is death!" (T 80)

Koestenbaum interpreting Heidegger expresses the same difficulty:

> "What mental image is present when I think of the real meaning of the death of myself? Honest analysis will disclose that there is then no image of the world left." (K 28)

Of course, the logic here is not quite acceptable. To know that there will be no image left is still to have an image. One could, however, more carefully say that my death can neither be imagined or spoken of, nor not imagined or spoken of. It is not within my experience and I have no access to what might *be* outside of my experience. It would have been helpful if Heidegger would have simply stated such a view, because it leads to some interesting clarifications which will be discussed in the chapter on Wittgenstein. But he did not.

According to Heidegger death is not meaningful to one as an event that will occur, because the observer himself dies. This position could be clarified by observing that my death is not an event for me because "event" will have no use or meaning or context for me when I am dead. But this presupposes one already knows what it is like to be dead. How does Heidegger know that death is not meaningful to me, even presupposing that the observer dies? In addition it is contradictory to say, "Death has no meaning to me because I will be dead," because to say "I will be dead" presupposes one knows what death is. Again we are confronted with category-mistakes, naming-fallacies and misuses of language.

Heidegger says, "As long as Dasein *is* an entity, it has never reached its 'wholeness.' " (H 280)

"There are many who, proximally and for the most part, do not know about death." (H 295)

"One *knows* about the certainty of death, and yet 'is' not authentically certain of one's own." (H 302)

The authentic view for him is that death is a "to-be-going-to die," only an anticipation or a "running before" not an actuality. Yet the "to die" part of this expression seems to express the view that it is known. The statement is a paradox. We cannot know death yet we can anticipate death even though we do not know what it is. The paradox or oxymoron is produced that death is a possibility that is inevitable. Compare this to a statement like, "Heidegger anticipates nothings." How could he "anticipate" such?

He uses special terms to represent his view. Death is my "ownmost," "non-relational," and "not to be outstripped." A translation of these terms might be something like this, "My awareness of death reveals that I am going to die and that I will die alone." Certainly I must die my death, assuming I know what "die" and "death" are, but each person always does and must experience all of his own experiences and so in this sense it is as uninteresting to say I must die my own death as to say I must eat my own breakfast. If one accepts unquestioningly another's beliefs or another's theory, even an existentialist theory, then one is not, in one sense, thinking one's own thoughts. One must accept one's own existentialism. But then existentialism is no more, for one's existentialism might then turn out to be ordinary-language philosophy. I can recommend that. The topic of "my death" will be further discussed in section 8.

One interpretation of Heidegger's view is that since we cannot experience death it is only possible. But here we run into equivocation regarding what is and what is not "possible." He is saying that death is a possibility that is inevitable. This is a strange use of the term "possible." "The possible is inevitable," is an oxymoron or contradiction in that possible implies that something could not be the case. In any case to speak of death as a fact or as inevitable must be argued for and the concept of death must be clarified. This Heidegger does not do. He in effect says, "Death is that which I cannot imagine which I can imagine." A paradox and an oxymoron in this case, however, may be useful in rendering a paradoxical situation. We must face death yet we are not too clear about what it is we have to face. We know death only in conscious life and have no experience of death as such, and the concept has a uniqueness requiring further clarification. In general Heidegger reveals to us an aspect of the problem rather than a contribution to a solution.

Sartre makes a distinction between "being-in-itself" and "being-for-itself." It is never quite clear what is meant by either of these metaphysical expressions, however, we may by making a conscious category-mistake render them in ordinary-language as follows: The "for itself" is the way we interpret and see the world and ourselves. The "in-itself" is reality as it is, which we can never know. One may draw a parallel to Kant's view that all man knows is appearance or phenomena, and man himself imposes categories on reality or partly constitutes reality by his categories. He sees reality only in terms of cause-effect, space-time, substance-quality. But we can never see the *Ding-an-sich,* that is reality-in-itself. The obvious objection is that if we only know what the "for-itself" produces, and appearances, how can we know there is an "in-itself" or "reality-in-itself?" Sartre's own view would be a mere appearance, a mere expression of the "for-itself," not the actual case. But it is best not to criticize the terminology or views of Sartre. They are perhaps best left alone.

Sartre represents his position that one cannot imagine one's own death:

> "Since the for-itself is the being which always lays claim to an 'after,' there is no place for death in the being which is for-itself." (S 540)

What is the meaning of this statement? My interpretation will go wrong, it cannot be right. And the Sartrean critics will have their way, for they cannot be wrong. I think the above statement may be translated from the metaphysical to the everyday context (which is illegitimate) as meaning that the consciousness conceives of death, and for the consciousness itself to be dead is to no longer be able to interpret or conceive of death. One difficulty with this view is that it presupposes death. Sartre sometimes seems to assume that one can get outside of the for-itself, get outside of language, and at other times that there is an outside to get into even though one cannot get into it. Thus when he speaks of ontology he seems to mean to refer to the "in-itself," to the "thing-in-itself." He says that death is not an ontological structure of my being insofar as my being is "for" itself, not "in" itself.

> "There is no place for death in being-for-itself; it can neither wait for death nor realize it nor project itself toward it." (S 547)
> "Thus death is not my possibility in the sense previously defined; it is a situation-limit as the chosen and fugitive reverse side of my choice." (S 547)

For Sartre death is unrealizable. (S 548) It is the inapprehensible limit of my freedom, and choice, possibilities, although it is nevertheless limited by others. "Freedom," "choice," "possibilities," are none too clear or helpful here. For example, "freedom" to do what? "Freedom at all?" Why not freedom to refute Sartre's philosophy and his view of death? Why is death a "situation-limit"? Perhaps because it ends all possibilities. But why speak of possibility in such an ambiguously open and general way and how does he know it is a "limit"? The difficulty in assuming a "reverse side" has already been discussed. Compare: 1) A book has a reverse side. 2) A choice has a reverse side. Compare: 1) The room is the limit of the event. 2) Death is the limit of the event.

If death is to be spoken of as a limit one should give a clear model of how limit is to be used. It is not adequate to say death is a situation-limit, any situation at all. Death is not the limit of the situation in which we find that we have clarified the concept of death such that our view of it as a limit (of this or that specific kind) can no longer be maintained. But, as was said, Sartre's technical terminology does not matter. It does raise problems and questions. What is a paradigm for limit if death is to be regarded as a limit? Is it like a speed limit, the limit of a city, the limit of knowledge, the limit of a line, the limit of a function of a living organism, the limit of a limit, etc.?

6. *Life as a Planned Whole, a Continuum from Beginning to End.*

In terms of death, one conceives of his life as a fixed span of time (i.e., activity or change).

> Tolstoy writes of Ivan, "Even when he was at the School of Law he was just what he remained for the rest of his life." (T 69)
> "He lay on his back and began to pass his life in review in quite a new way." (T 90)
> Ivan says, "Maybe I did not live as I ought to have done." (T 88)
> Sartre says above, that death is a "situation-limit." "Death is a boundary." (S 531) One plans one's life in terms of goals.

For Heidegger the wholeness of a life attains great significance. Koestenbaum interprets Heidegger's view in writing.

> "The thought of her death enables her to see her life as a total project." (K, a 36) "He will see every action of his life in the light of a total plan." (K, a 36)

For Heidegger, Dasein must be considered in terms of being for a whole.

"Everydayness is precisely that Being which is 'between' birth and death." (H 276)

"The possibility of Dasein's having an authentic potentiality-for-Being-a-whole emerges, *but only as an ontological possibility.*" (H 311)

Dasein's being as care, depends on temporality, on the future, because there is "constantly something to be settled." (H 279) The dying of others cannot substitute for such wholeness or temporality. Death gives us a complete or total perspective of human existence, from birth to death.

7. *Facing Death Forces One to More Realistically Evaluate and Live Life*

Tolstoy shows how Ivan in the light of impending death gradually begins to reevaluate his life.

"Ivan Ilych considered his duty to be what was so considered by those in authority . . . from early youth was by nature attracted to people of high station as a fly is drawn to the light. . . . He succumbed to sensuality, to vanity . . . but always within limits which his instinct unfailingly indicated to him as correct." (T 69)

"The thing was to exclude everything fresh and vital, which always disturbs the regular course of official business, and to admit only official relations with people, and then only on official grounds." (T 74)

"But suddenly Ivan Ilych was conscious of that gnawing pain, that taste in his mouth and it seemed ridiculous that in such circumstances he should be pleased to make a grand slam (in bridge). . . . and what was most awful was that he saw how upset Mikhail Mikhaylovich was about it but did not himself care." (T 78)

"But strange to say none of these best moments of his pleasant life now seemed at all what they had then seemed . . ." (T 88)

"All that had then seemed joys now melted before his sight and turned into something trivial and often nasty." (T 88)

"And the further he departed from childhood and the
nearer he came to the present the more worthless and
doubtful were the joys." (T 88)

"Maybe I did not live as I ought to have done." (T 88)

Ivan at the end of the story finally does experience an
authentic or close relationship with his servant, Gerasim, and it
then seems to him that it made his life meaningful for once in
his life. It is ironical that he should have such an experience and
reevaluate his life meaningfully just at a time when it is to end.
But this perhaps small but genuine experience was so powerful,
and contrasted so much with the others he had witnessed, that
it was enough to allow him to face death. He thus says, "And
death . . . where is it?" (T 92)

Tolstoy's description of Ivan's last moments may be
compared with post-reformation *Ars moriendi* (books on the art
of dying) such as Lewis Bayly *The Practice of Pietie* (1612):

"One houre well spent, when a man's life is almost
outspent, may gaine a man the assurance of eternall life:
Sooth him not with the vaine hope of this life, lest thou
betray this soule to eternall death." (O'Connor 208)

Tolstoy is still in the religious tradition.

A closer consideration of the story may reveal that Ivan
wasn't facing death really honestly. There were no
considerations or clarifications of death given except that he did
not know what death is. He never really examines the question.
His problem was in fact a rather strange one. He thought that if
he lived well he would not be afraid of death. He then has one
humane experience with Gerasim and feels he can therefore face
death. But ethics and the way one lives has little or nothing to
do with understanding death. Death is in no way clarified by
understanding our attitudes about how we live. When he asks,
"And death . . . where is it?" it is absurd that he should be
looking for it in terms of how he lived.

Tolstoy's story is really about how one should live and only
slightly and incidentally about the nature of death or an inquiry
into death. It perhaps should be entitled, *The Life of Ivan Ilych*
or *The Life and Dying of Ivan Ilych*. The irony of dying when

he has just learned how to live honestly, may suggest the absurdity of life and thus make death not at all something one can be ready for. There is an absurdity in Tolstoy's suggestion that because one lives well death is easier to face. Death may be quite irrelevant to how one has lived. It is a religious dogma that one may be punished for his sins in an afterlife. It is optimistic to think there is an afterlife, but mainly it is not honestly argued for. It is an instance of "bad faith."

Heidegger's major observation about death appears to be this view that the thought of death forces us to reevaluate our life:

> "The end of Being-in-the-world is death. This end, which belongs to the potentiality-for-Being . . . limits and determines in every case whatever totality is possible for Dasein." (H 277)
> "Death *is* only in an existential *Being-towards-death.*" (H 277)
> "Death, in the widest sense, is a phenomenon of life." (H 290)

In effect Heidegger is saying that we must accept death so as not to be surprised by it or confused by it. But since Heidegger never clarifies the nature of death one would still have to remain in confusion about it. He wrote,

> "When, by anticipation, one becomes free *for* one's own death, one is liberated from one's lostness in those possibilities which may accidentally thrust themselves upon one . . . Anticipation discloses to existence that its uttermost possibility lies in giving itself up . . . " (H 308)

Although little insight is given into the nature of death, death can supposedly serve as an ultimate evaluator. One tends not to be insincere when he faces death. But is this true? It would seem to be one of the most false observations one could make. When faced with death we create myths, fictions, religions, rationalizations, and are often more dishonest than ever. Heidegger himself is quite metaphysical, dogmatic and obscure regarding an analysis of death. Death then is not necessarily the ultimate evaluator though Heidegger is suggesting that it ought to be. One faces death with the limits of his knowledge and ability to inquire. If these are limited or obscure his confrontation with death may be ineffective. What Heidegger seems to have failed to see is that honest inquiry into one's concepts, including the problem as to the nature of death, is what is needed, not a mere emotive "anticipation" or new-coined metaphysical terminology.

Heidegger's view could be used to support a travel advertisement directed at the elderly: "See the world before you leave it." A reevaluation of one's life if inquiry and search for knowledge is not included as a part of it, as it is not on Heidegger's theory, would miss the point. On his view one might simply in the face of death change from stamp-collecting to alchemy or astrology as many are in fact now doing. The perspective given life by death is that of interpreting and assessing life, but no help is given as to how that might be done or what criteria for such might be. It is not adequate to simply say that confrontation with death is needed to make one reevaluate. One may decide that he should in the face of death be a bank robber or drop an H-bomb somewhere. Facing death may only make one like bananas more. But it may make one lose his appetite altogether.

In addition, confrontation with death need not be singled out as the only important or motivating force which may stimulate one to a reevaluation of one's life. One may instead witness an accident, face disappointment, be insulted, etc. But these are merely emotional contexts which may lead to neurosis. Perhaps one can rather best reevaluate his life by rational inquiry involving a careful philosophical clarification of his concepts, more careful perhaps than Heidegger's. This would involve becoming acquainted with clarifications given in ethics, philosophical psychology, careful discussion, and confronting one's ideas with counterexamples and alternative views. A reevaluation of this sort would put one in the position of saying, "It is as if I had been reading the wrong books for many years." When confronted with the problem of death Sartre and Heidegger would have to be eliminated from the shelf.

Koestenbaum interprets and modifies Heidegger's theory to include this view which I suggested above that confrontation with death and with the problem of death must drive one to inquiry, not just to emotive or undirected or uninformed reevaluation. The existentialist stress on the individual, on first person experience (often uncritical and self-righteous thoughts), and therefore on emotions, especially negative ones such as dread, or nausea, makes everything subjective and places stress on the irrational. Koestenbaum corrects this to stress that which is rational and involves honest inquiry rather than so-called "authentic" feeling or emotion. Koestenbaum writes.

"The person who is aware of his death and the consequent limit to his time on earth will thereby concentrate on essentials. Recognizing his death, man is prompted to get immediately to the point of his life — and to stay there." (K, a 36)

"This insight prevents man from *drifting* into situations." (Ibid. 37)

" 'What do I really want out of life?' 'What is the purpose of my human existence?' " (K, a 37-38)

(Here we may ignore the misleading phrasing that assumes that there is a purpose, but rather read this in the sense that one needs to consider goals and various alternatives to one's objective.)

"It follows that the thought of death is not morbid or depressing. On the contrary, it is revitalizing, it will lead the student directly to the path which will make him an educated person. He will learn quickly how to distinguish essential knowledge from essential frills." (K, a 38)

Koestenbaum does not tell us which experiences are better than others, are "essential," but does at least stress reason, inquiry, and education. This is shown in the following. It is also shown how rigid the theory is held with its fixed stages and a singular perspective of human thought and behavior. The model is, nevertheless, sometimes relevant to actual behavior.

"Our response to death follows four clearly delineated stages. First, we repress the thought of our own death by projecting it onto external realities (such as onto the stage in plays, the newspapers, etc. Also we flirt with death – in war or daring acts – to prove that death cannot assail us). Second, when we recognize the reality of the death of myself, we experience anxiety. In fact, death, as the symbol of my finitude, may well be the source of all authentic, i.e., ontological, anxiety. Third, after the anxiety of death has been faced, the anticipation of death leads to courage, integrity, and individuality. Finally, by opposing, contradicting, and fighting death, man feels his existence and achieves some of his greatest glories – in art, religion, and self-assertion." (K, a 39)

To say this is to assert that one in the face of death has more energy to work at any task whatsoever. This view may inspire a great criminal. It suggests that anything is as good as anything else. Koestenbaum makes this relativity and arbitrariness of activity clear in his statement:

"Every man must commit himself personally to whatever values he chooses to consider highest. . . . What the decision is, or should be, about the meaning of life is . . . a burdensome individual decision." (K, 1 40)

The view presented here perhaps could be rendered in terms more poetic than metaphysical. Death is like trying to find fresh, red strawberries buried deep beneath the frozen wintery snow. The confrontation with death may thus yield a vitality of life. This point is certainly an important one and, as I would wish to interpret it, the confrontation with death may, but need not necessarily make one aware that one of the most important goals in life is to inquire honestly in an attempt to determine the answer to his problems and his nature, including the problem as to the nature of death.

Inquiry is therapy. To clarify one's concepts is to allow one to better adjust to and understand himself and his world. Koestenbaum gives several examples of such therapeutic effect:

"The student who sits in the library and falls asleep instead of studying his assignment might find help in conquering his problem if he has learned to see his present moment in relation to his eventual death." (K, a 35)

"In seeing her human existence 'from the aspect of eternity,' she recognized that breaking off the engagement would be but a passing ripple in the totality of her life." (K, a 36)

But although death, whatever it is, may provide one model for the reinterpretation of our lives it is only one perspective, one model among a great many others. It does sometimes provide the necessary shock value needed to start some people inquiring.

On Sartre's view, death only tells us something about ourselves and our inability to conceive of our own death. It is outside of our conscious possibility or awareness. He renounces Heidegger's being-toward-death: Death is not my possibility but a contingent fact. Death is not a proper possibility of mine. It is to adopt the view of another.

"To contemplate my life by considering it in terms of death would be to contemplate my subjectivity by adopting with regard to it the other's point of view." (S 545)

"Our attitudes to death can be neither authentic nor inauthentic because we always die in the bargain." (S 548)

Death only tells us about ourselves, about our consciousness and that we cannot conceive of our death. Death humanizes us.

"By admitting my death can be revealed in my life we see that it cannot be a pure arresting of my subjectivity." (S 545)

"Death reveals to us only ourselves and that from a human point of view." (S 533)

Death is the absence of meaning but in a "derived sense thousands of shimmering, iridescent relative meanings can come into play upon this fundamental absurdity of a 'dead' life." (S 541)

For Sartre, death reveals that man is condemned to be free. In existential psychotherapy this is interpreted to mean that freedom to act in the now "being in the world" is necessary to mental health.

Frankel has presented such an existential psychotherapy which he calls "logotherapy." It stresses the fact that by facing death, by existential crisis, one becomes more humanistic and gains purpose in life, thereby dispelling the feeling of meaninglessness. This, of course, assumes that by facing death one will become more humanistic, that it will give one a purpose in life and dispel meaninglessness. These results may not obtain and the reverse may often or even usually be the case. This therapy assumes that there are new sorts of emotions and anxieties such as dread, existential anxiety, existential meaninglessness. But one does not usually or perhaps ever have a problem with Being or "existential" problems, unless perhaps he is a metaphysician or has been told by an existentialist that he has such problems. People do often have a lack of purpose or direction. But this is not an "existential" lack of purpose or direction. It would, it seems, be rather neurotic to have the existentialist's dread, anxiety, nausea, etc.

Gardner Murphy states that not all facing of death necessarily represents a gain in mental health. (Feifel 73) Salvatore Maddi states that the normal, healthy, intelligent person does not need existential crisis or confrontation with death and that it will do little if anything to improve him.

In existential psychotherapy there are, following the views of Sartre and Heidegger, three existential anxieties:

1. anxiety of having to die,
2. anxiety of guilt,
3. anxiety of lacking something in life.

A neurosis is associated with each anxiety. This list of models and analysis is extremely narrow and restrictive. Nor is much if any clarification given into the nature of anxiety. Norman Brown wrote, "Anxiety about death does not have ontological status, as existentialist theologians claim."

The psychologist, Theodore Sarbin, recently gave a clear analysis according to which "anxiety" is an extremely misleading and unhelpful concept.

Certainly sometimes and in some ways the patient as well as the average normal person is concerned with death and it plays a part in his life and the way in which his concepts become organized. But what is mainly needed is a clear analysis of how death plays a part in our thought. Such analysis, I would suggest, may be gained by a careful critical examination of the way death and death concepts are used and conceived of in our language. Our thought is constituted by and inextricably bound up with our language and so the starting place of inquiry ought to be not into mental states or mental fictions such as anxiety but into the actual language used by the normal person as well as by the abnormal patient. The meaning of death related words is determined by their uses in language-games. We need then to examine closely what such uses are, to pay careful attention to what one says and how death terms arise out of one's situation and in one's life. This view would be an attempt to make intelligible Sartre's general and vague notion that death concepts depend on one's situation "in-the-world," that they are situational. One might rather say they depend on a context, on a language-game. To advance psychotherapy, then, a careful and specific clarification of the language-games we play regarding death, must be given.

Frankl approaches such inquiry when he attempts to treat phobias by means of "paradoxical intention." (Sahakian 528) One may think of this as a rhetorical device, an oxymoron or antithesis. It involves putting the patient in the very situation he fears. If one fears heights he may then be subjected to being placed in a high place. If one fears the idea of death he is then confronted with death or the dying. That is, the oxymoron metaphor combines opposites such as "Life is death," "Hot is cold," so "paradoxical intention" has the patient doing the opposite of that which he wishes to do. Our normal experience of death is such a paradox.

The dogmatic nature of the fixedness of the existentialistic model of Heidegger is revealed in Feifel's statement,

"The notion of the uniqueness and individuality of each of us gathers full meaning *only* in realizing that we must die." (62)

The existentialist view that facing death and experiencing dread help one to lead a better life is questionable. One sort of life many have been led to as a consequence of existentialist thinking has been described by Norman Mailer in "The White Negro" (*The Long Patrol*):

"The American existentialist . . . is to accept the terms of death, to live with death as immediate danger, to divorce oneself from society, to exist without roots, to set out on that uncharted journey into the rebellious imperatives of the self. In short, whether the life is criminal or not, the decision is to encourage the psychopath in oneself . . . the life where a man must go until he is beat . . . where he must be with it or doomed not to swing."

According to Mailer, the "hipster," now called the "hippie," smokes pot, has his own "in" jargon, excludes all who don't do or talk as he does or are over thirty, stresses emotion as self-justificatory, thinks that whatever he feels like doing is right, wants total freedom, is selfish, lacks knowledge of cause and effect of his actions, is irresponsible, sees things almost solely from the point of view of leftist rhetoric, lives (as does the neurotic or psychotic) only in the present, desires to rebel, cannot restrain his violence, favors strong or violent emotions, thinks all these qualities make him interesting, is bored, opposes reading and rational inquiry, stresses the dare or courage, stresses action or doing rather than understanding or intelligent planning, is as Mailer says, "hopelessly incommunicative," thinks he has an absolute right over the bodies of others yet wants total freedom for himself.

In short, the hippie is confused. He is confused about emotions and so instead of gaining more freedom by his stressing emotions, he becomes a slave to them. By viewing everything as absurd and meaningless he fails to learn about how things work, about cause and effect, about himself and his environment, and so becomes a slave of his ignorance. His stress is on mystic, felt experience only. This excludes the more positive and enlightened feelings one might have. It reveals a deficiency in the ability to feel. "The mystic's inner experience of the possibilities within death is his logic. So, too, for the existentialist. And the psychopath." Their goal, Mailer says, is only "their knowledge that what is happening at each instant of the electric present is good or bad for them . . . " That is, the stress is on their own selfish uninformed interests and feelings of the moment. Mailer says,

"Consider the hipster a philosophical psychopath. . . .
The psychopath at his extreme is virtually . . . incapable of
restraining his violence. . . . The psychopath seldom knows
any reality greater than the face, the voice, the being of
the particular people among whom he may find himself at
any moment."

Mailer quotes Robert Lindner's statement from *Rebel Without
A Cause* that the psychopath

"is incapable of exertions for the sake of others. All his
efforts, hidden under no matter what disguise, represent
investments designed to satisfy his immediate wishes and
desires. . . . The psychopath, like the child, cannot delay
the pleasures of gratification . . . he must rape . . . His
egoistic ambitions lead him to headlines by daring
performances."

The hippie language stresses pleasure for oneself. He lives as
long as he has energy to compete for immediate pleasure which
he is always seeking. He would put it, as Mailer says, " 'Well,
now, man, like I'm looking for a cat to turn me on. . . .' " Their
main goal is said to be to have a good orgasm and they advocate
absolute sexual freedom.

The possible result of the views held by the American
existentialist hippie are that,

"The hipster lives with his hatred, that many of them
are the material for an elite of storm troopers ready to
follow the first truly magnetic leader whose view of mass
murder is phrased in a language which reaches their
emotions. . . . The hipster is equally a candidate for the
most reactionary and most radical movements. . . . "

In response to Mailer's support of the hippie, which turns
out to be more of an argument against the hippie, Jean
Malaquais says that to think the hippie has a new kind of
knowledge is false. The hippie's knowledge is only a very
narrow practical knowledge of how to survive momentarily in a
back alley, nothing more. Ned Polsky, another commentator on
Mailer's article in the same volume (*The Long Patrol*) states,

"The new Bohemia's inferiority shows up clearly in its lack of intellectual content. Most hipsters scarcely read at all not because they can't but because they won't. The closest thing to an intellectual discussion is their chatter about the pseudo-profundities of contemporary jazz; they don't even know − worse, don't want to know − that the things they praise were achieved by art − music composers years ago. As for the few who can be said to read they . . . select what is in large part trip − a compound of Rexroth and Rimbaud, Henry Miller and *Mad Comics,* Sartre and science fiction, jazz magazines and jerkoff magazines. Their own literary productions are few, and what there are of them . . . have almost no literary merit whatever. . . . Hipsters are not only more 'psychologically' crippled than most people but sexually likewise − they are not sexually free and have no chance to become so. . . . Mailer confuses the life of action with the life of acting out."

The above account applies as well today as it did a few years ago when Mailer wrote. It applies not to every existentialist but to a certain number who have directly or indirectly been influenced by them. Every college student has to take several English courses and is exposed to existentialistic literature or criticism. One of the main consequences of holding the existentialist viewpoint has been presented. Whether or not the account is absolutely true of the American existentialist, or hippie, or leftist liberationist − at least the account is suggestive. The existentialist does not seem to be of much help in telling us how we may live our lives better, and to tell us that we must confront death and experience anxiety, dread and meaninglessness may do more harm than good.

I do not wish to assume that existentialist philosophers are hippies. In fact, I think it is important to consider existentialism as sympathetically as possible. Some of their views and the consequences of them must be found to be helpful and interesting. It is important to take an educated view of existentialism rather than merely a critical view. It is equally important not to take a sympathetic view of it without also a critical view.

8. *My Death*

The existentialists, in conjunction with their emphasis on the individual, subjectivity, and emotion, stress the fact that one's own death is of a different sort than the death of another. Tolstoy also gives instances of this:

> "And he had to live thus all alone on the brink of an abyss, with no one who understood or pitied him." (T 79)
> " 'We can ease your sufferings.' 'You can't even do that. Let me be.' " (T 90)

Each dies his own death because one's experiences are only his own:

> "His mental sufferings were his chief torture." (T 90)

Perhaps the following paragraph best shows the import of one's own death:

> "The syllogism he had learnt from Kitzewetter's Logic: 'Caius is a man, men are mortal, therefore Caius is mortal,' had always seemed to him correct as applied to Caius, but certainly not as applied to himself. That Caius — man in the abstract — was mortal, was perfectly correct, but he was not Caius, not an abstract man, but a creature quite quite separate from all others. He had been little Vanya, with a mamma and a papa, with Mitya and Volodya, with the toys, a coachman and a nurse, afterwards with Katenka and with all the joys, griefs, and delights of childhood, boyhood, and youth. What did Caius know of the smell of that striped leather ball Vanya has been so fond of? Had Caius kissed his mother's hand like that, and did the silk of her dress rustle so for Caius? Had he rioted like that at school when the pastry was bad? Had Caius been in love like that? Could Caius preside at a session as he did? 'Caius really was mortal, and it was right for him to die; but for me, little Vanya, Ivan Ilych, with all my thoughts and emotions, it's altogether a different matter. It cannot be that I ought to die. That would be too terrible.' " (T 81)

On Heidegger's view an inauthentic they-self is contrasted with an authentic self. My death must be considered as a possibility rather than an actuality, for only others have actually died. One is not buried from his own point of view. In this sense my death is "non-relational." It is different than objective biological death or the death of others. He speaks not of biological death but of existential - ontological death or consciousness of death.

> "We cannot compute certainty of death by ascertaining how many cases of death we encounter." (H 309)
> "Death is in every case mine, in so far as it 'is' at all." (H 284)
> "Dying is not an event; it is a phenomenon to be understood existentially." (H 284)
> "If idle talk is always ambiguous, so is this manner of talking about death. Dying, which is essentially mine in such a way that no one can be my representative is perverted into an event of public occurrence which the 'they' encounters." (H 297)

Since death is supposedly the end of our own possibility it is non-relational. It is indefinite.

Heidegger would have us focus our entire life on the fact of our own death. We must find the answer to it for ourselves, on his view. It is not, however, clear why one cannot accept another's answer to death especially if it is found acceptable and well-founded. It is trivial, in a way, to say that I have to die my own death. As Sartre stated, I always must do whatever I do. If I take on a false theory it is I who take on a false theory. Certainly we may accept other's views uncritically and we must make other's views meaningful to ourselves rather than take them on as slogans or fads, even existentialism. But if this is all that is meant, Heidegger and Sartre should have said so. Either their position is trivial because I do everything I do, or the simple point is made that I need to accept the death of others or their views of death critically.

A further problem arises. How do I know my death is unique and entirely different from that of others? If I cannot know what death is for me how can I know what it is for another so as to distinguish it from my own? We often learn of our own "death" by observing what happens to others. Our language, including our language about death, is intersubjective not private, and so my death is not my death as a private experience. The problem of private states arises. What evidence is there of our having unique, internal, hidden private states or a private language? By means of an intersubjective language we learn to speak and theorize about death. Without ever having learned a language we do not know how we would think and so do not know how death would be revealed if at all. It is not known what animals and insects know, and not known if they are aware of death. We can only describe such a situation, e.g., the dog walked around the recently killed dog. He sniffed, looked away then back again at the still body. After a short while he walked away. What the dog might have "thought" is unknown even if he had yelped or whimpered at the death of his master. It could be that he just "noticed" that his master was behaving differently. He may not have been "surprised" to find that the next day his master was again throwing a stick to him. Perhaps this is why some dogs remain "faithful" or stay by their master even after death. They were simply conditioned to act in a certain way and they are not "aware" of the nature of death.

Not only might we learn of our own death by means of and in terms of intersubjective language and phenomena, but if we can know of another's death we can by analogy relate his death to our own. If we assume, as we usually do, that consciousness depends on a physical body functioning normally then we can assume that the death of another will be no different than the death of oneself. I am not asserting that this is or is not the case but merely that if Heidegger is to maintain that one's own death is unique he must show that it in fact is unique. To say it is unique because one dies alone, is merely to say one dies.

Even to speak of one's own consciousness ceasing assumes an intersubjective language by means of which we conceive of, categorize and so constitute a self. The alternative is to wonder how a dog "thinks" of himself. Heidegger presents his view as follows:

"Death is Dasein's *ownmost* possibility. Being towards this possibility discloses to Dasein its *ownmost* potentiality-for-being, in which its very Being is the issue. Here it can become manifest to Dasein that in this distinctive possibility of its own self, it has been wrenched away from the 'they.' " (H 307)

For Sartre also, death shows that life is unique, that one only really experiences his own death. But he makes the objection against Heidegger that although no one can die my death, no one can do anything else for me either. Sartre stresses one's freedom to choose one's death, that it must subjectively arise out of the consciousness of each person. Death is not that which gives life its meanings, as Heidegger believes. (S 539) We know of our deaths by others' deaths as a sign of our own:

"Death . . . does not remain simply human, it becomes *mine.* By being interiorized it is individualized. Death is no longer the great unknowable which limits the human, it is the phenomenon of my personal life which makes this life a unique life." (S 532)

"Death is never that which gives life its meanings." (S 539)

"Not only does death disarm my waiting by definitively removing the *waiting* and by abandoning in indetermination the realization of the ends which make known to me what I am — but again it confers a meaning from the outside on everything which I live in subjectively." (S 544)

9. *Emotion Toward Death*

Tolstoy mentioned various emotions regarding dying and death: The "death chill" (cf. Leveton "Ego-Chill"), despair, fear, etc.

"A chill came over him." (T 80)

"Ivan Ilych saw that he was dying, and he was in continual despair." (T 81)

"There was no fear because there was no death." (T 94)

There is at the present state of knowledge little agreement about the nature of emotions. This allows new theories to develop and new emotions to be created without much clear criticism. The topic has been advanced recently by writers on contemporary philosophical psychology. (See W. Shibles, *Emotions*) It is often thought that an emotion is an inner feeling or mental state, that it is an individual, personal, private state. It is seen upon analysis that an emotion is found to be a pseudo-category which stands for more specific phenomena. B. F. Skinner wrote,

"The emotions are excellent examples of the fictional causes to which we commonly attribute behavior."

One cannot "have" an emotion but there is rather a specific configuration of events. "Emotion" does not name a specific state. An emotion involves and partly describes a specific context, relationship between persons and/or objects, evaluations, and often some feelings. It is not itself a feeling although it may involve feelings. "I envy his technique," may merely be an evaluation, a way of saying "he has a good technique," without involving any special internal feeling whatsoever. Jealousy is not just a feeling or a special kind of feeling, but largely an assessment of a situation such that, for example, one has something someone else wants and does not wish to give it up. Feelings may be involved but they need not be the same in every instance of jealousy and they may change from moment to moment. In any case it is not just a feeling. The jealous person tells of his jealousy by describing an external event or situation. Jealousy involves a context and part of what we mean by jealousy is a description of that context.

Thus an emotion does not have an object but rather the object and context is included in what is meant by the emotion in the first place. One does not just fall in love, one falls in love with someone. The following dialogue seems strange:

"I fell in love"
"With whom?"
"No one, I just fell in love."

Now, the existentialists have presented a model of reality which gives (epistemological) primacy to emotions. Nietzsche stressed emotions such as struggle, overcoming, being unpopular or unliked, suffering; Kierkegaard stressed dread, Heidegger meaninglessness, care, anticipation, despair, *Angst* or anxiety, and dread; Sartre, alienation, anxiety, nausea, meaninglessness, emptiness and similar emotions. Nearly all of these emotions are negative, undesirable, or neurotic. It is in the religious tradition that such emotions as "despair" have been stressed. In the *Ars moriendi* or Craft of Dying books of the fourteenth and fifteenth century one of the five temptations of the dying is temptation to despair. This is a sinful thing for a Christian and requires inspiration against despair. (O'Connor 7-9) The idea is that if one faces death and despair it will make him more religious. Heidegger uses this device to try to suggest that facing death can change one's life. Here is another instance that the existentialist view is just another restatement of Christian dogma and techniques. Reality is viewed metaphysically through the model of such emotions. Emotions are thought of as individual, private, personal, situational, certain, immediate. Thus they cohere with the stress placed on the subjective individual, rather than with an intellectual inquiry and reason or areas of knowledge involving laws or rules. There is a great emphasis placed on the self-justificatory or self-righteous nature of emotions. One "does one's own thing" on the basis of his emotions or on the basis of how he feels in the situation. In Camus' *The Stranger,* a man feels like shooting another and so he does so. "It seemed all right at the time."

The existentialists often treat emotions as if they were feelings and so think that emotions justify themselves. One supposedly just "has" an emotion which "comes over him" and so can do nothing about it but satisfy the passion. But if negative emotions, as I have suggested, rather involve descriptions of contexts and assessments as well as sporadic feelings, then emotions are partly rational. As rational, they can be reconsidered, clarified, and dissipated due to their unreasonableness.

One's passion for revenge may be seen to help no one, to be quite ineffective in correcting the cause of the original wrong. Instead of revenge one might see that the better policy is to try to understand what the cause of the wrong is and correct it intelligently. The emotion of revenge may then be found to be a useless "getting back for its own sake" and so dissipate to the point where one no longer experiences it. One will no longer have the feelings which usually are involved with revenge.

The difficulties which arise with emotions as they are presented in the metaphysics of Sartre (who has also a small book on emotions) and Heidegger are mainly these:

1. the nature of emotions is either assumed without analysis or inadequately presented.
2. emotions are often treated as private, and mental, and confused with feelings.
3. emotion terms are misused because they are combined with obscure metaphysical terms thus creating category-mistakes.
4. new emotions are stipulated to exist which lack objective, descriptive foundation.
5. emotions are thought to be self-justificatory.
6. emotions are obscure in these ways yet are made the very foundation of existentialistic metaphysics.
7. emotions are often thought to have objects which do not exist. This is a misconception of the nature of emotion.

For Heidegger the authentic emotion regarding death is dread or anxiety. These emotions relate to possibilities rather than actualities, that is, in a sense, are objectless. The inauthentic emotion of fear of death regards death from the viewpoint of another and so as an object. Anxiety is not fear.

"The 'they' does not permit us the courage for anxiety in the face of death." (H 298)

"The state-of-mind which can hold open the utter and constant threat to itself arising from Dasein's ownmost individualized Being, is anxiety. (*Angst*) In this state-of-mind, Dasein finds itself *face to face* with the 'nothing' of the possible impossibility of its existence. Anxiety is anxious *about* the potentiality-for-Being of the entity so destined, and in this way it discloses the uttermost possibility." (H 310)

I cannot "fear" my own death as my own death because death is not an actual object and, on his view, fear required that there be an object. It's not at all clear why this must be so. We say we "fear" the unknown. It does not seem that dread or fear can be adequately characterized merely in terms of having or not having an object. As was earlier mentioned, an emotion is in part a description of a situation and context. It is not just an internal feeling directed at an external object as an arrow is directed at a target. Nor are these emotions necessarily feelings one must have naturally. They may be culturally determined, created, or even be pseudo-emotions. Heidegger may be stipulating emotions which one never has, which never arise. The emotional dread or anxiety may be created by him in the sense that if one assesses or sees the situation regarding death as he does then one will experience these emotions. Emotion is partly rational. Heidegger himself seems to recognize this for he does not make a clear separation between reason and emotion. Understanding "is always accompanied by a mood." (H 296) He seems to be stipulating the existence of new emotions which accord with his metaphysical analysis of death. They are in a sense "metaphysical emotions."

If anxiety or dread of death will lead one to a meaningful life it may be only because we believe Heidegger that it will do so. Great anxiety *may* lead to a more meaningful life but not necessarily. Paul Schilder states about Heidegger's view of death and nothingness as constantly before man giving life meaning,

"Heidegger offers as proof of this assertion merely his intuition. According to my opinion, such theories are merely based upon the misunderstanding of words." (80)

Anxiety may rather lead to suicide or neurosis. This may be especially the case when "Life is not your friend." Heidegger is saying, as Koestenbaum represents it, "I despair totally, therefore exist necessarily." (K, b) Heidegger makes emotions the foundation of his metaphysics. He writes, "Being-toward-death is essentially anxiety." (H 310) Unfortunately, the first statement above does not follow or is trivial. That is, to say "I despair therefore I exist," can only legitimately mean "I despair therefore I despair." To say I despair therefore I exist in some other sense does not follow, e.g., "I despair therefore I exist in the next room." "Being" and "exist" are naming-fallacies.

Jacques Choron (1964) wrote,

"We cannot expect assistance from the existentialist philosophers . . . since these either want man to remain in the state of death anxiety or categorically declare the meaninglessness and absurdity of life."

People too often let negative emotions be the solution to death. It is as if life only gains its values through destruction of itself.

The negative emotions of dread, despair, anxiety, thus seem to reveal what is sometimes meant by Being or existence. But to say they lead to one's being and existence would mean he would have to reveal what being or existence means in the new context. When anxiety gives us Being, *what* does it give us? Being is empty here as elsewhere. It either refers to everything and therefore makes no distinctions, or else it refers to one or another thing so equivocally or trivially that it is dangerous.

Another possible interpretation is that our intellect just objectively contemplates death but we only really confront death when we find that we experience such emotions as dread or anxiety. But since emotions are partly intellectual or rational our emotions may be constituted merely by confused rational assessments just as those of a "mental" patient who thinks some one is out to get him. In brief, if one is confused about death or fills himself with metaphysical and mystical views about death his emotions, which are partly comprised by such views, will be unreliable and misleading. Emotions are not self-justifying. They can be criticized in a way similar to that in which rational statements are. We often say, "You shouldn't have felt that way," or "You have no reason to feel anxious."

Walter Kaufmann suggests similar difficulties with Heidegger's view of anxiety:

"It is true that human beings occasionally experience anxiety without being able to say of what they are afraid, but Heidegger has not shown at all that either in many or in any of these cases people are afraid of 'Being-in-the-world.' . . . Tolstoy's indictment of an unchristian, unloving, hypocritical world cannot simply be read as a fair characterization of humanity. Nor is it true that 'Being-toward-death' is essentially anxiety, and that all illustrations to the contrary can be explained as instances of self-deception and the lack of 'courage for anxiety of death.' " (44, 47)

Sartre's view is that our consciousness of freedom gives rise to dread and anguish. We must choose, make decisions and by so doing be responsible for these choices even though we have no control of their future outcome. We supposedly suffer anguish because it is our inner nature to express nothingness Fear is from without, anguish is from within. Anguish is the apprehension of nothingness.

But here again since nothingness is a confused notion, as has been shown earlier, it is not clear how anguish can be an apprehension of it. To suffer anguish about nothingness is like suffering emotion over oneness, universal mind, absolute truth, being, existence, goodness, as such. To do so would create a great many new emotions. To do so would seem to be arbitrary stipulation.

A meaningful life may depend on one's likes and attitudes, on being conceptually free so as to be able to enjoy life. Facing death allows one to free himself of some shortcomings (not in Sartre's metaphysical sense of freedom), but it may also give him new shortcomings. One may be able to face death quite honestly yet still not enjoy or organize his life. If one faces death he may have to overcome his fear and by so doing may gain strength and courage. But it would seem that the most effective way of overcoming the fear of death would involve inquiry, clarification of the notion of death, and getting after the problem of death and possible survival as much as possible. The threat of death ought then to push one into inquiry rather than merely into an emotion of some sort. Emotion will not help to solve the problem of death. For Sartre, man is a "useless passion."

It is not satisfactory merely to say that death is a fact, accept it, do not inquire into it. Man has never really accepted that. He has been dishonest about death and been afraid to face it. He has failed to inquire into the problem of death because it is a difficult problem, one that seemingly allows us no possibility of conquering it. But this would just mean that one must keep inquiring, keep attempting to learn more and more about its nature. To accept death is to ignore man's greatest challenge, to dogmatically accept total defeat without inquiry or with mere emotion, a wimper. To accept death is like failing to see that there is disease in the world or that humans have sexual needs. Such inquiry may be an ongoing thing, but it is an adjustment and offers hope. It is an attempt to do something about the problem of the nature of aging, survival, prolongation of healthy life, which gives real adjustment rather than blindly accepting a vagueness we call death or finding ways to divert one's attention from it. Heidegger and Sartre both treat death and emotions too dogmatically as fixed parts of fixed natures. To think of death as a fixed end is useful for the purpose of helping us plan our lives, but we need no metaphysics to do that.

On the existentialist view since "emotion" and feeling are valued more highly than reason or intellect their concern might be to keep a hospital patient alive as long as body sensations are present after rational consciousness has ceased. The consequence would be that of keeping humans alive after irreversible brain death, thus yielding human vegetables. But as was indicated a clarification of emotion precludes this consequence.

10. *Death as Absurdity (Antithesis, Paradox, Oxymoron).*

Death may reveal the absurdity of life, that there is a great contrast between life and death or that there is death in life and life in death in some way. These accounts stress 1. oxymoron or metaphorical contrasts of opposites, 2. nothingness, absurdity, meaninglessness. The existentialists themselves do not speak of metaphor or oxymoron but rather seem captivated by their own metaphors.

Tolstoy presents many of such situations. He presents absurdity, trival events, and contrasts:

"That drawing room where he had fallen and for the sake of which (how bitterly ridiculous it seemed) he had sacrificed his life — for he knew that his illness originated with that knock." (T 82)

One often wants only to die for great causes and over important matters. But much of this is outside of one's control. One is to a large extent the subject of chance. It is a kind of absurdity to die for nothing at all or die from a fish bone. Of course, to die from a fish bone can show how really important fish bones are.

"What is it all for?" (T 82)

"It really is so, I lost my life over that curtain as I might have done when storming a fort. Is that possible? How terrible and how stupid?" (T 82)

Ethics seems to have little or nothing to do with our dying or our death. Ivan is worried by the fact that he did not live as he ought to have lived, though he did everything "properly." Tolstoy writes,

"He tried to defend all those things to himself and suddenly felt the weakness of what he was defending. There was nothing to defend." (T 90)

It thus seems absurd that death and dying are irrelevant to the sort of life we live. To think death is some kind of punishment is to anthropomorphize death.

" 'Why these sufferings?' And the voice answered, 'For no reason — they just are so.' Beyond and besides this there was nothing." (T 89)

"He wept on account of his helplessness, his terrible loneliness, the cruelty of man, the cruelty of God, and the absence of God. 'Why hast thou done all this? Why hast thou brought me here? Why, why dost thou torment me so terribly?' He did not expect an answer and yet wept

because there was no answer and could be none." (T 88)
"Then what does it mean? Why? It can't be that life is so
senseless and horrible." (T 88)

The image of Gerasim holding Ivan's legs high in the air, an
almost comical picture, shows the absurdity of life and death. It
is ironic that it is almost the one thing which, though seemingly
comical, Ivan finds most meaningful in his life.

"It seemed to Ivan Ilych that he felt better while Gerasim
was holding up his legs." (T 83)

The following juxtapositions of opposites are also absurd,
yet at the same time suggest life-death opposites. Ivan, while
suffering, is confronted by the vivacious, sensuous presence of
his wife. His wife was herself a contradiction in looking so
attractive, for she was cold and lacked understanding:

"After dinner, at seven o'clock, Praskovya Fedorovna
came into the room in evening dress, her full bosom
pushed up by her corset. . . ." (T 86)

Ivan's son, while appearing pathetic, nevertheless, had more
understanding than most of the others:

"His son had always seemed pathetic to him, and . . . It
seemed to Ivan Ilych that Vasya was the only one besides
Gerasim who understood and pitied him." (T 87)

The most expensive furniture is contrasted with its having
some of the poorest qualities. The following statement also
symbolizes man's deterioration.

"Morocco is expensive, but it does not wear well." (T 89)

In this last quotation we may also see how an attempt is
made to somehow relate death by analogy to our experiences,
to try to find analogies which disclose the nature of dying. It is
we who are expensive Morocco, it is we who are fragile, who do
not wear well.

A contrast, antithesis, oxymoron, or seeming juxtaposition of opposites is provided by:

"It is as if I had been going downhill while I imagined I was going up?" (T 88)

"She began to remind him of his medicines. 'For Christ's sake let me die in peace!' he said." (T 90)

Here life-giving medicine is contrasted with death. He says in effect, "Don't disturb me with life-giving medicine, can't you see I am dying." A paradoxical view perhaps but not when one sees that contemporary medicine cannot cure one of death, and so life-death is a paradox. Medicine cannot yet cure one of death, only put it off for awhile.

In "For Chirst's sake let me die in peace!" if taken literally, there is the paradoxical view that one dies for Christ, and so without the hope of medicine. In addition it is suggested perhaps that medicine is of no help when what is needed is a miracle, like Christ's resurrection. But such suggestions are faint. It may mean "For Christ's sake let me die in love."

One of the keys to what Heidegger does, though without explicitly presenting it as a technique or showing that he is aware of it, is to use oxymoron, antithesis. Out of this arises an absurdity, a meaninglessness, paradox. Life is death, death as revealed in life, is the paradox we are in. He appears to be struggling to say this in his own metaphysical way:

"Dasein is dying as long as it exists." (H 295)

"Death, in the widest sense, is a phenomenon of life." (H 290)

Koestenbaum echos this view:

"And paradoxically, the most vitalizing fact of life is the utter inevitability of death!" (K, a 35)

Heidegger says that death is a possibility that I cannot avoid. This is paradoxical. How can an inevitability be only a possibility? He paradoxically holds that great anxiety alone leads to a meaningful life. Only not-to-be gives sense of to be. Being is nothingness. The notion of being is again misused here. What is it to mean, and if it means everything it means nothing. If it means everything nothing also may be included in it. To talk of Being as such or Nothing as such is unintelligible because these terms are so open and vague that they cannot include anything at all. They make no differences. They do not matter.

Some misleading views may be left from metaphysics' view that death gives rise to dread of nothingness or that nothingness is a thing. Wenkart points out that the schizophrenic child is afraid of an absence or a void. He is afraid when food disappears from the plate because it is eaten. He sees and fears absence. The existentialist view may be a metaphysical or intellectual schizophrenia of this sort insomuch as nothingness is in itself feared. It is quite a different thing to fear the loss of something, than to fear nothingness itself.

Heidegger in attempting to argue for being, first assumes death or nothingness and then states that being is not that. But this will not do because nothing only makes sense in relation to being, not being-as-such, anyway. By being, Heidegger sometimes seems to imply that he means the emotion of dread or anxiety. Nothing or non-being would then refer only to lack of emotion. He states that not facing death with dread is not to be really alive, not to have being. But "nothing" here cannot be nothing at all. Nothing is relative to our experience and still within our experience. It is having an empty case when it could be full, not like having an empty case when we cannot know what it would be like for it to be full. Nothing is a certain configuration of things.

The device of paradox and oxymoron are useful in forcing us to explore a concept by juxtaposing it with unlike concepts thereby creating tension, and forcing us to consider closely and revise the previous categories and association involved with such concepts.

Sartre speaks of Being and Nothingness on the metaphysical level but he does treat death or nothingness, at times, as being involved in or determined by a conscious living process only. This reveals the absurdity of thinking of death as being only a living process and at the same time as being an unknown to us:

"It [death] is a being which belongs to an existent process
and which in a certain way constitutes the meaning of the
process. Thus the final chord of a melody always looks on
the one side toward silence — that is, toward the
nothingness of sound which will follow the melody; in one
sense it is made with the silence which will follow the
melody, in one sense it is made with the silence since the
silence which will follow is already present in the resolved
chord as its meaning." (S 531)

The paradigm for nothingness or death here seems to be
silence. They are seen as analogous to silence. But the analogy
fails because silence is still something. It is just a different
configuration than noise. One may think silence is nothing
because it is seen as the opposite of noise — but that is just a
linguistic problem. One can put "not" in front of anything.
That does not create an entity, Nothingness. Silence is not an
entity. But there is a configuration of events such that we hear
nothing, or very little, but where we still see, feel, think, etc. To
have silence is not to have no experience whatsoever. It is
merely to change the configuration and quality of one's
experience. We can enjoy silence. Whether there can be absolute
nothingness is still a question. It may or may not be a
meaningless question.

Sartre says, "Death, in fact, is only on its negative side the
nihilation of my possibilities." (S 540)

Here death is defined as the end of possibilities. I assume
"possibility" does not include the possibility of being dead for
if it did it would not end *all* possibilities. Stated differently
Sartre uses "possibility" in a vague, unintelligible or at least
equivocal, open-context way. How does Sartre know that death
ends all possibilities? Does he know what death is or that an
afterlife is not possible? He has not argued his case but merely
stipulated it *a priori* in an oracular way.

While he says that death ends possibilities still it is not for
him just a fixed end which gives one's life meaning, as Heidegger
believes. It is in a way created by us and tells us only about
ourselves. This seems to put death back into experience rather

than outside it. We cannot know reality (being-in-itself) but only appearance and perspectives which we create (being-in-itself).

> "The absurd character of death. In this sense every attempt to consider it as a resolved chord at the end of a melody must be sternly rejected." (S 533)

> "Death is never that which gives life its meaning." (S 539)

Death is absurd because created by our consciousness yet never understood by it, and because we never know when it will happen. It haunts us as chance. We may prepare to die courageously in some way, but before we can we find we absurdly die of a fishbone, a cold, or from stepping on a banana peel.

> "What then is death? Nothing but a certain aspect of facticity and of being-for-others — i.e., nothing other than the given. It is absurd that we die." (S 547)

> "It (death) is in no way distinguished from birth, and it is the identity of birth and death that we call facticity." (S 545)

Here is another instance of the metaphor, oxymoron or paradox of "Birth in death." This metaphor may reveal some insights into both of its terms, but Sartre mainly just presents the juxtaposition.

Frankl, as was mentioned earlier, stresses "paradoxical intention," which means that the patient is encouraged to do or wish to happen the very thing he is afraid of. Frankl's "paradoxical intention" may be made more clear than he makes it by conceiving of it in terms of antithesis, of oxymoron, and on the model, "life is death," and "death is life." The center of Frankl's therapy is to show the significance of the experience of death for therapy, for living a meaningfull life. To experience meaningfulness one must experience meaninglessness. But his view is more like the view of Sartre than Heidegger. "Paradoxical intention" relates to Sartre's view of death as an absent presence, and to absurdity.

11. *Death and the Self*

The problem of what death is depends on what the self is because it must be determined just what it is that dies. If the self is regarded as body and soul, as the mystical religious tradition would have it, then the body dies but the soul does not. Heidegger speaks of the self as Dasein, being-there in the world. But as long as Dasein *is,* it is not yet, and as soon as Dasein dies, it is no more. This parallels the Epicurean "If death is there, you aren't; if you are there, death isn't." The self is defined as a not-yet. To dread is to be a self. The awareness of death can lead one to fully exist and so be an authentic self. Death and dread reveal the self and the alienation involved. The self is defined in terms of death, for Heidegger. Emotion, e.g., anxiety, reveals the true self as well as the world. Self is emotion is world, is part of Heidegger's view. The self is defined metaphysically as it is for Sartre who speaks of it in terms of "being-for-itself" and "being-in-itself." As we have seen, the view one takes of self determines in part the view one takes of death.

Tolstoy speaks of the various selves of Ivan: his childhood self, his culturally determined self, his newly awakened self which arises from his apprehension of death, etc. He writes, for example,

"But the child [Ivan] who had experienced that happiness existed no longer, it was like a reminiscence of somebody else." (T 88)

In considering what dies when the self dies we often make such distinctions as:

1. death of cerebrum or higher brain center or death of consciousness
2. death of motor controls of back of brain
3. death of heart

etc.

It is a question as to when a person dies, because we are not sure how to conceive of a person or self. Many would say that if a person's higher brain centers are permanently damaged so that he will not regain consciousness he is no longer a person or self even though his body may be kept alive. (If consciousness is not lost but if the body fails to function, the heart and other organs may be able to operate by or be replaced by machines. Body failure may not determine death even if such machine dependence is permanent. If many of the parts become replaced a problem of identity may even develop.) It is an unsolved medical and moral question as to when a person is dead, partly because decisions need to be made as to what a person or self is. (See chapter on the medical definition of death and the definition of a "person" in the chapter on abortion.)

12. *Analogies, Symbols and Metaphors of Death and Dying.*

Tolstoy's story depends heavily on these devices. He presents the following analogy, and very beautiful image of flight:

"And the example of a stone falling downwards with increasing velocity entered his mind. Life, a series of interesting sufferings, flies, further and further towards its end — the most terrible suffering. 'I am flying. . . .' " (T 89)

"Flying" is a marvelous image because it suggests that we are ignorant of death, cannot really know of it, so we try a fantasy or fictive image which we know is fictive. We are not really flying, yet we can represent by this image our hope and our lack of knowledge at the same time. It is thus that we are all flying. We fly towards death.

Light has been an important symbol of knowledge, of life. The sun gives life, and light allows man to live and see.

"Ivan Illych fell through and caught sight of light. . . ." (T 91)
" 'Death, darkness?' " (T 85)
"In place of death there was light." (T 92)

The light here is mystical. How are we to conceive of it? It is not exhausted by the notion of a beatific vision. Can death or the experience of it only be rendered by a metaphor? Do our models and metaphors of death *create* death rather than describe or illustrate it? How could they illustrate death if we do not know what death is? What is needed is a more thorough analysis of the notion of death. James Olney's recent article (1972) on metaphor in Tolsloy's story of Ivan Ilych gives only a religious interpretation of metaphor as symbol or transcendent. (See sections on the review of D. Z. Phillips book and the review of Vernon's *Sociology of Death* for an analysis of symbol.)

Small events often stand for, symbolize, actually serve as analogies, or examples of what we mean by death. We may think that death is pain.

> "His ache . . . acquired a new and more serious significance . . ." (T 77)
> "But then, when he was moving something himself, his wife would say: 'Let the servants do it. You will hurt yourself again.' And suddenly *It* would flash through the screen and he would see it." (T 82)
> "He was terrified by what he saw, especially by the limp way in which his hair clung to his pallid forehead." (T 85)

Mirrors, especially, serve as signs or magical models of aging, dying, and death. Mirrors involve the revealing of the self in a metaphoric way. And one views oneself as older. Artists have at times painted pictures of men looking in a mirror only to see there their future fleshless skull. Don Quixote was shocked to a certain kind of reality by means of mirrors.

Witnessing an accident can symbolize one's own destruction. It is really that I crash when the cars collide. Heidegger states, "Death in the widest sense, is a phenomenon of life." (H 290)

Koestenbaum interprets Heidegger in giving a number of instances of symbolic death:

> "Death . . . is a cornucopia of clues about the meaning of life." (K, a 32)

"A symbolic death is the collapse of the particular world towards which our energies and goals are directed. The collapse of his business is a symbolic death for the businessman." (K, a 33)

"A personal slight is a further example of symbolic death. To be ignored by others, especially by those whose attention we prize and esteem, is to be thought dead. . . . To refuse to speak to the person . . . we act as if that person were dead." (K, a 33)

He almost quotes Heidegger's statement above (H 290) in saying "Death is a fact of life." (K, a 40)

Sartre uses symbols such as stickiness, nausea, guilt, through which to view the world. He stresses the stare, or the surprise face in the window. Both he and Heidegger use metaphors of negative emotions as well as metaphysical notions such as being and nothingness. Sartre says nothingness lies in the heart of being, like a worm, (a pathetic fallacy or sinking metaphor) but also sees the world through emotions of anxiety and alienation. For these writers, not living fully symbolizes death in life, a symbolic death. They do not, however, clarify the nature of symbol and metaphor. (See Shibles *Metaphor*)

Poets have at times given us emotionally suggestive models or analogies by means of which to view death. They seem persuasive. One may observe a glistening snowflake which implicitly yields a certain feeling of mystery – hidden within the snowflake a vague suggestion that we must die.

13. *Man Creates His Own Death*

Man creates his own death by his interpretation of it. If he misconceives of it he must live with his misconception. If he thinks there is punishment after life he must live in the torture of such an idea whether or not such is in fact the case. If we hold views which are circular, are category-mistakes, or if we fail to clarify our concepts associated with death we determine, though in a mistaken way, what death is. I would want to suggest that the nature of death is determined by the limits of our language and limits of our metaphors of death. We see death through our models of death. Such metaphors and models to a large extent constitute death. Dylan Thomas wrote "Death is all metaphors." ("Alterwise by Owl-Light") The existentialists, however, fail to talk of models and metaphors, but are rather captivated by their own fixed metaphors and jargon.

Sartre, quoting Kafka, presents this as follows:

> "We may recall here a fable of Kafka's: A merchant comes to plead his case at the castle where a forbidden guard bars the entrance. The merchant does not dare to go further; he waits and dies still waiting. At the hour of death he asks the guardian, 'How does it happen that I was the only one waiting?' And the guardian replies, 'This gate was made for you.' . . . *Each man makes for himself his own gate."* (S 550)

> "I become responsible for *my* death as for my life." (S 532)

For Sartre I make myself what I am, I am responsible for the character of finitude which causes my life and my death. I make myself because I select out choices or possibilities, and so limit myself. The matter may be put in this way: The gates we make are made from our metaphors of death.

The existentialist, Karl Jaspers, states similarly,

> "Man and only man produces languages, tools, ideas, acts, – in short, he produces himself." (22)

One's language affects and partly determines the way one views reality. It partly constitutes reality.

Wenkart suggests this also by saying that we adjust to the world by means of language. We even create nothingness by means of our language and imagination:

> "Communication is the most decisive participation in what transpires between man and man. Silence as absence of communication is an overwhelming threat. . . . Where language as the greatest and most meaningful source of coexistence fails, isolation spreads. Nothingness prevails between man and man." (87)

On Heidegger's view we do not choose our death but are thrown into it. On the other hand it is meaningful depending on how one looks at it. Sartre and Heidegger stress the individual's interpretation of reality and death when they stress the possible, or choice, rather than the actual.

Koestenbaum, reflecting Sartre's and Heidegger's view, states that man constitutes the world. (K, a 32) Each man creates his own world to structure his life and viewpoints around, e.g., a business world. "Every man lives in a self-centered world." (K, a 32)

The meaning of existentialistic self-creation is merely that man chooses certain things and not others. It is not an account or clarification of how one gains knowledge and so does not add to such knowledge. No insight is given into the nature of or relation between thought, meaning, words, objects, nor are symbol and metaphor clarified.

14. *Death As An Absolute Fact*

Heidegger regards death as an absolute fact. Sometimes, however, he asserts that we cannot really know death, as was mentioned in the section on whether one can imagine one's own death. Following Heidegger, Koestenbaum wrote,

"No meaningful existence is possible without the honest recognition of the unadulterated facts of human existence. . . . One of the most important of these facts is that of my own inevitable death." (K, a 30)

"Authentic success and happiness in human existence demand uncompromising realism: we must understand and acknowledge the facts of life." (K, a 35)

"He must see the consequences of the knowledge that he is mortal. He must never let go of this insight." (K, a 35)

"A fraudulent promise: that of symbolic immortality." (K, a 35)

"Think of one's eventual death as an absolutely necessary aspect of human existence . . ." (K, a 37)

"All of us have been condemned to die." (K, a 39)

"Man cannot escape death — real *or* symbolic. He must construct his life . . . with the full and clear realization of that fact." (K, a 39)

"Death is a fact of life." (K, a 40)

"The essence of human existence is its mortality." (K, a 41)

Thus the view presented is:

1. Death is an absolute fact, absolutely necessary.
2. It is a fact of life.
3. We must always contemplate death.
4. There is no alternative to death, no immortality, no escape from death.
5. Everyone is condemmed to die.
6. The very essence of human existence is death.

Some obvious objections arise. How do we know that death is absolutely necessary and can never be conquered? If death is an absolute fact what is that fact? We do not seem to be clear about what death is, whether some sort of afterlife is possible, etc. Thus it seems dogmatic merely to assume that a vagueness is an absolute fact. Why must we always contemplate death? It would seem better to inquire into it to try to advance knowledge about it, than to accept it as a fact and merely emotionally relate to "it." To say everyone is "Condemned" to die is to suppose a value judgement. Who condemns? This presupposes also that death is a bad thing, whereas supposedly it is a thing to contemplate and make life rich with. To say the very essence of human existence is death, sounds like a statement made during a bombing or H-bomb attack. We are very destructive people. But this is not what is meant here. Why is not the essence of man rather to inquire, solve his problems, find ways to live longer, understand death better and perhaps even overcome it in some way in the future. Descriptively, however, most men both avoid death and avoid honest, non-superstitious inquiry into death.

For Sartre death removes the one who contemplates it, removes all his possibilities and meaningfulness. Since it removes my possibilities it is outside of my possibilities. Yet he maintains that it is a given, pure fact. This may be contrasted with his view of the inability to imagine one's own death.

> "Since death does not appear on the foundation of our freedom, it can only *remove all meaning from life.*" (S 539)
>
> "Dogmatic realism was wrong in viewing death as *the state of death* — i.e., as transcendent to life — the fact remains that death such that I can discover it as *mine* necessarily engages something other than myself." (S 545)
>
> "We must conclude in opposition to Heidegger that death, far from being my peculiar possibility, is a *contingent fact* which as such on principle escapes me and originally belongs to my facticity." (S 545)
>
> "Death is a pure fact as is birth." (S 545)

The difficulty of maintaining both that death is a fact and that we lack evidence of death yields a contradiction as may be seen in the following statement by Bugenthal:

> "Life is, period. It is not a matter of [Freud's life-] instinct, it is a matter of fact. Death is, just is, period. Again, not a matter of [Freud's death-] instinct, but of fact." (332)

But then he continues with

> "We have no phenomenological evidence of what death means, only external observation. All our evidence is inferential." (332)

These two statements seem contradictory.

Norman O. Brown. *Life Against Death* New York: Vintage 1961

J. Bugenthal. *The Search for Authenticity* New York: Holt 1965

Arthur Carr. *Tolstoy's Ivan Ilych with Commentary* New York: Health Sciences 1973

Jacques Choron. *Death and Western Thought* New York: Macmillan 1964

–––––. *Modern Man and Mortality* New York: Macmillan 1964

Herman Feifel. "Death-Relevant Variable in Psychology" *Existential Psychology* R. May, ed., New York: Random House 1961

Martin Heidegger. *Being and Time* J. Macquarrie & E. Robinson, trans., New York: Harper & Row 1962

Karl Jaspers. *The Perennial Scope of Philosophy.* Quoted in R. Winn, *A Concise Dictionary of Existentialism* New York: Philosophical Library 1960, p. 22

Walter Kaufmann. "Existentialism and Death" *The Meaning of Death* H. Feifel, ed., New York: McGraw-Hill 1959

Peter Koestenbaum. "The Vitality of Death" (a) *Confrontations of Death* F. Scott and R. Brewer, eds., Oregon State University 1971

–––––. "Death and Finitude" (b) *The Vitality of Death* Westport, Conn.: Greenwood 1971

Alan Leveton. "Time, Death, and the Ego-Chill" *Journal of Existentialism* 6 (1966) 69-80

Salvatore Maddi. "Existential Neurosis" *Psychopathology Today* W. Sahakian, ed., Itasca, Illinois: Peacock Publishers 1970, pp. 130-143

Sister M. O'Connor. *The Art of Dying Well* New York: Columbia University 1942

James Olney. "Experience, Metaphor, and Meaning: The Death of Ivan Ilych" *Journal of Aesthetics and Art Criticism* 31 (1972) 101-113

Vance Randolf. "Death and Burial" *Ozark Magic and Forklore* New York: Dover 1947, pp. 301-327

Richard Ruiz. "Death in the Philosophy of Jean-Paul Sartre" *Death and the College Student* E. Shneidman, ed., New York: Behavioral Publications 1972

Gilbert Ryle. *Concept of Mind* New York: Barnes & Noble 1949

William Sahakian, ed., *Psychopathology Today* Itasca, Illinois: Peacock Publishers 1970

Theodore Sarbin. "Anxiety: Reification of a Metaphor" *Essays on Metaphor* W. Shibles, ed., Whitewater, Wisconsin: The Language Press 1972

Jean-Paul Sartre. *Being and Nothingness* H. Barnes, trans., New York: Philosophical Library 1956

Paul Schilder. *Goals and Desires of Man* New York: Columbia University Press 1942

Warren Shibles. *Emotions* Whitewater, Wisconsin: The Language Press 1973

—————. "Linguo-Centric Predicament," "Timelessness," *Philosophical Pictures* 2nd revised edition, Dubuque, Iowa: Kendall-Hunt 1972

—————. *Metaphor: An Annotated Bibliography and History* Whitewater, Wisconsin: The Language Press 1971

B. F. Skinner. *Science and Human Behavior* New York: Free Press 1935

Leo Tolstoy. *The Death of Ivan Ilych* in *Confrontations of Death* F. Scott, R. Brewer, eds., Oregon State University 1971

Antonia Wenkart. "Death in Life" *Journal of Existentialism* 8 (29) 1967, pp. 75-90

Ludwig Wittgenstein. *Philosophical Investigations* 3rd edition, G. Anscombe, trans., New York: Macmillan 1958

Shakespeare

Shakespeare presents a number of pictures of death, images of death, but also a death rhetoric. These pictures, this rhetoric, will be examined. His treatment of death is more than this. It is also dramatic and developed in the context of an entire play or plot. But it is the pictures and rhetoric which are of special interest here. Tragedy and even comedy may have deaths. Death is easy to come by. But style, rhetoric and pictures of death often contribute to action and plot rather than depend on it. The Elizabethans had a special interest in emblem, imagery, rhetoric, and death.

Tragedy obviously has a concern with death but so also does comedy. Tragicomedy became popular in Shakespeare's day. (Shapiro) This is comedy which has in it deaths, threats of death, supposed deaths (where the deceased is found to be in fact alive), and/or metaphorical death (e.g., death considered as a birth.) "Cymbeline," though a comedy, was titled "The Tragedy of Cymbeline." The comedies usually involve catastrophe revolving around marriage. Death and marriage are often metaphorically juxtaposed, e.g., death is regarded as one's bride or groom. References to death may be found in all of Shakespeare's plays and in his sonnets.

1. *Macbeth*

Malcolm: "Nothing in his life
Became him like the leaving it; he died
As one that has been studied in his death
To throw away the dearest thing he ow'd,
As 'twere a careless trifle." (I, iv, 7)

147

Style and rhetoric are central here as in all of Shakespeare. What is said depends on the way in which it is said. The metaphors are:

a) to think the best thing one does is to die well. There is irony in this as well as a juxtaposition of opposites, e.g., to *die* is the best thing in *life*.

b) to be praised for dying.

c) to have to study death, to advance oneself by studying how to prevent advancing oneself. There were many art of dying books at this time (*ars moriendi*) which were religious superstitious books showing woodcuts of the devils which would attend one at the moment of death if he did not conform to the various beliefs of the church. Such books were "studied," and they revealed the horrors of a sinful death. These books may only indirectly be implicated here.

d) to throw away or treat as a trifle that which is most important is also an antithesis, oxymoron, or conceit. Death here is rendered by antithesis, irony, conceit. Implicit is the view that there is no reason for one to die peacefully.

Macbeth:

> "Tomorrow, and tomorrow, and tomorrow,
> Creeps in this petty pace from day to day,
> To the last syllable of recorded time;
> And all our yesterdays have lighted fools
> The way to dusty death. Out, out, brief candle!
> Life's but a walking shadow; a poor player,
> That struts and frets his hour upon the stage,
> And then is heard no more: It is a tale
> Told by an idiot, full of sound and fury,
> Signifying nothing." (V, v, 19)

Our yesterdays, man's acquired knowledge has not conquered death but merely sped him on his way. In regard to the inquiry into and conquest of death we are seen to be fools. Every sign suggests our demise, each moment, each day, the snuffing out of a candle. Death is depicted in this way. All conquests are trivial compared to the conquest of death. Without overcoming death or attempting to do so we are unreal, not really human, mere actors who "strut and fret" and then die. Life is meaningless if one accepts death as inevitable. Though man takes himself seriously and his accomplishments as important, they are in fact, because of death, unimportant. This is an oxymoron or antithesis: The important is unimportant. And this oxymoron like the others reveals paradox and mystery.

Macbeth:

> "I will not be afraid of death and bane
> Till Birnam Forest come to Dunsinane." (V, iii, 59)

This is a hyperbole and a hypothetical conditional. "If Birnam Forest comes to Dunsinane, then I will be afraid, " is like "If the impossible happens, then I will be afraid." The hypothetical is at this point a conceit originating from the mouths of witches who foretell of Macbeth's death in riddles and paradoxes. Hecate says, "To trade and traffic with Macbeth/In riddles and affairs of death." Later we find that the incredible and absurd does happen, the metaphorical riddle becomes literal truth as the Forest comes to Dunsinane carried as camouflage by enemy soldiers. It happens as if by fate, as if one can only powerlessly observe one's own demise. Macbeth's messenger reports, "I looked toward Birnam, and anon methought the wood began to move." Soon Macbeth's head is off. Hecate, goddess of witchcraft, had earlier stated:

> "He [Macbeth] shall spurn fate, score death, and bear
> His hopes 'bove wisdom, grace, and fear:
> And you all know, security
> Is mortal's chiefest enemy." (III, v, 30)

Death is seen as a paradoxical, necessary absurdity.
The following is also a conceit or oxymoron and suggests health in death.

> "Who wear our health but sickly in his life
> Which in his death were perfect."   (III, i, 108)

2. *Hamlet*

Hamlet:

> "To be, or not to be — that is the question: —
> Whether 'tis nobler in the mind to suffer
> The slings and arrows of outrageous fortune,
> Or to take arms against a sea of troubles,
> And by opposing end them. — To die, — to sleep, —
> No more; and by a sleep to say we end
> The heartache and the thousand natural shocks
> That flesh is heir to — 'tis a consummation
> Devoutly to be wished. To die, to sleep,
> To sleep — perchance to dream. Aye there's the rub,
> For in that sleep of death what dreams may come
> When we have shuffled off this mortal coil,
> Must give us pause. There's the respect
> That makes calamity of so long life . . . .
> Who would fardels [burdens] bear,
> To grunt and sweat under a weary life,
> But that the dread of something after death,
> The undiscovered country from whose bourn
> No traveller returns, puzzles the will,
> And makes us rather bear those ills we have
> Than fly to others that we know not of?"
>
> (III, i, 56)

These lines, perhaps too famous to comment upon, reveal much about one view of death. He speaks of suicide, as the existentialist Camus does in *Myth of Sisyphus*. Camus asks why one should not commit suicide since life is absurd or meaningless. Camus concludes that an absurd life is still better than death. Shakespeare thinks of the outrages man must experience in life. This makes long life seem undesirable and death a welcome end. Death is here, as often, regarded as a sleep. But this need not comfort for death is a mystery, an unknown and one often prefers life to that of which he knows nothing. In one sense, to die is to sleep no more. Even though death may be pictured as a sleep it is not like the sleep we know. It may be accompanied by crazed and horrible "dreams."

Death is "the undiscovered country." It "puzzles the will" for in the face of death one does not know how to act, what to do, how to live. Perhaps faced with death one is rather forced to the action of inquiry into death and life. Hamlet, however, has not taken this step but sees in death a further reason for inaction. It is to say if death is a confusion or unknown we do not know what to do in life. He did not see that if death is an unknown, unconquered, confusion that one should by inquiry clarify it. Anxiety toward death may lead to maladjustment and confusion.

At the beginning of Act 5 gravedigger clowns sing and joke as they dig and toss up skulls. Hamlet holding the skull of Yorick, the King's jester, says:

"Alas, poor Yorick! I knew him, Horatio —
a fellow of infinite jest, of most excellent fancy.
He hath borne me on his back a thousand
times, and now, how abhorred in my imagination
it is! My gorge rises [in nausea] at it.
Here hung those lips that I have kissed I
know not how oft. Where be your
gibes now? Your gambols? Your songs?
Your flashes of merriment, that were wont to
set the table on a roar? Not one now, to mock
your own grinning? Quite chop-fallen?
Now get you to my lady's chamber and tell
her, let her paint an inch thick, to this
favor [facial appearance] she must come — make
her laugh at that."   (V, i, 201)

Jest is contrasted with death, and so life with death. The gravedigger clowns pun, joke, and sing in the grave also as a behavioral metaphor or contrast of life and death. The lively warm jester carrying Hamlet on his back is pictured and contrasted with the skull bone Hamlet now sees and holds. The skull grins, as they did in the prevalent dance of death and art of dying books. The skull's death grin is contrasted with the once lively clown's mocking grin. Here is humor about death, pictorial horror, pictorial captivation and rendering of death, contrast of life and death. "Chop-fallen" means downcast as well as a pun on "chapless," i.e., without jaws. The jaws have fallen from their grin. Hamlet tells the dead clown to now have the lady paint an inch thick with makeup, with flesh, to evoke laughter as Yorick once painted his face to amuse his audiences. It is all as contrast.

Further contrast is presented when Hamlet speculates that even the famous Alexander may wind up as part of a stopper for a beer barrel:

Hamlet:

"Alexander returneth into dust;
the dust is earth; of earth we make loam;
and why of that loam, whereto he was
converted, might they not stop a beer barrel?"
(V, i, 232)

and

"Imperious Caesar, dead and turned to clay,
Might stop a hole to keep the wind away.
Oh, that that earth which kept the world in awe
Should patch a wall to expel the winter's flaw!"
(V, i, 236)

The contrast here is between the noble and famous, and the trivial. The dance of death pictured death as a skeleton which served as a democratic leveler taking rich as well as poor, upper class as well as lower. There is here a further leveling of animate to inanimate and man in the end is filtered into dust. Hamlet utters "Pah!" to the skull's unpleasant smell. A man, a warm friend, becomes merely an ugly odor. This may be compared with the following:

King: "Now, Hamlet, where's Polonius?"
Hamlet: "At supper."
King: "At supper! Where?"
Hamlet: "Not where he eats, but where he is eaten. A certain convocation of politic worms are e'en at him. Your worm is your only emperor for diet. We fat all creatures else to fat us, and we fat ourselves for maggots.

Your fat king and your lean beggar is but variable service,
two dishes, but to one table. That's the end . . . .
A man may fish with the worm that hath eat of a king,
and eat of the fish that hath fed of that worm."   (IV, iii,
17)
The dead become one with nature. It is a naturalistic picture.

One may contrast this jesting-serious scene with
Shakespeare's epitaph at Holy Trinity Church, Stratford on
Avon. His stone reads:

> "Good friend for Jesus sake forbeare,
> To digg the dust encloased heare!
> Bleste be ye man yt spares thes stones,
> And curst be he yt moves my bones."

Whoever wrote these words did not want them mocked as in
the above gravedigger scene. There was grave robbery at this
time. Often there were no gravestones and the bones were later
dug up and put in a charnel house until decayed. Thus the dead
were often only buried temporarily.

3. Measure for Measure

Claudio:

> "Aye, but to die, and go we know not where,
> To lie in cold obstruction and to rot,
> This sensible warm motion to become
> A kneaded clod and the delighted spirit
> To bathe in fiery floods, or to reside
> In thrilling region of thick-ribbed ice −
> To be imprisoned in the viewless winds,
> And blown with restless violence round about
> The pendent world, or to be worse than worst
> Of those that lawless and incertain thought
> Imagine howling − 'tis too horrible!
> The weariest and most loathed worldly life
> That age, ache, penury, and imprisonment
> Can lay on nature is a paradise
> To what we fear of death."
>   (III, i, 118)

As a naturalist, as one believing one becomes one with nature, and as one who sees death as an unknown, death is fearful. The worst life is preferable to death. Again we are reminded of Camus.

> Duke: "Be absolute for death. Either death or life
> Shall thereby be the sweeter. Reason thus with life:
> If I do lose thee, I do lose a thing
> That none but fools would keep. A breath thou art,
> Servile to all the skyey influences
> That dost this habitation where thou keep'st
> Hourly afflict. Merely, thou art death's fool,
> For him thou labor'st by thy flight to shun,
> And yet runn'st toward him still. Thou art not noble,
> For all the accommodations that thou bear'st
> Are nursed by baseness. Thou'rt by no means valiant,
> For thou dost fear the soft and tender fork
> Of a poor worm. Thy best of rest is sleep,
> And that thou oft provokest, yet grossly fear'st
> Thy death, which is no more. Thou art not thyself,
> For thou exist'st on many a thousand grains
> That issue out of dust. Happy thou art not,
> For what thou hast not, still thou strivest to get,
> And what thou hast, forget'st. Thou art not certain,
> For thy complexion [humors] shifts to strange effects,
> After the moon. If thou art rich, thou'rt poor,
> For, like an ass whose back with ingots bows,
> Thou bear'st thy heavy riches but a journey,
> And death unloads thee. Friend hast thou none,
> For thine own bowels [offspring], which do call thee sire,
> The mere effusion of thy proper [own] loins,
> Do curse the gout, serpigo, and the rheum
> For ending thee no sooner. Thou hast nor youth nor age,
> But, as it were, an after-dinner's sleep,
> Dreaming on both; for all thy blessed youth
> Becomes as aged, and doth beg the alms,
> Of palsied eld. And when thou art old and rich,
> Thou hast neither heat, affection, limb, nor beauty,
> To make thy riches pleasant. What's yet in this
> That bears the name of life? Yet in this life
> Lie hid moe thousand deaths. Yet death we fear,
> That makes these odds all even."
>
> (III, i, 5)

"Be absolute for death" means be certain of death. If one is resolved to it one lives in less hope or question about its inevitability and so can accept it stoically. "Be absolute for death" may also be a pun or parody of the prevailing "absolution for the dead" (short prayers after mass). One supposedly becomes absolved of his sins. Death itself would be easier to take on the Duke's view. Death is made more welcome by a condemnation of the conditions of life. Life is seen to be only what a fool would value. (cf. Hamlet's "All our yesterdays have lighted the way to dusty death.") Life is subject hourly to mere chance, to astrological influence of stars, to sudden death at every moment — we are death's fool, i.e., death's clown to be called to perform our death at all times. Life is subject to death though we put forth all effort to shun it. Death is at the basis of all things, of life, of love, of wealth and objects we regard as most precious. We lack genuine strength of mind to encounter danger for we fear death and the decomposition of our body. According to the Duke we ought not fear death for it is but a sleep and sleep is good and welcome to man. His arguments thus far are unconvincing. However, one should try to conquer death rather than give up on the task as would a weakling. It would rather seem one would be a "fool" to unquestioningly accept death. That all must die and that pleasure is ended by death hardly allows one to accept death or deny pleasure. Of course, he is right in that as yet neither research nor money have been able to conquer death. But they have both helped to conquer disease and they are now just beginning to make contributions to slowing aging. The argument that death is sleep fares no better. It is a naive and misleading analogy. We have no reason at all to think death is sleep and rest, and so to seek it as we would seek sleep.

The Duke continues that we are not ourselves for we are just so many grains of dust, so much inanimate matter. The view is that of the atomists and stoics. We return to nature, belong to nature and are not separate from all its processes. Thus at death one cannot give up what one never possessed. But this argument equivocates in regard to possession. We are more than particles or grains of dust. We have consciousness and this we may indeed lose.

He says that life is lacking because we are not satisfied with what we have and are not yet in possession of what we want, always desire more. Our very desires, knowledge and decisions are often at the mercy of our physical condition. One's own children curse diseases and symptoms of their aged parents and hope for their parents' early death. In these many ways "death" is found throughout our life. Thus, the Duke concludes, death should not be feared for it brings an end to all the "deaths" we experience in life.

To say this is again to equivocate. It is to suggest that one can cure a disease by killing the patient. It is also to assume that, because a number of things are unpleasant about life, all is wrong with life. It is similar to the stoic view, and to the view of Lucretius. In synecdoche one may erroneously substitute the whole for what is merely one part, one instance. It is faulty overgeneralization.

4. *Shakespeare's Metaphors and Imagery* (cf. Spurgeon)

a) Death is regarded as a marriage or romance (cf. McClelland):

"The stroke of death is a lover's pinch,
Which hurts, and is desired."
Antony and Cleopatra V, ii, 298

"I will be a bridegroom in my death,
and run into't as to a lover's bed."
Antony and Cleopatra IV, xiv, 99

"If I must die, I will encounter darkness as
a bride, and hug it in mine arms."
Measure for Measure III, i, 83

"Oh, love! Oh, life! Not life, but love in death!"
Romeo and Juliet IV, v, 58

"O son, the night before thy wedding day
Hath death lain with thy wife. See, there she lies,
Flower as she was, deflowered by him.

Death is my son-in-law, Death is my heir,
My daughter he hath wedded. I will die,
And leave him all − life, living, all is Death's."
Romeo and Juliet IV, v, 35

"Shall I believe
That unsubstantial death is amorous,
And that the lean abhorred monster keeps
Thee here in dark to be his paramour?"
Romeo and Juliet V, iii, 102

"I do think there is mettle in death
which commits some loving act upon her,
she hath such a celerity in dying."
Antony and Cleopatra I, ii, 147

"The next time I do fight
I'll make death love me, for I will contend
Even with his pestilent scythe."
Antony and Cleopatra III, xiii, 193

"I had rather be married to a death's-head with a bone in
his mouth."
Merchant of Venice I, ii, 55

"O my accursed womb, the bed of death."
Richard III IV, i, 54

The lover's pinch, the marriage, the bride or groom, the
lover's bed, the meeting of a loved one after death, jealousy of
death, are all analogies and conceits suggesting that death may
be desirable. As love has risks and torments so death has the
most of all yet *may,* like love, be worth it and reveal some great
though now unknown erotic-like mystery and benefit. It is,
however, a far-fetched conceit yet it contains within itself some
irreducible element or truth which, like a metaphor, cannot be
entirely reduced to literal language or refutation. Marriage, a
joyful and creative loving act, is juxtaposed with death to yield
a tension of opposites which gives insight to each of the two
terms. The Shakespearean critic, Katherine MacMullan wrote:

"There is no greater tribute to Shakespeare's art than the consummate fascination evoked by the spectacle of the dying queen [Cleopatra], garbed in all the verbal apparel of seductiveness and death."

Shakespeare's great conceits yield great insights. Romeo can see the aspect of death as lover, and even be jealous of death. One still today often expresses the view that he will meet his mate or lover after death. He thinks this, perhaps, though he may have never said so. The confirmed bachelor is still left after death to "play the field."

b) Death is pictured or metaphorized in various ways. But Shakespeare in *Cymbeline* presented his own caution regarding such pictures, as follows:

"Your death has eyes in's head then; I have not seen him so pictured: you must either be directed by some that take upon them to know, or to take upon yourself that which I am sure you do not know, or jump the inquiry on your own peril: and how you shall speed in your journey's end, I think you'll never return to tell one."
Cymbeline V, iv, 184

On this view all we have is metaphors for death and so should not pretend to know what death itself is like. Such metaphors which we take seriously are often found to be as humorous as the statement:

"I had rather be set quick i' the earth
And bowl'd to death with turnips!"
Merry Wives III, iv, 91

With this caution the following images are presented in various plays:

c) Death is a sleep, But though this image is often used there are also cautions against it:

"Shake off this downy sleep, death's counterfeit,
And look on death itself!"
Macbeth II, iii, 81

"A man that apprehends death no more dreadfully but as a drunken sleep."
Measure for Measure IV, ii, 148

"O sleep, thou ape of death, lie dull upon her!"
Cymbeline II, ii, 31

Here sleep is only a mock death or suggestion of death. Death is not a sleep.
Death is an end or banishment.

"Well, death's the end of all."
Romeo and Juliet III, iii, 92

"Welcome, destruction, death, and massacre
I see, as in a map, the end of all."
Richard III II, iv, 53

"World's exile is death: then 'banished' is death mistermed."
Romeo and Juliet III, iii, 20

d) Death is seen as a personified skeleton as it appeared in dance of death woodcuts, skull rings, decorations, etc.

"Do not speak like a death's head; do not bid me remember mine end."
II *Henry IV* II, iv, 255

"The jaws of death."
Twelfth Night III, iv, 394

"Prosperity begins to mellow
And drop into the rotten mouth of death."
Richard III IV, iv, 1

Almost direct from a dance of death book seems:

"By medicine life may be prolong'd, yet death
Will seize the doctor too."
Cymbeline V, v, 29

Other personifications are:

> "The seaman's whistle
> Is as a whisper in the ears of death."
>
> > *Pericles* III, i, 9

> "This fell sergeant, Death,
> Is strict in his arrest."
>
> > *Hamlet* V, ii, 347

He speaks of death as arrest elsewhere:

> "What fell arrest
> Without all bail"
>
> > Sonnet 24

> "I will die
> And leave him all — life, living, all is Death's."
>
> > *Romeo and Juliet* IV, v, 39

e) Death is seen in terms of the concept of certainty.

> "Death is certain."
>
> > II *Henry IV* III, ii, 45

> "The worst is death, and death will have his day."
>
> > *Richard II* III, ii, 103

> "Certain, 'tis certain, very sure, very sure.
> Death, as the Psalmist saith, is certain to all,
>   all shall die."
>
> > II *Henry IV* III, ii, 41

> "And nothing can we call our own but death
> And that small model of the barren earth
> Which serves as paste and cover to our bones."
>
> > *Richard II,* III, ii, 152

> "It seems to me most strange that men should fear,
> Seeing that death, a necessary end,
> Will come when it will come . . ."
>
> > *Julius Caesar* II, ii, 36

"We were born to die."
                    Romeo and Juliet III, iv, 4

"Sir Toby: "But I will never die."
Clown: "Sir Toby, there you lie."
                    Twelfth Night II, iii, 115

f) Death is a night, shutting out of light.

"Thy eyes' windows fall,
Like death when he shuts up the day of life."
                    Romeo and Juliet IV, i, 100

g) Death is regarded often as a cure. One should welcome death in his old age.

"He had rather groan so in perpetuity than be cured
By the sure physician, death."
                    Cymbeline V, iv, 7

"Come, sir, are you ready for death? —
Over-roasted rather; ready long ago."
                    Cymbeline V, iv, 153

"What of a death too,
That rids our dogs of languish?"
                    Antony and Cleopatra V, ii, 41

Shakespeare speaks of "timeless death," "dusty death," "engrossing death," "living death," death as nature in "He's walk'd the way of nature," death as non-being in "He quit being." "Ripeness [readiness] is all" (*King Lear* V, ii, 11), and "He's not prepared for death," (*Measure for Measure* II, ii, 84) reveal the influence of the Christian tradition and art of dying books according to which if one does not profess one's faith before death and repent his sins devils carry off their souls. Barnadine even claims he cannot meet death because he has been drinking all night and so "is not fitted for it." (*Measure for Measure* IV, iii). The Duke responds,

"Unfit to live or die. O gravel heart! . . . A creature unprepared, unmeet for death, And to transport [execute] him in the mind he is were damnable."

On the other hand, death is presented as irrelevant to sins or the way one lives: "Live how we can, yet die we must." III *Henry VI;* IV, 2, 28. And Shakespeare rebukes those who are driven to a belief in immortality because of a fear of death, those who "want nothing of a god but immortality." *Coriolanus* V, iv. The art of dying books stressed illumination at the moment of death and the Platonic tradition stresses the blinding light when one faces truth. In spite of such fabrications there is reported to be a euphoria just before death. This is suggested in the following:

"How oft when men are at the point of death
Have they been merry, which their keepers call
A lightning before death."
Romeo and Juliet V, iii, 88

David McClelland. "The Harlequin Complex" *The Study of Lives* R. White, ed. New York: Atherton Press 1964 pp. 95-119

Gloria Shapiro. "Death in the Shakespeare Comedies" Ph. D. diss. Brandeis University 1961

Caroline Spurgeon. *Shakespeare's Imagery* Cambridge University Press 1935

Emily Dickinson

Emily Dickinson spent her life exploring death by means of poetry. She grew up in a climate of religious dogma and puritanism. She explored religion in an attempt to believe in it, and tried to experience conversion but found she could not honestly do so. She attempted to overcome and cope with the religious concepts prevalent around her which she could not understand. This inquiry into death was not made openly and directly, as she had first in some way to cope with the seemingly puzzling and obscure religious notions of immortality, God, afterlife. death, etc. She did not accept Christ, rejected religious orthodoxy, and stopped attending Church. Emily Dickinson was not a theoretical philosopher and did not create a systematic philosophy. Her exploration was more subtle, more concrete, more by suggestion. It was by means of poetry. Thomas Ford (1966) wrote, "Poetry filled the gap left by her inability to 'experience' religion through the orthodox channels of her day." (p. 130)

What characterizes poetry is that it juxtaposes the familiar and the strange, the abstract and the concrete. This brings abstraction and obscurity down to the level of the concrete and intelligible. It is a way of opposing theory, or attempting to see if it can be made clear. The result is that many of Dickinson's metaphors relate the elevated with the everyday, a process called "sinking a metaphor." Metaphor exposes much. The contrast is often humorous as well as telling. Humor provides release of tension as well as insight. "The truth I do not dare to know/I muffle with a jest." (III 1715) It also produces tension or paradox and allows for expansion of the meaning of the terms explored. Metaphorical exploration allowed her to break

163

out of the religious conceptions and categories imposed upon her. Metaphorical juxtaposition broke down old meanings creating new more diverse and more suggestive ones. It allowed her to cope with death by means of poetic inquiry, ongoing inquiry, and so escape from narrow dogma in a delicate, indirect and subtle way. It avoided a head-on collision with the language inherited but wore it beautifully away with the commonplace observations and verbal juxtaposition of objects as seen from the kitchen window. Dickinson deviates from usual grammar. Articles, prepositions, auxiliary verbs are often omitted. She relates things commonly unrelated and deviates from convention and custom. All such deviations of rule, custom, and the familiar are metaphors.

Metaphor allowed her to render a world which seemed to be full of contradictions and paradoxes the greatest paradox of which is death. Metaphor, because it has many interpretations, allowed her to avoid fixed dogma. If death is regarded as a lover, many meanings are possible. Emily did not hold to a literal organized system of ideas but explored each idea, each metaphor separately. She was thus able to honestly inquire into death and was saved in her comabt with it by means of poetry.

The absurdity of having to think of death in terms of life, to think of loss of consciousness by means of consciousness is struggled with often by means of conflict. The philosopher, Unamuno (*The Tragic Sense of Life*), says that because of conflicts such as reason-emotion, peace-war, life-death, love-hate, there is agony and this yields a necessarily "tragic sense of life." By tragic all that is meant is oxymoron, conceit or antithesis. His view is thus rooted in the tradition of upholders of the conceit, namely those such as Gracian, Tesauro, Marino. The view of the tragic sense of life is thus based on extravagant, tensive, insight-giving metaphor. With intense feeling one tends to think in terms of metaphors, in terms of opposites. Jose Ferrater-Mora (*Being and Death*) is in the same Spanish tradition. He calls himself a "dialectical empiricist" and stresses tensions, strong contrasts without synthesis. Nature, spirit, consciousness are regarded not as absolute but as limiting relative concepts. He says, "No single concept can ever perform the 'integrating' task," (p. 9) and "We cannot conclude once and for all that a higher organism dies inevitably and necessarily." (p. 140)

To be alive and not inquire into and be concerned with the problem and fear of death is to miss perhaps the greatest challenge of being alive. To do less, to avoid death, is to deny one's very humanity.

Emily became increasingly aware of the prevailing lack of inquiry into death, and lack of inquiry in general. She wrote, "My Mother does not care for thought." (II, 404) And Ford wrote, "In a mood of despair she wonders if she is the only thing in the universe disturbed about death." (p. 164)

Analysis will proceed from her early poems. Ford divides her poetry into three periods. Such divisions must be largely arbitrary because such devices as "periods" are metaphors and so transcend narrow classifications. The periods he gives are: 1. Before 1861, apprenticeship; 2. 1861-1865, her most creative and mature period; 3. after 1865, a few poems, and elegies written for friends. (pp. 68 ff.)

Emily often personifies death and regards it perspectively. It is seen as a marriage, bride, king, tyrant, sleep, darkness, night, weight, immobile, silence, timid, bold, lover, murderer, brigand, democratic equalizer, thoughtful coachman, wild beast, comforter, a parting, rest, security, traveler, riddle, great mystery, etc. Her early poetry, Ford says, is especially descriptive of the physical, medical or clinical aspects of dying and death. "Her primary motive in observing the dying and the dead had been the hope of receiving some hint of what happened after death." (Ford p. 152) She speaks of the "Extasy [sic] of death." (I, 165) This seems to derive from the Catholic view that at the moment of death the soul leaves the body and gains all knowledge and unlimited vision and so has a beatific vision. Emily, however, found no evidence for such visions nor did the dying reveal the secrets of death.

In the following poems the "I" in the poems does not necessarily refer to Emily's own views. The "I" may be regarded as a fictive "I." Nevertheless, the views presented through this fictive "I" are here treated as if they were her own. It may not be far off to assume that, at least in some respects, what one writes is what one thinks. What other criterion for thought would there be? W. H. Auden: "How can I know what I think till I see what I say?"

166

VOLUME I (*The Poems of Emily Dickinson*)

"Mortality is fatal."   (3)

A perfectly circular or redundant statement showing by its repetition that death is solid, final, dangerous. Though fatally serious the surprising circular juxtaposition of the obvious creates humor. Humor provides a release from problems and tension and can in some cases give insight.

"Death, but our rapt attention
To immortality."   (7)

If we take the view that death does not name an entity, death is our present experience of thinking of it or of unending life. And our very concern with death is what death is. It is what we imagine it to be.

"We lose − because we win−
Gamblers − recollecting which
Toss their dice again."   (21)

It makes no sense to win unless it makes sense to lose. To lose is then to affirm winning or the concept of winning. Similarly it makes no sense to live unless it makes sense to die. To die is then to affirm living or the concept of living. We then toss our dice again in the risk, in the game of life and death. Death gives meaning to life and vice versa.

"Ah Little Rose − how easy
For such as thee to die!"   (35)

The price of man's consciousness is his thinking that he will die.

"We who saw the launching
Never sailed the Bay!"   (43)

We are aware of the death of others but have neither evidence of nor know what our own death will be like. Our vision and concepts of death may, with the advancement of our scientific knowledge, show that our present concepts are mistaken. To be careful we must say that we do not know what death is like because we have not experienced it in our own case. Though to die may be not to experience.

The following poem uses and comments on the use of euphemism and metaphor in our representation of the dead. Dickinson suggests the inhumaneness of sobbing at funerals. Death is quieter than sleep, nameless, unknown, and is like a "fled" bird. The poem reads like a riddle. Poem 50 refers to death as "The Riddle," and she writes "Can I expound the skies?/How still the Riddle lies!" (89)

> "There's something quieter than sleep . . .
> And will not tell its name."
> "It has a simple gravity
> I do not understand."
> "I would not weep if I were they —
> How rude in one to sob!"
> "We — prone to periphrasis,
> Remark that Birds have fled!"   (45)

> "If I should die
> And you should live —
> And time sh'd gurgle on — "
> "Tis sweet to know . . . "
> "That Commerce will continue —
> And Trades as briskly fly —
> It makes the parting tranquil
> And keeps the soul serene —
> That gentlemen so sprightly
> Conduct the pleasing scene!" (54)

This "sinks" the seriousness of death to the level of everyday active business and trading of wares. It produces humor and irony by the great contrast between active business, "gurgling" time, and inactive, timeless death.

That it is sweet to know commerce will continue is covertly suggestive that one is immortal, because it suggests that one will be around to know that commerce will continue. That one will be a skeleton after death can also covertly comfort one for it suggests one will still know a skeleton survives. This is the problem of the self. We are not clear as to what the "I" is. It may end up being different than we now think and so give us a different picture of the world. Perhaps we cannot separate ourselves from objects. One could say the world thinks in me. Some such picture might suggest that we endure as long as objects do. Thus it is nice to know a tree will grow in the cemetery, that my skeleton will survive, or that commerce will continue. That is to suggest or serve as a covert proof that the tree still thinks in me and so I will not die. Also if matter derives from the conscious somehow, then death doesn't necessarily mean such experience will cease when the body dies.

> "Dust is the only Secret —
> Death, the only One
> You cannot find out all about
> In his 'native town.' " (153)

Though in a small town one knows the people and all about its happenings, though one's native town or oneself should be best known to one, as regards one's death in the "native town" of the cemetery we find that that "native" phenomenon we know nothing of. We know little of the atomic nature of our body and the dust it becomes.

> "It's such a little thing to weep —
> So short a thing to sigh —
> And yet — by Trades — the size of *these*
> We men and women die!" (189)

We treat the dying and death by means of trades, like any other trades, but they are not. Trades of the living are used to represent trades of dying; such things as sighs and weeping are much too lively and too insignificant to do justice to challenging sighless death.

> " 'Tis not that Dying hurts us so —
> 'Tis Living — hurts us more — " (335)

Death is not the same as dying. Death may be painless, dying may not be. Dying, in the sense of approaching death, may not hurt as does the pain experienced. It is also our views of death, our fears and imagined fictive picture of death which may be painful. The contrast between dying and living is here a combination of opposites, a conceit or oxymoron, that life which is usually thought good is seen as bad.

"After great pain, a formal feeling comes —
The Nerves sit ceremonious, like Tombs — "

"This is the Hour of Lead —
Remembered, if outlived,
As Freezing persons, recollect the Snow —
First — Chill — then Stupor — then the letting go —" (341)

The first line, perhaps one of Dickinson's finest, says much more than can be said in any other way. Pain is an experience, formal is not. Formal-feeling seems a contradiction. After pain, one returns to normal (one sense of formal here). After life one returns to normal, death. Formal is both normal and static. The line is almost a casual explanation or law according to which death is explained as being as desirable as the normal condition which often follows pain. An especially pleasurable feeling comes when pain is overcome. Here, after life and pain comes a release and with it a static formal state. Death is covertly made to seem desirable and the line therefore seems to give hope. These lines may be compared with those of her later poem: "There is a finished feeling/Experienced at Graves —/A leisure of the Future —/A Wilderness of Size." (II 856) Is death vast? When dead does one become very old? Or does death lack duration? We say one is dying not one is deading. Death is no process and does not take time — it may be more like an achievement ("finished feeling") verb like "to win." To win is not a process and does not take time. Is death then an achievement or rather a process, a vastness, a "wilderness of size"?

The "Hour of Lead" refers to the lead enclosure that one is buried in but also to a heavy silence. It is the "Hour of silence" and the "Hour of death." It is the formal release and "letting-go." The analogy may be that just as release or ecstasy follows cessation of pain, so if one could experience death it would be "remembered, if outlived."

> "Much Madness is divinest Sense —
> To a discerning Eye —
> Much Sense — the starkest Madness — "   (432)

We often learn most from deviating, by means of poetry and metaphor, from literal language and traditional models and categories. Such deviation seems mad but can give more knowledge than can the familiar, normal, or ordinary. In addition "much sense" may in fact be the mere captivation or blindness caused by holding to be literal and absolute what is really a disguised metaphor. Mark Van Doren said similarly, "There should be two kinds of words, *knowing* and *awareness.* We know death, but the only way to *know* short of dying is to drive the nail in as far as it will go through poetry." (W. Eaton, 1965)

> "We cannot put Oneself away."   (443)

One ordinarily speaks as if he can witness his own funeral. He imagines and has a picture of himself as lying in a coffin with people standing around. To imagine such things is to know more than we have evidence for. It is like putting oneself away. Theologians in this respect often speak as if they can perform their own autopsies. Dickinson's view is that "consciousness is the only home of which we now know." (II, 634) Also putting someone away implies that one is mad. One cannot put one's consciousness away as one can put a madman away. One can, however, go mad.

> "I heard a Fly buzz — when I died — "
> ". . . uncertain stumbling Buzz — "   (465)

The buzzing fly is an impressive image connoting the weakening of the senses when organized sounds and speech become mere noise and buzzing, the contrast of buzzing with the stillness of death, the contrast of a quite common and ordinary unimportant thing, such as a fly, with death. It is a metaphorical contrast or "sinking" of a metaphor. In this last connotation the fly becomes important. Flies often are associated with decomposing flesh. The image of the buzzing fly shows even more, gives one an experience of death or dying. A fly is death.

> "We do not play on Graves —
> Because there isn't Room — "
> "And People come —"
> "And put a flower on it —
> And hang their faces so —
> We're fearing that their Hearts will drop —
> And crush our pretty play —."   (467)

Innocent, joyful play of children is contrasted with the negative, destructive, and serious emotions of adults toward death. Perhaps emotions such as grief are unnecessary and adults could attain once more the joyful innocence of children. There perhaps should be room for such play. Life should be stressed not negative emotions at death. She wrote elsewhere, "Endow the living — with the tears —/You squander on the Dead."   (II 521)

> "I had no time to Hate —
> Because
> The Grave would hinder Me
> And Life was not so
> Ample I
> Could finish — Enmity —"   (478)

Facing death makes one examine his life more carefully. The metaphorical deviation or conceit is to think one cannot hate enough whereas hating is usually thought undesirable. The point is made by reducing the situation of hating to a hyperbole and absurdity. She elsewhere says "Death reorganizes estimate."

VOLUME II

"This world is not conclusion."
"And though a riddle at the last
Sagacity, must go —
To guess it puzzles scholars."   (501)

"Conclusion" in a way does not apply. It is a technical term. Death appears to surpass all of our arguments and all conclusions. The scholar's tools are not appropriate to investigate death with. The world we know now seems not to be all the world one can know.

"Narcotics cannot still the Tooth
That nibbles at the soul —"   (501)

Death must be honestly faced without evasion of drugs or dishonest denials.

"Men die — externally —
It is a truth — of Blood —
But we — are dying in Drama —
And Drama — is never dead — "   (531)

We die our metaphors. Our death is what our dramatic living consciousness and imagination determine it to be. She writes elsewhere, "Life — is what we make it —/Death — we do not know —" Again, she says, "Unable are the loved to die/For love is Immortality."   (809)

"I've seen a Dying Eye
Run round and round a Room —
In search of Something — as it seemed —
Then Cloudier became —
And then — obscure with Fog —
And then — be soldered down
Without disclosing what it be
'Twere blessed to have seen — "   (547)

The eye provides an impressive image. It is dramatic. The eye of a bull is large like an inanimate globe seemingly incapable of allowing an animal to see with. The eye of a bull provides a metaphorical contrast to the eye of a man. So also what is expected of an active, darting, living eye is contrasted with the eye of a dead man. The usual associations are gone. We read the eyes of a living person but of the death stare we notice a great abnormal change. A "death stare" is a fiction. It is merely a new experience for us and so just a metaphorical juxtaposition, as is the surprise face suddenly appearing in a window. The death stare serves as such a surprising deviation from normal that it causes fear and the dead man's eyes are customarily closed and sealed. We tend to ask questions such as "What does a dead man see?" And confusions about the nature of death can raise fearful speculations.

"Afraid! Of whom am I afraid?
Not Death — for who is He?"   (608)

If we do not know what death is how can we fear or have any other emotion toward it?

"Because I could not stop for Death —
He kindly stopped for me —
The Carriage held but just Ourselves —
And Immortality."
"I first surmised the Horses Heads
Were toward Eternity — "   (712)

If one is active with life, death can be forgotten, death stops for one. The first two lines at the same time suggest that death will come, thus yielding an antithesis or conceit. The last line treats "Eternity" as an abstraction. It is an obscure notion. By sinking it or relating it to a horse's head a critical tension is created, whether intentionally or not. There is perhaps no intelligible model for "eternity" within our experience. It is an unfounded or metaphysical concept resting on a faulty analysis of time or "infinite" time.

VOLUME III

> "Is Heaven a Physician?
> They say that He can heal —
> But Medicine Posthumous
> Is unavailable —
> Is Heaven an Exchequer?
> They speak of what we owe —
> But that negotiation
> I'm not a Party to — "   (1270)

Again by relating theoretical and abstract terms to the concrete, by contrastive juxtaposition religious speculation is exposed. Emily Dickinson here shows herself to want no part of such religious speculation for it appears too much like a business negotiation or bribe, it appears irrelevant to human needs and a healthy mind and body. Her disbelief is clear. She wrote,

> "God is indeed a jealous God —
> He cannot bear to see
> That we had rather not with Him
> But with each other play."   (1150)

And she states, "Believing what we don't believe / Does not exhilarate."   (1741)

> "To die is not to go —
> On Doom's consummate Chart
> No Territory new is staked —
> Remain thou as thou art."   (1295)

We speak of "going," "departing," in our everyday contexts such as departing or leaving a room. One may think then that it makes the same kind of sense to depart from or leave life. This is a category - mistake. In leaving life "no territory new is staked." Thus it is left for us only to deal with what we do know, our normal usages, to remain in that domain of language and knowledge where things still make sense. We have little choice.

She herself misuses words like "nothing" and "eternal," using them abstractly while seeming to treat them as if they were terms used in everyday concrete situations. For example, " 'Nothing' is the force/That renovates the World." But absolutely "nothing at all" must be unintelligible to us. "Nothing" only makes sense in the limited circumstance in which there *could* be a certain thing, e.g., an empty refrigerator. She herself speaks of infinity but suggests its limitation in a conceit or oxymoron: "finite infinity." (1695) Still "no territory new is staked."

"Seed — summer — tomb —
Whose Doom to whom." (1712)

One's death is another's life. This is the principle of eating and nutrition. Our death brings life to other things which live and grow as well as those which do not. We tend to look at death only from our own perspective.

"As subtle as tomorrow
That never came,
A warrant, a conviction,
Yet but a name." (1713)

We think of death in terms of models which are subtle, persuasive and captivating: tomorrow, beyond, possible, eternal, warrant, conviction, etc. These sound as though they describe or explain. Yet upon analysis they are seen to be naming - fallacies, mere names.

W. H. Auden. "Squares and Oblongs" *Poets at Work* C. Abbott, ed., New York: Harcourt, Brace & World 1948 pp. 171-81

Winifred Eaton. "Contrasts in the Representation of Death by Sophocles, Webster, and Strindberg." Ph.D. diss., Syracuse University 1965

Thomas Ford. *Heaven Beguiles the Tired: Death in the Poetry of Emily Dickinson* University of Alabama Press 1966

Thomas Johnson, ed. *The Poems of Emily Dickinson* 3 vols. Harvard University Press 1958

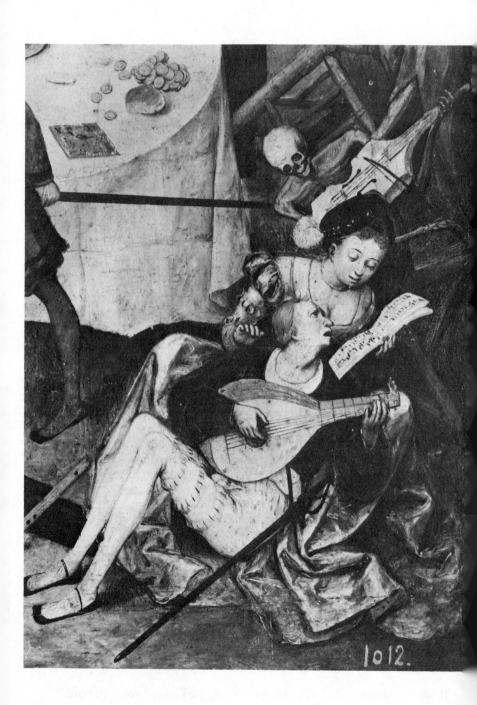

Dylan Thomas

1. *When Once the Twilight Locks No Longer*

"When once the twilight locks no longer
Locked in the long worm of my finger
nor damned the sea that sped about my fist,
The mouth of time sucked, like a sponge,
The milky acid on each hinge,
And swallowed dry the waters of the breast."

Twilight is a central image. It combines light and dark, night and day, and in this poem, dark womb and the light experienced at birth, as well as life and death. At twilight there is a special light, a setting sun, a mist, a transition, a blend defying clear-cut categories. Twilight locks suggest embrace and romance at dusk, one's curly hair. And locks are locks of the womb, and locks aiding the transport of ships. "The twilight locks no longer/Locked in the long worm of my finger" suggests the release of sperm and freedom for a writer to write and create. "Worm" may mean both phallus and the worm which devours the corpse. Like "twilight" it has a dual meaning. Such dualistic words suggest life in death and death in life — a synthesis of polar concepts. The sperm is not damned, in several senses of damn, but "sucked" or absorbed by the "mouth of time," the womb. "The mouth of time" also absorbs or changes the life of man and brings on aging, sucks up life, the "milky acid." Milk nourishes, acid destroys, and so milky acid is an oxymoron or antithesis synthesizing life and death. The milky acid is the semen as well as the poet's creative ink. The womb or "mouth of time" "swallows dry the waters of the breast." That

177

is, it absorbs the semen and gives it up again at birth. Swallow
dry is another antithesis or "twilight" word — a seeming
contradiction. It's a statement that life is death and death is life.
To swallow dry is also to dry up, to kill. The "waters of the
breast" is mother's milk and amniotic birth fluid. The ink, the
"milky acid," reveals the truths of the emotions of the human
breast and dries and dies (is "swallowed") on the paper. The last
lines of the poem are:

"Awake, my sleeper, to the sun,
A worker in the morning town,
And leave the poppied pickthank where he lies;
The fences of the light are down,
All but the briskest riders thrown,
And worlds hang on the trees."

This seems to suggest in terms of the poem that one forget
the false dreams, religion, and myths of creation, etc., forget
tomb and womb and live in the world, make the most of it,
"awake to the sun." Awake to new creation and awarenesses.
There is light now, one is born, the poem revealed and revealing
new light. "And worlds hang on the trees," refers to the view
that the world hangs on and depends on words. The world is
rendered and constituted by words, poetic creation, metaphors.
Though there be tomb in womb, a darkness in every light, and
death in all life we create our world by our words and it is this
which we, or some of us, are driven to to transcend a dim
reality of death.

Other poems (or every Thomas poem) elaborate the
life-death theme:

"I see the boys of summer in their ruin"
(summer, or life, contrasts with ruin and death.)

"Let us summon/Death from a summer woman."

"And doublecrossed my mother's womb."
(Being born is the doublecross of being born to die and the
double cross of religion [the cross].)

"I sit and watch the worm beneath my nail
Wearing the quick away."

"And what's the rub? . . . The thistle in the kiss."

"Joy is the knock [sexual] of dust [death], Cadaver's
shoot."

"I dreamed my genesis in sweat of death."

"Hands hold you poison or grapes?"

"After the first death, there is no other."
(That is, after birth there is no other birth; one can only die
once; after death we live forever; after the first death there is no
"other.")

W. Tindall (*A Reader's Guide to Dylan Thomas* p. 183)
spoke of "His [Thomas'] two beliefs: that life is eternal and
death, final. The believing unbeliever, at once holy and secular,
hopeful and desperate, believed what he knew to be untrue."

"Love in the Asylum" ends with the poet's relation with "a
girl mad as birds" and it is ironic that the madness of the insane,
poet, philosopher should be the very thing which yields most
insight.

"And taken by light in her arms at long and dear last
        I may without fail
Suffer the first vision that set fire to the stars."

(This also suggests that love yields death, that death is in life in
various ways. Poetic creation gives birth to insight as sexual
creation yields birth of offspring. "I *may* without *fail*," is an
oxymoron treating certainty as mere possibility. The poet
creates certain hypotheses by means of the word. Death is best
rendered by poetic metaphorical paradox.)

Tindall states (p. 194) about the poem "Unluckily for a
Death":

"Unluckily for the death that awaits him, the lucky, holy
poet seems trying to say, resurrection is possible, although

the woman, its agent, is a problem: hot, cold, constant, inconstant, and unawakened . . . No hot chill on her 'clay cold' mouth can assure the constancy of this sensual stature, however dedicated. . . . Hot and cold, clay and flesh, cloister and hearth, love and lust, and all the other incompatibles reveal the poet's problem."

Thomas' continuation of the life-death theme is in:

"Lie down, lie down and live
As quiet as a bone." (A reference here to romance and death)

"Time held me green and dying
Though I sang in my chains like the sea."

"The oak is felled in the acorn
And the hawk in the egg kills the wren." (This tomb-womb theme tends to fatalism.)

"And the flood flowers now."

2. *A Process in the Weather of the Heart*

"A process in the weather of the heart
Turns damp to dry."

There is a process within us which, like nature, weathers. Scientists speak of cells being allergic to themselves and of one's body causing its own destruction because of its built-in self-destructive control system and genetic structure (e.g., DNA, RNA forces). That the "weather of the heart" may be the cause of drying may suggest voodoo death or, more intelligibly, those who have a predilection to death thereby psychosomatically bringing on a shock-like state causing their own death. "Damp" and "dry" are terms suggestive of the humoral theories in the history of medicine. There were the four roots: earth, air, fire, and water. These were hot, cold, wet or dry. The humors were phlegm, black bile, yellow bile, sanguine (blood). It was thought that old age was caused by a becoming dry or drying up. Our expressions still reveal such theories, e.g., "Dry up!" Recalling the four-root schemes of ancient and medieval medicine hint at our present ignorance of adequate knowledge in these matters.

Dampness, or water, and dryness serve as open-similes or models to be expanded. Water is a life-giving fluid, a life principle, and a metaphor to be expanded and made intelligible in terms of such things as chemistry, thirst, and its antitheses such as death and dryness. Wet and dry are central models for investigation. But also the process

> "Turns night to day; blood in their suns
> Lights up the living worm."

Cells reproduce themselves, keep the body alive and if "suns" suggests "sons," man is immortal in his offspring. Blood keeps the body alive. Blood represents life as well as violence. Blood in sons is hot as blood in suns.

Now this and what follows served as an insightful scientific hypothesis:

> "A process in the eye forwarns
> The bones of blindness; and the womb
> Drives in a death as life leaks out."

> "A darkness in the weather of the eye
> Is half its light . . . "

It appears there is a biological *memento mori* in the bones, a biological death instinct. Because death is built-in, to give birth to a child is to give death to a child. We are ignorant of such processes but he projects them as hypotheses. Metaphors may be regarded as hypotheses for exploration. "A darkness in the weather of the eye" may be "half its light" because we know so little about perception, yet it is our very ignorance which may save us. If what we see death to be is true the picture is quite dim, but our ignorance about much of the perceptual process gives us some hope, some "light." (It is that of which we are now ignorant which gives us hope. These are clarifications and hypotheses to be explored.) Also it requires darkness to see and it requires death to live. Perception involves the model of an internal and a separate external world. But a clear distinction between inner (or pseudo - psychological) mental events and external events has never been clearly made out. Just as the distinction between inner and outer breaks down to some extent so also does the distinction between life and death. An absolute difference between such terms is apparent not real.

The distinction between internal and what consoles about hypotheses is that they allow us to escape the narrowness of our present categories. They allow for new insight and advance. Metaphors please and are significant in the face of death for they are intelligent ways of coping with an analysis of death. They yield scientific clarifications and hypotheses. It is for this reason that one can marvel at this poetry and can carry it forward to understanding when traditional and literal statement has ceased.

"A weather in the flesh and bone
Is damp and dry; the quick and dead
Move like two ghosts before the eye."

The distinction between life and death ("the quick and dead") has not carefully been made out. What we regard as life appears to be reducible to inanimate particles, electrons, etc. The "quick and the dead" are alike electrons or "like two ghosts before the eye." Inanimate objects, crystals, etc. form complex changing systems as do "living" cells. It is not that live things move and inanimate ones do not. All objects, all atoms are in constant motion and change. (W. Shibles "A Defense of Animism") Thus "the quick and dead move like two ghosts before the eye" because the distinction between inner-outer, life-death is hypothetical and not clear.

In addition the "quick and dead" "move like two ghosts before the eye" because both depend on the eye, i.e., depend on perception. We see the living and we see the dead. They are equally products of our consciousness, and objects of our seeing. How we are to understand such seeing is in question. For example, we investigate seeing circularly by means of seeing. If observation is the criterion of our scientific method then we would be investigating observation by means of having assumed observation. Thus the "quick and dead" are "ghosts" or fictions of our perception. "Quick" also suggests moving, and dead still. But motion and stillness are also fictions of or determinations of our perceptual perspective. "Dead" is a further fiction because all we usually think it is is determined by our perception. But knowledge of our perceptual process leaves much to be desired. (W. Shibles "I See Blue") These are our ghosts of knowledge, our ghosts of vision, our ghosts of inquiry.

"A process in the weather of the world
Turns ghost to ghost; each mothered child
Sits in their double shade.
A process blows the moon into the sun
Pulls down the shabby curtains of the skin;
And the heart gives up its dead."

Ghost turns to ghost as the world's electrons and particles interact. To call this a "process" or force, power, mass, inertia are all equally metaphysical. "Process" may even be used here as an irony, for there is no specific process. It is a naming-fallacy. "Mass" and "inertia" are two very confused terms ("ghosts") in physics. (M. Jammer) But "process" here may serve as a fiction, hypothetical entity, a mystery, to be made clear.

The very nature of a particle is today in question. The most elementary particles are not particles at all, but theoretical inferences from bubble chambers and concepts such as inertia. Inertia refers only to change and relations of changes so that it is not at all clear how a subatomic, non-visible "particle" can be derived from observable change. The nature of elementary particles is yet to be fully explored. Some physicists even speak of the "spontaneous generation" of particles. (K. Ford) Thus we may think of the most elementary particles, for the time being, as little question marks. There is in addition the dispute as to whether certain phenomena such as the propagation of light is best explained by waves or by particles, two seemingly contradictory entities. Particles then are seen as the mysterious ghosts responsible for the weather of the world. Life is as mysterious a ghost as death.

"Each mothered child/Sits in their double shade" suggests a breaking down of distinctions of life and death but also a fatalism. "Mothered child" has the ring of "smothered child." It is a gentle suggestion of life and death in a single word. Not only is death in life but life comes to death. Thomas suggests that we are born to die, it is in us to die. The ghost of life shifts and weathers. "A weather in the flesh and bone/Is damp and dry" suggested sterility. The "double shade above" suggests life and death. Life seems to be unnatural and contain, built-in, its death. But, not quite. For life and death here are the processes of the world, all the world and the life-death process is one. Life does not become death for there is no life but only life-death or death-life. The following lines suggest this transcendence of polar opposites to yield a oneness, a single process:

"A process blows the moon into the sun,
Pulls down the shabby curtains of the skin;
And the heart gives up its dead."

When moon and sun meet all becomes one and life and death are transcended. We transcend even the twilight of the poem "When Once the Twilight Locks No Longer." "The heart gives up its dead" as death is surpassed by means of the life-death process. Life can no longer go to death because death is already in life and life is in death. The heart, or sexual nature of man, and womb of woman give birth to death, release the child, and are also now freed from the child, death. Death is then biologically and perceptually within not outside of man where "within" and "without" are ghostly and "shabby curtains of the skin." The skin suggests the sensuous and psychological death-in-life called love which transcends death. The oneness, mystery of process, the poet's metaphors or models, and love surpass a narrow view of dogmatic seeing of the dead, in favor of insight into death.

Though we speak of forces and processes we have yet to learn how our body chemistry, and physiology is translated into language, how cells can speak. The above themes are further represented in the following poem:

3. *The Force That Through the Green Fuse Drives the Flower*

"The force that through the green fuse drives the flower
Drives my green age; that blasts the roots of trees

Is my destroyer.
And I am dumb to tell the crooked rose
My youth is bent by the same wintry fever.

"The force that drives the water through the rocks
Drives my red blood; that dries the mouthing streams
Turns mine to wax.
And I am dumb to mouth unto my veins
How at the mountain spring the same mouth sucks.

"The hand that whirls the water in the pool
Stirs the quicksand; that ropes the blowing wind
Hauls my shroud sail.
And I am dumb to tell the hanging man
How of my clay is made the hangman's lime."

"And I am dumb to tell the lover's tomb
How at my sheet goes the same crooked worm."

4 . *Light Breaks Where No Sun Shines*

In itself this metaphorical line may mean many things:
a) Light is destroyed if one has no offspring.
b) Sperm is released into the womb.
c) A child is born into the light from the darkness of the womb.
d) The dead body fertilizes the soil to become part of plant life.
e) There is no light or knowledge where there is no sun, none in the coffin, none in the womb.
f) In the unfertilized womb there is no son.
g) Dawn comes up.
h) There is light or knowledge of a sort where there is darkness, mystery or ignorance.
i) Antitheses or combinations of opposites yield insight, e.g., there is light where there is none.
j) One may have visions with one's eyes closed.
k) There are no negative statements. "Where no sun shines" describes a positive configuration of events.

The last suggestion (k) is supported throughout the poem:

> "Light breaks where no sun shines;
> Where no sea runs, the waters of the heart
> Push in their tides;
> And, broken ghosts with glow-worms in their heads,
> The things of light
> File through the flesh where no flesh decks the bones."

Further events happen "where no seed stirs," "where no wax is," "where no cold is."

We cannot think of death as nothing at all, an absolute negative because "nothing" and "negative" refer to conscious positive configurations of events within our experience. There are no absolute negative statements as such. Negative statements describe positive events. "There is no sea," refers to a certain positive relationship of objects..

> "Where no sea runs, the waters of the heart
> Push in their tides"

An interpretation of this is that all is action. There is no emptiness as such. Sperm is released in the womb. It is there "where no sea runs," where the sea of sperm now does run. The conceit is that sea is where it is not. This is the paradigm for: life is where life is not, and death is where death is not. This is the oxymoron and antithesis to suggest the view that there is no nothing, and death cannot be nothingness for nothingness is not within our experience. Negation yields a positive statement and is part of our active experience. Death then is also a part. All we know is action and conscious experience. Death breaks out in life. And since negations are positive things and part of life, life breaks out in death and negations, "dawn breaks behind the eyes." The poem explores many such conceits or oxymora.

The conceits break down our more narrow logics and reveal that there is yet mystery — that death is nothingness will not do:

> "When logics die,
> The secret of the soil grows through my eye,
> And blood jumps in the sun."

In other poems also the notion of negation, and nothingness is explored poetically:

a) "The world's turning wood . . . will . . . undie . . . "

"Turning wood" may refer to the poet's craft which remains immortal. To "undie" means to live, to go from death to life, to create, and it also is a revealing contradiction.

b) "undead water"

c) "What's never known is safest in this life."

d) "Who could hack out your unsucked heart,
   O green and unborn and undead?"

e) "No Time, spoke the clocks, no God, rang the bells"

5. *And Death Shall Have No Dominion*

These words are from St. Paul, *Romans* 6:9. In this poem as well as in "When Once the Twilight Locks No Longer" he refers to and rephrases "The sea gave up the dead," from *Revelation* 20:13. But Thomas does not give a Christian account. He rather presents a poetic account and his insights transcend religious dogma.

Dominion means supreme authority, domain, absolute ownership. Death shall have no dominion because:

a) "Dead men naked they shall be one
   With the man in the wind and the west moon." (All will become one with nature.)

b) Madmen are made sane by becoming one with nature. This is put in the form of a contradiction or oxymoron: "Though they go mad they shall be sane."

c) "Though they sink through the sea they shall rise again" as part of nature.

   d) "Though lovers be lost love shall not."

   e) "Faith in their hands shall snap in two,
       And the unicorn evils run them through;
       Split all ends up they shan't crack."

Religious faith is irrelevant. One becomes one with nature.

   f) "No more may gulls cry at their ears
       Or waves break loud on the seashores;
       Where blew a flower may a flower no more
       Lift its head to the blows of the rain;
       Though they be made and dead as nails,
       Heads of the characters hammer through daisies;
       Break in the sun till the sun breaks down,
       And death shall have no dominion."

Another reason why death has no dominion is because men have failed to inquire into it honestly or forcefully. They have rather taken on mythical fictions to pacify themselves with. It has no dominion also because our knowledge of death is always in terms of living and living consciousness.

6. *Do Not Go Gentle into that Good Night*

The poem contains reverse ritual, that is, whereas religion stresses ritualistic repetition in an attempt to hypnotize one into belief in miracle, repetition is used here to stress honest inquiry and praise of life and nature. The typical Christian view is that one should accept death, not inquire into it or try to avoid it. All is in God's hands. The recent book by Glenn Asquith, *Death Is All Right,* takes this position.

The existentialists hold the same view, that death is not to be inquired into but accepted as an absolute fact. On these views all we can do is live better or more religiously or dogmatically. Medieval views represented in the *Art of Dying* books state this view in terms of a temptation by devils to resist death at the moment of death. This temptation they say must be resisted; one must learn to die well, to die in ignorance perhaps, but to die in accord with the dogma or faith. The church and existentialism sought and seek to drive men to belief in their philosophies by exaggerating the evils, demons, dread and anxiety of dying and death. Thomas opposes the dishonesty of this and he opposes a mere quiet sheep-like giving-in to death as if death is good, as if death is a mere goodbye, or departure, or sleep at night:

"Do not go gentle into that good night,
   Old age should burn and rave at close of day;
Rage, rage against the dying of the light."

One should "not go gentle into that good night" because:

  a) Raging against death is one way of affirming life.

  b) One's knowledge and ability to inquire may have been dull, irrelevant, or superstitious:

"Because their words had forked no lightning they
Do not go gentle into that good night."

  c) "Good" men, who follow traditional, religious or dogmatic rules blindly have not learned how to live and have failed to contribute to knowledge or the world:

"Good men, the last wave by, crying how bright
Their frail deeds might have danced in a green bay."

  d) Fools, those who live dangerously without thought or consciousness, those who have not thought of death, all learn too late that their behavior, their grief or worry, and dissatisfactions brought their own death. They regret the lives they lead:

"Wild men who caught and sang the sun in flight,
And learn, too late, they grieved it on its way."

  e) Those who are serious ("grave men"), perhaps philosophers, those who are dying; those having illuminating visions at death; those literally blind; even those who are already in the grave — all should rage against dying:

"Grave men, near death, who see with blinding sight
Blind eyes could blaze like meteors and be gay."

"Grave men" may refer to undertakers, now called "funeral directors," who instead of encouraging people to have expensive, "proper" or "correct" funerals to pacify all concerned (business and family) should rage against death and dying – treat it as the blast and violent thing that it is. "Grave men" may be those men who think "nothing" awaits them after death. Serious men should see that one can rejoice in life and in facing death and inquiring into it. Anything else would be dishonest escape. "Blind eyes" by becoming part of nature can take part of nature's processes of burning, dissolving, breaking and so range against death and dying. "See with blinding sight" is a combination of opposites. Light which usually makes seeing possible now makes it impossible. The source of life is the source of death. Those who "see with blinding sight" are often poets, artists, philosophers, brilliant scientists who by conceit, and new creative models and metaphors see what hitherto could not be seen or has not yet been discovered.

f) Dylan's father, like Dylan, did not believe in religion. Dylan faced death honestly and explored it by means of poetic insight. It was always more than he knew, more than anyone knows, more than poetry could tell yet poetry could tell more than most. His poetry could tell him more than he could know. A metaphor tells us more than we can literally say in prose. Metaphor cannot be reduced to literal statement without remainder. Thomas faced death in a bloody, raging confrontation, where raging nonacceptance is the proper adjustment and where the challenge of death is most aesthetic because the most challenging. It is to fight blind but a fight which is necessary and which dwarfs all other confrontations. Thomas out-Hemingway's death. Death is that ugly, rugged mountain which one would be a fool and inhuman not to challenge. It is a mountain which is within us, man's iron and metal, the red berries in our blood, the fox and fern within us. No challenge surpasses this. The poem ends:

"And you, my father, there on the sad height,
Curse, bless, me now with your fierce tears, I pray.
Do not go gentle into that good night.
Rage, rage against the dying of the light."

For Thomas, ethics is irrelevant to death. The way one has lived is irrelevant to death and there is no afterlife for ethics to be relevant to. There is no "final judgment." Good and bad apply to living men and small boys. They apply only for living purposes:

> "Good and bad, two ways
> Of moving about your death . . .
> Blow away like breath . . .
>
> And all your deeds and words,
> Each truth, each lie,
> Die in unjudging love."

Time is explored in an attempt to cope with death. If all time is transcended by non-temporal or aesthetic experience of the moment or of miracle then death is overcome. But time is change and, for Thomas, man becomes one with nature. As earth, man changes and time is irrelevant to man as scattered about as part of nature:

> "The moment of a miracle is unending lightening"

This line suggests dialectically that a moment is unending, that great moments or miracles make death seem irrelevant, that the life-death cycle continues endlessly. There is the miracle of birth, of love-making, of death, of becoming alive in nature. We are "saved" as long as plants come up, which is as long as nature is. All this adds up to a paradox of a fixed time or moments as opposed to an endless eternity. Time, man as one with nature, paradox is explored in:

> "Time sings through the intricate dead snowdrop. Listen."

> "And she rose with him flowering in her melting snow."

Thomas is a poet. And so it is natural that he should turn his inquiry into death into metaphors — for metaphors:

1. are aesthetic and allow aesthetic release from difficult or insurmountable problems.
2. render wonder and paradox.

3. dissolve traditional categories and limitations, thereby promoting insight and inquiry.
4. unite diverse elements such as
   a) opposites, e.g., life-death.
   b) poetry, love, language, death, all of which may inextricably involve one another.

And all this Thomas elaborates. He addresses the paradox, mystery and wonder:

> "These were the woods the river and sea
>   Where a boy
>   In the listening
> Summertime of the dead whispered the truth of his joy
> To the trees and the stones and the fish in the tide.
>   And the mystery
>   Sang alive
> Still in the water and singingbirds."

"There could I marvel/My birthday/away . . . "

We begin with wonder and inquiry and even to think or know about creation or death language is presupposed:

> "In the beginning was the word . . .
> The word flowed up, translating to the heart
> First characters of birth and death . . . "

Creation is derivative from our knowledge and our knowledge derives from language and from the language of poets. This is the language of metaphors:

> "I would be tickled by the rub that is:
> Man be my metaphor."

To be a complete man, to live fully is signified here. And man's perspective is taken as a metaphor for all the world. Man is all, a metaphor for all. This is the drunken sobriety of his ability. It is successful in rendering serious humor and the absurd. We live and die our metaphors.

We live and die the demons and hells we ourselves create. We live our views of death. If our language is vague we hypnotize and psychologize ourselves into belief by vagueness and delusions as with the words eternity, timeless, god, afterlife, other world:

"Were vagueness enough and the sweet lies plenty,
The hollow words could bear all suffering
And cure me of ills."

And this Thomas put in one short line:

"Death is all metaphors."

Glenn Asquith. *Death is All Right* Nasnville: Abington Press 1970

Kenneth Ford. *The World of Elementary Particles* New York: Blaisdell 1963

Max Jammer. *Concepts of Mass* Harvard University Press 1961

Warren Shibles. "A Defense of Animism" *Philosophical Pictures* 2nd revised edition, Dubuque, Iowa: Kendall-Hunt 1972

—————. "I See Blue" *ibid.*

Psychiatry, Psychology,
and Philosophical Psychology

In each of the following cases mentioned the entire article and its experimental conditions and contexts should be consulted for complete accuracy. Only what seemed to be the more interesting findings are presented here. What characterizes nearly every study is that it rests on a certain amount of general or incompletely understood terminology such as measurements of "liberal views," "anxiety," "guilt," "grief," "fear," "death," etc. The experiments and studies can be no more precise than the terms used in them. What is needed prior to making such surveys, studies, and statistical correlations is a conceptual clarification of the terms involved. Thus a clarification of emotions is included here.

I BEREAVEMENT AND EMOTION

Lindemann presents a psychiatric view. He attempts to show that acute grief has a definite immediate or delayed syndrome and results in psychiatric and bodily disorder. The syndrome commonly involves:

1. body disturbance: body distress lasting in waves of 20 minutes to one hour, tightness of throat, choking or shortness of breath, sighing, empty feeling in abdomen, lack of muscle power, tension, loss of appetite, food tastes bad, lack of saliva flow.

2. distorted or unrealistic pictures or preoccupation with pictures of the deceased. Patient may tend to walk or act like the deceased or seem to have the same ailments.

3. guilt, e.g., for not having been more kind to the deceased.

4. hostile reactions. Patient is active, restless, irritable, angry.

5. loss of patterns of social interaction and adjustment, e.g., indecisiveness, lack of initiative, strong dependence, unsociability, loss of interest.

6. Especially in delayed grief reactions, in addition to the above, are found overactivity with a sense of loss, altered electrocardiograms, mechanical behavior, self-destructive behavior such as giving away all of one's possessions or losing one's friends and professional standing, or suicidal behavior, depression, appearance of psychosomatic conditions such as colitis, rheumatoid arthritis, asthma, inability to sleep. It was found that 33 of 41 patients with ulcerative colitis developed their disease soon after the loss of a person important to them.

The above data is interesting but it would be wrong to conclude that the reactions are solely due to the loss of an important person or that the funeral ceremony can serve as therapy for such grief. The funeral ceremony cannot be simply regarded as a cure-all. Also, to be concerned with grief alone is to ignore one's other feelings and reasoning. Lindemann, in fact, mentions that shock treatment is sometimes used to relieve the sense of guilt. He recommends not a funeral ceremony but rather, proper psychiatric care. The analysis he gives also would require a philosophical clarification of guilt as well as of grief. It is, for example, misleading to say "grief" or any emotion is an entity which *causes* something else.

His stress on the distortion of one's pictures is quite suggestive. It may be fruitfully related to the view that scientists see their data in terms of "pictures" (models, images, metaphors). Scientists are said to have altered perception due to a new "seeing-as" brought on by a change of models. We tend to see things and "understand" them in terms of pictures, diagrams, maps, charts, etc. just as a poor child might see a half-dollar as larger than a rich child sees it.

We "envisage" death. We speak of death in terms of the most solid, unchanging visual things we know, e.g., a rock. A rock is used to replace shoddy reasoning. That we are in a visuo-centric predicament may provide an escape from the dogmatic view that death or dead people are just what we see them as. We do not fully understand perception and how it works. There is a circularity in trying to explain perception in that we see ourselves; the criterion of investigation, observation, is at the same time the very object of investigation. When perception is better understood, death will be better understood.

Both scientist and the bereaved may be captivated and misled by such pictures. Both may take them literally rather than as the metaphors they are. In any case, such a notion as picture distortion is not an argument for open-casket ceremonies which are said to produce "memory-pictures." "Memory-pictures" may even be disturbing because they are artificial, doctored-up, and metaphorical deviations from the normal, natural and real.

Lifton reports on the psychological effects of the atomic bomb on Hiroshima which caused the death of from 63,000 to 240,000. The survivors, even years after, feared delayed effects on genes, or expected sudden death from leukemia or other diseases. Men with high radiation exposure were found to have fewer daughters, and exposed women were found to have fewer sons than normal. A sociological phenomenon developed that the survivors most highly radiated were discriminated against in employment and marriage. Instead of "daughter of so and so" a woman would be called "A-Bomb maiden." A new identity with the dying was created. They had now to continually face the threat of death. This resulted in fatalistic illusions, apathy, guilt and shame. The existentialists believe that facing death makes one a better person and more alive. Although Lifton did not discuss this, such was found not to be the case in Japan. However, Lifton creates for us a new emotion similar to the new emotions such as "dread," created by the existentialists. Lifton calls it "psychological closure." It is such that when faced with an overwhelming threatening stimuli such as an atomic explosion we fail to act or react, become apathetic, and we find our knowledge, beliefs, and values completely violated. One might call it an "A-Bomb Emotion." To hypostatize such a new emotion is to create a myth, and shows a failure to understand the nature of emotions. He compounds this mistake by adding also a belief in "existential guilt" and "injured being" (after Buber). To create such unfounded entities can only prevent the progress of our ability to improve "mental health." It may also be pointed out that one may experience the same sort of "atomic" shock in view of everyday activities. One may be demoralized and shocked at the sorts of violent and unintelligent things people say and do every day. Philosophers may sometimes withdraw when overwhelmed with irrationality and superstition. Perhaps philosophers have a special awareness of such things and so we may create a "Philosopher's Emotion" of "philosophical closure." But it is a creation.

Shoor and Speed in a psychiatric paper conclude that mourning at a funeral may be an important need for a person. When mourning is absent the grief is thought to result in deliquency, alcoholism, mental illness, depression, neuroticism, obesity, anti-social activity, radical change in behavior, promiscuity. It is stated that psychiatrists are not certain whether or not children are able to mourn. One conclusion given is much too strong for the evidence given, that is the statement, "Had these youngsters been encouraged to mourn such distortions would not have evolved."

Barry in a psychiatric analysis asserts that the death of the mother is more likely than the death of the father to cause subsequent psychosis in a child, especially for children under eight. He stresses the view that there are thought to be multiple, not single, causes of psychosis. This may be seen as a corrective of the last conclusion reached by Shoor and Speed above.

One cause of severe bereavement is a formerly great dependency on, or extreme attachment to the deceased. Awareness of the possibility of loss through death may help one to avoid the shock of grief. If death is feared because of fear of loss of friends perhaps one ought not to become so attached to others. On the other hand, friendship may be made more realistic and beautiful because of the knowledge that we and our friends alike must die. Death casts an amazing, mysterious and bloody shadow on life.

Emily Post in *Etiquette* (1934) gives the following funeral practices: It is acceptable that no women appear at the grave.

This contrasts with the present view that even children now attend funerals. Evidently the grief was thought to be adequately dealt with without being present at the grave. She notes that the present tendency is toward sincerity in funeral practice. However, she says that an elderly widow is expected to mourn for life, deep mourning with crepe veil one year, black the second year, possibly colored veil thereafter. A young widow is expected to mourn for a year at least. Deviations from these mourning practices are said to be improper and show lack of feeling. A widower must not attend a dance for a year, a son may not attend for six months, and a brother for three months.

Such views treat emotions as if they were feelings and treat emotions and feelings in terms of mechanical, rigid, or fixed formulae or ritual, rather than with sincerity and reason.

Teicher, in a Freudian account, claims that we all have an oedipus complex, a sense of guilt deriving from a fantasied murder in the past. Such a statement appears as a highly metaphorical myth. That is, it is as the psychologist Theodore Sarbin put it, a metaphor-to-myth fallacy. It is questionable whether anyone has experienced such guilt.

Teicher's view is also that an adult's neurotic illness is due to unresolved infantile conflicts. Again, a highly questionable assertion. It implies a determinism and suggests a fatalism as well. He also states that the basic motivation of man is to preserve himself. Again, many exceptions may be found to this. For example, the very fact that man has done little to conquer death and has hardly begun to inquire into the cause of aging belies the statement. Certainly, generally, one wants to preserve himself but it is not necessarily the basic motive of all or much of his behavior. Teicher's statements generally are "all" type statements, e.g., all men have guilt, all have oedipal complexes, etc. His conclusion comes easy, then, that guilt and the oedipal complex are the bases of combat fatigue (which he terms "death anxiety neurosis"). More interesting and less of an all statement is his assertion, "Every combat soldier reacts according to how his previous psychologic patterns have prepared him." I think this may be put also as, "We live and die our metaphors," even our Freudian ones.

An excellent study on grief is Dr. George Engel's "Is Grief a Disease?" Engel shows that grief has a definite syndrome and predictable symptomatology and course. (Lindemann, above, also presented grief as having a definite syndrome.) Grief is like a disease and should be considered therefore as something one can treat and cure. Grief generally is characterized by the following pattern: a) initial shock, disbelief, attempt to deny loss, b) awareness of loss and experiences, negative emotions of shame, sadness, guilt, helplessness, crying, anorexia, sleep disturbance, somatic symptoms, loss of social interest and interest in one's work, c) recovery stage and resumption of mental health. This pattern is similar to that presented by the psychiatrist, Kübler-Ross. Engel argues as follows against the common prejudices which view grief not as a disease but as normal or necessary:

1. Grief is no more a natural reaction to a life experience than a wound or burn is a natural response to a physical trauma. Rather, grief is a pathological state.

2. To support grief because it is familiar or commonly experienced is no argument but merely shows man's failure to cope adequately with his experience. "One may escape both measles and grief."

3. In opposition to the view that grief is a self-limiting process requiring no medical attention it is argued that medicine has not yet properly recognized grief as an abnormality or disease, just as epilepsy, alcohol, and mental diseases were at one time not regarded as diseases. The physician treats grief as outside of his domain and patients fail to think grief is a disease and so do not complain of it. They complain rather of some physical ailment. Grief may be a disease whether it requires medical attention or not.

4. Grief is a deviation from the state of well-being and so should be regarded as a disease.

5. To the view that grief is a purely subjective psychological experience he asserts that we may find out that there are bodily changes occurring during grief.

(Other studies, e.g., Lindemann; Shoor and Speed, show there are definite physical and mental abnormalities resulting from grief. Compare also the section on psychosomatic events in this chapter. Hyperparathyroidism was thought to be a subjective experience at first.

6. To the argument that no one ever dies of grief he replies, a) it may nevertheless be a disease, and b) we do have evidence that grief may lead to death. (See section on psychosomatic events.) There is often death of the spouse shortly after the funeral of his or her mate. Grief can lead to fatal shock. Grief has been recognized as a cause of disease from Hippocrates on. Literature frequently reports the phenomenon of dying from grief.

7. To suggest that some grief is pathological while some is normal is false and misleading. All grief is negative and an abnormal detriment to health. Often grief is absent, delayed, disguised, apparently normal, but nevertheless can be found later to lead to organic or mental disease. ["Mental disease" is, of course, a misnomer. There is no mind to be diseased. "Psychological disorder" and "emotional disturbance" are similar misnomers.]

8. To the view that grief is necessary or a health adaptation he states that this would be like saying that a wound is a healthy adaptation. We may or may not survive the wound or the grief.

9. Is not grief a natural response of a healthy person to loss? He responds that we may be mislead that because a person is healthy in other ways he is healthy in all ways. Grief, however, is unhealthful.

He thus recommends that research and practice should be directed to studying and treating grief as a disease. Such study has already been begun in this book and in a recent book on emotions. (W. Shibles *Emotions* 1973)

The philosopher, A. Ewing, wrote about the emotion, hatred, "Hatred is never justifiable." (*Proc. Arist. Soc.* 31) I would like to suggest that all negative emotions are for the most part unjustifiable and should be eliminated by means of philosophical clarification or, as Ellis calls it, "rational psychotherapy." This involves reassessing one's beliefs and statements to make them more intelligent and realistic. The assessment must be done both in advance and at the time one experiences the negative feelings. Death must not be avoided but inquired into in advance. This helps one to avoid confusion and shock when faced with death. We may note that we often do not grieve when an elderly person dies. This suggests that perhaps grief may be arbitrary. Also we do not grieve for people who are distant from us.

Honest open inquiry in advance, assessment at the time, and communication are essential for avoiding negative emotions. Assessment when one has the negative feeling or emotion is necessary because it is at this time that one must change one's previous patterns of behavior. One must at this time be able to quickly assess so as to dissipate the negative feeling. In the case of shock it is too late to reassess at its initial stage. This is why advance assessment is needed. To have negative emotions is to be a slave of one's ignorance and to be less than human, less than a full human being. At the time one has negative emotions he must, however, accept that he has them and not regard them as being "bad."

Some of the implications of the above theory of emotions regarding death and dying are:

1. If the funeral ceremony is an irrational ceremony attempting to release emotions of grief, etc. it is misguided.

2. It does not seem to be the case that the present typical funeral ceremony properly deals with human emotions.

3. Grief, bereavement and similar emotions are seen to be unnecessary and avoidable in the first place. They may be prevented rather than encouraged. Positive emotions may be more easily induced than was previously possible.

4. Once it is seen that shock can cause death, and often does in the case of the surviving spouse, one is encouraged to inquire into death and dying in advance to avoid shock.

5. Our knowledge or ignorance of death and dying will

determine the feelings we have when confronted with them. Thus the more informed we are about them the better we will be able to cope with them.

6. Once one understands how guilt works it is seen that guilt experienced at the death of someone close can be avoided.

7. Analysis of anxiety, dread, and emotions supposedly uniquely experienced regarding death, may now be clearly analyzed.

In regard to the first point above it now will be shown that the funeral ceremony does not release emotions. In the chapter on the funeral industry and the chapter on funeral customs it is shown that the typical funeral ceremony is an irrational activity — although that may be obvious.

It was seen that emotion, e.g., grief, is not just an internal feeling. Yet many people, including psychiatrists, and funeral directors think that one must express his emotion because if he doesn't it will become "stored up" within him causing mental damage and frustration. Howard Raether (NFDA) commits this mistake of thinking of an emotion as a feeling. He states, "Grief is a feeling." (Columbia Univ. Symposium, Nov. 1972) Such a view treats anger as an entity, something which can be "stored up." It is the technical Freudian language made common. The picture is entirely misleading because the "entities" "stored up" have never been located.

There is recent evidence that the release of pent-up emotions or "energy" may be harmful. Robert Trotter in *Science News* reports that psychological and psychotherapeutic work opposes the release of violent emotions because:

"in the long run, the patient may be learning aggressive responses that are repeated and used outside of the therapeutic session. . . . The patient accepts the approval and learns that he will not be punished for his violent actions. Experiments in behavior theory, says Berkowitz, indicate that such reinforcement heightens the likelihood of aggression in other settings. . . . Reward that tends to strengthen a broad spectrum of aggressive responses."

This picture of anger or grief can do much harm because it suggests that emotions are passive (cf. "passions") and that one's beliefs are not the cause of them. It suggests that one is not responsible for them, that one's grief and anger are just feelings one is born with. The picture is a deterministic, fatalistic one. If the psychiatrist or others ask the patient to release his emotion, e.g., anger, whenever he "feels" it, it may well lead to the patient simply becoming an angry, violent person. This is because "releasing emotions" does not get at the cause of the emotion. The cause of the emotion, if we exclude physiological damage, is faulty assessment. Emotion is assessment which guides feeling. If the assessment is unrealistic, faulty, or confused, then negative feelings will most likely be induced. The patient may, however, be asked to "release his emotions" once just so that he may begin to clarify what is bothering him. It may allow him to begin to speak of his problem and situation and so assess it when he otherwise might find it too painful to face or express. The patient's cure will come from the clarification of his beliefs, not from "release of energy," "release of emotions," or other fictive or magical "psychic forces." If the funeral ceremony is for the purposes of "releasing emotions" it is misguided. It should rather be for the purpose of clarifying one's assessments. Each clarified assessment is like taking an immunity shot to keep one healthy.

A typical account of grief which commits the errors indicated above is that of G. Westberg in his pamphlet, "Good Grief." He states the following:

1. "Faith plays a major role in grief of any kind." It is not clear how this could be the case for the non-religious person.

2. "Grief is a natural part of human experience." This does not, however, mean that it is a necessary or desirable part of human experience. Diseases are also natural. Certainly if one is experiencing grief he should not deny that he is doing so, or think that it is wrong to grieve.

3. He speaks of "emotional release": "Emotion is essential to man and to try to repress it is to make him less than a man." The objections to the release of emotions are indicated above. Also, it would rather be the case that if one became violently emotional or angry all of the time one may say that he is causing harm to himself as well as to others, and is less rather than more of a man. He is a slave of his emotions.

4. "We ought to allow ourselves to express the emotions we actually feel." This confuses emotions with feelings. It also leads to an often held view that one's goal in life is only that of having someone to mourn for him. A funeral without mourning was thought to be a bad thing. But why should it be a major consideration to have mourners?

The funeral director often stresses grief therapy, and this may seem also to be a justification for the necessity of having complete or elaborate funerals. Although the terms "grief therapist" pervade funeral literature Harold Ruidl (Wisconsin F.D.A.) wrote to the author, "Funeral directors do not claim the role of 'grief therapists.' " Howard Raether (National F.D.A.) also wrote to the author, "The rank and file funeral director does not lay any claim to being a grief therapist, at least not that I am aware of." He supports the view that the funeral's function is to alleviate grief, guilt, etc., but wrote elsewhere, "This is not to say that the funeral director should practice psychiatry or psychology." (*Omega* 2, 1971)

The Marketing Service of the *American Funeral Director* offers cards to funeral directors which read, "The funeral director more than most people, has a sympathetic understanding of the nature of grief." The funeral director claims the role of grief therapist without having the required psychiatric training. As grief therapist he may even charge for the role of exhibiting sympathy. But alienation often characterizes the funeral rather than release of grief. Real grief therapy cannot be adequately handled by a salesman or under the conditions specified in the chapter on the workings of the funeral industry. George Marshall wrote,

"The undertaker's [funeral director's] services are needed and important, but as a counselor, he is not the man. It is a rudimentary principle of counseling that the counselor must be conversant with the values involved in the situation, and the undertaker's art is not derived from the principles of religious liberalism. Hence, the family is counseled according to the undertaker's experience with the values of the majority of people in regard to death. Because of his repeated experience he may honestly believe that everyone wants excessively priced mahogany, bronze or walnut caskets (that will decay in a few months); that the body should be dressed in the best clothes; that jewelry may be buried (to corrode in the ground); that the body must be embalmed to preserve it (when it is impossible to preserve it)."

Sidney Parnes, Professor of Creative Studies at Buffalo, presents the view that:

"the death of a loved one might be an opportunity . . . We rely on the learned rituals and traditions surrounding death, but fail to create new ways of dealing with bereavement . . . Problem-solving principles are potentially useful for training a client to serve as 'his own therapist.' "

He proceeds to specify a number of ways in which one might take a positive, adjustive stance when facing bereavement. These are a few realistic assessments which may guide positive rather than negative feelings. He suggests, for example, that we consider:

"In what ways might I commemorate the person through pleasant experiences rather than through traditional 'mourning' experiences?"
"In what ways might I enjoy new-found freedom?"
"In what ways might I honor his or her death in a constructive way?"
"In what ways might I make his or her memory bring me happiness in my future activities?"
"In what ways might I channel all of my grief into constructive energies?"

As was mentioned in the chapter on the funeral, it is irrational and harmful to experience guilt. Of course, one must accept the guilt if he already is experiencing it. One way to alleviate guilt is to inquire into the cause of aging and contribute to or engage in an analysis of the nature of death. Guilt, then, forces one into inquiry. One feels guilty sometimes because he has done nothing to prevent, clarify, accept, or delay death. Guilt derives from unrealistic or irrational assessments. It is like repeating to oneself "I am bad," "I am blamed." "I am no good," etc. These are non-adjustive, self-defeating irrational assessments which lead to feelings of inferiority, depression, and guilt.

The question is what is the funeral for in the first place? So that the soul will go to heaven, so that one will increase his social status, so that the emotions of the onlookers will be assuaged? If one is not clear about the nature of emotions then one will not know what a "proper" or "the best" funeral will be. "Proper" and "best" are ethical terms and as such are open-context terms which are in themselves meaningless. "Best" may refer to many things. If one has not thought about death he may in the absence of any other criterion think the "best" is simply the most expensive. A careful look at the nature of death is needed before determining what a proper funeral would be. In an increasingly non-religious society religious ritual becomes unintelligible. *Rational* symbolic ritual is, however, not being opposed here. A look at R. Habenstein and W. Lamers *Funeral Customs the World Over* would show that funeral customs the world over are based on local superstition and compulsive behavior due to the confusion about the nature of death, although the authors try to defend such practices. For example, in Tibet one custom is for the Lama to remove a hair from the scalp to allow the soul to escape from the pore. This is similar to the Western practice of opening the windows so the soul can escape, or religious rites to guide the soul on its way. In Bali a bamboo tube is put in a buried body to allow the soul to escape. Funerals as usually performed are seen to be irrational and superstitious. They therefore are not honest inquiries into the concept or nature of death nor do they offer a clarification of one's assessments which guide feelings. They do not allow one to adequately cope with one's situation in regard to death and dying. If the bereaved person "feels" guilty the funeral ceremony is irrelevant. The bereaved needs rather to reassess why he is guilty, what he can do about his guilt. One reason for guilt is that one wishes he could have done something to prevent death or to prolong the deceased's death. The thing to do would be to give money to health research and medical causes or to the philosophical study of the nature of death. It would be irresponsible to leave money to the Church to compensate for guilt. To hold a religious or dogmatic view of the nature of death can be a form of death denial. The Bible is not a study of or inquiry into the nature of death. The Bible has rather to do with suggestions as to how to live life. Unfortunately people tend to think that if they join a religion they will find out more about death or literally live an afterlife. This is not the case. There is no substitute for open, honest, ongoing investigation of death.

Because of the irrational and irrelevant nature of the typical funeral great emotional harm rather than help is the result. If one thinks he has to sacrifice all or much of his money for a funeral to overcome his guilt he is misled. Sacrificing money for a funeral is like burying money. Also the emotions will be adversely affected when one finds he has no money left to live on. What is needed at the time of death or dying is an intelligent and verbal assessment of the situation, its causes and consequences. The acts performed should be ones which get at the causes of the difficulties rather than merely at the symptoms as funerals do. To think a typical funeral ceremony is a therapeutic device is to think a good drunk will be a lasting solution to one's problems. Many funeral customs involve heavy drinking. It is only a temporary distraction. Distractions do not suffice to cope with emotions. An important caveat is needed here. Since many people do not inquire and cannot become clear about their assessments, a typical irrational or superstitious ritual may offer temporary relief, especially if it is customary and sanctioned by society. It may function as a placebo or self-suggestion. On the other hand, such superstitions may also make one compulsive, fanatic and unable to cope with his grief, guilt, and negative emotions. Certainly such practices have a negative emotional effect on intelligent people who see them as irrelevant, death-denying, barbaric, commercial practices. Such people tend to join memorial societies providing low cost funerals with dignity and reason.

Guilt, grief and negative emotions experienced regarding death and dying can be dissipated and avoided. This very study has the value of preassessing such situations and so helping to prevent shock. Good emotions help one to age less fast and avoid early death. Negative emotions have the reverse effect.

To think that grief is necessary may lead to the often held view that one's goal in life is mainly that of having someone mourn for him. A funeral without mourners was thought to be a bad thing. But why should it be a consideration whether one has mourners or not? Kant says in *Critique of Aesthetic Judgment,*

"Take the case of the heir of a wealthy relative being minded to make preparations for having the funeral obsequies on a 'most imposing scale, but complaining that things would not go right for him, because (as he said) the more money I give my mourners to look sad, the more pleased they look."

In our study it has been found that negative emotions are unnecessary, and may be dissipated by means of an inquiry into the nature of emotions. Negative emotions, although common, are largely a result of confusions in reasoning. Such confusions lead to other kinds of physical and psychological disorders.

In addition to the view that a clarification of emotions will show that grief is unnecessary it may be the case that grief behavior, as other negative emotive behavior, is simply culturally imposed and learned. It can be a learned kind of role behavior and so can be unlearned. Such behavior is not necessary or inherent in one. Cultural differences show that what one grieves about, another is joyful about. In one culture it is thought to be harmful for children to attend funerals, in another the child plays games at funerals and enjoys it with no harmful aftereffects. As we learn to act bored, revengeful, angry, we may learn to grieve. There is strong evidence that grief is an arbitrary act, not a necessary one. It is not intelligent behavior.

Rational assessment in regard to death depends upon our knowledge of death. We see death in terms of our metaphors for death, e.g., sleep, nothingness, journey to heaven, etc. If we do not think carefully about death we may fear it as an unknown or create superstitions about it. That is, in order to create better emotions concerning death we must become clearer about what death is. The present inquiry into the concept of death is a step in this direction.

We fear death without a clear knowledge of what it is we fear. It is an emotion without a clear object. Thus this emotion is sometimes called anxiety. It may also involve depression, dread, etc. The psychologist, Theodore Sarbin recently gave an analysis of "anxiety" showing that it is not an internal state and that it is an extremely misleading and unhelpful concept. According to my analysis of emotions, anxiety is a descriptive assessment which guides feeling, but in this case one's assessment cannot be too clear because people know very little about death. This means that to attempt to cope with anxiety concerning death one must find out more about death. It forces us to inquire into death. If one has confused, unintelligent or superstitious views about death then his emotions about death will most likely be negative or precarious. The prevailing views concerning death are superstitious or philosophically inadequate. There is death-denial rather than open, honest, inquiry into and clarification of the concept of death and dying. We, for example, have just become secular enough to begin to bother inquiring into the cause of aging, the cause of which is as yet unknown. Thus to improve our emotions regarding death and dying we must improve our knowledge and rational assessments by inquiring into, and clarifying these concepts. We must act on the findings of such inquiry. Dying patients must be allowed and helped to communicate and clarify their thinking about death and they may be helped by use of a more sound view of emotions such as the one presented here.

Funeral songs and poetry are also traditional ways of attempting to represent or express grief and emotion. As representations they are cultural ritualistic devices. As expressions, the question arises as to whether poetry and song express emotions. The aesthetic theory that art expresses emotions, is unsatisfactory because it assumes an unexamined theory of emotions. Poetry is largely based on metaphor. It is a use of language. We have no direct evidence for psychological entities such as internal atomistic "ideas" or "emotions" as such. The poem itself is the expression or emotion. For the aestheticians, Benedetto Croce and R. Collingwood, the intuition or emotion is the expression. The expression does not just represent emotions or express separate internal emotions. To extend this view, intuition and emotion may be thought of as the metaphorical language or poem. In this respect poetry may help one to clarify his ideas about death, as well as to adjust to it. Such was the case with Emily Dickinson, Dylan Thomas, John Donne, and many other poets and novelists. It is important for the bereaved or the patient to communicate his views about dying and death or to communicate to a sympathetic, careful listener. Communication is perhaps the most important form of therapy both for the normal as well as the abnormal person.

In view of the preceding argument the following may be recommended:

1. The adoption of the view of emotions as assessment which guides feelings.

2. The employment of this view of emotions to effect changes in present funeral practices. This would make them more rational practices and bring more dignity to man as an intelligent human being rather than as an irrational person unable to consciously cope with his problems.

3. The employment of this theory of emotions in treating the bereaved as well as the dying patient. This would involve open, honest, discussion with the patient. Because thought is mainly language use, careful attention should be paid to the language and captivating metaphors of the patient.

4. Because emotions are descriptive, empirical assessments it forces us to promote and engage in further inquiry into death, aging, dying. Death may itself perhaps be found to be only a disease.

5. Negative emotions should be regarded as diseases or forms of sickness which can and should be eliminated.

Without a full scale clarification of our ideas concerning emotion, death and dying we become a slave of our ignorance. We live and die our metaphors. We die a thousand deaths before our own, live in fear of fictions, and erect monuments to our lack of inquiry.

II. DEATH AND EMOTION*

Emotions are relevant to death and dying, in a number of ways. One may experience grief, sorrow, guilt, shock, etc., at the death of others. The thought of "death" and "dying" often makes one anxious and fearful. Dying hospital patients and their attendants, as well as the bereaved, experience a great range of emotions concerning death and dying. Funeral directors now often refer to themselves as grief therapists and think of the funeral ceremony partly as functioning to meet the emotional needs of the bereaved.

In order to properly understand the function of emotion in relation to death and dying one must first be clear about what an emotion is. This clarification will be seen to be relevant to our present therapeutic and funeral practices and will indicate a revision of such practices.

What is the status of our knowledge of emotions? A few representative statements follow:

"Examination of current treatments of emotion reveals a discouraging state of confusion and uncertainty." J. Brown and I. Farber *Psychological Bulletin* 1951

"Exactly how emotional experience arises is still a mystery." C. Morgan *Physiological Psychology* 1965

"The 'emotions' are excellent examples of the fictional causes to which we commonly attribute behavior." B. F. Skinner *Science and Human Behavior*

"The psychology of affective processes is the most confused chapter in all psychology. Here it is that the greatest differences appear from one psychologist to

*Most of this section was delivered as a paper by the author at the Symposium, "Philosophical Aspects of Thanatology," Columbia University, College of Physicians and Surgeons and Foundation of Thanatology, May 1973.

another. They are in agreement neither on the facts nor on the words." Ed. Claparede in *Feelings and Emotions* (Wittenberg Symposium 1928)

"Our knowledge of the topic of emotion is much less complete than our knowledge of the other topics in the field of psychology." *Encyclopaedia Britannica* 1955

If, then, our knowledge of emotions is confused this would affect our ability to understand and treat so-called "emotional disorder." If Skinner is right that there are no emotions as such, then one cannot have "emotional disorders" as such. But there is some important work now being done in philosophy in the area of philosophical psychology and in psychiatry which is not yet widely known about and which helps to clarify the nature of emotions. I will now discuss some of these findings and present what I consider to be a useful theory.

Traditionally emotion is regarded as an internal state of feeling, e.g., we say, "I *feel* sad." It is thought to be opposed to reason and it is thought that emotions are an unchangeable part of one's given basic nature. The following analysis rejects all of these views. Emotion is not merely an internal state, it does involve reason, and it can be changed.

In order to correlate an emotion with a physiological event one must know what an emotion is. But since emotion will be seen here to partly involve a description of a situation, one cannot find a physical correlate for the belief or description. Moreland Perkins *(Philosophical Review* 75, 1966) states,

"It is the emotion as a whole that gets 'named,' not the bodily feeling which enters into it. Emotions get fixed as facts as a consequence of the abiding presence in language of common names for them."

A physiological correlate for an emotion would have to involve physiological correlates for our language as well. Emotions are not just fixed responses or internal states in a certain part of the body, as is the case with visceral agitations. B. F. Skinner states *(Science and Human Behavior),*

"In spite of extensive research it has not been possible to show that each emotion is distinguished by a particular pattern of responses of glands ana smooth muscles," and "It has not been possible to specify given sets of expressive responses as characteristic of particular emotions, and in any case such responses are not said to *be* the emotion." He concludes, "As long as we conceive of the problem of emotion as one of inner states, we are not likely to advance a practical technology."

Psychologists and others instead of clarifying the concept of emotion have tended to simply presuppose that there are emotions and then try to find an objective scientific physiological correlate for them. The procedure is question begging as well as inadequate. William Hunt put the matter in this way (*Psychological Bulletin* 5(1941),

"The amusing result is that psychologist, physiologist, and neurologist alike show preference for the objective approach through a study of behavior, neurohumor, or thalamic lesion; yet no sooner do they find some unique aspect of their material than they proudly offer it as the possible basis for the experience of emotion, an experience whose existence, uniqueness, and characteristics are still largely a matter of supposition."

On the view I wish to present, emotion is a rational assessment which guides feelings. These terms need to be defined.

a. By "rational" or reason is meant language use or saying things aloud or silently to oneself, or writing. Reason, thought, and ideas are synonyms. We have no evidence that there is thought or ideas as such. We do not catch an idea or see one. That we have ideas is based on the substance-quality doctrine, or mind-mental quality doctrine according to which we have a mind and we think with it, that we have ideas in our minds. But there is no more evidence for a mental substance called "mind" than there is for ideas. "Ideas" were derived from atomism in the form of the principle of the association of ideas. It was thought that just as atoms are associated so also ideas are associated. This was called mental "chemistry." But again there was no evidence for these mental idea atoms. William James even spoke of a "stream of consciousness" instead of atomistic ideas. Reason, thought, ideas as mental entities are pseudo-psychological entities.

"Reason," "idea," "thought," have a great many uses in language and not merely the use of attempting to describe an internal entity of some sort. In examining the use of such terms it is seen that what we mainly mean by "He thinks well," "He reasons well," "He has a good mind," is not that he has mental processes and entities but rather that he speaks or writes well or has abilities such as being able to swim. Reason or thinking largely refers to language ability. We do not know what it would be like to have a wordless idea. All of this is to say that language, not thought or reason, has epistemological primacy. (See W. Shibles *Philosophical Pictures* for further support of this.) Thus to say that emotion is a rational assessment which guides feeling, is really to say that emotion is or reduces to linguistic formulations which guide feelings. This is exactly what the therapist Albert Ellis *(J. of General Psychology* 1958) states when he says that emotional disorders are caused by repeating unintelligent things to oneself, and that one should "practice saying the right kinds of sentences to oneself." The actual language used is extremely important in understanding and correcting "emotional disturbance." This is why communication is especially important in grief therapy, and treatment of the dying patient.

b. By "assessment" is meant a description of the context and situation. Jealousy, for example, is not an internal feeling but largely a description of a situation. If someone says he is jealous we do not ask him how it feels, but rather about the situation. We say, "Tell me about it," "What happened?" or "Who got involved with whom?" That is, we ask about the context and the situation. "Jealousy" is a word which partly describes an assessment of a situation. It may or may not involve a feeling also. If feelings are involved they may be different every time one "feels" jealous. But because emotion is partly a description of a context or situation it is not just a feeling. It is thus a category-mistake to say "I feel x," where x is an emotion. One cannot *feel* jealous. One cannot *feel* grief. Emotions are not feelings. In opposition to the traditional view, emotion is not irrational but rather is largely constituted by reason. Emotion is reason. The statements one utters or writes may be true or false. False beliefs often induce negative feelings. Thus the rational or descriptive beliefs often induce negative feelings. Thus the rational descriptive statements which go to make up an emotion may be true or false.

c. By "feeling" is meant such experiences as we refer to as "bodily sensations." They involve such concrete experiences as pain, warmth, tickles, nervousness, "butterflies" in one's stomach, the feeling of blood rushing to our cheeks, tenseness, etc. If one sees an unjust act, he assesses the act as unjust and this may induce negative feeling in him such as that which accompanies increased blood pressure. Perhaps some of the above points may be expressed by the following "tale."

The King and the Cat: A Tale of the Passions
Consider the following statements made by the king:
1. "I fear the bear." (in the presence of a bear)
2. "I fear the possible revolution."
3. "I fear that I am mistaken."

In statement No. 1 the fear may be referred to as occurrent. It is an immediate response to danger. This expression may be replaced by the fear-behavior of running away. Both king and cat may perform the same act. Instead of "I fear the bear," the king may utter "Watch out," and the cat a concerned "meow."

In statement No. 2 the king may be concerned with future events, possibilities, hopes. He may have emotions regarding governments, and entities cats can know nothing of. It would seem that cats cannot fear revolutions nor can they fear possible or future revolutions, for what is future time or any time to a cat? And without our language it cannot have the sorts of fears we have. It cannot hope, and perhaps cannot experience despair of his future death as can man. Not even church mice can have religious awe. We may refer to type No. 2 statements as dispositions or conceptual assessments.

To say "I fear a possible revolution," is not necessarily to report an internal state or feeling. One may have instead said, "I think there will be a revolution." One can fear a revolution without feeling anything. Or, stated differently, the king is here using the word "fear" metaphorically. It would be equally metaphorical (a "pathetic fallacy") to speak of the cat smiling, as for instance, Lewis Carroll's Cheshire cat. That the smile of his cat was all that was left after the cat disappeared may suggest how stereotyped, abstract and unfeeling a smile can be.

The king can assess in a way the cat cannot and so can have fears the cat cannot have. This is the price he must pay for being a king. It is the price one pays for consciousness, especially if one misconceives of or is ignorant of how to control one's emotions.

The cat cannot fear future death as we conceive of it, and this is a great price we pay for our consciousness. Schopenhauer pointed out that man is worse off than animals because with man's greater cognitive power goes greater susceptibility to pain.

In "I fear a possible revolution," "fear" may function as an evaluative term. The king suggests by it that it would be a bad thing if a revolution took place.

The third statement, "I fear that I am mistaken," again seems not to regard fear as an emotion word at all. He could have instead said, "I think that I am mistaken." "Fear" here may be used merely as a stylistic device suggesting much the same idea as does the word "mistaken." No one wishes to make a mistake. But no "fear," as such, need be experienced. In this, the king and the cat could agree even if the cat could talk. Although, of course, a cat cannot be mistaken.

Although emotions are usually regarded here as assessments preceding feelings, two other cases should be mentioned. The feeling may come at the same time as the assessment. This may especially be the case with shock. If one has not thought in advance about the death of someone close to him he may experience surprise, confusion and negative bodily feelings at the same time, and so experience shock. The third case is where the feeling comes before the assessment. This happens especially when the feeling itself is being assessed as in the case of illness, drunkenness, hangovers, tiredness, or reports of drug reactions.

The observer determines emotions by the circumstance or situation. An emotion word seems to be an elliptical word covering both feelings and the contexts involved. Geldard wrote,

"The role of context is beautifully illustrated by some of the early experiences in film production. The Russian directors Kuleshov and Pudovkin took a closeup of the face of the actor Mosjukhin, while in a quiet pose, which they joined in three different combinations. The same close-up was followed by a) a picture of a plate of soup, b) one of a coffin in which lay a dead woman, and c) one of a little girl playing with a funny toy bear.

'When we showed the three combinations to an audience which had not been let into the secret the result was terrific. The public raved about the acting of the artist. They pointed out the heavy pensiveness of his mood over the forgotten soup, were touched and moved by the deep sorrow with which he looked on the dead woman, and admired the light, happy smile with which he surveyed the girl at play. But we knew in all three cases the face was exactly the same.' " (Geldard *Fundamentals of Psychology* p. 46)

Emotion, then, is not merely a feeling. C. D. Broad (J.A.A.C. 1954) states that all emotions are cognitions. George Pitcher wrote, "A change in knowledge can, by itself, result in the restraint or the removal of an emotion." A. I. Melden (*Mind* 74), R. Peters (*Concept of Motivation* 1958), W. Shibles (*Emotions* 1963), and E. Bedford (D. Gustafson, ed., *Essays in Philosophical Psychology*) treat emotions as forms of judgment. Melden provides one of the clearest statements regarding the rational nature of emotion:

"Whatever else anger may be, it cannot be an internal feeling or state conceptually unrelated to the functions of intelligence in the social circumstances in which it occurs . . . Nothing less than our status as rational and social beings in situations of enormously varying degrees of complexity

— as the whole human beings that we are — must be involved in order to provide any reasonable adequate account of the role of emotions in our lives." (*Human Action* T. Mischel, ed. pp. 216, 221)

Errol Bedford offers support to the analysis of emotions as being largely assessments: "Emotion words form part of the vocabulary of appraisal and criticism." (p. 89) His main view is that emotion words do not mainly report internal states, but rather are appraisals. They presuppose social relations, moral, aesthetic, and legal judgments. Ashamed and shame apply only if the act is subject to criticism. Vain, envious, resentful are terms of appraisal or censure. In "I envy Schnabel's technique," "envy" may serve not to describe a feeling but rather as a term of praise.

He holds that emotion is not just a feeling and so cannot be a cause of actions. On this view it is wrong to say, "I did it out of jealousy." Jealousy cannot be a cause. He states, "An emotion is not any sort of experience or process." (p. 77) To report an emotion is not just to report a feeling but is rather to report the context of our behavior. If we know our emotions better than others do, it is not just because we know our feelings better but because we know the context of our behavior better. Often, however, others know more about our emotions than we ourselves do. Bedford says, "If an emotion were a feeling no sense could be made of them at all." (p. 91)

Now because emotion is not just a feeling but rather a rational activity we can condemn and justify them, e.g., as in "You ought not to be envious."

Moreland Perkins agrees with Bedford's view and states that "what we feel when we feel angry is not to be explained simply or even mainly by telling what we feel in our body when we feel angry." But Perkins stresses the fact that emotion terms often do involve some reference to bodily feelings.

A specific example may help to illustrate the nature of emotion as well as to show that and how negative emotions may be changed and dissipated. By "negative emotion" is meant ordinarily undesirable ones such as revenge, anger, jealousy, grief, dread, and anxiety.

One often thinks that revenge is a natural emotion to experience and one often, in one way or another, takes his revenge. A friend pours molasses on your books. You know this is more than a joke, that he has gone too far, and take your revenge. You pour molasses on his books in the traditional "tooth for a tooth" fashion. You immediately feel relieved, but after a while you begin to feel as if you had yourself done a mean act. In addition, it may turn out that your friend has been mistreated by his parents and friends and did the above act in his misery and confusion at a time when he needed friends most. Your revenge was the worst thing you could have done to him, and it drove him to a neurotic condition. When you realize this you wish you had not gotten revenge.

In any case, revenge has no purpose or point except an immediate unintelligent act on the part of the harmed party. Revenge does not get at the cause of the problem. We may regard one as not being well or as being ignorant or unintelligent, if he does harm to another. It does not help for such a person to get revenge. It does not help many criminals to merely lock them in prison for a certain number of years. They often come out worse than when they went in. What is needed is correctional action directed at that which caused the person to do the harm in the first place.

Thus in the case of a harmful act by another, one might realize that revenge has no intelligent function. In the preceding example one might instead go to one's friend and ask why he poured the molasses and how things have been going for him. After acting in this way on a number of occasions one can find that one has a pleasant feeling of helping another human being, and eventually one will no longer experience revenge. This is because emotion is a rational description or assessments and beliefs which guide feeling. If the rational aspect is changed the feelings change. One no longer has the emotion of revenge or at least one immediately overcomes that emotion. No outburst or release is needed, only common sense and intelligence regarding cause and effect.

A similar argument, or example, may be offered for anger, hatred, grief and guilt. They are not innate necessary forms of behavior, but may be considered as expressions of inability to understand, adjust, or act in a certain situation. They can be overcome both when they occur and, more important, one finds that such emotions eventually can even stop occurring. Psychiatrists often say one of the greatest deterrents to successful therapy is the patient's view that he cannot change his emotions and his behavior when, in fact, he can. Albert Ellis wrote,

"What are some of the major illogical ideas or philosophies which, when originally held and later perpetuated by men and women in our civilization lead to self-defeat and neurosis?" He gives as one of these the following: "The idea that one has virtually no control over one's emotions and that one cannot help feeling certain things — instead of the idea that one has enormous control over one's emotions if one chooses to work at controlling them and to practice saying the right kinds of sentences to oneself." (1958)

The average person holds also that emotions are, or are like, feelings and so are inevitable and cannot be changed. Rather one can change one's emotions and to a large extent determine and encourage some while eliminating others. Thus the negative feelings are not induced.

III AN ANALYSIS OF KÜBLER-ROSS ON DEATH AND DYING

Kubler-Ross is one of the most influential writers on the subject of dying. Her great concern and effort in this area deserve appreciation. The following criticisms are given only as a balance to her otherwise fine work. She based her book on a course she taught for medical and theological students. It involves interviews with terminally ill patients. The book would thus seem to be well-based on an empirical description of what actually occurs. It is no good to say, "But I have seen these patients and they have said these things and acted this way." Such is not the case. Her description is rather based on her own theories as indicated by the following. In the philosophy of the social and natural sciences it has become evident (T. Kuhn, L. Wittgenstein, Mary Hesse, N. Hanson) that our description of reality is largely determined by our models or metaphors. Even seeing is a "seeing-as," not merely direct, immediate seeing of objective fact. Models and metaphors partly constitute reality. However, to take a model or metaphor literally is to commit what the psychologist, T. Sarbin, and others have called the "metaphor to myth" fallacy. (See W. Shibles *Metaphor: An Annotated Bibliography and History*.) Kubler-Ross seems to take her descriptions literally and so to commit this fallacy.

Her descriptions commit the metaphor to myth fallacy of assuming the existence of an unconscious mind (Freudianism). She states, "In our unconscious mind we can only be killed, it is inconceivable to die of a natural cause or of old age." How do we know this is the case if we never have access to our so-called "unconscious mind"? (cf. MacIntyre *The Unconscious*) Certainly man often covertly denies that he will die but speaks and acts as if he will not be killed. She continued, "Our unconscious mind cannot differentiate between the wish to kill somebody in anger and the act of having done so." Again a description of overt statement and behavior would be preferable. The description need not even be strictly behavioristic. Statements one makes to oneself and even imagery may be included. Her analysis does not account for the basic complex way in which we think, viz., language use, imagery, abilities, but rather assumes simplistic, inaccessible, mentalistic entities. She goes on, "In our unconscious we cannot perceive our own death and do believe in our own immortality, but can conceive of our neighbor's death . . . " (12) (37) This statement combines the existentialist's stress on individuality and subjectivity, with Freud's statement, "Our unconscious is . . . inaccessible to the idea of our own death . . ." *(Civilization, War and Death)* In any case the statement produces a kind of necessary and essential built-in denial. Although we often do deny, lie, and are dishonest in facing reality it is not *necessary* that we do and be so. There are philosophical arguments by L. Wittgenstein and others which explicate what it could possibly mean for even the *"conscious mind"* to comprehend death. Rather than an entity there may be some concrete usage which is referred to by "conscious" or "unconscious." It may be more difficult to understand the unconscious than it is to understand death.

Kübler-Ross presents the following stages which the dying patient supposedly passes through: 1. denial and isolation, 2. anger, 3. bargaining, 4. depression with a great sense of loss, 5. acceptance, 6. hope. The stages overlap but do not replace each other. Hope usually persists through all stages and is maintained up to the end.

Her model of stages, if treated as a model or metaphor, may be suggestive but if taken as a literal description of reality it commits the metaphor-to-myth fallacy. "Stages" is a metaphor, as are the names of each stage. Stage 1, "denial and isolation," is based on Freudian views of unconscious denial and thus is theory laden. Also it is a natural and intelligent reaction of a patient told he has a fatal illness, to check out the facts. Many people were told of having a fatal illness only to find it was diagnosed incorrectly or that is is really not fatal. Patients have even survived after all of the usual criteria indicate that they should be dead. Thus what is called denial may well be simply a concern to verify the facts. Certainly there is often an attempt at denial as well. Such denial may in part be the base of religion which assures an afterlife. Kübler-Ross found that religious patients did not face death more easily than did non-religious patients.

The stages are too procrustean, narrow and fixed, even though they overlap, to adequately account for all of the thoughts, images, perceptual and motor abilities which a person has regarding dying. The stages a patient "passes through" are more diverse and complex than are those included in her analysis. To put it differently, the stages purport to tell us how the patient thinks and, if so, they can be seen to be inadequate. Perhaps because stemming from the Freudian tradition, Kübler-Ross is alert to some of the more concrete ways in which we do think, namely, in terms of defense-mechanisms. I would prefer to call these language-games or rhetorical devices because it is more descriptive of how we think to do so, and because the so-called "defense-mechanisms" usually do not really defend but rather are self-defeating and unrealistic. Also "mechanism" implies a mechanical device, yet none are presented. For example, she presents the interesting cases of those who try to challenge death by driving fast, by destructive activity such as war, riot, crime, mountain climbing. Such activities as well as Hemingway's bullfighting would seem to be irrational ways of understanding or coping with death. She also notes the paradox of killing in order to avoid the reality of death. This language-game or rhetorical-device is a clearer paradigm than her Freudian explanation of it in terms of the unconscious. I would wish to argue that the specific language-games, the metaphors and models one has, have more to do with one's thinking during dying than do the stages mentioned. Kübler-Ross herself quite correctly stresses the need to have the patient communicate his own thinking, and to communicate with the patient. It is doubtful if it would console the patient if he were told he is passing through stages. It may depress him. He may go through stages not mentioned, or skip stages, etc.

The stage system is too neat. "Now, I'm at the anger stage, next comes bargaining." "Acceptance is over, only hope is left." The stages are general enough and so they could apply to every case in some way or other, but how would it help to know that one is in the depression stage? What are we to do about it? Her view is that we should face death and accept it as a necessary reality. The goal seems to just be to see that people die less fearfully. But what is the point of that?

An analysis of the stages in terms of emotions will help clarify the issue. I wish to define emotions as largely assessments and descriptions which guide feelings. The stages may be thought of as attempts at assessments, some of which are realistic and rational and others of which are unrealistic, dishonest (denial), or irrational. (See W. Shibles *Emotions*) Irrational or unrealistic assessments lead to negative emotions, such as stage No. 2 – anger, stage No. 4 – depression. It is rational to accept what is the case and what it is not in one's power to change. The acceptance stage may involve this. The average patient may in fact become dishonest, angry, irrational and depressed but this does not mean that he must do so or that such a reaction cannot be largely prevented. What the average patient does, need not be what he should do. If one's assessments are rational, honest and clear from the start, negative emotions can be avoided or greatly diminished. One may, then, not need to go through these stages, but be better able to accept death from the start. Kübler-Ross is describing for us the typical irrational way in which one copes with dying.

She says about her book, "It is not meant to be a textbook on how to manage dying patients." (Preface) Supposedly it is just a description of the stages a dying patient goes through. But, nevertheless, her book is taken to be the basis on which one manages dying patients. If they go through certain stages we may supposedly help them through such stages. Kübler-Ross does in fact present her theories as ways of managing the dying patient.

One assessment which the author has is, like Freud's, that death is an absolute natural necessity. She stresses a more human life more than a prolonged life. But, logically, we do not in fact know that death and old age cannot be conquered. Thus one way of coping with dying and death is to promote research on the biology of aging, disease, and clarification of the concept of death itself. This will also help to alleviate guilt due to feeling one has not done anything to help the aged or the dying. We often have negative emotions concerning death and dying because we have superstitions, confused and irrational ideas concerning them.

Sigmund Freud. "Our Attitude Towards Death" *Civilization, War and Death* John Rickman, ed., London: Hogarth Press 1968 pp. 14-25

226

Norwood Hanson. *Patterns of Discovery* Cambridge University Press 1968

Mary Hesse. "Scientific Models" *Essays on Metaphor* W. Shibles, ed., Whitewater, Wisconsin: The Language Press 1972

Elizabeth Kubler-Ross. *On Death and Dying* New York: Macmillan 1969

Thomas Kuhn. *The Structure of Scientific Revolutions* University of Chicago 1962

Alasdair MacIntyre. *The Unconscious* New York: Humanities 1958

Theodore Sarbin. "Anxiety: Reification of a Metaphor" *Essays on Metaphor* W. Shibles, ed., Whitewater, Wisconsin: The Language Press 1972

Warren Shibles. *Emotions* Whitewater, Wisconsin: The Language Press 1973

IV ATTITUDES TOWARD DEATH AND OLD AGE

Alexander, Colley and Adlerstein, by means of word association and galvanic skin response tests, conclude that people, although they normally avoid the subject of death, nevertheless respond to death words more emotionally than to other words. They conclude that death is an underlying, motivating force in human behavior.

Although this analysis is suggestive the terms "emotion" and "motivating" should not be taken too seriously in this experiment. A more careful analysis of these terms is needed.

Swenson asserts about the attitudes toward death of the aged:

1) Religious elderly people face death better than non-religious ones. [This view has been corrected by G. Vernon and others in Vernon's *Sociology of Death.*]
2) Those in nursing homes fear death less than those in their own homes unless they live alone in their own homes.
3) The less educated avoid death.
4) The unhealthy fear death more than the healthy.
5) Inquiry into attitudes toward death may be best determined directly rather than by metaphysically delving into the "unconscious."
6) The aged are seldom conscious of death. They repress it, fear it normally, or look forward to it.
7) Chronologic age has little or no value in predicting thought concerning death.

These results are, of course, extremely general and of limited value. Contradictory results could be easily found. The results are valid only with reference to the specific situations reported and methods used. The results can be no more concrete than the abstractness of the terms used, e.g., the terms "death," "religious," etc.

Adolf Christi in an interview of one hundred acute psychiatric geriatric patients found that all but two were very upset about death. Christi used the criterion that the longer the time spent to associate death words the greater is the anxiety about death. He found that death words took longer to associate than other words. This criterion appears wholly unsatisfactory. It may just show that one is confused about death. But the time taken may mean nothing significant at all. Christi found evidence against Feifel's view that a religious person does not fear death as much as a non-religious person. But both investigators were dealing with different sorts of patients, circumstances and assumptions. This makes it unacceptable to merely compare one's findings or conclusions with another's.

Christi found that terminal psychiatric patients were relieved to discuss death with someone, and he therefore recommends that the physician attempt to discuss death with the patient.

Diggory and Rothman note that college students fear snakes, cancer, and death of loved ones — even more than their own death, thus supporting the view that death should be thought of in terms of one's interests, goals, self-esteem, that is, in terms of one's life activities. A negative definition is thus given of death. Death is not drinking, not enjoying, not thinking, etc. One's fears of death can best be thought of in terms of one's goals, hindrance to completion of tasks or activities, etc.

Shrut states, "There is a comparative lack of scientific writing on death." He finds that all of the aged show at least mild "anxiety" concerning death. ["Anxiety" perhaps should always be put in quotes, because it is a term of questionable meaning.] He says that fear of death is universal and that all fear is essentially fear of death. That all fear is or is based on fear of death is an interesting statement in need of further clarification. But insufficient support is given for the view that all fear is fear of death, though some psychiatrists such as Frankl have a similar view.

Shrut says that death may be regarded as a tool for achieving certain goals, a passage from one state to another, a biological end. For him death as an end cannot be experienced, and so we can never encounter it.

His findings are that among the aged, apartment residents had better health than those in Central House institutions; a permissive setting makes the aged socially alert and productive; those residing in an environment like pre-institutional homes reveal minimal fear of death. He presents the important point that subjects who live in settings like their former ones, whether apartment or home, show less fear of death than those who live in dissimilar environments.

Some of the findings and assertions of Kalish (1963) connected with a study of 220 college students are that approval of birth control, abortion, and euthanasia correlate highly with one another; and belief in God, afterlife and approval of capital punishment are significantly correlated. The latter correlation expresses a sense of punitive justice. He notes that those who most fear death are most opposed to abortion and that those who are religious are less humanitarian, less liberal, and favor capital punishment.

Kalish (1966) asserts that death is subjectively perceived, e.g., as social death which may then cause physical death. Desertion of a friend or parent may bring about social death leading to withdrawal and despair. "Psychological death" is when a person is no longer aware of himself and his environment. Kalish's main point is that what we perceive as the death of another is not just biological deaths, but social deaths, psychological deaths, or we may perceive social immortality in the sense of living on in one's memory. Kalish's categories could perhaps be better termed metaphorical kinds of deaths.

Howard and Scott present the view that attitudes toward death are mainly the result of cultural themes. They agree with Wahl that death is regarded as symbolic for many sorts of things. We, for example, react to death as if it were dying or pain, a defeat of man and medicine by nature, separation from friends, inactivity. These symbolic views often conflict or are unresolved in an individual. In support of this study it may be pointed out that by becoming aware of the nature, logic and functioning of metaphor in our beliefs and thought we can be better able to understand and resolve such conflict. We may, for example, find that some of our models are taken literally when they are in fact metaphors. As metaphors our models may be expanded to gain insight. It is often seen that, as Robert Frost once wrote, "All thinking is metaphorical." To comprehend death then involves understanding metaphor.

Kastenbaum mentions the mechanism of *"thanatomimesis"* which is death feigning leading one to think one is dead. Spiders and animals "play dead" or "play possum." Man also exhibits such behavior without being completely aware of his doing so. It may be culturally induced. One may learn to play such roles as boredom, swoon, catalepsy, trance, ecstasy. J. Schneck, (1951) spoke of the death feint and discussed its relations to the state of hypnosis or the hypnotic suggestive state. The yoga practitioner seems to feign death, and children "play dead." The dying and elderly may often feign death. They may experience an isolation or social death which leads then to physical death. In feigning dead the person does not communicate with others, or he communicates mechanically or only in terms of what is expected of him. One may similarly be given the "silent treatment," and so regarded as dead.

The attempt in the above account is to define death in terms of consciousness, not in terms of vegetative life. When this is done it is seen that our roles and cultural beliefs, or games we play, determine whether we are alive or not. Death occurs not just in a person but between one person and another, as with social death. That is, death is not just internal but is a situation, context, involving cessation of communication and response. One criterion of death is failure to communicate, or respond. If we have lost consciousness, lost enjoyment in living, or play dead, we may in a most important respect be dead. There are as many deaths as there are thoughts, situations, responses, and perspectives.

In support of Kastenbaum's views, we find advertisers even asserting that toothpaste has sex-appeal and that soda will make one "come alive." This is our general mechanism of not accepting things for what they are, but rather regarding them as something else. The author states, "Neither psychology nor any of the other behavioral and social sciences have done much to clarify the nature of psychological aliveness." One answer to this problem is to critically clarify one's concepts. An examination of the nature of metaphor would also be helpful.

Sudnow showed that the young receive deferential treatment in hospitals (Vernon 105). Similar treatment of the aged may be found in regard to exclusion from jobs, and life-saving machines. In support of Sudnow it may be noted that in 1967 no one over age 45 was eligible for use of an artificial kidney machine. (Vernon 98) The aged are often denied psychiatric care and even education. Little research has been done on aging. A liberation movement for the aged may be indicated.

Ohara and Reynolds discuss the attitude toward death of love-pact suicide. This may be compared with *Romeo and Juliet* and Shakespeare's view of death as lover, bride or bridegroom. There is the thought or image of being united after death. Japanese literature often involves love-pact suicide. It is ten times as common in Japan as in England and Wales combined. Love-pact suicides took place in romantic, scenic settings. One researcher, Dr. Komine, found such suicides to be usually due to inability to marry, non-marital sexual relationships, economic problems, and family discord, in order of decreasing frequency. For males over age 30 the cause was usually trouble over a mistress or another's wife. There were also murder-suicide love pacts. Some love-pact suicides were caused by homosexual problems.

Mary Williams surveyed the change of attitudes toward death in psychological literature from 1931 to 1961. There were only a few more articles on the subject in 1961 than in 1931. She concludes,

"Psychoanalysts have worked like moles, hardly interested in what goes on above ground, and sociologists, surveying the earth with their measuring apparatus, have hardly noticed the tremors from below. Few have yet attempted a synthesis."

She found that death remained a rather taboo subject and that this repression expresses itself in other forms such as war or suicide. She states,

"Perhaps one of the most important rediscoveries in this agnostic age has been the enormous psychic need for immortality . . . The search for proof of survival has become almost respectable in recent years with the advent of parapsychology as a science."

Elliott Jaques' "Death and the Mid-Life Crisis" presents the view that around age 35 men of genius often die, one's work becomes very creative or comes to an end, one becomes aware that he has not much time to live and tends to fulfill needs or desires hitherto denied. The analysis given is largely Freudian.

Statements made here such as, "The unconscious is not aware of death *per se*," seem strange since supposedly the unconscious cannot by definition be conscious or aware of anything. The analysis given depends upon whether or not one accepts Freudian explanations. It is found that if one has by mid-life not achieved some success or a satisfactory self-image, gradual depression and psychological disturbance can be expected. At middle age one tends to lie about his age, be hypochondriacal over health and signs of aging such as grey hair, become more concerned with religion [although Shneidman showed there was less religious concern], lack genuine enjoyment of life, become sexually promiscuous to prove one's youth and potency [this would need to be demonstrated], there is intellectual dishonesty [though this seems common at any age], and increase in arrogance and ruthlessness. The view presented is that one must be able to mourn for one's self and for one's lost youth. Jaques' view here uses "mourn" in a new way and it becomes a metaphorical use. How can one mourn for oneself? That depends upon what mourning for another is. For Jaques it suggests the Freudian assumption that what happens in childhood determines one's life, and since that childhood is now gone or "dead" we may mourn for it.

In opposition to Jaques' view, an analysis of emotions would show that such a metaphor or model is unfounded and does not allow one to deal in a realistic way with the actual cause and effect and rational factors involved in the situation. The mid-age crisis can perhaps be best explained not as an inherent property, principle, or emotion, but rather as the rational assessment of one's situation. This rational assessment plus contextual description which guides feeling is what the mid-life crisis reduces to. By "crisis" in mid-age crisis is meant a radical change in one's emotion. If emotion is thought of as an internal state one may draw the conclusion that the emotion is a necessary, inherent property or principle. An analysis of the way emotion terms work, as presented earlier, shows that this is not the case. The mid-age crisis emotion is not an inherent or internal emotion, but rather the rational assessment of one's situation involving descriptive contextual factors which guide feelings. No one or group of specific feelings need be present and no feelings need be present at all. The mid-life crisis then reduces primarily to a change in one's assessment of his situation. This means that by intelligent reasoning one may avoid incurring negative feelings which may result from confusion of one's situation and one's goals, or from an unrealistic knowledge of cause and effect. The "mid-life crisis" as a crisis is quite avoidable. A clearer and more honest analysis of death and dying and its relation to living can help to avoid such a sudden but confused realization which the mid-age crisis is.

In regard to the attitude of the abnormal toward death, the *Merck Manual* states that the schizophrenic depersonalizes, and his nihilistic ideas increase until he feels dead or feels he no longer has a body or that there is no world. The "Involutional Psychotic Reaction" is said to involve preoccupation with death. This fear is projected in symbolic forms such as feelings of unworthiness. This account presupposes a questionable and Freudian analysis of how the abnormal person thinks.

V ATTITUDES TOWARD FUNERALS

According to Shneidman's study (1971), 80 percent of 30,000 people surveyed report that funerals are very much overpriced, 62 percent that funerals should cost less than $300, 2 percent that a reasonable charge may exceed $600. [The average funeral costs close to $1,000.] Only 2 percent desire a funeral as large as possible, one third want no funeral at all. Twenty percent of the religious, and 63 percent of the anti-religious, do not want funerals. Those who are anti-religious unanimously reject large, formal funerals. Forty-seven percent believe funeral rituals and wakes are important for the survivors. Eighteen percent say such rituals are unimportant.

Only 6 percent approve of lying-in-state at the funeral. Seventy percent do not wish to lie in open caskets. [This figure is significant in view of the funeral director's argument that the memory-picture and its grief-therapy is a necessity.] Women especially, are against lying in open caskets. Ninety-one percent of the anti-religious group disapprove of display of their corpses. More Roman Catholics approve of open casket (12 percent) than any other group.

Thirty-two percent would donate their bodies to medical schools or science if they had their own choice. Eighty-two would donate their hearts. The very religious usually refuse to give their hearts (25 percent). Protestants are more likely to donate their bodies or choose cremation than are Jews or Roman Catholics. Fifty-two percent of the anti-religious prefer cremation to burial. Eighty-three percent do not mind having autopsy. Shneidman concludes,

> "All these results point to one of the main findings of the questionnaire, namely that – over the past generation or two – there has been a tremendous secularization of death."

One might add that ritual often takes the place of rational thought, intelligence, and genuinely aesthetic experiences. Emily Post in her Etiquette (1934) surprisingly states,

> "It is strange that long association with the sadness of death should seem to have deprived an occasional funeral director of all sense of moderation. Whether the

temptation of 'good business' gradually undermines his character — knowing as he does that bereaved families ask no questions — or whether his profession is merely devoid of taste, he will, if not checked, bring the most ornate and expensive casket in his establishment. He will perform every rite that his professional ingenuity for expenditure can devise. He will employ every attendant he has. He will order vehicles numerous enough for the cortege of a President. He will even, if thrown in contact with a bewildered chief-mourner, secure a pledge for the erection of an elaborate mausoleum . . . And it is not unheard of that a small estate is seriously depleted by vulgarly lavish and entirely inappropriate funeral expenses."

Mitford notes that this caution is omitted in more recent editions.

L. Boros in *The Mystery of Death* states, "The philosopher will get no assistance [insight into death] from those who are professionally concerned with dying."

William May, Professor of Religion, presents the following in Liston Mills *Perspectives on Death*:

"The attempt to cover up death in the funeral service is an unmitigated disaster for the Church, preceded and prepared for by the Church's failure to reckon with death in its own preaching and pastoral life."

Joseph Mathews (1967) gave an account of his experience at his father's funeral. He first was quoted $100 for a casket but then found the price was $275 and up and that the $100 was said to be only for paupers. The pauper coffin was kept outside of the showroom. The director finally agreed to $100. Later the 92-year-old body was cosmetically beautified to look like age 52. The author was horrified at the deception of such lifelike makeup, and he himself removed the cotton stuffed in his cheeks, the powder, rouge and the rest of the makeup. The banks of flowers were removed and the artificial grass carpet rolled back. The words said about the deceased were said by one who knew him well and they were true representations of the person's life. This contrasts with the typical praise of the dead by one who does not know him.

The words used at a funeral I attended were "This person was well liked as evidenced by the flowers present." Such evidence is rather a faulty guide especially, as in this case, when said by someone who had no knowledge of the deceased. Mathews' experience ended, however, with ritual of a religious nature. He threw the, numerologically correct, three portions of dirt on the coffin, and uttered ritualistic and symbolic religious words.

VI PSYCHOSOMATIC EVENTS: SUDDEN DEATHS FROM UNKNOWN CAUSES (AND VOODOO DEATH)

The term "psychosomatic" is widely used. It is, however, a misnomer. It derives from the Greek word which means life, breath, soul, and especially, mind. But contemporary philosophical psychology has shown (G. Ryle, et al.) that there is no evidence for mind. The container theory of mind though held by the majority of people has not a bit of evidence to support it. Psycho-somatic is mind-body, and as there is no mind so psycho-somatic is a naming-fallacy. If we let "psycho" stand for thought we are still in difficulty, for what evidence do we have for an "idea" or a "thought"? These are pseudo-psychological entities. Thought reduces to ability to do things, and for the most part to our ability with language. Thought is not an epistemological starting point but language is. We need not "think" in order to present a theory but we must write or speak. Thus "psychosomatic" should for accuracy and clarity be changed to "linguo-somatic." To study a patient's thought we study what he says. His other behavior should not be excluded. Schizophrenia as well as other abnormal as well as normal behavior is being studied mainly by the kind of language one uses, and the statements one says to oneself and becomes captivated by.

The American Psychiatric Association lists a number of categories of psychosomatic disorders:

1. cardiovascular reaction
2. respiratory disorder (asthma, overbreathing, etc.)
3. gastrointestinal disorder (ulcer, colitis, etc.)
4. anorexia nervosa (loss of appetite due to emotional reasons)
5. genitourinary reaction (frigidity, impotence, etc.)
6. dysmenorrhea (painful menstruation)
7. endocrine reactions (e.g., anemia)
8. musculoskeletal reaction
9. psychophysiologic disorders of the organs of special senses

Helen and Harold Kaplan report, "In the field of

psychosomatic medicine, no single theoretical model is considered entirely satisfactory at present."

One way of conceiving of psychosomatic involves the very definition of emotion presented throughout this book. Emotion is largely assessment which guides feeling. This may alternately be called psychosomatic, i.e. *psyche* is assessment which guides *soma* which is feeling. Psychosomatic becomes another word for emotion. Assessment (or psyche) may be thought of as physical processes which guide feelings also. When one makes an assessment certain physical events are taking place and these events lead to others, e.g., to feelings.

Lindemann found that 33 of 41 patients with ulcerative colitis developed their disease soon after the loss of a person important to them. Unresolved negative emotions are seen to bring about bodily disturbances.

In an interesting article by Weisman and Hackett concerning predilection to death, the following suggestive cases are presented:

1. Patients who are extremely anxious about their impending surgery, are firmly convinced of their dying during the operation, and look forward to dying, are often not operated on because such an attitude is found to bring about their death.
2. People who are told by a fortune teller [or perhaps astrologer], or even a friend, that they will die at a certain time are found to fulfill the prophecy. [One may relate this to the self-suggestive biblical prophecy that "The wages of sin is death." It brings on shock reaction which may cause death.]
3. "Psychic" death is reported whereby patients correctly predict their own death, and there is found no organic cause of death.
4. Some await God's punishment by being killed, or feel they live at the expense of other's lives, or believe in *Liebestod*, i.e., that lovers reunite after death.
5. Predilection patients commonly had, in effect, "died" socially. They had no remaining interest in human relationships. It is theorized that they welcome death by phantasied survival after death.

6. Those patients who are suddenly isolated or disowned, or rejected by family or friends may as a result of this "social death" bring about their physical death. One man died after he found out none of his six children would give blood to help him. No organic cause of his death was found.

All of the cases Weisman and Hackett present are similar to the cases of "voodoo" death prevalent among tribal cultures. The result in all such cases appears to be social rejection bringing about the self-destructive behavior of starving oneself, withdrawal, etc., leading to conditions ever more suitable for shock to occur. Shock is largely responsible for such deaths, as Cannon (1942) observes in his study of "voodoo" death. Because shock is the cause no organic causes are easily found after death. Presumably one could find organic causes in all such cases of death by shock or "voodoo" death. This theory still leaves more to be explained as to the psychosomatic mechanisms involved.

Weisman and Hackett suggest some possible mechanisms. They state, " 'Death' is personified as is 'life' — It thus lends itself to many metaphors, mystic abstractions, etc." The authors are alert to the importance of metaphor in regard to understanding the nature of death as well as our adjustment to it. They point out that we adjust to death by means of fantasy. We view life in terms of various concepts and our notions of death are seen in relation to them. Our language and metaphors construct a complex world for ourselves and so cannot be adequately rendered by a single sentence or metaphor. The authors assert, "Life as it is lived has more parameters than there are laboratory methods available to use them; death encompasses the human personality as much as life does." They note that our view of death depends upon our view of our selves, [our metaphors for ourself]. In fearing death we are often fearing loss of what we conceive to be our self. Fear of death may come with a new situation which forces a new view of the self upon us. [We must prepare ourselves for new metaphors of ourselves, and of possible situations which we might find ourselves in. Metaphor may in this way be used as a way of coping with death.]

An example is given of some fixed or stereotyped metaphors used to "explain" all things: "After a certain age every vague complaint, in the absence of surgically localized disorders, is attributed to either 'menopause' or the 'infirmities' of old age." They point out that "I," after death, and "When I am dead" are not acceptable uses, and assert that one cannot imagine his own death even metaphorically: "A phantasy of absolute subjective death is impossible to imagine."

It is also indicated how one thinks of fear of death or dying. It is often "seen-as," seen as an it, pain, oncoming insanity, one's self dying, disintegration of body, accumulation of regrets, fear of others, fear of rejection, fear of one's past misbehavior. Fear of death may be confused with fear of dying. One may die in one perspective rather than in another or confuse perspectives. A pregnant coed may commit suicide not thinking she will die but only that she is getting rid of her problems. Also abandonment is represented metaphorically by drawn shades, hushed voices, different ways of speaking, etc.

Weisman and Hackett then point out that in order to understand the dying patient we must find out something about him, how he views life, himself, his environment, others. To state their view in terms other than those the authors use, we must find out the metaphors and models the patient lives by; every phrase one uses tells a great deal. Once this is known, the authors point out, we will know what would constitute an appropriate death for a patient. They state that the criteria for the therapy to bring about an appropriate death are: 1) conflict reduction, 2) the patient must be properly understood in terms of the image he has of himself, 3) important social relationships must be restored, 4) his wishes must be satisfied as much as possible. Dr. Alex Comfort, a biologist, presents a similar view when he states,

"Continuance of active work, retention of interests, of the respect of our fellows, and of sense of significance in the common life of the species, apparently makes us live longer — loss of these things makes us die young." (p. 193)

Elie Metchnikoff in 1908 stressed the fact that old people should be kept mentally alert, learn how to avoid stress and worry. This and other psychosomatic arguments presented in this chapter are strong arguments for the view that the most important goal in life must be active inquiry into oneself, one's environment, and basic critical philosophical inquiry, e.g., into the nature of emotions, death, etc. To fail to engage in such inquiry is seen to lead to one's death.

What was said above in regard to second person (you) or third person (him) therapy may perhaps also apply to the first person case. That is, the more clear one is about his emotions, his life, his conceptual fantasies, his models and metaphors, the more clear will be the kind of death desired and adjusted to. Along these lines we find the authors stressing the necessity of open discussion with patients. This helps patients to come to a clearer understanding of themselves.

Although the authors present their goal as getting the patient to die with dignity, or as they put it, "The purpose of living is to create a world in which we would be willing to die," this can rather only be the goal of the psychiatrist. To die quietly seems to be a very limited goal. The philosopher wishes to always find out more about death and dying and it will not do to simply hold such views that will lead us to "want to die."

In regard to psychosomatic phenomena Le Shan found that poor social experiences are highly correlated with development of cancer. Forty-two out of 45 cancer therapy cases, but only one out of 30 control therapy cases had a background of childhood feelings of isolation, or rejection, loss of a central relationship and sense of great despair. (Vernon pp. 100-101)

In Shneidman's survey of the 30,000 readers of *Psychology Today* 92 percent were found to firmly believe (56 percent), or tend to believe (36 percent), that psychological factors can influence (or even cause) death. Forty-three percent thought that most deaths have strong components of conscious or unconscious participation by the persons who die.

Barber in his article, "Death by Suggestion," rejects the view that voodoo death is in fact caused by voodoo, sorcery, witchcraft, magic, or suggestion. He found that in most cases poisoning could have been the cause, that often the victim does not eat or drink enough for survival, and that organic disorder may have been the cause in some cases. However, he fails to mention shock as the main cause. Barber rejects, as premature, explanations of such deaths as being based on overstimulation of the sympathicoadrenal system (Cannon's view) or overstimulation of the parasympathetic system.

Ashley Montagu in discussing the nature of psychosomatic medicine points out that feelings were regarded by F. Dunbar as related to bodily functions, that Selye's work on stress and endocrinology also suggests psychosomatic relationships, as does the phenomenon of "voodoo" death. Montagu recommends observation of anthropological phenomena for additional clues and instances, e.g., adolescent sterility varies from culture to culture and may be due to cultural beliefs and factors rather than physiological factors alone. The main point is that "psychosomatic" involves a number of integrated factors such as somatic, psychic (which was criticized earlier in this chapter), social, and cultural.

Asthma is seen to be related to the fear of death. (M. Williams) This may be due to overprotectiveness of the mother.

Kalish (1966) asserts that social death may cause or enhance physical death. He calls this "psychosomatic death."

Walter Cannon of Harvard Medical School, in his article, "Voodoo Death," concluded that voodoo death is not magical death but death by shock. The test of such shock is rapid pulse, cool and moist skin, high red blood cell count, low blood pressure, increased blood sugar. Lack of food and water causes excitement of the sympathico-adrenal system. Great fear produces physical changes. Fear serves to prepare the body for action and if no action follows, the body is harmed. Cannon's view involves the Darwinian teleological assumption that all our experience has the purpose of survival.

Soldiers who were in shock due to war wounds died from the shock rather than from the wound. It may be pointed out that the existentialist's stress on the necessity to experience dread and anxiety can be similarly detrimental, possibly leading to shock or suicide and so bring about one's death. Cannon cited a number of scientifically reported instances of so-called "voodoo death" throughout the world. Although he does not say so, some cases approach the nature of hypnotism, e.g., some Brazilian Indian tribes accept what is told them, thus when the medicine man tells them they will die they may by shock do so. It would be interesting to investigate whether one by hypnosis can be caused to go into fatal shock. Some instances involve self-conviction, e.g., that demons determine one to die. Statements in the Bible are similar: "The wages of sin is death."

When one finds out that the thing he did was taboo even long after the act, he can go into shock and die within 24 hours of finding this out. Often a bone is pointed at the victim and the victim thinks that he is thereby due to die. Such spells are negated only if the victim is told it was a mistake, or the bone pointer undoes the spell. Such spells lead to abstinence of food and water and social rejection by the community, that is, one starves oneself making shock more likely, and he also experiences social death. The condemned person is regarded as if dead. Cannon asserts that voodoo death applies to very ignorant people, but in view of other findings in this chapter it affects people thought to be intelligent, e.g., death caused by death of someone close. It may be noted that, according to Strehler (1957), the widowed and divorced have higher mortality rates than the single or married. Death may be due to shock or psychosomatic causes.

Albert Cain and Irene Fast found that a seven-year-old girl developed her first asthmatic attack a day after her asthmatic sister died of such an attack. The attacks recurred each anniversary of her sister's death. The researchers attribute these attacks to family encouraged identification with the deceased, e.g., the child may be made to worry lest she die as her sister had. (*Science News* 12-18-71, p. 409)

Francis Bacon (1561-1626) was aware of psychosomatic relations. He noted that men die from great and sudden grief, fear, or even from joy.

In the Ibo tribe of Nigeria one may die as a result of a false oath. In legal disputes a "black oath" is, e.g., "If my assertion is wrong let this oath take away my life." If the person is living after a year he is freed of all guilt. In a number of cases the man, perhaps from feelings of guilt, hangs himself, or kills himself by carelessness within the year. (Noon)

It is not satisfactory to assert that death may be caused by self-suggestion or hypnosis, without an analysis of the nature of suggestion and hypnosis. Such analyses show that we are clear about neither process although we can somehow effectively "induce" (a word derivative from magnetism) hypnosis. (Gordon)

William Godwin (1756-1836) (Gruman 1966) once thought that one could prolong life by gaining voluntary control over the emotions, and over bodily functions. According to him, clear thinking and proper emotions can increase life. Bad news may cause disease or death. Cheerfulness leads to a longer life. His view is that reason can help create a more happy person and so increase length of life. His stress on reason is similar to that of the contemporary view of Albert Ellis in *Reason and Emotion*. Ellis calls his own view "rational psychotherapy." Godwin concludes that we become diseased and die partly because we consent to and because we think we will.

Elie Metchnikoff had the view that sleep and death are both types of self-intoxication. Death is not necessary and inevitable but rather is partly caused by self-suggestions. (Cochrane)

The following account is also suggestive of psychosomatic phenomena. The *Merck Manual* (1961) states about warts:

"Psychotherapy (hexing): In young children, suggestion accompanied by impressive but meaningless manipulations, such as painting the lesion or touching them with unusual objects or exposing them to heat lamps, is often remarkably successful."

This need not deny naturalistic explanation and is not meant to suggest that magic is being performed. One's assessments or beliefs involve nerves and chemistry, and affect feelings and other physiological states. Beliefs have physical consequences.

Freud's "death instinct" may be con..dered as a psychosomatic bringing about of one's own death. What Freud meant by "death instinct" is another matter, but if seen as one's tendency to destroy himself in one way or another it appears to involve psychosomatic factors, e.g., accident proneness, engaging in dangerous activities, failure to inquire or educate oneself thus leading to unhealthful emotional and physical circumstances, etc.

Edwin Shneidman (1966), who has done extensive work on suicide, labels as subintentioned suicides or death-hasteners ("psyde-hasteners") those who are ignorant, or those who have extreme or confused emotions. Thus strong emotions and emotions such as fear, anxiety, hate can lead to one's death or suicide. Ignorance here may be regarded as a failure to inquire. Failure to inquire into, for example, ethics, philosophical psychology, or critical philosophy may lead to one's lack of realistic knowledge of how things work and lack of a knowledge of cause and effect generally, thereby leading to conceptual confusion, maladjustment, and so death. By means of careful and critical philosophical clarification one may no longer be at the mercy of his metaphors, category-mistakes, naming-fallacies, circular statements, confusions regarding ethics, etc. By misusing ethical language or mistakes in judgment and assessment, one may be led to perform actions which bring about his own death needlessly, and to induce negative emotions which speed aging leading to shock and death.

I. E. Alexander, R. S. Colley, and A. M. Adlerstein. "Is Death a Matter of Indifference" *Journal of Psychology* 43 (1957) 277-283

Francis Bacon. "History of Life and Death" *The Works of Francis Bacon* J. Speeding and R. Ellis, eds., London: F. Frommann 1963 pp. 213-335

T. Barber. "Death by Suggestion" *Psychosomatic Medicine* 23 (1961) 153-155

Herbert Barry, Jr. "Significance of Maternal Bereavement Before Age of Eight in Psychiatric Patients" *Archives of Neurology and Psychiatry* 62 (1949) 630-637

W. B. Cannon. "Voodoo Death" *American Anthropologist* 44 (1942) 169-181

Adolf Christi. "Attitudes toward death among a group of acute geriatric psychiatric patients" *Journal of Gerontology* 16 (1961) 56-59

A. L. Cochrane. "Elie Metschnikoff and his theory of an *instinct de la mort*" *International Journal of Psychoanalysis* 15 (1934) 265-270

Alex Comfort. *The Biology of Senescence* London: Routledge and Kegan Paul 1956

J. C. Diggory and D. Z. Rothman. "Values Destroyed by Death" *Journal of Abnormal and Social Psychology* 63 (1961) 205-210

246

Albert Ellis. *Reason and Emotion* New York: Lyle Stuart 1962

G. L. Engel. "Is Grief a Disease?" *Psychosomatic Medicine* 23 (1961) 18-22

Jesse Gordon. *Handbook of Clinical and Experimental Hypnosis* New York: Macmillan 1967

Gerald Gruman. *A History of Ideas About the Prolongation of Life: The Evolution of Prolongevity Hypothesis to 1800* Philadelphia: American Philosophical Society 1966 pp. 85 ff.

A. Howard and R. Scott. "Cultural Values and Attitudes toward Death" *Journal of Existentialism* 6 (22) (Winter 1965-1966) 161-171

E. Jaques. "Death and the Mid-Life Crisis" *Int. Journal of Psychoanalysis* 46 (1965) 502-14

R. A. Kalish. "A Continuum of Subjectively Perceived Death" *Gerontologist* 6 (1966) 73-76

—————. "Some Variables in Death Attitudes" *Social Psychology* 59 (1) (1963) 137-145

Helen and Harold Kaplan. "Current Theories of Psychosomatic Medicine" *Comprehensive Textbook of Psychiatry* A. Freedman, and H. Kaplan, eds., Baltimore: Williams & Wilkins 1967

R. Kastenbaum. "The Psychological Death" *Death and Dying* Pearson, ed., 1969 pp. 1-27

Elisabeth Kübler-Ross. *On Death and Dying* New York: Macmillan 1969

Robert Lifton. "Psychological Effects of the Atomic Bomb in Hiroshima: The Death Theme" *Daedalus* 92 (1963) 462-497

Erich Lindemann. "Symptomatology and Management of Acute Grief" *American Journal of Psychiatry* 101 (1944) 141-148

George Marshall. "Before a Family Faces Death" Boston, Mass: Unitarian Universalist Association (1972)

Joseph Mathews. *The Modern Vision of Death* Scott ed., Richmond, Virginia: John Knox Press 1967

Elie Metschnikoff. *The Prolongation of Life* New York: Putnam's Sons 1908

Ashley Montagu. "Contributions of Anthropology to Psychosomatic Medicine" *American Journal of Psychiatry* 112 (1956) 977ff.

John Noon. "A Preliminary Examination of the Death Concepts of the Ibo" *American Anthropologist* 44 (1942) 638-654

Ohara and Reynolds. "Love-pact Suicide" *Omega* 1 (3) (August 1970) 159-166

S. Parnes. "Freedom from Death" Paper presented at the Symposium "Philosophical Aspects of Thanatology" Columbia University, May 1973

Emily Post. *Etiquette* New York: Funk and Wagnalls 1934

Theodore Sarbin. "Anxiety: Reification of a Metaphor" *Essays on Metaphor* W. Shibles, ed., Whitewater, Wisconsin: The Language Press 1972

Jerome Schneck. "The Unconscious Relationship Between Hypnosis and Death" *Psychoanalytic Review* 38 (1951) 271-275

Science News 100 (5) (Dec. 18, 1971) p. 409

Warren Shibles. *Emotions* Whitewater, Wisconsin: The Language Press 1973

Edwin Shneidman. "The Deaths of Herman Melville" *Melville and Hawthorne in the Berkshires* H. Vincent, ed., Kent State University Press 1967

————. "You and Death" *Psychology Today* 5 (1) (1971) 43-45, 74-80

Mervyn Shoor and Mary H. Speed. "Death Delinquency and the Mourning Process" *Psychiatric Quarterly* 37 (1963) 540-558

S. D. Shrut. "Attitudes Toward Old Age and Death" *Mental Hygiene* 42 (1958) 259-266

Bernard Strehler, ed. *The Biology of Aging* Symposium, Tennessee 1957. Washington D.C.: American Institute of Biological Science, Publication No. 6, 1960

248

Wendell Swenson. "Attitudes Toward Death Among the Aged" *Minnesota Med.* 42 (1959) 399-402

C. F. Teicher. "Combat Fatigue or Death Anxiety Neurosis" *Journal of Nervous or Mental Disorders* 117 (1953) 234-243

Robert Trotter. "Let it all out: yes or no?" *Science News* Oct. 14, 1972 p. 254

Glen Vernon. *Sociology of Death* New York: Ronald Press 1970

C. Wahl. "The Fear of Death" *Bulletin Menninger Clinic* 22 (6) (1958) 214-223

Avery Weisman and T. Hackett. "Predilection to Death" *Psychosomatic Medicine* 23 (1961) 232-256

G. Westberg. *Good Grief* Philadelphia: Fortress Press, rev. 1971

Mary Williams. "Changing Attitudes to Death: A Survey of Contributions in Psychological Abstracts Over a Thirty-Year Period" *Human Relations* 19 (4) (Nov. 1966) 405-422

Freud

The following words by Freud may summarize his statements on death as presented in *Civilization, War and Death,*

"Our unconscious is just as inaccessible to the idea of our own death, as murderously minded towards the stranger, as divided or ambivalent towards the loved, as was man in earliest antiquity."

1. This view is often rendered by the statement that we cannot imagine our own death but unconsciously think we will live forever. This is incorrect. Nothing in this statement denies that we can *consciously* imagine our own death. He is not holding the more contemporary view that no matter how hard we try to imagine our own death we see that we instead survive as spectators, nor that one can imagine the death of another person but not of himself. Seeing that a loved one dies suggests to one that he too will die. The dead person "belongs" to us as a part of ourself. Death cannot be thought of because our use of language gains its meaning from contexts involving life. But death has no context because it is the end of contexts. One's death is not even a mere blank, for to think it is is to assume one can imagine one's death.

But Freud is rather presenting the more obscure view that a) we have an unconscious mind, and b) the unconscious cannot know of one's own death. The "unconscious mind" is found by contemporary philosophical psychologists and perhaps most psychologists to be a fictive entity. It is a metaphor erroneously taken literally. Thus statements made about whether the unconscious thinks it will live forever, or be unable to imagine its death are unintelligible.

Our "unconscious" supposedly knows no denials or negatives and since death is negative it cannot know death. Freud says, "No instinct we possess is ready for a belief in death." Heroism is based on our inability to imagine our own death. Our dread of death is mainly a feeling of guilt.

2. The unconscious (not the conscious) is ambivalent about a loved one and perhaps also about death. Death is thought to be an end yet we treat it as if it were a beginning. Freud said, "Consideration for the dead, who no longer need it, is dearer to us than the truth, and certainly, for most of us, is dearer also than consideration for the living." The dead are the metaphors of the living.

The loved one who dies is both a part of ourselves and not ourselves. This gives rise to ambivalence about death. We, like some primitives, are often hostile to the death of someone close. There is, on this view, hate-gratification behind our grief.

Our unconscious supposedly hates and wishes to kill everything which stands in its way:

> "And so, if we are to be judged by the wishes in our unconscious, we are, like primitive men, simply a gang of murderers. . . . We owe the fairest flowers of our love-life to the reaction against the hostile impulse which we divine in our breasts."

In killing others or in being a hero we tend to deny our own death. We think that death is quite appropriate to the "enemy." Freud thought war is inevitable: "There will be, must be, wars." Killing is regarded as a basic part of our unconscious. We must recognize it is there and accept it. "Illusion can have no value if it makes this more difficult for us. . . . If you would endure life, be prepared for death."

In this article Freud suggests that remembrance of the dead is the basis for the erroneous thought that a soul survives. Perhaps this might be rendered by saying that soul only refers to our memory of a dead or absent person.

In his article, "Mourning and Melancholia," Freud regards mourning and grief as morbid pathological conditions which require medical attention. The bereaved person is confused about all that he has lost. Freud's view here is important because most believe that grief and mourning are simply natural and necessary activities. It is also interesting that grief is regarded as a confused state in view of more contemporary analyses of emotion discussed in this book. It may be suggested that what the "unconscious" sometimes refers to is just lack of conceptual clarity. Freud seems to say we can never know the "unconscious" but possibly all that is really meant is that we are confused and not knowing (being confused), we cannot know what we don't know. This is merely a suggested possible meaning for "unconscious" as it may sometimes be used. It at least avoids the error of thinking of the unconscious as an entity, as Freud often does.

Death may be an important factor in what we say and do. What we mean by the unconscious is what we say and do. We may build a solid stone house because we unconsciously think, that is, confusedly say to ourselves, that it will protect us against death. A mathematician may seek death — seek to attain a reality where numbers do not matter, seek to escape reality by the study of abstract number, or tersely explore the question of whether or not there is infinite number — whether or not numbers go on and on even after one's death. Mathematics and logic can both be escapes from facing reality. The symbolic logician, A. N. Whitehead wrote, "Logic, conceived as an adequate analysis of the advance of thought is a fake." All application of number is metaphorical application. There is death's worm in every concept and object.

In "The Theme of Three Caskets" Freud again shows our ambivalent attitude toward death. It is puzzling how the unconscious becomes conscious on Freud's analysis. In *The Merchant of Venice* Portia has her suitors choose between three caskets of gold, silver, and lead, and she agrees to marry the successful chooser. Love is here tied in with death. Love is related to death, opposites replace each other. We thus react with hate when we feel love. Three relations of roles of woman are also given. Woman is mother, provider and comforter, and also as mother-earth — destroyer. Freud says again here that death is inevitable and it is no use to struggle against it: "The silent goddess of Death, will take him into her arms." Death is here related to woman and life. There is death in life and life in death. King Lear seeks woman's love as he falls into the arms of

Death. Man creates illusions for himself regarding death, e.g., religious, mystical or metaphysical views: "Man makes use of his imaginative faculty (phantasy) to satisfy those wishes that reality does not satisfy."

We are psychologically out of balance with death. Either we should prepare for death or fight it. At present we do neither honestly or well. Even scholars and professors stay clear of critical subjects such as philosophy of natural and social sciences, philosophical psychology, etc., and avoid learning about death. Our ambition and pride often thrive on not looking too far into the future. For the average man there is no problem of death. He rationalizes and constructs a fiction or lie for himself. Writers on death seem hardly to touch on the problem. It is as if they by their writing wanted to write what is expected of them — something nice. We accept views of death on authority, because of tradition, or because those around us accept such views.

The duality of life-death, love-hate is similar to the dialectic or dualites of the ancient Greeks. For Aristotle death is due to the constant interplay of dualities. One quality takes the place of the other as life becomes death and death life. After funerals we often have feasts. Suicidal people are sometimes seen to have an ambivalent love-hate paradox, e.g., they want to slit their throats and yell for help at the same time. But Freud thinks there is a life instinct (*Eros*) and a death instinct (*Thanatos*). This conflict supposedly results in ambivalence and leads to neurosis and sadism — an extravagant view. He explains our killing of others as being an outer projection of our own death instinct. Norman Brown, though he gives a Freudian account, says Freud's death instinct is not only a mere metaphor but also a confusing metaphor.

The conflict between Freudian life and death instincts supposedly brings about guilt. Fear of death is really the result of guilt feelings. Death is seen as guilt. Freud thought that man invents spirits, religion, and demons because of his guilt over the death of someone close. This may be modified to suggest the following paradigm. Demons, spirits, etc., were invented as entitative embodiments of one's guilt. Guilt also needs a more contemporary analysis and may be found to reduce to confusions of assessments. It is an error to treat guilt as a thing.

Freud's greatest error was to hypostatize entities such as id, ego, superego, unconscious, energy, etc. Thus both Freud and the believer in demons commit a naming-fallacy by assuming entities where there is no evidence for them.

A. C. MacIntyre, in an excellent book on Freud's notion of the "unconscious," pointed out that although Freud's concrete practices of finding out what people say and do in firsthand contact with the patient are valuable, his belief in id, ego, unconscious, etc., as entities is unfounded. Such entities are due to taking mechanistic metaphors literally. Freud treats the "mind" as a hydrolic system with "psychic energy" instead of water, flowing through the mental compartments and pipes in accordance with the principle of the conservation of energy. If id is full, energy is less in the ego and superego. If superego is large there is less energy for the id and ego, etc. Freud thinks of the parts of the mind as things or entities and, as MacIntyre shows, there is no evidence for such things. Freud simply was captivated by his early mechanistic neurological metaphors. (See also W. Shibles "An Examination of the Subconscious")

In 1920 Freud formulated the "death instinct." In 1923 he found that he had cancer of the mouth and subsequently had thirty-three painful, life-saving operations. The "death instinct" even in Freud's own case was supposedly balanced off by the "life instinct." It is not that we have merely an instinct to die.

"Instinct" (L. *instinctus*) means impulse, push, urge on, incite, move, or stimulate to action. It need not be thought of as a thing or an inborn "nature" or "essence." "Instinct" is partly based on two obsolete and unsupportable doctrines: 1) substance-quality doctrine according to which if some quality is seen that quality must be part of or inhere in a substance. The name, "instinct," is meant to label such a substance. But we have no evidence for such substance and, in addition, the substance-quality doctrine involves a metaphysical, invisible substance and such substances are found to be unintelligible except mainly among Catholic metaphysicians. (See Shibles "Linguo-Centric Predicament") "Instinct" is a naming-fallacy. A. J. Levin wrote,

"The failure to separate the source of the terrors [of death] easily leads one to ascribe the terrors to a single general cause. The next step is to give a teleological [end or purposive] basis to death — to call it an instinct."

Freud himself late in his career saw that the death instinct is a myth and in fact the basic stress in his overall view may be on love rather than on death. (Ver Eecke)

2. The doctrine that for every effect there must be a cause. Thus because someone does something it is thought that some thing must have caused it. We may thus say that whenever anyone does anything at all he has an instinct to do it. It is circular reasoning. The reader, for example, would then have an instinct to read or an instinct to learn to read, etc.

Seneca spoke of "libido moriendi" or "death-drive." Drive may be analyzed in the same way "instinct" was. "Libido" means passion, desire, appetite — all vague terms requiring analysis in terms of a clarification of emotions. Freud's "Todestrieb" is a death drive. Death drive is also spoken of as a death-wish.

To speak of death-wish may yield a circularity. If someone drives fast we may say he has an unconscious death-wish. But one may drive fast simply because he enjoys it or is ignorant of cause and effect relating to the speed of automobiles and likelihood of accident. He may not think he will have an accident. On the "death-wish" view one could maintain that whenever one is in danger, has any kind of accident or illness, he therefore has a death-wish. This reasoning is circular.

And to assert that it is an "unconscious wish" is contradictory. A wish by definition is conscious. The phrase would read "unconscious conscious wish." The paradigm of what could be meant by "unconscious wish" is activities such as: a) one does not admit to himself or others that he desires something, b) one finds himself doing things he was not aware that he wanted to do, etc. But there is no unconscious as such and no entitative wish or "force" in it. "Force" and "energy" in psychology, as well as in physics, must always be reduced to some concrete piece of behavior or a specific operational definition. If this were done it would be found that "force" and "energy" do not name entities as such and in this respect are naming-fallacies. Such terms can be used as elliptical for concrete operations, but more care is needed in using the terms in this way than is usually encountered.

The idea of a death-wish may, then, be reduced to such behaviors as that of war, violent behavior, drinking alcohol, taking drugs, dangerous sports, and destructiveness, the manufacturing and use of unsafe automobiles, failure to inquire in general. There would almost seem to be, on this argument, an "ignorance instinct" or instinct to remain ignorant, for after thousands of years there has been extremely little inquiry into aging and death. But such activities do not mean we have a "death-wish." They mean only that we do things which are unintelligent. The search for a "death-wish" is a search for an "essence" or "quintessence" of the mediaeval theological variety.

Even Freudians often reject the "death instinct." Otto Fenichel wrote,

"The clinical facts of self-destruction . . . do not necessitate the assumption of a genuine self-destructive instinct. . . . The concept of a death instinct is neither necessary nor useful. . . . There is no necessity to assume that either of these two pairs of opposites [life and death drives] represents a genuine and unconditioned dichotomy, operative from the very beginning."

Freud's theory appears to be a rigid kind of determinism. All of one's actions are said to be determined by one's childhood and his actions in later life are spoken of as if literally in terms of childhood activities, e.g., if one does not get the "point" of something he may be said to have suffered breast withdrawal in childhood. (Sharpe) Fenichel stresses, as we did earlier, that the concern should not be with "natures" or fictitious entities but with the situation and behavioral patterns involved. A. J. Levin states,

"The death instinct is a fiction. . . . By making death an instinct, Freud added another 'fate' to the human struggle . . ."

One of Freud's most recent accounts of "death instinct" is contained in his article "The Economic Problem of Masochism." (1924) Masochism is a form of death instinct. Freud says, the death instinct aims "to lead our throbbing existence into the stability of an inorganic state." The inorganic state is a Nirvana-like stability or resolution of tension of the oxymoron "Life is death." One of the meanings the "death instinct" could have is that of being a reality principle. That is, perhaps one of the things meant by the "death instinct" is only that we must not be so concerned with seeking pleasure that we fail to see that we age and die. In addition, the oxymoron "Life is death" is a rhetorical device we use or language-game we play.

On Freud's theory the tendency to repeat, the repetition compulsion, is more basic than the pleasure principle. The repetition compulsion relates to death supposedly because it seeks to return everything to its original state, the inorganic dead state out of which it arose. Freud says the repetition compulsion is the "tendency innate in living organic matter impelling it towards the reinstatement of an earlier condition." In *Beyond the Pleasure Principle* (p. 50) Freud wrote, "The goal of all life is death." Freud's view is not original. It had been expressed by Schopenhauer (1788-1860) who said, "Dying is certainly to be regarded as the real aim in life," and "Each individual is really only a special error, a false step, something that had better not be." (Choron) Montaigne (1533-1592) had stated similarly, "The goal of our career is death. It is the necessary object of our aim...."

This view is illegitimate or circular. Because one sees that all things die does not mean that a) they must do so, or b) that it is the goal of life. Living things change form and they do not have as a goal one part of the ongoing process more than another. To say the goal is death is to say there is a goal or there is a "higher" purpose given man by a "higher" being. But Freud was an atheist and on this view there are no purposes given men by fictitious or hypostatized spiritual beings. Also if the goal of life is death one may ask what the goal of death is.

Freud's view suggests that death and aging are absolute and cannot be conquered. It is to say that life is unnatural and so temporary. This is a dogmatic view. People once said that disease is natural and must be accepted as a part of life. But we have found that, however "natural," disease can be "naturally" conquered such that it is no longer necessary. Freud, too, dogmatically closes the door on our ability to inquire into and conquer aging and death.

Perhaps more insight into death would have been gained if Freud had rather just applied his defense-mechanisms of projection, denial, introjection, rationalization, withdrawal, overcompensation, etc., to our views of and attitudes toward death and dying. Rhetorical devices and language-games have more to do with attitudes toward death and dying than do pseudo-psychological mentalistic entities.

Norman O. Brown. *Life Against Death* Middletown, Conn.: Wesleyan University Press 1959 pp. 77-134

Jacques Choron. *Death in Western Thought* New York: Collier 1963

Otto Fenichel. *The Psycho Analytic Theory of Neurosis* New York: Norton 1945 pp. 59-61

Sigmund Freud. "Our Attitude Towards Death" *Civilization, War and Death* John Rickman, ed., London: Hogarth Press 1968 pp. 14-25

A. J. Levin. "The Fiction of the Death Instinct" *Psychiatric Quarterly* 25 (1951) 257-281

A. MacIntyre. *The Unconscious* London: Routledge 1958

Michel de Montaigne. "To Philosophize is to Learn How to Die" *Complete Essays* D. Frame, trans., Stanford University Press 1958 Chapt. 20

Ella Sharpe. "Psycho-Physical Problems Revealed in Language: An Examination of Metaphor." *International Journal of Psychoanalysis* 21 (1940) 201-213 Summarized in W. Shibles, *Metaphor: An Annotated Bibliography and History* 1971

Warren Shibles. "An Examination of the Subconscious" *Philosophical Pictures* 2nd ed. Dubuque, Iowa: Kendall-Hunt 1972

–––––. "Linguo-Centric Predicament" *Philosophical Pictures* 2nd ed. Dubuque, Iowa: Kendall-Hunt 1972. Also *Sophia* (Rome) 36(1968)

W. Ver Eecke. "Myth and Reality in Psychoanalysis" Paper presented at Symposium "Philosophical Aspects of Thanatology" Columbia University, May 1973

Child's View of Death

How children view death — children who press buttons which blow up the world, who drown in a glass of water, see how close they can come to a snake's tongue, children who lie in the tub — the water blurring their faces — and let the waves flow in and out of their mouths.

Simon Yudkin wrote, "We still know very little about how children think of death." (1969) One of the most detailed, complete accounts based on observations, though not necessarily experimental observations, is that of Gesell and Ilg. Their views form a large part of the following analysis. Rabbi Grollman's book is also cited. The age groupings given are not rigid and may overlap or not be applicable to a particular case. "Stage" is merely a metaphor here, or helpful fiction. On my analysis it is not so much growth stages that the child goes through but primarily stages in the development of his use and understanding of figurative and literal language.

Ages One-Four There is hardly any understanding of death. At age four there may be a vague idea of death. (Gesell)

The child comes into the world and for a long while lacks even a roughly clear understanding of cause-effect, self, other, object or their relations. At the end of life when one is ill, or senile one also again lacks such understanding. Memory may fade or distort and turn everything into chaos again. One comes into the world as a babe and often leaves it as a babe. In old age the tendency to chaos may help us adjust to death and the chaos of death.

Although one may speak of children as not being able to understand the notion of death, this assumes that adults can understand it. Nearly all available evidence shows that adults do not understand death. They seem to regard it as either a taboo or a mystical-religious subject. Children often have more insight into death than do adults. A child may make the issue quite refreshingly clear by asking upon seeing a dead bird, "Will that happen to me?" The child like the ordinary-language philosopher has an ability to look and see in a concrete manner what in fact the situation is. The child is often developing uses of words in specific cases and the ordinary-language philosopher reduces obscure abstraction back to such uses and specific cases.

Cousinet (Vernon 284, 285) says a child first denies death, then accepts a reversible death, then finally arrives at a view of death. The child still does not understand but nevertheless accepts. This would seem to be the way dogma and prejudice get started.

Maria Nagy (Vernon 285) gives the following developmental stages regarding death:

Ages 3-5: Death denial or subjective views on death,

ages 5-9: acceptance of the death of others but not his own death,

ages 9-10: he now accepts his own death. (Vernon 285)

The Freudians present the view that the child goes through a narcissistic, self-love stage, or egoistic stage from age two to four; love for parents from age four to seven; and no particular love development from seven to twelve. (Drake 8) If this were true then the loss felt when a parent dies would possibly be different at each stage.

C. Izard (208) cited a study by R. Spitz (1946) according to which a child under age five who was deserted by his mother for more than five months is certain to become depressed. He also notes that F. Brown (1961) found that of 216 hospitalized depressed patients 41% lost a parent by age 15. Izard also mentioned several studies showing that there is not a significant relationship between early parental loss and adult bereavement. The experiments yield conflicting results.

Age Five A summary of Gesell and Ilg's account follows:

a) Death is regarded as an end and it is recognized that old people die.
b) If told by adults that the dead go to heaven, he may ask why they do not fall out.
c) There is interest in one's posture when one dies.
d) In games he plays being killed or shot.
e) He may enjoy killing animals, bugs, etc.
f) He does not think he or others really die. Death is thought to be reversible.
g) He is unemotional about death.

This account seems in some ways more honest than that of adults. The child does not take fictive metaphors, e.g., of heaven and hell, as literally as adults do in their attempt to deny or avoid death. The child may innocently question such beliefs. His inquiry into death takes the form of actual experimentation with things which die around him. He does not take death seriously perhaps because he has not experience it. Neither have adults experienced it but they conceive of their own death by analogy to other humans who die. The child is not yet emotional about death because his assessments of death are not yet clear. He is just beginning to construct a view of self as it relates to the world, often by physical means. At this point he seems to be seeing death only in terms of life and his own living awarenesses and activity. To arrive at a concept of death would require abstraction, analogy, symbolization which he has not yet learned.

G. Rochlin wrote,

"What is remarkable is not that children arrive at adult views of the cessation of life, but rather how tenaciously throughout life adults hold to the child's beliefs and how readily they revert to them." (Gesell 63)

Regarding the question, "If people go to heaven why do they not fall out?" the expansion of the heaven model is thus disguised nonsense reduced to patent nonsense and even shows that many of our explanations of death are in fact disguised jokes.

Since the child of five has only a limited knowledge of cause and effect (and of concern for others) he has a limited knowledge of good and bad. Good and bad as with other ethical or moral terms depend upon an empirical and descriptive knowledge of cause and effect. Thus the child is not yet entirely aware that killing is bad. He may kill living things just to see what will happen. Initially he learns that if he attempts to kill someone he will be punished, and with increased knowledge he learns what the undesirable consequences of killing are. Complex patterns of such beliefs develop. In America killing people is one of our oldest established institutions. It is only now beginning to be seriously questioned. Unfortunately it is doubtful if attempts will be seriously made to entirely eliminate killing people. Vernon says the child of six to ten is also ready to kill, at least in play, and fear of his own death is rare. (284)

It is especially at ages 3-5 that death is conceived of entirely subjectively and metaphorically, e.g., a person who leaves may be thought dead. The metaphor is often taken literally – the Irish considered a relative who left for America as dead, and performed a funeral ceremony. The Orthodox Jew treated one who married outside the faith as "dead" and here also a funeral ceremony was performed.

One child was told that in order to live one must eat. Since her father died after she missed breakfast she concluded that not eating caused her father's death. (Gesell 22) This is to confuse cause and effect but also to misunderstand that for her to live she must eat. It is also a *post hoc* fallacy, i.e., that because something occurs before another it is not necessarily its cause.

From age five to ten death is metaphorically personified, regarded as a "death man" or person. (Gesell 102) The child sometimes hides to avoid "him."

Age Six This age is characterized as follows (Gesell):

a) Susceptibility to teaching about the devil.
b) Emotional about death
   1. May dream about pictures of dead children he has seen.
   2. Dislikes idea of being buried.

3. Preoccupation with objects associated with death.
4. Fears his mother's death.
5. Should often be protected from death experiences.
6. Unable to easily forget dead animals seen.
c) Exploration of causes of death.
d) Death is regarded as reversible.
e) Other people are thought to take the dead person's place, e.g., puppies take the place of dogs, children of parents. If someone dies he needs to think of a substitute, e.g., an aunt.
f) Death is thought to be mainly the result of aggression or violence.

These views suggest that the child is becoming more aware of the analogical view of death according to which he sees that because other animals die he will lose those he depends on such as his mother, and that he too will die. His knowledge of causation is limited and egocentric in terms of his needs, thus resulting in confused interpretations. For example, he thinks that if someone dies someone will take the place of the deceased. This is a perspective from the point of view of his needs. The child is very dependent upon his mother and seems to need to find a substitute should something happen to her. Adults in many cultures have been found to believe that the soul of a dead person goes into a baby as its new body. Beliefs about soul and resurrection if taken literally seem to be based on a lack of knowledge of cause and effect or an interpretation of the situation solely in terms of one's needs.

The child conceives of death in terms of violence probably because the major factor in his life is the punishment he experiences as he attempts to exercise the limits of his powers, abilities, and freedom. He may then think of death as punishment. He may think that his misbehavior caused the death of his mother or father and so feel guilty. The mother's death before the child is eight is found to contribute to later psychological disturbance (Vernon 289) Some report that this is also the case especially for children ages 8-12. (Vernon 291) Guilt is thus seen to be based upon a lack of knowledge of cause and effect. The biblical statement, "The wages of sin is death" also bases death on the model of punishment.

This lack of knowledge of cause and effect may also cause the various emotions indicated above (b, 1-6). In accordance with the view of emotions presented in this book, if one is confused in his rational thinking and assessment negative or undesirable emotions (feelings guided by assessment) will probably result. Here the child is barely becoming aware of his death. At such a time, because of unclear thought about death, one might well expect damaging emotional responses. This may be one reason why a child should be told about death honestly and be given a realistic appraisal about it. (Bertrand Russell) Superstition, talk of hell, the devil, or monsters, can be traumatic or even make the child depend on religion for security from such evils. It is apparent especially at this age or before that the church does its work. This was the point of the Christian art of dying and dance of death books which showed death horribly represented as a worm, snake, toad-eaten body, and monsters which seek to snatch up the soul at the moment of death. Fear was put into man in order to drive him into religion. This is more fully documented in the chapters on religion, art of dying, and dance of death.

The child's fears are produced and explored by those of the adult as seen in the following description by W. Wallis in his book *Religion in Primitive Society:*

"In some parts of Europe, as late as the last century, universal suicide was preached by fervent missionaries who represented it as the only means of escape from the snares of Antichrist, the only assured way of eluding earthly sins and sorrows and securing the eternal joys of heaven . . . Priests, monks and laymen preached salvation by flame. They seduced children [into suicide] by promises of gay clothes, apples, nuts, and honey in heaven . . . Thousands of men, women and children rushed into the flames and were destroyed." (Vernon 284)

Children are taught to fear God and they think that God can kill them. (Vernon 284)

That pictures of dead children and sights of dead animals are vivid, lasting and haunt the child's dreams shows how one interprets events imagistically and how pictures may be captivating and persuasive. Pictures may be thought of as models or types of seeing-as. The chemist and philosopher of science, Norwood Hanson, and others have argued that the pictures we have and our very perception is partly determined and altered by our theories or rational assessments of a situation. (1961) If this is the case then the pictures of the dead which fixate, captivate and haunt the child are partly a result of his assessments or in this case confusion about death. Should his assessments be made clearer his pictures would lose their terror-inducing powers.

Another way of putting this is that when "emotional" problems arise one begins to hallucinate or experience distorted imagery or pictures. The analysis of emotions as assessments can, however, show how such pictures may be avoided and corrected.

In view of the above analysis the funeral director's stress on the necessity of a lasting memory picture appears misguided. It gives no rational insight into death and since emotions are largely based on assessment, would not serve to improve negative emotions or create positive ones except by fiat or creation of a false impression. The memory-picture practice may be related to the practice of having a child kiss the corpse. This was found to be a traumatic experience. (Vernon 288) The "memory-picture" view may rather create negative emotions in adults as well as in children. In defense of the funeral director, this is a deceptive analysis in some ways because a large number or even a majority of Americans might well be found to experience positive emotions as a result of a memory-picture regardless of the rationality of the reason for their doing so. It may be due merely to self-suggestion that the memory-picture sometimes has a beneficial effect. The funeral director's argument, "Don't intellectualize just ask what the bereaved think," is based on this common reaction.

Thus the memory-picture in itself may have nothing especially to do with such emotions. A photograph would do just as well should it become a culturally accepted practice. Also any object relating to the deceased may help one to more rationally communicate and express his unclear thoughts about the matter. If the ritual is irrational it will result in negative emotions of a mild or quite serious nature. Pictures can drive fear and death itself into man. The escape is to note that they are merely metaphors or models, that they can suggest unclear thinking, and that what is rather needed is a rational assessment and more intelligible and beneficial images. (cf. Chapters on psychiatry and funeral industry.)

To guide children regarding death we need to know of their fantasies. This involves talking with them openly and honestly about death without imposing on their views. Clarifying their fantasies allows them to communicate and clarify their thinking. We may then discuss where the fantasy is ill-founded or based on a mistake. Some parents will, of course, be willing to say that the fictions are true, especially in the case of religious fictions.

Yudkin also recommends communicating with the child openly about death. The child should not be told fairy tales about death or beliefs the adult does not himself accept. (Grollman) This view is in opposition to the "I'm OK, You're OK" view of therapy. Grollman suggests that an honest statement of ignorance is better than a falsehood: "Why not admit the lack of understanding in this mysterious area of life." (Grollman 12)

If the child is told that the deceased mother has "gone away" he may think the mother has deserted him, punished him, or think that maybe she will come back. Adults often think the dead will return, and again there is no clear separation of child and adult views of death.

The child, like the adult, may regard death metaphorically as a sleep (cf. "slumber room") or in terms of things like food which simply seem to disappear, become "all gone." One regards death as other than what it is. A child who regards death as sleep may not be able to sleep for fear that he will die. A prevalent view of various cultures is that if the soul goes too far away from the dreaming person death may occur.

Age Seven

The views of the seven-year-old are similar to those of the six-year-old and are characterized further as follows (Gesell):

a) Death is not just a result of punishment but thought to be due to old age, overeating, etc.

b) Unemotional interest in objects associated with funerals.
c) Unable to accept death as a biological process. Denies he will die.
d) In general, is more realistic and has a better understanding of death.

The lack of the emotional reaction at age seven as compared with that of age six may be due to the fact that the rational understanding is improved. This would support the theory of emotions presented earlier.

Age Eight
The following characterizes age eight (Gesell):

a) Unemotional view of death (unless person is very close).
b) Less interest in objects associated with funeral.
c) Interest in what will happen after death.
d) May understand that he and others die.

Age Nine
At nine the child (Gesell):

a) is realistic. He, for example, does not believe in Santa Claus. Death is due to natural causes.
b) closely associates death with dying.
c) has transient unemotional questions about death, e.g., why one has no pulse, how one stops breathing, or what it means to be "not living."
d) may say, "I wish I were dead," without meaning it.

The model for death is dying and pain, even for adults. It is a process of letting one aspect of a situation be the situation itself. This is the metaphoric process of synecdoche: "Death is pain," or "Death is dying." In "I wish I were dead," death is being used as a tool for power and as a threat. This is part of the complex rhetoric of suicide.

Age Ten This age is similar to age nine but there is a clearer separation of animate and inanimate (Gesell).

Inanimate and animate are arbitrary labels and scientists are still not in agreement about whether certain objects are animate or inanimate. (Shibles) The stages presented here are from the point of view of an adult who regards his view as correct. The child is presented as coming to a supposedly more and more mature view of death. This is because children are often erroneously regarded only as immature adults. But if no clear analysis of death has yet been given it seems strange to speak of having a gradually more "mature" view of death. We do not arrive at *the* correct concept of death but rather there is a continuous process of inquiry into death.

In general one needs to find out what the child actually thinks about death and related subjects. It is important to find out what images he has of death and also what metaphors he uses regarding death. We must communicate with him about death openly and honestly without imposing unproven theory, dogma or evasion. We do find that children who attend Catholic schools nearly all have the same metaphysical view of death based upon the teachings of the school. (Vernon 278) This involves a closed method of indoctrination resulting in poor adjustment, poor therapy, and unrealistic thinking.

The child's view of death, like the adult's may be partially determined by culture, what those around him say and do. Until he is taught such beliefs he is often found by his questions to expose a culture's irrational beliefs and practices. He may ask, "Why do they throw three handfuls of dirt on the coffin?" "How can the soul leave the body?" "How do we get a 'new body' after death as they say we do?" Relevant to this, Glenn Vernon says, "The average parent is of but little help to the child in search for answers about death." (Vernon 275) A child brought up alone and without language would not have our views of death.

Concern with death may be the cause or consequence of other problems a child may have. It may result from being captivated by a picture or misleading abstract terms and expressions in language. Death and dying are not subjects isolated from other aspects of one's life. They are greatly affected by one's general understanding and by one's ability to analyze and solve his problems.

Negative childhood experiences with death have been connected with later or immediate psychological problems. Viktor Frankl and others think that nearly all such problems have some close relation to death. This view, however, seems like a generalization from a particular case or a narrowly simplistic solution to all problems. A closer look at the particular language involved is needed and avoidance of turning our metaphors into myths by taking them literally. Grollman states, "Man defines the world in which he lives and patterns his behavior according to the definitions he has developed." (29) The child may think of death as a flame that went out, or in terms of the model "all gone," or an empty glass. To find out what a child's view of death is one must mainly examine his language as well as his perceptions and actions. It is unacceptable to regard all dream and adult activity in terms of metaphors for three childhood stages or birth activity as Freud and the astrologers, respectively, deterministically do. If someone "does not get the point" the Freudian says it is probably due to breast withdrawal in infancy. (Sharpe) This "explanation" shows a failure to understand how metaphors work and how they can captivate one who does not understand them.

The suggestion sometimes made that the child should mourn (Vernon 292) may be supported to the extent that mourning may help a child begin to communicate his thoughts about death, especially when no one will talk about it. But it is only a temporary, possibly harmful, means of communication and rationally coping with the problem of loss and death especially if the mourning, guilt, and anger persist without assessment and communication. A rational analysis is needed. A substitute for reason yields only a temporary distraction. One may try to solve a mathematical problem by a ceremony, ritual, and dancing but although one may feel better for a short while the problem will not be solved. It will still haunt. Similarly the funeral ceremony is an irrational ritual which offers temporary distraction rather than more permanent adjustment and understanding.

Vernon wrote,

"It would be wrong to conclude that *any* ritual and *any* funeral service will automatically produce the results [needed] . . . Ritual participation may also produce anxiety." (297)

The kind of ceremony needed is one which stresses communication of a reasoned view regarding death and dying. Children and adults should not be encouraged to attend funerals until funeral ceremonies improve. M. Diskin and H. Guggenheim point out that small children especially should not attend funerals, because of the child's irrational associations. (Grollman) The question may also be raised as to how much the funeral ceremony is also irrational. Some attempt to defend the ceremony, maintaining that it is irrationality that is needed. Lucian long ago wrote,

> "At funerals . . . they simply commit their grief into the charge of custom and habit . . . [It is a] superfluous practice. Regarding grave-mounds, pyramids, tombstones, and epitaphs, all of which endure but a brief space, are they not superfluous and akin to child's play? . . . You will find, if you take note, that these things and others still more ridiculous are done at funerals . . ."

This view is not presented as a proof or argument but does raise an important question: Does the funeral ceremony help a person adjust to the problems which confront him regarding death?

One thing about the religious ritual involved in guiding the righteous soul into the next world, is that it can never fail. And without an ability to fail it is not clear how it can succeed.

Fairy-tales are similarly irrational and a dangerous means of communicating with children or allowing them to understand their world. Fairy-tales often involve death-denial, e.g., the princess or hero either never dies or comes back to life, and only the wicked really die. (Heuscher) The child may partly in this way have learned to associate death with punishment or see death as reversible. Fairy-tales and novels do reveal (and determine) how intricate, metaphorical and subjective our views of death are. Death is often regarded merely as some kind of failure in life. A relevant expression is, "He is death to women." In "The Goose-Girl" the false bride has as punishment to be placed naked in a barrel lined with sharp nails, and rolled and rolled until dead. (Heuscher)

Raleigh Drake. *Abnormal Psychology* New Jersey: Littlefield, Adams 1954

Viktor Frankl. *The Will to Meaning* New York: World 1969

Arnold Gesell and F. Ilg.*The Child From Five to Ten* New York: Harper 1946

Earl Grollman, ed. *Explaining Death to Children* Boston: Beacon Press 1967

Norwood Hanson. *Patterns of Discovery* Cambridge University Press 1961

Julius Heuscher. "Death in the Fairy Tale" *Diseases of the Nervous System* 28 (1967) 462-67

Carroll Izard. *Patterns of Emotions* New York: Academic Press 1972

Lucian. "On Funerals" *Works* 8 vols. A. Harmon, trans. Harvard University Press 1925 vol. 4 pp. 113-131

Bertrand Russell. "Your Child and the Fear of Death" *The Forum* 81 (1929) 174-178

Ella Sharpe. "Psychophysical Problems Revealed in Language: An Examination of Metaphor" *International Journal of Psychoanalysis* 21 (1940) 201-213

Warren Shibles. "A Defense of Animism" *Philosophical Pictures* 2nd ed. Dubuque, Iowa: Kendall-Hunt 1972

Glenn Vernon. *The Sociology of Death* New York: Ronald Press 1970

Simon Yudkin. "Death and the Young" *Man's Concern with Death* Arnold Toynbee, ed. New York: McGraw-Hill 1969 pp. 46-55

Sociology of Death

I. AN ANALYSIS OF GLENN VERNON'S *SOCIOLOGY OF DEATH**

This book briefly surveys the contemporary literature on death and dying, which relates to the field of sociology. It is the most comprehensive sociological analysis, though not the most comprehensive analysis, available on the subject, and each particular account is somewhat brief. This suggests its use as a survey text for a sociology course. An attempt is made to keep the analysis of each account objective. This is not always done but the critiques are nevertheless straightforward and helpful. To this extent it is an excellent and useful beginning survey. As he points out, the study of death is a taboo topic and the study of death has been somewhat neglected in sociology. V. R. Pine writing in the *American Journal of Sociology* has recently shown that many of Vernon's paragraphs are almost identical with those of original sources. In these cases he should have quoted original sources.

The author has had the insight to deal at least briefly with some aspects of death which are ignored by most others, e.g., the treatment of death in motion pictures, death and humor, the obituary, cryobiology, and the symbolic nature of concepts relating to death and dying. There are, however, some difficulties with the text. They center around the nature of the methodological and conceptual approach to death.

Vernon defines sociology as the study of man's behavior involving more than one individual. Such a definition would hardly distinguish sociology from behaviorism, psychology, psychiatry, history, philosophy, or nearly any other subject. Much of the data he uses is from the field of psychology.

*Reprinted from *Journal of Value Inquiry*.

273

He divides the data of scientific analysis into, a.) empirical referents (ER), b.) non-empirical referents (NER). These are said to involve only symbols and have no empirical referent. He then states, "A method restricted to the empirical is incapable of reaching decisions about the superempirical. The scientific method, then, cannot be used to secure answers to all types of questions in which man is interested, such as value questions and questions about the supernatural (superempirical)." (p. 5) This view runs through the entire book. Although he makes claims to be completely scientific this first and major methodological statement is subjective.

Vernon could have rather maintained that people often hold a spiritual or superempirical view, as he did on pages 33, 55 and following, and that, as a sociologist, it is important to study the nature and extent of such beliefs. Vernon, however, claims that such beliefs are valid.

Vernon's definition above involves covert assumptions about value, a superempirical world, a theory of language or symbols, the view that science just deals with what is objective.

In speaking of symbols he assumes a theory of language which he does not discuss or argue for. The result is that it is not clear what a symbol is, much less a symbol which does not even relate to the empirical. He states, "A symbol is something which stands for or represents something else (the referent). It is something to which meaning is attached." (p. 5) But contemporary philosophical and psychological analyses of "meanings," e.g., by Gilbert Ryle (1949), Ludwig Wittgenstein (1968), Warren Shibles (1971), and the work of B. F. Skinner in psychology, show that there is no evidence for "meanings" as such. It is a pseudo-psychological or mentalistic concept for which we have no evidence. There are no meanings any more than there are small atomistic "ideas" within us associating as a kind of mental chemistry. In speaking of "attaching meaning" Vernon assumes a mentalism. He seems to hold the old view of meaning, according to which words have "meaning" or stand for "ideas." To think that all words represent things, ideas, meanings is a naming-fallacy. It is a naming-fallacy to think that "meaning" refers to a mental entity. Words may be regarded as uses in a language context and behavioral situation. They may also refer to operations and processes. In every case they should be able to be reduced to some concrete and intelligible process, event, object or use. In this sense all words have empirical referents. Thus to speak of a symbol as having no empirical referent is to invoke a spiritual or mystical world. What we have access to is behavior, what people say, write and do, not spiritual or mental states. Vernon does state that he is not concerned with internal phenomena, but his language and theories nevertheless presuppose them.

If a symbol cannot be reduced to a clear paradigm, operation, or example it may be regarded as unintelligible, not as being the sign for something spiritual. Vernon's concept of symbol seems to be rendered by one of the principles he mentioned as characterizing the child's view of death, namely, "A tendency toward undue generalization of limited knowledge." (p. 284)

It is thought that just as a word can represent the empirical world, so also a word can be a symbol of an ideal world or spiritual entity. An examination of the concept of symbol shows that there are conflicting theories as to its nature. One of the most central theories is that symbol is not a representation of the sublime or transcendent, but is merely one type of metaphor. (W. Shibles *Metaphor: An Annotated Bibliography* pp. 362-63) A survey of over a hundred accounts of symbol shows that it is closely related to metaphor or is merely one type of metaphor. For example, Wellek and Warren in *Theory of Literature* state that symbol is an often used metaphor. "Symbol" derives from the Greek meaning, "throw together."

As a metaphor, a symbol is a juxtaposition of two terms or a synecdoche, a substitution of one term or object for another. We may symbolize death as a skeleton with a scythe, or state metaphorically, "Death is a skeleton with a scythe." One reason why one may be led to think that the symbol allows one to represent the nonempirical is because the symbol as a metaphor has certain suggestive characteristics. A metaphor has many interpretations and so cannot be reduced to a single one without loss of meaning. Metaphor also provides paradox and tension. But any one interpretation of a metaphor must be concrete, empirical or intelligible. Because there are many possible meanings of a metaphor, does not mean it represents a higher spiritual or religious reality. This is one result of the still current confusion about the nature of metaphor, imagery and symbolism. The archetype, symbol, sublime, and the anagogic are metaphors taken literally or taken as something more than metaphor. The symbol is not more. Recent books on the subject of metaphor must be examined as a corrective of Vernon's assumptions and statements as to the nature of symbol.

Vernon's stress on the relation of individual behavior (I), to symbol (S), to audience (A), to situation (S), which he refers to as I-S-A-S, is useful in that it includes context and situation as ingredients rather than "meanings." This is, however, only a model or metaphor and the danger is not to take a simplistic, procrustean model or metaphor as literal truth. Formulae such as S - O - R (stimulus - organism - response) or S - R (stimulus-response) or R vs E (reason versus emotion) are similarly captivating. Nearly all use of formulae and mathematics is metaphorical. I. A. Richards stated, "What we have to do is to watch metaphors at work tricking us and our fellows into supposing matters to be alternatively much simpler and much more complex than they are." Symbolizing may lead to a kind of self-hypnosis or becoming captivated by a model or metaphor. Though these models may mislead they may be suggestive also and Vernon does mention that the phenomena involved are multi-dimensional.

To say that science cannot deal with symbolic phenomena is in part to claim that since science forms a universe of discourse separate from other areas such as religion, science cannot refute religion and religion cannot refute science. Such is not the case. Science is a bogus category. It includes all kinds of insights, concepts, methods, objects. There is no one scientific method as such, as Max Black (1954) and others have shown. Vernon seems to erroneously imply that there is such a discrete method and universe of discourse.

We may assume that each universe of discourse, e.g., sociology, poetry, has its own methods, acknowledged language, criteria of truth, etc. and that because these are peculiar to that universe of discourse they cannot be used against or refute different universes of discourse. This is not the case. To say this is to say each universe of discourse is immune from criticism. We find that certain universes of discourse, e.g., fortune telling, astrology, alchemy, mythology, religion, and even "science," often wear away by means of change from within. The concepts and formerly acknowledged meanings are seen to be unintelligible or confused and communication within that area of knowledge breaks down. Our scientific theories are much different than they once were, and scientific revolutions are constantly taking place, as Thomas Kuhn pointed out. (1962) In addition, counterarguments and examination of one's methods are always relevant to any universe of discourse. It is not enough to defend a universe of discourse simply because its speakers acknowledge and speak its language. Its language may consist mainly of misuses of language or vague abstractions.

Sociology, both its methods, concepts and the phenomena dealt with, is seen to rest heavily on metaphors (models, diagrams, as-if roles, or parts played, etc.). Thus Vernon's view, if modified to state that man's behavior is largely determined by his language, is one of the most important observations to be had about human behavior. Perhaps this is the reason he comes back to the symbol again and again throughout the book.

Vernon asserted above, that one area which cannot be reduced to scientific analysis is that of value. Again, this is not the case. Vernon has assumed the common dogma that "science" cannot deal with symbol and value. The logic of the use of ethical terms shows them to be characterized as being abstract, open-context terms. (Shibles "Ethics as Open-Context Terms" 1972) They mean nothing in themselves but covertly imply empirical, descriptive situations. To say, "That act is good," says nothing. One must, to make it intelligible, substitute an empirical or descriptive statement for "good." By "The act is good," one may mean that it accords with the law, with tradition, with religion, or with what one's friends think. Value terms such as good, bad, right, wrong, ought, ought not, are all characterized as being open-context terms with a loosely limited range of substitution instances. Such instances may be circularly reduced to other ethical terms but ultimately imply descriptive and empirical statements if they are to make sense. Thus the realm of value is not an ideal realm somehow separate from the world of science or from everyday description. Because value does reduce to descriptive empirical statement the following statement is unacceptable: "Sociology is not concerned with providing moral or value answers about death or any other subject." You "should" do this, means often, "If you do not do this such and such will happen, and you do not want that to happen." To point out consequences is scientific and many if not all laws are of such an if-then nature. To describe wants is certainly a descriptive and empirical matter. Thus any study of consequences and empirical descriptions deals with values because values reduce to such things. To be moral is merely to know descriptively how things work, what consequences are involved and what wants are present and relevant. This is perhaps why we find Vernon, in spite of his attempt to be objective, giving criticisms pointing out such consequences or suggesting certain courses of action. To do so can be entirely justifiable — that is, as long as it is not done with misused or confused ethical terms.

Vernon states that "there is nothing about dying or death objects which dictates that some particular evaluation be applied." (7) If this were so there would be no point in reading his analysis. In view of what was said earlier about value, to do an analysis is to point out existing attitudes and the consequences of our beliefs and actions. It can then, for example, be shown that our practices do not cohere with our desires or that our desires are confused or that our less important desires are being satisfied at the expense of our more important ones. Vernon himself suggests that man is often led by societal pressure and roles, thereby disallowing more intelligent behavior. Thus quite particular recommendations can be made.

His statement that nothing here dictates a particular evaluation may be put more clearly by saying that beliefs are ultimately arbitrary. They may be ultimately arbitrary but they are quite absolute when regarded as the present or prevailing beliefs and priority of wants and desired consequences at a particular time. One can then discuss and recommend courses of action in terms of such existing beliefs. As Shakespeare put it, nothing is either good or bad, it is only thinking that makes it so. Vernon, elsewhere, does speak of harmonizing beliefs and behavioral patterns of society. (p. 9)

In numerous places in the book, death and dying are treated as if they are exclusively social or biological phenomena and as if no other analysis is possible. He states that *the* nature of death and dying is a social phenomenon: "Dying is a social phenomenon" (p. 96), "The major premise of this chapter is that dying is social in nature" (p. 112), "Dying is a social as well as a biological process. The fact that death is biologically inevitable, however, does not determine the conditions of actual death. Social factors do" (p. 126), "Man is a social being." (p. 151)

There is, however, no question but that social patterns, pressures and practices do greatly influence and determine one's behavior. Although Vernon does not mention it, inquiry into death may be set back and distracted by our social-political concern with war, just as war often distracts one from other domestic problems. But Vernon's stress on the symbol (language) shows that there are other important influences as well. One may choose not to follow social customs and rituals. It may also be noted that by stressing social role and custom as determinative, it is harder to convincingly assert, as Vernon sometimes does, that one dies his own personal and individual death.

A few further observations may be made. The book *Funeral Customs the World Over* by Haberstein and Lamers, is referred to as a scholarly work. Mitford, *The American Way of Death* (p. 150), points out that it was written in cooperation with and support from the National Funeral Directors Association, for promotion purposes. James Whittman (1968) in his review of another book by the same authors regards it as "an excellent source book on funeral practices," but adds, "The authors have several themes that are developed . . . The most apparent one is stated on page 5, 'The "decent funeral" is a universally accepted part of American thought and life, and the funeral director 'belongs.' It is taken for granted that his services are to be used in the burial of the dead.' " All that the *Funeral Customs* book shows is that people everywhere have cultural patterns which they follow. This does not mean that the patterns followed are intelligent. Nor does it mean we should follow our cultural rituals any more than that we should follow those of other people. A reading of the Haberstein-Lamers book shows a lack of the sort of scientific methodology which a philosopher or social scientist would require. The book presents nearly every culture as believing in a "soul." But besides the fact that many theologians and ministers reject the notion of soul and also reject the concept as being supported by the Bible, it is hard to believe that everyone means the same thing by soul. More care should be required before imposing one's views on other cultures. The scholarship of *Funeral Customs the World Over* is at least suspect, but perhaps no more than other books or articles on these subjects.

It is interesting to note Vernon's stress on death as a neglected, taboo subject. He points out how in movies the American audience is almost never allowed to identify with the murdered or dead person. He observes that one cannot in an intelligible way conceive of or imagine his own death or afterlife, because there are no antecedent probabilities, and because such matters can only be approached in terms of living experiences. He also mentions the inadequacy of the view that we have a death-instinct (cf. Freud), that we were necessarily created to die, and he avoids concern with an "unconscious." He condemns Malinowski for holding that death is the supreme crisis of life, because no criteria of "supreme" are given. He notes that our discussion of death depends upon our analysis, research, and clarity of terms concerning life. We often even use death as a form of punishment of ourselves and of others as in revenge suicide. The suicide victim may be seen as the victim of society rather than as an evildoer. He notes how the factor of self, identity, and self-definition are related to the concept of death. Some murderers merely wish to be well-known, to have their picture in the paper. The philosophical problem of the self is relevant to the problem of death.

Vernon correctly sees that death is regarded "as" a number of different things, although he could have established a better developed theory if he had seen that this is a metaphorical activity. We see death metaphorically. Then the characteristics of metaphor such as tension, paradox, juxtaposition, synecdoche, multi-meaning, humor, insight, release, hyperbole, metonymy, oxymoron, substitution, etc. could be brought to bear on the analysis. He discusses death as escape, as entertainment, as revenge, as reinforcement of social status, as a means of social control, as sex, as underlying artistic behavior, as lover, as reward or means to obtain reward, as punishment, as sleep, as a social rejection. He points out that social death can be a cause of physical death.. Our way of seeing death, our metaphors of death, may lead to our death.

In opposition to the view that mourning and funeral rites are necessary in order to overcome guilt feelings and bereavement, Vernon correctly calls attention to the fact that "one particular behavior pattern does not have identical consequences for all people under all conditions." (p. 168) Funerals in some cases may do harm. The particular factors of each case must be considered, and generalizations to the effect that funeral ceremonies are necessary or not necessary must be avoided. He states, "The meaning of death is never rigidly established at any given time for the society or for the individual." (p. 272) In regard to the funeral director's practice of "grief therapy," it is pointed out that the funeral may sometimes do more to produce grief than relieve it. (p. 171)

After an analysis of the various studies relating to religion and death he concludes, "If one is concerned solely with testing the hypothesis that a religious solution to the problem of death is more effective for reducing anxiety than a non-religious solution, the answer is that there seems to be no real difference in anxiety levels." (p. 200). "No clear-cut picture emerges from this review of relevant research. There does seem to be sufficient evidence to question seriously the premise that religion serves to reduce fear of death." (p. 203) While other texts and articles conclude one way or the other on this controversial religious topic Vernon, in spite of his stress on the non-empirical, gives the more objective conclusion that in view of the evidence the question cannot yet be resolved. It can, however, be easily seen that one who believes in sin, guilt, hell, etc. could die a horrible death.

Vernon also, though most likely unintentionally, hints that perhaps fear, guilt and other negative emotions regarding death and mourning may be unnecessary and may even be done away with. Such fears can be socially determined. If so, they can perhaps be eliminated by rejecting those present social practices which are unintelligent. He quotes Feifel and Heller to the effect that "we need to subdue irrational fears and guilt sentiments associated with death." (p. 190) Vernon states, "The lower classes had the least control of their emotions following a bereavement — with little show of emotion among the upper classes." (p. 262) Clergymen are reported to hold that the funeral intensifies grief. (p. 264) These statements are not arguments but are quite helpful in accustoming one to begin to accept the idea that our emotions are not a fixed part of our nature but are able to be changed, dissipated, and replaced by more positive emotions. An examination of the nature of emotions in the light of our present knowledge of philosophical psychology would reveal how one may do this.

Vernon offers the criticism, "It would be wrong to conclude that *any* ritual and *any* funeral service will automatically produce . . . [effective results] . . . The convictions of the major ritualists involved in funeral behavior may reflect decisions of many types which are not supported by the scientific evidence." (p. 297) In addition it may be added that such arguments as that unresolved or incompleted mourning leads to emotional disturbance, do not necessarily lead one to conclude that therefore present funeral practices are able to properly resolve and complete it.

This book presents a brief summary of a great number of statistical, psychological, and sociological research studies by a number of researchers. Such studies supposedly represent a scientific objective account. This is deceptive. The studies for the most part should only be taken as suggestive or as hypotheses rather than as conclusive scientific findings. Such studies often leave out much, depend on imprecise language, employ undeveloped or unsupported models, lack adequacy or broad overall perspective, and the conclusions given are often more guesses by the author than findings derived from the research. The contemporary philosopher, Ludwig Wittgenstein, put is this way, "In psychology there are experimental methods and *conceptual* confusion." (1968) This is not, of course, entirely true. Much excellent and sound work is being done in psychology and sociology. It is, however, a needed qualification and it points to the fact that we need not just statistical surveys of beliefs, etc., but we need a philosophically sound and clear analysis of concepts related to death and dying. That is, in addition to sociology, economics, and psychology, a philosophical analysis of death and dying is needed. Philosophical psychology, the philosophy of language, and the philosophy of science cannot be overlooked in this regard.

Max Black. "The Scientific Method" *Problems of Analysis* Cornell Univ. Press 1954

Thomas Kuhn. *The Structure of Scientific Revolutions* University of Chicago Press 1962

Gilbert Ryle. *Concept of Mind* New York: Barnes & Noble 1949

Warren Shibles. *Metaphor: An Annotated Bibliography and History* Whitewater, Wisconsin: The Language Press 1971

—————. *Philosophical Pictures* Dubuque, Iowa: Kendall-Hunt 1972

Glenn Vernon. *Sociology of Death* New York: Ronald Press 1970

Rene Wellek and Austin Warren. *Theory of Literature* 3rd ed. New York: Harcourt, Brace and World 1956

James Whittman, Jr. "Review" *Sociological Symposium* I (Fall 1968) 95-96

Ludwig Wittgenstein. *Philosophical Investigations* 3rd ed. New York: Macmillan 1968

II. ROBERT FULTON ON DEATH

Dr. Robert Fulton, a well-known writer on the sociology of death, has done research for the National Funeral Director's Association (NFDA) and read papers at their meetings and elsewhere.

In one study involving over 1,400 funeral homes he found that in 1969 as compared with 1966 there was a trend toward a private service, no viewing of the deceased, immediate disposition of the body, a memorial service, and toward no service at all. In his report of this at an NFDA seminar in January 1971, as stated in *The Director* (Feb 1971), he presented also what the NFDA called "positive developments": It was reported by funeral directors that clergymen are showing more interest in the funeral as grief therapy, and that more children are attending funerals. Whether these are positive developments, however, needs to be evaluated.

In his article "On the Dying of Death" he presents the following view: Death is ignored by contemporary existential man. It is avoided, denied and treated as if it were avoidable or a result only of accident. Thus the title: "The dying of death." After pointing out that grief can result in asthma, colitis, rheumatoid arthritis, antisocial behavior, psychosis, psychosomatic and somatic disorders, and psychoneurotic illness, he states that deritualization of mourning and supression of grief are harmful trends in the United States. He believes that the funeral *if properly responsive* to the needs of the survivors can prevent such disorders caused by grief.

But in opposition to Fulton's view the question of whether or not the funeral does and can do this and whether or not it is the best way of alleviating grief still needs to be answered. It may be the best method in view of the confusion about grief and death and our present beliefs and practices. It may not be the best method in terms of a more enlightened view of death and emotions. The question is whether our present practices are based on reason or superstition. Fulton's escape clause above is, if the funeral is "properly responsive."

In another article (1964) Fulton condemns the euphemistic terminology of the funeral director and the coffin manufacturer, e.g., he opposes stressing a "water-tight" vault, in favor of a program of facing death and learning how to better serve the social and psychological needs of the bereaved.

Perhaps Fulton's best known study is "The Sacred and the Secular: Attitudes of the American Public toward Death, Funerals, and Funeral Directors" (1965). Two groups were surveyed: 1) 10,000 householders, 2) members of memorial societies.

Of the householders, 69 percent believe in God or a Creator, 19 percent that death is an end, 12 percent that the purpose of the funeral is religious, the majority that the funeral serves its purposes.

Of the memorial group, 22 percent believe in God, 53 percent that death is an end, 16 percent that the funeral has no purpose at all, and the majority that the funeral service does not serve its purpose or serve to aid the bereaved. In fact, three-fourths of this group think changes are needed in the funeral ceremony to make it more simple, less expensive, shorter, more personal and more emotionally realistic. The majority of both groups oppose government handling of funerals.

A survey of this sort, however, only tells what people think. It should not be taken as an argument that what they want is well-informed or that it is in some sense best for them. They most likely are not at all familiar with government operated funerals in France and Switzerland which some have praised for their clearly published practices and prices (cf. Mitford, and Harmer). That the majority believes in a certain thing does not establish its truth or make it informed inquiry. It can, however, be suggestive of needed change.

In his discussion, Fulton points out that the study revealed that sacred and traditional ceremony is regarded as being wasteful, meaningless, and artificial. This is especially true of the memorial group which was more rational, better educated, and more pragmatic, more willing to contribute body organs for the benefit of others and for medical research.

Fulton's conclusion from, or discussion of, the data collected does not at all seem to follow. Perhaps the discussion section is supposed to be more speculative than the rest but if so it may be misleading in being mistaken for a conclusion. He says that ceremony relates man to God or the sacred, by means of sacrifice. Ceremony links the sacred society and the individual.

Ceremony is also said to allow needed expression of anger and hostility and lessen guilt and anxiety. Although in "Widow in America" he states, "For the most part, medical practitioners and the clergy know next to nothing about grief and bereavement." But in his study there was no analysis of anxiety, guilt, or ceremony. It was only a survey of what people think generally about funeral practices. He does not give an analysis of the nature of emotion yet concludes regarding certain emotion. Irrational ceremony may rather be a form of bad adjustment and not allow us to get at the cause of our grief and confused emotions concerning death. In the first place emotions are largely rational. There are no emotions as such, but emotion reduces to a rational assessment which guides feelings and includes a description of a situation or context. Emotions are often confused because our rational assessments are confused. This means that with a change to more clear rational assessments and descriptions concerning the nature of death our negative emotions concerning it can be dissipated and we can better move in the direction of improving our inquiry into death and aging. The way to alleviate our negative emotions is, then, not by means of irrational ritual or other escape methods. Whereas Fulton claims that we do not face death, the claim may be brought against his view that he does not allow us to face the cause of our negative emotions honestly. To promote ritual and mysticism can hardly be a scientific or intelligent approach to knowledge.

Fulton also claims that desire for cremation might be the result of anger, e.g., of the rejection felt by the elderly. Certainly he is correct in asserting that the elderly in our society are in many ways poorly treated. But the desire for cremation may be rather due to anger toward the irrational and superstitious reality-denying rituals, religious practices, and superstitions prevalent in our society. In any case, many who desire cremation are not at all angry, but desire it, wish to avoid high funeral costs, wish land to be put to other than burial use, etc.

Fulton also asserts that the funeral director's practice of charging according to the ability to pay, is in fact a benefit not to the director but to the purchaser. This may often be the case.

However Mitford's point cannot be denied that it may work so that the charge is in accordance with the insurance, or other money available, thus depleting all of one's savings. This criticism of the director is also stressed by Sidney Margolius in the Public Affairs Pamphlet on funeral costs.

In view of Fulton's defense of existing funeral procedures it is surprising to note that Jessica Mitford cites Fulton's studies as undermining the funeral industry. He did find that a hard core of 23 percent of each religious group studied, felt that the funeral director takes advantage of the public; and more than this expressed reservations. He also said, "Clergymen, and in particular Protestant clergymen, are gravely disturbed over those aspects of the funeral program which in their eyes are neither necessary nor proper." (Mitford p. 210)

Robert Fulton. "Death, Grief and Social Recuperation." Paper presented at The Gerontology Institute, Wayne State Univ. 1969. Published in *Omega*

—————. *The Director* 41 (Feb. 1971) 3-4

—————. "On the Dying of Death" *Explaining Death to Children* E. Grollman, ed., Boston: Beacon Press 1967 pp. 31-47

—————. "The Sacred and the Secular . . ." *Death and Identity* Fulton, ed., New York: Wiley 1965 pp. 89-105. (Originally published Milwaukee, Wisc: Bulfin Press 1963)

—————. "Widow in America" Revised version of speech given at Harvard Medical School 1970

—————, and Eric Markusen. "Childhood Bereavement and Behavior Disorders: A Critical Review" *Omega 2* (1971) 107-117

—————, and Julie Fulton. "A Psychosocial Aspect of Terminal Care: Anticipatory Grief" *Omega 2* (1971) 91-100

—————, Julie Fulton, Roberta Simmons. "The Prospective Organ Transplant Donor." Prepared for the Second International Conference on Social Science and Medicine, Aberdeen, Scotland, Sept. 7-11, 1970

288

––––––, and Phyllis Langton. "Attitudes Toward Death" *Nursing Forum* 3, 1 (1964) 104-12

Ruth Harmer. *The High Cost of Dying* New York: Crowell-Collier 1963

Sidney Margolius. "Funeral Costs and Death Benefits" Public Affairs Pamphlet No. 409, 1967

Jessica Mitford. *The American Way of Death* New York: Fawcett World Library 1963

Medical-Psychological
Definition of Death

When does death occur? Is it when the body ceases to function without external mechanical help, when consciousness ceases? Often both consciousness and physical functions can be restored with the help of physicians. How death is medically defined depends on one's purposes. Traditionally the physician kept the patient alive in almost any condition and circumstances as long as time, energy and expense allowed. One may define death as that condition which is beyond the point at which medical science can in any way revive the body. If the patient has irreversible loss of consciousness the question arises as to whether the patient should be kept alive as a "human vegetable" to be cared for by elaborate machines and attendants. The question which arises is a philosophical question: What is a person? This is the problem of the self. If a person is only a physical body then death refers to cessation of the physical body. If a person is also consciousness, death is cessation of consciousness. The question is whether one must be dead in all possible ways to be considered dead or whether irreversible cessation of consciousness is sufficient. How we are to conceive of a person depends upon our own purposes, as well as on our knowledge of human behavior. An analysis of philosophical psychology involves a clarification of the nature of "person," "self," "action," "consciousness," "thought," etc. This clarification is needed before one can decide what it is that dies. It is inhumane and harmful to assert without evidence that the body dies and the soul lives on. The view we have of the self determines what it is which dies. In addition, the view we have of elementary "particles," electromagnetic "forces," and physical matter (as opposed to animate organisms) will determine whether anything really dies at all. In summary, when one speaks of death he must know the specific context and paradigm which is involved. Death does not refer to a single context or example, but has a great many meanings. It is not a single instantaneous process. And it seems not to be a process at all. "He is dead," is therefore an equivocal statement. One was thought to be legally "dead" if he joined a religious order or became a monk. Orthodox Jews regarded a child who married outside the faith as "dead," and a funeral was performed. One may be regarded as "socially dead." Non-philosophers may be regarded as "dead" to open inquiry and critically examined knowledge. This is suggested by the saying, "The unexamined life is not worth living." A sound medical and philosophical definition of death leads to a sound legal definition of death.

Arthur Winter (1969) presents the following definitional conclusions of a symposium regarding the determination of the "moment of death":

1. Total lack of response to external stimuli, even pain.
2. Absence of spontaneous muscular movements, especially breathing.
3. Absence of all reflexes, including full dilation of the pupils, absence of response to ice water in ears, and absence of deep tendon reflexes. Muscles respond to electrical stimulation after several hours.
4. Total collapse of arterial blood pressure.
5. Flat electrocardiogram.
6. Flat electroencephalograph tracings. Electrical response of the brain stops after approximately thirty seconds. Exceptions to these are in cases of severe drug intoxication or hypothermia. (Barbituate poisoning may result in flat EEG.) Accurate medical definitions have the value of avoiding premature death. One 18th century physician listed fifty-two cases of persons who were buried alive, and seventy-two with incorrect death certificates. A Professor of Medical Jurisprudence, A. Louis, reported in 1752 a case of a monk who had intercourse with a dead girl. Just before burial the girl was revived and nine months later gave birth. (Mant, Toynbee 1969)

The five criteria of death established in 1968 by the Council for the International Organization of Medical Science are: (1) loss of response to environment, (2) cessation of reflexes and muscle tone, (3) cessation of spontaneous respiration, (4) sudden fall in blood pressure, (5) a flat EEG. Dr. Hadassah Gillon, however, found a brain injured patient who satisfied these criteria yet lived. (1969) He proposes an added test be oxygen consumption in the brain. There may be oxygen consumption even with a flat EEG.

Henry Beecher gives the following definition (1970):

1. Deep unconsciousness with no response to external stimuli, nor internal need.
2. No movement or breathing (unless artificial).
3. No reflexes (except occasional spinal reflexes).
4. A flat (isoelectric) electro-encephalogram (EEG). The EEG is not essential in the diagnosis of brain death.

He excludes those under CNS depressants, e.g., barbiturates, and people whose internal temperature is below 90 degrees F (32 degrees C). The four criteria must be present for at least 24 hours. Beecher's criteria would adversely affect the donation of organs to needy patients. However, he proposes that the respirator and other "life" sustaining machines may be turned off when there is irreversible brain damage. This would allow for heart and organs to be transplanted to other patients. (Ladimer)

One additional test of death given is to inject uranine, and if the blood is still circulating mucus membranes will turn yellow. (Battesta)

Joseph Still stresses the fact that the determination of death depends on the determination of life. He suggests the following five levels and adds that one level should not be confused with another:

1. Cellu-vegetative death. Some body cells can be kept alive outside of the body indefinitely. Rigor mortis stiffening is due to cellular metabolism which continues after the other body functions cease.
2. Organ death.

3. Organismal death, e.g., heart and lungs stop.
4. Psychic death. Cerebral brain cells are permanently destroyed in about five minutes after breathing ceases. This produces a permanently vegetative state. The body may be kept "alive" by heart, lung, and kidney machines. Relevant to abortion it is not clear when psychic life begins. Electroencephalograph waves appear only after the embryo is forty-three days old. Self-consciousness begins only after several years.
5. Vegetative death. The cells of the vegetative controlling part of the brain die after eight minutes.

Pope Paul's encyclical "Of Human Life" states that there is one soul for each life, it enters the fertilized egg at conception and leaves at death. Still says that this view does not indicate at which of the five deaths the soul leaves. If it leaves with the psychic death then one cannot consistently hold that the soul enters the egg at conception. In any case, the soul dogma can offer no criterion for the beginning or existence of life or of death. The only criteria are empirical criteria such as fertilization of the egg and observable behaviorial criteria including descriptions of "consciousness."

Edwin Shneidman, who has done extensive work in the area of death and suicide, states, "The word 'death' had become a repository for persuasive logical and epistemological confusions — 'Idols of the Dead.' " He proposes a revision of our present classifications of death. Death is not just a biological event but should depend on our consciousness. Shneidman points out that of the 137 causes of death mentioned by the International Classification of the Causes of Death, there are only four modes given, namely, 1. natural death, 2. accident, 3. suicide, 4. homicide. "Natural" is seen to be an arbitrary category. Why is death by virus natural, rather than accidental? An analysis of such terms is not given here but it would lead to a clearer understanding of our use of "natural" and "accidental" in these cases of the rules which guide such uses. If death is regarded as unnatural there could be no such thing as a natural death.

He further points out that death should not be thought of as an "act," because it is not something we can do, it is not an experience. We can only perform the act of dying. Thus the emphasis is put on what we think we are doing when we commit the "act" of suicide or of killing ourselves.

Shneidman presents a complex classification which especially stresses conscious and social experience. A distinction is often made between "clinical death" whereby the person is medically pronounced dead, and "biological death" whereby cells or organs are still functioning or able to function. Shneidman proposes a distinction between "cessation" and "termination." "Cessation" refers to the irreversible stopping of any conscious experience. Thus we are asked to speak of "cessation" rather than death. Shneidman does not notice that "cessation" cannot be experienced any more than death can be experienced.

By "termination" he refers exclusively to the stoppage of physiological processes. Thus one can "cease" before he "terminates." This terminology seems to substitute "cessation" or "conscious stoppage" for "clinical death," and "termination" for "biological death." The latter two terms mean the same thing. A suicidal might think he can terminate without ceasing. He might think that he is just getting rid of his conscious problems yet his body will remain alive, i.e., cease to some extent but not terminate.

Shneidman gives the following classification:

1. Cessation.
2. Termination.
3. Interruption. A temporary conscious cessation, e.g., sleep.
4. Continuation. Desire both to live and to die. Continuation may involve a range from no thought, fantasy, fleeting concern, obsession, or deliberate performance or suicide. Thus an adequate understanding is needed in order to determine the kind of cessation involved.
   a) rescue fantasies, gamble with death, cry for help.
   b) feel hopeful or hopeless with psychological impotence.
   c) feel self-righteous, indignation, defeat, ennui, inner resourcefulness.
   d) orientation toward next temporal interval whether

one of blandness, inertia, habit, interest, demand, expectation, anticipation. [Anticipation, expectation and blandness especially characterize the existentialist view.]

The categories given here involve emotion classifications which are overvague and subjective. No analysis of emotions is given. A philosophical clarification of emotions is needed before such categories can be made workable. The classification which would result would differ from Shneidman's in that it would have to include 1. language used, 2. contextual description, 3. objects involved. An analysis of emotions, including those of anticipation and expectation, is given elsewhere in this book.

Four subcategories are given regarding how an individual sees his own death, at least sometimes, or at the time of death:

1. Intentional death. (psyde means cessation)
   a) Psyde-seeker. Desire to end conscious experience where rescue is unlikely.
   b) Psyde-initiators. Knows he will die soon so he initiates his own death with pills, pulling out tubes, etc.
   c) Psyde-ignorers. Die thinking his psyche will live on or he will meet friends after death. (This appears to be close to the Christian view.)
   d) Psyde-darers. Bets on his chances to survive.
2. Subintentioned death. That is, covert intention such as carelessness, ignorance, foolhardiness.

Anxiety, hate, and fear also lead to one's death. (cf. 2 c below) This classification is interesting in that it regards ignorance or lack of intelligent inquiry in general, and lack of emotions specifically, as leading to one's own death. This category may then apply to everyman insofar as he has avoided inquiry into death and the problem of aging. It means that those who fail to inquire into ethics, emotions, philosophical psychology, the philosophy of science, etc. are bringing about their own death. The contemporary ordinary-language philosopher Ludwig Wittgenstein spoke of philosophy as being therapy. This is an excellent instance of such therapy. One soldier for example argued that he ought to fight in a war because it is his "duty," but failed to see that the statement, "I ought to do my duty" is circular and so meaningless in itself because "duty" means "what I ought to do." The statement would then read, "I ought to do what I ought to do." One may give up his life on the battlefield as a consequence of his confession about how ethical terms and statements work. As most people are, without question, disinterested in knowledge or inquiry they may be classified as "psyde-hasteners" or "subintentional death hasteners." Most people then are slowly or quickly committing suicide.

Subintentional death is classified as:

Psyde
a) —chancer. One leaves it up to chance or gambles with death. The Christian, in effect, does this when he performs a dangerous act and says, "It is God's will," or one says "When my time is come, that will be it."
b) —hastener. Most people insofar as they fail to engage in critical inquiry into themselves and environment may be said to be hastening their own death. The use of alcohol, tobacco, lack of care in driving, disregard of hygiene and nutrition, etc. lead to one's own death.
c) —capitulator. Strong emotion such as fear and anxiety may lead to one's death. One may because of such emotion give in to death.
d) —experimenter. One seeks new drug and alcohol ·experiences which lead to one's death or to a life-long vegetative state. This is extremely common among teenagers and college students.
3. Unintentional death. This is "natural," accidental or homicidal death.
Psyde
a) —welcomer
b) —accepter
c) —postponer
d) —disdainer (denies death)
e) —fearer

4. Contraintended death.
   a) feigner. One only pretends to commit suicide.
   b) threatener. Threat of death is used as a tool or power to achieve some goal.

The above account stresses the intention thus allowing special attention to be paid to the way in which one views death, especially those who are suicidal. The classifications, though very interesting, nevertheless seem vague and general. They should rather be more carefully based on the actual causes of one's death. The system is more refined than the traditional one in including intention. But one reason intention was perhaps not previously included is that it is difficult to determine what was or is intended and also what an intention is. For a clearer analysis of intention, recent work in philosophical psychology should be examined. (c.f. W. Shibles "Intention") Once this is done a clear statement about "intention" should be given before a classification is based on it. It may then be seen that "intention" is a pseudo-psychological category as is "consciousness," "thought," and "idea." It is an appeal to a private, internal state for which we do not have evidence, as the contemporary philosophers Gibert Ryle, and Ludwig Wittgenstein have shown. In summary, a medical, psychological or scientific classification of death and approaches to death is not yet, but ought to be, careful and precise enough so that it is philosophically sound and adequate.

O. A. Battesta. "What Happens When You Die?" *Science Digest* May 1964, pp. 80-84

Henry Beecher. "The New Definition of Death" AAAS Meeting, Chicago 1970

H. Gillon. "Defining Death Anew" *Science News* 1969

Erving Ladimer. "The Challenge of Transplantation" Public Affairs Pamphlet, No. 451, 1970

A. Keith Mant. "The Medical Definition of Death" *Man's Concern with Death* A. Toynbee, ed., New York: McGraw Hill 1969 p. 16

297

Edwin Shneidman. "Orientations Toward Death" *International Journal of Psychiatry* 2 (1966) 167-190. Reprinted in *The Study of Lives: Essays on Personality in Honor of Henry Murray* R. White, ed., New York: Atherton Press 1964 pp. 200-227

Warren Shibles. "Intention" *Wittgenstein, Language and Philosophy* Dubuque, Iowa: Kendall-Hunt 1971

Joseph Still. "The Levels of Life and Semantic Confusion" *ETC* 28 (1971) 9-20

Arthur Winter. *The Moment of Death: A Symposium* Springfield, Illinois: Charles Thomas 1969

Abortion

It is difficult to determine the exact moment of death or the exact moment of life or even what life is. That it is difficult is not determined by value or moral considerations. This is because value terms such as good, bad, right, wrong, responsible, irresponsible, should reduce to empirical descriptive statements. Such terms are open-context terms and have no meaning in themselves – or rather are elliptical. "Abortion is wrong," is in itself meaningless. "Wrong" here implies, but does not state, a loosely limited range of substitution instances. It may mean abortion has certain harmful consequences, is not efficient enough, is illegal, is against religious doctrine, etc. But until the specific substitution is made the meaning is incomplete. What characterizes value terms is merely that they are vague, are meaningless in themselves, and that to give them meaning we must substitute concrete descriptive and empirical instances for them. (See W. Shibles "Ethics as Open-Context Terms") To say that "X is wrong" means "X is not in accord with religion," is a substitution but one needing further clarification to determine whether the religious model is intelligible. Ethical terms reduce to statements about consequences of actions in relation to one's desires, needs and understanding. To say "X is right" ultimately reduces to "X is in accord with my understanding, needs and desires." Needs and desires are empirical. To say, "X is right in itself," is a category-mistake, and failure to comprehend the logic of ethical language. "Abortion is in itself wrong," or "Abortion is in itself right," are misuses of language. There is no independent "realm" of value. Thus the abortion question is not a moral question, it is a question of examining the facts, actions and consequences for the needs and beliefs of oneself and others in society. There are no ultimate or absolute values of good or bad. Shakespeare accordingly said that nothing is either right or wrong but it is only thinking that makes it so. Socrates stated that one only does wrong acts out of ignorance. It is a descriptive empirical question of knowing the consequences of one's actions for certain desired purposes. To be ethical is to be intelligent, to inquire, to question.

The determination of the moment of life and the moment of death, then, is relevant to one's purposes. Abortion is neither good nor bad in itself. What is important is to see what the consequences are of having an abortion or not having an abortion. Neither the mother, father, nor society have any obligations, responsibilities, or rights as such. We may, however, specify certain courses of action which produce results we desire. We have no "obligations" as such to the unborn and the unborn have no "rights" as such. It is no argument to say that "life in itself is valuable," or there is a "sanctity of life." Rather clarification of these terms is needed. I would want to say that killing man is wrong in the sense that it leads to consequences not meeting the purposes, desires and needs of myself and others. But it is not wrong in itself. It is wrong in the sense that it is usually unintelligent and self-defeating behavior.

The abortion question is difficult because people are not clear as to what their beliefs and desires are. Whether abortion is right or wrong depends on one's desires, goals, needs, purposes and one's knowledge of consequences, causes, and effects. But if one is not clear about these he cannot clearly decide the issue. One may not be able to decide about whether abortion is right or wrong because he is not clear as to what his goals are. The religious person has his answer dictated to him by religious doctrine but, as will be seen, religious authorities disagree. Whether we regard the embryo as a "person" or "human being" or not depends on our purposes. If one is confused about how ethical terms work or if one has confused concepts of "person," "life," "death," "killing," etc., then the question of abortion will not be effectively and realistically resolved.

It is important that the pregnant woman have the choice of whether or not to have an abortion rather than have the choice imposed upon her arbitrarily or by those who hold superstitious, unenlightened or unintelligent beliefs. Catholics attempt to impose their view of abortion on everyone and make it into universal law. Their view is usually based on a belief in the existence of metaphysical entities and essences such as soul, being, person, goodness, rightness, truth, etc. An examination of the legal aspect of abortion may serve as a guide to the relevant desires, technical aspects and consequences of various beliefs and practices.

Legal Considerations

In 1873 a Federal statute, the Comstock Act, prohibited obscene literature as well as the importation of contraception devices and literature. In 1958 the laws of 33 states still opposed giving contraceptive information or displaying it. In several states even physicians were not allowed on any grounds to give such information. (Conn., Mass.) California prohibited the use of any materials for the prevention of contraception. (Calderone 196) This law had the consequence that many thousands of women found themselves with unwanted pregnancies. In 1965 the Supreme Court declared state birth control laws unconstitutional because they deprive married people the right to the use of contraceptives and the right to marital privacy. (Griswold vs. Connecticut, 381 U.S. 479)

Beginning in the 1830's all states passed laws prohibiting abortion except when it would be necessary to save the mother's life. Before the 19th century common law in England (1327-1803) and America (1607-1830) allowed a woman to terminate pregnancy at will. Early strict abortion laws are said to have been passed because abortion was dangerous in times when modern antiseptic techniques were not available.

"Restrictive abortion laws, passed originally for medical considerations are being retained today for religious reasons. Separation of church and state is . . . fundamentally involved." (NARAL Summer 1972)

Until several years ago the laws of 45 states required that abortions be performed only when necessary to preserve the life of the mother. Six of these states also permitted therapeutic abortion to save the life of the unborn child. Two states also permitted abortion if it "prevents serious or permanent bodily injury." (Calderone 33, 34, 187) The penalty for *intending* or attempting to procure an abortion was up to 14 years imprisonment. The woman could be punished even if she were not pregnant at the time of the attempt or intention. These state laws were enacted beginning in the 1820's and were the first abortion laws. There was no federal abortion law except a ban on interstate advertising. Mississippi (1966) allows an abortion in the case of rape or incest. Massachusetts (1845) allows it to preserve a woman's life or health. Pennsylvania forbids abortions performed unlawfully but neither the courts nor the legislature has defined "unlawfully." Since 1967 twelve states passed laws allowing abortion when there is danger to maternal health, risk of fetal deformity, or a history of rape or incest. In all cases a medical review board is required, thus forcing the woman or her doctor to defend her qualification for abortion.

The qualifications or stipulations for procuring an abortion are as follows: (They are given here according to pregnancy time limit, residency requirement, age for consent): Arkansas (not stipulated (NS), 4 mos., age 16), California (20 weeks, none, 18), Colorado (16 weeks for rape — otherwise NS, none, 18), Delaware (20 weeks, 4 mos, —), Georgia (NS, state residents only, 14), Kansas (NS, none, 18), Maryland (26 weeks, none, 16), New Mexico (NS, none, 16), North Carolina (NS, 4 mos, 16), Oregon (150 days, state residents only, 16), South Carolina (NS, 90 days, 16), Virginia (NS, 120 days, 16). California does not permit abortion when there is risk of fetal deformity. Oregon allows that determination of the physical or mental health of mother may include the present or future total environmental situation.

It should be pointed out that the duration of pregnancy is determined from the first day of the last menstrual period even though the conception took place two weeks later.

In 1970 four states passed laws permitting abortion for any reason at all. In these states a woman need only ask for the abortion. The states and their legal restrictions are:

Alaska ("nonviable fetus," 30-day residence, age 18),
Hawaii ("nonviable fetus," 90-day residence), Washington
(4 lunar months, 90-day residence), New York (24 weeks,
no residency requirement). "Nonviable fetus" generally
means twentieth week of pregnancy. A 1971 Supreme
Court ruling allowed D. C. to interpret its abortion laws to
allow abortion easily.

The reform laws of the 1960's were partially based on the
1959 recommendation by the American Law Institute. This
proposal reads:

"A licensed physician is justified in terminating a
pregnancy if:
1. He believes that there is substantial risk that
continuance of the pregnancy would gravely impair the
physical or mental health of the mother or that the child
would be born with grave physical or mental defect, or the
pregnancy resulted from rape by force or its equivalent . . .
or from incest . . .; and
2. Two physicians, one of whom may be the person
performing the abortion, have certified in writing their
belief in the justifying circumstances . . ."

One of the consequences of laws based on this proposal was
that over 90 percent of abortions were performed on the
ground of damage to mental health. (Hall 1971) A group for the
Advancement of Psychiatry Committee wrote, "Most abortions
now performed legally by licensed physicians were performed
by stretching the concept of 'psychiatric grounds' to the
breaking point." (*The Right To Abortion* p. 11) Psychiatrists
were not clear about what the psychological consequences of
aborting would be. After three years of study the Committee on
Psychiatry and Law stated,

"We recommend that abortion, when performed by a
licensed physician, be entirely removed from the domain
of criminal law. We believe that a woman should have the
right to abort or not just as she has the right to marry or
not." (Ibid. p. 12)

The American Civil Liberties Union in 1967 stated the following position:

"It should not be deemed a crime for a woman to seek, and for a doctor to perform, the termination of a pregnancy in accordance with generally accepted community standards of medical practice. The ACLU believes that all criminal sanctions should be removed from the area of abortion, and that the laws and standards governing this medical procedure be the same as those which govern the performance of all medical procedures. The Union views present abortion laws as unconstitutional because:

1. They are unconstitutionally vague;

2. They deny to women in lower economic groups the equal protection of the laws guaranteed by the Fourteenth Amendment, since abortions are now freely available to the rich but forbidden to the poor;

3. They infringe the constitutional right to decide whether and when to have a child, as well as the marital right of privacy and the privacy of the relationship between patient and physician;

4. They impair the constitutional right of physicians to practice in accordance with their professional obligations, in that they require doctors to refrain from a medical procedure whose failure to perform would, except for the abortion laws, amount to malpractice in many cases, and;

5. They deprive women of their lives and liberty, in the sense of deciding how their bodies are to be used, without due process of law." (*American Civil Liberties Policy Guide* 1967)

On January 22, 1973, the U.S. Supreme Court ruled in the case of *Roe v. Wade* (Texas) and *Doe v. Bolton* (Georgia) that the existing restrictive state abortion laws are unconstitutional. The Supreme Court ruled in the Texas case that a woman may for any reason have a physician-performed abortion within the first three months of pregnancy. The decision is to be made only by the woman and her physician without the previously required necessity of an examining board. During the next three months the state may regulate standards to protect the woman's life but may not prohibit abortion. Thus the individual states may arbitrarily prohibit abortion after the first six months except when the mother's life is threatened. The physician need not perform an abortion at any stage if his judgment or religious beliefs are against it. After six months the state may but need not protect the life of the fetus by prohibiting abortion, unless it is necessary to preserve the life of the mother. Some of the reasons given in coming to the decision were:

1. The Constitution does not define "person" and the common legal and non-legal use of the term is that it only applies postnatally. The fetus is not a "person" before birth and does not have full legal rights. Justice Blackmun said, "The unborn have never been recognized in the law as persons in the whole sense." [This is in direct opposition to the Catholic position.]

2. Mortality of the mother due to abortion during the first three months is less than mortality due to childbirth. Also the child is not viable, cannot live on its own outside the womb, during this period. [It may sometimes survive after the fifth month. In New York it was found that abortion in the first 24 weeks was only 12 percent as dangerous to a woman's life as is childbirth. Illegal abortions kill 400 women a year, and 350,000 women are admitted yearly to hospitals due to damage done by illegal abortions.]

3. The women's rights view that an abortion may be terminated at any time at all and for any reason, was rejected. Rather a number of factors and consequences should be considered such as emotional, physical, familial consequences, age of mother, whether unwed, whether or not the child is unwanted, etc.

4. The right of privacy and personal liberty guaranteed by the 14th Amendment can include a woman's freedom to have an abortion. (Also 1st, 5th and 9th Amendments and Bill of Rights.)

It may be noted that the following countries have very liberal abortion laws: Scandinavia, Japan, Soviet Union, Hungary, England, Czechoslovakia, Poland, Rumania, Bulgaria,

Iceland, East Germany. In addition, over three hundred tribal or cultural groups practice abortion. Among the Mataco every first pregnancy is aborted. (Devereus) In Japan about 50 percent of all pregnancies result in abortion. In Scandinavia one in five is aborted. (Hall 1971)

Since the January 22, 1973 Supreme Court Decision various states have enacted legislation which is either unconstitutional or not in the spirit of the Supreme Court Decision. The state laws require blanket waivers allowing even public state hospitals not to perform an abortion (e.g., Utah, Tennessee, Georgia, Idaho, Louisiana). All physicians and assistants may exempt themselves from performing an abortion. (Indiana, Utah, Tennessee, Georgia, South Dakota, etc.) This may in fact mean that no abortion at all could be performed in such states. Some states require that abortion can be performed after the first or second trimester only if it endangers the life or physical (but not the mental) health of the mother. (Indiana, Rhode Island, Tennessee) States which do allow for the health of the mother may in the second or third trimester interpret "health" to mean only physical health. A number of states also prohibit advertising or aiding and counseling regarding abortion, thus making it unknown or inaccessible. (Nevada, Louisiana, Rhode Island, Utah) In Utah consent of the husband or father must be given and a judicial hearing must take place before the abortion is performed. In addition, because no doctor or hospital need participate in Utah and because during the first 90 days abortion may only be performed if necessary to preserve the life, physical or mental health of the mother, abortions are extremely difficult to obtain. Rhode Island's law even regards the fetus as a person from the moment of conception and prohibits abortion unless necessary to save the life of the mother. (Source: NARAL June 6, 1973) Such state abortion laws are being challenged, e.g., Rhode Island's law by Civil Liberties Union.

At present, Senators James Buckley (NY), D. Bartlett (Okla.), W. Bennett (Utah), C. Curtis (Neb.), M. Young (N.D.), H. Hughes (Ia.) are introducing an amendment to the Constitution to prohibit all abortions unless the evidence shows the certainty that the death of the mother will result from giving birth. The amendment also defines the embryo at all stages as a person.

Catholic organizations are putting great effort in an attempt to outlaw abortion for all and to undo the January 1973 Supreme Court Decision. Their effort includes attempting to encourage hospitals to not participate in performing abortions. In Montana the Federal District Court forced a Catholic hospital in Billings to allow sterilization, because the hospital receives public funds. (NARAL 6-6-73)

Discussion

A. Inconsistencies

Strict abortion laws are inconsistent with actual practices in the United States, as well as with those in other countries where abortion is legal. Legalization of abortion would allow the poor to afford an abortion and would allow qualified physicians to do the abortion. Abortion is often objected to by those who favor capital punishment and killing such as in a "just" war. Catholics usually hold this position. Those who encourage animals to be hunted or killed for food oppose abortion. Catholics use the metaphysical argument that animals do not have souls. Killing born animals for food may be more violent than aborting the unborn.

If it is killing to abort an embryo it may be killing to amputate, or destroy tissue. Cells of living beings may be derived from such tissue. The biologist would be a murderer.

If abortion is killing it is not clear why causing a mother psychological anguish by refusing abortion is not killing. Psychological harm may lead to illness, social death and actual death.

If a psychiatric examination is needed before having an abortion, why not rather administer a psychiatric exam before a woman becomes a mother to see if she would be a suitable mother? We screen prospective adoption parents thoroughly but not prospective mothers. The question is not just "Is it wrong to have an abortion?" but also "Is it right to give birth?"

If having an abortion is killing why not rather regard as murderers the makers of inferior automobiles which do not yet have adequate bumpers and safety devices, or those who pollute the environment? Because of the consequences it would often be killing not to abort.

If abortion is a crime it would also be a crime to use now widely employed contraceptive devices which interrupt pregnancy after conception. (Hall 1971)

Abortion is sometimes allowed for incest and rape and deformed fetuses. On the premise that to have an abortion is to kill, it is not clear why this also would not be regarded as killing. To be raped by a man and then forced to have the child would appear to be a double rape.

Other inconsistencies may be found based on material presented elsewhere in this account. But pointing out inconsistencies does not solve problems. The purpose of presenting them here is merely to point up existing confusions of beliefs, desires and goals.

B. *Consequences*

Some of the consequences of not allowing abortion are as follows: the 1964 rubella (German measles) epidemic caused 30,000 American children to be born mentally retarded, with cardiac deformity and with cataracts. (Hall 1971) Mongoloids, detectable in the 20th week of pregnancy, have been born. Numerous additional cases can be mentioned of births of mentally and/or physically deformed children. Those born deformed or without parents often become the burden of society. Everyone must contribute to their care. And there is also overpopulation.

Children are born without fathers, without there being financial support to care for the child, with little or no possibility for being adopted (especially black children). In 1961 of the three million illegally born children in the United States under 18, only 31 percent had been adopted. Adopted children often feel adopted rather than part of the family.

Perhaps one of the most significant consequences of disallowing a woman to have an abortion is the emotional harm done to herself, her child, and her family. A committee of the Group for the Advancement of Psychiatry reports,

"The adverse consequences of maternal rejection have long been recognized by psychiatrists as one of the major contributing elements of human psychopathology. In fact, some psychiatrists believe that one of the most important goals of preventive psychiatry is the prevention of 'unwanted offspring'; such prevention was declared by Dr. Stephen Fleck to be 'preventive psychiatry's single most effective tool.' " (1970 p. 31)

The 1968 *Diagnostic Manual of Mental Disorders* lists the classification "Psychosis with childbirth." Certainly if abortion were liberally allowed women could be more interested in and able to achieve and provide sexual satisfaction and emotional and physical closeness to other human beings. It would be one corrective of the prevalent alienation and of sexual and emotional frustration. Fear of pregnancy is one well-known cause of sexual frigidity. (Drake 56) If a woman is worried about being pregnant, or if having a child will make her emotionally frustrated her sex life and her other relations with others will most likely also be impaired. Some women, of course, by having a child are more fulfilled than they would be in any other way.

The consequence for one's emotions depends on the nature of emotions. Emotion may be defined as an assessment which guides feelings. (See W. Shibles *Emotions*; E. Bedford, A. Melden, A. Beck) By assessment is meant a description of a context or situation. Emotions are not just internal states or feelings but largely consist of rational or irrational descriptions of contexts. Jealousy, for example, is an assessment of a situation which leads to negative bodily feelings. But the feeling is not the emotion. It is a category-mistake to say "I *feel* emotion." Because emotions are largely determined by assessments, if one's assessments are uninformed, unintelligent, or confused, then one will experience negative feelings – or such emotions as fear, guilt, depression. These emotions lead to physical and mental damage in the form of ulcers, physical malfunction, shock, neurosis, psychosis, suicide, as well as to failure to enjoy living. Such conditions, in effect, bring on actual and social death. By not allowing a woman to have an abortion we may, in effect, be aborting the woman.

Thus one consequence of being misinformed, confused, or unable to exercise intelligent choice in the matter of abortion is that one will thereby create negative emotions for himself and

others which lead to mental and physical harm, social as well as
actual death of the mother. Such consequences result from not
being allowed to have an abortion, being forced to have an
unwanted or deformed child, fear of the possibility of having a
pregnancy which it is illegal to terminate, fear of examining
boards, confusion about the status of the soul or whether or not
an embryo is a human being, having to raise a child when one is
not able to or does not want to, being forced to marry, social or
religious stigma, etc. One may mistakenly confuse having a child
with an act of nature, sex, the love of God, love of life, etc. and
so feel guilt, or be told she should feel guilty. One may desire to
have children because of psychological inadequacies, emotional
imbalance, desire for immortality, etc. She may want a child
because she is unhappy or bored. One should be clear about
what is meant by asserting, "A woman *needs* a baby." L.
Wittgenstein once asked, "Do we have children because it
pays?"

G. Ulett and D. Goodrich in their book on contemporary
psychiatry state,

"Pregnancy brings not only the internal stress of
dramatic physiological changes but also the external
stresses of new social responsibilities and emotional
readjustments within the family. It is a natural breaking
point for women with vulnerabilities of personality and is
the situation in which up to eight percent of psychoses in
women occur."

"History reveals the onset of irritability, crying spells,
insomnia, somatic complaints, and seclusiveness beginning
in the first trimester. . . . In a sizeable percentage the child
is basically unwanted or even illegitimate. . . . It is a good
rule to avoid leaving the mother alone with the new baby
if the patient is delusional, as infanticide is not rare. . . .
Some authorities have recommended sterilization as a
preventive measure."

Fatherhood may also bring on mental illness. One may also
suffer negative emotions if confused about the nature of ethical
terms, such as erroneously thinking that "Abortion is in itself

wrong," is somehow an argument, instead of an open-context statement which is in itself meaningless. Abortion is today "right" if what is meant by "right" is determined by the Jan. 1973 Supreme Court decision. If one assesses the consequences of having an abortion he may also find it to be "right." Several unclear conceptions regarding abortion remain to be clarified.

It may be believed that "Abortion is wrong" in the sense that it is not "natural." But "natural" is both an obscure term and a value term here. If man is "natural" why is not everything man does "natural"? Man "naturally" grows, cuts down, and eats food. He controls his environment. To have children is to control nature as much as to have an abortion. Also it is not clear that whatever is natural is therefore "good." Certainly what is natural is not "good" in itself. For example, disease is natural. It is not adequate to say that having children is a natural female sexual development. There are females who would assert that having an abortion is a natural female development and that it allows woman to be more sexually adequate and emotionally fulfilled.

One reason why abortion may seem "wrong" is because we are used to people giving birth and wanting to give birth. "To give birth is right," and by "right" they mean, "We are used to it," or "It is traditionally done." But to argue that on the basis of what one is accustomed to or on the basis of what is a traditional or long cultural practice, commits a logical fallacy. Such reasoning would justify war because we have traditionally gone to war. Some things seem right because they are familiar, and wrong if they are new or unfamiliar. People are used to babies. To argue that abortion is wrong because it is not familiar, not a familiar practice, is therefore unjustified. We cannot logically argue that war is right merely because it is a familiar practice.

Another argument concerns the definition of an embryo as a person or human being. This argument fails, as was seen in the Supreme Court decision, because the differences between an embryo and a person or human being are too great. This is in part the "private states" problem or the problem of whether or not there are other "minds." If an embryo is a person why not also our evolutionary ancestor, the chimpanzee? The latter likeness to man is greater. Those who maintain that the embryo is a human being sometimes do so by analogy, but the analogy is based on only a few superficial material and physical characteristics. The fallacy is committed of substituting the part, or the few characteristics, for the whole, a full human being. If a dying man has irreversible brain damage and so becomes a "human vegetable" dependent on life-prolonging machines he is often regarded as dead and the machines are unplugged. The status of the embryo is similar. As will be seen even some Catholics argue that an embryo only has a vegetative soul. That an embryo is potentially a human being is discussed in a following paragraph.

"Person" has been defined by Aristotle as a "rational animal." But no acceptable definition was given of reason. Thus we may propose an empirical and descriptive definition. By reason or thought is meant use of language and abilities. What we mainly mean by intelligence is ability with language and sometimes manual or visual skills. These are the sorts of things which make man human and make him a person. (See W. Shibles *Philosophical Pictures*) These are also the sorts of things which an embryo does not have.

An embryo may be thought to have abilities but only in the sense that any tissue has abilities. In this sense insects, plants, animals and even inanimate objects may be said to have abilities. It may be added that electroencephalogram readings are inadequate tests of thought or consciousness. EEG readings may be found even in plants, unconscious people, and parts of the body other than the brain. EEG brain waves are found only after the embryo is 43 days old. But a person is not a brain wave. EEG has little value in psychiatry. (Ulett) The relation between animate and inanimate will be discussed later, as will the Catholic view of what is meant by "human being."

It is important to understand whether or not an embryo is a person or human being because if it is, then one who has an abortion may feel she is a murderer or feel guilty and grieve for the deceased. If the embryo or fetus is not a person or human, then there is no murder, and need be no guilt or grief.

One reason why it has been found difficult to determine whether or not the embryo is a person is that "person" is an obscure attribute. To ask if the embryo is in itself a real "person" or "human being" is to ask a misleading question. It assumes that "person" or "human being" name entities in themselves and that by certain procedures we can discover if the names fit. These terms are rather naming-fallacies. We tend to think that all questions must have answers. But it may rather be that it is the question which is confused. To solve the problem we must dissolve the question. We mean certain things by "person," "being," and "human being" in ordinary use. People often mean by "person": "someone who is nice," "one who believes certain things," "one who acts in a certain way," etc. We may use these terms in a new metaphorical way, for example, to refer to a corporation as a person. But this does not mean that a corporation is a person in the same way that we are. It does mean that it is we who arbitrarily determine what is to be a person and what is not to be a person. We may regard anything as a person or human being if we wish. We do so to suit our purposes. If we look closely we may find our own paradigms, e.g., a person is someone who acts like I do, someone who has compassion, etc. We simply stipulate that an embryo is or is not a person or human being. But it makes no sense to say that an embryo must descriptively be defined as a person. An embryo may not be defined as a person descriptively but only metaphorically and stipulatively. It is definitional. The question of whether or not an embryo is a human being has gone unanswered because the distinction was not made between description and stipulation, and between naming as a description and naming as a use. It is a naming-fallacy to assert that "person" must name an entity. But "person" does have uses in linguistic and situational contexts. It may name a configuration of events. We use the word "person" or "human being" arbitrarily and for our own purposes. It is not even clear in what sense we may refer to a mature man as a person. We say about someone, "He is not a real person," or "He is not really human." "Person" often describes one's actions and behavior. "Being" is even more abstract and metaphysical. To find out the use of these terms they must be reduced to concrete paradigms or examples in concrete situations. Their meaning is there, not elsewhere. To apply "person" to new uses or situations is to personify. To apply "human" to new uses or situations is to humanize and anthropomorphize. Thus because an embryo is not in itself a person or human being, one need feel no guilt or grief in aborting. If one takes his metaphors literally he may, because of this delusion, feel guilt and grief. And this is only to say that we live in accordance with our metaphors. Another argument is that the embryo is a potential life. Is aborting like chopping down an acorn? To look at it this way is to impose a kind of physical, mechanical determinism or fatalism on man. Suppose there is a bomb ready to demolish the enemy in a "just" war. (Some regard both "just" wars and life as "good.") Then suppose the fuse is lit. The "potential" argument would have it that we cannot put out the fuse because it is already "lit." Such mechanical determinism fails to consider the "potential" for living men. If a woman's life will be emotionally and physically painful or if the consequences are adverse for others in society then the potential life of the fetus is sustained at the expense of the potential life of the parent or of the lives of the members of the whole society. Somehow abstract and obscure metaphysical principles seem to take the place of concern for the living.

Emotional harm is often worse than physical abuse. Anger, guilt, depression, etc., may cause one to be in effect mentally and socially dead. Those aspects of our society which contribute to such emotional damage may be thought, in many ways, to produce a greater crime than physical damage to property or body.

The suicidologist, Edwin Shneidman wrote, "Practically all suicidal behaviors stem from a sense of isolation and from feelings of some intolerable emotion on the part of the victim." (1970 p. 430)

The following facts are also relevant. When abortion was legalized in New York a) maternal mortality dropped, b) there was a sharp drop in hospital admissions for "botched" abortions, c) infant mortality dropped, d) out-of-wedlock births declined (and infant mortality rate for illegitimate children is double that of other children), e) abortion itself became safer. ("50 Physicians Evaluate Legal Abortion in New York" NARAL)

Emotional cruelty may itself be thought of as a crime. It is, of course, understood that one who objects to abortion may suffer negative emotions by aborting — but in this case no one is forcing her to abort.

A word may be said about the husband's role. He is affected by the emotional and physical life of his wife. Often an abortion may make the wife a better person and better wife because she may then be able to lead a more fulfilled life. And she may at a later time decide to have a child or adopt one, If the husband prefers to adopt a child or does not want another or any children, abortion may help strengthen the marriage and family. And an unwanted child would not keep together a bad marriage.

It would seem that ultimately the male has no control over whether or not the woman should have an abortion. It is her body and her decision and he is not a father until the child is born. But if she is concerned about her husband's wishes, or wants to have him support the child, his wishes would have to be considered. Nor does a husband have a given right to force his wife to have a child. Nothing says the purpose of marriage is to have children and in perhaps all marriages some kind of birth control is practiced. Abortion can either strengthen or break a marriage. It is no argument to say the purpose of marriage is to have children. Marriage is entered into for many reasons and having children may not be one of them. One often marries for sexual and emotional companionship.

Although it would seem that the women liberationists' demand for an abortion anytime is as absolute as the Catholic's opposition to any abortion, there are arguments in favor of the former view. First, of course, is that the consequences for the woman and society of not having the abortion are adverse. Second, physicians supposedly serve society and do so in a medical capacity. Why shouldn't a woman then demand an abortion even after the first three months assuming she is aware of any risk to her life which may be involved? It would appear that women are not being allowed to have an abortion after three months under the guise that it interferes with sound medical practice. Medical practice has nothing to do with it. After three months there is more risk to the life of the woman but if she understands this and chooses to take the slight extra risk why shouldn't she have the choice to do so? We do not condemn or refuse help in giving birth just because there is normally some risk involved. Thus when the various states adopt new abortion laws it is important for them to consider allowing abortion anytime after as well as before the first three months.

C. *The Catholic Position*

1. According to the Catholic, what makes man human is his soul. Human embryos have souls and therefore are human and furthermore have the rights of humans. To medically abort an embryo is to kill a human and deny it its rights. Pope Pius XII said,

"Even the child, even the unborn child, is a human being in the same degree and by the same title as its mother."

Second Vatican Council (1965): "Abortion and infanticide are unspeakable crimes."

According to Pope Paul's encyclical "Of Human Life" there is only one soul for each life and it enters the egg at conception and leaves at death. It is not on his account clear if the soul leaves at psychic death or at biological death.

In order to understand what is meant by soul or in order to agree with what is asserted here, one must accept certain metaphysical, religious or mystical views that man has a certain kind of soul. Few, if any, non-Catholics would be willing to accept these views and many would be unwilling to do so. Clear, intelligible and objective evidence is needed for the soul model and it is not forthcoming. Wittgenstein wrote,

" 'The separation of soul from body' . . . If he says this, I won't know yet what consequences he will draw. I don't know what he opposes this to." (69)

To assert that embryos have rights is to misuse the term "right" or to use it in an open-context way. Souls have no rights, stones have no rights. Even to say that men have rights as such is, as was mentioned earlier, to misuse the term "rights." Therefore it is not clear what is meant by saying that the embryo has rights. It does not have a "right" as such, e.g., it has no "right to life" as such. But we may or may not have a right to give life in accord with civil law or some other standard we develop. The embryo has no wants or desires. Or at least there is a problem here of private states and the problem of other minds. Also the circumstances and contexts of an embryo and man are so different that to speak of them as having "rights" in the same sense is to create a category-mistake.

But on the religious view it is a given absolute principle and God-given "right to life" which the embryo has. The principle derives from metaphysical and religious principles. It is not a concern with empirical description or consequences of one's actions. The mother, it is believed, should be allowed to die, rather than harm the embryo. Dr. Robert Hall (1970) stated that this view "consists in observing a moral law regardless of the consequences for individual human beings." (p. 425) He states that the view is "one-dimensional" stressing that the embryo be saved at any cost, without a full consideration for society or the life of the person involved.

The Catholic view that killing the embryo is wrong is inconsistent. The Catholic, as St. Thomas Aquinas believed, accepts the just war as well as capital punishment. R. Kalish (1963) in a study of 220 college students, found that approval of birth control, abortion, and euthanasia correlate highly with one another; and belief in God, afterlife and approval of capital punishment are significantly correlated. He notes that those who most fear death are most opposed to abortion and that those who are religious are less humanitarian, less liberal, and favor capital punishment.

2. The Catholic view is that either there is a real human being at conception or there probably is, or we cannot be certain if there is or not. (O'Donnell) It is assumed that there is a soul at conception. For example, the Catholic Hospital Association has the principle,

"Every unborn child must be regarded as a human person, with all the rights of a human person, from the moment of conception." (Hall 1970 p. 419)

This view has some curious consequences. Since about one out of three fertilized eggs never becomes implanted in the uterus but is released at menstruation, each of these released eggs would be a person.

This view that soul is independent of body or matter opposes another Catholic position that the soul is only the form or function of completely formed matter (hylomorphism).

What is significant about the above view is that the Catholic admits having insufficient evidence for a soul in the sense that the time when the soul enters the unborn child is difficult to determine.

The question partly rests on the view of animism. What are we to regard as animate and what as inanimate? The distinction can only be arbitrarily determined on the basis of one's purposes. Certain cases may be seen as animate or as inanimate (See W. Shibles "A Defense of Animism") The embryo only has a vegetative soul and is not human until it has a human shape.

But to suggest that cells are people is to go far beyond the animate-inanimate question into the area of personification and anthropomorphism. A homunculus was thought to be a man the size of a cell which just grows larger in the womb.

We often erroneously think that because the embryo has some characteristics like ours, it has all the characteristics of a human being. This commits the fallacy of substitution of part for whole.

The Catholic technique of presenting greatly magnified pictures of the fetus for shock effect may be offset by the horror pictures of mothers who die because of illegal abortion or childbirth, beaten or murdered unwanted children, mothers and children who commit suicide or become psychotic due to having unwanted children, monstrous births, etc. Horror pictures could also be shown of the rabbit, chicken or butchered cattle which we eat. There may be more reason to protect living animals than unborn humans.

If the embryo is a human being it is certainly not like any of the human beings or persons we usually know. Nevertheless the Catholic seems to find a resemblance.

But assuming there is a soul what difference would it make? A soul supposedly cannot be killed. There are for the non-believer no consequences of souls. Though there are consequences of a belief in souls. The stress on the next life seems to have the effect of producing a lack of concern for this life of living men.

It is argued that only God can take life or create life. Is this true? First, man can and does create and destroy life. Second, the Catholic encourages man to destroy life in the case of a just war or capital punishment. There is also a long history of the Inquisition whereby thousands of non-Catholics were killed. Today Irish Catholics war with Protestants.

The Catholic may defend the just war on the basis of self-defense. But a) self-defense is almost never an acceptable reason for war. There are too many untried options available to man to call his actual bombing of the enemy self-defense (e.g., Viet Nam, Korea, etc.), b) if self-defense can justify killing in war, it can also justify abortion. The embryo may be thought of as an unwanted aggressor whose birth and necessary care would both psychologically and physically shorten the life of the mother who desires an abortion.

3. A more liberal view is that of the Catholic philosopher, St. Thomas Aquinas: (hylomorphic or "the form of physical matter" view). The soul is merely the form or shape of matter once the latter is formed or well-developed. On this view the soul does not enter the embryo at birth but only at some hard to specify later time when the fetus is more fully developed. It may be noted, since women are of the concern of abortion, that Aquinas also held, "As regards the particular nature, woman is defective and misbegotten . . ." *Summa Theologica* I, Question 92 art. 2. The Catholic Council of Vienne of 1312 held the hylomorphic view and did not allow baptism of premature births unless the fetus had a human shape.

In holding this view the Catholic Jesuit philosopher J. Donceel wrote,

"I feel certain that there is no human soul, hence no human person, during the first few weeks of pregnancy, as long as the embryo remains in the vegetative state of its development."

After this there is a soul. But one might extend his view to point out that even at birth the baby is dependent and not complete.

Thus it is seen that the definition of an embryo as a human being is controversial even within the Catholic faith. It is hard to get metaphysics right.

Both Senator Edward Kennedy and President John Kennedy, though Catholic, opposed the imposition on all members of society a religious view concerning abortion. It was thought that to do so is to ignore separation of church and state.

4. All abortion is murder of the innocent. Abortion or directly destroying the embryo or fetus to save the mother's life is murder. The mother's life can only be saved if an operation on her is required, such as removal of a cancerous uterus. Then the abortion is regarded as an adjunct to the operation and is not really abortion. The Catholic view is not concerned with the consequences for man. If by aborting one embryo the rest of mankind would be saved from destruction then they would still favor not aborting that embryo.

In the first case to call an embryo "innocent" is to personify, misuse language and give a value judgment. "The embryo is innocent" is like "The cells are innocent," or "the innocent wind." In any case, it may not be innocent. If humans are guilty of original sin then at conception the embryo would be guilty and so not innocent — "the guilty embryo." The personification argument is carried to the extent that some Catholics have presented the argument that it is presumed that the unborn child would want to sacrifice his life for the life of the mother. In this case a weak argument may have desirable consequences.

5. Pope John XXIII wrote, "Human life is sacred — all men must recognize that fact. From its very inception it reveals the creating hand of God. Those who violate His laws . . . offend the divine majesty . . ." (*Mater et Magistra*, May 15, 1961)

What is striking about the Catholic view is its absolutism. It is absolute because based on divine authority. We should not "offend the divine majesty." But man must accept the responsibility, accept the consequences of his actions. To put the burden of responsibility on God is to avoid responsibility and avoid using one's intelligence to make decisions. The Catholic does, however, seem willing to accept the consequences of his views on abortion regardless of the harm they might cause.

One of the most important aspects of the religious controversy about abortion is that a minority of Catholics who do not wish to have abortions wish to impose on the majority of people a law which prevents anyone from having an abortion. This is a modern form of religious Inquisition involving review boards and lifelong suffering or the death of the mother. The American Civil Liberties Union states that constitutional abortion laws "are possibly violative of the First Amendment clause forbidding the establishment of religion [by the state] and guaranteeing the separation of church and state." (*The Right to Abortion* p. 21)

It may be noted that no non-religious association favors restrictive abortion laws but all of the major legal, medical, social, religious, etc. institutions oppose restrictive abortion laws. National Medical Assoc., United Church of Christ, American Psychological Assoc., American Health Assoc., and at least 60 other such organizations which are religious or non-religious oppose restrictive abortion laws. (NARAL 1972)

In fact, many or most Catholics themselves seem to favor abortion. The Catholic theologian Dr. Mary Daly stated that the Pregnancy Counseling Service in Boston advised 17,000 – 20,000 women seeking an abortion, and about 40 percent of these were Catholic. Dr. Daly herself favors the repeal of prohibitive abortion laws. (*National Catholic Reporter* 4-2-71) Many Catholics think abortion should be merely a matter of conscience. The President's Commission on Population Growth found that 39 percent of Catholics favor abortion, 50 percent believe that it should be performed under some circumstances, and 9 percent oppose it under any circumstance. A 1972 Gallop Poll shows that 54 percent of the Catholics interviewed think the decision to have an abortion should be up to the woman and her physician. There is even an 800-member Roman Catholics for Repeal of Abortion Laws organization in Pennsylvania.

One is in effect asked to accept Catholic and metaphysical belief. Consider a non-Catholic woman before the abortion examining board saying, "I would like to have an abortion because I am poor, ill, without a husband and supporting eight children," and receiving the reply, "We must now examine the theological and metaphysical question of the nature of being and the soul."

Catholics are prohibited by threat of excommunication, from performing or having abortions. Because this restriction would not allow Catholic physicians to carry out lawful legal procedures, perhaps their practice, in areas involving pregnancy and giving birth should be limited to Catholic patients. Catholic physicians are not even allowed to recommend another physician for the purpose of abortion. A woman on an operating table may learn too late or not at all, that her physician is a Catholic who believes in monstrous births, or that the fetus should live even at the expense of the mother. If legal penalties for having or performing an abortion are required, they perhaps should apply only to those who object to abortion.

Conclusion

The attempt has been made to present the various views of the abortion question. It was seen that the issue revolves around a number of unclear concepts such as life, death, person, emotion, soul, right, wrong, responsible, potential, natural, etc. It cannot be said either that an embryo is a person or is not a person. The goal here was only to present clarifications of these terms. One must be clear about what he in fact means by "person" or "human being." He often means by "human being" such things as "someone who is kind," "someone who behaves in a certain way," "someone I like." If one is not clear about which paradigms he holds, he may be involved in category-mistakes, naming fallacies, or take his metaphors literally. What view of "human being" an individual takes is up to him but there are consequences and intersubjective criteria.

It was argued that ethical statements ultimately rest on descriptive, factual and empirical considerations such as wants, needs, and one's objective knowledge of cause and effect. One's view about abortion can only be as clear as his view about these other concepts. Because values are ultimately determined in terms of the individual's own knowledge and desires he must determine for himself, on the basis of what has been said, what conclusion he wishes to draw. It is hoped that women will also be allowed to have the sort of intelligent free choice which will allow them to be potentially and actually emotionally fulfilled, intelligent and complete human beings. I do not wish to conclude that a woman should or should not have an abortion. But whatever decision or choice is made she and others will have to accept the consequences of her beliefs and actions.

Aaron Beck. *Depression* Univ. of Penn. 1967

Errol Bedford. "Emotions" *Essays in Philosophical Psychology* D. Gustafson, ed. New York: Doubleday 1964

Mary Calderone, ed. *Abortion in the United States* New York: Hoeber-Harper 1958

George Devereus. *A Study of Abortion in Primitive Societies* New York: Julian Press 1955

Joseph Donceel, S.J. "A Liberal Catholic's View" *Abortion in a Changing World* R. Hall, ed., New York: Columbia University Press 1970 pp. 39-45

R. Drake. *Abnormal Psychology* New Jersey: Littlefield 1966

Robert Hall, ed. *Abortion in a Changing World* New York: Columbia University Press 1970

Robert Hall. *A Doctor's Guide to Having an Abortion* New York: New American Library 1971

R. A. Kalish. "Some Variables in Death Attitudes" *Social Psychology* 59 (1) (1963) 137-145

A. I. Melden. "The Conceptual Dimensions of Emotions" *Human Action* T. Mischel, ed. New York: Academic Press 1969 pp. 119-211

National Association for Repeal of Abortion Laws (NARAL) (6-6-73 Bulletin) 250 West 57th St., New York, New York 10019

Thomas O'Donnell, S.J. "A Traditional Catholic's View" *Abortion in a Changing World* R. Hall, ed. New York: Columbia University Press 1970 pp. 34-38

The Right to Abortion Group for the Advancement of Psychiatry, New York: Scribner 1970

324

Warren Shibles. "A Defense of Animism" *Philosophical Pictures* 1971

————. *Emotions* Whitewater, Wisconsin: The Language Press 1973

————. "Ethics as Open-Context Terms" *Philosophical Pictures* 1971

————. *Philosophical Pictures* Dubuque, Iowa: Kendall-Hunt 1971

Edwin Shneidman. "Preventing Suicide" *The Psychology of Suicide* New York: Science House 1970

George Ulett and D. Goodrich. *A Synopsis of Contemporary Psychiatry* 4th edition, Saint Louis: Mosby Co. 1969

Ludwig Wittgenstein. *Lectures and Conversations on Aesthetics, Psychology and Religious Belief* C. Barrett, ed. Oxford: Basil Blackwell 1966 pp. 53-72

Religion

I CONTEMPORARY THEOLOGY

Religion involves statements, visions, perceptions, actions, objects, and behaviors. These easily become confused by overabstraction, category-mistake, or simple lack of thought. Ian Ramsey wrote,

"Too often have men talked as if the way to solve theological problems was by great familiarity with God, when what was needed was a patient and thorough examination of the language being used about him." (1967 preface)

Religious language such as "God," eternal life," etc. seem to name entities, we want them to name entities. But we never find what they are supposed to name. Why? The answer given here is that they name performances and activities experienced at the moment, have a meaning only in the linguistic and situational context of the moment, and that use of such words is their meaning. To think they name things is a naming-fallacy as unfounded as thinking that mind or time name objects in themselves. "Eternal," means on this view, only to point to such things as loneliness, despair, separation. For Ramsey, "Hell" is not a place, not a place, for example, with tables and chairs, not a place at all. D. M. MacKinnon in *New Essays in Philosophical Theology* wrote,

"One cannot if one is honest, ignore the extent to which metaphysical arguments, like those concerning immortality, have gained plausibility from a refusal to attend to the logic of our language." (p. 262)

Ramsey's approach to religion is very close to that of ordinary-language philosophers. The meaning of a term *is* its use in a language-game (i.e., as part of a language context and a certain situational context). To desire God may then mean only to wish one were more secure and less fragile. Ramsey further sees that metaphor especially, characterizes religion. In his chapter "Models and Qualifiers" in *Religious Language* he discusses God and God's attributes, e.g., the attributes "immutable," "perfection," "simplicity," "first cause," "infinitely wise," etc. Paradigms, characteristic situations, models or specific ordinary-language contexts are found in an attempt to elucidate these notions. In his *Models and Mystery* he presents the view that models and metaphors give us a unique insight into reality. No single metaphor can exhaust a subject matter. There is no single literal interpretation of a religion. In a metaphor two ideas cooperate in an inclusive meaning-giving "mystery" generating an insight or "disclosure" which is geared to the context of that insight and arises out of it: "A metaphor is always a signpost of some disclosure," "What is not verbally odd is void of disclosure power." Death may then be examined by exploration of metaphors.

John Wisdom also offers significant contributions toward the clarification of religious language. The following is an account in his article "Eternal Life." He begins,

"I fear that you will be disappointed in what I have to say. For I am going to talk about . . . those who when they speak of eternal life give to their words a meaning which carries no implication as to whether there is a life after death . . ."

This is to say that most think that "eternal life" names a state or entity or place somewhere. To think so is a naming fallacy. Thus it is feared the reader will be disappointed. Wisdom's approach is more basic. It is simply to look and see how the words "eternal life" are used in a specific, actual, living situation. How they are used will then constitute their meaning. Whether such words have an implication for there being a life after death "both are seeking a remedy against a sort of despair which comes not merely from the thought of death but from a disappointment with life together with the thought that it ends in death." This then is one use or meaning of talk of eternal life. "Eternal life" may mean one wants to avoid disappointment with life and avoid the thought that life ends in death. It does not mean that after death there is life or that it makes sense to talk of anything as being "eternal." We have perhaps no instance of anything within our experience which may make sense of the notion "eternal." It is as unfounded a notion as that time exists in itself. Time is merely change of objects. (Shibles, "Timelessness") There is no "eternal life" as such. There is only what comes from a close examination of what we say in specific contexts. "Eternal life" as an entity or name of a state or place offers us no intelligible context, and so not a desirable context or "place to be." The average man and the religious person are extremely metaphysical.

Again one may speak of "eternal life" if one is the sort of person who does not find the sort of contentment or pleasure he is looking for. The religious person often says that life on earth is not perfect, whereas life after death is. Wisdom gives us a description of such a person:

"He has tried many things and has found some pleasure in some but never the contentment he was looking for. He no longer expects to find it. He sees all things under the shadow of death which he believes to be the end of a man. His despair is expressed in the refrain 'All is vanity.' It is against such a pervasive despair that . . . those who when they speak of eternal life . . . have sought to present a remedy."

To expand this model may be suggestive. Desire for heaven and hell may be seen to be a selfish goal, and to be an excessive desire for pleasure. A "feeling of eternity" is merely a special feeling of well-being, security, beauty, etc. The feeling of immortality may also be a kind of pretending. This is what "hope" partly is. It is similar to William James' notion of a "will to believe." Pretending, however, can only make certain psychological things come true.

Also it may be seen that to view life under the perspective of
"eternity" is after all just *one* perspective. It has no more force
than another, but less, because both "eternity" and "life after
death" are obscure concepts. To speak about "eternal life" may
be like saying, "Look at it in the long run." The conclusion may
be reached that the ultimate good is staying alive.

At the end of discussions about "God" or "eternal life"
there are always a few who say, "Now I don't care what the
arguments are, I still believe in these things." This may only
mean "I'm tired of thinking," or "Let's go on to something
else."

Wisdom's method of reducing religious terms to concrete
actual usages in our everyday experience is represented by the
words of Buddha which he quotes:

"Accordingly, Malunkaputta, bear always in mind what it
is that I have not elucidated . . . I have not elucidated,
Malunkaputta, that the world is eternal . . . I have not
elucidated that the soul and the body are identical, I have
not elucidated that the soul is one thing and the body
another; I have not elucidated that the saint exists after
death, I have not elucidated that the saint does not exist
after death: I have not elucidated that the saint both
exists and does not exist after death . . . And what,
Malunkaputta, have I elucidated? Misery, the origin of
misery . . . the cessation of misery . . . The path leading to
the cessation of misery have I elucidated."

To talk of "eternal life" is talk of avoiding misery. "Eternal
life" means "avoidance of misery." It is not to talk of a length
of time of a world, a soul "surviving" a body, or a special place
with gardens one will travel to. "Eternity" in this sense has
nothing to do with time. And since time is change, "eternity"
has nothing to do with changes of objects or experiences.
"Eternal" and "forever" only refer to things like long roads,
interesting vistas, the length of a ball of kite string one does not
intend to completely unwind. Wisdom wrote about Spinoza's
confused concept of "eternity" or "under a species of
eternity":

"It is worth thinking of a very clear instance of this so that we are better prepared to recognize less clear instances of it."

Wisdom states that one may not know what he means by certain statements yet still find a use for them, e.g., "speed at an instant," "God exists." We *may* find a use, any use, but we may also be misled. We have used the word "time" usefully but it has also greatly misled us into thinking of it as an entity in itself. Also, Wisdom's example of "speed at an instant" may easily be reduced to intelligible relations and paradigms of changes which are clear to us. On the other hand, even false theories or religious concepts can be helpful in *some* respect or other, just as the cruellest war may have *some* desirable effects. Wisdom's point seems to be in part that religious terms have a use rather than a naming function. They play a part in a person's life. Both "damn," and "God" have such uses. In speaking of "ghost" we may really mean our memory of a person. Or ghost may be the crude vision of that of which we are ignorant, the unknown. That is, our use of ghost may suggest that we mean by it a memory of our ignorance of the nature of something. The mind is now called the "ghost in the machine" by Gilbert Ryle *(Concept of Mind)*. The container theory of mind, or mind thought of as an entity, are rejected except by the average person — for him the body is still haunted.

One use or meaning which "God exists" may have in our lives is that of saying that we are ignorant and must inquire. I do not mean to suggest that religious persons inquire, but to speak of "God exists" may reflect at least some desire to. In looking to see what we are actually saying when we use language, we must consider subtle concrete kinds of analogies and contexts. Such statements as "God exists" are seen to be useless as descriptions. They only have meaning as a use in terms of our concrete experiences. Contemporary theologians now attempt to make obscure religious terms meaningful by reducing them to concrete experiences which are intelligible. "There is eternal life," then, refers to a wide range of experiences and uses none of which is a description. To take "eternal life" literally rather than as a use or to take it as metaphorical is to create a myth as well as to ignore what the person who uses the term is really experiencing. Of course, one often speaks of "eternal life" because he has learned to, and he may think that somehow it refers to something. He has in this sense already created or taken on the myth.

The terms "beyond" and "transcend" are especially relevant here. They lead to false analogies. But "There is a house beyond the hill" is not like "There is a life beyond death," or "There is something beyond our experience." We become captivated by the model of "beyond." We do know what it is like to go beyond a hill or a present moment, but the misuse comes in when we speak of going beyond time, beyond life, beyond experience, beyond consciousness (we are even *conscious* of having dreamt and having been unconscious). And it is no good to speak of "the beyond," as such. It is no place. Still when having a certain aesthetic experience one is tempted to say he has a feeling of the beyond or that by viewing the beauty of nature he transcends or feels that there is something beyond. Beyond and transcend here, however, only refer to the aesthetic or elevating experience one is having at the time. It does not refer to or describe a beyond. The experience may more accurately be called an aesthetic experience than a feeling of the beyond. The experience is such that for a moment one imagines that there is some wonderful thing or person he has not yet seen. Beyond means beyond our past experience, a new experience. An aesthetic experience can be so fulfilling that one wants to hang onto it, to walk into the sunset forever, into the beyond. Why not? The poet Wallace Stevens wrote that everything depends on experiences such as seeing a duck on a pond at sunset. One has the feeling of transcending, of going "beyond." It is the experience of being on the brink. If only, or with the right help, one might transcend into that which is beyond. It can in a sense be very simple to do. Dylan Thomas, for example, would simply raise his arms beside him and fly, fly out of the window and over the barnyard, welsh towns and sea.

Now, in speaking of "eternal life," Wisdom says that we are sometimes referring to experiences of the sort expressed by saying "Time seemed to stop," or "Time stopped." He describes this experience as follows:

"There have been times when in an extraordinary degree I have seen things in that way. At such times I have felt a joy, a contentment, which no regrets for the past nor fears for the future could take from me."

One may similarly have the feeling at times of having great mental power, of having supreme ability and knowledge. But if we accept such experiences honestly and at face value we find they are experiences like others, very pleasant, but revealing nothing mystical, metaphysical, or religious. They are not special contacts with a "beyond." Of this Wisdom adds,

"But what truth, over and above the truth that he has had a certain sort of experience, did he learn from that experience? What truth is he trying to convey to us? I can't say. I don't know."

To argue that one has a mystical truth it does not help to say "This is an ineffable truth." It misses the real use of the experience. No truth was had. What is meant by "I have an ineffable truth" is merely a certain feeling or emotion. Scotch and drugs may produce similar "truths" or "feelings of eternity." As experiences they cannot be denied, but to consider them descriptive statements or truths is another question.

When confronted with and trying to understand a writer who was asserting that "there is a way to eternal life," Wisdom wrote,

"I was in difficulty . . . At first I thought of my difficulty as like that of one who is confident that someone has given a new meaning to old words but is not clear what that new meaning is."

The theologian, Paul Tillich, in his article "Eternal Now" makes most of the mistakes discussed above. His errors are these: 1) He treats time and eternity as if they name entities in themselves, whereas they only refer to relations of changes of objects and experiences. In opposition to Tillich's view, there is no time or eternity as such. 2) He does not see that time words and religious terms have concrete intelligible paradigms, that is, he does not look carefully to see how language works and so becomes captivated by it, takes his metaphors literally. Tillich makes the following statements:

1. "Praying means elevating oneself to the eternal." Here eternity is regarded as naming an entity, "the eternal."

2. "There is no other way of judging time than to see it in the light of the eternal." "Eternal" *means* time, and so time is to be judged in terms of time. This is a circular statement. It also shows that he thinks that time names an entity. In part it restates the religious model of attempting to regard each moment as subsumed under a species, or from the perspective or point of view of eternity, and then giving primacy to this perspective. But this assumes we know what eternity is.

3. "If we were totally within time, we would not be able to elevate ourselves in prayer, meditation, and thought to the eternal."

Time is change and so we cannot be within or outside of time, nor do we change in time. We change without time. Time is merely elliptical for various changes such as the movement of the hands of a clock. Tillich is now captivated by the almost unnoticeable word "within." It is a metaphor he takes literally.

4. "We speak of time in three ways or modes: the past, the present, and future. Every Child is aware of them, but no wise man has even penetrated their mystery."

If time is mysterious then one can, it is thought here, relate it to religious mystery such as suggested by "eternal," "God," "beyond," "transcendent," etc. But this is an argument from ignorance. Two unknown things are alike, alike because we know little about either one. Lewis Carroll's Alice says that the things she saw were all alike in that she did not know what any one of them was. One meaning of "eternal" is that we are ignorant of certain things. But the assumption that "no wise man has ever penetrated their [time, the past, present, or future] mystery," is false. There is no past, present, or future as such, for the same reason that there is no time in itself. The past is not a place or entity, nor can the future become the present or the past. Nor can time "pass" or go "on and on" to yield eternity. The past is merely a certain kind of change, for example, that which we can do nothing about, and Tillich suggests something like this when he says, "We can make the past remain nothing but *past*. The act in which we do this has been called 'repentance.' " He states that we thus "discard them [elements of one's experience] into the past as something that no longer has any power over the present." The future is not time, but changes we can bring about. The present is the changes and experiences we are engaged in. To think the future becomes the present and the past, is to hold a misleading literal picture: ⌿Past ⁄ Present ⁄ Future ⁄ One would then ask how long the present is, that is, how thick must be the line separating the future from the past. When is the present? How can a future become a present? Such questions show that the model misleads. It misleads because the past, the present, and the future are thought to name entities. In addition if they name entities it is not clear what evidence we have for such entities, or how one of them, e.g., the future, can "pass" to become another, e.g., the past, or why future does not just become past without the thin line of the present. Tillich does say at one point that there is for Christ no historical past, but that He is beyond or above time. But we are *all* above time because time does not exist. We live in a timeless world, but nevertheless a changing world. The "eternal present" use of "I am" suggests this.

He also sees a difficulty with how the future can become the past, but is unable to resolve it. This is because he assumes that there is a past, present, and future as such. He states,

"The mystery of the future and the mystery of the past are united in the mystery of the present. . . . Is not the present moment gone when we think of it? Is not the present the ever-moving boundary line between past and future? But a moving boundary is not a place to stand upon."

He then gives up on the question as a mystery:

"The riddle of the present is the deepest of all the riddles of time. Again, there is no answer except from that which comprises all time and lies beyond it — the eternal."

The general point, in opposition to Tillich, is time words may be seen clearly as reducible to relations of changes without a residue of mystery. Time does not pass, rather objects change. One does not become old as such, he rather changes in certain ways. To see what time is is not difficult. One need only look at what we do when we tell time and use time words. To break away from what people usually and misleadingly say about time is very difficult, e.g., that "time passes," "time marches on," "time flies," "save time," etc. Such expressions are usually taken literally when they are actually metaphors or disguised jokes. Tillich's view of time rests on a disguised joke: the "eternal now." The expression is also in one sense a contradiction, paradox and oxymoron. This is why he calls it a mystery. But metapnors based on confused time words cannot yield an interesting mystery.

5. "We come from the eternal ground of time and return to the eternal ground of time."

6. "The eternal stands above past and future."

Now, eternal begins to mean something other than time. Christ said, "I am the alpha and the omega, the beginning and the end." The "eternal now" begins to refer to a person and to his present experiences. We should have knowledge of the end of our lives to give insight into our present experiences. Thus, in effect, Tillich's model for time is to reduce it to experiential changes and relationships. What he said earlier about eternity, time, past, future, etc. is irrelevant now. The view that time is an experience is a defensible model, although Tillich is not aware that this is the model he is using. He is, without knowing it, reducing time to experiential change. He will, however, go on to struggle with and try to bring us back to the notion of a mysterious time in itself.

7. "We have a beginning as we have an end."

There is no context for such a statement. Beginning and end of what? "Everything comes to an end which has a beginning," might be a circular statement. It only means we see things in terms of the model of beginning and ending, each term implying the other. Can we have a beginning or end as such and in itself? The beginning and end cannot be in time for there is no time. If there is no time then knowledge is only of the moment and since death is supposedly an event in "future time" we cannot know death.

Death is only a certain kind of presence. Our present feelings as present have no limits. Feuerbach wrote,

"Immortal life is the full life, rich in contents . . . Every moment of life is of infinite importance and significance, for its own sake, posited by itself and fulfilled in itself, an unlimited affirmation of its own self, every moment of life is like a draught which empties completely the cup of infinity." (Choron 1963 p. 191)

If time is observed change, when observed change ends, time ends. Time is nothing to a stone. A stone to itself cannot grow old. Nor can it grow old to us. To speak this way is to personify. Thus we do not, after we die, become very old. Death is not a state. It does not begin or end. One cannot be early or late for death. It makes no sense to ask how long death lasts. It may in one sense be like an achievement word such as "to win" or "to lose." It takes no time to die, win, lose. They have no duration.

"We have a beginning" might only mean something like "I now consciously contemplate that I was born." that is, that this birth is a certain kind of change I am led to think of. To say "I was born" seems to suggest that I was there to witness the event. I am imagining a picture. The picture I imagine is now. I do not have the knack of going back in "time," nor can I compare yesterday's image with today's. Yesterday's image is only available today and so can only be today's image.

The same arguments apply to an end or our death. One speaks about his death as if he can witness his own funeral, his own lack of consciousness. It seems easy enough: my body is lying there, there are flowers and people gathered around. But this overlooks one fact. I cannot be there to picture it, I cannot imagine my inability to imagine. I have in one sense nothing within my experience to relate that experience to, just as there is no intelligible model for infinity *within* our experience. It makes no sense to talk of the beginning or end of the world in the same sense that we might talk of, for example, the beginning and end of a storm. Evidence and clarification is needed for such a beginning or ending. In another sense I can have and fabricate all kinds of analogies and pictures.

8. We should speak about the eternal which is neither timeless nor endless time. The mystery of the future is answered in the eternal of which we may speak in images taken from time. But if we forget that the images are images, we fall into absurdities and self-deceptions. There is no time after time, but there is eternity *above* time."

He sees that eternal may be spoken of metaphorically by analogies to time words. Thus eternal is now treated as non-temporal. If eternal is not a time word, he could speak of it as a concrete experience of change, or as a mysterious, religious, transcendental event. Here he chooses to do the latter and to speak about being "above time." The question is, is there evidence for such an eternity above time? The eternal is here just an assumed or presupposed synonym for God. In the next quote he refers to it as a "power."

9. "Each of the modes of time has its peculiar mystery . . . Each of them drives us to an ultimate question. There is *one* answer to these questions – the eternal. There is *one* power which surpasses the all-consuming power or time – the eternal: He who was and is and is to come, the beginning and the end. He gives us forgiveness for what has passed; He gives us courage for what is to come. He gives us rest in His eternal presence."

Tillich's arguments rest on our confusions about time and time words such as present, past, future. Because we are ignorant of such things, it might help to look at time from the point of view of the eternal, where eternal is somehow above time. The argument is circular and assumes that the eternal is God. It also applies only to those who are as confused about time as is Tillich — however, he does at places struggle with the concept. He gives some insight when he attempts to reduce time words to experiences, for example, in speaking of the past in terms of repentance and forgiveness.

He takes the eternal God to be what time means whereas what time is is the very experience one now enjoys, the experience of change. The "eternal now" is not God, it is merely a certain kind of experience. It is, of course, "above" or outside of time because there is no time as such.

Tillich's view in this article illustrates the logical consequences of being confused about time and about how our language works. He becomes captivated by his language and by taking his metaphors literally. The result is self-deception. One must, however, be sympathetic with Tillich's attempt for it is a great task to overcome one's previous views as well as common beliefs.

338

II. REVIEW OF D. Z. PHILLIPS *DEATH AND IMMORTALITY**

D. Z. Phillips' book, *Death and Immortality,* is a healthful book in most ways. It is correctly claimed that this is more than a survey. It is argued that "the notions of the survival of non-material bodies, disembodied spirits or new bodies, after death, all seem open to fatal logical objections." (xi) Phillips further argues that immortality is the antithesis of moral concern. Much of what is said here was said in, for example, Wisdom's "Eternal Life" in *Talk of God* (Vol. II 1967-1968). His views explicitly follow those especially of Wittgenstein, A. Flew and Peter Geach in the tradition of ordinary-language philosophy. He seems, however, to modify such views right away for he says that there can be thought without language or action: "Not all the thoughts that pass through his mind issue directly in word and deed . . . There is no question of doing or saying anything about the changes brought about by contemplation . . ." (p. 9) He, without evidence, presupposes that there are thoughts as such, and that there can be thoughts without language, word, object, or image. We have no evidence for such thoughts or ideas. By thinking we mean using language (even without speaking or writing it, i.e., silently) or doing something. We must use language even to speak of or use the word "thinking." Phillips uses a statement by Rush Rhees to support his view about private thought but even Rhees says in that quote, "None of this [thinking] would be possible without language; and the lover's thoughts are in the language of love." (10)

Because of Phillips' disregard of language he maintains that there is a private "inner" life of thought and assumes that thoughts and ideas are some kind of inner entity. He does admit that thought must be connected with common outer activity and a common language but this does not save his view of the independence of thought. (W. Shibles "Linguo-Centric . . .")

Phillips says, "Death is not an experience, but the end of all experiences, and one cannot experience the end of experience."

Reprinted from *Southern Journal of Philosophy* 10, no. 3 (1972) 391-394

(13) But perhaps it would be more careful to say merely that the "end of experience" has no use for us, that we are simply ignorant of what it would mean to speak of the end of experience. And he himself gives this correction in a following paragraph: "Our language, it might be said, is too confined to tell us anything about the world beyond the grave." (14)

A significant contribution to clarification concerning the concept of death is given by pointing out that our language concerning it is largely based on misleading or unfounded analogy, such as Saint Paul's simile of the corpse as a planted seed which will rise to grow again. It is misleading and fallacious to assert the likeness:

a) If you plant a seed a flower will appear.
b) If you plant a human body a new resurrected body will appear.

The observation is also made that "life after death" is a contradiction and in any case is not an assertion which can be true or false. The question is rather whether it is meaningful at all. (15) The conclusion is reached that belief in immortality as a belief in the existence of a non-material body is "riddled with difficulties and confusions" and "rests not only on one mistake but on a large number of mistakes." (17) In addition, it is pointed out that if there is not afterlife then moral strivings or punishments based on an afterlife are to be rejected. (19) He then considered "life after death" not as literal statement or statement about soul separating from body etc., but metaphorically, though he does not speak of metaphor. He quotes MacKinnon ("Death" *New Essays in Philosophical Theology*) to the effect that the expression "life after death" really means something which is characteristically human, and "takes shape through such expression," and it is suggested that the expression communicates something which cannot be expressed. But need there be a secret in this? "Life after death" seems not to be intelligible as a descriptive use and so may make sense as some other sort of use, e.g., to express hope. Phillips attempts to give the phrase a new paradigm or meaning by regarding it as a comment on the kind of life a man is leading. (44) Thus the soul for him is not descriptive of an entity or incorporeal substance. To ask about one's soul is only to ask about what kind of life a man is living. Thus expressions involving soul are not literal descriptive expressions and entities but metaphorical statements about one's behavior.

Such statements *show* their use in their context. They do not literally or tersely describe or tell their use. God is not an entity but serves a function in such contexts as that of prayer.

Phillips similarly sees that "eternal" is an obscure term and he suggests that it be only regarded as referring to our lives considered in light of certain moral and religious beliefs. Eternity as such does not exist. It is not an extension of our present life. (49) He does, however, slip into Platonism in stating, "Eternal life is the reality of goodness . . ." (48) Goodness needs also to be reduced to a clear concrete paradigm. What could absolute, contextless "goodness" be? In any case, for him immortality, soul, and eternity are terms having a use concerning only this our life and our way of living it. Such terms supposedly refer to our self-renunciation, as there is no necessity that man should live. His paradigms of God are only things like forgiving, thinking, loving, etc., in the contexts of contemplation, attention, renunciation. There is no God as such, or reality of God.

Phillips states the paradigms which apply to language about the dead. "Eternal" as applied to immortality only means things such as the fact that "the will of the dead cannot be changed." One's state is fixed forever. But we do not know what it is not to change at all, to be "fixed forever." Such fixing is only relative to one perspective not all. There is no known absolute zero of change. One may no longer speak, but nevertheless his body continues to change.

Flew is attacked for assuming one can "picture" one's own funeral in a literal sense. A correction is offered to the effect that statements such as, "I can picture my own funeral," have no intelligible descriptive literal use but do have intelligible paradigms or metaphorical uses. By envisioning one's own funeral, as for example, Scrooge did, one may give a new perspective to his life. This perspective is, then, one possible use or meaning of "I can witness my own funeral." It allows one to consider his life as a whole. One takes religious and metaphysical questions as metaphorical and mythical statements reducible to some present contextual meaning and use. This is how we take fairy tales, and traditional myths. We see what meaning they might have for our lives. Frazer's work on myths is, therefore, here appropriately discussed. What strikes us as terrible in the myths is itself what gives birth to the myths. The myths make us fearful. The story gives rise to certain views and this is all that is meant by them. This is the ordinary language view that a) the meaning of a word, e.g., God, is its use in a language-game, and b) to find out the full use one must examine its context. But it could be that Phillips allows too much here. The use could be based on a schizophrenic or fanatic religious view or on a fallacious assessment. One may "live by" religious terms, but these terms may be fallacious or misguiding as paradigms of usage. That is, we need not assume that all terms have healthful or intelligible paradigms and uses. Perhaps much of religious language is language which does not. Perhaps also there are better paradigms according to which one may organize his life. He sees this objection, however, when he states, "I am not saying that religious beliefs are never confused . . . Perhaps more often than not the believer's faith is a complex tangle of beliefs and confused accounts of those beliefs." (69-70)

Phillips' account rests heavily on the concept of "universe of discourse," although he does not use the expression. He states that some speak religious language and some do not. Those who do not cannot contradict the religious speaker. W. M. Urban in *Language and Reality* explored and developed the theory that each universe of discourse has its own criteria of truth, meaning, and intelligibility. This view is here rendered in terms of language-games, contexts, and uses. Nevertheless, a universe of discourse, e.g., of religion, changes from within, and in addition may be found later to be unintelligible language. Certainly the speakers of a certain universe of discourse *think* they are making sense, but they may be shown that they are deluding themselves. Phillips, then, in stating "the man who has no use for the religious picture is not contradicting the believer," may be wrong. (76)

One may point out conceptual confusions, and the religious believer may come, as I think he often has, to give up much of his religious language and paradigms of religious terms. Phillips' own account is a fine example of just such revision of religious language. It gets the religious person or theologian to cease taking religious language literally and to begin finding some more intelligible paradigms for such language. This perhaps cannot always be effectively done, and one may begin to see that other metaphors, models, or "pictures" may be more intelligent, honest, and useful. Phillips at times suggests this: "A religious picture loses its hold on a person's life because a rival picture wins his allegiance." (74)

His assumption that religious disagreement is like disagreement of evaluative judgment rests on a mistake. The mistake is the implication that ethical, moral or evaluative statements are in themselves meaningful. They are not. Ethical terms such as "good," "right," "ought," etc., are open-context terms which imply a great many substitution instances but in themselves say nothing. One person could mean by "x is good" what another person means by "x is bad." All ethical or evaluative terms reduce to descriptive non-ethical terms such as statements about likes, wants, consequences. To say "x is good" may mean "I like x," or "x is in accordance with the law," etc. As naturalistic descriptions, then, evaluative situations *can* be argued. One evaluative statement, then, by clarification and reduction to descriptive terms, is seen not to be as "good" as another or as useful as another. It is the specific wants, contexts, consequences, etc., alone which need to be rationally examined. The inquiry should be adequate, but it is rational inquiry in any case. Thus, against Phillips, the disbeliever can contradict the believer, and evaluative or moral judgment can be resolved.

A "universe of discourse" is self-justificatory as long as there are speakers of it. Phillips utilizes Wittgenstein's notion of a "form of life" to express the givenness of such universes of discourse, and of religious language-games. Certainly our language is given, in terms of having an epistemological primacy. But fallacy and category-mistakes are uses given too. They also are language-games. And one may become captivated by a model.

He says that if a moral or religious picture goes in decline there is often no substitute for it. (77) This would perhaps be better put in terms of the logic of metaphor. A metaphor cannot be reduced to literal statement without remainder, and since religious language is highly metaphorical this would also be true of religious language. He speaks of a new "seeing-as." Certainly metaphors do say something, something given, which can be said no other way. This is the stuff that poets are made on. This book is excellent in reducing religious language to concrete paradigms of actual ordinary language uses and language-games, but the gain for religious language as self-justificatory is not attained.

III. RELIGIOUS ANALOGY

The religious approach is often presented in terms of analogies. These presuppose already accepted religious beliefs, otherwise they would appear entirely unfounded. Glenn Asquith offers a typical presentation in his book, *Death Is All Right.*
He says death is all right because it is:

1. an adjournment. As we depart from friends so we depart from life.
2. one common experience. As we share with some so in death we may share with all for all must die regardless of class or wealth.
3. a return to our source. It is assumed that since objects we make have sources, we too have a source.
4. the other end of things.
5. reparation. As a doctor stops pain so death does also. [This seems like curing a disease by killing the patient.]
6. restoration. As a building may be restored, at death a new body is restored from the old one.
7. the place of answers. As we learn answers from books, at death we will learn the answers of life, e.g., who really wrote Shakespeare, etc.
8. the redemption of promises. Death is all right because just as an author of a mystery story reveals the solution, so at death the mystery of life will be revealed.
9. the opened storehouse. Death will be like an opened department store at Christmas. God wouldn't have us experience part of such goods in this life without opening up the rest at death. [Asquith's materialistic side]
10. a focus. Death is like getting new glasses enlarging our vision so that everything is constantly and clearly in focus.
11. the reason for life's preparation. Life is a preparation for death and the next life.

12. a glad encounter with God. Death is "God's final benefit." "Think of death as coming from an icy night into a warm lighted room where someone has prepared every cheer and comfort."

This last analogy may be reinterpreted such that instead of speaking of death and afterlife as a warm, cheerful room, we may let the room be what we in fact mean by a religious view of afterlife. That is, "eternal life" only means "a warm, cheerful room" we now experience. All of the above analogies are obviously imagined and baseless. They are not honest inquiries into what one knows or has evidence for. They are not arguments although they are often taken to be such. One may say that just as we plant a flower seed in the ground, a flower will grow, so when we plant or bury a body a new body will be resurrected. This is a dishonest and misleading analogy, not an acceptable argument. It already presupposes the doctrine of resurrection. It is important then to see when one is using an analogy and a metaphor so as not to be captivated by them, or regard them as arguments when they are not.

The view above (No. 7) that death is "the place of answers," that at death one will have all knowledge, appears false. Death is not a state or experience as such. We do not say, "Yesterday I had a problem with death." Death has no duration, does not begin or end. "You cannot know what death is until you die." Compare this with "I know what it feels like to be a rock." Feuerbach: "Don't be snobbish, condescend to the stone, get the feeling of that which is deprived of feeling." It is not the case that at death one becomes more intelligent. Death is not a way of observing things. If death were a place of answers perhaps it would make more sense to become religious after rather than before death.

IV. DEATH IN THE BIBLE: THE OLD TESTAMENT

According to the Greek view, at death the soul or shades enter the earth, wait for initial judgment, cross the river *Styx.* Then the guilty take the left road to Tartarus over a river of fire, the *Pyriphlegthon.* The righteous take the right road to the Elysian Fields. Those not yet purified return to earth in new bodies. The *Old Testament* (OT) presents somewhat similarly the view that the dead are in a lower world, *Sheol* and are shades, shadows, or ghosts. Generally, there is no view of an afterlife. Afterlife is simply an unknown. In several places there is brief mention of a resurrection but it is otherwise absent: Isaiah 26.19 "Thy dead shall live, their bodies shall rise," and Daniel 12:12. The dead do come up for the necromander, however (I Samuel 28:13). The deceased joins his ancestors in Sheol in a kind of vague shadow-life. It is not like the Christian view of personal immortality. Although the Greeks, e.g., Plato and Aristotle, presented a dualism of body and soul whereby the soul survives intact after the death of the body, the OT makes no such distinction. Man does not have an immortal element, a soul, but is just one unified total person. *Nefesh* refers to the total person not to soul. It may at times mean "I," "self," or "principle of life," but not a soul separate from body. In general, the OT regards death as an unknown. Very little is said to make it intelligible. The same is true of the *New Testament* although it adds the doctrine of resurrection. In the OT there was only community survival, survival of Israel. Death is regarded as a rather natural event. The following statements characterize the *Old Testament* on death:

Job 17:14 "I have said to corruption, thou art my father: to the worm, thou art my mother, and my sister."

Man is seen to become at one with nature (especially after a difficult life).

Job 17:26 "They shall lie down alike in dust, and the worms shall cover them."

The stress on worms as representing death plays a significant role in art and poetry.

Psalms 144:4 "Man is like to vanity: his days are as a shadow that passeth away."

This is depicted in "vanity" scenes in paintings. A man is seen with a lit candle and skull which reminds him of his transience and fate.

Eccl. 5:15 "As he came forth of his mother's womb, naked shall he return to go as he came, and shall take nothing of his labor, which he may carry away in his hand."

This again stresses the view that life is short and all must die. It places stress on the avoidance of doing and acquiring trivial things in this life.

Eccl. 9:4 "To him that is joined to all the living there is hope."

Immortality is often thought of as only the survival of the community or one's ancestors. The emphasis is on relations in society not on another life.

Eccl. 9:10 "Whatsoever thy hand findeth to do, do it with thy might, for there is no work, nor device, nor knowledge, nor wisdom, in the grave, whither thou goest."

Death is final without divine enlightenment. Therefore live now.

Prov. 10:25 "The years of the wicked shall be shortened."

This suggests that those who do deeds harmful to society are, like those violating a social taboo, thereby bringing about "voodoo death." They will feel guilt, and tend to be unhappy, nervous and so psychosomatically cause their own early death. The OT places stress on moral social living rather than on an afterlife. Some tribes give vows such as, "If I wronged this man may I die within a year." Deaths sometimes follow such vows.

Ezek. 18:4 "The soul that sinneth, it shall die."

"Soul" means whole person. The person who chooses to oppose society creates for himself a social death which leads to a physical death. He dies also in that no one will remember him. Similar passages are:

Proverbs 10:2 "Righteousness delivers from death."

Proverbs 12:28 "In the path of righteousness is life, but the way of error leads to death."

This view also relates to ancient medicine or faith-healing. If one thinks he will get better it may help him do so in the case of certain diseases of a psychological sort. It also relates to belief, as in the following passage:

Psalms 68:20 "Our God is a God of salvation; and to God, the Lord, belongs escape from death."

One may rephrase this. *If* one believes in God, he will be saved. This works as does hypnosis. If one believes in it, it works. It is not an argument for truth but more like hypnosis. If you *think* or *believe* you will be saved then you will because of your very belief. In this sense it would be true that if you believe in a God of salvation, you will be saved.

The meaning of God and Death in the OT has more to do with moral behavior of the living than with statements about an afterlife or the nature of death. The terms "God," "death," etc. have meaning only for social behavior, faith healing, and have some relevance to ancient medicine.

Sheol and death may be thought of as analogous to human social injustices and situations rather than as descriptions of places. Judaism which bases its beliefs on the OT has no dogmatic belief about an afterlife.

V DEATH IN THE NEW TESTAMENT

With the New Testament (NT) comes an increasing belief in resurrection of the individual instead of just a communal resurrection of Israel. On some interpretations the doctrine of the soul was added and is sometimes interpreted to carry on the Greek belief in the soul. The Catholic view interprets the Bible according to St. Thomas Aquinas who adapted Aristotle's philosophy, including form-matter, soul-body distinctions to religion. The view that man has a separate soul appears to be more Greek than biblical. A popular child's prayer goes, "If I should die before I wake, I pray the Lord my soul to take." Mention of death is stressed even for children. In the Sunday school tract, "A Child's Guide to Holiness," we find the apologetic words "Fear not, thou dying child, though life's day is drawing to a close . . . Life on earth is misery compared to the joy that shall be yours in heaven." There is an unclear notion of heaven and hell. Some think everyone will be saved, others only a few.

About the view of resurrection, Tertullian wrote, "The Son of God died; This is believable because it does not make sense. And after he was buried, he rose again, this is quite certain, because it is impossible." (Choron p. 86) Some views of death presented in the NT are as follows:

I Cor. 15:26 "The last enemy that shall be destroyed is death."

Death is a major concern of the Bible yet little insight is given into the concept.

I Cor. 15:55 "O death, where is thy sting? O grave, where is thy victory?" 15:56 "The sting of death is sin."

By the belief that one will be saved death is thought to be conquered.

Rev. 20:12 "And I saw the dead, small and great, stand before God . . . and the dead were judged . . . according to their works."

One is judged according to his moral behavior. It is a statement about life not death. And it is not clear what death has to do with one's moral behavior. One is judged here in order to make society better, it would seem. The judgment takes place at resurrection:

I Cor. 15:52 "For the trumpet shall sound, and the dead shall be raised incorruptible, and shall be changed."

I Cor. 15:51 "Behold I show you a mystery; We shall not all sleep, but we shall all be changed."

The analogy is often presented that the righteous will attain a new body after death just as a seed planted becomes a plant.

The emphasis on resurrection is also a deemphasis on this life. There is contradiction here. Most biblical terms have reference to our moral actions in this life, e.g., sin, yet we are told that this life is of little importance:

Phil. 1:21 "For me to live is Christ, and to die is gain."

And the OT states:

Eccl. 7:1 "The day of death is better than the day of one's birth."

In the Middle Ages and Renaissance this became the Christian slogan, "*mors melior vita*" (death is better than life). W. Wallis wrote in his book, *Religion in Primitive Society* (1939),

"In some parts of Europe, as late as the last century, universal suicide was preached by fervent missionaries who represented it as the only means of escape from the snares of Antichrist, the only assured way of eluding earthly sins and sorrows and securing the eternal joys of heaven . . . Priests, monks and laymen preached salvation by flame. They seduced children [into suicide] by promises of gay clothes, apples, nuts, and honey in heaven . . . Thousands of men, women and children rushed into the flames and were destroyed." (p. 281)

Members of the Christian sect Circumcelliones, often jumped from cliffs to their death on the rocks below. Albigensian heretics brought about their own death by Endura which is the hastening of death by fasting and bleeding.

As with the OT, the NT presents the view that if one believes then he will be saved. As was pointed out, this is a circular statement or one which works as does self-hypnotism:

John 5:24 "He that heareth my word, and believeth on him that sent me, hath everlasting life . . ."

An alternate version of this is,

Rev. 21:8 "All liars, shall have their part in the lake which burneth with fire and brimstone . . ."

It may seem that the religious person believing as he does in fictious myths or make-believe and taking it for truth, is himself a dishonest liar. But it does not make sense to lie where it does not make sense to tell the truth. But as a form of circularity and self-hypnosis the statement appears true, i.e., *if* one does not believe he will not be saved.

The Bible is in a long tradition of primitive medical and religious practices, rituals, customs. One of these is the tribal custom of eating the flesh of the deceased in order to gain the person's power of knowledge. It is a type of cannibalism. The tradition is suggested in the following:

John 6:51 "I am the living bread which came down from heaven: if any man eat of this bread, he shall live forever: and the bread that I will give is my flesh . . . " John 5:53 "Then Jesus said unto them . . . Except ye eat the flesh of the Son of man, and drink his blood, ye have no life in you."

Taken metaphorically this may mean that one should act in a moral way in society.

Rom. 5:12 "Wherefore, as by one man [Adam] sin entered into the world, and death by sin; and so death passed upon all men, for that all have sinned."

This and eternal punishment is perhaps the most cruel proclamation passed upon mankind. When a man is born he is already found guilty. The strangeness of this suggests that we must have mistranslated this passage or be taking it the wrong way. Talk of sin is usually talk of sex. Even marriage is prohibited by some parts of the Bible. (Luke 20:35) That man is guilty of seeking and needing sex often causes much psychological harm. Certainly man's sexual desire is strong, and it often leads him to his downfall, but this does not mean that he should abstain from sex (sin) entirely. It may rather be that society does not as yet adequately meet his needs. Put differently, it is hard to see what one's sexual activity has to do with death if such activity does no one any harm. Why is sex regarded as sinful in itself?

Rom. 8:16 "To be carnally minded is death."

This could mean that it can lead one into socially harmful situations.

I Tim. 5:6 "But she that liveth in pleasure is dead while she liveth."

It would be strange to object to pleasure. But this statement may relate to the fact that one may sometimes seek only selfish pleasure at the expense of others. It is also in the Platonic tradition of a denial of the body in favor of a release of a "pure" soul. "Pure" functions in a strange sense here because there is no evidence for a soul or spirit, except an outdated medical view that life is caused by breath (or spirit). The case against sin is put clearly:

Rom. 6:23 "The wages of sin is death."

As with the OT one's concern with the violations of social taboos may bring about one's [voodoo-like, or psychosomatic] death. This is exemplified by:

2 Corinthians 7:10 "Worldly grief produces death."

It is thought that Christ died so that man may live, that this was the biblical miracle. Even today men are pronounced dead but later found to be alive. This may have happened with Christ and it may have then appeared as a miracle. An analogy is then used that Christ has died and arose, so man will die and be resurrected:

Rom. 6:5 "For if we have been planted together in the likeness of his death, we shall be also in the likeness of his resurrection."

Another instance suggesting that biblical statements be taken in a moral or ethical rather than in an ontological naming-fallacy sense is seen in the following:

I John 3:14 "We know that we have passed out of death into life, because we love the brethren. He who does not love remains in death."

Death here is merely social death, moral death. To be dead is to have no concern for one's fellow man. To have concern with one's fellow man is a kind of immortality, but nevertheless an odd kind. We may be misled in thinking that a man's money survives his death. Dignity alters in a way money does not. "Christ" could in this sense only mean to love one's fellow man, not to name a person or entity, "Christ." Religion, as it involves obscure terms, naming-fallacies and category-mistakes, may be regarded as a worship of names rather than a worship of God.

It is usually thought that the Bible gives the only answer to death and immortality. But it is seen to give no analysis or clarification of the concept of death at all. Its concern is mainly to induce man to live according to the social laws of his community and the Ten Commandments. Talk of God, eternal life, heaven, hell, etc. are metaphors for man's living relationship to man. Some give metaphysical interpretations of soul, etc. but such views are not made intelligible to us, nor is the view of a new resurrected body intelligible, outside of the explanation of its being a product of self-hypnosis (belief or faith).

Choron states that it is vain to seek in the OT comfort and consolation for the fact of death in terms of belief in immortality. (p. 81)

It is as if when one needs shoes he goes to a shoe store, if groceries to a grocery store; so also if he is worried about death he goes to church. But the Christian does not have the answer to death.

Glenn Vernon states (1970 p. 247)

"Concern with death is in fact, one of the major *raisons d'etre* of religion . . . Relationships between the religious and the legal norm definitions have been changing, as the whole society has become increasingly secular in nature." (p. 247)

The Christian has never honestly inquired into the concept of death and the Bible says almost nothing about it.

Liston Mills says in connection with a Vanderbilt Divinity School seminar on death,

"Until recently death has been largely the domain of the Christian church in the western world . . . Religiously, modern man no longer speaks with the assurance he once did of meeting God and of eternal life . . . This world and its woes were . . . often neglected in a preoccupation with the next world and its bliss." (pp. 7-8)

As part of this seminar Leander Keck wrote that there is no such thing as *the New Testament* view of death. It is too diverse to yield a single view. He says,

"The biblical statements themselves presuppose ideas shared with the ancient world. . . . This systematized doctrine of death [is] as alien to us as are its biblical roots, if not more so . . . Death is a problem today partly because the language we inherited to talk about it no longer says what we think about it. . . . If today death as such poses no moral problem, then we have no more than historical interest in the New Testament or in the vast ancient tradition with which it shares this concern." (Mills pp. 96-97)

John Killinger presented a similar view as part of this theological seminar on death. He says,

"The church of our time [is] . . . characterized by a general confusion of belief heavily inclined toward agnosticism, or not knowing whether we believe anything at all." (Mills)

Again, another participant in the seminar, William May, states,

"Despite traces of contemporary belief in the immortality of the soul, the minister is ill advised to rely on it in the presence of death. Nowhere is the bankruptcy of the doctrine so evident as in a certain type of Protestant funeral service in which the minister strains to give the impression that the person 'lives on'. . . . The minister gives the sad impression that he has a repertory of three or four such 'personalized' services, designed like Sears Roebuck seat covers to fit any and all makes and models of cars." (Mills pp. 171-176) He also speaks of "the church's failure to recon with death in its own preaching and pastoral life."

Ninian Smart (Toynbee pp. 120-121) speaks of a contemporary demythologizing of death, that some, like Schleiermacher, had believed in a universal salvation for everyone and that now there is a loss of interest in afterlife. The stress is, among Protestants, on a this-worldly ethic. Smart also notes that this trend is partly a result of scholarly work on the *New Testament,* revealing that it is symbolic, mythic and metaphorical and so unable to support traditional literal interpretations, e.g., concerning hell and punishment. The stress is on reform rather than on eternal damnation. The Protestant stress then is on life and experience here and now. Some of Tillich's statements suggest this view also. Prof. Smart in another article states,

"The *New Testament* does not have a systematic doctrine of survival and . . . it is not so easy to hold to a belief in a

356

mind-body dualism which would render immortality intelligible," and he speaks of "a rather general scepticism about the possibility of life after death," The problem of death "has been approached, on the whole, obliquely in recent theology, as elsewhere." (Toynbee pp. 133-137)

Smart in a third article (Toynbee pp. 138-144) is even more clear. It is asserted that a non-Catholic, (Catholics are more dogmatic on such issues) cannot give comfort to the dying or bereaved because their views of an afterlife are very much in doubt. Biblical mythology about death and afterlife lacks foundation as a result of historical criticism of scripture.

"In these circumstances it is hard to know how specifically Christian convictions can be incorporated into the expression of the rituals of death." "Traditional beliefs and practices connected with death do not attract public agreement."

As a result Prof. Smart suggests that in religion

"the 'solution' therefore is to treat death in a minimal and rather informal way."

Prof. Fred Gealy writes,

"Quite generally biblical man is uneasy and uncomfortable in the presence of death." (p. 35)

The sociologist Glenn Vernon after an analysis of the relation of religion to the fear of death states,

"No clear-cut picture emerges from this review of relevant literature. There does seem to be sufficient evidence to question seriously the premise that religion serves to reduce fear of death."

There is good reason why Christians have not contributed to an understanding or clarification of the notion of death. In the first case the Bible is in the mythical not the scientific tradition.

Secondly religious statements are held dogmatically or on faith. It is thought that whatever the Bible says about death is the truth and so there is no need for further inquiry. Religion in this way held back inquiry and investigation into the concept of death. In the Middle Ages and Renaissance, physicians were condemned by the church for interfering with God. It was thought that the only cause of disease is sin and the only cure is to be religious. Gradually the church began to accept medical practice. It is only now beginning to accept honest, open inquiry into the concept of death. Biologists are often religious, the community of which they are a part is religious and so there is little interest in and almost no research done on, the inquiry into the nature of aging and death. Religion has supposedly answered the question *a priori.* Thus we today do not know the causes of aging and only with recent secular and scholarly research of the Bible has a more serious and honest inquiry into the concept of death begun. If one's concern is with the concept of death or immortality it is found not sufficient to compulsively attend mass or church on Sunday to hear a confused and dogmatic biblical approach which advertises salvation but has little to say about the nature of death. Rather one's Sundays could be better spent in honest, open inquiry. Biologists can no longer be weekday scientists and Sunday dogmatists.

The Bible's opposition to inquiry is suggested also in the following:

Ecclesiastes 1:18 "For in much wisdom is much grief, and he that increaseth knowledge increaseth sorrow."

Not only does the Bible oppose open inquiry, but, in addition, the penalty of knowledge is death. This is made clear in the first book of the Bible:

Genesis 2:17 "But of the tree of the knowledge of good and evil, thou shalt not eat of it: for in the day that thou eatest thereof thou shalt surely die."

One interpretation of this passage is not just to show that it is anti-inquiry but that it is circular. If death is evil and one knows of good and evil then he will know that his death is evil, that is, that he will die. Thus knowledge of good and evil leads to knowledge of one's death, to knowing one will die. If one knows good and evil he will be ashamed (Genesis 3:7). But to be ashamed means to know good and evil.

If man had not partaken of the tree of knowledge of good and evil he certainly would not know anything is either good or evil, he would not know that to die is good or evil, he would not know he would die and so in this sense not die. Perhaps animals are in this state of not knowing good, or evil, or death. The penalty man has to pay for consciousness is that of being aware that he will die. This may be a significant message of the caution against partaking of the tree of knowledge.

It is claimed by Christians that man because of Adam's sin is guilty, even from birth. One should rather only be guilty of failure to adequately inquire into life and death.

The penalty of not obeying the command not to partake of the tree of knowledge of good and evil is to be punished by death. To obey, however, one must know already of good and evil. If one has no knowledge of good and evil he can neither obey nor disobey. That is, duty, ought, obedience, are moral or ethical terms. Thus Adam could not obey or disobey and it makes no sense to punish him for what he knew nothing of. He could not say it was good to eat of the tree of knowledge of good and evil unless he already knew what good is.

The knowledge of death as a penalty for being conscious may lead to the view that, because we know we must die, we must make more of our lives. Since we do have knowledge of good and evil the emphasis is on living justly and well. This appears in:

Psalms 90:12 "So teach us to number our days, that we may apply our hearts unto wisdom."

By wisdom is meant partly or mainly knowledge of living justly.

The religious emphasis on immortality may be seen as a flight from death as a death-denial. Miguel de Unamuno (1954) states that the flight from death is the heart of all religion. It is put in the form that one must die in order to live, that is, it is not immortality so much as resurrection, but death nevertheless is denied. We become victorious over death. But the victory comes by leading a good life. It is perhaps more a victory over life than a victory over death. Death is used as a threat to try to make man more moral. Walter Kaufmann wrote,

"Christianity has on the whole used its vast influence to make men dread death." (P. 61)

This is the view especially maintained in the Christian art of dying books of the Middle Ages and later.

The tree of knowledge stands as a curious image. The unknown or that of which we are ignorant is made concrete by representing it by a visible object. This is the sort of metaphor which renders the abstract, by means of the concrete. But this type of metaphor may also misrepresent or make a fallacious or confused notion seem true by giving a concrete analogy or representation. In any case the model for knowledge of life after death, soul, God is really ignorance. We do not know what they are so we find them represented by analogies and metaphors. The images are nevertheless striking: a tree of knowledge, Christ on a cross – a striking deviation from normal funeral rites, death as an angel sent by God, death as a rider on a pale horse. Our view of death is often rendered and constituted by a model such as the sprouting of a flower in spring, or dancing skeletons which grin and even hold hands. God is seen as light. Perhaps this is because the nature of light is one of the most obscure and mysterious things of all. Such images fix themselves in us and seem to guarantee truth. They are interesting images, ones which may be explored in various ways. They may also misguide and mislead if taken as proofs or arguments. Talk of knowledge or the tree of knowledge is especially curious because religious concepts usually reduce to mystery, or are based solely on ignorance. We cannot know God yet we are asked to know God. By "soul" we often mean that about us of which we are ignorant. Religion is sometimes regarded as an "opiate of the masses." John Dewey wrote,

"Of belief in immortality more than of any other element of historic religions it holds good, I believe, that 'religion is the opium of peoples.' " (Lamont 1965)

Lou Silberman points out that Sheol is only used as an analogue to human experiences, and death as an analogue for the various weaknesses man experiences in his relations with his fellow man. (Mills pp. 23ff) William May also suggests this by saying that God should not be mentioned directly, but only indirectly by one's reaction to crises, friendship, calmness. (Mills p. 196)

The religious person often confuses 1. man as an ethical creature, and 2. man as a social creature. This leads to the naming-fallacy of taking the Bible and religious terms as if they name entities, rather than moral relations between people. Thus a soul was thought of as a thing, something to account for the fact that man's body dies, and the desire for immortality. Soul means often "desire for immortality," "that about me of which I am ignorant," etc.

Soul was thought of as being form without matter and therefore eternal. Such arguments fail, for if this were true, number and logic, which are said to be form without matter, would also be eternal.

The Catholic view is that at the moment of death the soul leaves the body and a beatific vision or ecstasy is experienced. The soul is often thought of as being rooted throughout the body and thus pain is experienced when the soul leaves and its roots are pulled out. But the ecstasy experienced is not as the dogma would have it that we at death are pure soul and can see God. Physicians have shown that rather the anesthetic action of carbon dioxide on the central nervous system and the effect of toxic substances produces such ecstasy. ("Death" *Harvest Years* 1969)

But St. Thomas Aquinas as well as nearly all others who have presented arguments, proof, or evidence for the existence of a soul admit that such arguments fail, that one must simply "believe" in a soul or have "faith" that there is one. Since nothing rational or intelligible can then be said about a soul or God, there is a question as to whether even the believer can know what it is he believes in. Secondly, there are difficulties with the nature of belief.

To know requires evidence. But the religious person often wishes to say "I believe," as if it means "I know," e.g., "I know that my redeemer liveth." But belief is not knowledge. Belief is a hope or guess. It is by definition excluded from truth, fact, or knowledge.

One cannot know by means of faith or belief. One can only believe by means of belief. Equivocation is not an argument for the existence of soul or God.

The argument given here for soul and such religious terms has been that they reduce to concrete uses in everyday situations. For example, "I have a soul" may mean, "I am ignorant about how I work or function." Soul here refers to my ignorance, not to a thing within me called a soul. Similarly "God" often means "I am in trouble," or "I wish things were different." Always find out how "knowledge" of death, afterlife, immortality, soul, etc. was acquired, how such terms are actually used. They will then be seen to fail to be the descriptions we imagine they are.

There is a great deal of evidence that "God" does not exist. One can no longer say that there is no evidence that "God" does not exist. A. Freedman and H. Kaplan (1972) show that, "The ecstatic states occuring in acute schizophrenia are related to the ecstatic transports of religious mysticism." They state that mystical experience represents psychological regression at its most extreme.

Should one take religion literally, many problems or counterexamples arise in addition to those presented above:

1. There is no contradiction in the view that there is a God and no survival or afterlife, even if God were somehow made into an intelligible concept. Camus: "Secret of my universe: imagining God without human immortality."
2. If man is immortal why are not June bugs immortal? Do they have souls?
3. Is personal survival like whistling in a box?
4. If we have a religion protecting us from death, why not one protecting us from birth?
5. Theologians seem to be those who think they can perform their own autopsy.
6. God is immortal because nothing can be immortal.
7. To speak of the next life, or another life is still to speak of this life.

8. What survives in religion is religion itself. To have one's ideas continue they must be made into a religion. Even science must do so to have followers.

9. The reason one believes in reincarnation and afterlife is because they are too much, are absurd, and suggest that about such things we must remain silent.

10. Death is not a sin, good, or bad.

11. Behavior seems irrelevant to death. One could equally say "If you do not do X you will live forever," or "If you do X you will live forever."

12. To think that one can be religiously horribly punished after death is optimistic.

13. Wherever there is an ignorance, an empty space, man will fill it in anyway, with myth and fiction.

14. The inability of the Christian to cope with death leads to guilt because he thinks morals have something to do with death. They don't.

15. Why does the "soul" need a ritual in order to leave the body — or is the "soul" merely the ritual and nothing more?

16. Do we have metaphysics and religion because people dishonestly defy death?

17. What the "soul" is, if anything, depends on whom you talk to.

18. Theognis of Megara (and common Christian view):

   "The best thing is not to be born at all. The next best thing is to escape this miserable existence as soon as possible." (Also Eccl. 7:1 "The day of death is better than the day of one's birth.")

19. Soul is one of the least pure, i.e., least intelligible ideas in the world.

20. If after resurrection one gets a new body why wouldn't it be the body of an ant, or elephant?

21. If one rejects abortion why not also condemn abstinence and not having children. It would be killing not to have an unlimited number of children.

22. Love of God and love of man may be a way to close one's eyes to inquiry into death.

We may end with Amos Wilder's statement,

"The secular witness today is all the more necessary because dogmatic answers have become so unrelated to our experience."

The man who is dead is the man who fails to inquire, who is not yet aware of honest, open, inquiry into himself and his environment. What survives in religion is religion itself. Man is superstitious. Therefore, even to make honest inquiry into death acceptable it must be made religion. This inquiry must then have its rituals, myths, poetry, music. We might light a candle for inquiry.

Jacques Choron. *Death and Western Thought* New York: Macmillan 1963

"Death: The Way of Life" *Harvest Years* 9 (April 1969) 19-34

Alfred Freedman and H. Kaplan. *Diagnosing Mental Illness* New York: Atheneum 1972

Fred Gealy. "The Biblical Understanding of Death" *Pastoral* Psychology 14 (1963) p. 35

Walter Kaufmann. "Existentialism and Death" *The Meaning of Death* Herman Feifel, ed., New York: McGraw Hill 1959

Corliss Lamont. *The Illusion of Immortality* New York: Ungar 1965 (1935)

William May. "The Sacral Power of Death in Contemporary Experience" *Perspectives on Death* Liston Mills, ed.

Liston Mills, ed. *Perspectives on Death* Nashville, Tenn.: Abingdon 1969

D. Z. Phillips. *Death and Immortality* London: Macmillan 1970

Ian Ramsey. *Models and Mystery* New York: Oxford University Press 1964

————. *Religious Language* New York: Macmillan 1963

–––––. *Talk of God* Royal Insitute of Philosophy Lectures Vol. II London: Macmillan 1967-1968

Gilbert Ryle. *Concept of Mind* New York: Barnes & Noble 1949

Warren Shibles. "Timelessness," and "Linguo-Centric Predicament" *Philosophical Pictures* 2nd revised edition, Dubuque, Iowa: Kendall-Hunt 1972

Lou Silberman. "Death in the Hebrew Bible and Apocalyptic Literature" *Perspectives on Death* Liston Mills, ed., Nashville, Tenn.: Abingdon Press 1969 pp. 13-22

Ninian Smart. "Death and the Decline of Religion in Western Society" *Man's Concern with Death* A. Toynbee, ed., pp. 138-144

–––––. "Death in the Judaeo-Christian Tradition" *Man's Concern with Death* A. Toynbee, ed., New York: McGraw Hill 1969

Paul Tillich. "The Eternal Now" *The Meaning of Death* H. Feifel, ed., New York: McGraw-Hill 1959 pp. 30-38

Miguel de Unamuno. *Tragic Sense of Life* New York: Dover 1954

Glenn Vernon. *Sociology of Death* New York: Ronald Press 1970

Amos Wilder. "Mortality in Contemporary Literature" *Harvard Theological Review* Vol. 58, no. I

John Wisdom. "Eternal Life" *Talk of God* Royal Institute of Philosophy Lectures, Vol. II London: Macmillan 1967-1968

John Donne

Donne (1572-1631), both poet and religious preacher, exemplified the concern with death prevalent especially since the Middle Ages. He devoted his life to trying to overcome death. He was like death's worm crawling inside of life and preached half worm, half religion with his total concern with death. His *Biathanatos* deals with the justification of suicide. For Donne what really exists is death, all else is appearance and a degree of death. One poem reads,

"O strong and long-liv'd Death, how camest thou in? . . . .
How could I thinke thee nothing, that see now
In all this All, nothing else is, but thou.
Our births and lives, vices and virtues, bee
Wasteful consumptions, and degrees of thee.
For wee, to live, our bellows weare and breath,
Nor are we mortall, dying, dead, but death."

He feared the nothingness he thought death to be. (See the critique of "nothingness" in the chapter on existentialism.) Donne wrote, "For to be Nothing, is so deep a curse . . . . It is impossible that any man should wish himself Nothing." (*Essays in Divinity*)

His poetry was full of death conceits or extravagant metaphors. The conceits stress paradox. He explores the paradox of death. He wrote, "Enter into the grave, thy metaphoricall . . . . " (1919 p. 195)

He says in "Death's Duell,"

365

"We have a winding-sheet in our mother's womb that
grows with us from our conception, and we come into the
world wound up in that winding-sheet; for we come to
seek a grave. . . ."
Death is throughout related to birth.

"Doth man die even in his birth? . . . Hath any man here
forgot today, that yesterday is dead? And the bell tolls for
today, and will ring out anon; . . . We die everyday, and
we die all the day long; and because we are not absolutely
dead, we call that an eternity, an eternity of dying." (p.
197)

He gives as images for death: death's head, coffin, groom,
death-cart, bell, embalming, light, worm, year's end, sickbed,
and the world as a graveyard. "This whole world is but a
universal churchyard, but one common grave." The bridal bed is
"virginity's grave." (Rugoff 1962; Humphreys 1948) The image
of a bell appears in: "Never send to know for whom the bell
tolls, It tolls for thee."

The worm is one of the most often used images of death.
Donne was preoccupied with the sensual aspects of physical
death and even of jellied putrefaction: "To see the brain
produce nothing but swarmes of worms . . . . To see great men
made no men." But the worm was not Donne's idea, it was the
tool of the Church, and it also may cover what we now call
cells, germs, and even the worm-like chromosomes which some
think self-destruct our cells to cause aging and so death. Man is
also less than worms, for worms eat him; Nature has her chance
to eat back man. The contemporary existentialist, Sartre,
continues the theme of the worm in speaking of the "worm" in
the "heart of being." This is a continuation of the biblical view,
though Sartre claims to be an atheist.

The medieval and Christian view that death is a leveler is also
presented:

"The angel that shall call us out of that dust, will not
stand to survey who lies naked, who in a coffin, who in
wood, who in lead, who in fire, who in coarser sheet."
(Sermons)

The funeral objects are no indication of the person who died. In death all become dust: "The ashes of an Oak in the Chimney, are no Epitaph of that Oak, to tell me how high or how large that was." The clergymen of today still use this same argument against the elaborateness of funerals. Like the Christian, Donne had condemned this life in favor of the next. He calls life "a week of deaths, seven days, seven perils of our life spent in dying." ("Death's Duell")

Donne often pictures himself as dead.

> "When I dyed last, and Deare, I dye
> As often as from thee I goe, . . . "

Everything in this world is merely a reminder of one's own death.

> "Everything is a remembrance, everything is a Judge upon me, and pronounces, I *must* dye."

In *Paradoxes and Problems* he sees that we bring about our own death psychosomatically and because of our confused emotions of grief: "All things kill themselves . . . . We daily kill our bodies with surfeits, and our minds with anguishes." Melancholy was thought by many to be a possibly fatal disease. For Donne a wrinkled brow is our grave.

Death is regarded as a subject of ignorance. Man has hardly inquired or gained much knowledge into himself or the nature of death:

> "Poore soule, in this thy flesh what doest thou know? Thou know'st thy selfe so little, as thou know'st not, How thou didst die or how thou wast begot. Thou neither know'st, how at first cam'st in, Nor how thou took'st the poyson of mans sinne."

But Donne's view was still, often, traditionally Christian. He states, "Sin is the root, and the tree, and the fruit of death; the mother of death, death itself, and the daughter of death." Love is linked with death.

While experiencing strong emotions we tend to think in opposites such as love and hate, life and death. For Donne love must involve or even consist of a balanced body and soul, just as the humors or elements had to be balanced in medieval medicine. If there was balance one could conquer death, if not, not. If lovers part it is like a death but if in harmony, then there can be no death. Love can, in a way, conquer physical death. A token from the lover may even prevent decomposition of the body. Love also is a death for the benefit of the species: "For that first marriage was our funeral, We kill our selves to propagate our kinde." *(An Anatomie of the World)* "Love mee, that I may die the gentler way." *(Poems)*

Neither his views on love, Christian denial of the flesh, nor his belief in a soul allowed him to believe in immortality. He thought of the soul as smoke, vapor, a bubble, and something which might be, in the grave, ignored by God. He did, as a Christian, now and then think that the soul is destroyed by sin. He never could really accept the doctrine of resurrection. His final view was one of doubt. He wrote in Sermon 29, "What is there in the nature and essence of Man, free from death?" For him the soul is not immortal. He even feared resurrection: "Rather dead than changed."

Donne thought we should constantly think of death. To prepare for death we must die a little bit each day. "He that takes a dram of death today, may take an ounce tomorrow, and a pound after." He thought denial of pleasures today would also help one prepare for death, the greatest denial of all.

John Donne. *Donne's Sermons* Logan Smith, ed., Oxford: Clarendon Press 1919

Mary Jane Humphreys. "The Problem of Death in the Life and Works of John Donne" Ph.D. diss. Cornell University 1948

Milton Rugoff. *Donne's Imagery* New York: Russell & Russell 1962

Art of Dying

Ars moriendi refers to a number of medieval religious, especially Catholic guide books on how to die. (See sources at end of chapter and end of book) The art of dying books are full of horrors and degrading questionings put to the religious person just before death. It was hoped that such terrors would drive one into the Catholic faith. The devils make frightening, strange noises, have faces like angered lions and are reported to be too terrible for man to look upon before death. All of one's sins are supposedly seen flashing before him at death. This is perhaps one of the sources of the view that at death all of our life runs before our eyes. The grinning devil tortures the sinful with red hot flesh-hooks. Frederick Weber wrote,

> "It was in Mediaeval Europe under the auspices of the Catholic Church, that descriptions and representations of the terrors of death and hell began to take on their most horrible aspects."

The black plague or black death from 1348 until 1350 killed a fourth of the population of Europe thus creating an almost unequalled catastrophe. (W. Langer) There were after this, frequent outbreaks which in some parts of the world continue even today. In such circumstances the medieval man turned to religious superstition and witchcraft. The disease was thought to be God's punishment for human sin. The present religious view still is that physical death is the result of original sin (*Romans* 5:12). The disease is caused by the organism *Bacillus pestis* and has the forms a) pneumonic (lungs affected), b) bubonic (lymph gland swelling), c) septicemic (blood poison). It is called the "black death" because black patches appear on the skin due to hemorrhage. The disease is carried by the fleas of black rats and other rodents. There is fever and pain. Death follows in five or six days. There was at this time great stress on the art of dying books to protect one from devils, and people were suspected of being witches and were tortured to confession. Some were put on a wheel and spun until the devils in him were forced out. For an account of these sorts of superstitions see T. Boase *Death in the Middle Ages* and P. Haining *Witchcraft and Black Magic*. Haining wrote, "It was the Christian Church which detailed all the horrors of devil worship as later times came to understand it." (p. 14) The church would tolerate no other religions and so began its centuries of persecution. The Inquisition to punish "false doctrine and heresy" began around 1233 by the Catholic Church. In the late 16th century 30,000 executions took place. In Germany there were eventually 100,000 executions of witches. In Britain the Witch Act condemning witches was not repealed until 1951. The atmosphere of the times is suggested by Haining as follows:

> "Wherever one went the tales of horror [of the Inquisition] mounted, and no one could be sure of his life from day to day. A careless word, a strange action, and death could be just a whispered word away. Once begun, the system was to continue for 200 years – and leave a blot on the story of humanity which can never be erased." (p. 29)

The Dominican priests, Jakob Sprenger and Heinrich Kramer, published in 1486 "The Hammer of the Witches" (*Malleus Maleficarus*) which served as the inquisitors text and was based on the Bible, esp., *Exodus* xxii. 18 "Thou shalt not suffer a witch to live."

The Catholic view is still that at death one sees God, the next world, the above mentioned horrors, or a great light. This view was in part based on Plato's philosophy according to which the truth is too bright to look at directly. There is supposedly for the Christian a feeling of beatitude. It may actually be a kind of sun worship. According to the *Tibetan Book of the Dead* the brilliant light of ultimate reality is supposedly seen. But scientists explain this feeling as mere elation or light-headedness caused by lack of oxygen and toxic substances in the blood stream. The experience involves recollecting one's past life, and great rapidity of thought and imagination. One in such a state in fact is ready for death and does not naturally experience fear or pain. Also light was associated with good, and darkness with evil. Candles were lit to keep away evil spirits. The art of dying books consist usually of the following six parts:

1. Commendation of death and knowledge of how to die well. Ecclesiastical writings on death present the view that man's death is better than his life. Death is only like a release from prison, thus one should give up his soul willingly and gladly. A typical sermon went, "What is man . . . but a stynkynge slyme, and after that a sake ful of donge, and at the laste mete to worms" (Owst). Other similar church writings are given from the 13th and 14th century writings.

Joan Huber, in 1967, dedicated her dissertation on death to Jesus Christ and presented her view that this life is merely subordinate to the next.

2. Five temptations by the devil test the faith of the Christian. This is the "moment of truth" when the fate of the soul is decided — when the soul thought to be rooted in the body is painfully pulled out by the roots and released to heaven and hell. The Comper book states:

"Know all men doubtless, that men that die, in their last sickness and end, have greatest and most grievous temptations, and such as they never had before in all their life. . . . The devil with all his might is busy to avert fully a man from the faith in his last end . . . to deceive him with some manner of superstitious and false errors or heresies."

The five temptations were depicted in woodcuts showing horrible monsters ready to snatch the soul of the dying man. These woodcuts were among the first, and nearly any history of woodcuts will show pictures of the five personified monster-like temptations from medieval books. In fact, the *Ars moriendi* books were the first and perhaps the most prevalent books printed. The temptations are to: a) disbelief b) despair c) impatience d) vanity e) avarice. The woodcuts also depict five corresponding "inspirations": faith, hope, love, humility, and detachment. One is driven to these fine inspirations partly out of fear. St. Gregory wrote much about deathbed temptations by the devil.

It may be noted that "despair" was treated much as the existentialists treat "dread" today. Despair and dread supposedly drive one to Christianity or make one live a better life. What a "better" life means depends on the theory or particular religion adopted.

There was a great fear of sudden death because, on the Catholic view, then one would not be able to have last rites and would be snatched off by black devils and sent to purgatory. This may be one source of Shakespeare's statement, "All's well that ends well." If one's sins are forgiven all is well on the Christian view. On a non-Christian view, just because life ends well by no means means that all is well. Not all is determined by the last moment of death. St. Christopher supposedly protected the Catholic from sudden death and plastic magnetic statuettes are still seen in automobiles in spite of this outmoded practice.

3. Interrogations of the dying. Many questions are put to the dying person to be answered correctly if he is to be "saved." He is asked if he has faith in God, loves God, etc., and is asked to repent and forgive his enemies. Some books allowed acceptance of deathbed repentance and others condemned it.

4. The dying man is told to die as Christ did and short prayers are given him to say.

5. He is told how to act toward his friends and so how to die. A warning is given against giving false assurances of one's recovery. O'Connor wrote,

> "The warning against giving bodily aid for a sick man precedence over spiritual aid received wide circulation in the Middle Ages and is one of the most frequently repeated directions in the Protestant books on dying in the sixteenth and seventeenth centuries."

The Christian view was that all disease is caused by sin and therefore no physician is needed. Even in the 17th century one was advised to send for a minister, not a physician, for the dying person.

6. Prayers are given to be said for the dying.

Luther said, "For the conclusion of our life is the touchstone of all the actions of our life. . . . For the art of dying well is the science of all sciences, the way whereunto is to live well, contentedly and peaceably." (O'Connor, p. 205)

In the Middle Ages man was preoccupied with death generally. Preachers' favorite topic was death. One was taught to constantly think of death or remember death (*memento mori*). "Memento mori" was inscribed on rings, cups, plates, chimneys, buildings, churches and could be found almost anywhere. Skeletons were brought to banquets as was the practice also in Greece and Egypt. Prostitutes in the Middle Ages wore rings with skulls or death heads on them, as did many others. Drinking cups would be inscribed with "Drink for you will die." Luther wore a gold death's-head ring with the motto, "Think often of death." In the 16th century Ignatius Loyola meditated on a skeleton as a spiritual exercise. In Spain, Christians often still possess skulls and use them in church ritual, and in Catholic Mexico All Souls Day reveals skulls and skeletons everywhere.

The horror of the art of dying books was extended to representations of decomposing flesh. Skeletons were pictured with flesh being eaten by long snakes and toads. A decomposed skeleton was called a "Hautskelett" in Germany. The motto was "memento mori" or "Such as I am, so will you be." Cardinal Lagrange in 1402 had a funeral monument representing him as half decomposed. The Plague of 1348 made death very well known.

The "remember death" theme of ancient Greece and Rome stressed living pleasurably and fully now while we can. The motto *"carpe diem"* meant "Enjoy the day" or "Enjoy life while you can." The Christian message was to remember and fear death so that one becomes Christian, repents his sins and rejects this world in favor of the next. In India some "fakirs" paint a skeleton on their skin as a sign of their religion. Death was a favorite topic of poetry, songs and plays. There were "Vado mori" ("I must die") poems in the 13th century that began and ended with these words. A fool would in a play attempt to escape death and, by trying, bring himself yet closer to it.

The art of dying books are like the Egyptian or Tibetan Book of the Dead according to which the soul is conjured out of the body and guided into heaven. It is hard to believe that the soul, even if there were one, is so unintelligent that it needs all the guidance accorded it. For Aristotle it is the *rational* soul which survives.

The art of dying books suggest that there is a correct or best way to die. But "correct" and "best" are interpreted in terms of a specific religious belief. To die well one rather needs an adequate knowledge of the concepts of death and dying. In itself it makes no sense to say death is appropriate or inappropriate, correct or incorrect, proper or improper, done well or not done well, tragic or comic. One cannot *a priori* say man's death is more tragic than the death of a dog or an insect.

T. Boase. *Death in the Middle Ages* New York: McGraw-Hill 1972

Frances Comper. *The Book of the Craft of Dying* London: Longmans 1917

R. S. Ellis. "The Attitude Toward Death and the Types of Belief in Immortality" *Journal of Religious Psychology* 7 (1915) 466-510

P. Haining. *Witchcraft and Black Magic* New York: Grosset Dunlap 1972 (Bantam book 1973)

Joan Huber. "Chaucer's Concept of Death in the Canterbury Tales" PhD diss. University of Pittsburg 1967

William Langer. "The Black Death" *Scientific American* 210 (Feb. 1964) 114-121

Sister Mary, O'Connor. *The Art of Dying Well* New York: Columbia University Press 1942

G. Owst. *Preaching in Mediaeval England* Cambridge 1926

Theodore Spencer. *Death and Elizabethan Tragedy* Harvard University Press 1936, Chapt. I

Frederick Weber. *Aspects of Death and Correlated Aspects of Life in the Art, Epigram, and Poetry* 3rd rev. ed., New York: Hoeber 1920

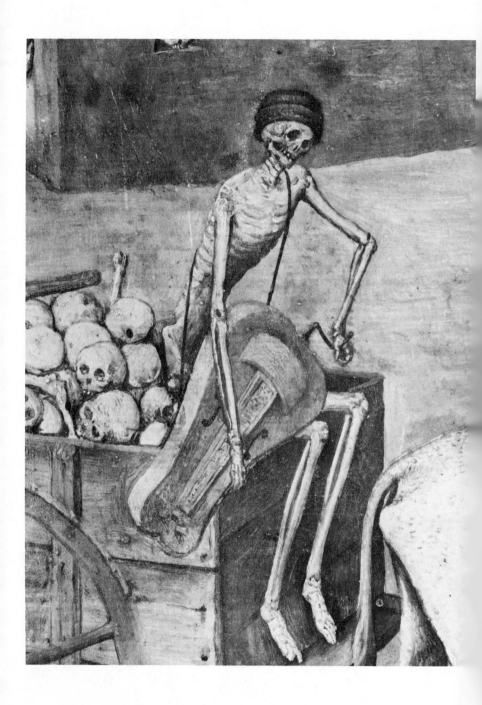

Death in Art

I. *The Dance of Death*

It is not clear where the dance of death originated. In France it was called *danse macabre,* in Germany, *Totentanz.* It appeared in religious morality plays and in art. A 1424 fresco was one of the first illustrations. Rabbi Santo's poem "Danze de la Muerte" of 1360 is one of the first dance of death poems. Several factors seemed to be responsible for the institution of the dance of death, or to have continued it:

1. In the Middle Ages people often danced in the open.

2. Vigorous dancing especially with drinking can produce elation which is mistaken for being possessed by a "spirit." The spirit supposedly caused one to dance. This is another example of the consequence of a belief in a soul. The Salem Witch Trials is another. Similarly insane people were thought possessed. Perhaps the reverse is rather the case: only those who believe in souls or spirits are possessed, their bodies haunted. Belief in souls and spirits is perhaps as common today as it ever was. In religious cults the "whirling dervish" (and there was also a Mohammedan "howling dervish") would spin and dance in circles shouting cries to Allah. The very religious person was often by religious fervor led to dance wildly, a practice commonly seen in churches in southern United States.

3. The Black Plague or Black Death of the 14th century (e.g., 1347-1359) may have caused people to try to dance off the plague thinking it to be due to a spirit which possessed them.

4. St. Vitus's dance is another name for the disease, chorea. "Chorea" derives from the Latin word for dance. It is a nervous

disorder involving spasmodic movements. The name "St. Vitus' dance" was first applied to epidemic dancing mania because it was supposed to be cured with the aid of St. Vitus.

5. Dancing mania in the 1500's in Italy was supposedly caused by the spider bite of the Tarantula. The "Tarantella" may be connected with this.

6. In the 14th century there were epidemic dancing manias, e.g., in 1347. It seems to be partly a socially induced, ritual-like phenomenon.

7. The Church encouraged the dance of death to turn people to the faith.

8. The dance of death became associated with the tradition of representing death by means of a skeleton. Thus it became a dance of skeletons.

9. An ancient tradition still existing today in some cultures is that of holding a feast and dances in cemeteries. It was thought the departed soul shared in the feast and ate some of the food.

10. On the All Souls' Day of the Catholic religion the dead were and are thought to rise out of the grave at midnight and perhaps dance around. The dancing skeletons lured the living into the dance. The skeletons often tear men away without allowing repentance.

11. Music was thought to entice the living to join the dead. (Stegemeier) A later children's version of this is the Pied Piper of Hamelin (1888) which shows rats being enticed by music, leading to their death. Music was thought also to lead one into sin, according to the tradition.

12. Holding wild dances for the dead is an old folk custom. It was thought to chase away evil spirits.

13. "Dance of Death" was also a social game played especially at weddings. One dancer plays corpse and is blindfolded. The members of the opposite sex kiss him and dance around him.

14. Medieval plays have the call to death theme, e.g., "The Pryde of Lyfe," "Everyman," "The Castle of Perseverance," "Slaughter of the Innocents."

The best known woodcuts depicting the dance of death are those of Hans Holbein the Younger (1497-1543). Holbein even designed an alphabet of death. A recent book republished his dance of death woodcuts. (Holbein 1971) The woodcuts first appeared at Lyons in 1538. Holbein made the drawings in 1523 and 1526 and Hans Lutzelburger made them into woodblocks. The drawings are said to be merely images (*simulachres*) or metaphors for death since no one has ever seen death. It often appears to be assumed that death is visualizable and so a naming-fallacy is produced. Each scene depicts death in an emblematic metaphor. Pictures were used because most of the common people were illiterate.

"Dance of death" has special appeal because it is an antithesis or oxymoron. Dance suggests life and so opposites are juxtaposed and combined yielding "Life of death." The dead seem to be made alive as a covert type of death-denial while death dances life away. The woodcuts show a) the universality of death, or death as democratic, for all must die regardless of social class, age, or sex; b) caprice, for death comes often suddenly when least expected. The skeletons surprisingly display a great range of emotions including glee, haste, friendship, lust, anger, contemplation, sympathy. They do not all merely grin.

The forty-one woodcuts begin with creation in *Genesis* and the temptation according to which Eve deceived Adam into eating the forbidden fruit thus making all men mortal and doomed to die. A snake is shown in the garden and this may be why snakes and long worms were thought to be or represented as feeding on dead bodies. Also *Ecclesiastes* says that when man is dead, snakes and worms eat him. A skeleton is, then, depicted as leaving the garden with Adam and Eve. The skeleton holds a guitar. Then Adam is seen condemned to till the soil in sorrow until he becomes dust ("Unto dust shalt thou return.") Here a skeleton is shown hard at work with Adam. There is an hourglass by their feet and Eve nurses a child in the background. The next cut shows a skeleton drummer, skeleton buglers and the bones of all men, for here all have died. The remaining woodcuts illustrate a skeleton dragging a member of each profession off to death, for no one is exempt. The professions are: the Pope, emperor, king, cardinal, empress, queen, bishop, duke, abbot, abbess, nobleman, canon, judge, advocate, senator, preacher, priest, monk, nun, old woman, physician, astrologer, miser, merchant, seaman, knight, count, old man, countess, lady, duchess, peddler, ploughman, child. The next to the last illustration shows a judge of men who will decide the fate, heaven or hell, of each man according to his sins and virtues. The last picture shows a man and woman with a skull shield between them. The skull shows a snake coming out of its mouth as if it were a tongue. Above the shield are skeleton arms holding a rock over an hourglass. The message given is from *Ecclesiastes* 7:36 "Remember the end, and thou shalt never do amiss." The point is that to always think of and prepare for death will supposedly help one lead a sinless life. This is also largely the point made by the contemporary existentialist. The existentialist though he claims to be an atheist, is in fact carrying on the mediaeval Christian tradition. Both views stress constant reminders of death, despair, dread, and guilt. Existentialism is merely a new form of Christian belief in this respect.

The skeletons romp, yank violently, tug, play a musical instrument, wear a crown, hold an hourglass, toll bells, and in general mimic and dress like the one about to die. They count money, preach, hold a physician's urine bottle, drive a lance through the knight, etc.

Above each woodcut is a biblical saying such as the following:

"And he that is today a king, tomorrow shall die." (Eccl. 10:10)

"I will smite the shepherd, and the sheep shall be scattered." (Mark 14:27)

"He shall die without instruction; and in the greatness of his folly he shall go astray." (Proverbs 5:23)

"What man is it that liveth, and shall not see Death?" (Psalms 89:48)

"Behold, the hour is at hand." (Matthew 26:45)

"I myself also am a mortal man, like to all." (Wisdom of Solomon 7:1)

"There is a way which seemeth right unto a man; but the end thereof are the ways of death." (Proverbs 14:12)

"Death is better than a bitter life or continued sickness." (Eccl. 30:17)

"Physician, heal thyself." (Luke 4:23)

"For when he dieth he shall carry nothing away." (Psalm 49:17)

"Man that is born of a woman is of a few days, and full of trouble. He cometh forth like a flower, and is cut down; he fleeth also as a shadow, and continueth not." (Job 14:1,2)

A modern version of the dance of death is R. Dagley's *Death's Doings* which contains thirty etched illustrations readapted to modern occupations. Some variations of the dance of death are Dance of Death of Women, and of Angels. The Bliss history of woodcut shows the following illustrations:

a) The doctor and the lover with their own dead selves, from Verard's "Danse Macabre" (Paris 1485).

b) The bride, the daughter of Joy and their dead selves from Verard's "Danse Macabre des Femmes" (Paris 1486).

c) A picture of the story of the three dead and three live young men as told in the 13th century. A duke, a count and a king's son ride out with a hawk. They meet three skeletons and try to escape. The skeletons which were of a Pope, cardinal and papal notary plea for them to repent — which they then do. The story has also a version whereby the three meet skeletons of themselves.

Baudoin de Conde has a poem, "The Three Quick and the Three Dead." The three noblemen face three skeletons and the nobles see the skeletons as what they too will become.

Arthur Hind's history of woodcut contains the following illustrations:

a) "Impatience" a temptation from the *Ars moriendi* books. The dying man knocks over a table, and monsters appear under the bed. (I, figs 94, 95)

b) "Doten dantz" (dance of death) (I, fig. 155, ca. 1492) A semi-skeleton with a horn has a worm or snake coming out of its body and a toad at its feet. Some onlookers are horrified and others are smiling and content.

c) "Death on Horseback" (I, fig. iii, ca. 1463) A semi-skeleton on horseback aims an arrow at men riding horses, and another skeleton with a scythe mows people down.

d) Dance of death scenes are shown from *Danse Macabre* (Lyon ca. 1499), *Danse Macabre des Hommes* (Paris ca. 1491),

Danse Macabre des Femmes (Paris 1492), *The Book of Hours* (Paris 1488, 1496, 1527). *The Book of Hours* is a calendar which was widely distributed throughout the population. It contained pictures of the dance of death, the seven sins, the virtues, the tale of the three living and the three dead, etc. (Vol. II)

II. *The Triumph of Death*

Francesco Petrarch's poem "The Triumph of Death" (1470) inspired representations of chariots driving over men. Skeletons are seen around the chariot. Often the three fates are in the chariot. There are triumphs of Love, Chastity, Fame, Time and Eternity as well as of Death. Petrarch though he inspired this tradition, himself stressed living and worldly accomplishments rather than the next life. The name "Triumph of Death" may also refer to the religious notion of resurrection. Several "Triumph of Death" paintings are by: Gamelin (British Museum), Della Bella (private collection), Breughel the Elder (Madrid, Prado Museum). Breughel's painting illustrated at the beginning of this book, shows death triumphing over all in every conceivable way. It is a magnificent representation of the climax of the dance of death and triumph of death themes.

III. *Tomb Sculpture*

The *memento mori* theme was represented in funeral ceremonies and objects. A *"gisant"* monument is one showing the body as it looks in life with its material signs of wealth and status, and below or above that, the body is shown as it looks in or after decomposition. The result is a striking and shocking metaphorical juxtaposition contrasting life and death. In 1393 Guillaume de Harcigny's tomb represented him as half corpse, half mummy. Rene de Chalons in 1547 had his body be represented as it might look three years after death. Ligier Richier had a skeleton carved which still showed some flesh on it. The epitaph was often something like "You too will be like me, food for worms." In the early 1500's Jeanne de Bourbon of Auvergne had a tomb sculpted showing her decomposing body with worms crawling over her breast and in and out of the cavities. The tomb of Johannes Gmainer (1482) shows a skin skeleton with long worms. The tomb of Cardinal Lagrange (1402) shows a half decomposed body. Early 16th century church statues were of partly decomposed corpses and warned "You too will die." The head of the effigy of Frances I de La Sarra shows four large toads eating eyes and mouth, with long worms in arms and shoulders. (Panofsky) The tomb of John Fitzalan (1435) shows in four dimensions (including time) a knight in armor and below this, the knight as he actually looks in death. The tomb of Valentine Balbiani by Germain Pilon shows a beautiful clothed woman leaning on her elbow reading a book, with two cherubs on each side of her. Below is her actual appearance after death. The tomb of Pope Alexander VII, (St. Peter's Rome) done by Gian Lorenzo Bernini, shows an extremely elaborate sculpture of seven, three-dimensional figures with the Pope featured praying and in his full robes. A skeleton is seen below coming out of a canopy with hourglass in hand. (Panofsky) It is interesting that such expense and effort was taken as an attempt to show humility. A contradiction is apparent here.

Similar to this tradition are the Citapati, the lords of the graveyard in Tibetan Buddhism. They are shown as dancing skeletons waving entrails and holding eyeballs. (H. Daniel) Buddha is represented as a skeleton, due to fasting.

IV. *Vanity Paintings*

The vanity theme is a reminder by the church that one should not be vain for we must die.

Skulls were included in the portraits of even the most elaborately dressed persons. This was the practice especially in the 16th and 17th century. Some examples are the following: "Portrait of a Gentleman" by Naron (Dulwich Gallery); St. Jerome is shown in his study contemplating a skull in a Durer painting of 1510. Cezanne did several paintings of the vanity sort. One contains a skull, candle and closed book; another a youth contemplating a skull. Picasso also did vanities. A skull also appears in scenes where a mother nurses a child or is juxtaposed with a sleeping baby, (e.g., Barthel Beham, British

Museum). Holbein's painting of Sir Brian Tuke shows a skull and an hourglass (Munich). Bocklin did a portrait of himself in 1872 showing death as a fiddler behind him.

V. *Other Art*

Durer's work includes paintings of Apocalypse showing the biblical pale rider on a pale horse (Rev. 6:8), "King Death on a Horse," "Knight, Death and Devil," "Death as a Ravisher," "The Promenade" (skeleton grins behind a tree at a pair of lovers), "Death and a Fool," "Three Knights and Three Skeletons" (1491), "Death of a Soldier" (shows Death riding a lean horse and carrying a scythe. The inscription says "ME[M]ENTO MEI"), "Escutcheon of Death" (shows an old man as Death satyr-like with a young pregnant woman. The woman feeds Death by giving birth), St. Jerome is shown in his study contemplating a skull.

Interesting variations of all of the preceeding themes may be found in a book by Sanchez-Camargo on death in Spanish painting. Skeletons are represented from the Middle Ages up to the present times.

John of Calcar engraved a "Thinking Skeleton" for Vesalius' *Anatomy*. Wiertz has a painting showing a woman passively and contentedly facing a skeleton. Munch has a striking painting of a woman passionately kissing a skeleton. Hans Balding-Grien has a picture of a skeleton kissing a terrified voluptuous woman. Nikolaus Manuel-Deutsch in his "Death the Soldier Embracing a Girl" shows the skeleton's hand under the dress of a girl. It is a striking metaphorical juxtaposition of sex and death. Mathias Gothart-Neithart's "Pair of Lovers" shows long worms, flies, dragonflies, toads, and snakes which are crawling in and out of the bodies of two lovers.

Regarding death in modern art each individual work would have to be examined and discussed. The religious unity of thought from the old tradition is now beginning to diminish. For a statement on death in modern art C. Gottlieb's article, "Modern Art and Death" may be consulted.

Other themes and traditions in art would involve a close look at the particular art works of the culture. The Greeks for example personified death by a gentle, winged youth

(Thanatos) armed with a sword. In peasant Poland death is represented by a tall, thin, white woman. The Trivi of North Australia make funeral poles 20 feet high and 3 feet wide. Each pole is smoked and painted with beautiful and individual designs. The cremation effigies to be burned by the Balinese are elaborate and immense, requiring perhaps seventy-five people to carry. The effigy for a nobleman is a bull, noblewoman — cow, king or queen — winged-lion, soldier — deer. In Santa Ana in the Solomon Islands an artistic skull receptacle is made in the shape of a bonito fish.

Art as it relates to the modern American funeral should include comment on polished cherry caskets and the richness and color of its velvet lining as well as all the other items associated with a funeral. Forest Lawn Memorial Cemetery is also an art museum. They hire master cosmeticians and plastic surgeons to beautify the dead and make an art of making them look beautiful, natural and alive. Michelangelo's "David" and "Moses" statues in St. Peter's Church in Rome were copied at great expense and are displayed in Forest Lawn. Sometimes an art show is held in a mortuary "slumber" room. Forest Lawn is said to have more art works than the Louvre. Statues and art objects are on display throughout the cemetery and may be purchased and placed near one's own plot. Rose Moretti, a stained-glass-window artist, did a thirty-four by fifteen foot replica of Da Vinci's "The Last Supper." It was and perhaps still is unveiled every hour for observers. Jan Styka's "Crucifixion" is displayed in a million and a half dollar Hall of Crucifixion at Forest Lawn and was or still is seen seven times a day. The painting is so large that the largest stage in Los Angeles was not wide enough for it. (Mitford) An "Art Guide to Forest Lawn" describes the art objects throughout the cemetery.

Douglas Bliss. *A History of Wood-Engraving* London: Dent 1928

Manuel Sanchez-Camargo. *La Muerte y La Pintura Espanola* Madrid: Editora Nacional 1954

Richard Dagley. *Death's Doings* 2 vols. London: J. Andrews 1908

386

Howard Daniel. *Devils, Monsters, and Nightmares* New York: Abelard-Schuman 1964

Carla Gottlieb. "Modern Art and Death" *The Meaning of Death* H. Feifel, ed., New York: McGraw-Hill 1959 pp. 157-188

Arthur Hind. *The Dance of Death* A complete facsimile of the original 1538 edition of *Les simulachres & historiees faces de la mort* New York: Dover 1971

Jessica Mitford. *The American Way of Death* New York: Fawcett World Library 1963

Erwin Panofsky. *Tomb Sculpture* New York: Harry Abrams 1964

Henri Stegemeier. "The Dance of Death in Folksong" Ph.D. diss. University of Chicago 1939

Psychic Phenomena and Death

Nietzsche says, "Timelessness and immediate rebirth are compatible once the intellect is eliminated." But once the intellect is eliminated, the question of death and all other questions are eliminated. It is a way of dissolving the question. Schopenhauer sees certain experiences as revealing or being immortality:

> "The momentary cessation of all volition which takes place whenever we give ourselves up to *aesthetic contemplation,* as pure will-less subject of knowledge . . ."

may become permanent. (Choron 181) However such aesthetic experiences remain only that — aesthetic experiences. The poet Wallace Stevens thought that certain experiences allow us to transcend or surpass this life somehow. On seeing a duck floating on a pond there is life and hope, and everything depends on it — its yellow beak shaped as it is. But again the aesthetic experience is only what it is, not something else, not a vision into an "afterlife."

William Hocking (1957) has written on psychic experiences as they relate to death and a possible afterlife. He states, "I am personally little impressed by the proofs which have been offered for the immortality of the soul."

The soul would not provide the basis for an afterlife. Someone says, "The soul goes to another world." Then think of the "places" a soul can "go" — into an animal, into a tree, into the sky, into a leaf, into a stone. Suppose we say it goes "into" a different world. How does it go "in"? Is a "different world" one unlike the one we know? Does it have different rules and a different nature? Can one tell that this is the case? If so what in our experience can show us that it is the case?

Hocking states similarly,

"If there is another life, there must be another nature. . . . We seem to ourselves to mean something by the phrase 'other world' only by illicitly drawing an imaginary boundary about this world." (26, 27)

Ducasse (1951) wrote,

"Our examination of the reasons commonly given for asserting the impossibility of survival has revealed that they are logically weak — far too much so even to show that survival is more unlikely than likely."

His view is that it is dogmatic to think that only matter is real. Matter is only one way of looking at the world, a way having a specific purpose. He thinks that consciousness may survive death, but he fails to clearly describe consciousness and even speaks of the survival of mind. Contemporary analyses show that mind is an unfounded and unintelligible concept; that we do not have minds. Mind was erroneously thought of as a metaphysical substance or container for ideas. This outdated view is now called the "container theory of mind." Thus it makes no sense to say the mind might survive the body. Mind cannot die because mind cannot live.

Ducasse quotes evidence from the reported psychical experience of Sir William Crookes whose scientific accuracy and honesty was supposedly beyond question. Crookes wrote,

"On one occasion I witnessed a chair with a lady sitting on it rise several inches from the ground. On another occasion, to avoid the suspicion of this being in some way performed by herself, the lady knelt on the chair in such manner that its four feet were visible to us. Then it rose about three inches, remained suspended for about ten seconds, and then slowly descended."

This instance contradicts all we know about the laws of physics. But the experience is easily accounted for on the basis of auto-suggestion and hypnotism. The witness may be "honest" and "accurate" in reporting but what he is reporting is really a self-hypnotic experience not a chair rising. Psychic experiences are relevant to death because it is claimed that one can communicate with the dead, or one can have "out-of-body" experiences. Ducasse, while admitting that such experiences involve trickery, thinks that some are genuine.

Another type of example Ducasse gives is from the accounts of Gardner Murphy. Some have correctly reported (or had apparitions of) a person dying or having died though the person was not seen and not known to be ill. But these sorts of reports may be explained in better ways. If one knows a person well, he knows something of his actions and failings. There is much evidence for having an apparition or thought that someone is ill or dead. For example, the person is careless, drinks in excess, deviates from his usual behavior, has not written or called as he usually does, is getting to an age where disease is more likely, etc. This can account also for determining roughly when the person will become ill or die. The "apparition" seems as if it just came to the person but may rather be due to putting together a number of subliminal or small suggestive details without consciously or clearly being aware that one is doing so. In addition, the chances that a person will be ill or die are quite high generally. This allows correct prediction much of the time.

Another experience Ducasse reports is "cross-correspondences" whereby two mediums at great distances from one another report unintelligible messages which only when put together make sense. But any two sentence fragments may be put together somehow to make an intelligible sentence. What is learned here is only something about making a sentence, not special communications from the underworld.

Gardner Murphy says, "We have *direct evidence* that this process of filching and sifting among the minds of the living does actually occur." (Ducasse 471) The view that the medium reads the minds of those present or those absent is unacceptable in that it erroneously assumes that there are minds. The medium may, however, gain some knowledge from observing the behavior, and the objects worn by those present. There is no evidence for mind and so minds cannot be "read."

Nor is it intelligible to explain psychic experience by means of "spirit," "force," "energy" or "soul." These terms seem to name entities but do not. They are elliptical for concrete operations. "Energy" and "force" are not names of entities, but of relationships between objects. "Iron filings go toward a magnet," is the sort of thing we mean by "magnetic force" or "energy." There is no force or energy as such, and none is observed. "Spirit" is elliptical for what we do. It refers to a piece of behavior. If it is thought to refer to an entity in itself it is a naming-fallacy. "Spirit" derives from the word for "breath" and breath is associated with being alive. It makes no sense then, to say, "Spirit survives life." It is like saying, "Breath survives breathing," or "When there is no action there is action." "Force," "energy," "spirit," "soul" are metaphysical terms some of which only sound scientific. Being obscure terms they tend to be used as explanations for obscure phenomena, or those things of which we are ignorant. The terms were so used in the history of science and medicine when causes of events were frequently unknown. Before the discovery of the germ theory of disease and even afterward, sin or impurity of soul was thought to be the cause of all disease. The solution was to purify one's soul. Whole theories of metaphysics and religions can grow out of these sorts of naming-fallacies and mistaken views of science and medicine. It is like the child who said, "The wind is making it dark. That's the magic trick outside."

Ducasse has a weak thesis about survival. It is that something or other in some state or other may survive death. For example, some state of consciousness may survive. He thinks that reports of memory and dream argue for immortality. There are reports of dreams in which one claims to have met Shakespeare. Plato spoke of one's remembering solutions to geometrical problems known from a previous life. Such arguments or descriptions are unacceptable. One reason is that it is not clear what could be meant by "previous life," another that the reports do not show where the phenomena dreamt or remembered came from. Also our present views of dreaming and memory are in great need of clarification. (Shibles; N. Malcolm) For example, it is not clear that memory is of the past rather than the present. How do we compare the present image with a past image if all we have access to is the present? In regard to dreaming, because when one is dreaming he is asleep (and so not conscious) he cannot know he is dreaming, the evidence for having a dream is only the report of it when one wakes up. Dreaming may then be a report of our conscious state. The psychologist's rapid eye movement tests do not give evidence for dreams but merely assume that we have them and then correlate reports of dreams with eye movement. The common views of both memory and dreaming are in need of clarification before they can be used as evidence for survival.

The reincarnationist's statement that he can "remember dying" and the view that one can die in a dream, need examination. To say that death is sleep or a dream is an argument from ignorance insofar as we are not clear, except superficially, what sleep and dreaming are.

Both dreaming and memory imply time and because time may be analyzed into a relation of changes there is no time as such. Thus memory which is only of the past, and dreams which only can be reported in the past tense, must be revised to refer only to present relations of changes. There is no time, no past or future as such, but only a relation of changes. Thus Ducasse's view that dreams and memory might survive, needs clarification. His arguments do not support his attempt to refute the view that "no life after death both possible and significant can be imagined."

Rosalind Heywood in her writing on psychical research stated,

"The nature of death is not yet settled . . . the nature of death is still an open question." She quotes Jung, " 'We cannot visualize another world ruled by quite other laws. . . . [The question of immortality] is so urgent, so immediate and so ineradicable that we must endeavour to form some sort of view about it.' "

However, Jung's view that the self might exist outside of space and time is based on the obscure metaphysical terms "space" and "time." No clear analysis of time or space is given. If time is change how can one exist outside of change? What is space? Is it an object in itself? How can one exist in or outside of space?

Heywood speaks of out-of-body experiences in terms of the feeling that one has left one's body, e.g., by drug, dream, ritual, or altered states of experience. William James took Nitrous Oxide and reported seeing his whole body, and everything in a house at once. LSD, great aesthetic experience, transcendental meditation, mountain climbing, religious experience, artificial stimulation of the semicircular canals which affect our sense of orientation, may give one an out-of-body experience or sense of a loss of self or "I."

Certainly experiences are had, but how they are to be interpreted is another question. To think one left one's body is not to leave it. Under LSD one may report taking out one's mind, washing it and putting it outside the house. But because it has been shown that there is no evidence for having a mind, such activity is unfounded. It is rather seen to be the case that one's confusions and beliefs are simply magnified by certain drugs. Drugs often produce an artificial schizophrenic state. This provides no evidence for leaving one's body. But the experience of thinking one does is not deniable.

If one goes mad so also does the world and everything one does in it. One has a new body in a new world. This is a simple way to attain an out-of-body experience, a "transcendent immortality."

Transcendental meditation states are accompanied by a specific EEG brain wave response change. That something is experienced in such meditation is undeniable. The confusion arises in describing or claiming to experience certain things. The meditator often claims to experience consciousness, cosmic consciousness, mind, astral bodies, soul, nothingness, etc. He then asserts that he knows his consciousness will survive bodily death. Sri Ramana Maharishi says that his body dies but not his consciousness, not his real "I." He does not identify himself with his body. The statements made by Maharishi are obscure and metaphysical. They only point to a certain feeling he has and give no evidence for mind, cosmic consciousness, survival after death, survival of consciousness, etc. Such statements are unjustified. They should rather be reduced to the actual experience one has, e.g., certain feelings. The transcendental meditationist is captivated by his misuse of language.

Indefiniteness, though a fallacy, seems to allow us to escape death. One may have certain feelings or visions by starving oneself, taking drugs, holding one's breath, or experiencing something beautiful. To then call such experiences visions of mind, God, another world, etc. is unfounded. It is one thing to have feelings or visions, it is another to understand and describe them. When pleasant feelings are had we want to claim that they are something other or more than what they are. To experience a sunset is not to experience a soul or afterlife. We want to say they "transcend." One thinks he can transcend, think beyond, though he does not know where or what thinking is in the first palce. To "think beyond" does one blow a hole in the sky, through the blue?

Although one may be often in disagreement with the positivism of A. J. Ayer he seems correct in stating in *Language, Truth and Logic,*

"The mystic, so far from producing propositions which are empirically verified, is unable to produce any intelligible propositions at all. And therefore we say that his intuition has not revealed to him any facts. It is no use saying that he has apprehended facts but is unable to express them. For we know that if he really had acquired any information, he would be able to express it."

Psychic research revolves around the notion of perception, the self, and consciousness. These need to be examined by careful philosophical and scientific analysis. Such work will lead to a revised view of the nature of life and therefore also of the nature of death.

A number of perceptual deviations appear in abnormal behavior or slightly abnormal behavior which tend to account for some psychic phenomena. "Depersonalization neurosis" involves a feeling of unreality and one also feels estranged from the self, body, or environment. Self-hypnosis and suggestion account for many phenomena but there is also wish-fulfillment, and hallucination. There are visual, auditory and somatic "hallucinations," experiences of having one's thoughts controlled, delusions, hearing one's own thoughts, spreading of one's thoughts to others, experience of being controlled by the outside. The schizophrenic may perceive more visual stimuli in a given unit of time than do other persons and he may think he is reading others' minds due to his loss of ego boundaries. When he is being controlled by others he is vulnerable to accepting psychic phenomena beliefs. There is a derealization or loss of contact with reality. The schizophrenic irrationality may be only temporary as in a special psychic phenomena encounter, but then leave soon after with the person resuming his rational self. If schizophrenics can hear the voice of God they may also think they can hear the voice of a deceased relative or other person. The schizophrenic often feels he has arrived at a revelation and is certain of new "facts." He just "knows" certain things are somehow true. He often develops an exotic or non-communicative language of his own. Normal individuals often have the sensation that when they are in a place, hear something, see something or think something for the first time, that they had that experience before (*deja vu*). This gives some the idea that they must have had the experience in a previous life. Psychological explanations of psychic phenomena as poor logic, suggestion, mental sets, neuroticism, etc. are very persuasive. (Drake)

In an attempt to account for reports of psychic phenomena, one may also add the defense mechanisms and avoidance mechanisms which usually form a part of our thinking.

Jacques Choron. *Death in Western Thought* New York: Collier 1963

Raleigh Drake. "Spiritistic Phenomena" *Abnormal Psychology* New Jersey: Littlefield, Adams 1954

C. J. Ducasse. *Nature, Mind and Death* Lasalle, Illinois: Open Court 1951

Rosalind Heywood. "Attitudes to Death in the Light of Dreams and Other 'Out-of-the-body' Experiences," and "Death and Psychical Research" *Man's Concern with Death* A. Toynbee, ed. New York: McGraw-Hill 1969 pp. 185-218, 219-250

William Hocking. *The Meaning of Immortality in Human Experience* New York: Harper 1957

Norman Malcolm. *Dreaming* New York: Humanities Press 1959

Warren Shibles, "Memory" *Wittgenstein, Language and Philosophy* Dubuque, Iowa: Kendall-Hunt 1970

Maharishi Mahesh Yogi. *The Science of Being and Art of Living* New York: New American Library 1963

Death in Various Cultures

In anthropology cultural views of death are treated mainly under the heading of "primitive religions." It is not clear how one religion can be more "primitive" than another, superior to another, or more true than another. The way death is approached depends largely on religious beliefs. What is said in the chapter on religion and death is relevant here. In the following a number of practices, beliefs, and attitudes toward death and funerals will be mentioned because of their interest, radical deviation from our own customs, or because of some methodological interest. By presenting such contrast one may be in a better position to ask why he has the practices he has rather than others. Alternatives or even counterexamples to one's beliefs are thereby suggested. There are ways of doing things which may be more intelligent than our own. By examination of other cultural practices we may put in perspective our own practices.

Nearly all of the cultural beliefs reported show a lack of knowledge of cause and effect, faulty analogies, or category-mistakes. Such beliefs are, however, adjusted to and may serve to temporarily meet psychological needs. They are also sometimes indicative of well-founded patterns of behavior.

Rotuma Island is 300 miles north of Fiji. In general, death is regarded by the Rotuman as follows (Howard and Scott):

a) death is a rest or sleep.

b) Christian or religious dogma regarding death is not closely adhered to.

c) there is little stress on afterlife though they believe the ghost of the deceased remains active.

d) the funeral is passive, unemotional, and it involves play and joking.

397

e) very hazardous things are done casually.

The point that Howard and Scott make about Rotuman views is that these people fear death less than we do, accept it naturally, and therefore live a better, more free life. The author's point that death must be faced and that negative emotions are hardly necessary is an important one. They contrast this society with that of the United States. Their account, however, is suspect. Americans view death as sleep also, and we speak of "slumber rooms." Our own views of afterlife are confused and religious beliefs and practices not strongly adhered to. In the United States we drive automobiles fast and casually, yet it has caused as many deaths as has military combat. One may add the dangers of mountain climbing, alcohol, hard drug intake, smoking, etc. In general, a very careful and specific analysis of all of the customs, language usages, etc., would be needed in order to adequately assess the attitude toward death of the Rotuman. Care should be taken to avoid imposing our views on them or to render their concepts as if they were ours also. For example, it is not clear what they mean by "ghost." In many cases it is not clear what we mean by our terms, e.g., death, soul, God, time, eternal, etc. Most accounts given of the beliefs of other cultures share these methodological difficulties. In this particular case the authors seem to want to point out merely that death is more accepted by the Rotuman and he can therefore live a more happy life than can the American because the American denies, avoids and fears death. Here a very small population is contrasted with a very large population. Allowances should be made for this difference. The viewpoint is that of an existentialist, the theory of which is questionable. (See chapter on existentialism)

The views of death of the Ibo tribe of Nigeria are characterized as follows (Noon):

a) Death is by the Gods. (cf. the Christian view that only sin causes disease and death.) The cure is for the "doctor" to take over the disease by the patient. (This may be compared with "sin-eaters" in Britain and the Catholic practice of confession.)

b) Death by *Uke* (spirits of misfortune). Marital fighting and discord is thought to sometimes cause the death of the child as a sign to the parents to stop fighting. Names should properly describe one's life. If wrongly named, the spirit can give the individual poor health or death. The Uke love grieving and so if parents grieve over a child the Uke soon cause the death of another child.

c) Failure to wash one's hands after handling the corpse may make one become like the corpse, and have short memory. (This is identification with and personification of the corpse.)

d) Death is caused by taboo, oaths, duties.

Violation of a taboo was seen to lead to asthma and/or death, e.g., a boy's playing with a dog is taboo in one clan. If a taboo is violated one's protective spirits leave and the person takes on the character of the taboo object. One such boy died of a cough ("bark"). This is suggestive of pyschosomatic causes of death.

e) Twins and albinos are thought abnormal. They are exposed at birth. (This may be related to our attitudes supporting abortion.)

f) In a dispute one utters the "black oath": "If my statement is wrong let this oath take away my life." If the person is alive after a year he is freed of guilt. A man hanged himself within six months after uttering this oath. This is relative to social and psychosomatic causes of death. It also suggests that death is the result of antisocial activity as does the following view.

g) Suicide may be caused by an "oath of the world" whereby usually a beautiful woman takes an antisocial oath to deceive all who are nearest her, and then she commits suicide on them. The husband is thus prevented from having a child and the bride price is not returned. The woman is thought to be possessed by a spirit.

h) Their view that a man may die because he has the spirit of recklessness in him seems circular.

The views presented above are, of course, rough generalizations about a culture. If accepted they suggest that when a cause is not known it is attributed to a spirit. By spirit we may mean "ignorance of a cause." Thus, the circularity of "If a person is reckless he has a spirit of recklessness." It is not clear why people are reckless. The cause is often largely unknown. It is also seen that death may result from antisocial behavior, a view held in common with the Bible. Psychosomatic causes of death are also suggested. In general, nearly all of these patterns may be found to prevail in our own society.

The Ibo and Christian view of "sin" and "purification" may be contrasted with other views of sin and purification. For the Christian, to be virgin is to be sinless and pure. For those of northern Haiti a girl who dies a virgin becomes a wandering spirit (*Diablesse*) and cannot reach heaven. Thus after her death a ritual intercourse is arranged and performed with a wooden or other object. Here it is a sin not to have intercourse.

The Nayars of Malabar often become drunk on arrack at funerals and are thought to be possessed by a lineage ghost. They then perform frenzied dances. (Gough) This seems relevant to one possible origin of the dance of death. It is thought that there must be a spirit which causes one's behavior. The "spirit" is something one can name as if it names an entity. This may be called a naming-fallacy. One's language may mislead him into thinking that words must name entities. Its use may, however, only refer to an unknown. One cause of such entities may be simply the effect of the alcohol. Drugs similarly produce such "spirits."

Vance Randolph presents a number of interesting views about death and dying in Ozark culture. Nearly any small event may foretell of death: a window closing at night, an object breaking when no one is near it, a picture falling from the wall (one who picks up the picture will die within a year), imagining hearing glass break when it doesn't, breaking a mirror, unusual clicking of a clock, a stopped clock which begins to strike, sound of rattle of "death bones" before someone's death [the "death rattle" heard at death is probably due to mucous accumulation]; raps, knocks, ticks or bells heard when no one is near; death tick or snap, ringing in the ears (called "death bells"), sweeping the floor after dark, burning oil to the last drop, burning firewood which pops or crackles a lot, imagining one sees the face of an absent friend in the mirror, imagining one sees a coffin-shaped object reflected in the water, transplanting cedars, allowing a child less than a year old to see his reflection in a mirror, cutting a baby's fingernails with a metal blade (mothers thus bite the nails off); some claim to "smell death"; if a dog won't eat bread touched to its lips the death of someone will soon occur; the one whom the dying man's gaze last falls on will die earlier than the others present; people die often when the clock strikes the hour; stopping of a clock by itself when a corpse is in the house, seeing oneself in a mirror in the house of the deceased, cats going near or sniffing the dead, leaving a grave open overnight, counting vehicles at funerals, crossing or colliding with a funeral procession; it is thought that deaths come in threes (cf. three is a holy number in Christian religion, e.g., three handfulls of dirt are thrown on the grave in modern ceremonies); a sudden chill indicates a rabbit or animal is walking over a spot which will ultimately be his grave; taking flowers out of cemeteries.

One man in Missouri asked to be buried on his side because he always slept that way. Another was buried with his rifle and colt revolver loaded and cocked. Such practices seem little different than the practice of being buried in polished cherry or mahogany with an adjustable bed and velvet lining. The Ozark resident often buried the body in a cloth wrapping and the burial was at once handled by the family rather than by a funeral business agency. Sometimes a funeral was held later at a church without the body present. There was no open-casket service. And hillfolk think it a bad sign if the body is somehow preserved or fails to decay. It should, they think, return to dust.

Various things are done to symbolically punish the murderer, e.g., hold down the top of a tree with a stone, throw pawpaw seeds into the grave. It is thought that a light rain is a good omen and will do more to comfort the bereaved on the day of the funeral than will preacher's words. Nature has almost always been found to be pacifying. This provides an interesting perspective on "grief therapy." The non-Christian was given a non-Christian burial.

Practices vary from feeding children popcorn at funerals, and yelling, kicking and jumping in the grave, to completely silent ceremonies. It was sometimes thought that noise disturbs the sleep of the deceased. In 1972 in Wisconsin a local law was being considered to require snowmobiles when near cemeteries to make less noise. Often slow auto speeds are required when near cemeteries. Such vehicles are allowed to make louder noises near places where people work and live. There may in this regard be more concern for the dead than for the living.

In the Ozarks, as elsewhere, there were objects which the deceased wanted to be buried with. It is as if certain objects will somehow protect or save him. It may be a cocked rifle, a religious cross, gold, silver, etc. Expensive coins are placed on the eyes of the deceased. (This custom may relate to avoidance of the death stare as well as payment for "passage" of the soul. The Greeks thought the soul had to cross the river, Styx.) In general, Ozark practices are very much like those found in peasant Poland, Rumania, and Hungary.

The facts used in the following accounts are largely from Habenstein and Lamers *Funeral Customs the World Over.* This book, according to Mitford's *American Way of Death* (p. 150) was written in conjunction with the National Funeral Directors Association as a part of a promotion campaign for the funeral industry.

James Whittman in his review of Habenstein and Lamers, *History of American Funeral Directing,* regards it as "an excellent source book on funeral practices" but adds,

> "The authors have several themes that are developed. . .
> The most apparent one is stated on page 5, 'The "decent
> funeral" is a universally accepted part of American
> thought and life, and the funeral director 'belongs.' It is
> taken for granted that his services are to be used in the
> burial of the dead.' "

All that the *Funeral Customs* book shows is that people everywhere have cultural patterns which they follow. This does not mean that the patterns followed are intelligent. Nor does it mean that we should follow our cultural rituals anymore than that we should follow those of other peoples. They mention that embalming is rarely practiced in Ireland, and that in Poland one is not allowed to bargain for a coffin or buy it in advance. The latter practice may tend to support our present funeral practice but the former would not.

Habenstein and Lamers are fair in bringing out the point that the funeral director in England is legally obliged to mention the minimum service provided for a fee equal to the amount given under the National Health Service Act. Twenty-five pounds is the amount their National Health Service pays for funeral expense.

Not all of the customs presented here are still widely practiced today. The cultural analysis and terms used are general and should be regarded as tentative only. Those writing about other cultures tend to impose our language and terms on them. Much more philosophically sound work is needed than is now available in anthropology, anthropological linguistics, transformational and structural grammar. Work done in contemporary ordinary-language philosophy may be especially helpful in anthropological work. This has been attempted recently by the anthropologist, Annamarie Simko "Death and the Hereafter." (*Omega*) A careful analytical philosophical explication of each term is needed as well as a critique of methods used.

If one holds that mind, idea, emotion, and meaning name entities (and those who write about other cultures almost always do), it will seriously negate their findings. One's view of how thinking and language work affects his analysis of how other people think and speak. If time is regarded as an entity or a word naming something in itself, it again will affect the objectivity of the analysis of other cultures. Time does not name an entity as such, but is merely a change or relation of changes. (Shibles "Timelessness") The concept "time" is often misused in our culture and theories. It cannot without clarification be used to interpret the views of people in other cultures. "Eternity" as another time word, also needs clarification.

A term specially requiring clarification is "soul" or "spirit." It is misleading to say or suggest that the members of nearly every culture believe in a soul or spirit. These terms need to be carefully analyzed. It is pointed out by Lamers and Habenstein that the Duna Indians of Panama speak of "purba" which means "shade" or "shadow." More and more detailed analyses of this sort are needed. *Funeral Customs the World Over* may, then, be regarded as a popular account of funeral customs. It is with these qualifications that the facts given in the above book are used below. The following very brief account is meant to be suggestive only. It is by no means an adequate analysis.

Here ancestor worship is prevalent. There is father-son identification. It involves the metaphorical process of substitution and identification of different things or persons. The son often builds his parents' coffins and the parents are honored to have it ready. The view is presented that the Chinese are very ritualistic. Their practices involve paid mourners, loud wailing, food for the dead, belief in three souls, and ceremonies to accommodate the souls, e.g., a "soul chicken" is placed on the coffin to induce the soul to accompany the body. The wicked are thought to become rats or worms. Habenstein and Lamers present the view that in China the funeral ceremony is the most important event in a man's life and that a man's entire estate may go toward his funeral costs. They also point out that the modern Red Chinese burial is more practical, efficient and less superstitious. Cemeteries are turned over for agricultural use. The authors appear to disapprove of the latter practices.

It was thought by the Chinese that if one's children die soon after one another there must be ghosts in them. After death the second child to die is slapped with shoes and thrown into a lake in order to drown the ghost. The child's face may be smeared with soot so the ghost will not recognize him. His body may be hung from a tree to avoid reincarnation.

In Mongolia the body is often left open for scavengers. (It may be noted that the vulture is one of the longest lived animals with a 117-year life-span.) They say the eagle is the nomad's coffin. This is in striking contrast to American burial practices. Under age ten a deceased infant's or child's body is buried without ceremony.

In Tibet Buddhist beliefs prevail. The *Tibetan Book of the Dead* is meant to help the soul pass on its way from the body. One custom is for the lama to remove a hair from the scalp to allow the soul to escape from a pore. This is the same as Western practices of opening the windows so the soul can escape, and Christian religious funeral rites to guide the soul on its way. Astrologer lamas are used to determine the details of the funeral. The dead are feared. If the ceremony is not proper it is thought that the dead will do harm to the living. This belief is prevalent in nearly every culture. Funerals are in accordance with the four elements: Earth, air, fire, water; i.e., earth burial, open air, cremation, lake or stream burial. As in Mongolia, open-air burial was most common. The flesh is separated from the bones, bones are ground and kneaded with barley. The body thus goes up in the sky as it is eaten by birds. In contrast, our own burial practice appears possessive in that we want to possess the body intact, enclosed in a sealed box and plot. Our practice takes up useful land space and money for cemeteries. The Tibetan practice is neither possessive, nor is land space taken up, nor is great expense incurred. The soul is thought to have left the body at death. There is a theologian's question here: Which of two contradictory ceremonies really does release the soul — or how is one to "succeed" in releasing the soul?

In Laos, funerals are happy affairs. Death is not mourned. The deceased is thought reborn to a better life, to Nirvana or to Buddha. "Nirvana" means a "blowing out" or extinction of a flame. The implicit analogy is that at death we go out as does a flame. In *Alice in Wonderland* we find the question, "Where does the flame go when the flame goes out?" There are funeral feasts and games lasting for six days and nights.

In Lamet, northwest Laos, coffins are often made for sitting positions. The contemporary new art painter, Magritte, has created one also. In China coffins are sometimes round. After the Lamet funeral and Buddhist ceremonies the family of the deceased would jump, scream, wail, and carry torches in an attempt to chase the spirits of the dead from the house. Also as they believe there is a soul in the head and a soul in the knees, a stone is placed over each such position on the grave.

The Zoroastrians of Persia and India have elaborate purification rites. Only certain people may touch the body. If the wrong person touches it he must go through nine days of purification which involves bathing in cow urine.

The dead are left for vultures to eat, in open "towers of silence" in the mountains. Three circles are drawn around the body. Magic numbers appear here as in Christian beliefs. It is thought that demons are around the body in the form of flies. This is close to the Catholic view of the moment of death when demons appear to attempt to snatch the soul.

As in Tibet, earth, air, fire and water are regarded as basic elements and as having a basic purity, and open-air burial is regarded as least contaminating. The body, as in most Christian religion and platonism, is thought of as being impure and, as the authors says, "the ultimate of defilement."

The four roots, earth, air, fire, and water appear in the works of Aristotle and earlier. With each of them is associated a combination of properties such as hot, dry, cold, moist. It was thought that these should be kept in balance for health. These

were related to the four humors, black bile (melancholy),
yellow bile (choleric), blood (sanguine) and phlegm
(phlegmatic) and their corresponding temperaments. Sanguine
people were too hot and blood letting was practiced. This was
also related to the planets in astrology and one was born under
an earth, air, fire or water sign. The signs were also related to
parts of the body. All one's activities were determined
ultimately by the four roots and the astrological signs. Some of
these beliefs seem applicable to the Tibetan and Zoroastrian
practices as presented by Habenstein and Lamers.

In Turkey, where the Koran is the guide, death is said to be
desired rather than feared. It is not clear whether this is an
experimental finding or a deduction from the religion. In
Turkey it is not usually proper to show grief.

Embalming is prohibited by the Moslem religion. Various
parts of the body are each washed three times. Number magic
also is evident in that each man or passerby must carry the
coffin for at least seven steps. Death is seen as a lover in the
symbolism of draping the coffin of a young girl with a scarf. It
is thought that she is married to death and so, after death, will
have all of her desires fulfilled. Women are not allowed at
funeral ceremonies at the mosque. This is not totally unlike
American custom. Emily Post commented that women need not
attend funerals. Similar to American custom, the deceased is
said to be a good person whether he or she was or not. The
Turks also think there is a light or illumination when the soul
departs, which mourners may see. This is similar to the Catholic
view. (Light is also a powerful metaphor of afterlife in Celon
and other countries.)

Iran also follows the Koran. Here, unlike Turkey, death is
greatly feared. They react violently at funerals. They roll on the
ground, rip their shirts, pull out their hair, scratch their skin,
put dust in their hair. They wash the body three times, draw
seven lines on the grave and mourners take seven paces. The
authors say that there is still a belief in ghosts in Iran. This
statement assumes that such beliefs are not common or that in
the United States such beliefs are no longer held. But
Christianity is based on such spiritual beliefs, e.g., the Holy
Ghost or the soul which leaves the body. In Iran the ghost is
sometimes thought of as a revengeful half-shrouded skeleton.
Again this suggests the dance of death books. (See chapter on
dance of death.)

The Ashanti of West Africa believe, as Christians did and often still do, that disease originates in supernatural beings. Food is offered to the dead three times. There is funeral dancing, singing, playing, and intoxication. At one time slaves were sacrificed.

The Navaho tie a "death knot" around the dead body. The knot is never to be untied. Only a knife is allowed to cut the knot and when cut the knife is thrown away. The Navaho have great fear of death and contamination from the dead. They skip, hop and take a roundabout path in their return from the grave to avoid being caught by an evil spirit.

Spirits supposedly almost always defy observation by the average person. The Tiwi of North Australia, for example, claim that the spirits are black by night and white by day. The Tiwi funeral dance includes young girls. The Tiwi often crawl into the grave, slash themselves, jump high in the air and fall flat. They may also eat grave dirt. The Catholic practice of taking a wafer in church seems similar to the eating of grave dirt. The jumping seems to be a physiognomic reaction. Like children they express themselves and react to the world largely in terms of bodily movement. Dancing is a similar means of expression. "Grief therapy" takes this form in this culture. Funeral dancing may be considered as a possible means of therapy in addition to our usual practices. That such practices may seem barbaric is only because they are not familiar to us. To them our practices may seem barbaric. They also make elaborate and very artistic funeral poles for the dance ceremony, which are twenty feet high and three feet wide. Each pole is made differently. Art has often in our culture been employed as a temporary sort of grief therapy.

The Menabe tribe of Madagascar believes the soul of a king passes into a large snake, and thinks the soul is a double for the body. They allow deceased criminals and sorcerers to be eaten by dogs. This is similar to our former practice of not burying those who commit suicide or are criminals. The question arises as to why graves should be marked at all, why one should even keep an ash of a cremation. It seems to be because there is a great desire on our part for possession. But one cannot take others' graves with him when he dies. Their ashes become mixed with one's own. In this respect it is we who belong to the dust rather than the other way around.

The Salish Indians did not mark the grave if one of them died in a foreign land. This was due to the fear that the enemy would find it and scalp the remains. The dead are in this way animated and personified so that they are thought of as being still somehow alive. The dead are thought to communicate with and have power over the living. Such a view is based on personification or the "pathetic fallacy" of treating inanimate things as if they have feelings. It is metaphorical to talk to a corpse: "Why don't you say something?" Prayer is also similarly metaphorical.

The Ikongo suspend the coffin in a meeting house. The Sioux Indians practice suspension also but by tree burial. The Ikongo do not mark their forest graves though others are marked. In our own culture marked graves led to tomb and grave robbing. Shakespeare's stone appeals to the reader not to disturb his bones. The Ikongo funeral procession is noisy, involving screaming, yelling, wrestling and games. There is little grief in the usual sense.

Bali, in Oceania, has one of the most elaborate funeral ceremonies. In their more ancient practices parts of the body of the deceased may have been eaten in the belief that one thereby gains magical powers. This is now done symbolically by allowing water to drip over the body into rice. The rice is then cooked, shaped into the figure of a man and eaten. This again seems similar to the Catholic practice whereby the wafer is eaten and regarded as the body of Christ. Haberstein and Lamers suggest that the funeral is the largest and happiest celebration the Balinese have. They point out that the people are thrifty yet will give all their savings for a funeral.

The body is cremated in an elaborate ceremony and the soul is thought to return to earth in another human body. The Christian belief is similar but different in that for the latter there is a resurrection of a new body and not so much a transmigration into another existing body. The Balinese also think the soul may wander from the body in dreams, escape through the mouth and refuse to return. A bamboo tube is put in a body temporarily buried until cremation, to allow the soul to escape.

That views about life are carried over to views about death is indicated by the practice of beginning the funeral ceremony with the corpse naked except for the sexual parts which are covered. In Turkey only those men not eligible to marry the deceased woman were allowed to place the body in the grave. In Lebanon a holy man is not allowed to wash the body of a woman. This may be partly due to the fact that women are regarded as impure. In Israel and India only women can attend deceased women. The dead are thus personified and sexual taboos are seen to apply even after one is dead.

In Bali pieces of broken mirrors are put on the eyelids, steel on the teeth, a gold ring with a ruby is put in the mouth, Jasmine flowers are put in the nose, and iron nails put on the arms and legs. An egg is rolled over the head which is covered with a white cloth. The priest writes on paper tickets for use in the afterlife. The above is like our practice of burying the dead with coins or jewels. (In Japan coins are put in the hands of the deceased so he may pay his way to eternity.) The personification involved is so much a part of our tradition, that the soul will take a journey, etc., that we are hardly ever aware that it is a metaphor taken literally.

In Bali food is fed to the deceased. (cf. "soul food") Gigantic animal effigies are built, in which the dead are to be cremated. The animal effigy chosen depends on the social class of the deceased. It is for a nobleman, a bull; noblewoman, a cow; King or Queen, a winged lion; soldier, a deer. It may require seventy-five people to carry it. The practice of effigy burning is partly a result of the metaphorical substitution or identification of the person with the effigy.

Little reverence seems to us to be shown to the body when it is carried. There is staggering, clowning, and fireworks are set off. The bearers seek out rough spots and mud holes to go through. Some of these practices are supposedly to confuse the spirit so it will not return to the house. After the body is set down there is a fight over its possession. People climb over the tower to obtain precious ornaments. The burning body is poked carelessly or its parts strewn around and the body may be scolded for not burning fast enough. Small boys seek treasures in the ashes left from the cremation. The funeral is treated in general as we treat Christmas. That small children are actively present and seeking treasures may suggest that the ceremony may be appropriate for children. It would be equivalent to our providing presents and candies to children at funerals. Shock from childhood bereavement may be lessened. But such shock may be primarily induced or learned as a cultural pattern in the first place. That is, one may learn to grieve when he wouldn't have normally done so. The cultural requirement for mourning is indicated by the fact that there are paid mourners in many cultures.

Sometimes Balinese widows jumped into the flames to die also. This decision was left up to the woman. It was an acceptable form of euthanasia until the Dutch stopped its practice.

Unlike religious practices elsewhere, in Bali a test is made to find out how successful the ceremony has been. Thus an attempt is made to communicate with the dead person to see if he was cremated properly. Magical tests are provided for magical practices. In the Christian religion even magical tests seem to be absent. We never do know if the Christian ceremony "worked." If some mistake has been made, for example, if someone took six steps instead of seven, or performed an act two instead of three times, what would happen?

In Lebanon there is a Moslem ceremony. No vehicles were used, all was on foot. There are paid mourners. Women may be banned from the funeral march. Cemeteries are regarded as unclean. They are purposely neglected as they are regarded as a form of idolatry. This is in contrast to the American cemetery practice and the Christian view that cemeteries are holy. The Lebanese dead are questioned by angels before being admitted to Paradise, and this is like the Catholic view of questioning the dying regarding their genuineness of belief.

In Israel the windows are opened when someone dies, perhaps so the soul may escape. Mirrors are covered. There are rigid regulations governing all procedures. Only women could attend a woman's body, the body may not remain unburied overnight, no coffin is to be used, there are seven days of mourning of which the first three are to be work-free, children must pray for the dead parent annually, etc. That there is no mourning for the infant who does not live thirty days suggests that the child is not yet regarded as a person. This belief may be used to support the acceptability of abortion in Western culture.

In Ethiopia there is bitter funeral weeping, hair is pulled out, faces scratched. One must weep in accordance with how close a relative the deceased is. Every reminder of the deceased must be reacted to with much grief. One is supposed to mourn for seven days. This shows again that grief is partly a culturally prescribed activity rather than a necessary, natural, or intelligently chosen activity.

Eskimos of Victoria Island joke about death and the authors say death for them is regarded unemotionally. The Eskimos may say casually, "The foxes have eaten so and so." Nevertheless they have rigid taboos suggesting a fear of death and those who keep vigil are called "those who are afraid." Unwanted children are simply strangled at birth.

In Japan the funeral practices are largely those of Buddhism and Shintoism. They have ritual practices, e.g., seven services, each one at seven-day intervals, etc., but also some less usual beliefs. The dead are thought to listen and pallbearers laugh and talk as they work around the grave. After the funeral, relatives hold a drinking party. Cremation was prohibited in 1875 but is almost universal today. Perhaps most important is the Japanese view that one should not display negative emotions. To do so is thought to be an imposition on others.

In India, ceremonies are largely Hindu. When death approaches a journey is made to a sacred river to live there until death. There a Brahmin has the man's sin transferred over to himself. They believe the soul is trapped in the skull and so during cremation the skull is made to burst. If the fire fails to do it a club is used. Bones are thrown into a sacred river by a professional priest bone thrower. Thus bones are seen to line the sacred rivers. All of this often uses up the entire savings of the family. The practice of *suttee,* throwing oneself on the funeral pyre to be cremated with one's husband, was made illegal in 1829 though it still sometimes occurs. There are sometimes paid mourners.

Russian funeral customs are significant especially because of the way in which they have changed. Their old practices involved ancestor worship, loud wailings and shouting, overeating, drunkenness, games, dance, stealing, animism, cults of the dead, etc. Around 1930 the ceremony became more secular, rational, and utilitarian. Cremation is stressed except for certain heros of state who are permanently embalmed and displayed.

The metaphorical process of thinking is represented among all Christian views of death and afterlife. It is reflected especially well also by Polish peasant beliefs and practices. Poland is largely Catholic. Some of their folk views are: death is personified as a tall, thin, white woman; on All Saints' Day the dead return to their former house, the souls visit the church at midnight causing a great light there, a drawing of straws at Christmas determines how long one will live, the first to leave the Christmas table will die within a year (cf. death by suggestion), on All Souls' Day one must walk carefully and blow on the bench before he sits down so as not to crush a spirit, nothing should be twisted after sunset to avoid entangling a spirit, Holy Week is a good time to die because the graves are opened then, God may be begged off from death for awhile. The following are signs that God is present: creaking floor, dog's growl, crowing, dream indications, a white spot under the small finger of the left hand. A sudden change of the weight of the body shows that the soul has departed. Doors and windows must be left opened and often a hole made in the roof to allow the soul to escape, murderers have no shadow because they have no soul, the eyes of the corpse must be closed or they will cast a spell, the lips and jaw of the corpse are closed so that he will not turn into a vampire and bite people, mirrors are covered so reflection of the dead or death will not be seen, the cattle and bees of the dead man must be first told of his death so they will not also follow him in dying, orchards and farm buildings are also told, singing through an "empty" night provides protection against spirits, sins are thought to hide in the seams of clothes, sewing or pounding may bruise the soul of the dead person, the house may not be whitewashed for nine months as it may close in the soul, use of the comb of the dead may cause baldness, a pillow is omitted from the coffin so the stay in purgatory will be short, a coin is put under the head so the dead will not steal from the living, candles must be lit so the soul can find its way to eternity, money should be left in the coffin to pay the way into heaven, the body is kissed and regarded as if it were alive, the coffin must be touched three times on the inner step of the house and three times on the outer step, one cannot bargain about a coffin or buy it in advance, the driver should start or run his horses three times, if one gives a backward glance at the·

grave it might cause the soul to follow him. Modern funeral ceremonies are similar, but diverse, more modern practices are found. They are often Catholic practices. Practices in peasant Hungary and Rumania are similar.

An analysis of singing and funeral dirges and poems could have been done for each culture. In Rumania lamentations take the form of ritual chants and grief dirges. Singers are hired. Songs are sung in a tone they refer to as "griefless." Four well known ritual songs are "The Great Song," "The Rooster," "The Dawn," "The Song of the Fir Tree." A thirty-foot fir tree is planted at the head of the grave. Funeral ceremony is treated like Christmas. There are games, jokes, stories, candles and a candy decorated fir tree. The fruit is distributed at the ceremony. Rumanians once danced around the grave. This may have been one of the sources for or consequences of the mediaeval dance of death. In Hungary and elsewhere burial feasts had been held by the grave.

In Mexico All Souls' Day, Nov. 1st, is celebrated as perhaps the major holiday of the year. The entire city is devoted to honoring and celebrating the dead. The practice is based on Catholic religious views. It is a complete festival and carnival of the dead. They feast in cemeteries. There are grinning skull cakes, skull candies, chocolate caskets, sugar coated tombstones. A skull may be put at the center of the table with candy in its eyesockets. Skeletons are seen and skeleton costumes. Well-known men are represented in the newspaper by means of pictures of skulls. The whole event is a gigantic tensive metaphorical oxymoron. The most lively and joyous is juxtaposed with the most ugly and dead. The result is humor, high excitement, and violence.

Octavio Paz also presented an account of All Souls' Day in Mexico. He wrote,

"The word death is not pronounced in New York, in Paris, in London, because it burns the lips. The Mexican, in contrast, is familiar with death, jokes about it, caresses it, sleeps with it, celebrates it; it is one of his favorite toys and his most steadfast love."

Paz states that life and death are inseparable and that when life lacks meaning, death lacks meaning. This may be better put, as above, in terms of an oxymoron, the conceit, or reciprocal metaphor, that is, "Life is death." There is death in life and life in death. Each term becomes modified by the other in creating a tensive, absurd, humorous, and paradoxical insight. The striking juxtaposition also yields the surprise due to combination of opposites yielding a release and freedom from narrow categories and apparent escape from the problems regarding death and life. At the fiesta the Mexican explodes. This analysis may help explain why Paz goes on to say,

"We kill because life – our own or another's – is of no value. Life and death are inseparable, and when the former lacks meaning, the latter becomes equally meaningless."

Paz continues to build up the fact that the fiesta becomes the highest point in the Mexican's life, and then speaks of the "grandeur" of murder: "Through murder we achieve a momentary transcendence." This view shows that the synthesis of the metaphorical antithesis "Life is death," or "Death is life," is "Murder is grandeur." The opposites are reconciled. Paz's interpretation is one-sided. It is not clear that murder does reconcile the opposites. However, his main point about reconciliation or synthesis is interesting. The antithesis "Life is death" may have been resolved in a great many other ways, perhaps more fulfilling, and more intelligent ways. Murder seems too extreme to serve as synthesis. It seems rather to serve as the pole of chaos or wild confusion. One might also relate the "Life is death" metaphor to the Spanish bullfight. The fiesta is wild and irrational. It transcends and deviates from behavioral restrictions and categories. It is free. Paz thinks that such freedom allows us to see that our traditional categories and behavior are masks of falsehood.

The Cuna Indians of Panama believe that if the soul wanders too far from the body or too far away while asleep the person will die. The dead are greatly feared and never mentioned by name. (Name magic is part of Christian customs as are our euphemisms for death. One does not speak of the "corpse" but rather of "the loved one" or "Mr. Jones.") A death chant is sung which lasts about twenty hours. They have no fear of the cemetery and may even eat and sleep there.

The Jivaro of the eastern Andes do not believe that death is natural. It is thought to be due to some man or witchcraft. Every death is regarded as murder. In Western Christian tradition disease and death were and are thought to be caused by God, and one may say, "It is up to God when I will die." Thus it is God who kills the Christians or inflicts him with disease. (Death may, however, be a kind of self-murder if it is found that old age and death can be prevented.) The relatives of the Jivaro do not inherit the belongings of the dead man but rather his possessions are distributed among others. This may be equivalent to our willing our money to research and seems to be an intelligent practice more beneficial to society than giving great sums of money to one's offspring or a relative. They also remove the head of the deceased, shrink it to a sixth of its original size and keep it as a sign of honor or vengeance.

The Kaingang of Brazil are said by Habenstein and Lamers to have a "pathological" fear of the supernatural world and to "invent" bloodthirsty, ferocious spirits. The authors' account here is biased and slanted in favor of Christianity. Rather it would seem Christians are quite similar. They have been told they ought to fear hell, and eternal fire, and they "invent" evil demons and devils to tempt and punish "evil" ones. Beliefs of Kaingang seem no less pathological or invented than those Christian religious beliefs now still prevalent in our society and, as was indicated, especially by witch trials and art of dying books and visions of hell. A criterion is needed for one to say that one religion is better than another, yet no objective one is given or found. The ferocity of religious belief is presently being seen in the violent Protestant - Catholic wars going on in Ireland. That the various cultures invent or believe in such horrifying spirits means they must live and die their horrifying beliefs and defend such beliefs. That is, one lives and dies his metaphors.

In Ireland a wake is, as elsewhere, a "watch" of the dead, perhaps to protect the dead from evil spirits, perhaps also to see if the person is in fact still alive. (Kane) The wake was often characterized by drunkenness and there was also much brawling. Sometimes the money raised for a wake by the poor is spent first on drink. There is also drinking and smoking in the graveyard. Kane claims that since the Irish are very superstitious the funeral ceremony has a beneficial therapeutic result.

An examination of funeral practices in different cultures reveals the following:

1. Funeral practices depend largely on cultural patterns and religious beliefs.
2. Great divergence of practice is found from culture to culture.
3. Cultural patterns are usually believed in regardless of how irrational they may seem to those of a different culture.
4. As believed in, such cultural practices may be found to be therapeutic.
5. If cultural funeral practices, including Christian and American practices, are questioned or examined they are found to be irrational and unintelligent.
6. Existing funeral practices do not contribute to inquiry or increase our knowledge of death or dying.
7. Emotions are not clarified by existing funeral practices but if the ritual is believed in it may help placate emotions. In some cultures grief seems not to be experienced.
8. For many cultures the very young child is unceremoniously disposed of even months after birth. Abortion would seem not to be objectionable and is practiced by nearly every society. (See chapter on abortion)
9. There is a belief in spirits or souls in perhaps every culture but the beliefs about such souls are diverse, contradictory, or confused. Some think there are four or a great many souls, others that there is just one. The soul is often taken literally and is expected to escape through a hole in the roof, the pore of a hair or a straw. Spirits or souls rule the world, haunt the living, or go to a good or bad world. They must be fed, guided to the next world, talked to, or appeased in other ways.
10. Death is regarded as a tool for punishment of antisocial or "bad" behavior.

11. Magic numbers, especially 3, 7, 12, play a large part in funeral ceremony. This superstition or belief is closely tied with religious belief.
12. Most of the rituals and beliefs, however barbaric seeming, which are found in other cultures are found also in Christian and other American funeral practices.
13. In many cultures there is funeral sacrifice of lives and/or of one's entire possessions. This may result from the inability to rationally cope with or understand emotions such as grief and guilt, and the lack of rational inquiry into the nature of death.
14. Mourning behavior may be absent or violent among different cultures.
15. Mystical symbol, metaphors taken literally, and false analogies regarding death and the funeral are prevalent in every culture.
16. Details of an afterlife are often entirely metaphorical but are nevertheless taken literally.

E. K. Gough. "Cults of the Dead Among the Nayars" *American Anthropologist* 71 (1958) 446-478

Robert Habenstein and William Lamers. *Funeral Customs the World Over* Milwaukee, Wisconsin: Bulfin Printers 1960

Alan Howard and Robert Scott. "Cultural Values and Attitudes Toward Death" *Journal of Existentialism* 6 (22) (1965-1966) 161-171

John Kane. "The Irish Wake" *Sociological Symposium* 1 (Fall 1968) 11-15

Jessica Mitford. *The American Way of Death* New York: Fawcett 1963

John Noon. "A Preliminary Examination of the Death Concepts of the Ibo" *American Anthropologist* 44 (1942) 638-654

Octavio Paz. "The Day of the Dead" *The Labyrinth of Solitude* L. Kemp, trans., New York: Grove Press 1961 pp. 47-64

Vance Randolph. "Death and Burial" *Ozark Magic and Folklore* New York: Dover 1947

418

Warren Shibles. "Timelessness" *Philosophical Pictures* 2nd ed., Dubuque, Iowa: Kendall-Hunt 1972

Annamarie Simko. "Death and the Hereafter" *Omega* 1 (2) (May 1970) 121-135

James Whittman. "Review of Habenstein & Lamers *The History of American Funeral Directing*" *Sociological Symposium* 1 (Fall 1968) 95-96

Mark Twain

The Art of Inhumation

I encountered a man in the street whom I had not seen for
six or seven years; and something like this talk followed. I said:
"But you used to look sad and oldish; you don't now. Where
did you get all this youth and bubbling cheerfulness? Give me
the address."

He chuckled blithely, took off his shining tile, pointed to a
notched pink circlet of paper pasted into its crown, with
something lettered on it, and went on chuckling while I read,
"J. B., UNDERTAKER." Then he clapped his hat on, gave it an
irreverent tilt to leeward, and cried out:

"That's what's the matter! It used to be rough times with me
when you knew me – insurance-agency business, you know;
mighty irregular. Big fire, all right – brisk trade for ten days
while people scared; after that, dull policy-business till next fire.
Town like this don't have fires often enough – a fellow strikes
so many dull weeks in a row that he gets discouraged. But you
bet you, *this* is the business! People don't wait for example to
die. No, sir, they drop off right along – there ain't any dull
spots in the undertaker line. I just started in with two or three
little old coffins and a hired hearse, and *now* look at the thing!
I've worked up a business here that would satisfy any man,
don't care who he is. Five years ago, lodged in an attic; live in a
swell house now, with a mansard roof, and all the modern
inconveniences."

"Does a coffin pay so well? Is there much profit on a
coffin?"

"*Go*-way! How you talk!" Then, with a confidential wink, a
dropping of the voice, and an impressive laying of his hand on
my arm: "Look here; there's one thing in this world which isn't

419

ever cheap. That's a coffin. There's one thing in this world which a person don't ever try to jew you down on. That's a coffin. There's one thing in this world which a person don't say — 'I'll look around a little, and if I find I can't do better I'll come back and take it. That's a coffin. There's one thing in this world which a person won't take in pine if he can go walnut; and won't take in walnut if he can go mahogany; and won't take in mahogany if he can go an iron casket with silver door-plate and bronze handles. That's a coffin. And there's one thing in this world which you don't have to worry around after a person to get him to pay for. And *that's* a coffin. Undertaking? — why it's the dead-surest business in Christendom, and the nobbiest.

"Why, just look at it. A rich man won't have anything but the very best; and you can just pile it on, too — pile it on and sock it to him — he won't ever holler. And you take in a poor man, and if you work him right he'll bust himself on a single lay-out. Or especially a woman. F'r instance: Mrs. O'Flaherty comes in, — widow, — wiping her eyes and kind of moaning. Unhandkerchiefs one eye, bats it around tearfully over the stock; says:

" 'And fhat might ye ask for that wan?'

" 'Thirty-nine dollars, madam,' says I.

" ' It's a foine big price, sure, but Pat shall be buried like a gintleman, as he was, if I have to work me fingers off for it. I'll have that wan, sor.'

" 'Yes, madam,' says I, 'and it is a very good one, too; not costly, to be sure, but in this life we must cut our garment to our clothes, as the saying is.' And as she starts out, I heave in, kind of casually, 'This one with the white satin lining is a beauty, but I am afraid — well, sixty-five dollars *is* a rather — rather — but no matter, I felt obliged to say to Mrs. O'Shaughnessy —'

" 'D'ye mane to soy that Bridget O'Shaughnessy bought the mate to that joo-ul box to ship that dhrunken divil to Purgatory in?'

" 'Yes, madam.'

" 'Then Pat shall go to heaven in the twin to it, if it takes the last rap the O'Flahertys can raise; and moind you, stick on some extras, too, and I'll give ye another dollar.'

"And as I lay in with the livery stables, of course I don't forget to mention that Mrs. O'Shaughnessy hired fifty-four dollars' worth of hacks and flung as much style into Dennis' funeral as if he had been a duke or an assassin. And of course she sails in and goes the O'Shaughnessy about four hacks and an omnibus better. That *used* to be, but that's all played now; that is, in this particular town. The Irish got to piling up hacks so, on their funerals, that a funeral left them ragged and hungry for two years afterward; so the priest pitched in and broke it all up. He don't allow them to have but two hacks now, and sometimes only one."

"Well," said I, "If you are so light-hearted and jolly in ordinary times, what *must* you be in an epidemic?"

He shook his head.

"No, you're off, there. We don't like to see an epidemic. An epidemic don't pay. Well, of course I don't mean that, exactly; but it don't pay in proportion to the regular thing. Don't it occur to you why?"

"No."

"Think."

"I can't imagine. What is it?"

"It's just two things."

"Well, what *are* they?"

"One's Embamming."

"And what's the other?"

"Ice."

"How is that?"

"Well, in ordinary times, a person dies, and we lay him up in ice; one day, two days, maybe three, to wait for friends to come. Takes a lot of it — melts fast. We charge jewelry rates for the ice, and war prices for attendance. Well, don't you know, when there's an epidemic, they rush 'em to the cemetery the minute the breath's out. No market for ice in an epidemic. Same with Embamming. You take a family that's able to embam, and you've got a soft thing. You can mention sixteen different ways to do it. — though there *ain't* only one or two ways, when you come down to the bottom facts of it, — and they'll take the highest-priced way, every time. It's human nature — human nature in grief. It don't reason, you see. Time being, it don't care a d——n. All it wants is physical immortality for deceased, and they're willing to pay for it. All you've got to do is to just be ca'm and stack it up — they'll stand the racket. Why, man, you can take a defunct that you couldn't *give* away; and get your embamming traps around you and go to work; and in a couple of hours he is worth a cool six hundred — that's what *he's* worth. There ain't anything equal to it but trading rats for di'monds in time of famine. Well, don't you see, when there's an epidemic, people don't wait to embam. No, indeed they don't; and it hurts the business like hellth, as we say — hurts it like hell-th, *health,* see? — our little joke in the trade. Well, I must be going. Give me a call whenever you need any — I mean, when you're going by, some time."

In his joyful high spirits, he did the exaggerating himself, if any had been done. I have not enlarged on him.

With the above brief references to inhumation, let us leave the subject. As for me, I hope to be cremated. I made that remark to my pastor once, who said, with what he seemed to think was an impressive manner:

"I wouldn't worry about that, if I had your chances."

Much he knew about it — the family all so opposed to it.

Hygiene and Sentiment (excerpt)

In an address before the Chicago Medical Society, in advocacy of cremation, Dr. Charles W. Purdy made some striking comparisons to show what a burden is laid upon society by the burial of the dead:

One and one-fourth times more money is expended annually in funerals in the United States than the Government expends for public school purposes. Funerals cost this country in 1880 enough money to pay the liabilities of all the commercial failures in the United States during the same year, and give each bankrupt a capital of eight thousand six hundred and thirty dollars with which to resume business. Funerals cost annually more money than the value of the combined gold and silver yield of the United States in the year 1880. These figures do not include the sums invested in burial-grounds and expended in tombs and monuments, nor the loss from depreciation of property in the vicinity of cemeteries.

For the rich, cremation would answer as well as burial; for the ceremonies connected with it could be made as costly and ostentatious as a Hindoo *suttee*; while for the poor, cremation would be better than burial, because so cheap (Four or five dollars is the minimum cost.) — so cheap until the poor got to imitating the rich, which they would do by and by. The adoption of cremation would relieve us of a muck of threadbare burial-witticisms; but, on the other hand, it would resurrect a lot of mildewed old cremation-jokes that have had a rest for two thousand years.

I have a colored acquaintance who earns his living by odd jobs and heavy manual labor. He never earns above four hundred dollars in a year, and as he has a wife and several children, the closest scrimping is necessary to get him through to the end of the twelve months debtless. To such a man a funeral is a colossal financial disaster. While I was writing one of the preceding chapters, this man lost a little child. He walked the town over with a friend, trying to find a coffin that was within his means. He bought the very cheapest one he could find, plain wood, stained. It cost him *twenty-six dollars.* It would have cost less than four, probably, if it had been built to put something useful into. He and his family will feel that outlay a good many months.

The Funeral Industry

In a brochure entitled "What About Funeral Costs?" the National Funeral Directors Association gives a concise account about funeral costs in the following section:

I FUNERAL COSTS

A. Four Separate and Distinct Categories of Charges Make Up the Cost of a Funeral:

1. Those which specifically involve the funeral director including his professional services and those of his staff; the use of the facilities and equipment he has available; and, the casket and the vault selected.
2. Those dealing with the disposition of the body. If earth interred, there is the cost of the grave (if no cemetery lot is previously owned) and the charge for opening and closing same. If cremated, there is the charge for the actual cremation, plus the cost of an urn if one is desired in which to place the cremated remains.
3. Those for memorialization, such as a monument or marker for the grave or a niche for the urn of cremated remains.
4. Those miscellaneous expenses paid by the family directly or through the funeral director. These include such items as: flowers, newspaper death notices, additional limousines, burial clothing and out-of-town transporation of the body.

B. Important General Considerations

Anyone seeking information in advance of need on funeral and burial costs can secure such data from a funeral director.

Experience dictates that it is difficult to be specific about over-all expenses without knowing when, where and under what circumstances death will occur. The funeral is usually selected by the family of the deceased. Their needs, desires and demands must be considered. Their decision is often rooted in religious and ethnic customs, family preferences and traditions, and of course, the customs and usages of their particular community. Then, too, the economy of an area has its effects on funeral prices just as it does on the cost of other services and commodities.

C. Cost of Services and Merchandise Provided by the Funeral Director

1. Methods of Pricing or Quoting Prices
   There are various methods of quoting the prices of the services and merchandise provided by the funeral director. The following is a brief explanation of the various methods used:
   a. Single Unit or Standard
      This method establishes a single price based upon the standard and/or necessary and/or requested items of service to meet the needs and customs of individuals in a given locality and the casket selected.
   b. Bi-Unit or Services and Facilities Plus Casket
      This method of quoting a funeral price is made up of two basic figures. One is for the professional services and use of the facilities to meet needs and customs. The other is for the casket.
   c. Functional or Itemization
      This method lists the various facets of the funeral service according to function or use including various services of staff and items of facilities, equipment and merchandise and the price of each.
   d. Supplementary Data for All Pricing Methods
      With all pricing or quotation methods there are some items which are or may be priced separately. This is especially true when the single unit or bi-unit methods are employed. Items such as outer receptacles (vaults), urns, clothing, and the like are

listed, and priced separately from the funeral service as such. Most times the itemized or functional method will include these under merchandise. Sometimes, however, a separate portion of the funeral agreement form or invoice is devoted to them.

D. Some Statistics Regarding Services Selected in 1971 and Some Expense Data

The National Funeral Directors Association conducts an annual nationwide survey among its members which shows how much people are paying for the funerals they select. The most recent survey indicates that in 1971, Americans paid $983 for the "average" regular adult funeral they selected.

When all services conducted were considered the amount paid was $858. This latter statistic, in addition to regular adult funerals, includes funerals for children and indigents and partial services where death occurred other than where the funeral and/or burial was held and two funeral homes were involved.

Of all funeral services selected: 6.8% were priced between $200 and $499; 19.2% between $500 and $799; 28.5% between $800 and $999; 16.2% between $1,000 and $1,199; 8.9% between $1,200 and $1,499; 3.4% between $1,500 and $1,999; and 0.7% over $2,000. The remaining 16.3% included funeral services for children and indigents or partial services.

Keep in mind these figures do not include vault, cemetery or crematorium expenses, monument or marker, or miscellaneous items such as honoraria for the clergyman, flowers, additional transportation charges, burial clothing or newspaper notices.

Families choose the casket to be used as part of the funeral they desire from a selection displayed by the funeral director. While all funeral directors do not use the same method of quoting prices as indicated above, the funeral director's total charge includes not only the casket, but also an amount to compensate him for the services he renders and the facilities and equipment he provides to conduct the funeral.

It should be noted that every funeral director has a substantial investment in facilities and equipment. In 1971 the investment range of those participating in the study was from an average of $119,697 for funeral homes which conducted less than 100 funerals that year to $620,028 for those that had more than 300 services.

The major expense item for a funeral home is salaries. Personnel, facilities and equipment must be available 24 hours a day to serve the public.

The following percentages reflect expenses involved in providing the average funeral in 1971: salaries (29%); burial merchandise available from the funeral director (20%); building and occupancy (9%); items secured as an accommodation to the family (11%); supplies, services, collections and promotion (8%); automobile (6%); general expense (5%); and taxes (4%). This leaves the profit margin at 8%.

Burial Enclosures. For earth burial, many people wish the casket and remains to be placed in an outside enclosure. Outside enclosures, providing protection against the elements, are known as burial vaults. They are made of concrete, steel, fiberglass and solid copper. Burial vaults will range in price from about $175 up, and are generally sold through funeral directors.

For those who do not use a protective vault, many cemeteries require the use of some type of outside enclosure to reduce the possibility of a grave cave-in. These can come in the form of a sectional concrete enclosure most of which sell for about $90 or more. Some cemeteries will permit a wooden outside enclosure which will be sold starting at about $50.

E. Interment or Cremation

Interment or cremation charges are in addition to those paid to the funeral director for the services and goods he provides. In most cemeteries the cost of an individual grave space ranges from about $75 to $350. Costs of opening and closing the grave are approximately $40 to $200, and any other cemetery charges which will be itemized. Prices for individual crypts in indoor mausolea start at about $600. Outside garden crypts begin at about $350.

The cost of a cremation ranges from $35 to $150. Urns to hold a single cremated remains run from $50 to over $250. Urns intended for more than one cremated remains sell for $100 to over $500. Columbaria niches to hold such urns range from $35 to $750, with the price depending on the size, location and quality of the niche.

F. Monument or Marker

When earth burial is utilized, most people wish to memorialize their dead and mark their graves. Although most markers or monuments are purchased from monument retailers, some are bought from cemeteries. In certain parts of the country, funeral directors sell them for the convenience of those they serve. Bronze markers vary in price from $75 to $300, and stone monuments start at about $75. The cost of either can run considerably higher depending upon the size, materials, design and craftsmanship of the memorial.

G. Miscellaneous Expenses Including Cash Advances

The cost of flowers, burial clothing, transportation of the body — if burial or cremation is to be at a place other than where death occurred — additional limousines or flower cars, honorarium for the clergyman, and newspaper death notices make up some of the miscellaneous items paid through the funeral director or directly by the family. Because most of these items involve the discretion of the family, they must be dealt with individually and separately.

Some of these expenses are not associated with the services or facilities of the funeral home. However, most funeral directors will advance monies for their payment at the pleasure of the family.

These include crematory and cemetery charges; honoraria for personal services of other individuals such as clergymen and musicians; paid newspaper death notices; long distance telephone calls; certified copies of death certificates; air or rail transportation and flowers. There may also be times when a funeral home accepts the responsibility for charges made by an out of town funeral establishment for any services or merchandise provided in the forwarding or transferring of remains.

H. Suggestions For Family-Funeral Director Relations After Death Occurs

Before the family selects the funeral service, the funeral director should explain the various aspects of the funeral and the costs thereof as to the services and the merchandise he provides and as to that obtained from others such as cemeteries and florists. This should be done before the family goes into the casket selection room. The funeral director should make clear the range of prices of funerals he has available. Also the funeral director should welcome any questions or discussions as to what is or is not required by laws and/or regulations to such laws.

The funeral director should review for the family the various death benefits and/or burial allowances that may be available to them such as those involving Social Security, the Veterans Administration, labor unions, fraternal and other organizations. He will assist in the preparation and filing of the necessary forms to secure these benefits and allowances for the family. Where further professional assistance is required he should suggest that the families seek the advice of other professionals.

Because the total price of the funeral as to the funeral director is in some way affected by the casket selection, there should be a card or brochure in each casket in the selection room. Such card or brochure should outline the services offered by the funeral home. Services and merchandise not included where a single unit or standard price method is used should be listed on the card or brochure as separate items or given in a verbal explanation.

When a family decides on the kind of service desired, the funeral director should provide a memorandum or agreement for the family to approve or sign, showing (1) the price of the service that the family has selected and what is included therein; (2) the price of each of the supplemental items of service and/or merchandise requested; (3) the amount involved for each of the items for which the funeral director will advance monies as an accommodation to the family; and (4) the method of payment agreed upon by the family and the funeral director.

(The above was published by the National Funeral Directors Association.)

II A CRITIQUE OF THE CRITICISMS OF MITFORD AND HARMER

Jessica Mitford's *The American Way of Death* became a number one bestseller. It has been reviewed as "A brilliant . . . case against the whole funeral industry." (*New Yorker*), "The best ever written on the subject." (Harry Golden), "A well-documented expose . . . she effectively exposes the commercialization, the unnecessary extravagance, and the maudlin deception of the modern funeral." (*New York Times*) Mitford's views are very similar to the views in Ruth Harmer's *The High Cost of Dying*. Mitford's arguments against present funeral practices will be presented and evaluated in the following account:

1. According to Mitford, business and merchandising methods apply to the funeral industry leading to excesses and unfair exploitation. There is an emphasis on keeping prices high and the person who is in need of a funeral director does not usually think it proper to compare prices. This and funeral practices result in a non-competitive or perhaps a price-fixing situation, according to Mitford. The prospect is "sold" on goods he does not want, due to such merchandising, display, and exploitive sales techniques. Caskets are displayed to stress higher priced ones. Organized professional salesmen exploit by memorizing and delivering a fixed "pitch" or sales talk. Competition tends to lead to having a funeral better than one's neighbor's. One needs the best car, a Cadillac, as a hearse; the deceased body must look as if it were alive and be dressed in the best clothing; the casket must be the best polished mahogany or 18 gauge lead coated steel (which merchandisers call "the Classic Beauty"); etc. There are drive-in funeral homes with mortuary display windows so that one need not leave his car. The funeral business is overcrowded thus increasing selling and merchandising pressure. Even disinterments are encouraged in order to sell new, metal or different caskets and so lead to "repeated business." Funeral directors often compete with cemeteries so that each charges the other high fees for services rendered. Forest Lawn cemetery, the largest, now handles all aspects of the trade of the funeral director and performs marriage ceremonies as well. The tax-exempt, non-profit Forest

Lawn even has a museum, art galleries, displays throughout its property, and it features the "Crucifixion," the largest oil painting in the world. Salt and pepper shakers, cups, platters, music played to the deceased for eternity, etc. are sold. Many such items are in the shape of the cemetery art works or show views of the cemetery. Forest Lawn has earthquakeproof, bombproof vaults. The cost for a funeral at Forest Lawn usually ranges up to $15,000. Irving Thalberg has an $800,000 tomb there. (Harmer p. 44) One cemetery, Pet Haven, even merchandises plots for animals. The pets are even sometimes embalmed. The animal is usually a dog or cat (but perhaps a fish, ant, or mouse plot will soon be found). Parakeet ashes may be put in $2500 gold urns. Harmer notes that Franco has a multi-million dollar monument in the Guadarrama Mountains. (p. 44) (One could add the many enormously extravagant memorials, such as the Taj Mahal which is a memorial to one wife of Shah Jehan.) It is pointed out that trade associations lobby for pro-funeral legislation and keep funeral costs high. They oppose memorial societies which are set up to provide an inexpensive funeral. Their trade magazines are monolithic as spokesmen for what the funeral director should think and do.

Funeral directors take the views of Mitford and Harmer to be poorly supported and in many instances wrong. Guidelines for funeral practices are presented at the beginning of this chapter and there it states that the funeral director "should explain the various aspects of the funeral and the costs thereof" quite candidly and openly. It is part of his stated code of ethics. The first portion of this chapter also serves to respond to a number of objections made by Mitford and Harmer. The funeral director in general appears to keep within acceptable business practices. There is an attempt to avoid competition of funeral directors with cemeteries and various state laws regulate the relationship. The developer of Forest Lawn is Dr. Hubert Eaton. His idea now is that because people leave their money to various libraries, hospitals, etc., and because these are memorials, such institutions or "co-memorials" should be located within the cemetery. This would make Forest Lawn into a city within itself. This would revise the Latin word for cemetery, *necropolis*, "city of the dead," to include "city for the living." It may be noted that in Wisconsin (156.12) it is illegal to operate a mortuary or funeral establishment within a cemetery. Forest Lawn is certainly an exception to the average cemetery or funeral establishment. For example in Wisconsin (156.12) "No licensed funeral director . . . shall, directly or indirectly, receive or accept any commission, fee, remuneration or benefit of any kind from any cemetery, mausoleum or crematory . . . in connection with the sale or transfer of any cemetery lot. . . ." Funeral trade associations promote pro-funeral legislation but not necessarily to keep funeral costs high. The funeral director does not necessarily oppose memorial associations, but rather he is the one who supplies services for such associations. There does seem to be a tradition and cohesiveness of ideas as presented in the trade and funeral journals, but this means also that there are certain ethical standards adhered to. There is also a constant interchange with medical, legal, religious and other organizations. Through such interchange there is a responsiveness to changing views.

One of the great difficulties with Mitford's arguments is that they are often based on single instances only. What applies in California may be quite unlike what happens elsewhere. The accusations are not always fully or adequately dealt with or supported. The book is suggestive and does indicate what some of the actual practices are but falls short of indicating what is the case for the great majority of funeral directors. More organized evidence is needed here than she presents. Such an extensive detailed analysis remains to be done and goes beyond the scope of this book.

The Association of Better Business Bureaus states that there is "Questionable advertising, high pressure sales tactics and serious malpractices by a small minority such as exists on the fringe of any business or profession. They victimize bereaved families and create public distrust out of all proportion to their numbers." (1961)

Howard Raether (NFDA) quite fairly agrees and regarding Harmer's work states, "There are unscrupulous funeral directors as Mrs. Harmer writes. This is to be deplored as is the uncontestable reality that there are also unprincipled and dishonest politicians, physicians, clergymen . . ." (1971) He further adds that the role of the funeral director must be adaptive. Raether, however, defends the elaborate funeral and argues that its ritual value is especially necessary. Nevertheless the attack on funeral directors could perhaps be made on nearly any modern American business equally well. They should not be singled out as being the only offender, nor should it be claimed that all funeral directors are unscrupulous.

That other selling techniques take advantage of the public does not justify the funeral director who uses them, but on the other hand, he would have to go against established American business practices to change it. He was taught such methods in his business dealings within his community. The director is caught in a large ongoing system which permeates every aspect of his culture. He cannot be blamed for the system. He can, however, attempt to change the system and reevaluate funeral policies. There are, as was seen at the beginning of this chapter, codes of ethics, fair practices and guidelines which the director attempts to live up to.

There is great social pressure in any community to conform to existing beliefs and practices. If the director fails to conform he will be unpopular and bankrupt. This is the one thing which is behind what Mitford says is the attack of some funeral directors on their critics as being communists, atheists, and un-American. What is being asked for by Mitford is not, then, merely a reform of the funeral director but, if one expanded the argument, a reform of our very culture, our society, and our inherited and unexamined views about the nature of ethical terms and about death itself. The blame for such confusion may be placed on the shoulders of the members of society and not merely on the shoulders of the funeral director.

One may argue that the present funeral services are good for the community. Good is an open-context term and although it is often used as if it has a specific meaning, it may not. "Good" has no meaning in itself, but to be intelligible must be reduced to some concrete substitution instance. "Good" may mean "It works," "It pays well," "We are used to it" (i.e. it is traditional), etc. It is not intelligible to produce the greatest "good" for the greatest number, as the utilitarian would suggest, unless one specifies what "good" means here. (See Shibles "Ethics as Open-Context Terms.")

Similarly one is told that he should have a "proper" funeral, or "I know you would want to do the right thing." What is a "proper" or "good" funeral? It is meaningless to say "X is just good in itself." The prospective buyer is often confused about death and so does not know what a good or bad funeral would be. Thus he, for lack of a better criterion, may assume that an expensive funeral is the "best" funeral. The effect of the obscure open-context terms "good," "proper," "best," "ought," "duty," "bad," "right," "wrong" is that of confusing or exploiting. This is one instance of how one may be misled by language, and one of the consequences of not examining the way in which ethical terms work.

Cremation is also affected by commercialization. Paul Irion in his book *Cremation* says that crematoriums have a commercial emphasis and the staff is urged to "talk less about cremation, crematory, incineration, and more about columbaria, memorials, chapels. . . ." Expensive caskets are encouraged just as with regular burial. He states that funeral directors are "less than enthusiastic about cremation." In some states the funeral directors have legislation requiring a licensed funeral director to secure the death certification and permission to cremate. Irion adds that they are thus not excluded from the cremation process though they do not stand to gain the profit they would from burial.

The strewing of ashes is opposed, Irion states, because it detracts from profits. He quotes the Cremation Association of America, "Let's sell memorialization. . . . This will promote the sale of urns, nitches and our garden plots as well."

However, the body could be cremated into a fine powder such that not even strewing is needed. This is frequently done in England. To argue that it is desecration to reduce the remains to a fine powder after having gone through an intense burning process would be a strange argument. The Catholic opposition to cremation is no longer supportable. Pope Paul sent instructions to all Catholic Bishops that cremation is acceptable under certain circumstances. God can just as "easily" resurrect a body from ashes as from bones. (*Time* June 12, 1964, p. 85) Orthodox Jews often oppose cremation as being a desecration of the body. In Wisconsin law it is stated (H 18.07) "Cremation of a dead human body shall be considered as a final disposal of that body." The practice of incompletely cremating the body seems to be partly or largely to encourage urn and other

expenses. The memorial value of the dust remains questionable
and this issue is best treated in those sections of this book
dealing with emotional attitudes toward death.

2. The existing funeral practices are defended as being
founded on the "American Tradition." (Note: the headline in
the *Wisconsin State Journal*, May 2, 1970: "Psychiatrist Backs
'American Way of Death.' ") Mitford points out that this is a
poor argument because funeral ceremonies were once more
simple and meaningful than they now are. There was a plain
pine box used and friends and neighbors did the burying. To
speak of "Valley Forge" caskets plays upon one's patriotism
and desire for heroism. Forest Lawn cemetery, Mitford states,
has a "Court of Patriots" or "Court of Freedom" corner.

Certainly Mitford is right if the only argument for a practice
is that it is based on tradition. Argument from tradition is one
of the basic informal fallacies in logic. In addition, part of the
American tradition involves exploitation. War also has been part
of the American tradition but that does not justify war. We are
trying to change that particular tradition of fighting and
bloodshed. "The American Tradition" may to the extent that it
is critical, rather support not the status quo, but the insight to
question, reevaluate and change. But as was mentioned above
(no. 1) it is socially difficult to depart from the present culture
and ways of doing things which the majority of people believe
in. One can understand why the funeral director may wish to
support the status quo.

George Marshall in connection with the Unitarian
Universalist Association voices opposition to the traditional
American way in the following statement:

> "Families must be prepared for the issues arising in
> death. Otherwise, one falls back on the hackneyed phrases
> of the commonplace in seeking to render help to those
> who are bereaved, and they rely upon the judgments of
> funeral directors, or seek to follow the customs and
> conventions of such funerals as they may have attended.
> In doing so, people whose lives have been signally
> distinguished by a resolute striving for independence and
> rational action, close out the most individual and enduring
> memory of life with a commonplace mediocrity which

oftentimes falls very short of the life that should be commemorated. Surrendering their independence of judgment, at the time when it is most called for, they seemingly surrender the expression of the virtue of life, so that the death stands out all the more glaringly as a rude wrenching at the roots of life, rather than as the serene and beautiful fulfillment of one who, needing no apology, wraps the garments of a life about him and lies down to rest."

Malcolm Wells (1972) argues that a better type of funeral than we now offer would be natural-burial which opposes embalming, the use of caskets and vaults, waxen lifelike bodies, plastic flowers, etc. He proposes organic burial instead – the return of our bodies to the living land and the life-death-life cycle. The body again becomes part of trees, flowers, soil, etc. if buried wrapped in simple burial cloths. One's blood pulses through the earth. The cemetery would be a garden of life, filled with growth and animals instead of metal, plastic and concrete. Death is not stone, steel or diamond. The funeral director need lose no profits by organic burial for he could offer this sort of burial as is now being done in Philadelphia by a large funeral home. Wells quotes Walt Whitman:

> "I bequeath myself to the devil
>   to grow from the grass I love,
> If you want me again
>   look for me under your bootsoles.
> You will hardly know who I am or what
> I mean,
>   but I shall be good health to you
>   nevertheless,
> And filter and fiber your blood.
> Failing to fetch me at first keep
> encouraged,
> Missing me one place search another,
> I stop somewhere waiting for you."

There is a kind of immortality in plants, rust, and bones.

3. Mitford objects to the funeral directors' argument that they only give the public what the public wants. One objection is that partly as a result of merchandising and selling methods of modern business, the public is sold and has little choice in what it wants. Often a family with no wage earner spends the entire insurance money on a lavish funeral it was talked into having. One is encouraged to use expensive metal caskets for cremation even though they will be discarded before cremation takes place. Mitford cites numerous examples in which the average person is seen to want but unable to obtain a very inexpensive, simple, quiet funeral. Mitford notes that one indication that the National Funeral Directors Association has not adequately served the public is that it requires as a qualification for professional membership, membership in the white race. (p. 188) Harmer refers to "the barbaric and ostentatious funeral practices in which we indulge. . . . People are getting the kind of funerals they have also been persuaded to want." (p. 212)

Mitford's statement about NFDA membership is no longer correct. The constitution of the NFDA does not now have a qualification for membership having to do with race, creed, color, or national origin and there has been no such qualification since 1963. Mitford is certainly right in condeming funeral overspending. But it is partly due to public demand that people overspend. At the beginning of this chapter it is pointed out by the NFDA that the funeral director himself is aware of this and that he should discourage such practices. The director would seem to support the Unitarian's statement, "We agree with the social workers that funeral counseling should help families conserve their resources rather than spend recklessly." (G. Marshall)

Mitford may not be entirely fair in opposing the view that the director just gives the public what it wants. Certainly there are abuses in meeting the needs of everyone, and a complex economic and religious system cannot be expected to work absolutely perfectly. The average person is not a philosopher. He is not ·clear about nor does he inquire into the nature of death. In short, he usually does not really know what he wants. Thus it is hard to condemn the funeral director for failing to meet needs. The director offers what is available and what is demanded. The most common type of funeral demanded by the public is a religious funeral, and the director has attempted to serve this need to the best of his ability in the cultural system he is in. He shares the values of most people and does attempt to meet such needs. On the other hand, this does not mean that the values of most people are intelligent and beyond revision. That they are rather in great need of revision is not the sole responsibility of the funeral director, though it is part of his responsibility. An intelligent public must be more clear in indicating to the director what it wants, and not do things just because they are usually done that way. Memorial societies arose out of an attempt to meet needs which were not being met by the funeral director. Hopefully the director will meet such needs and make such memorial societies less necessary.

4. Mitford presents the view that the funeral director stresses the necessity of a "memory picture" of the deceased on inadequate psychiatric grounds. The stress on the memory-picture supposedly justifies the often unnecessary practice of embalming, and lifelike makeup necessary for viewing the body, and so leads to the increased costs and services of an elaborate funeral. Mitford quotes Prof. Volkart, Professor of Sociology at Stanford University and Director of the Program in Medicine and Behavioral Sciences, "I know of no evidence to support the view that 'public' viewing of an embalmed body is somehow 'therapeutic' to the bereaved." (pp. 75-76) [Ernest Morgan in "A Manual of Simple Burial" also opposes viewing. (pp. 7-8)]

It may be argued against Mitford that one could quote from a great number of professional people to the effect that the memory picture is useful and therapeutic. Quotations are, of course, informal fallacies or arguments from authority. They have a certain persuasive value but, though they are used throughout this book, they should not be substituted for the arguments themselves. They often are merely used to indicate what people think or that there are differences of opinion. With this caution one may note that Paul Irion is one who does support the value of public viewing: "It can be very helpful for a bereaved family to see their loved one in repose. Viewing the body is another means by which the whole situation is focused on reality. Often it is helpful in relieving painful memories of a lingering illness or a terrifying accident." ("Quotes" 1970)

It may be that a photograph may suffice in place of an embalmed and cosmetically prepared body. In China and elsewhere the picture of the deceased was carried along with the casket. In any case, more evidence is needed for the necessity of a memory-picture than is given. The bereaved may be simply talked into believing it is necessary or be guided by custom. It may be added that memory-pictures may even be disturbing, because the body after being prepared and altered is an artificial deviation and metaphorical deviation from the natural, normal, and real — and the viewer knows it.

Imagery may haunt a person because it is a very unnatural or dreaded object or because one may not know what happened in a particular death situation and would like to see some concrete evidence. If the image is of a dreaded subject what is needed is a reassessment of the reasons it is dreaded. Once these are clarified, along with the realization that it is irrational and self-defeating (though not bad in itself) to have negative emotions, one will not be troubled by such imagery. Public viewing of the body is something which may have to be overcome rather than something which may help one overcome grief. One's assessments will determine whether or not public viewing will be helpful. Seeing a corpse does make one face the reality of death but it does not help one to come to terms with death. Assessments are needed for that. In short it is not the memory picture which is of importance, as if the picture or image had some magical power. Rather it is the rational thinking which must be done about the deceased and about death which is of importance. The stress should be on rational assessment rather than on the magic of pictures or imagery. What one imagines should be realistic and not be a source of negative emotions, but this is a different matter than that involved with public viewing. Public viewing and vigils might help those Christians who imagine the devil might try to snatch the soul away at death. (cf. Art of Dying section)

It is a therapeutic device to imagine in advance, one's own possible illness or death so that when it happens one will not induce shock or extreme negative emotions. This is one of the values of *memento mori*, remember death. If you imagine it coming it will not take you by surprise. One's game of darts and basketball may supposedly be improved just by imagining playing these games.

The imagery of death is, at present, destructive rather than realistic or constructive imagery. On the one hand one is asked to imagine superstitious entities such as souls, angels, heaven, devils, hell. Or one is asked to look at a prepared dead body in a beautiful box — a seeming contradiction. If one is confused about death and dying he does not know what to imagine. If these concepts were more clear and more realistic one's imagery would also be more clear. One's thinking is largely verbal but does to some extent involve one's images and one's abilities and habits. The issue of a memory picture is really the issue of what part imagery plays in our thinking. It is not an adequate answer to say that a memory picture is needed, anymore than it is adequate to say a memory picture is not needed. What is needed is the right (intelligent) sort of imagery not necessarily just memory imagery. What is needed is mainly a clarification of our assessments or beliefs which are responsible for our imagery.

5. Mitford presents the view that funeral directors deceive in attempting to present funerals which deny death. The body is made to look lifelike. Caskets are made of polished cherry wood, with adjustable beds and are sealed as if to say that the dead are somehow still alive and will be preserved forever. Funeral terminology and euphemisms suggest this trend. The undertaker is now called a "funeral director," coffins are "caskets," hearses are "coaches," corpses are "loved ones" (even if disliked) or "Mr. Jones." The room in which the corpse is put is called a "slumber room," the death certificate is a "vital statistics form," "deceased" or "expired" is used in place of "dead." The word death is avoided wherever possible. Foreverness symbols such as "rock of the ages" are used to suggest one will live forever. [It may be noted that there are some brain damage disorders which involve similar denial. Anosognosic patients may show a language disorder (paraphasia) involving the use of neologisms, word substitutes, inappropriate words, which deny illnesses, e.g., thermometer may be called a "gradient," wheelchair may be called a "chaise." Use of third person regarding death denies the first person use of "my death" or "I will die."] An artificial grass mat conceals burial earth. For the earth-scattering ritual a metal Earth Dispenser may be used, thus not requiring one to even touch the earth. Cemeteries are purposely located in places

which have an ocean view. Death denial is revealed in the singing radio commercial put out by the Chambers funeral home (p. 162):

"If your loved ones pass away
Have them pass the Chambers way.
Chambers' customers all sing:
'Death, oh death, where is thy sting?' "

Regarding Mitford's view here it seems to be the case that the funeral director both does and does not deny death. He explicitly encourages one to consider death, view the body, etc. On the other hand some practices, advertising and language used does seem to cover up the reality of death. Howard Raether (NFDA) stated to the author that the body is not made to look lifelike but rather made to be acceptable for viewing. Advertisements, however, speak of "lifelike" fluids, etc. In addition, even if the goal is viewing the body the latter is still make lifelife for the purpose of viewing. Cemeteries may be located with ocean views but not necessarily so the dead will have a pleasant view. They are sometimes so located out of respect for the dead. How rational it is to respect the dead is another question.

6. According to Mitford the funeral director plays on the guilt feelings of the bereaved. He asserts that to alleviate such guilt sacrifice is needed. By sacrifice is meant financial sacrifice. She quotes the *National Funeral Service Journal* (Aug. 1961), "It seems highly probable that the most satisfactory funeral service for the average family is one in which the cost has necessitated some degree of sacrifice."

In opposition to Mitford's statement I suspect that the average funeral director does not consciously and deliberately play on the guilt feelings of the bereaved. He does often stress the need to eliminate guilt, the virtue of sacrifice, emphasis on ritual. The question may be rather whether guilt is properly dealt with by means of the funeral. Guilt may in some cases be temporarily distracted by such sacrifice especially if the bereaved thinks it will be. But guilt is often a result of wanting to have done something to prevent someone's death without having done so. One way to alleviate guilt is to inquire into the cause of aging and contribute to or engage in an analysis of the nature of death. Guilt forces one into inquiry. One feels guilty sometimes because he has done nothing to prevent, clarify, accept, or delay death. There are other causes of guilt such as not having been kind to the deceased. But guilt derives from unrealistic, non-adjustive assessment, lack of assessment, or confused assessment. An examination of the nature of emotions (see psychiatry chapter) shows that guilt is not a desirable or necessary emotion and that by realistic assessment of one's beliefs one can avoid and dissipate guilt. Guilt and grief are sicknesses to be prevented, avoided, and dispelled. And one need no longer feign grief or hire mourners.

The funeral director is not alone in regard to the enhancement or mismanagement of guilt. Both existentialism and religion have stressed the fact that man's nature is to be guilty. Nietzsche condemns this imposition on what man's nature must be, and states that the Christian view that man is guilty of Adam's sin makes man a mere inferior shadow of a human being. Guilt of this sort is fictive. To have such negative emotions is to be a slave of one's emotions. It is to be less than human.

7. Mitford presents the view that the funeral director plays on the religious prejudices of the bereaved. The Jewish are by religion to be buried in Jewish cemeteries. Forest Lawn was established as a Christian cemetery and made much of itself as being pro-Christian yet, according to Mitford, it opened a Jewish cemetery without letting its Christian bias be known. Herbert Eaton, founder of Forest Lawn who advertises himself as "God's True Believer" said, "Christ in business is the greatest thing that can happen to business." (p. 124) He said, "Let every salesman's motto be: *Accent the spiritual!*" (p. 127) But it is found that all of the major Christian and Jewish religions stress a simple, inexpensive, funeral, one unlike the average funeral one sees. If one must spend money the churches often recommend giving to education or research, rather than spending it on elaborate funerals. It would seem that a lavish funeral might rather prevent one from getting into heaven. (Harmer states that the Archbishop of Paris declared that since all are equal before God only a single type of funeral will be offered in Parish churches. (p. 57)) The funeral director often

takes the position that the funeral service is and must be a religious and mainly Christian service. The director may in fact be imposing his own view of what a religious service is. The stress on Christianity leaves out those who are not religious and not Christian.

Harmer quoted one funeral director as saying, "The funeral ceremony is a religious service and the idea of a quick disposal of the body will go a long way toward eliminating any observance of faith in God, in the hereafter, and in the immortality of the soul." (p. 25)

In regard to the above criticisms it should be mentioned that Paul Irion, Corliss Lamont and others have developed a humanistic funeral service. Such services are available from most funeral directors. Some directors stress the Christian service more than others. There is an emphasis on the Christian funeral service, however. It seems to be part of our cultural tradition. An examination of death in religion is presented in other chapters. The funeral director and his employees usually join a number of religious and service organizations, and his firm often sells funeral services to them. The stress on Christian funerals may serve as a way to convert people to Christianity. H. Eaton of Forest Lawn seems to suggest that the Christian has a better chance of getting into heaven if one is buried in his cemetery. He speaks of his cemetery as the "first step up toward heaven." Business does seem to be confused with, as well as a part of, religion, and religion used for business purposes.

God is imposed in a number of ways: in school, on coins, by religious pressure of the community and even at death. We find the reaction to this on a number of tombstones. (Wallis 1954) The tombstones read:

Joseph Coveney 1897: "The Christian religion begins with a dream and ends with a murder." (The townspeople and relatives chiseled and sandblasted these words off.)

Jeremiah Hacker 1895: "The angry, wrathful, Bible God is a Myth."

George Spencer 1808: "Beyond the universe there is nothing and within the universe the supernatural does not and cannot exist. Of all deceivers who have plagued mankind, none are so deeply ruinous to human happiness as those imposters who pretend to lead by a light above nature . . . Religion has murdered millions for doubting or denying her dogmas, and most of these [dogmas] have been false."

Cy Deeter for the grave of his wife: "There is no God. Man has no soul. Life ends forever at death. The human race has advanced, not on account of the Church, but in spite of it . . . I hope there is a hell for all those hell fire preachers." (The words on this stone are now chipped away.)

Alvin Lusk 1858: "No good nor ill by supernatural cause. . . . Known truth not fantom faith gives real bliss."

That these stones were erected by members of the funeral industry indicates that either they were not altogether stressing religion, or that they had little choice in the matter.

George Marshall expresses the Unitarian concern in the following:

"The dull insensitive materialistic arrangements for caskets, for the public display of the body, painted and waxen, have been determined. In a word, the emphasis has been shifted away from the spiritual values and life back to the material and physical aspects of it, in the very hour when we need to accept the transitory aspects of physical life . . . Although funeral directors have good intentions, they deal almost constantly with orthodox and conventional concepts of death, and are not prepared by experience to understand the concepts of the religious liberal."

That the Church stresses inexpensive funerals, if true, is certainly not always true. A number of dignitaries in the Church had extremely expensive and elaborate funerals.

8. According to Mitford the funeral director plays on the social status-seeking role of the bereaved. Black people are often

not allowed to be buried in white peoples' cemeteries. Until 1958 Forest Lawn was restricted to Caucasians. A 1958 law prevented such segregation. The poor or those in a low class are told or it is implied, that they will improve their status with a magnificent funeral. Their first ride in a Cadillac will be after death. Caskets are often nicer than what we have to live in. It is a form of obtaining what one wants when he no longer needs it. Mitford quotes the *National Funeral Service Journal*:

> "Buying habits are influenced largely by envy and environment. Don't ever overlook the importance of these two factors in estimating the purchasing possibilities or potential of any family. . . . Envy is essentially the same as pride . . . It is the idea of keeping up with the Joneses. . . . Sometimes it is only necessary to say, '. . . Here is a casket similar to the one the Joneses selected' to insure a selection in a substantially profitable bracket." (p. 182)

Status-seeking and merchandising is based partly on the American way of life, and partly on confusions the average man has about his emotional needs. It may be condemned in every corner of our society not alone with funeral directors. Certainly not every funeral director consciously and deliberately takes advantage of status prejudices, and it may be that the majority of them do not.

9. Mitford states that the prices of the funeral director are seldom advertised and are hard to obtain. The same casket costs are found to differ greatly with different funeral establishments. The Washington funeral director, W. Chambers, is quoted as testifying before a Congressional Committee in 1947, "The funeral industry has no standard prices; whatever can be charged and gotten away with is the standard rule." (p. 35) When firms advertised inexpensive funerals they were expelled from funeral directors' associations. (p. 43) These practices may be contrasted with those of the French who had in 1962 ten classes of advertised fixed prices, e.g., from $10 up: class 6 is $30, class 1 is $3000.

In opposition to Mitford's statements above, it has been pointed out at the beginning of this chapter that the code of professional practices of funeral directors states, "The funeral director should explain the various aspects of the funeral and the costs thereof . . . The funeral director should make clear the range of prices of funerals he has available." There may, of course, be a difference between ideal standards and actual practices. Another reason prices may not be advertised is that, according to the Council of Better Business Bureaus, "Most funeral directors do not consider it ethical to advertise prices." ("Facts" 1961)

Mitford claims that, as one of the possible results of her book, prices of funerals declined. It would be quite difficult to determine if a decline was due to her book, but in any case there was an increase rather than a decline. In 1963 the average for the funeral service portion only was $763; in 1971 it was $983. Prices increased each year since 1963. The U.S. Bureau of Labor Statistics indicates that from Dec. 1963 to April 1972 all items in the Cost of Living Index rose 41.3%, but "funeral services, adult" rose only 32.1%.

10. According to Mitford, the funeral director often misinforms the public about burial laws. He frequently states that caskets or elaborate services are needed for cremation when they are not, that embalming is required when it is not, that one cannot bury the deceased when, in fact, he can. Mitford states, "In no state is embalming required by law except in certain special circumstances, such as when the body is to be shipped by common carrier." (p. 24) Although when a body is bequeathed to a medical school the survivors are in most states bound to carry out these directions, a mortuary science book states that the survivors may dispose of the body in other ways. (p. 24) Also it is pointed out that the laws of California (in 1963) do not require that a casket be used when a body is cremated, even though several funeral directors claimed otherwise. Vaults are not required by law but cemetery salesmen often claim that they are. (p. 25) Directors often erroneously say that only a licensed funeral director can move or dispose of a body. Whereas most state laws permit ashes to be scattered or privately buried, one is told that this is not legal.

In regard to the statement about bequeathal being rejected by the survivors, Wisconsin law (155.06), for example, states, "A parent of an unmarried decedent under 21 years of age [changed in 1971 to 18 years] may revoke the gift," and ". . .

unless the surviving spouse gave consent to the donation in writing prior to the donor's death, the surviving spouse of the decedent may revoke the gift." As part of his code of ethics as presented at the beginning of this chapter, the funeral director "should welcome any questions or discussions as to what is or is not required by laws and/or regulations to such laws." This is a standard which presumably Mitford would agree with. It is the practice or the following of this standard which Mitford finds exception to. In regard to vault requirements cemeteries often require them to prevent cave-ins. According to H. Raether (NFDA), courts tend to uphold the practice of requiring a vault. That there might be a better way of doing all of this must certainly be indicated — for example, Malcolm Wells' natural organic earth burial.

Laws should be accurately stated and cited, and to misrepresent them for the sake of a sale or due to one's own value preferences, is irresponsible. If there are relevant considerations other than legal ones they should be discussed openly.

11. There is, on Mitford's view, faulty advertising regarding the nature of the funeral, merchandise, and services. Cemetery salesmen are misleadingly called "Memorial Counselors." Some crypts are referred to as "Judgment Proof." Forest Lawn sells a brochure stating that this cemetery is a "first step up toward heaven." Mr. Eaton of Forest Lawn attempted to convince the public that they have a "Memorial Instinct."

In regard to the "memorial instinct" Eaton can be condemned along with the psychologists who claim we have death instincts and other instincts. Certainly man has in fact spent great amounts of energy, time, and wealth on monuments, though that is no argument for an instinct. The "first step up toward heaven" though it may suggest a special method, perhaps objectively means merely that one must die before he goes to heaven. In Wisconsin (156.12) the funeral director and others are prohibited from "false, misleading or fraudulent advertisement," and are prohibited from soliciting funeral services or the right to prepare a dead human body. But advertising is generally persuasive and often deceptive. Advertising in the funeral industry tends to be like advertising in nearly every other aspect of our society.

The following typical advertisements appear in the *American Funeral Director* (Jan. 1972):

"A Con-O-Lite Vault Protects Forever."
"Suggest the very best, Lewis Burial Garments."
"It is finishes of the highest gloss and softest satin ever achieved, revealing the warm beauty of the finest hardwoods grown."

Casket and Sunnyside (Aug. 1971) shows a 1971 Concrete Vault Cover Girl. Doric Burial Vaults advertises "Timeless Protection," Conwed Caskets advertises, "Only the best is acceptable." The "best" is an open-context term and here may mean only the most expensive or most elaborate, not necessarily that which clarifies one's assessments or alleviates grief.

12. Mitford states that the lavish use of flowers in a funeral is of questionable value. Since florists' businesses are sometimes even more than 50 percent devoted to funeral flowers, extra expenses of this sort may be encouraged and practices such as "P.O." (Please Omit Flowers") discouraged. A *Florist's Review* (June 1, 1961) headline reads: "Wisconsin Florists, Morticians Cooperate to Fight P.O."

The value of flowers ties in to the questions concerning emotions, e.g., grief. How much do flowers serve as the right sort of therapy? Do they serve only as temporary release or do they help get at the genuine cause of grief? Certainly at least some flowers in some cases can be beneficial. Some people may prefer and receive more satisfaction from contributing to worthy causes instead.

13. According to Mitford, the funeral director is often not honest and open in his presentation of the need for embalming. It is usually not required by law, health reasons, or sanitation yet the director uses all these reasons to support embalming. The purpose of embalming is mainly to allow brief preservation of the body for the purpose of displaying it for viewing, or because there is a 48 hour waiting period before cremation is allowed. The bereaved is almost never asked whether he wants an open-casket ceremony, thereby necessitating embalming and extra expense. Mitford quotes Dr. I. M. Feinberg (the *National*

Funeral Service Journal): "Sanitation is probably the farthest thing from the mind of the modern embalmer. We must realize that the motives for embalming at the present time are economic and sentimental, with a slight religious overtone." (p. 66) Dr. Jesse Carr, Chief of Pathology at San Francisco General Hospital was quoted, "Public health virtues of embalming? You can write it off as inapplicable to our present-day conditions." (pp. 66-67) He states that one is better off with a shroud than a casket. (If embalming or spreading ashes is opposed because it is unsanitary, it may be noted that animals are not embalmed but often just left lying in the road. One can drop the cremated ashes of a dog over Calfornia but not the ashes of a person. (Harmer p. 168)

Paul Irion states that members of the Cremation Association of America have managed to pass anti-ash scattering laws in at least three states. (1972)

14. Funeral directors and certain state laws are said to impede medical work. Autopsies are discouraged because it makes embalming harder and it is harder to sell an expensive casket for an autopsied body. Because of delay due to time consuming autopsy required in some states, e.g., New Jersey, vital organs cannot be used for transplant to living patients. [Actually the time may be determined by the pathologist.] Also, because bodies are given for medical research there is no funeral for the funeral director to perform. He may therefore discourage such practices. Mitford quotes from Howard Raether's speech to the National Funeral Directors Association, "The ultimate of all these programs is to give the entire body to medical science. With no body there is no funeral. If there are no funerals, there are no funeral directors. A word to the wise should be sufficient." (p. 222)

These statements are not entirely correct. When the body is given for medical research or for organ donation the funeral can often be performed in nearly the same way as usual. In some cases services may be performed before or after the body is donated, and in others without the presence of the body. Also Howard Raether is even responsible for some of the wording on the Uniform Donor Card. Mitford quotes a speech Raether gave over 15 years ago.

The Uniform Anatomical Gift Act has been adopted by nearly every state and has the effect of promoting organ and body donation for medical research. Certain laws do still impede medical work and some of these will be discussed later.

In general the funeral directors associations have information concerning body and organ donations for medical research, and have donation forms for this purpose. These organizations meet with members of the medical profession in an attempt to determine the need and method of such donations. The methods of donation must be improved a) because organs must often be removed immediately after death and b) because of changing conceptions of the definition and time a person may be considered dead. Individual funeral directors are in a good position to help in the process as well as to suggest means by which it can be accomplished. The director may be one of the most important people to distribute literature and recommend that organs and body be donated to needy patients and medical science. This would gain them a certain respect in their community as rational and concerned members of the society. One would guess that, upon entering a funeral establishment, in only a rare case is such literature now displayed and readily available. The director could also, as part of his advertising, recommend that one's organs and body be donated and add that the funeral service need not be dispensed with or interrupted in so doing. The argument that organ transplant is often only in the research stage and so one need not donate is not an acceptable argument against donation. (See section on organ and body donation.)

15. Mitford presents the view that funeral directors in some ways clash with clergy. They often resent the clergy accompanying those wishing to choose a casket. The clergy tend to choose inexpensive ones because they often believe elaborate merchandise and services do not truly represent religious views. Also the funeral director often wants services held in his own chapel thereby seeming to more and more take over the function of the clergy. Clergymen often reject the death-denying practices of lifelike cosmetic preparations and euphemistic terminology used in connection with the funeral, e.g., "slumber room," "the loved one," etc.

The attitude of clergymen is partly discussed in the chapter on religion. The National and local Funeral Directors Associations often meet with clergymen to discuss the issues objected to above and there is an attempt made to resolve such conflicts.

16. Mitford states that the funeral industry opposes memorial societies and often refuses to supply them with needed caskets and materials or refuses to cooperate with them. Legislation is promoted to prohibit the establishment of memorial societies.

A memorial society is a non-profit organization which makes advance arrangements to provide a person with a simple dignified funeral at a reasonable, fixed price to be determined in advance of need. (See section on memorial societies.) A number of states do not now have memorial societies and one might find that present legislation is unfavorable to them or prohibits them by law. On the other hand, it is the funeral director who does supply and cooperate with the existing memorial societies. The NFDA position is, "Memorial societies expect funeral directors to provide . . .special services at special prices. These prices are . . . unrealistic." (*The Director* April 1971 p. 5) Some organizations have to supply their own caskets and materials. Hopefully funeral directors will serve the needs of those who now find funeral practices inadequate and so make memorial societies less necessary.

17. The views of Mitford and Harmer have not basically changed since 1963 but have, if anything, been reinforced. Recent statements are contained in *Omega* (1971) and *Atlantic Monthly* (1965). They even report that and how the funeral industry has violently attacked and tried to suppress their ideas and how it has investigated their personal lives. Harmer states that the college where she teaches was advised to fire her for her exposure of the funeral industry.

Such may be the case with certain people connected with the funeral industry and these practices should be exposed. In my own experience I have found the directors of the National and Wisconsin Funeral Directors Associations to be quite helpful in responding to objections, providing literature, and in devoting a great deal of time to commenting on a first draft of this chapter. They also are deeply involved with medical, religious, and other organizations in attempting to cooperate with them.

Conclusion

Harmer and Mitford have raised important questions about and provoked inquiry into the existing practices of the funeral industry. I have here tried to give both sides to the criticisms they have made. Generalizations concerning any industry leave much to be desired, including Mitford's attack on the funeral industry. One of the reasons for the funeral directors' negative reaction to Mitford's book may be due to the fact that she seems to condemn *all* funeral directors. In addition, there are questions as to the truth and adequacy of statements made. On the other hand, one would hope that funeral directors would only welcome valuable and accurate criticism of the less ethical aspects and practices of their trade. Mitford and Harmer have been at least of some service to them in this way.

Mitford mainly attacks funeral practices, without presenting the stated ethical goals and standards of the funeral directors associations. There is an attempt of the latter to be fair and responsive to the needs of the public.

Mitford's attack on the funeral industry does not allow for the fact that the funeral director reflects the values of our present culture and common beliefs. The present funeral ceremony in part grew out of the beliefs and desires of the average person. The director is condemned for having grown up with such beliefs. He is no more critical of such things than are most people. She seems to attack the funeral director alone, when her arguments apply equally to American business, culture, and values in general. She and Harmer often themselves appeal to and agree with such common values, without argument or examination. Mitford's analysis is excellent in presenting some of the sicknesses in our culture and values, as revealed by the funeral industry. Certainly with changing values more adaptive funeral directors are needed. Her book does not give us the insights we need into death so that funeral practices can be made more intelligent, but mainly points to our economic confusion about death. If we do not know what to think about death we will not know what kind of funeral to have or how much, if anything, we should pay for it. The economics of the funeral thus depends upon our understanding of the nature of death. The reader may erroneously get the impression after reading her book that he is clearer about death. The book is not a clarification of dying or death. It is an excellent book only if combined with counterarguments and supportive arguments offered by the funeral directors, economists, philosophers, psychologists, and others in relevant professions.

Harmer's conclusion is that our present funeral ceremonies are expensive and barbaric. She suggests that funerals should be inexpensive and yet meaningful, and that money cannot buy meaning. The money saved can be better spent on the basic needs of the living, such as food, education and medical care. It could also be spent on the advancement of medical science. It may be added that some of the money saved or willed could best be spent on inquiry into the very concept of aging and death itself. Such inquiry or contribution to inquiry might be a better way of consoling the bereaved and lessening the guilt often felt at the loss of a friend. It allows one to help prevent the early loss of other friends. Perhaps it is for these reasons that Harmer takes the position that, ultimately, elaborate funerals do not really help the bereaved or make families and communities more close. Families could become more close by talking to one another rather than by sending money to each other. Elaborate or commercial funerals merely encourage irrational responses and unrealistic thinking on the part of the survivor. (p. 225) It would seem that funeral directors for the sake of continued business would want people to be superstitious, prejudiced, confused, emotional, and unrealistic in their thinking. But it is doubtful that they consciously wish to do this.

To act and give one's savings intelligently to worthwhile causes can produce genuinely meaningful emotions and adjustments. A funeral can still be "good" and "proper" if only one person attends, if it costs $10, and is indeed very small. Harmer states quite correctly that the economic questions she raised only lead to questions of the meaning of death; they do not attempt to answer it. Mitford's book also deals almost solely with the economic aspect of death. An understanding of the nature of death and dying remains to be established. Unfortunately while most are interested in how much a funeral costs, they seem much less interested in a careful examination of the concepts of death and dying.

III GENERAL LEGAL CONSIDERATIONS AND SUGGESTIONS

A constant reevaluation of laws relating to the funeral industry is needed to keep them in line with contemporary developments in philosophy and psychology and other areas, as well as in medicine. A few suggestions may be indicative. (Laws must be checked in the individual states for currentness and accuracy):

1. If the body is first removed from the casket before cremation the casket must not be used again according to some state laws. Perhaps the same casket could be used over and over so as to avoid unnecessary expense. The same oven is used over and over. Inexpensive disposable caskets could be encouraged when used for this purpose.

2. Should cemetery land be tax free as it now is? Cemeteries are now set up as non-profit organizations such as the thriving Forest Lawn cemetery. The seemingly irrational use of land merely for the purpose of burial may be discouraged by the imposition of taxes. (cf. No. 18)

3. Laws often restrict noise near cemeteries, require one to drive especially slow near them, and restrict access to the areas in or around cemeteries. It is not clear why such rules should apply here rather than elsewhere. The dead would not mind, and respect for the living should apply everywhere. New York Times Service (Dec. 10, 1972) reports,

"Across the country in recent months, a number of cemeteries have been opened up to cyclists, picnickers, joggers, baseball teams, fishermen, nature enthusiasts, and others simply anxious to flee if only briefly, the neighboring noise and bustle of urban life. 'The trend is clear,' said John Philbin who directs 37 Catholic cemeteries in the Chicago archdiocese. 'Cemeteries will increasingly have more than one use. They have to. It's just good citizenship. In many areas the cemetery is about the last open green space left.' "

4. States not allowing for the establishment of memorial societies may reconsider such laws.

5. The funeral charge is one of the first legal charges which may be made against the estate of the deceased. As there are reports of one's entire savings being used for funeral expense of the loss of a breadwinner it may be desirable to put a legal maximum on the amount allowed toward the funeral. The Uniform Probate Code states, for example, that the funeral expenses must be reasonable and responsible. This is perhaps too vague. Adoption of such laws could place greater stress on living needs and prevent compounding grief with financial worry.

6. Perhaps a maximun limit of the cost of an average funeral should be specified for burial insurance. A few states limit funeral expenses, for persons without immediate relatives, to amounts suitable to his standard of living. Some states do not allow burial insurance at all. Burial insurance is often restricted due to certain past abuses which were encountered. It may be noted that in Wisconsin the law (206.49) prevents a funeral service-insurance tie-in.

7. Although, perhaps not related to the funeral industry directly, legislation is needed to allow the dying not to be kept in a vegetative, unconscious state endlessly. It may be noted that suicide is not a crime in Wisconsin though under English common law suicide is a felony and may involve forfeiture of property. One may sign a statement in advance to the effect that if he has irreversible brain damage he does not want to be kept alive in a vegetative state.

8. Some laws favor or discriminate against women such as in regard to inheritance, social security, having to risk life in military draft. These and those concerned with funeral practices should be reconsidered. In Wisconsin one law (H 17.04) reads "Upon request of the family or its representative the presence of a female shall be permitted [to witness the embalming] in cases of a female corpse." This, though trivial perhaps, appears a discrimination in favor of the female.

9. Disinterment of the dead in Wisconsin (155.10) carries a fine of up to $500 or not more than three years nor less than one year in jail. Rather the penalty should involve psychological correction of the thinking of the transgressor. To fine or put someone in jail does not get at the cause of the difficulty.

10. Wisconsin law (979.20) requires reporting of death "when there was no physician, or accredited practitioner of a bona fide religious denomination relying upon prayer or spiritual means for healing in attendance . . ." This may involve a religious bias.

11. Some states do not allow interstate transportation of a corpse across their borders. This practice should be reconsidered because, for example, some states have an excess of bodies for medical research while other states are needy. The prohibition may also have relevance for preventing organ donations to the living.

12. Some states do not permit funds for dialysis, and transplantation of organs under Medicare and Medicaid for all or part of the costs. These laws may be reconsidered. As of July 1, 1973, Medicare has been extended experimentally to cover kidney transplants and dialysis for those of any age who require it.

13. There seem to be practices which require various people concerned with death and the dying to be religious. For example, one nurse stated that at a Madison hospital (Wisconsin) one of the first atheists was admitted to the nursing program in 1961. Religious belief is still today a question to be answered on admission forms and it pressures applicants to answer so as to gain admittance. These practices should be examined.

14. Laws should be considered to provide for burial by kin or friends. In Wisconsin H 17.12 states, "These rules shall not prevent any person from preparing for burial or conducting the funeral, of any deceased member of his family when such procedure is found desirable." H 17.05 states that a metal or metal lined casket is not required for local interment. H 17.10 states that embalming is not required. 69.45 states, "Any person who personally prepares for burial and conducts the funeral of any deceased member of his immediate family may obtain and file" a certificate of death with the registrar and secure a burial permit. Michigan law once stated and perhaps still states that the next of kin "can bury the corpse in any manner he sees fit, so long as it does not outrage public decency or amount to a public nuisance." (*Michigan Law Review* Vol. 23 1924-1925 p. 274 ff.)

A doctor certifies a person's death, and makes out a death certificate. The next of kin or a religious organization may take the death certificate to the county health office to obtain a transit permit. The body may then be taken to a medical school, crematory or cemetery. A burial permit is also required if the deceased is to be buried. The laws regarding specific procedures vary from state to state.

15. Laws relating to body donation for medical and other research and laws relating to transplantation of organs need reconsideration. The next section deals with some of these issues.

16. Sidney Margoluis in a Public Affairs Pamphlet entitled "Funeral Costs and Death Benefits" reports that a 1964 New York State law was publicized as requiring an itemized statement of prices of items involved in the funeral. The law, he points out, only actually requires a list of services and materials, not prices. The law may have been changed since Margoluis wrote. Both list and prices may in the future be required in states where funeral directors do not adhere to the funeral industry ethical recommendations to provide such information automatically.

17. Margoluis notes that some states have had to enact laws requiring that money paid in advance for pre-need cemetery plots, etc., be placed in trust so the promoters do not leave with the purchaser's funds.

18. Margoluis also mentions that cemeteries, though nonprofit, may pay their employees high wages and yield high profits. The question is raised as to whether and under what conditions cemeteries should be allowed to be nonprofit organizations.

19. Some states such as Michigan (E. Morgan, *A Manual of Simple Burial*) are said to have restrictive laws making it difficult for memorial societies to develop. Morgan and Margoluis both indicate that legislation promoted by the funeral industry tends to favor the industry rather than the general public. Morgan wrote,

> "Funeral directors' organizations are often able to put through laws whose ostensible aim is to protect the public but which really promote the interests of the industry at the expense of the public."

He cites as examples, a state law forbidding anyone but a funeral director from owning a mortuary (thereby excluding a price conscious union from starting its own mortuary), an attempt by Florida morticians to make embalming compulsory (they did get a law passed requiring embalming if the body is held longer than twenty-four hours), a Florida law requiring that a body not be cremated in less than forty-eight hours, a few states prohibit the scattering of ashes, some states do not allow funeral contracts or price quoting before death, misrepresentation of funeral laws and restrictions on how bodies may be disposed of. (Morgan himself offers some correctives of his accusations, pointing out that many directors do itemize bills and that the NFDA has "an excellent report" on organ donation.) Such accusations need more careful evaluation and analysis.

IV. ORGAN AND BODY DONATIONS

In 1963 Harmer noted that in 21 states the laws did not allow persons to bequeath their bodies to education and science. (p. 186) Laws should be reexamined which now make it illegal to so donate one's body. The 1968 Uniform Anatomical Gift Act (e.g., Wisconsin 155.06) has allowed that regardless of which state death occurs in, one's body or its parts may be left for medical or other research or for use by patients in need of organs. This act should be considered for full adoption by every state not now adopting it, viz., (as of April 1970) Alaska, Arizona, Delaware, D. C., Kentucky, Mass., Mississippi, Nebraska, New York, Virginia.

Laws preventing the release of vital organs, and laws requiring time-consuming autopsy in cases of accidental deaths thereby prohibiting use of vital organs, should be reconsidered. Cornea extraction, for example, must be done within three to four hours after death. The laws may be effective only if they allow and encourage immediate use of organs from accidental deaths, for these provide one of the most favorable sources of organ transplant.

For heart transplants, fresh hearts are needed but religious views sometimes oppose heart transplants. Such views and relevant laws should be reevaluated.

Some states require a higher age than 18 for body or organ donation. This should be reconsidered. Meanwhile, sometimes those under 18 may carry donation cards signed by their parents. The following states as of April 1970 require that one be 21 years of age: Delaware, Iowa, Maryland, Mississippi, Penn., Phode Island, Utah, Virginia.

According to the *Milwaukee Journal* (Jan. 29, 1969) Attorney Harold Ruidl of the Wisconsin Funeral Directors Association said, "A person's survivors should have the right to revoke a gift [of entire body] after death occurs. Under the bill survivors could make a donation, but could not cancel a previous gift." Ruidl also stated, "For the emotional recovery of those who have lost a relative this option would be desirable." The Wisconsin State Medical Society opposed Ruidl's amendment. In addition, the Funeral Directors Association tried to raise the age, for those able to donate, from

18 to 21 years. The executive secretary of the legislative council held that the survivors should not cancel a donation and that the body should not be conceived of as the property of the survivors.

One Wisconsin law (155.06) states, "A parent of an unmarried decedent under 21 years [changed in 1971 to 18 years] of age may revoke the gift," and "the surviving spouse of the decedent may revoke the gift." This appears to seriously undermine the wishes of the deceased. The surviving spouse may, however, give written consent before the donor's death. The survivor could be persuaded to have an elaborate funeral to serve as "grief therapy" and forgo body donation. The arguments against such "grief therapy" have been presented in the chapter on psychiatry and emotion. It would seem that grief resolution might be better served by making the donation so as to promote research to combat aging and death itself.

To donate a body or organs one need only fill out a Uniform Donor's Card, sign it and have two witnesses sign it (three in New Hampshire) for it to be a legal document. Relatives, family physician and close friends should be notified of your desire to donate. The card must be carried with you because organs are only useful if removed immediately after death. Parents may donate organs or bodies of deceased minor children. You may specify that all usable organs be donated. The Donor Card reads as follows:

UNIFORM DONOR CARD

OF_____
Print or type name of donor

In the hope that I may help others, I hereby make this anatomical gift, if medically acceptable, to take effect upon my death. The words and marks below indicate my desires.

I give: (a) _____ any needed organs or parts

         (b) _____ only the following organs or parts

_____
Specify the organ(s) or part(s)

for the purposes of transplantation, therapy, medical research or education;

        (c) _____ my body for anatomical study if needed.

Limitations or
special wishes, if any :_____

462

The Donor Card and information may be obtained without charge from the following:

Your local hospital or medical school.

American Medical Association, 535 N. Dearborn St., Chicago, Illinois 60610

Continental Association, 59 E. Van Buren St., Chicago, Illinois 60605

Deafness Research Foundation, 366 Madison Avenue, New York, N. Y., 10016 (Donations to research by people with hearing defects.)

Eye-Bank Association of America, 3195 Maplewood Ave., Winston-Salem, North Carolina 27103 or 315 Park Ave. So., New York City

Falconer Foundation, Inc., 66 W. 87th St., New York, N. Y. 10024 (Information on radiation research donations.)

Living Bank, 6631 South Main, P. O. Box 6725, Houston, Texas 77005

Medic Alert, Turlock, California 95380 (Also a source for doctors to obtain health information of its members in case of emergency)

National Kidney Foundation.

National Pituitary Agency, Suite 503-7, 210 West Fayette St., Baltimore, Maryland 21201

National Transplant Information Center, 135 Flower Hill Road, Huntington, New York 11743

National Association of Patients on Hemodialysis and Transplantation, P. O. Box 60, Brooklyn, New York 11203

Tissue Bank, U. S. Naval Medical Research Institute, Bethesda, Maryland 20014 (Write for information, not donor card.)

United Health Foundations, Inc., 150 Fifth Avenue, New York, N. Y. 10011

You may specify that the body not be used for military medical research, police sciences, mortuary science, atomic radiation research, etc. But young people are encouraged to donate their bodies, in case of accidental death, to radiation research. (See Falconer Foundation above.) Often the only way medical and other valuable research is done is through military funding, police and mortuary science. You may also specify that you do not wish prayers or a religious ceremony. Some funds may be left for charges for transportation to the medical school. In some or all states, the body of one who dies of smallpox, diptheria or scarlet fever is not accepted. (Wisc. 155.03) Deaths due to cholera (Asiatic), diptheria, polio, plague or scarlet fever require quarantine of those exposed. The body after research may be cremated or buried as you wish. The medical school will often dispose of the body for you, with no funeral expense being involved. If cremated, one may specify that no ashes are to remain, thus avoiding problems of disposing of the ashes.

Eyes may be left for the 35 thousand or so people who could see if corneas or fluids were made available to them. There is a great need for these. They may be donated even if one wears glasses, because only the corneas are transplanted. They must be removed within two to four hours after death. For information one may contact the Eye Bank for Sight Restoration, 210 East 64th St., New York City or the Eye Bank Assoc. of America (address above). Eyes may also be left for research. Lions Clubs, Elks Association and other service organizations have been especially helpful in promoting eye donations. Airlines often donate free transportation.

About twenty-five different kinds of organs and tissues such as bones, skin, nerve tissue, heart, kidney, liver, spleen, lung, thymus and pituitary tissue, nerves, arteries, veins, ear parts, etc. may be donated to the living. Some of those parts are, of course, donated also by the living to the living, e.g., kidney, sperm, bone marrow, etc. The U. S. Naval Tissue Bank in Bethesda, Maryland, freeze dries and otherwise preserves nearly all kinds of body parts, except that vital organs can usually only be preserved for 12-24 hours. The kidney may now be kept viable for up to 70 hours in a special medical unit. Kidney transplants would, if available, extend the lives of about 10,000 people. To make these available there would have to be one hundred million card carrying kidney donors. There are only five percent of such prospective donors. Each year 59,000 persons die from kidney disease. The American College of Surgeons, National Institutes of Health Organ Transplant Registry reveals the following number of transplants as of Aug. 1, 1972 (for all institutions): kidney 10,245 (est.), liver 166, lung 30, pancreas 27, heart 194, bone marrow 300 (est.). Heart transplants cost about $18,700 with other organ transplants being even higher. Corneal transplants cost around $1,000. One can see the need here of encouraging willing money to the needy for life-saving operations and the advancement of research.

G. Engel. "Is Grief a Disease?" *Psychosomatic Medicine* 23 (1961) 18-22

"Facts Every Family Should Know About Funerals and Interments" 1961 Association of Better Business Bureaus

Ruth Harmer. "Funerals, Fantasy, and Flight" *Omega* 2, 3 (1971) 127-35, 150-54

————. *The High Cost of Dying* Macmillan 1963

Paul Irion. *Cremation* Quoted from David Berg and G. Daugherty, eds, *The Individual, Society, and Death* Baltimore, Maryland: Waverly Press 1972

Irving Ladimer. "The Challenge of Transplanation" Public Affairs Pamphlet no. 451, 1970

George Marshall. "Before a Family Faces Death" Boston, Mass.: Unitarian Universalist Association

Jessica Mitford. "Have Undertakers Reformed?" *Atlantic Monthly* June, 1965 pp. 69-73

————. *The American Way of Death* New York: Fawcett World Library 1963

Ernest Morgan. *A Manual of Simple Burial* Burnsville, North Carolina: Celo Press 1971 (Revised 1973)

"Quotes that may be considered in rebuttal to the letter of Allen Johnson, Jr. in *National Observer* for Feb. 9, 1970" sent to author by H. Ruidl (WFDA)

Howard Raether. "Comments on Ruth Harmer's 'Funerals, Fantasy and Flight,' " and "The Place of the Funeral" *Omega* 2, 3 (1971) pp. 157, 148

Warren Shibles. *Emotions: An Interdisciplinary Approach* Whitewater, Wisconsin: The Language Press 1973

——–. "Ethics as Open-Context Terms" *Philosophical Pictures* Dubuque, Iowa: Kendall-Hunt 1972. Also read at International Congress of Philosophy, Brazil Oct. 1972

Charles Wallis. *Stories on Stone* New York: Oxford University Press 1954

Malcolm Wells. "Undertaking With a Green Thumb" *Environmental Quality* 3 (Aug. 1972) 29-32

Memorial Societies

Because death is a universal human experience and because it has a profound emotional and social impact on the survivors, the customs and practices associated with it are very important.

We have learned by experience that a simple, dignified service held with a closed casket or, better yet, in the form of a memorial after the body has been removed, can effectively emphasize the deeper meaning of the occasion and, by stressing the enduring values of the life which has passed, bring inspiration and comfort to the survivors.

Also important, this simple procedure can ease the financial burden. Instead of $1500 or more, including cemetery costs, a dignified and satisfying service may be had for a fraction of that amount.

Because simplicity in funeral arrangements tends to be contrary to prevailing custom, families often have difficulty in knowing where to turn or how to proceed in order to get either simplicity of service or the moderate costs which properly should go with such simplicity.

Memorial Societies are organized to provide guidance and moral support in this matter to such families as desire it. The Societies are non-profit organizations, democratically controlled by their members. Their officers serve without pay. The following pages will give you further information about the Societies and about the simplicity which they advocate.

* Reprinted by permission from Celo Press.

Questions and Answers Concerning Memorial Societies

Q. WHAT IS A MEMORIAL SOCIETY?

A. A memorial society is a group of people who have joined together to obtain dignity, simplicity and economy in funeral arrangements by advance planning.

Q. IS IT RUN BY FUNERAL DIRECTORS?

A. No, it is a people's cooperative organization that assists its members in selecting a funeral director and in getting the services they want.

Q. HOW IS IT CONTROLLED?

A. It is a democratic organization managed by an unpaid board of directors elected from its membership.

Q. WHO ORGANIZES MEMORIAL SOCIETIES?

A. They usually are initiated by a church or a ministerial association; occasionally by labor, civic or educational groups; sometimes by a few concerned individuals.

Q. IS MEMBERSHIP LIMITED?

A. No. Even though a society may have been organized by a church or civic group, it is open to all regardless of creed, color, occupation or nationality.

Q. HOW ARE MEMORIAL SOCIETIES SUPPORTED?

A. Most have a lifetime membership fee of $10 or $15 plus a $5 records charge at time of death. Some receive bequests and other gifts.

Q. WHAT HAPPENS WHEN YOU JOIN?

A. The society lets you know what kinds of funeral services are available and at what cost. You talk it over in your family and decide on your preference, then fill out forms provided by the society.

Q. CAN THESE PLANS BE CANCELLED OR CHANGED LATER?

A. Certainly. Any time.

Q. HOW DOES PRE-PLANNING HELP AT TIME OF DEATH?

A. In several ways:

1. You know what you want, how to get it and what it will cost. You don't have to choose a casket or negotiate for a funeral.

2. Your family understands what is being done. Simplicity will not be mistaken for miserliness or lack of respect.

3. By accepting the reality of death in advance, and by discussing it frankly, you and your family are better able to meet it when it comes.

Q. DOES PLANNING REALLY SAVE MONEY?

A. The amounts vary greatly, but memorial society members usually save $500 or more on a funeral.

Q. WHAT IS THE BASIS OF THESE SAVINGS?

A. Simplicity. If you are not trying to demonstrate social status or compete with the neighbors, a dignified and satisfying funeral need not be costly.

Q. CAN THESE SAVINGS BE MADE WITHOUT A MEMORIAL SOCIETY?

A. As a rule, yes. But you generally have to search carefully and inquire widely to discover all the possibilities, something few families are prepared to do, especially at a time of death.

Q. HOW DO I JOIN A MEMORIAL SOCIETY?

A. Phone or write the nearest society and ask for their literature. They will send you information about the help they can give you and the membership fee.

Q. WHAT IF THERE IS NO SOCIETY NEARBY?

A. Write the Continental Association of Funeral and Memorial Societies, 59 East Van Buren St., Chicago, Illinois 60605, to find out if there is a society that serves your area or if one is being formed. In Canada, write the Memorial Society Association of Canada, P. O. Box 4367, Vancouver 9, B. C. If you are interested in helping start a society, the Associations will supply information and frequently local contacts as well. Nearby societies can often give experienced help.

Q. WHAT IF I MOVE TO ANOTHER PLACE?

A. There are memorial societies in more than a hundred cities in the U. S. and Canada. Nearly all are members of the Continental Association or of the Memorial Society Association of Canada. You can transfer your membership with little or no charge.

Q. ARE ALL MEMORIAL SOCIETIES ALIKE?

A. Being democratic, memorial societies vary in their arrangements and mode of operation. Their common characteristic is that they are democratic and non-profit. Now and then pseudo memorial societies are set up as "fronts" for funeral directors.

Q. HOW CAN IT TELL THE REAL THING FROM THE IMITATION?

A. In two ways:

1. Nearly all genuine memorial societies are members of the Continental Association or of the Memorial Society Association of Canada. Both associations screen their members with care.

2. A bona fide society has nothing to sell and rarely charges over $15 for membership. If an organization calling itself a memorial society asks a much larger fee, or if it tries to sell you a funeral or a cemetery lot in advance, you will be well advised to check with the Better Business Bureau.

Q. WHAT IS THE ATTITUDE OF FUNERAL DIRECTORS TOWARD MEMORIAL SOCIETIES?

A. Funeral directors generally try to give each family what it wants, expecting the family to choose service which will reflect its social and economic status. In line with their stated policy they often cooperate with memorial societies. At the same time they do have high overhead and do prefer to sell their "best" merchandise, whereas the societies encourage simplicity and economy. Hence funeral directors sometimes have a prejudice against memorial societies.

Q. ARE FUNERALS NECESSARY?

A. At a time of death the survivors have important social and emotional needs which should not be ignored. A funeral is one way of meeting some of these needs.

Q. ARE THERE OTHER WAYS?

A. Yes. The body can be removed immediately after death and a memorial service held later, at approximately the same time a funeral would have been held.

Q. WHAT IS THE DIFFERENCE?

A. In a funeral the center of attention is the dead body; the emphasis is on death. In a memorial service the center of concern is the personality of the individual who has died, and the emphasis is on life. In addition a memorial service generally involves less expense, and can be held in a greater variety of locations.

Q. WHAT ARE MEMORIAL SERVICES LIKE?

A. They vary, taking into account the religious customs of the family and the personal relationships of the one who has died. The distinctive thing about memorial services is that they stress the ongoing qualities of the person's life rather than his death. Each service can be worked out to meet the needs and circumstances of the particular family.

Q. IS EMBALMING MANDATORY?

A. If the body is to be kept several days for a funeral service, or is to be transported by common carrier, yes. Otherwise embalming serves no useful purpose and except in a few states is not legally necessary.

Q. WHY IS EMBALMING USUALLY PRACTICED IN THIS COUNTRY?

A. Unless otherwise advised the funeral director assumes there will be viewing of the body, and a service in its presence, and that embalming and "restoration" are desired. If this is not the case, and if the body is not to be held for a funeral service, he will omit embalming if so requested.

Q. WHAT APPROPRIATE DISPOSITION CAN BE MADE OF A BODY?

A. There are three alternatives:

1. Earth burial was once the simplest and most economical arrangement. With increasing population, rising land values, cost of caskets, vaults and other items usually required, it is becoming more and more costly.
2. Cremation, a clean orderly method of returning the body to the elements, is economical and is rapidly increasing in use.
3. Bequeathal to a medical school performs a valuable service and saves expense. In many areas there is a shortage of bodies for the proper training of doctors. Many public spirited people leave their bodies for this purpose. The eye-banks, too, need donors.

Historical Theories of Prolongation

Before discussing views of prolongation some background in ancient Greek philosophy will be reviewed. (See also W. Shibles *Models of Ancient Greek Philosophy*) Plato held the view that there are two worlds: a material world and a world of non-material pure ideas, a world of form and a world of matter. The world we see is illusory and only yields opinion and copies or shadows of the real world. The real world is the world of universal pure knowledge. It is called the world of Ideas and it is thought that the material world merely "participates" in the world of pure Ideas just as any particular good act participates in or is guided by some absolute standard of Good. This view stresses, (a) that matter is base and should be denied in order to reach more pure, immaterial, true knowledge; (b) that the particular and material world, the microcosm, is like an image of the Ideal world, the macrocosm. This belief leads to the view that there is a universal analogy of all things and so everything may be related (metaphorically) to everything else. Such views will be seen to be relevant to alchemy and other theories of prolongation. Plato sought a fixed, permanent, eternal, "pure" kind of knowledge or reality. The alchemical search had this goal also. Neither the alchemical position nor the view of Plato are completely intelligible.

Aristotle also believes in a world of form and a world of matter but sees them as inseparable from one another. The four elements of the universe are said to be earth, air, fire and water. The "heavenly bodies," or "intelligences," or planets are supposedly composed of a fifth element, quintessence, or aether. Alchemists often sought or claimed to have found this aether. Because it was thought to be most pure and most

473

permanent it was thought to give one long life. Each of the four elements was said to seek its own level, earth and water nearest the center of the universe; fire and air higher and farther away from the center. Thus the most pure elements were thought to have the least amount of matter in them. The substance of the outer planets was thus thought to be pure form or quintessence. What was sought was the permanent basis of the universe.

Each of the four roots has the following characteristic properties: earth – dry, cold; air – hot, wet; fire – hot, dry; water – wet, cold. These properties formed the basis for alchemy and medicine almost up to the present time. This system is still part of present day astrology. The four humors associate with the above properties of hot, cold, wet, dry as follows: blood: hot/moist; yellow bile (choleric): hot/dry; black bile (melancholic): cold/dry; phlegm (phlegmatic): cold/moist. This scheme had been held by Hippocrates (ca. 400 B.C.). The four ages of life were: 1. childhood: hot/moist; youth: hot/dry; adulthood: cold/dry; old age: cold/moist. In the mediaeval period this view predominated. Avicenna and Galen claimed that old age is cold and moist. Aristotle thought old age cold and dry but the views are very similar. We may compare this to our expression, "He is all dried up." For Aristotle old age and death are natural and necessary because the opposite qualities which compose all things constantly change and destroy each other. Thus fever involves excess of heat or blood (sanguine), and so restoring the proper balance to the four humors is necessary. Aristotle's view of longevity involves the above scheme. (Arist. 1963) Life involves humidity and warmth, and old age is due to one's becoming dry and cold like a corpse. Those living in warm countries are thought to live longer than those in cold countries. Since work produces dryness, and old age is dry, labor brings about old age. It is found that the laboring class in the United States has a higher mortality rate than other classes, though not necessarily for the reason given by Aristotle.

Although today and possibly also in Aristotle's day women live longer than men, he states, "By natural constitution and as a general rule males live longer than females, and the reason is that the male is an animal with more warmth than the female." Aristotle believes that death is always due to some lack of heat.

Heat is gradually breathed away by the time of old age. He says it is as if the heart had a tiny flame in it which is very easily put out. This may be compared to the religious term *nirvana,* which means "to blow out." Thus death in old age is painless and quick. It is mainly caused by the failure of organs to cool the body. The alchemists later stress "breath" or the life principles of substances. The word "spirit" derives from the word for "breath." Breath was often thought to be the cause of life rather than just an accompaniment. (Aristotle also characterizes life as that which has "soul.") From the foregoing views one could expect that to prolong life they would look for a "pure" substance, a permanent unchanging substance or "prime matter," a harmony of existing substances, and something which has "spirit" or "breath" in it. Aristotle's views were quoted throughout history and almost exclusively up until the 18th century.

The Alchemists

Gerald Gruman has written a history of attempts to prolong life. (1966) Much of the factual basis of the following may be found in his book. Gruman favors a progressive lengthening of the span of life. He says that the subject of prolongation of life is often

> "relegated to a limbo reserved for impractical projects or eccentric whims not quite worthy of serious scientific or philosophic consideration. One reason for this neglect is that there is, in philosophy, science, and religion, a long tradition of apologism, the belief that the prolongation of life is neither possible nor desirable. Another reason is that there are few subjects which have been more misleading to the uncritical and more profitable to the unscrupulous."

One may roughly divide alchemists into two groups:
1. *Mechanical alchemy.* This involved search for a basic substance which might prolong life because of its being a very stable, long-lasting substance. Such a substance seemed to them immortal and non-corruptible and thought it would make man similarly long-lived. For example, the Chinese Taoist alchemists

found that cinnabar (Mercury sulphide, $HgS + O_2$) when heated produces mercury (mercuric oxide $Hg + SO_2$). If mercury ($2Hg + O_2$) is heated it returns to a red substance, mercuric oxide ($2HgO$). They erroneously thought the red cinnabar is restored so that the process is a permanent and stable shifting from a red powder to a fluid mercuric metal and back again. It was regarded as an immortal chemical. "Immortal" as it is used here is used to mean only "stable" or "permanent" relative to other changing things, yet it seems to have been taken as metaphorically meaning "eternal" or "longevity producing." It is not clear what was actually thought but metaphors and analogies seem to have been taken as literal truths.

The more mechanical transformations were probably due to a lack of knowledge of the basic chemical elements or of how they combine. Nevertheless such early transformations led to modern chemistry. Many early chemists and scientists were also alchemists.

It was thought that all sorts of substances could be transformed or transmuted into gold and silver, which somehow give people immortality. The analogy is to the metamorphosis, transmutation, or transformation of a tadpole to a frog, or caterpillar to butterfly.

It was thought that base metal naturally evolves into gold but because it takes so long a catalyst or elixir is needed to speed up the process. This substance would transmute one metal into another and man (man's "metal") into immortality. The elixir was also called a "vital spirit" or "philosopher's stone."

2. *Internal alchemy.* This was mystical, spiritual and symbolic alchemy. It stressed purification of the soul to yield a pure life-giving substance and spiritual transmutation of one substance into another and so also a transformation of mortal man into immortal man. Our pure alcohol was "aqua vitae" or "pure water." Pure substances could purify the body. The Taoist alchemists thought that everything is made of breath of varying degrees of purity and so if the breath is kept one would live longer. This relates to Aristotle's view mentioned earlier that heat and breath are closely associated with or determine life. The Chinese, for longevity, advised eating the following substances because they were thought rich in "breath" (our

word today might be "energy"): eggs, peaches, turtle broth, and also things which live long.

Longevity foods and medicines were chosen by analogies of properties or "signatures." The relation of Platonic universal correspondence of all things is relevant here. A signature is based on a false analogy. The *Century Dictionary and Cyclopedia* (1902, Vol. 7) states about signature: "An external natural marking upon, or a symbolical appearance or characteristic of, a plant, mineral, or other object or substance, formerly supposed by the Paracelsians, and still by some ignorant persons, to indicate its special medicinal quality or appropriate use," e.g., yellow flowers to be administered for jaundice, or mandrake root useful and powerful because shaped like a man. In this way qualities thought to be especially powerful were shiny (mercury), translucent, fluid, wet, slippery, root-shaped like man, etc.

Pure substances were thought pure in other ways also by means of false analogy. One had to be morally pure in order to work with the alchemical life-prolonging substances. Also it was thought that if one ate out of gold or silver utensils it would prolong life. Gold foil is still today put in liquor, and names such as Goldwater suggest this practice. The Chinese add gold and silver to drinks, and our own silverware may derive from belief in its life-giving qualities.

The well-known Catholic theologian, St. Thomas Aquinas, who adapted Aristotle's philosophy as the official Catholic philosophy, accepted alchemical transmutation. Roger Bacon, who thought that death and old age are not inevitable, but rather only accidental, believed in alchemical and hygienic means of prolongation up to about 190 years of age. He sought pure gold for rejuvenation and chose especially substances rich in "breath" (called "virtue" or "vital spirit"). He thought the breath of a young virgin could help prolong life. It was a current opinion that headmasters of girls schools lived especially long. Elie Metchnikoff points to a similar view in the Bible (Kings I, chapt. 1): "Let there be sought for my lord the king a young virgin; let her stand before the king and let her cherish him, and let her lie in thy bosom, that my lord the king may get heat." This technique is called "gerokomy" and was used in ancient Greece and more recently in the 17th and 18th century. (p. 136)

Some of Bacon's arguments for life prolongation were:

1. Accounts of early men and biblical men are said to have lived extremely long. (Methuselah lived about 1000 years.)
2. soul is immortal
3. hygiene and exercise help longevity
4. ethical behavior helps longevity
5. there is evidence of a fountain of youth
6. certain animals live very long. They have instinctive knowledge of the powers of herbs and minerals.

Views of prolongation may be divided into those advocating it and those in opposition to it. The latter claim that we should not or cannot increase our life span and must therefore not try to do so, but that rather we must accept the fact that death is final. Alchemists, Taoists, Condorcet, William Goodwin, C. A. Stephens foresaw the possibility of the indefinite lengthening of human life.

The *Epic of Gilgamesh* shows that even a being similar to God cannot escape death. It is an apologist view suggesting that death is inevitable and must be accepted.

Hesiod has a myth of an "Age of Gold" when men never grew old. But due to decadence man gradually lost this capacity.

In "Hymn to Aphrodite" (8th cent. B.C.) Tithonus was granted eternal life by the Gods but not eternal youth and the result was a very decrepit human. The suggestion here was that one should not try to live forever.

In the Bible, Adam was created out of dust, water, and breath (compare with the "breath" of the alchemists). According to the Bible, death is final and necessary. Death was the result of sin, and the power of death is all in God's hands. Man must supposedly learn to believe that he is a very limited being and so must just humbly accept his fate. In the Bible there is little attempt to prolong life. The biblical stress on the fact that death is a result of sin is similar to Aristotle's view that erotic males do not live long. Behavioral studies, however, have now shown that the reverse is the case. But it is a common superstition that being an erotic person will cause one to become old early or die young. This view is based on the metaphysical view that the soul must be pure, rather than on an observation of what in fact is the case. The apologistic account opposes all attempts to prolong life, conquer death or inquire into such matters. (See chapter on death and religion.) Freud, Sartre, Heidegger, Epictetus, Epicurus, Cicero, Marcus Aurelius, and the average man as well as most psychiatrists, evolutionists, and biologists, are apologists claiming that death is a part of nature, is necessary, natural, and that we should submit and not oppose it. Lucretius and Malthus suggest that death is necessary to prevent overpopulation.

According to the Antediluvian Theory, before the flood people lived longer than they now do, e.g., Adam 930 years, Seth 912, Enosh 905, Kenan 910, Jared 962, Enoch 365, Methuselah 969, Lamech 777, Noah 950. This, as Roger Bacon noted, was thought of as a suggestion that our own life span can be increased. The argument however may only be suggestive to those who believe in the Bible. Bacon thought that our inability to live that long is due to our ignorance. St. Augustine (*City of God* Bk 15, 9-14) takes the antediluvian theory literally. Pliny speaks of Romans and Greeks who lived up to 800 years. In various cultures (Trobriands, Ainu, Banks Islands) people think their ancestors could rejuvenate by shedding their old body on the analogy that snakes shed their skins. This view is like the Christian view that at death one sheds his old body to obtain a new body at resurrection.

According to the Hyperborean Theory there are people in some parts of the world who live very long. "Hyperborean" means "beyond the north wind." Such places were Atlantis, Isle of the Blest, Avalon, St. Brendan's Island, Antilia. Columbus supposedly sought such a place. Now such places are thought to be parts of Russia, the land of the Hunzakuts in the Himalayas, or on another planet.

According to the Fountain of Youth Theory there is some substance which will give eternal youth. The alchemists sought such a substance but the theory is best known from Juan Ponce de Leon who is said to have discovered Florida in 1513 in his search for the fountain of youth. It is, however, not certain that he set out to look for a fountain of youth. Many health spas proclaim rejuvenating waters. The search may also take the form of health foods which are said to make one live longer, e.g., Greek ambrosia and nectar, honey, fermented juice of the soma plant, etc.

According to the Phoenix Theory some animals live much longer than man. The Phoenix is a mythical bird said to live 500 years in the Arabian desert and to rise rejuvenescent from its cremated ashes. It is a symbol of immortality. Hesiod states that a crow lives nine times as long as a human and the Phoenix 1,080 times as long. Studies of the life span of animals (e.g., by Alex Comfort) show that such is not the case although some animals live perhaps twice as long as man.

Sleeping Beauty, the Endymion Theory, suggest that a trance-like sleep will keep one youthful. Such theories and myths are perhaps based on the analogy to the hibernation of certain animals. That their body processes are slowed in such deep sleep may suggest they will age more slowly. A similar more recent view is that of Ettinger who suggests that freezing may preserve life. (See section on cryonics)

One of the first systems of prolongation was used by the Chinese Taoists. It involved sexual relations with a young woman especially between ages 14 and 19, without release of semen. Semen was thought to contain an ethereal substance, Ching, which can revive one's body and allow one to attain immortality. One of the models upon which they may have based this view is that in old age semen and menstrual fluid diminish and so it was thought that loss of fluid causes old age. This is an unproven assumption or a false analogy. Just as "breath" was associated with and so thought the cause of life, semen was thought to contain a life giving substance or "breath." In fact, if "breath" is added to the Ching it supposedly forms an embryo. Gruman wrote about this practice,

> "He who is able to have coitus several tens of times in a single day and night without allowing his essence to escape will be cured of all maladies and will have his longevity extended. If he changes his woman several times the advantage is greater; if in one night he changes his partner ten times, that is supremely excellent."

In China from the 2nd century up to the 7th century males and females had coitus in church groups to unite the female principle (yin) and the male principle (yang). The sexual means of prolonging life has continued in various other forms, for example, as a means of exercising by intercourse to keep healthy.

Such practices by the Taoists were strictly regulated. Fasting and abstinence were required for long periods of time. Also the Taoists thought that temperance promotes longevity. This seems to contradict the above practices as well as the following. They stressed what they thought was naturalness. It was often said that it is not desirable to live too long. Thus they both favored and did not favor prolongation.

Another technique for prolongation of life was by eating in a way that long-lived animals such as the crane and tortoise do. Again a false analogy is the basis of their thinking. They ate crane's eggs and tortoise soup. Foods from long-living trees such as pines and cypresses were also eaten. Dietary techniques could prolong life. One should eat only foods rich in spirit. Meat, wine, grains and many vegetables were prohibited. Foods were also eaten which kill the three harmful worms supposed to be in the body. Thus they ate cinnamon, licorice, ginseng and sesame.

In addition the Taoists tried to prolong life by means of retaining breath and by breathing as long-lived animals do. Air is more pure than other substances so it is thought to partake of the divine. This is similar to the place of air and quintessence in Greek philosophy. The Taoists sought to be nourished by pure air so that impure food would not have to be eaten. This view also suggests that aging is caused by impurities in our food. Thus air swallowing was practiced. Immortality was supposedly gained if one could hold his breath for 1000 respirations. "Embryonic respiration" was practiced according to which one could supposedly breathe through one's skin. One result of holding one's breath must have been anoxia or a euphoric light-headedness. After about three hundred respirations are missed one can no longer hear or see. We find that today, with training, the breath can be held for about four and one-third minutes.

One reason for the view that breath prolonged life is based on false causality regarding nourishment. The Taoists thought that digestion merely extracts breath from food and so it is really breath which nourishes. Air breath was thought more pure than food breath. The Taoists, alchemists, Greeks, medieval and ancient medicine, the Bible, all erroneously regard breath as the cause of life whereas it is only the accompaniment. They were not clear as to what function "breath" ("spirit") has in human physiology. "Soul" seems to name an entity which is responsible for life. It takes the place of what we call physiology today. But what we do not know about the cause of human experience and behavior may be called "soul." "Soul" means ignorance about ourselves. There is not soul as such, it is in some usages, not a thing or cause of anything. It is a statement about what we do not know. Their theories and practices are largely based on false analogy, lack of knowledge of scientific cause and effect, and their practice of taking their language and metaphors literally without being aware of how language actually works.

The Taoists also attempted prolongation by gymnastic methods. Rhythmical exercise supposedly overcomes obstructions of breath and sperm within the body. Osteopathy takes as part of its effectiveness freeing the nutritive fluids of the body to cure disease. Also harmful breaths are released. Exercise thus was thought to lengthen life and prevent disease. Although their knowledge of physiology and their picture of the entities involved was wrong it is still found that exercise helps prolong life and prevent disease.

Good hygiene was and still is an accepted means of prolonging life. Luigi Cornaro stressed temperance, proper diet, eating sparingly, avoiding hatred and upsetting emotions. He still believed in the four humors and thought temperance keeps them well-balanced. Regardless of the falsity of his picture, temperance does aid longevity.

Among prolongevists were Descartes, who thought a cure for old age possible and he hoped to live for 150 years, and Benjamin Franklin, who wished to be immersed in Madeira wine and later revived, as flies drowned in wine are sometimes later revived. Franklin wrote,

"All diseases may by sure means be prevented or cured, not excepting even that of old age, and our lives lengthened at pleasure even beyond the antediluvian standard." (Gruman p. 74)

Ettinger's view of freezing for later revival is a more recent development of this view.

William Godwin (1756-1836) thought that one could prolong life by gaining voluntary control over the emotions, and over bodily functions. He thought also that one could gain immortality. Clear thinking and proper emotions can increase life. Bad news may cause disease or death. Cheerfulness leads to a longer life. His view is that reason can help create a more happy person and so increase one's life. Negative emotions seem to cause stress, heart attacks, fast aging and death. Godwin's stress on reason is similar to the contemporary view of Albert Ellis in *Reason and Emotion*. Ellis calls his view "rational psychotherapy." Godwin concludes that we become diseased and die partly because we consent to and because we think we will. Sounder reasoning and emotions would help us stay healthier and prolong our lives. His view may be supported by recent research on psychosomatic medicine whereby one's attitude can even cause one's own death. Physicians find that one must have a will to live to survive operations or illness. Self-suggestion or hypnosis may also be relevant here. The body is seen to adapt or adjust to the direction given it. Also in view of contemporary analyses of emotions it is seen that rational inquiry into emotions allows us to dissipate the negative ones and strengthen the positive ones thus making it possible to lead a more satisfactory and so longer life.

Condorcet (1732-1794) thought that extensive prolongation of life is possible and he recommended an extensive research program on aging and prolongation. He wrote,

"A period must one day arrive when death will be nothing more than the effect either of extraordinary accidents, or of the slow and gradual decay of the vital powers; and that the duration of the interval between the birth of man and his decay will have itself no assignable limit. Certainly man will not become immortal."

One modern view suggesting prolongation, derives from Einstein's Theory of Relativity. His view is that there is time-dilation. It is often represented by the "twin paradox" according to which one man on a space vehicle leaves another and travels at such great speed that "time slows down" and he supposedly comes back younger than those he left behind.

According to the Fitzgerald-Lorentz contraction hypothesis used by Einstein the speed of light is assumed constant and to save the formula it is assumed that as speed increases objects contract, mass increases, and time itself slows down. But this is a great length to go to save the formulas because there is no time as such. Time is merely change. (See W. Shibles "Timelessness") For acceleration, $a = \frac{d(\dot{v})}{dt}$, distance is ($\frac{s}{t}$), and mass ($\frac{F}{a}$) and "a" involves time). Time can only have meaning in these formulas as a change of objects just as the hands of a clock are only changes but do not measure time in itself. Time as an entity is a fiction. Thus time dilation or time slowing down is unintelligible. A moving clock is found to go slower than a stationary clock. This only means that one clock might go slower if put in water. It does not mean that time goes slower. That time goes slower does not mean one does not age (change). Body action is slowed just as the fast moving clock may be slowed. But clocks do not become sick in the same way humans do. That objects may slow and contract at high speed seems true, that time slows is unintelligible. In no case does this appear to be a hope for immortality or for remaining young. If time dilation could keep one young one could supposedly not age at all if time stopped. In *Alice in Wonderland* this is exactly what happened. Because six o'clock is tea time and time has stopped the Hatter mistakenly thinks what is done at that time must stop also. That is, he sets a table with many places supposing that he must have tea over and over because time stopped at tea time. This is not unlike some of Zeno's paradoxes which confuse time with what takes place in time or which assume that time is something separate from the change of things or events. (See W. Shibles "Zeno" in *Models . . .)* One does not grow old in time. Time is change and one changes, becomes wrinkled etc., as clocks and other things change.

Aristotle. *The Works of Aristotle* J. Beare and G. Ross, trans., Oxford: Clarendon Press 1963 (1931) 4646-4806

Albert Ellis. *Reason and Emotion* New York: Lyle Stuart 1962

Gerald Gruman. *History of Ideas About the Prolongation of Life: The Evolution of Prolongevity Hypotheses to 1800* Philadelphia: American Philosophical Society 1966

Elie Metchnikoff. *The Prolongation of Life* New York: Putnams 1908

Warren Shibles. *Models of Ancient Greek Philosophy* London: Vision 1971

––––––. "Timelessness" *Philosophical Pictures* 2nd ed. Dubuque, Iowa: Kendall-Hunt 1972

Biology of Aging

I. THE STATUS OF RESEARCH: AGING AS A TABOO SUBJECT IN BIOLOGY

According to Bernard Strehler (1962) there is no inherent factor which automatically produces aging in animals and plants. After examining the various hypotheses of aging he states:

> "Unless a considerably more systematic attack on those fundamental areas directly related to the phenomenon of cellular aging is undertaken, it will be another score of years before we can even evaluate the feasibility of therapeutic measures directed toward slowing down this or that senescence process."

He calls for:

1. "A sufficient awareness of the part of biologists, biochemists, and biophysicists . . ."
2. "Sponsorship — moral, financial, and administrative — of a long-term program of research in this area. For too long has this area been regarded as a sort of step-child of other more legitimate areas. This has resulted in a near void where administrative leadership could have been exercised."

He supports the idea of establishing and funding a National Institute of Gerontology. Strehler predicts a 20 percent increase in life span by 1990.

487

Robert Kohn said,

"There are large gaps in our knowledge of basic processes."

"Many of the most interesting questions we might ask have received little or no attention."

"Very few of the explanations of biological phenomena that we accept as proved could actually survive a rigorously logical criticism."

"Aging has never been the major interest of the community of biologists."

"No textbook on aging exists." [1970]

"There are no reasons why aging processes will not be completely understood eventually, and methods devised for their inhibition."

"Agreement has not been the case; notions about causes of aging have generally followed the fashions of the times, and virtually every conceivable phenomenon has been proposed in the past, or is currently under consideration as a primary cause . . . Basic mechanisms of aging are currently at the level of hypotheses or theories."

For Kohn aging is regarded as a disease, but one which it is possible to cure at least to some extent: "Aging — the 100 percent fatal disease that everyone has."

A "disease" is a "lack of ease," an "uneasiness" and so is a deviation from our normal painless experiences. It refers to certain patterns of events, objects or experiences. But also it is a value term suggesting something which is undesirable, a *dis*-ease, something we would like to overcome or do away with. Although we know neither cause nor cure of perhaps fifty percent of mental and physical diseases (cf. *Merck Manual*) they nevertheless are classified as diseases. Dying, aging, and grief may also be regarded as diseases or uneasinesses to be overcome. Certainly negative emotions are seen to bring about aging and death. To value the present state of aging because it is "natural" is to overlook the fact that all diseases are "natural" also, yet we wish to, and have, overcome many diseases once thought incurable.

Alex Comfort's view of the present status of the study of

aging is that,

> "Relatively few [theories] are supported by any body
> of fundamental experiment. The devising of general
> theories of senescence has employed able men, chiefly in
> their spare time from laboratory research for many years."

He points out the great need to study the process of aging
and notes our past failure in this regard:

> "Insofar as biology is more than a branch of idle
> curiosity, its assignment in the study of old age is to devise,
> if possible, means of keeping human beings alive in active
> health for a longer time than would normally be the case
> — in other words, to prolong individual life. People now
> rightly look to 'science' to provide the practical realization
> of perennial human wishes which our ancestors have failed
> to realize by magic . . . Most people today would incline
> to prefer the prospect of longevity, which may be
> realizable, to a physical immortality which is not . . ."

He also suggests that it is religion and magical theories which
have prevented progress in the area of inquiry into aging, and it
may be added, into the concept of death as well:

> "The emotional preoccupation of former workers with
> magical rejuvenation did no good to the progress of
> science . . ."

In opposition to those who assert that we can never increase
the human life-span and therefore we need not do research on
aging, Comfort asserts, after a thorough examination of the
literature,

> "To the question 'Can the effective human life-span be
> prolonged artificially?' the most probable answer, based
> on all these possibilities [theories], would appear to be
> 'Yes.' "

The nature of elementary particles when it is better known
may also contribute to a knowledge of death. On the other

hand, physicists say the physical world is becoming more and more a mystery. Then our knowledge of life and death are becoming more of a mystery also. Death is the price we pay for the limits of our knowledge. Rosalind Heywood states,

"Perhaps we should keep on reminding ourselves that the science of today is not at the end of the road."

Dr. Augustus Kinzel, founding president of the National Academy of Engineering said, "We will lick the problem of aging completely." (*Newsweek* 4-6-70)
William Vrasdonk states,

"We simply do not know what the finality of death means and thus we cannot accept it as a creedal statement . . . If personal immortality is a hidden tendency in the biological makeup of man, then it is time that this aspect receives more consideration . . . Death should be refused as an everlasting solution to our situation."

The psychiatrist, Dr. Donald Prasser, M.D. has even established a "Committee to End Old Age and Death." (Bakersfield, California)
Dr. Arthur Galston, Professor of Plant Physiology at Yale University states, "Death isn't necessary." He gives several suggestive indications of the possibility of overcoming death:

1. Some plants whose sex organs are prevented from developing live indefinitely.
2. An individual cell of the mature carrot can be removed and reproduce a new carrot.
3. Organs and cells may be removed from an animal and kept alive in Petri dishes.
4. DNA can be transferred from one cell to another to improve the quality and functioning of the new cell.

For reasons such as these he concludes, "Here is man's dream of experimental immortality, and the path to immortality is now clear."

Should our modern age amount to no more than our being able to blow horns to warn ourselves of our own deaths? The English word "mort" refers to a note sounded on the hunting horn to announce the death of the hunted. In this case it, the hunted, is himself. One student said that death is like screaming at the top of your lungs with no one hearing.

II. CRYONICS

One attempt to achieve immortality is by the use of freezing bodies at death with the hope that medical science will advance to the point where the body can be thawed, revived, and cured of old age and disease. The most well-known advocate of freezing bodies at death is Robert Ettinger.

Bacteria have been revived which have been frozen for thousands of years. Eels have been frozen to 190 degrees Centigrade, and thawed to life undamaged. Frog and turtle hearts have been frozen (50% of body water frozen) and then revived. There is short term rivival (e.g., 24 hours) of frozen rabbits and primates. Human sperm, whole blood, corneas, lymphocytes, bone marrow, vaccines, bone, skin cartilage are frozen and later thawed for use. Over 400 normal children have been born by use of sperm stored by freezing. Bacteria, protozoa, yeast cells, insects, shellfish, dog kidneys, may also be frozen and revived.

In February 1972 there were at least thirteen frozen dead bodies including some quite prominent people. (*Chicago Sun Times* 2-6-72)

But the project of freezing bodies at death is as yet thought by many to be irrational. Dr. Callahan in an article in *Rational Living* (vol. 2, 1967) supports cryonics but the editors think of Ettinger's proposal as too theoretical. Dr. Robert Fulton states,

"Probably the most extreme expression of the impulse to deny the necessity of biological death in our society is the cryogenic movement."

Fulton is a defender of present funeral practices. The scientist Peter Masur (1970) states that bodies frozen with present methods will probably not be able to be revived.

However, the program of freezing with the hope of revival is more rational and has more evidence for success than the hope for a miraculous religious kind of resurrection of the body. The freezing program also has the virtue of promoting inquiry into cryobiology, research into how organs can be frozen and thawed without damage so they may be used for needy patients. It also sets a rational goal for us to aim at, to attempt to achieve immortality by rational methods, to study aging, prolongation. Such emphasis is greatly needed because of the general opposition and apathy to attempts to conquer death, and aging.

III. THEORIES OF AGING

The following is a report of the most common and current theories of aging. Each theory appears to be based upon one or several basic metaphors or analogies. For example, the wear-tear theory is based on the view that if something wears down it ceases to function any longer. The radiation theory is based on a view that age is correlated with amount of radiation, chromosome theory is based partly on the fact that longevity is inherited and that chromosomes program one's cell activity, growth rate theory is based partly on the discovery that reduced caloric intake in youth increases subsequent health and age span, the endocrine theory is partly based on the view that hormones can double the life of mice and rats. Each theory seems to provide merely a perspective, metaphor or model, and should not be taken literally as the model or cause of aging.

1. Brody-Failla Theory.
The Mortality rate is inversely proportional to vitality. "Vitality," however, is a vague term. (Strehler 1960)

2. Strehler-Mildvan Theory.
Death occurs when stress surpasses energy. (Strehler 1960) Vitality is the amount of energy needed to restore systems of the individual. This theory is also vague in that while defining "vitality," "energy" is vague. "Energy" is a pseudo-category and naming-fallacy. It seems to name something whereas its only meaning is the operational definition of its use in a particular context. It is misleading, for example, to say something ages "because its 'energy' is all used up."

3. Wear and Tear Theory.

Increase of damage, disease, and wear and tear causes aging. (Simms-Jones Theory) (Strehler 1960)

Comfort gives a list of over sixteen scientists who hold this theory. (7) He divides all theories of aging into a) wear and tear theories and b) toxic theories. Wear and tear theories stress cell colloid, tissue, nerve, endocrine, vascular and connective tissue deterioration. Accumulation of calcium and exhaustion of life-giving matter may cause aging. Immersion of rotifers in citric solution increases their life span, perhaps because it prevents certain of these accumulations or depletions. The cause of such correlations seems highly speculative and Comfort finds no evidence of a depletive senescence in mammals.

4. Radiation Theory.

Aging is due to radiation. It was found that aging or shortening of life is proportional to the amount of low dosage ionizing radiation given.

Irradiation causes arteriolocapillary fibrosis. (Kohn) Death occurs when physiological states such as breathing capacity fall below a certain level. (Strehler 1960) The theory was held by Sacher.

5. Somatic Mutation Theory. (Curtis in Kastenbaum)

Spontaneous, irreversible, increasing mutations in somatic cells curtail cellular function and cause aging. Chromosome aberrations (damage to the DNA molecule or protein synthesis which controls cell function) increase with age. It is pointed out that this theory is the best theory available but needs further testing. Non-dividing cells accumulate mutations causing aging, and dividing cells may, because of mutations, develop cancer. This theory is partly based on the radiation theory. After radiation, chromosomes have a more limited ability to repair themselves. It is found that offspring of old mothers have a short life, thus suggesting chromosomal damage. A test was devised to measure mutation rates, and also aging rates in mice.

Curtis' conclusion that "Death is necessary for the good of the species," is unfounded. (Weismann (No. 13) holds that view also.) It *assumes* that death is not a disease and that chromosome aberrations are not irreversible, when this is the very thing which is under investigation. It is like asking what pneumonia is and then asserting that it is a necessary disease for the good of the species. Also it is not clear what "good" of the species would mean except the survival of the species. But there seems to be no reason why the survival of the old would interfere with the survival of the species and no mystical, naturalistic, or ultimate reason why the species should survive. The point should be that we can make it survive. Giving an explanation in terms of a final purpose or cause (teleological explanation) is a metaphorical personification and anthropomorphism. It appeals to a view that someone decided the purpose of everything.

L. Jarvik also holds a chromosomal mutation theory of aging. (Kastenbaum) Cells having more than the normal 46 chromosomes increase with age and such aberrant cells cause aging. Such aberrations are chromosomally programmed as if the body were built to self-destruct. However, details of the process are lacking. We may also inherit a predisposition to certain diseases.

However, Kohn states that effects of mutations due to protein synthesis defect have not been found in cells of aging animals. Also irradiated mice survive and the percentage of chromosomal aberrations decreases. He concludes that such mutations do not cause aging.

Tumors appear in a regular pattern with increasing age. One may be born with a genetic predisposition to have tumors as exposure to mutations, viral infection, smoking, and radiation increases with age. (Kohn)

Molecular explanations for aging include inability of genes to repair themselves, error of protein self-replication, or blocking of cell replication. There is, for example, a selective loss of DNA from brain cells of aging dogs. (*Science News* 7-15-72; 12-30-72) Blockage of cell reproduction can be reversed by some immunosuppressant drugs. (*Science News* 11-4-72)

6. Autoimmunity Theory.

With age one's cells lose the ability to distinguish foreign invasion and its own cells, resulting in autoimmunity or immunity to one's own self, thus causing aging. This can produce inhibition of division of cells and the antibodies may produce harmful cross-linking. (See cross-linking theory). Autoimmunity is due to an increase with age, of serum globulins and auto antibodies. (Walford in Kastenbaum)

However, Kohn states, "The notion that autoimmunity is a major cause of aging in natural populations is tenuous."

7. Brain Weight Theory of Aging. (Sacher in Kastenbaum)

"The brain is the only organ or structure thus far known to correlate with longevity." Brain weight is stressed because Sacher believes that aging is the result of supramolecular functioning (or organized behavior) rather than due to properties of individual cells:

"The paradigm of molecular biology . . . is inadequate and insufficient as a research strategy for biological as well as psychological gerontology."

He does, however, accept a molecular and physical basis of human behavior, but this must be a hope or guess on Sacher's part for on his view experience has not yet been adequately reduced to chemistry and physiology. He seems to assume that the weight of the brain is a measure of its performance capability. He then comes to the conclusion,

"The more information the organism can acquire and utilize to control its own states the longer it will live."

If this were true it might support psychosomatic medicine and perhaps the view that the more effectively one inquires the longer he will live. It is often reported that the more active one is in old age the better is his mental and physical health. However true this may be it is a great assumption to make that ability correlates with brain weight. It ignores education, language ability and all of the factors we refer to when we speak of intelligence. On the other hand it is found that nerve cells do die when they have no function. (Kohn) James Birren, however, does hold the view that loss of neurons causes aging.

8. Multiple Cause Theory of Aging.

Sonneborn opposes the search for a single rather than a multiple cause of aging in different individuals and species:

"The research for a fundamental aging process and mechanism may well be doomed to eternal failure." (Strehler 1960)

Kohn holds that aging is not caused by a single organism:

"The view that aging is aging and that one can study any system and generalize to all systems is clearly not tenable."

It is suggested here also that aging as a name of a thing or entity is a naming-fallacy. One may ask what one thing aging could be? He points out that the death of a Mayfly is caused by starvation due to atrophy of the mouth, whereas mice die of disease. The cause differs.

In extending Kohn's view it may be added that death cannot be due to aging because aging is not a thing, or the sort of thing which can be a cause. One cannot die of old age but only of disease, etc. "Aging" in "to die of aging" is merely a term elliptical for a number of implied factors. However, as we have seen, we are not at all clear what these factors are. Thus the notion of aging at present must remain obscure. We must specify the model or paradigm we use for aging. We may mean by "the aged" that one has wrinkles and moves slowly. After his death could we then say, "He died of old age?"

According to Kohn, "The borderline between development and aging is frequently indistinct." In support of this it may be added that in some respects one "ages" faster in youth than in old age. There is greater cell division, etc., then. Such statements as, "As you age your processes slow," can be seen to be circular when what we mean by aging is slowing of processes. Many uses of "age" as a cause, may be seen to be circular. Aging often means or is elliptical for changes of various sorts. On this view one may alternately say, "One dies from aging," or "One dies from changes." Only certain changes are thought to cause death, e.g., a poor heart, not aging or change in general or as such. To say as Shock does, "Few people die of old age," implies that one can die of old age as such. To say "The body dies a little each day," lacks specificity.

Often, those who looked for a fountain of youth would postulate a single cause or cure of all aging. Alchemists thought gold could increase length of life. The Taoists thought retention of sperm could make one live longer. This may be based on an analogy to those organisms such as salmon which die or become vulnerable as a result of spawning. It was in fact found that in man continence increases rather than decreases mortality. (Comfort)

Comfort also holds that there is no one single cause of aging and that there is no single biochemical property of cells or tissues that can be called aged, or oldness. One specific objection he makes is, "The more elaborate the attempts to depict senescence in overall mathematical terms, the more intellectually disastrous they have proved."

Comfort quite correctly asserts that theories of aging must be cleared of "entelechies" [final cause, teleology, explanations in terms of survival of the fittest, final purpose as if determined by a creator] "inherent principles" [e.g., Freudian principles of "death instinct," etc.].

9. Cross-linking.

Cell membranes and myofilament components contain macromolecules which may change in the cross-linking or binding of small molecules. Permeability of cells might be adversely altered. However, Kohn states that too little study has been done on this to offer supportive evidence. Arteries could be thickened leading to further injury as a result of link-crossing.

Collagen makes up 25-30 percent of the total body protein and exists around the cells. It is the major fibrous protein. Cross-linking of collagen may cause stiffness and may prevent exchange of necessary materials. Some chemicals have been found which can interfere with collagen maturation, e.g., nitriles and penicillamine. These drugs were found unsuccessful in attempting to inhibit aging in mice. Nevertheless, Kohn says,

"Since it is this theory that is best able to explain aging in terms of current information, perhaps it should receive the highest priority for future investigations."

"It might be possible eventually to find an agent that will maintain the collagen in its optimal mature state by inhibiting the formation of additional cross-links."

An earlier theory of cross-linking was that of Heilbrun who thought aging was caused by dehydration or syneresis of colloids. (Kohn)

We are still not clear about the chemical nature of collagen cross-links, and the types of bonds formed by it in aging are unknown, though various insoluble substances are known to accumulate in cells which may cause disfunction.

Johan Bjorksten has attempted to find an anti-aging "pill" or retarding or age reversing substance based upon the cross-link theory. (McGrady) He is attempting among other things to find a substance which will unlink the cross-linked molecules which supposedly cause aging. He appears to be conducting experiments which seek micro-organisms which can subsist on cross-linked matter. He then extracts enzymes, precursors, or activators to be applied to human tissue and organs which are critically cross-linked. The result may be an anti-aging enzyme. Patrick McGrady, in a report on youth pills states,

"The feasibility of an anti-aging pill should no longer be doubted . . . Therapy based on any one of the major aging theories can probably extend our lives."

A Bjorksten pamphlet, "Dialogue on Death," gives perhaps the simplest account of the cross-linking process:

"In the body there is a kind of molecule known as a protein, and the proteins are the most important chemical part of the living body. These protein molecules are like long spirals of atoms, and in them all along the chain there are points which can tie in very easily with other molecules or atoms . . . In the body there are also a lot of chemical compounds which we can call cross-linkers which you can think of as small rods with a hook on each end, and they can hook into these sensitive points on the protein molecules and . . . bind the protein molecules together. When joined together they can't move as freely, can't do their job in the body."

Molecules having a deficit or surplus of electrons are subject to cross-linking with other molecules. Our bodies are said to contain approximately 10^{20} molecules of potential cross-linkers, 1.4 grams of a 155-pound person.

Cross-linking causes an accumulation of insoluble protein material in the various organs of man and animals, and such cross-linking increases with age. There is a resulting loss of elasticity, incapacity of cells and aging.

Bjorksten's theory is that "during aging, changes occur in large molecules in a manner which can be explained only by cross-linking."(*Chemistry* 7) Other theories of aging are said to be explained by this theory: the theory that overfeeding causes aging is really based on the fact that excessive eating causes increased cross-linking. The cross-link theory also adds to the somatic mutation theory by explaining how cells mutate. The ionizing radiation theory only accounts for a portion of aging cells and the aging of even these cells is due to cross-linking. The fluctuation of hormones in the hormone theory of aging may be explained by cross-linked molecules. Even pigments which are a sign of aging consist of cross-linked proteins. Hans Selye's theory that aging is caused by effects of calcium may be based on the fact that calcium is a cross-linking agent. Arthritis and arteriosclerosis are also said to be explained by Bjorksten's theory.

Bjorksten's recent research involves looking for hydrolic enzymes which he calls "gerolytic" enzymes, which can dissolve insoluble cross-linked macromolecular factions from organs of the aged (e.g., part of the cortex of an 80-year-old man was used). Thus a cross-link reversing or retarding agent is sought. Also from the above findings it would appear that one might increase longevity, somewhat, merely by not overeating.

It is argued that if all major diseases were cured, life expectancy would only increase fifteen or twenty years. But if aging were controlled slightly, even without the cure of these diseases, a greater gain would be made, such that the possible extension of life could approach two hundred years of age. As it is, a man of age sixty has about the same life expectancy as was had in 1789. (*The Relevant Scientist* 29) Also, because even minor diseases can cause death in the aged, research in aging to promote healthy life is supportive of research on disease.

Although the possible gain by research on aging is phenomenal as compared with the possible gain by doing research on individual diseases, almost no support is given to such research. Bjorksten wrote about this oversight:

"There's a certain mental block to be overcome. People think of getting old as inevitable — something that happens and can't be delayed." ("Dialogue on Death")

"Age and senility remain excluded from the mainstream of research to the degree that research touching on vitality has been hampered. . . . Any scientist aspiring to contribute decisively to research on retention of vitality still must be prepared to generate himself a major part of the money needed for this work and to face ignorance and lack of understanding, as have the discoverers of asepsis, vaccination, and sera." (*The Relevant Scientist* 32)

Some organizations have made contributions to the Bjorksten Research Foundation, e.g., Upjohn Company (over $500,000), Paul Glenn Medical Research Foundation ($2,100), Marcus and Bertha Coler Foundation ($1,000), etc. But they say continuing research funds are urgently needed. The Bjorksten Research Laboratory and Foundation of Madison, Wisconsin, is devoted exclusively to research on aging for the purpose of prolonging a healthy, active life. Other scientists are also in need of research funds. Geriatric and gerontological research is in great need of support and development. Perhaps the best approach to research on aging would be the establishment of a wide-scale non-profit organization funded by the U.S. government, and private donations, in connection with professionals in each of the major sciences, including philosophy, the humanities, and law.

Just as roads are partly paid for by means of tolls, if even a small percentage of the savings of each person who dies were given to research on aging and death the funds for such research would soon be adequate.

Dr. Richard Passwater is now, through the American Gerontological Research Laboratory, testing in various countries some anti-aging pills based on the theory that proteins are missynthesized. He accepts the cross-link theory. The pills being used contain such ingredients as vitamin E, a radiation protector, and a protein resynthesizer, an antioxidant. (McGrady)

Newsweek (9-15-72) reported several varieties of youth pill: 1. KH3, a capsule consisting of procaine or novocain; 2. Ribaminol, based on RNA which is considered a likely candidate for possible use as a memory enhancing pill; 3. GH3, an injected form of a youth pill. These pills were in 1969 not yet approved by the Federal Food and Drug Administration.

Although the article does not specify what GH3 is, I suspect it is Gerovital H3 which was developed in Rumania by Dr. Anna Aslan. Novocain and camomile seem to be used in her treatments.

10. Free-Radical Theory.

Free radicals, high energy sites caused by radiation, increase in the blood with age and produce injury causing aging. (Kastenbaum) The particular model which partly informs the free-radical theory is that there is an error in cell copying. Molecules perish as a result of attack by free-radical chemical agents.

D. Harman is testing antioxydants to increase longevity. It is believed these slow the activity of free-radicals.

11. Cell loss Theory.

Kohn gives the following objections to the view that aging is caused by cell loss:

1. Cell loss is not the same as cell aging.

2. We survive even with 40 percent of our liver, part of one kidney, one lung, and much brain damage.

3. Regeneration replaces mitotic cells.

4. Regeneration capacity has not been found to decrease with age.

5. There is nerve cell loss but this only explains loss of ability not aging.

He concludes from this and other evidence,

"The debilities of age cannot be accounted for on the basis of cell alteration or failure known to occur in any specific organ or system."

If the liver lobes are removed, cell division replaces most of the liver within several days. The rate of red cell formation and destruction does not change with age. But often the more specialized cells become, such as muscle and nerve cells, the less division tends to take place, and the fewer are the cell replacements.

12. Endocrine failure.

Aging is sometimes thought to be due to failure of the hypothalamus regulating hormones. (*Science News* 11-4-72)

Estrogenic hormone pills are often popularly advised for the delaying of aging in women, however some physicians suspect they may be cancer producing. (*Vogue* 8-15-65) Estrogen has, however, also been used to treat cancer.

There were transplantations of dog and monkey glands and hormone injections were given to prevent aging. The physiologist, Charles Brown - Sequard, in 1889 injected himself with the testicles of dogs and guinea pigs. He claimed that this rejuvenated him to some extent. (Wiles)

At present Dr. Paul Niehans of Clinique du Prairie at Clarens, Switzerland, is using cellular therapy, injecting cells from the organs of young animals (e.g., unborn lambs) into patients wishing to feel younger. This method is not yet approved by the Federal Drug Administration and his work is not usually accepted by the rest of the medical profession. (*Vogue* 1-15-66)

One of the basic models informing this theory seems to be the fact that hormones are found to double the life of mice.

Some think that it is a current fad to attribute all things to the relatively recent discovery of endocrine function and Kohn rejects the endocrine theory.

13. Weismann's Theory.

Weismann noticed that germ plasm can be kept alive indefinitely (but not soma). Unicellular organisms or protozoans need not age, though metazoa do age. Aging evolved, it is not intrinsic to all living matter. He holds an evolutionary theory, that is, the survival of the species argument that old people are harmful for they take the place of the young. (Comfort) Life is said to continue only long enough to aid perpetuation of the species. This is an unacceptable teleological view based upon the assumption of some high purpose or dogmatic statement of how things must be. This was discussed earlier. The "survival of the fittest" hypothesis fails also because man has not begun to inquire into death and how to prolong life. That is, he has hardly even tried to survive.

14. Toxic Theory.

Although not considered as the only cause of aging I would propose that aging may be caused in part by a gradual increase of various types of poisons in our food, air, and environment including the chemicals coming in contact with our bodies.

Other toxic theories stress different types of toxicity. Comfort lists the following types of toxic theories, without mention of food poison: Metchnikoff's theory that toxic intestinal bacteria causes aging and that overstimulated phagocytes destroy the nervous system; accumulation of metaplasm or metabolites; action of gravity; accumulation of heavy water; effect of cosmic rays; injury; metabolism rate; repletive theories relating aging to reproduction.

Metchnikoff's theory is partly based on the model that some birds absorb botulism but only a small amount in man's alimentary canal causes death. It may be added that Metchnikoff thought that religion and metaphysics were completely worthless and ineffective in solving the problems of death and of happiness. He thought life could be extended in man by scientific investigation. (Cochrane)

The view that aging is caused by toxins or poison in our food merely stresses a source of aging without specifying the ingredients or the specific mechanisms involved. But as has been shown our knowledge of basic processes is not adequate to give us detailed and complete explanations, even though many such mechanisms are generally known. In general much that the nutritionist and hygenicist tells us relates to the avoidance of toxic substances which affect heart, blood vessels, etc. There are also specific hypotheses based on balanced diet, intake of DDT and fats (cholesterol), etc. Adelle Davis wrote, "Vitamin A appears to delay the onset of senility and to promote longevity." She notes that America was in 11th place for life expectancy rate in 1949 but only 37th place in 1966. She attributes this largely to the intake of saturated and refined fats. Such hypotheses should, however, remain tentative until more conclusive and adequate research is available. One may consult, though with great caution, the research and textbooks on nutrition.

One of the main points of proposing a toxic theory of aging is to encourage investigation of the idea that perhaps aging is only a disease which can be cured. Should we be able to remove the poisons, once we can identify them, from our food we may find we are able to live a much longer and healthier life. The amount of poison allowed in our food seems now to be determined by how long we are expected to live on the average. In effect, this policy thereby determines how long we will live and that we will live no longer than expected. Again, the toxic theory is not taken to be the only cause of aging. One may add amount of x-ray exposure, amount and kind of medicine taken, amount of exercise, as well as some of the items presented in each of the other theories. Perennial plants are sometimes thought to live indefinitely and merely outgrow the accumulation of toxic materials.

15. Growth Rate Theory.

Minot believes that aging relates to decline in growth. When cells become more specialized or differentiated they cease to divide, grow, or repair themselves. Tissue growth rate slows down, causing aging. Certain fish, trees, unspecialized cells do not age, as long as they continue to grow. Some trees are one thousand years old. (Comfort)

Pearl holds that the rate of living or rate of metabolism causes aging. (Comfort) This view may be based partly on the observation that basal metabolism rate decreases with age. It does not, however, decrease very much. Shock states that at age 75 it is 84 percent of what it was at age 30.

However, according to Comfort, aging does not adequately correlate with metabolic rate. It is found, though, that a decrease in the caloric intake of some young animals results in increased subsequent health and increased life span. (C. McCay, Cornell Univ.) Rapid growth rate shortens life. The growth rate theory may be largely patterned after this model.

Antioxidants are found to slow aging processes. (Comfort) But this view depends upon the criterion for aging. D. Harman found that mice live twice as long as usual if they are fed antioxidants. (McGrady)

16. Additional Theories.

In regard to research on aging the following supposedly little explored areas are recommended as subjects for study (Strehler 1962):

a. the relation of temperature effects to aging.
b. search for possible latent human regenerative capacities.
c. lysosome synthesis and breakdown.
d. control of synthesis and degradation of cellular components.
e. biochemistry of cellular death.
f. longevity of subcellular structures.
g. factors controlling and linking all growth.
h. changes in immunological properties, e.g., autoimmunity.

IV. SOME CHARACTERISTICS OF AGING

A number of factors which characterize aging are (Strehler 1960):

Skin: Change in collagen and elastic fibers. Tendency to malignancy. Decreasing number of glomus units which regulate temperature and conserve body heat, slower healing, pigments and moles appear. Skin becomes dry, rough, wrinkled.

Taste and smell diminish. Hearing and vision become poorer. Cardiac output is decreased. Arteries become less elastic and vessels are calcified. There is change in the cholesterol in the walls of the large arteries. Speed of nerve impulse decreases. Nerve cells are irreplaceable once damaged but they last at least as long as the oldest person. Nerve cell loss takes place mainly between birth and maturity. They do not age or die from aging processes. (Kohn) Digital symbol ability and incidental memory decrease. One theory is that memory decrease is caused partly by a diminishing supply of RNA. Experimental work suggests that we may learn how to replenish this supply. Muscular strength decreases. The kidney efficiency declines with age. Bladder capacity and control diminishes.

Chromosome aberrations increase with age. (Curtis in Kastenbaum) One is less immune to disease and becomes more immune to his own cells. (Walford in Kastenbaum)

In a comparison by N. Shock of the average 30-year-old with the average 75-year-old the percentage of function or tissues remaining is as follows:

Brain weight (56) (that is, the weight of the brain is 56 percent of what it was at age 30), blood flow to brain (80), speed of return to equilibrium of blood acidity (17), cardiac output at rest (70), number of glomeruli in kidney (56), glomerular filtration rate (69), kidney plasma flow (50), number of nerve trunk fibers (63), nerve conduction velocity (90), number of taste buds (36), maximum oxygen uptake during exercise (40), maximum ventilation volume during exercise (53), maximum voluntary breathing capacity (43), hand grip (55), maximum work rate (70), maximum work for short burst (40), basal metabolic rate (84), body water content (82), male body weight (88). It should be noted, however, that man does not usually operate at maximum efficiency.

One cannot without a complete analysis draw conclusions about intelligence and ability from these figures. The following qualifications may be suggestive. The fact that brain weight decreases does not mean that one is less intelligent. The reverse may well be the case. That memory loss, especially short term memory loss, is experienced may be due partly to lack of interest and use or to suggestibility caused by the expectation that one's memory ability will be lost. It need not merely be the case that with age one's memory must degenerate or does so automatically. One may find also that in old age one has more free time than in middle age, but free time is not a necessary or sufficient condition for aging. It may also be noted that the young, as well as adults, forget a lot.

The number of taste buds decreases to 36 percent. But this does not mean that taste need be affected. One should not draw a simplistic mechanical picture. For example, with a physically normal eye one sees both more and less than meets the eye. We see 3D or we may have "psychic blindness." We do not see everything which falls on the retina. The eye is selective. In those cases where decrease in taste ability is experienced it may also be due to other factors such as smoking or general depression. Kidney deterioration may be partly due to toxic factors such as intake of coffee, alcohol, etc.

That there is less gonadal activity does not mean sexual interest is decreased. Rather sexual interest may stay the same or even increase. The increased interest in some cases may be due to a more permissive change in cultural values.

Burtrum Schiele discounts, to a large extent, apparently little cerebral and anatomical degeneration in the aged as the cause of deviant behavior and memory:

"Except in extreme cases there is poor correlation between the degree of brain change at autopsy and the behavioral disturbance that the patient may have shown."

On his view, in general, the old person has the same problems in old age that he had in youth. Older people are seen to be easily unbalanced and do tend to overvalue the past at the expense of the present and future. They tend not to eat properly thereby causing malnutrition, leading to personality disorder. He states, "The basic emotional needs of an older person do not change because he is old." Strehler (1960) reports that mental disease increases after age 55.

The EEG alpha rhythm or brain-wave frequency declines with age and may precede age changes in intellectual ability. (*Science News* 11-6-72, 9-23-72) It is thought that perhaps the elderly could be trained to increase alpha rhythm as youthful subjects have been trained to do.

Much work remains to be done in research into the nature of aging and finding ways to help the aged live more full and healthier lives.

V. LENGTH OF LIFE

A. Mildvan and B. Strehler (1960) present the following factors relating to life span:

Contrary to the Russian view that labor increases life span, it is found that laborers have the highest mortality rate.

The oldest age is around 110. The leading cause of death in descending order are: Heart, cancer, cerebral hemorrhage, accident, disease of infancy, pneumonia, flu, arteriosclerosis, congenital malformation, liver cirrhosis. Heart failure occurrence by age group is: 29% – age 25-44, 52% – age 45-64, 68% – age 65 and over. [Ladimer reported that kidney disease kills more people than automobiles do.]

From 1900 to 1956 in the United States, death from pneumonia and other infectious diseases, which caused death mainly before age 35, fell but deaths from cardiovascular-renal disease and cancer rose. The death rate of males exceeds that of females at every age. Married people have a lower death rate than single people; those widowed and divorced have high death rates. The major cause of death for women is diabetes and cancer. Longevity tends to be hereditary. But that one's lifespan appears to be inherited from one's parents is not a conclusive finding.

Comfort predicts that by 1990, if we do the research which is needed, lifespan of man will increase at least 20 percent. Rand Corporation predicts that given concentrated research significant life extension will be attained by 2023.

In *Scientific American* (Aug. 1961) Comfort, in an attempt to give some insight into the nature of aging, presented a study of the life span of animals. His findings are as follows: Warm blooded animals become senile and die at an early age. Our studies on longevity are mainly of man, the white rat, and laboratory mouse. Longevity research is almost completely lacking. He quotes Francis Bacon's words as being still relevant today:

"Touching the length or shortness of life in beasts the knowledge which may be had is slender, the observation negligent, and the tradition fabulous."

Ages of animals are often judged by counting annual growth rings of different sorts. Since birth certificates were only introduced in Britain in 1837 we can only verify the age of men up to 135 years. The oldest person known is 109 years. There are claims of older ages in Russia, England, etc., but these are unverified. Henry Jenkins is said to have lived from 1501-1670, and Old Paar from 1483-1635, but Comfort doubts these reports. The Bible (according to R. Bacon) speaks of the following ages: Shem 600 years old, Abraham 175, Isaac 180,

Jacob 147, Ishmael 137, Moses 120, Sarah 127. (cf. Antediluvian Theory in Prolongation of Life Chapter)

Comfort says elsewhere, "The longest-lived species is man," (1956) but in view of the figures he gives here this appears incorrect. Other now living things may have existed before man. The vulture lives over 117 years and the tortoise over 152. Also there are trees over a thousand years old. Some animal tissue and bacteria do not age and can be kept alive indefinitely. This is a suggestive finding in regard to longevity research.

Longevity in mammals, Comfort states, relates to size and reproductive rate. Cold blooded animals often live longer than warm-blooded. The tortoise and fish have a very long life which may be partly due to the fact that they continually grow. Death in many animals is caused simply by accident or predators. Three main environmental aging factors given are temperature, rate of food intake, radiation. Rapid growth rate may shorten life.

More research should be done on various animals in an attempt to determine the causes of aging. The findings may be suggestive for understanding aging in man.

Although our knowledge of the ages or lifespans of various animals has been little explored some of the tentative findings are as follows (figures refer to years):

Swallow	9	Halibut	60-70
Small bats	10-15	Large Salamander	50+
White rat	4+	Sponge	15
Harvest mouse	4	Chaffinch	29
Guinea pig	7+	(average is 6 months!)	
Shrew	2	Finch, parakeet	10-30
Queen bee	7+	Domestic pigeon	35
Silverfish	7	Seal	20-25
Large beetle	5-10	Sheep	15+
Earthworm	5-10	Rabbit	12
Sea horse	2	Frog	12-20
Guppy	5	Cow	30
Tortoise	100-150	Hoofed animals	20-35
Indian elephant	77+	Ant queen	19
Ostrich	30-40	Crocodile,	
Toad	36	Alligator	50-60
Mussel	50-100(?)	Horse	40+

Zebra	38+	Pelican, Crane,	
Carp	50+	Goose	40-55
Eel	55	Eagle Owl	68
Sturgeon	80-100+	Gray Parrot	73 (?)
		Cockatoo	70-85
Giant spider	20	Golden Eagle	80
Snakes, lizards	25-30	Vulture	117 (?)
Dog	24+	Man	115+
Lion	30-35	Chimpanzee, ape	30-40
Cat	27	Hippopotamus	49
Herring gull	40-45	Sea Anemone	60-80+
Dove	42	Swan	70

S. Bakerman. *Aging Life Processes* Springfield, Illinois: C. Thomas 1969

James Birren, ed. *Handbook of Aging and the Individual* University of Chicago Press 1959

Johan Bjorksten. "Approaches and Prospects for the Control of Age-Dependent Deterioration" *Annals of New York Academy of Sciences* 184 (June 7, 1971) 95-102

––––. "Cross-linkages in protein chemistry" *Advances in Protein Chemistry* M. Anson and J. Edsall, eds, New York: Academic Press 1951

––––. *Dialogue on Death* Madison, Wisc.: Bjorksten Research Foundation 1960

––––. "For Scientific Breakthroughs We Must Go Beyond Restraints" *The Chemist* 38 (May 1961)

––––, et al. "Study of Low Molecular Weight Proteolytic Enzymes" *Finska Kemists. Medd.* 80 (4) (1971) 70-87

––––. "The Relevance of Research to Preserve Vitality" *The Relevant Scientist* 1 (Nov. 1971) 29-32

––––. "Why Grow Old" *Chemistry* 37 (6) (1964) 6-12

D. B. Bromley. *The Psychology of Human Aging* Baltimore: Penguin 1966

511

Arthur Clark. *Profiles of the Future* New York: Harper 1962

A. L. Cochrane. "Elie Metchnikoff and His Theory of an 'Instinct de la Mort' " *International Journal of Psychoanalysis* 15 (1934) 265-270

Alex Comfort. *The Biology of Senescence* London: Routledge and Kegan Paul 1956 (contains an excellent bibliography)

Adelle Davis. *Let's Eat Right to Keep Fit* New York: New American Library 1954

Robert Fulton. "Widow in America" Paper delivered at Harvard Medical School 1970

Arthur Galston. "Death Isn't Necessary" *Science News* July, 1965 pp. 80-85

Rosalind Heywood. "Death and Psychical Research" *Man's Concern with Death* A. Toynbee, ed., New York: McGraw-Hill 1969 pp. 219-250

Robert Kastenbaum, ed. *The Psycho-Biology of Aging* New York: Springer 1965

Robert Kohn. *Principles of Mammalian Aging* New Jersey: Prentice Hall 1971

Irving Ladimer. "The Challenge of Transplantation" Public Affairs Pamphlet 1970

Peter Mansur. Reported in *Science News* July 22, 1970 p. 54

Patrick McGrady, Jr. "The Youth Pill" *Ladies' Home Journal* 88, 7 (July 1971) 72-74, 128-129

Burtrum Schiele. "Management of Emotional Problems in Aging" *Diseases of the Nervous System* 28 (1967) 35-39

Nathan Shock. "The Physiology of Aging" *Scientific American* 206 (1) (Jan. 1962) 100-110

Bernard Strehler, ed. *The Biology of Aging* (Tennessee Symposium 1957) Washington, D.C.: American Institute of Biological Sciences 1960

—————. *Time, Cells, and Aging* New York: Academic Press 1962

512

William Vrasdonk. "Beyond Thanatology: Immortality" *Journal of Value Inquiry* 6 no. 4 (Winter 1972) 280-285

Peter Wiles. "On Physical Immortality II" *Survey: A Journal of Soviet and East European Studies* 57 (Oct. 1965)

General Questionnaire Results

Three sources will be given:

1. Some of those reported by Vernon (1970) (V). Vernon's own 1968 study on attitudes toward death of 1500 college students.

2. The Shneidman survey (1971) of 30,000 readers of *Psychology Today* (PT).

3. The author's survey of college students enrolled in a philosophy "Seminar on Death." (See beginning of book.)

Association tests and statistical correlations can be quite misleading. We may, for example, find high correlations between death words and the names of trees or letters of the alphabet or sounds. Associations of these sorts are often based on analogy and metaphor just as the voice sounds are spoken of as being sharp, smooth, deep. The Rorschach test may even be regarded as more a test of metaphor ability than of personality. Thus death words may by the investigator be made to relate to entirely irrelevant phenomena. Such high correlations must be analyzed to determine what the relationship is. The sound "krick" is associated with sharp objects and "moang" with round objects. It is not clear why this is so. Also death is associated with unrelated objects. It is often related to the color black, to pain, to clouds, etc. What death is related to often depends on one's culture, particular experiences, what one has read, etc.

Of the replies given below it may be found that with discussion and clarification of the question and its concepts the results would be entirely different. Death is not often talked about or openly discussed even among the educated, so the results show only something like immediate responses rather than thought-out conclusions.

513

Often the choices given are entirely too restrictive. One must answer only yes or no, or possibly, or choose one of four or five possibilities. In my own questionnaire the above difficulties were avoided by asking essay questions. The results are, of course, harder to computerize. On the other hand they may be more meaningful.

I. Of 203 psychology students Kalish found more than a third would not allow a dying person to live in their immediate neighborhood, three of five would not want to employ them. (V 11)

Fulton found that 40 percent of his respondents to a general survey never or rarely thought about death. (V 11)

Vernon found that 64 percent of 1500 college students claim to have a transcendental belief in immortality and only 1 percent no belief in immortality.

A 1947 British survey by Mitchell of belief in afterlife showed 49 percent yes, 33 percent no, no opinion 18 percent. Of the religious people affirming belief were Catholics 62 percent, Church of England 46 percent, Jews 32 percent. Of the 49 percent believing in an afterlife most believe the spirit lives on or do not know what happens after life. (V 73, 74) This seems to support the view presented elsewhere in this book that if one's only evidence for a concept is faith or belief then he cannot know what it is he believes in. Here a spirit is a way of speaking of an unknown.

Of 277 Presbyterians, Nelson found that 15.9 were not positive about there being life after death and 1.4 percent thought there was probably no such thing as life after death. (V 73)

A 1966 Gallop poll about whether the soul lives after death showed affirmative results for 83 percent of the Catholics, 78 percent of the Protestants, 17 percent of the Jewish, (46 percent said no and 37 percent did not know), 37 percent Other and No Religion (42 percent said no and 21 percent did not know). (V74-75)

An American Institute of Public Opinion Poll of 1961 showed the following national differences in belief in afterlife. The United States was highest but Spain, Mexico, etc., were not mentioned. The results showing belief in afterlife are: USA 74 percent, Great Britain 56 percent, Switzerland 55 percent, West

Germany 38 percent (27 percent said "no"). (V76) The United States seems to be a much more superstitious or religious country than the others mentioned.

In Vernon's study most people when in mourning wanted to be left alone (38.2 percent) or were undecided (22.3 percent). (V 167)

Faunce and Fulton found that of 104 college students fear of death was more characteristic of the spiritually oriented group than of those not so oriented. (V 201)

Klopfer found that fear of death among residents in old age homes was greatly reduced when greater activity was possible. (V 205)

II. Some of Shneidman's results of his survey of 30,000 readers are as follows. (See also Shneidman's questionnaire used in his course at Harvard a modified version of which is in Thomas Shaffer *Death, Property, and Lawyers* New York. Dunellen 1970 pp. 59-68.)

Thirty-three percent reported that they do not recall any childhood discussion of death within their family. The response to "How religious do you consider yourself to be?" was: Very religious 11 percent, somewhat religious 32 percent, slightly religious 23 percent, not at all religious 24 percent, antireligious 9 percent. More women are religious than men. Thirty-eight percent of Protestants and 25 percent of Roman Catholics doubt or do not believe in the existence of life after death. Forty-eight percent reported that as children they believed in heaven and hell. As adults the response to belief in afterlife is: strong belief 23 percent, tend to believe 20 percent, uncertain 19 percent, tend to doubt it 22 percent, convinced it does not exist 16 percent. Fifty-five percent strongly wished there were a life after death. This last fact would suggest that they might support projects aimed to inquire into death and old age and attempt to conquer it.

Fifty percent of the respondents were Protestants and they made 53 percent of the suicide attempts. Thirty percent were Catholics and made 30 percent of the suicide attempts. Eleven percent were Jewish and made 6 percent of the suicide attempts. The 10 percent "other" made 11 percent of the suicide attempts. Although suicide is against the Catholic religion neither the prohibition nor the faith keeps a substantial number of them from attempting suicide.

Religion tends to push the antireligious away from traditional outlooks on death and had a negative effect on the views of the antireligious. Fifteen percent of the antireligious thus report that religion played a very significant (negative) role in their view of death. Of all respondents 42 percent claim religion played a very or rather significant role, 58 percent claim it played a less than significant role or no role at all. Most claim to be influenced by introspection and meditation (35 percent), and have been influenced most in their beliefs by existential philosophy (34 percent). Forty-one percent reply that no books influenced them. Thirty-five percent of the existential philosophers are nonreaders. The most influential works are the Bible, Albert Camus (especially *The Stranger*), Hermann Hesse (especially *Steppenwolf, Demian,* and *Siddhartha*). It is pointed out that though existentialists (such as Heidegger and Kierkegaard) stress death and anxiety 81 percent of the respondents reported feeling quite well and cheerful.

One out of seven persons aged 20-24 has had his attitude toward death significantly influenced by drugs.

As one matures it is found that one's religious beliefs become secular or scientized. After adolescence 35 percent see death as a final process of life or absolute end of consciousness.

The aspect of death found most distasteful was, in terms of the choices given, that one could no longer have any experiences (36 percent). Almost no Jews and only 1 percent of Catholics were most concerned about their dependents.

Fewer than one in ten think one should be kept alive in any circumstance.

Fifty-one percent state that the thought of their death makes them resolved to life or makes them feel pleasure in being alive.

Sixty-six percent would choose to die in old age rather than earlier, 29 percent just after the prime of life, 3 percent in the middle of the prime of life. Sixty-nine percent believe they will die in old age.

In terms of Shneidman's classifications (cf. chapter on medical definition of death), 39 percent are death-postponers, 42 percent are death-accepters, 14 percent death-fearers, 2 percent death-welcomers, 1 percent death-seekers or death hasteners. Over half of the death-welcomers feel cheerful. Eight out of ten would not want to know when they are going to die. If they had a terminal illness 7 out of ten would want to be told.

Thirty-eight percent would want a sudden death, 30 percent a quiet, dignified death. One in 20 would spend his few remaining days contemplating or praying, 20 percent would live as they have been, 19 percent would seek pleasurable activity such as travel, sex, drugs.

Of those age 35-39, 30 percent would not give their lives for any reason. Of the total group 58 percent would sacrifice his life for a loved one.

Thirty-three percent of the men want to outlive their wives and 18 percent of the women want to outlive their husbands. One reason for this might be that men are envious of the fact that women live longer than men.

Over 50 percent have wanted to die at some time in the past. Emotional upset was the most frequent cause. Thirteen percent actually attempted suicide. Perhaps this indicates that death is more often used as a threat or tool to accomplish one's purposes. Loneliness, illness and pain are the major reasons given for attempting suicide.

Only 15 percent believe that a person has a right to take his own life without being stopped. Sixty-nine percent say that if they were to commit suicide they would use barbiturates or pills. Eighty-three percent believe in life insurance [note that it is called life insurance rather than death insurance] Other results of his study are contained in the section of this book on attitudes toward funerals.

Shneidman concludes,

"All these results point to one of the main findings of the questionnaire, namely that — over the past generation or two — there has been a tremendous secularization of death."

Definitions and Etymologies

agathanasia (Gk *agatho,* good) a good death, death with dignity.

alive (ME on life, in life) conscious, alert, active, not dead. See entire book.

amort (MF *a la mort*) at the point of death.

amortality. Neither mortal nor immortal.

anger (ON *angr,* grief, sorrow; Gk *anchein,* to squeeze, strangle, hang; OE *enge,* narrow, painful) See section on emotions.

angst (Ger.) anxiety, dread.

anxiety (L *anxius,* solicitous, uneasy; cf. mourn) Apprehension caused by future certain or uncertain danger. Anxious is related to memory. To remember is to ponder over something. (A. Ellis states that neurotic behavior is due to the repeating to oneself of irrational statements.) The Greek word for memory, *mermeros,* means "causing anxiety, care, trouble." See section on emotion.

apatheia (Gk *apatheia,* without feeling) Lack of feeling, emotion, interest, or concern. [Actually no one can lack feeling but only certain assessments.] The stoics specified other definitions. See sections on emotions and stoics.

ars moriendi Art of dying. (See chapter)

519

Ataraxia (Gk calmness) A worry-free state making enjoyment of pleasure possible.

belief. Defined by *Century Cyclopedia* as "Persuasion of the truth of a proposition, but with the consciousness that the positive evidence for it is insufficient or wanting; especially assurance of the truth of what rests chiefly or solely upon authority." See chapter on religion.

believe (OE to allow, to believe; Ger. *Glauben,* to hold dear or valuable, be pleased with.) To trust without evidence. It is to hold a value judgment or opinion, to be persuaded, to hope, to make as if true − as a religious faith. It is "to credit upon the ground of authority, testimony, argument, or any other ground than complete demonstration." (*Century Dictionary*)

bereave (Ger. *berouben,* to rob; OE *bereafian,* to rob, plunder, ravage) To deprive as by violence, rob of, take away. (See section on emotion.)

casket (F. *cassette,* chest, box) coffin.

cemetery (L and Gk *coemeterium,* sleeping room, burial place)

ceremony (L *caerimonia* sacred usage) Religious observance, sacred rite, politeness, formality, symbol. (See "rite.")

coffin (ME, Gk basket) trunk, casket. Now, "casket" is the preferred usage.

conscious (L *conscius,* knowing, aware) Means waking rather than sleeping, animate rather than inanimate, having feeling, awareness of self, perceiving.

coroner (L *corona,* crown − originally one who watches over crown property) A public officer whose main duty is to inquire into the cause of any death which there is reason to believe is not due to natural causes.

corpse (L *corpus,* body) dead body.

cremate (L *crematus,* burn by fire)

dead, death, die (See entire book.)

deceased (L *decessus,* departure) Dead person.

dirge (L *dirge,* to direct; ME *dirge,* funeral service or hymn) A funeral hymn. It derives from a part of a service which is sung beginning "Dirige, Domine, Deus meus . . . ." (Psalms 5:9). "Dirge-ale," or "soul-ale" is ale served at a wake.

disease (OF *desaise,* uneasiness, pain, trouble; ME *disese,* lack of ease)

dread (ME *dreden,* fear, doubt) Dread means great fear and usually means dread of death. (See chapters on existentialism and emotion)

embalm (L *in* + *balsamum,* balsam, balm. To put balm (resin) in.) To treat a body to protect it from decay and odor.

emotion (L *emotion, emovere,* move away, stir up, agitate) See section on emotion.

endura (L *endurare,* to harden) Christian practice of hastening death by fasting and bleeding.

euthanasia (Gk *eu* + *thanasia,* easy + death) An easy death. a) inward euthanasia: freedom from psychological worry before death, b) outward euthanasia: freedom from bodily pain before death.

fear (ME *fere,* sudden danger; ON *far,* harm, distress, deception; L *periculum,* trial, risk, danger) See section on emotion.

geriatrics. Concern with the diseases and medical aspects of the aging of humans.

gerontology (Gk *Ger,* to become old, grow old) Study of the aging of plants, animals, humans.

grief (OF *grief,* burden, to wrong, encumber, oppress) See section on emotion.

instinct (L *instinctus,* impulse, incite, urge on, push, move, stimulate to action, instigation) See chapter on Freud.

keening (Irish *caoinim,* wail, cry of lamentation for the dead) A conventionalized Irish practice of sobbing for the dead. The virtues of the dead are praised in a high, plaintive key.

libido (L *libidinosus,* passion, desire, lust appetite) See chapter on Freud.

libido moriendi Death-drive. (Seneca) See chapter on Freud.

Liebestod (Ger.) View that lovers reunite only in death.

life (ME *lif,* Ger. *Leib,* body, continue, persist, remain, be left) See entire book.

macrobiosis. Prolongation of life (Hufeland 1796)

matador (Sp. *matador,* killer, murderer) One who kills bulls in a bullfight.

mourn (Ger. *murren,* grieve, murmur; OE *murnan,* to care for, be anxious about, lament over, remember)

memory, memorial (See anxiety.)

nascentes morimur "In being born we die."

necrobiosis (Gk *necros,* dead, death) Physical death of body cells.

necrolatry. Worship of or excessive veneration of the dead or spirits of the dead.

necrology. Register of deaths, obituary.

necromancer. One who practices necromancy.

necromancy. The attempt to contact the dead. It is a part of witchcraft and sorcery and often involves an attempt to reveal the future. Saul of the *Old Testament* contacted the Witch of Endor about a future battle.

necrophilism. An abnormal love of the dead. One lives by the corpse, kisses or mutilates it, exhumes it or practices cannibalism. (See chapters on religion, and funeral customs.)

necrophobia. Abormal fear of death or the dead body. Thanatophobia.

necropolis (L *necropolis,* city of the dead) cemetery. (Emily Dickinson spoke of "city of dead")

necropsy. Autopsy.

nirvana (Skt. *nirvanah,* blowing out a light) Joining the individual soul to a supreme spirit.

rite (L *ritus,* a custom; Skt *riti,* a usage, way. Gk *arithmos,* number) A prescribed form or manner governing action. Numbered steps as in numerology which may involve symbolic or magical meaning. Tends to be repetitious and compulsive.

ritual. A rite.

St. Vitus dance. The disease chorea. See chapter on dance of death.

spirit (L *spiritus,* breath)

taphophobia. Fear of being buried alive.

thanatology (Gk *thanatos,* death, plus *ology*) Science or study of death.

thanatomimesis. Imitation of the dead.

thanatophobia. Fear or horror of the dead. Necrophobia.

thanatopsis. View or contemplation of death.

thanatosophy. Philosophy of death.

thanatotropism. Being driven toward death.

Todestrieb (Ger.) Death drive (not death instinct). See chapter on Freud.

wake (ME *waken,* to wake, watch) Vigil or watch over a dead person.

Bibliography

Abrahamsson, Hans "The Origin of Death: Studies in African Mythology" PhD diss. Princeton University 1958

Adair, Maude *The Techniques of Restorative Art* Iowa: Brown 1948

Age and Aging (London journal)

Agee, James *A Death in the Family* New York: McDowell 1957

Aging and Human Development (Journal)

Aginsky, B. "The Socio-Psychological Significance of Death Among the Pono Indians" *American Imago* 1(1940) 1-11

Aitken, P. "The right to live and the right to die" *Medical Times* 95 (1967) 1184-7

Alden, Henry *A Study of Death* New York: Harper 1895

Alderstein, A. "The Relationship Between Religious Belief and Death Affect" PhD diss. Princeton University 1958

Aldrich, C. "The Dying Patient's Grief" *Journal of the American Medical Association* 184 (1963) 329-331

Alexander, Franz "The need for punishment and the death instinct" *International Journal of Psychoanalysis* 10 (1929) 256-269

Alexander, George "An unexplained death coexistent with deathwishes" *Psychosomatic Medicine* 5 (1943) 188-194

Alexander, Irving "Affective Responses to the Concept of Death in a Population of Children and Early Adolescents" *Journal of Genetic Psychology* 93 (1958) 1967-77

Alexander, Irving "Is Death a Matter of Indifference" *Journal of Psychology* 43 (1957) 277-283

Alexander, Irving and N. Farberow "Death and Religion" *The Meaning of Death* H. Feifel 271-283

Alexander, Irving and M. Adlerstein "Studies in the Psychology of Death" *Perspectives in Personality Research* New York: Springer 1960

Alvarez, Walter "Death with Dignity" *Humanist* 31 (1971) 12-15

Alvarez, Walter "Death often is not so difficult or painful" *Geriatrics* 18 (3) (1963) 165-66

Alvarez, Walter "Help for the dying patient" *Geriatrics* 19 (2) (1964) 69-71

Alvarez, Walter "Some aspects of death" *Geriatrics* 19 (July 1964) 465-66

American Cemetery (Journal)

American Funeral Director (Journal)

Anastaplo, George (On W. May's paper)Paper read at AAAS, National Academy of Sciences Symposium on "Problems in the Meaning of Death" 1970

Anderson, John "Changes in Emotional Responses with Age" *Feelings and Emotions* M. Reymert, ed. New York: McGraw-Hill 1950 pp. 418-27

Angrist, Alfred A. "A pathologist's experience with attitudes toward death" *Rhode Island Medical Journal* 43 (11) (1960) 693-97

Anthony, Sylvia *The Child's Discovery of Death* New York: Harcourt 1940

Anthony, Sylvia "A Study of the Development of the Concept of Death" (M.A. thesis abstract) *British Journal of Educational Psychology* 9 (1939) 276-77

Antitrust Aspects of the Funeral Industry U.S. Congress, Senate, Committee on the Judiciary Hearings before the Subcommittee on Antitrust and Monopoly, 88th Congress, 2nd Session on S. Res. 262, Part I. July 7, 8, 9, 1964 (Washington)

"Any man's death diminishes me" *New England Journal of Medicine* 278 (June 27, 1968) 1455

Archives of the Foundation of Thanatology (Journal) New York: Health Sciences Publ.

Aring, C. "Intimations of mortality. An appreciation of death and dying" *Annals of Internal Medicine* 69 (July 1968) 137-52

Aristotle *De inventute et senectate* ("On Youth and Old Age") G. Ross trans., W. Ross, J. Smith, eds. *Works of Aristotle* 12 vols, Oxford 1908-1952

Arnstein, Helene *What to Tell Your Child about Birth, Illness, Death, Divorce and Other Family Crises* Indiana: Bobbs-Merrill 1962

Ars Moriendi Books on the art of dying.

Art Guide and Forest Lawn Interpretations Glendale, Calif.: Forest Lawn Memorial Park Assoc. 1931 (1963)

Asbell, Bernard *When F. D. R. Died* New York: Holt, Rinehart & Winston 1961

Ashley-Montagu, M. "Contributions of Anthropology to Psychosomatic Medicine" *American Journal of Psychiatry* 112 (1956) 977 ff

Ashley-Montagu, M. *Immortality* New York: Grove Press 1955

Asquith, Glen *Death Is All Right* Tennessee: Abingdon Press 1970

Assheton, William *A Method of Devotion for Sick and Dying Persons; with particular directions from the beginning of sickness to the hour of death* London 1718

Aurelius, Marcus *Meditations* G. Long, trans. New York: Doubleday 1873

Austin, Mary *Experiences Facing Death* Indiana: Bobbs-Merrill 1931

Averill, J. "Grief: Its Nature and Significance" *Psychological Bulletin 70 (1968)* 721-748

"A Way of Dying" *Atlantic Monthly* 199 (1) (1957) 53-55

Ayers, Robert "Personal Survival of Death – An Analysis" *Modern Schoolman* 47 (1970) 331-39

Bacon, Francis "Of Death" S. Reynolds, ed. *Bacon's Essays* Oxford: Clarendon Press 1890 pp. 12-18

Bacon, Francis *The Historie of Life and Death* London 1638 pp. 213-335

Bailey, Orville "Death in Life" *Scientific Monthly* 58 (Feb. 1944) 117-128

Baker, J. and K. Sorenson "A Patient's Concern with Death" *American Journal of Nursing* 63 (1963) 90-92

Bakerman, S. *Aging Life Processes* Illinois: Thomas 1969

Banks, S. "Dialogue on Death: Freudian and Christian Views" *Pastoral Psychology* 14 (1963) 41-49

Barber, Hugh "The act of dying" *Practitioner* 161 (Aug. 1948) 76-79

Barber, T. "Death by Suggestion" *Psychosomatic Medicine* 23 (1961) 153-55

Barker, John *Scared to Death: An examination of fear, its causes and effects* London: Muller 1968

Barnouw, V. "Chippewa Social Atomism: Feast of the Dead" *American Anthropologist* 63 (October 1961) 1006-13

Barratt, Sir William *Deathbed Visions* London: Methuen 1926

Barry, Herbert Jr. "Significance of Maternal Bereavement Before Age Eight in Psychiatric Patients" *Death and Identity* R. Fulton pp. 206-215

Barton, E. "Old age and death" *Practitioner* 123 (Aug. 1929) 111-119

Basdekis, D. "Death in the Sonnets of Shakespeare and Camoes" *Hispania* 46 (March 1963) 102-5

Bataille, Georges *Death and Sensuality: A Study of Eroticism and the Taboo* New York: Walker 1962

Battesta, O. "What Happens When You Die?" *Science Digest* May 1964 pp. 80-84

Baxter, Richard *Christian Directory* 1673

Baxter, Richard *A Treatise of Death, the Last Enemy to be Destroyed* London 1672

Bayly, Joseph *The View from a Hearse: A Christian View of Death* Illinois: David Cook 1969

Bean, William "On death" *Archives of Internal Medicine* 101 (12) (1958) 199-202

Beatty, D. "Shall We Talk About Death?" *Pastoral Psychology* 6 (1955) 11-14

Beaty, N. *The Craft of Dying: A Study in the Tradition of the Ars Moriendi in England* PhD diss. Yale Univ. 1956; New Haven: Yale University Press 1970

Beberman, Arleen "Death and My Life" *Review of Metaphysics* 17 (1963) 18-32

Beck, Aaron *Depression* Univ. of Penn. Press 1967

Becker, E. *The Meaning of Birth and Death* New York: Free Press 1962

Becker, Howard "The Sorrow of Bereavement" *Death: Interpretations* H. Ruitenbeek pp. 195-216

Becker, Howard and D. Bruner "Attitudes Toward Death and the Dead and Some Possible Causes of Ghost Fear" *Mental Hygiene* 15 (1931) 828-837

Beckett, Samuel "Krapp's Last Tape" New York: Grove 1960 (other plays also)

Becon, Thomas *The Sick Man's Salve* J. Ayre, ed., Cambridge 1844 (1560)

Becque, Maurice and L. Becque *Life after Death* New York: Hawthorn 1960

Beecher, Henry "The New Definition of Death, Some Opposing Views" Paper read at

AAAS, National Academy of Sciences Symposium on "Problems in the Meaning of Death" 1970

Beigler, Jerome "Anxiety as Aid in the Prognostication of Impending Death" *Archives of Neurology and Psychiatry* 77 (1957)

Bellarmine, Saint Robert *The Art of Dying Well* John Dalton, trans. London ca. 1850

Bendann, Effie *Death Customs: An Analytical Study of Burial Rites* New York: Knopf 1930

Bereavement and Illness New York: Health Sciences

Berezin, et al., eds, *Geriatric Psychiatry: Grief, Loss and Emotional Disorders in the Aging Process* New York: International University Press 1965

Bergersen, Betty ed. *Distance and the Dying Patient* Missouri: Mosby 1967

Bertalanffy, Ludwig von *Problems of Life* London: Watts 1952

Bess, Joseph "Grief Is" *Death and Bereavement* A. Kutscher pp. 202-203

Bess, Joseph and G. Bartlett "Creative Grief" *Death and Bereavement* A. Kutscher pp. 317-18

Bess, Sandra "Behind the Veil, A Literary Mosaic of Grief" *Death and Bereavement* A. Kutscher pp. 328-342

Best, Pauline "An experience on interpreting death to children" *Pastoral Care* 1 (2) (1948)

Bichat, M. *Physiological Researches on Life and Death* F. Gold, trans. Boston 1827

Bierce, Ambrose *In the Midst of Life* New York: Putnams 1898

Biorck, G. "Thoughts on life and death" *Perspectives in Biology and Medicine* 11 (Summer 1968) 527-43

Bishop, R. *The Theme of Death in French Literature from Villon's "Grand Testament" to the Middle of the 16th Century* PhD diss. Princeton University 1943

Bjorksten, Johan "Approaches and Prospects for the Control of Age-Dependent Deterioration" *Annals of New York Academy of Sciences* 184 (June 7, 1971) 95-102

Bjorksten, Johan "Cross-linkages in protein chemistry" *Advances in Protein Chemistry* M. Anson, J. Edsall, eds. New York: Academic Press 1951

Bjorksten, Johan *Dialogue on Death,* Madison, Wis.: Bjorksten Research Foundation 1960

Bjorksten, Johan "For Scientific Breakthroughs We Must Go Beyond Restraints" *The Chemist* 38 (May 1961)

Bjorksten, Johan et al. "Study of Low Molecular Weight Proteolytic Enzymes" *Finska Kemists. Medd.* 80 (4) (1971) 70-87

Bjorksten, Johan "The Relevance of Research to Preserve Vitality" *The Relevant Scientist* 1 (Nov. 1971) 29-32

Bjorksten, Johan "Why Grow Old" *Chemistry* 37 (6) (1964) 6-12

Black, Max *A Companion to Wittgenstein's Tractatus* England: Cambridge Univ. Press 1964 "Death and Immortality" p. 373

Black, Stephen "The Scarlet Letter: Death by Symbols" *Paunch* 24 (1965) 51-74

Blacker, C. "Life and death instincts" *British Journal of Medical Psychology* 9 (1929) 277-302

Blackmar, Mary "Funeral Feasting" *Ladies' Home Journal* 80 (5) (1963)

Blackwood, Andrew *The Funeral* Philadelphia: Westminister Press 1942

Blank, Robert "Mourning" *Death and Bereavement* A. Kutscher pp. 204-206

Blauner, Robert "Death and Social Structure"*Psychiatry* 29 (1966) 278-94

Bluestone, H. and C. McGahee "Reaction to Extreme Stress: Impending Death by Execution" *American Journal of Psychiatry* 119 (1962) 393-96

Boase, T. *Death in the Middle Ages: Morality, Judgment, Remembrance* New York: McGraw-Hill 1972

Bogomolets, A. *The Prolongation of Life* New York: Duell 1946

Borkenau, Franz "The Concept of Death" *Twentieth Century* 157 (1955) 313-329

Boros, Ladislaus *The Moment of Truth* London: Burns 1965

Boros, Ladislaus *The Mystery of Death* New York: Herder 1965

Bosis, Lauro de *The Story of My Death* New York: Oxford University Press 1933

Bossard, J. *Ritual in Family Living* University of Pennsylvania (1950) 14-30

Bowers, Fredson "Death in Victory" *South Atlantic Bulletin* 30 (1965) 1-7

Bowers, M. et al. *Counseling the Dying* New York: Nelson 1964

Bowman, Leroy *The American Funeral: A Way of Death"* New York: Paperback Library 1964

Bowman, Leroy "On the Meaning of Death" *Humanist* 26 (1966) 54-61

Boyar, J. "The Construction and Partial Validation of a Scale for the Measurement of the Fear of Death" PhD diss. 1964

Boyd, Zachery *The Last Battell of the Soule in Death: Divided into eight conferences, whereby are showne the diverse skirmishes that are betweene the soule of man in his death-bedde and the enemies of our salvation* Edinburgh 1629

Bradbury, Ray (See Toynbee, 1972)

Brandon, S. *The Judgement of the Dead* New York: Scribner 1967

Brantner, John "Dialogue on Death" (tape cassette, 59 min.) Minneapolis, Minn: Center for Death Education and Research 1970

Brantner, John "Death and the Self" (tape cassette, 28 min.) Minneapolis, Minn: Center for Death Education and Research

Bratset, Richard "Review of Jessica Mitford *The American Way of Death*" *ETC* 23 (1) (1966) 102-108

Brewster, Henry "Separation Reaction in Psychosomatic Desease and Neurosis" *Death and Identity* R. Fulton pp. 216-225

Brickman, Harry "Psychedelic 'Hip Scene,' The Return of the Death Instinct" *Journal of Psychiatry* 125 (6) (1968) 766-772

Bridgman, Percy *The Intelligent Individual and Society* New York; Macmillan 1938 pp. 168-73

Bridgman, Percy *The Way Things Are* Harvard Univ. Press 1955 234-35

Brierly, J. et al. "Neocortical Death After Cardiac Arrest" *The Lancet* (Sept. 11, 1971) 560-65

Brill, A. "Thoughts on Life and Death or Vidonian All Soul's Eve" *Psychiatric Quarterly* 21 (1947) 199-211

Brim, Orville et al. eds. *The Dying Patient* New York: Russell Sage Foundation 1970

Brittan, R. and T. Marshall *The Disposal of the Dead* 1953

Broad, C. D. *Lectures on Psychical Research* New York: Humanities 1962

Broad, C. D. *Religion, Philosophy and Psychical Research* London: Routledge 1953

Brodsky, B. "Liebestod Fantasies in a Patient Faced with a Fatal Illness" *International Journal of Psychoanalysis* 40 (1959) 13-16

Bromberg, W. and P. Schilder "Death and Dying: A Comparative Study of the Attitudes and Mental Reactions Toward death and Dying" *Psychoanalytic Review* 20 (1933) 133-185

Bromberg, W. and P. Schilder "The Attitudes of Psychoneurotics Toward Death" *Psychoanalytic Review* 23 (1936) 1-28

Brooks, J. "Ways of Death" *Consumer Reports* 29 (1964) 40-43 (Review of Bowman, Mitford & Harmer books)

Brown, Charles "Reducing the High Cost of Dying" *Christian Century* 53 (October 21, 1936) 1391-1393

Brown, Norman O. *Life Against Death* New York: Vintage 1961

Browne, I. et al. "Emotional reactions to the threat of impending death" *Irish Journal of Medical Sciencs* 6 (Apr. 1967) 177-87

Browne, Thomas "The shame of death". Dawson, et al., eds. *The Great English Essayists* New York: Harper 1909 pp. 35-38

Browne, Thomas *Hydriotaphia Wine-Buriall* New York: Payson & Clark 1927 (1658)

Browning, Mary and E. Lewis *The Dying Patient: A Nursing Perspective* New York: American Journal of Nursing 1972

Bruehl, R. "The Time Tommy Died" *Voices* 5, 1 (1969) 55-57

Buchner, G. "Danton's Death" J. Holmstrom, tr., E. Bentley, ed. *The Modern Theatre* Vol 5 New York: Doubleday 1957

Budge, E. *The Mummy* London: Cambridge University Press 1894

Bugental, J. "Review of *Vitality of Death*" *Journal of Existentialism* 5 (20) (1965)

Bugental, J. *The Search for Authenticity* New York: Holt 1965

Bulger, R. "The Dying Patient and His Doctor" *Harvard Medical Alumni Bulletin* 34 (1960) 23

Bulletin of Suicidology (Journal)

Bullough, Vern "The Banal and Costly Funeral" *Humanist* 4 (1960) 213-18

Bullough, V. et al. "Longevity and Achievement in Eighteenth Century Scotland" *Omega* 1 (2) (1970) 115-119

Bultmann, Rudolf *Life and Death* London: Black 1965

Bunston, A. "German Idea of Death" *Living Age* 286 (Aug. 28, 1915) 523-9

Burmback, F. "A.B.C. Death" *Indep.* 112 (Jan. 5, 1924) 10

Burton, Arthur "Death as Countertransference" *Psychoanalysis and the Psychoanalytic Review* 49 (1962) 3ff

Burton, Robert *Anatomy of Melancholy* (1621) London: Chatto & Windus 1907 Part a. Sec. 3, Mem. 5, "Remedies against sorrow of death of friends and otherwise."

Byfield, N. *The Cure of the Feare of Death* London 1619

Cain, A. "The pre-superego 'turning-inward' of aggression" *Psychoanalytic Quarterly* 30 (1961) 171-208

Campbell, Anna *The Black Death and Men of Learning* New York: Columbia University Press 1931

Campbell, Ernest "Death as a Social Practice" *Perspectives on Death* L. Mills 209-230

Campbell, Ninian *A Treatise on Death* London 1630

Camus, Albert *A Happy Death* New York: Knopf 1972

Camus, Albert *The Myth of Sisyphus and Other Essays* New York: Vintage 1955

Camus, Albert *The Plague* New York: Knopf 1948

Camus, Albert *Resistance, Rebellion and Death* J. O'Brien, trans. New York: Knopf 1960

Canadian Funeral Director (Journal)

Cannon, W. "Voodoo Death" *American Anthropologist* 44 (1942) 169-81

Caponigri, A. "Reason and Death, the Idea of Wisdom in Seneca" *Proceedings of the American Catholic Philosophical Association* 42 (1968) 144-51

Cappon, Daniel "Attitudes of and Towards the Dying" *Canadian Medical Association Journal* 87 (13) (1962) 693-700

Cappon, Daniel "Attitudes on Death" *Omega* 1 (2) (1970) 103-108

Cappon, Daniel "The Dying" *Psychiatric Quarterly* 33 (1959) 466-489

Cappon, Daniel "The Psychology of Dying" *Death: Interpretations* H. Ruitenbeek pp. 61-72

Caprio, Frank "Ethnological Attitudes Toward Death: A Psychoanalytic Evaluation" *Journal of Clinical Psychopathology* 7 (1946) 737-52

Caprio, Frank "A Psycho-Social Study of Primitive Conceptions of Death" *Journal of Criminal Psychology* 5 (1943) 303-317

Caprio, Frank "A Study of Some Psychological Reactions During Prepubescence to the Idea of Death" *Psychiatric Quarterly* 24 (1950) 495-505

Carlozzi, Carl *Death and Contemporary Man: the crisis of terminal illness* Michigan: Eerdmans 1968

Carmichael, Benson "The Death Wish in Daily Life" *Psychoanalytic Review* 30 (1943) 59-66

Carnell, E. "Fear of Death" *Christian Century* 80 (1963) 136-37

Carpenter, E. "Eternal Life and Self-Definition Among the Aivilik Eskimos" *American Journal of Psychiatry* 110 (1954) 840-43

Carr, Arthur *Tolstoy's Ivan Ilych with Commentary* New York: Health Sciences 1973

Carr, J. "The Coroner and the Common Law III. Death and its Medical Imputations" *California Medicine* 93 (1960) 32-34

Carr, W. "Theological reflections on death" *North Carolina Medical Journal* 28 (1967) 461-4

Carrel, Alexis "The Mystery of Death" *Medicine and Mankind* I. Galdston, ed. New York: Appleton 1935

Carrere, J. et al. "Apropos of a case report. Reflection on death and paranoia" *Annales Medico-Psychologiques* 122 (1964) 408-10

Carrington, Hereward *Death – Its Causes and Phenomena* New York: Dodd 1921

Carstairs, G. "Attitudes to Death and Suicide in an Indian Cultural Setting" *International Journal of Social Psychiatry* 1 (1955) 33-41

Caruse, I. "A Contribution to the Study of Freud's Concepts of the Instincts for Death and for Aggression" *Bulletin of Psychology* 19 (1) (1965) 1-29

Casket and Sunnyside "The Authority of the Funeral Service Industry for 100 years" (Journal)

Cassell, Eric *Care for the Dying* New York: Institute of Society, Ethics and the Life Sciences 1970

Cassell, Eric "Is Aging a Disease?" *Hastings Report* 2 (April 1972) 4-6

Cattell, James "Psychiatric Implications of Bereavement" *Death and Bereavement* A. Kutscher pp. 153-162

Cavanaugh, John "The right of the patient to die with dignity" *The Catholic Nurse* 11

(Dec. 1963) 24-33, 68
Cemeterian (Journal)
Chadwick, Mary "Notes on the fear of death" *Psychoanalytic Review* 15 (1928) 102-103
Chadwick, Mary "Notes Upon the Fear of Death" *International Journal of Psychoanalysis* 10 (1929) 321-334
Chaloner, L. "How to answer the questions children ask about death" *Parents' Magazine* 37 (1962) 48, 49, 100, 102
Chaney, Edward, ed. *La Danse Macabre* England: Manchester University Press 1945
Chellam, G. *The Disengagement Theory: Awareness of Death and Self-Engagement* PhD diss. Western Reserve University 1964
Child, C. *Senescence and Rejuvenescence in Unicellular Organisms* U. of Chicago Press 1915
Choron, Jacques *Death and Western Thought* New York: Collier 1963
Choron, Jacques *Modern Man and Morality* New York: Macmillan 1964
Choron, Jacques *Suicide* New York: Scribner 1971
Christi, Adolph "Attitudes toward death among a group of acute geriatric psychiatric patients" *Journal of Gerontology* 16 (1) (1961) 56-59
Cicero *On Old Age and On Friendship* University of Michigan Press 1967
Clark, J. *The Dance of Death in the Middle Ages and the Renaissance* Glasgow 1950
Clark, Linda *Stay Young Longer* New York: Pyramid 1961
Clarke, John "Mysticism and the Paradox of Survival" *International Philosophical Quarterly* 6 (June 1971) 165-79
Clayton, Paula "Evidences of Normal Grief" *Death and Bereavement* A. Kutscher pp. 168-73
Cleghorn, Sarah "Changing Thoughts of Death" *Atlantic Monthly* 132 (Dec. 1923) 808-12
Clemens, Samuel "The Cost of Funerals," "Undertaker's Chat," "Coffins and Swell Houses," etc. *Writings of Mark Twain* 25 vols. New York: Harper 1899-1928
Cleveland, F. "The Dance of Death" *Journal of the American Medical Association* 176 (April 15, 1961) 142-43
Cochrane, A. "Elie Metschnikoff and his theory of an instinct de la mort" *International Journal of Psychoanalysis* 15 (1934) 265-70
Cohen, John "A Study of Suicide Pacts" *Medico-Legal Journal* 29 (1961) 144-51
Cohen, Sidney "LSD and the Anguish of Dying" *Harper's Magazine* (Sept. 1965) 69-78
Cole, David *Overcoming the fear of death* New York: Macmillan 1970
Cole, Fay "Relations Between the Living and the Dead" *American Journal of Sociology* 21 (5) (1916) 611-22
Cole, James *Of Death, a true description* London 1629
Collmer, Robert "John Donne's Interest in Death" M.A. thesis, Baylor University 1949
Collmer, Robert *The Concept of Death in the Poetry of Donne, Herbert, Crashaw, and Vaughan* PhD diss. Claremont Graduate School 1964
Collmer, Robert "The Function of Death in Certain Metaphysical Poems" *McNeese Review* 46 (1965) 25-32
Collmer, Robert "The Meditation on Death and its Appearance in Metaphysical Poetry" *Neophilologus* 45 (1961) 323-33
Comfort, Alex "To Be Continued" *Playboy* 18 (11) (1971) 113-14, 209-12
Comfort, Alex "The Life Span of Animals" *Scientific American* 205 (2) (1961) 108-119
Comfort, Alex *The Process of Ageing* New York: Signet 1964
Comfort, Alex *The Biology of Senescence* London: Routledge 1956
Comper, Frances, ed. *The Book of the Craft of Dying, and other Early English Tracts Concerning Death* London: Longmans, Green and Co. 1917 (Modernizes Douce's medieval *Crafte of Dying)*
Concept: The Journal of Creative Ideas for Cemeteries
Connell, E. "The Significance of the Idea of Death in the Neurotic Mind" *British Journal of Medical Psychology* 4 (1924) 115-124
Cooperman, Stanley "Death and Cojones: Hemingway's 'A Farewell to Arms' " *South Atlantic Quarterly* 63 (1964) 85-92
Corey, Lawrence "An Analogue of Resistance to Death Awareness" *Journal of Gerontology* 16 (1961) 59-60

Cornelius, Benjamin "Review of Ducasse *Nature, Mind and Death*" *Philosophical Review* 61 (1952) 551-56
Cosacchi, S. *Makabertanz* Meisenheim: Hain 1965
Coverdale, Myles "Treatise on Death" *Remains of Myles Coverdale* G. Pearson, ed. Cambridge: University Press 1846
Creegan, Robert "A Symbolic Action During Bereavement" *Death: Interpretations* H. Ruitenbeek pp. 217-221
"Cremation: Permissible" *Time* June 12, 1964 p. 85
Crooke, Samuel *Death Subdued, or the Death of Death* London 1619
Cumming, Elaine and W. Henry *Growing Old* New York: Basic Books 1961
Cunningham, Michael "To Live and to Die Humanly" *Religious Humanism* 3 (1969) 97-100
Curtis, Howard "Why We Grow Old (Cassette tape) American Chemical Society 1972
Cust, Lionel *The Master E.S. and the 'Ars moriendi'* Oxford 1898
Cutler, Donald, ed. *Updating Life and Death* Boston: Beacon Press 1968
Dagley, Richard *Death's Doings* 2 vols. London: Andrews 1827
D'Albe, Fournier *New Light on Immortality* London: Longmans 1908
Dallas, H. "What is Death?" *Living Age* 332 (Feb. 15, 1927) 354-9
Daniel, Howard *Devils, Monsters and Nightmares* New York: Abelard-Schuman 1964
Dastre, A. *Life and Death* W. Greenstreet, trans. London 1911
Davey, Richard *A History of Mourning* London: Jays 1889
Davidson, Bill "The High Cost of Dying" *Colliers* 127 (May 19, 1951) 13-15, 55-60
Davidson, G. *Basic Images of Death in America: An Historical Analysis* PhD diss. Calif.: Claremont Graduate School 1964
Davidson, Henry "Emotional precipitants of death" *Journal of the Medical Society of New Jersey* 46 (1949) 350-52
Davidson, R. "Let's Talk About Death to Give Care in Terminal Illness" *American Journal of Nursing* 66 (1966) 74-75
Davis, Kingsley "Death Customs and Rites" *Colliers Encyclopedia* 757-765
Day, Richard *Heroic Death, A Study from a Christian Point of View* Ann Arbor, Michigan: University Microfilm AC-1 No. 6597 1954
"Death," "Death Customs" *Encyclopedia Americana* J. Oppenheimer, J. Williams (legal aspects), D. Bidney (customs) Vol. 8, pp. 539-43
"Death" *Encyclopaedia Britannica* D. King (Biological), P. Jackson (Legal) 128-34
Death and Dying: Attitudes of Patient and Doctor New York: Group for the Advancement of Psychiatry, Symposium No. 11, 5 (1966)
Death and the Plowman (death from 1400) E. Kirrmann, trans. Univ. of North Carolina 1958
"Death Rites of the Camayura" (Film) 30 min. New York: American Broadcasting Co. 1960
"Death of Socrates" (Film, 16mm - 45 min.) New York: Peter Robeck 1972
"Death: The Way of Life" *Harvest Years* 9 (April 1969) 19-34
de Bary, R. *My experiments with death* London: Longmans 1936
de Beauvoir, S. *A Very Easy Death* P. O'Brien, trans. New York: Putnam 1966
Defoe, Daniel *Journal of the Plague Year* New York: Routledge 1884
de Hampole, Richard *Pricke of Conscience* ca. 1340
DeLuca, Peter *Dialogue of Dying Wel* R. Verstegan, trans. (before 1634)
Demos, Raphael "Review of Ducasse *Nature, Mind and Death*" *Review of Metaphysics* 6 (4) (1953) 563-82
Dent, Arthur *The Plaine Man's Path-Way to Heaven* London 1601
de Ropp, Robert *Man Against Aging* New York 1960
de Sade, Marquis "Dialogue between a Priest and a Dying Man" in *Selections from His Writings* P. Dinnage, ed., trans. New York: Grove 1953
Desoto, Anthony "Heidegger, Kneller and Vandenberg" (Reply to Vandenberg's July, 1965 article) *Educational Theory* 16 (July, 1966) 239-41
Deutsch, Felix "Euthanasia" *Psychoanalytic Quarterly* 5 (1936) 347-368
Devereux, G. "Primitive Psychiatry, Funeral Suicide and the Mohave Social Structure" *Bulletin of the History of Medicine* 11 (1942) 522-42
Devlin, William "Cremation" *Catholic Encyclopedia* vol. 4
Devos, G., H. Wagatsuma "Psycho-cultural Significance of Concern over Death and Illness Among Rural Japanese" *International Journal of Social Psychiatry* 5 (1959) 5-19

532

de Wind, E. "The confrontation with death" *International Journal of Psychoanalysis* 49 (1968) 302-5

de Wind, E. "Facing death" *Psyche* 22 (June, 1968) 423-41

D'Harcourt, Robert "Goethe et la mort" *Revue de Paris* no. 1 (1933)

Dibner, Andrew "Age, Personality and Health Correlates of Death Concerns in Normal Aged Individuals" *Death and Identity* R. Fulton pp. 123-30

Dickens, Robert "Unamuno on Tragedy, Agony and 'The Tragic Sense of Life' " *Journal of Existentialism* 8 (30) (1967-68) 161-77

Diggory, James and D. Rothman "Values Destroyed by Death" *Death and Identity* R. Fulton pp. 152-160

The Director (Journal of the National Funeral Director's Assoc., official publ.)

Diskin, Martin and H. Guggenheim "The child and death as seen in different cultures" *Explaining Death to Children* E. Grollman pp. 111-123

Doebler, Bettie *Death in the Sermons of John Donne* PhD diss. University of Wisconsin 1961

Doebler, Bettie "Donne's Debt to the Great Tradition: Old and New in His Treatment of Death" *Anglia* 85 (1968) 15-33

Donne John "Death Be Not Proud" *A Treasury of Great Poems* Untermeyer, ed. New York: Simon and Schuster 1955

Donne, John *Paradoxes, Problems, Essays, Characters* London 1652

Donne, John *Poetry and Prose of John Donne* A. Hawkins, ed. London: Nelson 1938

Dostoevsky, F. *The House of the Dead* New York: Macmillan 1915 (Also other novels.)

Douce, Francis *Holbein's Dance of Death* London: Bohn 1858

Douglass, W. *Death in Murelaga: Funerary Ritual in a Spanish Basque Village* Seattle: Univ. of Washington Press 1969

Dowd, Rev. Quincy *The Economics of Necrolatry* Univ. of Chicago Press 1921

Dowd, Rev. Quincy *Funeral Management and Costs* Univ. of Chicago Press 1921

Downing, A. *Euthanasia* California: Nash 1969

Draper, John *The Funeral Elegy and the Rise of English Romanticism* New York 1929

Drelincourt, Charles *The Christian's Defense Against the Fears of Death* London 1720

Drexelius, Hieremias *The Considerations of Death Upon Eternity* R. Winterton, trans. 1636

Drinnon, R. "In the American Heartland: Hemingway and Death" *Psychoanalytic Review* 52 (2) (1965) 5-31

Drummond, Eleanor, and J. Blumberg "How we discuss death in the adult health course for registered nurse students" *Journal of Nursing Education* 1(May-June, 1962) 21-28

Dublin, Louis et al. *Length of Life* New York 1949

Dubruck, Edelgard *The Theme of Death in French Poetry of the Middle Ages and the Renaissance* Hague: Mouton 1964

Ducasse, C. "Broad on the Relevance of Psychical Research to Philosophy" *The Philosophy of C. D. Broad* P. Schilpp, ed., Illinois: Open Court 1959 pp. 315ff

Ducasse, C. "Demos on 'Nature, Mind and Death' " *Review of Metaphysics* 7 (2) (1953) 290-98

Ducasse, C. *Nature, Mind and Death* Illinois: Open Court 1951

Ducasse, C. *A Philosophical Scrutiny of Religion* New York: Ronald Press 1953

Duckett, Eleanor *Death and Life in the Tenth Century* University of Michigan 1967

Duncan-Jones, Austin "Man's Mortality" *Analysis* 28 (3) (1968) 65-70

Dunton, John *The sickman's passing bell with the sighths and groanes of a dying man* 1684

Durkheim, E. *Suicide, a study in Sociology* Illinois: Free Press 1951

Easson, William *The Dying Child* Illinois: C. Thomas 1970

Eaton, Hubert *The Comemorial* California: Academy Press 1954 (See also A. St. Johns)

Eaton, J. "The Art of Aging and Dying" *Gerontologist* 4 (1964) 94-100

Eaton, W. *Contrasts in the Representation of Death by Webster and Strindberg* PhD diss. Syracuse University 1965

Eckles, John *Modern Mortuary Science* Philadelphia: Westbrook Publ. 1948

Edwards, Paul "My Death" *Encyclopedia of Philosophy* 416-419

Edwards, Phillip "The Danger not the Death: The Art of John Fletcher" *Jacobean Theater* 13 (1961) 159-77

533

Eisenthal, S. "Death ideation in suicidal patients" *Journal of Abnormal Psychology* 73 (April, 1968) 162-7
Eissler, Kurt "Death and the Pleasure Principle" *Death: Interpretations* H. Ruitenbeek pp. 11-18
Eissler, Kurt *The Psychiatrist and the Dying Patient* New York: International Universities Press 1955
Elam, Lloyd "A Psychiatric Perspective on Death" *Perspectives on Death* L. Mills 197-208
Eliade, Mircea *From Primitives to Zen* New York: Harper 1967 "Myths of the Origin of Death" pp. 139-144; "Death, Afterlife, Eschatology" pp. 321-419
Eliot, Thomas "Of the Shadow of Death" *Annals of the American Academy of Political and Social Science* 229 (1943) 87-99
Eliot, Thomas *Wasteland* New York: Harcourt 1962
Elliard, J. "Emotional reactions associated with death" *Medical Journal of Australia* 1 (June 8, 1968) 979-83
Elliot, Richard "The Funeral Business" *Barron's National Weekly* (April 11, 1955)
Ellis, Albert "Rational Psychotherapy" *Journal of General Psychology* 59 (1958) 35-49
Ellis, R. "Attitudes Toward Death and Types of Belief in Immortality" *Journal of Religious Psychology* 7 (1915) 466-510
Embalmer's Monthly
Engel, G. "Is Grief a Disease?" *Psychosomatic Medicine* 23 (1961) 18-22
Englebretsen, G. "Persons, Predicates, and Death" *Second Order* (forthcoming)
Epictetus *The Enchiridion* T. Higginson, trans. Indiana: Bobbs-Merrill 1948
Epicurus *The Philosophy of Epicurus* G. Strodach, ed. Northwestern University Press 1963 esp. "Letter to Menoeceus" pp. 178-195
The Epitaph-Writer Chester, England 1791
Erasmus, Desiderius *The Dyaloge called Funus* R. Allen, ed., U. of Chicago Press 1969
Erasmus, Desiderius *Preparation to Deathe* London 1543
Erskine, John "The Theme of Death in *Paradise Lost*" *PMLA* 32 (1917) 573-82
Escheverria, Jose "Reflexions metaphysiques sur la mort et la probleme du sujet" PhD diss Paris 1957
Eshelman, Byron *Death Row Chaplain* New Jersey: Prentice-Hall 1962
Ettinger, Robert "The Frozen Christian" *Christian Century* 82 (1965) 1313-1315
Ettinger, Robert *Man into Superman* New York: St. Martin's Press 1972
Ettinger, Robert *The Prospect of Immortality* New York: Macfadden-Bartell 1964
Ettinger, Robert "Science and Immortality" *Yale Scientific Magazine* 40 (7) (1966) 5-8, 20
Evans, William *Chemistry of Death* Illinois: C. Thomas 1963
Fackler, M. *Death: Idea and Image in Some Later Victorian Lyrists* PhD diss. University of Colorado 1956
The Facts of Life and Death Wash. D.C.: Public Health Service Publ. no. 600, 1965
Fairbanks, H. "Man's Separation from Nature: Hawthorne's Philosophy of Suffering and Death" *Christian Scholar* 42 (March 1959) 51-63
Farmer, J. Jr. "Death Education: Adult Education in the Face of a Taboo" *Omega* 1 (2) (1970) 109-113
Fassler, Joan *My Grandpa Died Today* Behavioral Publications 1972
Faulkner, William *As I Lay Dying,* "A Rose for Emily" and other novels.
Federn, Paul "The Reality of the Death Instinct" *Psychoanalytic Review* 19 (1932) 129-151
Feifel, Herman "Attitudes of Mentally Ill Patients Toward Death" *Journal of Nervous and Mental Disease* 122 (1955) 375-80
Feifel, Herman (Symposium on Death and Dying) American Psychology Association Convention 1956 (most papers are in his *Meaning of Death)*
Feifel, Herman "Death" *The Encyclopedia of Mental Health* A. Deutsch, ed. New York: Franklin Watts 2 (1963) 427-50
Feifel, Herman "Death - Relevant Variable in Psychology" *Existential Psychology* R. May, ed. Random House 1961
Feifel, Herman "The Function of Attitudes Towards Death *Journal of the Long Island Consultation Center* 5 (1) (1967) 26-32
Feifel, Herman *The Meaning of Death* New York: McGraw-Hill 1959
Feifel, Herman "Older Persons Look at Death" *Geriatrics* 11 (1956) 127-30

534

Feifel, Herman "The Problem of Death" *Death: Interpretations* H. Ruitenbeek pp. 125-29

Feifel, Herman "Scientific Research in Taboo Areas – Death" *American Behaviorial Scientist* 2 (1962) 28-30

Feifel, Herman "The Taboo on Death" *American Behaviorial Scientist* 6 (1963) 66-67

Feifel, Herman "The Meaning of Death in American Society" (tape cassett, 29 min.) Minneapolis, Minnesota: Center for Death Education and Research 1970

Feifel, Herman "Death" *Taboo Topics* N. Farberow, ed., New York: Atherton Press 1963

Feifel, Herman and R. Jones "Perception of Death as Related to Nearness of Death" *Proc. 76th American Psychological Assoc.* 3 (1968) 545-46

Feinberg, Gerald "Physics and Life Prolongation" *Physics Today* 19 (11) (1966) 45-48

Felder, B. "Some Thoughts on Living and Dying" *Voices* 5 (1) (1969) 79

Fellows, Alfred *The Law of Burial* London: Hadden 1952

Fenichel, O. "A Critique of the Death Instinct" *Imago* 21 (1938)

Ferber, Charles "Survivor - Benefit - Rights Under Social Security" *Death and Bereavement* A. Kutscher pp. 277-80

Ferrater-Mora, Jose *Being and Death* Univ. of California Press 1965

Fesbach, Sidney "Death in 'An Encounter' " *James Joyce Quarterly* 2 (1965) 82-89

Fiedler, Leslie "The Death of the Old Men" *Arts & Sciences* (1963-64) 1-5

Fiedler, Leslie *Love and Death in the American Novel* New York: Stein 1966

Finlay, Daniel "A Study of Form in *Anatomy of Melancholy*" PhD diss. Virginia 1967

Fisher, G. "Death, Identity, and Creativity" *Voices* 5 (1) (1969) 36-39

Flammarion, Camille *Death and Its Mystery Before Death* New York: Century 1922

Flesch, Regina "The Condolence Call" *Death And Bereavement* A. Kutscher pp. 236-248

Fletcher, Joseph "Euthanasia" *Morals and Medicine* Beacon: Boston 1954

Flew, Antony "Can a Man Witness His Own Funeral?" *Hibbert Journal* 54 (1955-56) eds., New York: Macmillan 1955

Flew, Antony "Immortality" *Encyclopedia of Philosophy* P. Edwards, ed., New York: Macmillan (4) 1967

Flew, Antony *A New Approach to Psychical Research* London: Watts 1953

Fliess, Wilhelm *Vom Leben und Tod* Jena: Diederichs 1919

Flügel, J. "Death Instinct, Homeostasis and Allied Concepts" *International Journal of Psychoanalysis* 34 (1953) 43-74

Fodor, N. "Jung's Sermons to the Dead" *Psychoanalytic Review* 51 (1) (1964) 74-78

Foelber, Paul *Bach's treatment of the subject of death in his choral music* Catholic Univ. of America Press 1961

Folta, J. "Social Reconstruction After Death" (tape cassette, 21 min.) Minneapolis, Minn: Center for Death Education and Research 1971

Ford, Thomas *Heaven Beguiles the Tired: Death in the Poetry of Emily Dickinson* University of Alabama Press 1966

Ford, Thomas *The Theme of Death in the Poetry of Emily Dickinson* PhD diss. U. of Texas 1959

Forest, Jack "The Major Emphasis of the Funeral" *Pastoral Psychology* 14 (1963) 19-24

"Forever Young" *Newsweek* Sept. 15, 1969 pp. 88-90

Forster, E. *Howard's End* New York: Vintage 1959

Foss, Martin *Death, Sacrifice and Tragedy* Univ. of Nebraska Press 1966

Fox, Jean "The Nurse Reflects" *Death and Bereavement* A. Kutscher 1969 75-83

Fox, W. "Inquiry into the History of Opinion Concerning Death" *Works* New Zealand vol. 7 213-63

Foxe, Arthur "Critique of Freud's Concept of the Death Instinct" *Psychoanalytic Review* 30 (1943) 417-27

Foxe, Arthur "The life and death instincts – criminological implications" *Journal of Criminal Psychopathology* 4 (1942) 67-91

Fraenkel, Michael *Death is not Enough* London: Daniel 1939

Francaviglia, Richard "The Cemetery as an Evolving Cultural Landscape" *Annals of the Association of American Geographers* 61 (Sept. 1971) 501-509

Frankl, Viktor *From Death Camp to Existentialism: A Psychiatrist's Path to a New Therapy* I. Lasch, trans., Boston: Beacon Press 1959

Frankl, Viktor "Psychiatry and Man's Quest for Meaning" *Journal of Religious Health*

1 (1962) 93-103

Frankl, Viktor *Psychotherapy and Existentialism — Selected Papers in Logotherapy* New York: Washington Square Press 1967

Frankl, Viktor *The Will to Meaning; foundation and application of logotherapy* New York: World 1969

Franz, Anne *Funeral Direction and Management* Florida State Board of Funeral Directors and Embalmers 1947

Frazer, Sir James *The Belief in Immortality* London: Macmillan 1913

Frazer, Sir James *The Fear of the Dead in Primitive Religion* 3 vols, London: Macmillan 1933-1936

Frazer, Sir James *The New Golden Bough* T. Gaster, ed., New York: Doubleday 1959. Part III "Death and Resurrection," Part IV "Dying and Reviving Gods"

Frazer, Winifred "Love as Death in 'The Iceman Cometh. " U. of Florida Monographs, Humanities Series No. 27 1968

Fredlund, Delphie "Death and the Family: From the Caring Profession's Point of View" (tape cassette 30 min.) Minneapolis, Minnesota: Center for Death Education and Research 1971

Freud, Sigmund *Beyond the Pleasure Principle* London: Hogarth 1950

Freud, Sigmund "The Economic Problem of Masochism" 1924

Freud, Sigmund "Mourning and Melancholia" *Collected Papers* New York: Basic Books 4 (1959)

Freud, Sigmund "Negations" *Complete Works* London: Hogarth Press 19 (1961)

Freud, Sigmund "The Theme of the Three Caskets." *Collected Papers* New York: Basic Books 4 (1959) 244-56

Freud, Sigmund "Thoughts for the Times on War and Death" *Complete Psychological Works of Sigmund Freud* London: Hogarth 14 (1957) 275-300

Friedlander, Kate "On the Longing to Die" *International Journal of Psychoanalysis* 21 (1940)

Friedman, David "Death anxiety and the primal scene" *Psychoanalysis* 48 (4) (1961-62) 108-118

Fulton, Robert "Attitudes Toward Death: A Discussion" *Journal of Gerontology* 16 (1961) 63-65

Fulton, Robert "A Psycho-Social Aspect of Terminal Care: Anticipatory Grief" (tape cassette, 32 min.) Minneapolis, Minn.: Center for Death Education and Research 1970

Fulton, Robert "Attitudes Toward Death in Older Persons: A Symposium" *Journal of Gerontology* 16 (1961) 44-66

Fulton, Robert "The Clergyman and the Funeral Director: A Study in Role Conflict" *Social Forces* 39 (May 1961) 317-23

Fulton, Robert *Creative Education and Social Crisis* New York: Wiley 1967

Fulton, Robert, ed. *Death & Identity* New York: Wiley 1965

Fulton, Robert "Death and the Self" *Journal of Religion and Health* 3 (1964) 359-68

Fulton, Robert *The Sacred and the Secular: Attitudes of the American Public Toward Death* Milwaukee: Bulfin Printers 1963

Fulton, Robert and W. Faunce "The Sociology of Death: A Neglected Area of Research" *Social Forces* 36 (1958) 205-209

Fulton, Robert and G. Geis "Death and Social Values" *Death and Identity* R. Fulton pp. 56-66

Fulton, Robert and G. Geis "Social Change and Social Conflict: The Rabbi and the Funeral Director" *Sociological Symposium* 1 (1968) 1-10

Fulton, Robert and P. Langton "Attitudes Toward Death: An Emerging Mental Health Problem" *Nursing Forum* 3 (1964) 104-12

Funeral Director (British Journal)

Funeral Directors Review (Journal)

Funeral Service Journal (British Journal)

Furman, Robert "Death and the young child" *Psychoanalytic Study of the Child* 19 (1964) 321-333

Galdston, I. "Eros and Thanatos, A Critique and Elaboration of Freud's Death Wish" *American Journal of Psychoanalysis* 15 (1955) 123-34

Gallwitzer, Helmut et al. *Dying We Live* New York: Pantheon 1956

Galston, Arthur "Death Isn't Necessary" *Science Digest* July 1965 pp. 80-85

Gannal, Jean *History of Embalming* R. Harlan, trans. Philadelphia: Dobson 1840

536

Gardiner, Alan *The Attitude of Ancient Egyptians to Death and the Dead* Cambridge University Press 1935

Gartley, Wayne and M. Bernasconi "The concept of death in children" *Journal of General Psychology* 110 (1967) 71-85

Gatch, Milton *Death: Meaning and Mortality in Christian Thought and Contemporary Culture* New York: Seabury 1969

Geach, Peter "Immortality" *God and the Soul* London: Routledge 1969

Gealy, F. "The Biblical Understanding of Death" *Pastoral Psychology* 14 (1963) 33-40

Gebhart, John *Funeral Costs* New York: Putnam 1928

Geertz, C. "Ritual and Social Change. A Javanese Example" *American Anthropologist* 59 (1958) 32-54

Geill, Torben "Old age, disease and death" *Excerpta Med.* 3 (20) (1960) 447-50

Geiringer, Erich "Fear of Death" *Spectator* 189 (Aug. 8, 1952) 179-180

Gerard, H. *The Relationship Between Religious Belief and Death Affect* Princeton University Press 1958

Geriatrics (Journal)

Geriatrics Digest (Journal)

Gero, F. *Death Among the Azande of the Sudan* W. Paxman, trans. Bologna: Editrice Nigrizia 1968

The Gerontologist (Journal)

Gibney, Harriet "What death means to children" *Parents' Magazine* 65 (Mar. 1965) 136-42

Gibran, K. *The Prophet*

Gibson, Paul "The dying patient" *Practitioner* 186 (4) (1961) 85-91

Giesey, R. "The Royal Funeral Ceremony in Renaissance France" PhD diss. Berkeley: U. of California 1954

Glaister, J. "Phantasies of the dying" *Lancet* 2 (Aug. 6, 1921) 315-17

Glaser, Barney and A. Strauss *Awareness of Dying* Chicago: Aldine 1965

Glaser, Barney and A. Strauss "Dying on time" *Trans-Action* 2 (4) (May-June 1965) 27-31

Glaser, Barney and A. Strauss *Time for Dying* Chicago: Aldine 1968

Glaser, Kurt "Attempted suicide in children and adolescents: psychodynamic observations" *American Journal of Psychotherapy* 19 (2) (1965) 220-27

Gleason, Robert "Toward a Theology of Death" *Thought* 23 (1957) 39-68

Glidden, Arthur "The American Funeral" *Pastoral Psychology* 14 (June 1963) 9-18

Gluckman, Max "Mortuary Customs and the Beliefs in Survival After Death Among the South-Eastern Bantu" *Bantu Studies* Johannesburg: Univ. of Witwaterstrand Press Vol. 2, 117-136

Golding, A. and G. "Anxiety and Two Cognitive Forms of Resistance to the Idea of Death" *Psychological Reports* 18 (1966) 359 ff

Goldsmith, C. *A Theoretical Analysis of Attitudes of Older People Toward Dying* PhD diss. Boston University 1969

Gonda, Thomas "Pain Relief, Addiction and the Dying Patient" *Death and Bereavement* A. Kutscher pp. 10-13

Goody, John *Death, Property and the Ancestors: A Study of the Mortuary Customs of the Lo Dagaa of West Africa* Palo Alto: Stanford Univ. Press 1962

Goody, John "Death and Social Control Among the Lo Dagaa" *Man* 59 (1959) 134-138

Gordon, David *Overcoming the Fear of Death* Baltimore, Maryland: Penguin 1972

Gordon, Rosemary "The death instinct and its relation to the self" *Journal of Analytic Psychology* 6 (2) (1961) 119-135

Gorer, Geoffrey *Death, Grief and Mourning in Contemporary Britain* London: Cresset 1965

Gorer, Geoffrey "The Pornography of Death" *Encounter* 5 (1955) 49-52

Gortley, Wayne and M. Bernasconi "The Concept of Death in Children" *Journal of Genetic Psychology* 110 (1967) 71-85

Gottlieb, Carla "Modern Art and Death" *The Meaning of Death* H. Feifel pp. 157-88

Gotz, Berndt "Sexualität, Erkenntnis, Tod" *Zeitschrift für Sexualwissenshaft* 17 (1931) 486-96

Gough, E. "Cults of the Dead Among the Nayars" *Journal of American Folklore* 71 (1958) 446-78

Gould, R. *Enigmas* London: Bles 1945

Graham, J. "Acceptance of Death – Beginning of Life" *North Carolina Medical Journal* 24 (1963) 317-319

Gray, Douglas "Two Songs of Death" *Neuphilologische* 64 (1963) 52-74

Gray, J. "The Idea of Death in Existentialism" *Journal of Philosophy* 48 (1951) 113-127

Greenberg, Irwin "Death and dying: attitudes of patient and doctor" *Group for the Advancement of Psychiatry* 5 (Oct. 1965) 623-31

Greenberg, Irwin and I. Alexander "Some correlates of thoughts and feelings concerning death" *New York Hillside Hospital Journal* 11 (2/3) (1962) 120-26

Greenberger, E. "Fantasies of women confronting death" *Journal of Consulting Psychology* 29 (June 1965) 250-60

Greenberger, E. "Fantasies of Women Confronting Death: A Study of Critically Ill Patients" PhD diss. Radcliffe College 1961

Greenberger, E. "Flirting with Death: Fantasies of a Critically Ill Woman" *Journal of Projective Technique* 30 (2) (1966) 197-204

Greene, Carlton *Death and Sleep: Their Analogy Illustrated by Examples* London: Elliot Stock 1904

Greenstock, David *Death – The Glorious Adventure* Westminster, Md.: Newman Press 1956

Gregory, Horace, ed. *The Triumph of Life* New York: The Viking Press 1943 (anthol. of elegiac poems)

Grief New York: Health Sciences

Griffin, Glen "Today's Funeral Director – His Responsibilities and Challenges" (tape cassette, 25 min.) Minneapolis, Minn: Center for Death Education and Research 1971

Grohmann, Adolf "Das Problem vom Leben und Tod in zeitgenossischer Literatur" *Zeitschrift fur Deutschekunde* (1930)

Grollman, Earl *Explaining Death to Children* Boston: Beacon 1967

Grollman, Earl *Talking About Death* Boston: Beacon 1970

Grosse, George et al., eds. *The Threat of Impending Disaster* Mass.: MIT Press 1964

Grotjahn, Martin "About the Representation of Death in the Art of Antiquity and in the Unconscious of Modern Man" *Psychoanalysis and Culture* G. Wilbur, W. Muensterberger, eds. New York: International University Press 1951 pp. 410-24

Grotjahn, Martin "Ego Identity and Fear of Death and Dying" *Journal of the Hillside Hospital* 9 (1960) 147-55

Gruber, Otto *When I Die* New York: Vantage 1965

Grugan, Arthur "Metaphysics and the Problem of Death: Review of Eugene Fink *Metaphysik und Tod*" *Research in Phenomenology* I (Oct. 1971)

Gruman, Gerald *A History of Ideas About the Prolongation of Life: The Evolution of Prolongevity Hypothesis to 1800* Philadelphia: American Philosophical Society 1966

Guardini, Romano *The Death of Socrates* B. Wrighton, trans. New York: Meridian 1948

Guardini, Romano *The Last Things, Concerning Death, Purification After Death, Resurrection* C. Forsyth, G. Branham, trans., New York: Pantheon 1954

Gutheil, Thomas "A Study of the Image of Death" *Harvard Medical Alumni Bulletin* 41 (3) (1967) 12-17

Guthrie, George "The Meaning of Death" *Voices* 5 (1) (1969) 99-103

Guttentag, Otto "The Meaning of Death in Medical Theory" *Stanford Medical Bulletin* 17 (1959) 165-170

Guttman, Allen "Love and Death and Dachau: Recent Poets" *Studies on the Left* 4(2) (1964) 98-109

Habenstein, Robert "Conflicting Organizational Patterns in Funeral Directing" PhD diss. Univ. of Chicago 1954

Habenstein, Robert and W. Lamers *Funeral Customs the World Over* Milwaukee: Bulfin Printers 1960

Habenstein, Robert and W. Lamers *The History of American Funeral Directing* Milwaukee: Bulfin Printers 1955

Hackett, Thomas and A. Weisman "Reactions to the imminence of death" *The Threat of Impending Disaster* G. Grosse, et al., eds. Cambridge: MIT Press 1964 pp. 300-11

Hall, G. "Thanatophobia and Immortality" *American Journal of Psychology* 26 (1915)

538

550-613

Hallowell, A. "Aggression in Salteaux Society" *Psychiatry* 3 (1940) 395-407

Hamlyn, P. *The Drawings of Holbein* London 1966

Harmer, Ruth *The High Cost of Dying* New York: Crowell-Collier 1963

Harrington, Alan *The Immortalist* New York: Avon 1969

Harris, Audrey *Why Did He Die?* 1965

Harris, R. *Outline of Death Investigation* Illinois: C. Thomas 1962

Harrison, E. *Death and Decadence in the Works of Klaus Mann* PhD diss. Harvard Univ. 1967

Hart, Hornell *The Enigma of Survival* London: Rider 1959

Hart, Hornell "Scientific Survival Research" *International Journal of Parapsychology* 9 (1967) 43-52

Hartley, William and Ellen "Your Kids May Live to Be 100+" *Science Digest* 63 (3) (1970) 38-42

Hastings Report (Journal) Institute of Society, Ethics and the Life Sciences

Havemann, Ernest "Are Funerals Barbaric?" *McCall's* (May 1956)

Havighurst, Robert "The Career of the Funeral Director" PhD diss. Univ. of Chicago 1954

Hazlitt, William "On the fear of death" *The Great English Essayist* W. Dawson; Coningsby, eds. New York: Harper 1909 55-64

Hazlitt, William "On the Feeling of Immortality in Youth" *Complete Works* P. Howe, ed. London: Dent 1934 Vol. 17 p. 189

Heinmann, Paula "Notes on the Theory of Life and Death Instincts" *Development of Psychoanalysis* J. Riviere, ed. New York: International Universities Press 1952

Heitz, R. "The Collective Representation of Death" *Death and the Right Hand* R. Hertz

Helton, Lyn (See Toynbee 1972)

Hemingway, Ernest *Death in the Afternoon* New York: Scribners 1932; *The Sun Also Rises* New York: Scribners 1954; and other novels

Henderson, Joseph and M. Oakes *Wisdom of the Serpent: The Myths of Death, Rebirth, Resurrection* New York: Macmillan 1971

Hepler "A Selected Bibliography on the Sociology of Death" *Sociological Symposium* 1 (1968) 85-91

Herter, Frederic "The Right to Die in Dignity" *Death and Bereavement* A. Kutscher pp. 14-19

Hertz, Robert "A Contribution to the Study of the Collective Representation of Death" *Death and the Right Hand* R. Hertz pp. 29-86

Hertz, Robert, ed. *Death and The Right Hand* R.&C. Needham, trans., Glencoe, Ill: Free Press 1960

Herzog, Edgar *Psyche and Death* Rolf and Cox, trans., New York: Putnam 1967

Heuscher, Julius "Existential Crisis, Death, and Changing 'World-Designs' in Myths and Fairy Tales" *Diseases of the Nervous System* 28 (1967) 462-67

Hickerson, H. "The Feast of the Dead Among the 17th Century Algonkians of the Upper Great Lakes" *American Anthropologist* 62 (1960) 81-107

Hilgard, Josephine et al. "Strength of Adult Ego Following Childhood Bereavement" *Death and Identity* R. Fulton pp. 259-271

Hinton, John *Dying* Baltimore: Penguin 1967

Hinton, John "Facing Death" *Journal of Psychosomatic Research* 10 (1966) 22-28

Hocart, A. "Death Customs" *Encyclopedia of Social Sciences* pp. 21-27

Hoccleve "Lerne to Dye" *Works* F. Furnivall, ed. London: Paul, Trench, Trubner 1892-1925

Hocking, William *The Meaning of Immortality in Human Experience* New York: Harper 1957

Hocking, William *Thoughts on Death* New York: Harper 1937

Hoffman, Francis "Grace, Violence, and Self" *Virginia Quarterly Review* 34 (1958) 439-54

Hoffman, Francis and M. Brody "The Symptom: Fear of Death" *Psychoanalytic Review* 44 (1957) 433-438

Hoffman, Fredrick "Theodore Roethke: The Poetic Shape of Death" *Theodore Roethke: Essays on the Poetry* A. Stein, ed. 1966 94-114

Hoffman, F. "Philosophy and Immortality" *Journal of Philosophy* 12 (1915) 409-416

Hohenschuh, W. *The Modern Funeral* Chicago: Trade Periodical Co 1900

Holbein, Hans *The Dance of Death* London: Phaidon Press 1947

Holbein, Hans *Les simulachres & histoires faces de la mort* Lyons 1538

Holden, Douglas *Death Shall Have No Dominion: A New Testament Study* St. Louis: Bethany Press 1971

Holland, J. et al. "Psychological Response to the Death of an Identical Twin by the Surviving Twin With the Same Disease"*Omega* 2 (3) (1971) 160-167

Holland, R. "Suicide"*Moral Problems* J. Rachels, ed. New York: Harper Row 1971

Hopkins, Edward "The Fountain of Youth" *Journal of American Oriental Society* 26 (1905) 1-67

Horst, O. "The Spector of Death in a Guatemalan Highland Community" *Geographical Review* 57 (1967) 151-67

Howard, Alan and R. Scott "Cultural Values and Attitudes Toward Death" *Journal of Existentialism* 6 (22) (1956-66) 161-71

Howard, Joseph "Fear of death" *Journal of the Indiana State Medical Association* 54 (12) (1961) 1773-1779

Howes, Elizabeth, ed *And a Time to Die* London: Routledge 1961

Huber, J. *Chaucer's Concept of Death in the Canterbury Tales* PhD diss. University of Pittsburgh 1967

Hufeland, Christopher *The Art of Prolonging Life* 2 vols. London 1796 (1905)

Hug-Hellmuth "The Child's Concept of Death" *Psychoanalytic Quarterly* 34 (1965) 499ff

Hughs, A. "The Triumph of Life" *Keats, Shelly Memorial Bulletin* 16 (1965) 12-20

Huizinga, J. *The Waning of the Middle Ages* London: Arnold 1952

Humphreys, M. *The Problem of Death in the Life and Works of John Donne* PhD diss. Cornell Univ. 1948

Hunsinger, George *Kierkegaard, Heidegger, and the Concept of Death* Stanford; Leland Stanford Jr. University 1969

Hunt, Leigh "Deaths of little children" *The Great English Essayists* C. & W. Dawson, eds New York: Harper 1909 pp. 64-69

Hunt, Vincent "Facing Death with the Patient — An Ongoing Contract" (tape cassette, 31 min) Minneapolis, Minn: Center for Death Education and Research 1971

Hutschnecker, Arnold "Personality Factors in Dying Patients" *The Meaning of Death* H. Feifel pp. 237-250

Huttler, M. *Ars Moriendi* Augsburg 1878

Huxley, Aldous *After Many a Summer Dies the Swan* New York: Harper 1939

Huxley, Laura *This Timeless Moment: A Personal View of Aldous Huxley* New York: Farrar 1968

Hyman, George "Medical Care During Bereavement" *Death and Bereavement* A. Kutscher pp. 295-96

Inge, W. "Death the Fulfillment of Life" *Chautauquan* 62 (April 1911) 254-60

Ingham, M. *Some Fifteenth-Century Images of Death and Their Background* PhD diss. University of California-Riverside 1967

Irion, Paul *Cremation* Philadelphia: Fortress Press 1968

Irion, Paul *A Handbook for the Humanist Funeral* (1971-1972)

Irion, Paul *The Funeral — An Experience of Value* Milwaukee, Wis.: National Funeral Directors Association 1956

Irion, Paul "The Funeral and the Integrity of the Church" *Pastoral Psychology* 14 (1963) 25-32

Irion, Paul *The Funeral and the Mourners* Nashville: Abingdon Press 1954

Irion, Paul *The Funeral — Vestige or Value* Nashville: Abingdon Press 1966

Isaacs, Bernard et al. "The Concept of Pre-Death" *The Lancet* (May 19, 1971) 1115-18

Jacks, L. "Challenge of Death" *Atlantic Monthly* 134 (Dec. 1924) 721-7

Jackson, Edgar "Attitudes Toward Death in Our Culture" *Death and Bereavement* A. Kutscher pp. 212-18

Jackson, Edgar *For the Living* Iowa: Channel Press 1963

Jackson, Edgar *Telling a Child About Death* Iowa: Channel Press 1965

Jackson, Edgar "The theological psychological and philosophical dimensions of death in protestantism" *Explaining Death to Children* E. Grollman, ed. pp. 171-95

Jackson, Edgar *The Christian Funeral* New York: Channel 1966

Jackson, Edgar "Grief and Religion" *The Meaning of Death* H. Feifel, ed. pp. 218-236

Jackson, Percival *The Law of Cadavers* New York: Prentice Hall 1950

Jacobs, Josef "The Dying of Death" *Fortnightly Review* (London) 1899

Jacobs, Paul "The Most Cheerful Graveyard in the World" *The Reporter* 19 (Sept. 1958)

540

Jacobson, David "Death" *Universal Jewish Encyclopedia* Vol. 3 New York 1943
Jacques, Elliot "Death and the Mid-Life Crisis" *International Journal of Psychoanalysis* 46 (1965) 506-12
Jaffe, Aniela *Apparitions and Precognitions* New York: University Books 1963
James, William *Human Immortality* Boston 1899 (Also in *Will to Believe*)
Jankelevitch, Vladimir *La mort* Paris: Flammarion 1966
Jeffers, Francis, et al. "Attitudes of Older Persons Toward Death" *Journal of Gerontology* 16 (1961) 53-56
Jelliffe, Smith "The Death Instinct in Somatic and Psychopathology" *Psychoanalytic Review* 20 (1933) 121-131
Jelliffe, Smith Review of the article, "Thanatophobia and Immortality" by G. Hall *Journal of Nervous and Mental Disorders* 45 (1917) 272-276
Jewish Funeral Director (Journal)
Johnstone, Henry "The Experience of Death and the Death of Experience" *The Problem of the Self* Penn. St. U. Press (1970) 93-102
Jonas, Hans "Life, Death and the Body in the Theory of Being" *Review of Metaphysics* 19 (1) (1965) 3-23
Jonas, Hans *The Phenomenon of Life* New York: Dell 1966
Jonas, Hans "Philosophical Reflections on Experimenting with Human Subjects" *Experimentation With Human Subjects* P. Freund, ed. New York: Braziller 1969
Jones, Ernest "On 'Dying Together' and an Unusual Case of 'Dying Together' " *Death: Interpretations* H. Ruitenbeek, ed., pp. 50-60
Jones, J. "Premonition of death" *British Medical Journal* 2 (1958) 1051
Jones, W. *Metaphysics of Life and Death* New York: Doran 1924
Journal of Cryobiology
Journal of Geriatric Psychiatry
Journal of Thanatology
Joyce, James "The Dead" *Dubliners* New York: Viking 1968 (Also funeral scene in *Ulysses*)
Jung, Carl *The Integration of the Personality* New York: Farrar 1939
Jung, Carl "The Soul and Death" *The Meaning of Death* H. Feifel, ed. 3-15
Juvenal *Satires* J. Mazzaro, trans., U. of Mich. 1965 (10th satire)
Kafka, Franz "A Hunger Artist" *The Penal Colony, Stories and Short Pieces* W. & E. Muir, trans., New York: Schocken 1949 (Also other stories)
Kaines, Joseph *Last Words of Eminent Persons* New York: Routledge 1966
Kalish, Richard "The Aged and the Dying Process: The Inevitable Decisions" *J. Soc. Issues* 21 (4) (1965) 87-96
Kalish, Richard "A Continuum of Subjectively Perceived Death" *Gerontologist* 6 (1966) 73-76
Kalish, Richard "The Effects of Death upon the Family" *Death and Dying* L. Pearson (1969) 79-107
Kalish, Richard *Death and Dying: A Briefly Annotated Bibliography* New York: Russell Sage Foundation 1970
Kalish, Richard "Experiences of Persons Reprieved from Death" *Death and Bereavement* A. Kutscher pp. 84-98
Kalish, Richard "Grief and Bereavement: A Selected Annotated Bibliography of Behavioral Science and Psychiatric Writings" *Death and Bereavement* A. Kutscher pp. 343-58
Kalish, Richard "Social Distance and the Dying" *Community Mental Health Journal* 2 (2) (1966) 252-55
Kalish, Richard "Some Variables in Death Attitudes" *Death and Identity* Robert Fulton pp. 170-80 *Social Psychology* 59 (1) (1963) 137-145
Kalish, Richard et al. *Death and Bereavement: An Annotated Social Science Bibliography* Los Angeles: California State College 1965
Kallan, H. "Perspective of Death" *Dial* 66 (April 19, 1919) 415-16
Kallen, Horace "Philosophy, Aging and the Aged" *Journal of Value Inquiry* 23 (May, June 1972)
Kane, John "The Irish Wake: A Sociological Analysis" *Sociological Symposium* 1 (1968) 11-16
Kapleau, Philip ed. *The Wheel of Death* New York: Harper & Row 1971
Kasper, August "The Doctor and Death" *The Meaning of Death* H. Feifel pp. 259-270
Kass, Leon "Death as an Event: A Commentary on Robert Morison" *Science* 173

(1971) 698-703

Kass, Leon "Problems in the Meaning of Death" *Science* 170 (Dec. 11, 1970) 1235-1236

Kass, Leon and E. Cassell (co-chairmen of Task Force on Death and Dying) "Program in the Ethical, Social and Legal Issues of Death and Dying" Hastings-on-Hudson, New York: Institute of Society, Ethics and the Life Sciences ca. 1970

Kastenbaum, Robert "Cognitive and Personal Futurity in Later Life" *Journal of Individual Psychology* 19 (1963) 216-22

Kastenbaum, Robert ed. *Contributions to the psycho-biology of aging* New York: Springer 1965

Kastenbaum, Robert "Death and Bereavement in Later Life" *Death and Bereavement* A. Kutscher pp. 28-54

Kastenbaum, Robert "Death as a Research Problem in Social Gerontology: An Overview" *Gerontologist* 6 (1966) 67-79, 125

Kastenbaum, Robert ed. *New Thoughts on Old Age* New York: Springer 1964

Kastenbaum, Robert "Psychological Death" *Death and Dying* L. Pearson (1969) 1-27

Kastenbaum, Robert "The child's understanding of death: how does it develop?" *Explaining Death to Children* E. Grollman pp. 89-108

Kastenbaum, Robert "Time and Death in Adolescence" *The Meaning of Death* H. Feifel pp. 99-113

Kastenbaum, Robert and R. Aisenberg *The Psychology of Death* New York: Springer 1972

Kastenbaum, Robert and C. Goldsmith "The Funeral Director and the Meaning of Death" *American Funeral Director* 86 (1963) April 35-37, May 47-48, June 45-46

Kaufman, Walter "Existentialism and Death" *The Meaning of Death* H. Feifel pp. 39-63

Kaye, Nancy "Fighting Fancy Funerals" *Medical Economics* (Jan. 29, 1962)

Keck, Leander "New Testament Views of Death" *Perspectives on Death* L. Mills pp. 33-98

Keeler, W. "Children's Reaction to the Death of a Parent" *Depression* P. Hoch & J. Zubin, eds. New York: Grune and Stratton 1954 pp. 109-20

Kellock, Katherine "Shopping for a Funeral" *Consumers Research Bulletin* April 1935

Kelly, William "Cocopa Attitudes and Practices with Respect to Death and Mourning" *Southwestern Journal of Anthropology* 5 (1949) 151-64

Kennard, E. "Hopi Reactions to Death" *American Anthropologist* 29 (1937) 491-94

Kephart, William "Status after Death" *American Sociological Review* 15 (Oct. 1950) 635-63

Kettlewell, John *Death Made Comfortable; or The Way to Die Well* London 1718

Kevorkian, J. "The Eye of Death" *Clinical Symposia* 13 (1961) 51-62

Keyes, E. "The Fear of Death" *Harper's Magazine* 99 (1909) 208-12

Kierkegaard, Soren *The Concept of Dread* W. Lowrie, trans. Princeton University Press 1968

Kierkegaard, Soren *Fear and Trembling: The Sickness unto Death* W. Lowrie, trans. Princeton University Press 1941

Killinger, John "Death and Transcendence in Contemporary Literature" *Perspectives on Death* L. Mills pp. 137-67

King, C. "Death as Depicted in Ancient Art" *The Gnostics and Their Remains* London 1887

Klaber, F. *When Children Ask About Death* New York: Society for Ethical Culture 1950

Klein, Donald and R. Blank "Psychopharmacological Treatment of Bereavement and its Complications" *Death and Bereavement* A. Kutscher pp. 299-308

Klein, Melaine "Mourning and Its Relation to Manic-Depressive States" *Death: Interpretations* H. Ruitenbeek pp. 237-67

Klemm, Frederick "The Death Problem in the Life and Works of Gerhart Hauptmann" PhD diss. Univ. of Penn. 1939

Kliman, Gilbert "The Child Faces His Own Death" *Death and Bereavement* A. Kutscher pp. 20-27

Klingensmith, S. "Child animism: what the child means by "alive" *Child Development* 24 (1) (1953) 51-61

Klopfer, W. "Attitudes Toward Death in the Aged" M.A. thesis, City College of New York

542

Kluckhohn, C. "Conceptions of Death Among the Southwestern Indians" *Culture and Behavior* New York: Free Press 1962 Chapt. 8

Knight, James and F. Herter "Anticipatory Grief" *Death and Bereavement* A. Kutscher pp. 196-201

Knight, James "Philosophic implications of terminal illness" *North Carolina Medical Journal* 22 (10) (1961) 493-95

Knower, Eve "Death Control" *Humanist* 8 (1935-1936) 139-42

Koestenbaum, Peter *The Vitality of Death* Westport, Conn: Greenwood 1971

Koller, Kathrine "Falstaff and the Art of Dying" *Modern Language Notes* 60 (1945) 383-86

Kramer, Heinrich and J. Sprenger *The Malleus Maleficarum* M. Summers, trans, New York: Dover 1971

Krant, Melvin "The Dying Patient — Medicine's Responsibility" *Journal of Thanatology* 1 (1971) 1-24

Krant, Melvin "The Physician of the Dying Patient" *Prism* 1973

Krant, Melvin "The Organized Care of the Dying Patient" *Hospital Practice* (Jan. 1972) 101-108

Krant, M. and E. Payne "Psychosocial Aspects of Advanced Cancer" *Journal of the American Medical Assoc.* 210 (Nov. 1969) 1238-1242

Krause, Anna *Jorge Manrique and the Cult of Death in the Cuatrocientos* Berkeley: U. of California Press 1937

Kreis, Bernadine and A. Pattie *Up From Grief* New York: Seabury Press 1969

Krieger, Wilber *Complete Guide to Funeral Service Management* New Jersey: Prentice Hall 1962

Krieger, Wilber *Successful Funeral Service Management* New Jersey: Prentice-Hall 1951

Kroeber, A. "Disposal of the Dead" *American Anthropologist* 29 (1927) 308-15

Kubler-Ross, Elisabeth "Dying: The Patient's Reaction, Language, Hopes" Paper read at AAAS, National Academy of Sciences Symposium on "Problems in the Meaning of Death" 1970

Kubler-Ross, Elisabeth *On Death and Dying* New York: Macmillan 1969

Kubler-Ross "The Searching Mind" *Today's Education* 61 (1972) 30-32

Kubler-Ross "Stages of Dying" (tape cassette, 32 min.) Minneapolis, Minnesota: Center For Death Education and Research 1971

Kurtz, Benjamin *The Pursuit of Death: A Study of Shelley's Poetry* New York: Octagon Books 1970

Kurtz, Benjamin "The Relation of Occleve's 'Learne to Dye' to Its Source"*PMLA* 40 (1925) 252-75

Kurtz, Leonard *The Dance of Death and the Macabre Spirit in European Literature* New York 1934

Kutscher, Austin ed., *Bereavement and Allied Fields* (An Annual) Articles from Archives of Foundation of Thanatology I, 1971, II, 1972

Kutscher, Austin *But Not to Lose: A Book of Comfort for Those Bereaved* New York: Frederick Fell 1969

Kutscher, Austin *Death and Bereavement* Illinois: Thomas 1969

Kutscher, Austin and A. Kutscher, Jr. *A Bibliography of Books on Death, Bereavement, Loss and Grief 1935-1968* New York: Health Sciences

Kutscher, Austin and L. Kutscher, eds. *Religion and Bereavement* New York: Health Sciences 1972

Kutscher, Heinemann et al., eds. *Emotional Care of the Cancer Patient* New York: Health Sciences 1973

Kutscher, Schoenberg et al., eds. *Loss and Grief* New York: Health Sciences

Labby, Daniel ed. *Life or Death: Ethics and Options* Seattle: Univ. of Washington Press 1968

Lake, Kirsopp *Immortality and the Modern Mind* Cambridge, Mass: Harvard Univ. Press 1922

Lamm, Maurice *Jewish Way of Death* New York: Jonathan David 1968

Lamont, Corliss "The Crisis Called Death" *Humanist* 27 (1967) 19-20

Lamont, Corliss *The Illusion of Immortality* New York: Ungar (1935) 1965

Lamont, Corliss ed. *Man Answers Death* (Poems on death) New York: Books for Libraries 1952

Lamont, Corliss "Mistaken Attitudes Towards Death" *Journal of Philosophy* 62 (2) (1965) 29-36

Landsberg, P. *The Experience of Death and the Moral Problem of Suicide* London: Barrie & Jenkins 1963

Laney, James "Ethics and Death" *Perspectives on Death* L. Mills pp. 231-52

Lange, J. "Modes of dying" *Pittsburgh Medical Review* 3 (1889) 27-34

Langer, William "The Black Death" *Scientific American* 210 (Feb. 1964) 114-118

Langlois, E. *Essai historique, philosophique, et pittoresque sur les danses des morts* 2 vols. Rouen 1852

Langston, Beach "Essex and the Art of Dying" *The Huntington Library Quarterly* 13 (Feb. 1950) 109-129

Lansing, Albert, ed. *Problems of Aging* Baltimore: Williams and Wilkins 1952

Larmand, Leon *Les Poetes de la Mort* Paris: L. Michaud 1910

Lasagna, Louis "A Person's Right to Die" *Confrontations of Death* F. Scott & R. Brewer pp. 109-110

Leake, C. "The care of dying older persons" *Geriatrics* 22 (Sept. 1967) 91-2

Le Comte, Edward *Dictionary of Last Words* New York: Philosophical Library 1955

Lee, Reuel *Burial Customs, Ancient and Modern* Minnesota: Arya 1929

Lehrman, Samuel "Reactions to Untimely Death" *Death: Interpretations* H. Ruitenbeek pp. 222-236

Lepp, Ignace *Death and Its Mysteries* B. Murchland, trans. New York: Macmillan 1968

Le Shan, Lawrence "Human Survival of Biological Death" *Main Currents* 26 (1969) 35-45

Le Shan, Lawrence "Psychotherapy and the Dying Patient" *Death and Dying* L. Pearson 1969 28-48

Le Shan, Lawrence and Eda "Psychotherapy and the Patient with a Limited Life-Span" *Psychiatry* 24 (1961) 318-23

Lessing, Gotthold "How the Ancients Represented Death" *Selected Prose Works* London: Bell 1879

Lester, D. "Antecedents of the fear of the dead" *Psychological Reports* 19 (Dec. 1966) 741-2

Lester, D. "Checking on the harlequin" *Psychological Reports* 19 (Dec. 1966) 984

Lester, D. "The fear of death of those who have nightmares" *Journal of Psychology* 69 (July 1968) 245-7

Lester, D. "Inconsistency in the fear of death of individuals" *Psychological Reports* 20 (June 1967) Suppl. 1084

Lester, D. "Attitudes Toward Death Today and Thirty-five Years Ago" *Omega* 2 (3) (1971) 168-73

Lester, D. "Choice of Method for Suicide and Personality: A Study of Suicide Notes" *Omega* 2 (2) (1971) 76-80

Lester, D. "Experimental and Correlational Studies of the Fear of Death" *Psychological Bulletin* 67 (1967) 27-36

Lester, D. "Fear of Death of Suicidal Persons" *Psychological Reports* 20 (1966) 1077 ff

Lester, D. "Religious Behavior and the Fear of Death" *Omega* 1 (3) (1970) 181-88

Lester, D. "The Concept of an Appropriate Death" *Psychology* 7 (4) (1970) 61-66

Lester, G. and D. Lester "The Fear of Death, the Fear of Dying, and Threshold Differences for Death Words and Neutral Words" *Omega* 1 (3) (1970) 175-79

Lester, Peter "Suicide as a Positive Act" *Psychology* 6 (3) (1969) 43-48

LeTourneau, Charles "A soliloquy on death" *Hospital Management* 96 (Nov. 1963) 58-60

Levin, A. "The Fiction of the Death Instinct" *Psychiatric Quarterly* 25 (1951) 257-81

Levin, Revella "Truth versus illusion in relation to death" *Psychoanalytic Review* 51 (Summer 1964) 190-200

Levin, Sidney and R. Kahana *Psychodynamic Studies on Aging, Creativity, Reminiscing and Dying* New York: International Universities Press 1967

Levinson, Boris M. And J. Kinney "The Pet and Bereavement" *Death and Bereavement* A. Kutscher 1969 270-76

Leviton, A. "Time, Death and the Ego-Chill" *Journal of Existentialism* 6 (21) (1965) 68-80

Leviton, D. "The Role of the Schools in Death Education" (tape cassette, 27 min.) Minneapolis, Minnesota: Center for Death Education and Research 1970

Leviton, D. "The need for education on death and suicide" *Journal of School Health* 39 (Apr. 1969) 270-4

Lewis, W. "A time to die" *Nursing Forum* 4 (1965) 7-26

Lieberman, M. "Observations on Death and Dying" *Gerontologist* 6 (1966) 70-72

Lieberman, M. "Psychological correlates of impending death" *Journal of Gerontology* 20 (April 1965) 181-90

"Life and Death, A Discursive Dialogue" *Fortune* 98 (1912) 698-708

"Life and Death" *Great Books (Britannica)* Syntopicon pp. 1013-1034 Includes detailed topical index and bibliography

Life Threatening Behavior (Journal)

Lifton, Robert *Boundaries* New York: Random House 1969

Lifton, Robert *Death in Life; survivors of Hiroshima* New York: Random House 1967

Lifton, Robert "Psychological Effects of the Atomic Bomb in Hiroshima: The Death Theme" *Daedalus* 92 (1963) 462-497

Light, James "The Religion of Death in 'A Farewell to Arms' " *Modern Fiction Studies* 7 (1961) 169-73

Likely, Wadsworth "Cancer and the emotions" *Science News Letter* (July 13, 1953) 366-68

Lindemann, Erich "Grief" *Encyclopedia of Mental Health* A. Deutsch, ed. New York: Franklin Watts 2 (1963) 703-6

Lindemann, Erich "Symptomatology and Management of Acute Grief" *American Journal of Psychiatry* 101 (1944) 141-148

Lipman, A. et al. "Preparation for death in old age" *Journal of Gerontology* 21 (July, 1966) 426-31

Lipson, Channing "Denial and Mourning" *Death: Interpretations* H. Ruitenbeek pp. 268-75

Little, J. *Law of Burial* 1902

Litvack, Stuart "Facing the Fear of Death" *Rational Living* 2 (1967) 20-21

Liveritte, Rudy "Some Thoughts on Death Anxiety" *ETC* 28 (1) (1971) 21-37

Lockyer, Herbert *Last Words of Saints and Sinners* Kregel 1969

Lodge, Sir Oliver *The Survival of Man* New York: Moffat 1909 Sect. 4

Lofland, John *Doomsday Cult* New Jersey: Prentice-Hall 1966

Lovatelli, Caetani *Thanatos* Rome 1888

Love, Elizabeth "Do all hands help ease the sting of death by tact and kindliness" *Hospitals* 18 (Dec. 1944) 47-48

Loveland "The Effects of Bereavement on Certain Religious Attitudes and Behavior" *Sociological Symposium* 1 (1968) 17-27

Lowry, Richard "Male-Female Differences in Attitudes Toward Death" PhD diss. Brandeis Univ. 1965

Lukic, Miodrag "Socrates and Indifference Towards Death" *Southern Journal of Philosophy* 9 (4) (1971)

Lupsets, Thomas *Treatise of Dieying Well* 1529

Lyons, Kristin "Death and the student nurse" *Tomorrow's Nurse* 4 (1963) 21-22

MacDonald, Arthur "Death-psychology of historical personages" *American Journal of Psychology* 33 (1921) 552-56

MacDonald, Arthur "Human death" *Medical Times* 56 (9) (1928) 232-41

MacDonald, Arthur "Human death" *Medical Times* (Aug. 1928) 206-16

MacDonald, Arthur "Systematic and scientific study of death in man" *American Journal of Psychology* 38 (1927) 153

MacGregor, Geddes "Death and Future Life" *Philosophical Issues in Religious Thought* New York: Houghton Mifflin 1973

MacKenna, Robert *The Adventure of Death* New York: Putnam 1917

MacKinnon, D. "Death" *New Essays in Philosophical Theology* A. Flew, and A. MacIntyre, eds. New York: Macmillan 1964

MacMullan, K. *Imagery of Death in Shakespeare's Plays* PhD diss. Bryn Mawr College 1960

Macphail, Andrew *Book of Sorrow* Oxford University Press 1916

Maddison, D. "The nurse and dying patient" *Nursing Times* 65 (Feb. 27, 1969) 265-66

Maeterlinck, Maurice *Death* T. Mattos, trans. New York: Dodd 1912

Maeterlinck, Maurice *Our Eternity* T. Mattos trans. (Extension on Essay on Death) London: Methuen 1913

Mahler, Margaret "Helping Children to Accept Death" *Child Study* 27 (1950) 98-99, 119-120

Malinowski, Bronislaw *Magic, Science and Religion and Other Essays* New York: Doubleday 1948

Malleus Maleficarum (See H. Kramer)

Mandelbaum, David "Social Uses of Funeral Rites" *The Meaning of Death* H. Feifel pp. 189-217

Marcel, Gabriel "My Death" *Tragic Wisdom and Beyond* S. Jolin, P. McCormick, trans. Northwestern Univ. Press 1973

Marcuse, Herbert "The Ideology of Death" *The Meaning of Death* H. Feifel pp. 64-78

Margolius, Sidney "Funeral Costs and Death Benefits" Public Affairs Pamphlet, no. 409, 1967

Marostica, Julia "The Role and Responsibility of the Nurse in Caring for the Dying Patient" M.A. thesis, Univ. of Utah 1965

Marriott-Watson, H. "Some thoughts on pain and death" *North American Review* 173 (1901) 540-53

Marshall, J. and V. Marshall "The Treatment of Death in Children's Books" *Omega* 2 (1) (1971) 36-45

Martin, D. and L. Wrightsman "The relationship between religious behavior and concern about death" *Journal of Social Psychology* 65 (April 1965) 317-23

Martin, D. and L. Wrightsman "Religion and fears about death: a critical review of research" *Religious Education* 59 (2) (1964) 174-76

Martin, Edward *Psychology of Funeral Service* Colorado: Sentinel Press 1962

Martin-Achard, Robert *From Death to Life* J. Smith, trans. Edinburgh: Oliver & Boyd 1960

Marvin, Frederic *The Last Words of Distinguished Men and Women* New York 1902

Maurer, Adah "The Game of Peek a Boo" *Diseases of the Nervous System* 28 (1967) 118-21

Maurer, Adah "Adolescent Attitudes Toward Death" *Journal of Genetics and Psychology* 105 (1964) 75-90

Maurer, Adah "Maturation of Concepts of Death" *British Journal of Medicine and Psychology* 39 (1966) 35-41

Maurer, Adah "On Bugental's Critique of Koestenbaum's 'The Vitality of Death' " *Journal of Existentialism* 6 (22) (1965-6) 223-24

Maurer, Adah "The child's knowledge of nonexistence" *Journal of Existential Psychiatry* 2 (1961) 193-212

May, Rollo "The daemonic: love and death" *Psychology Today* 1 (9) (1968) 16-25

May, William "The Sacral Power of Death in Contemporary Experience" *Perspectives on Death* L. Mills pp. 168-96

May, William Paper read at AAAS, National Academy of Sciences Symposium on "Problems in the Meaning of Death" 1970

Mayer, J. Sheridan *Restorative Art* Graphic Arts Press 1961

McCullen, J. Jr. "Ancient Rites for the Dead and Hawthorne's 'Roger Malvin's Burial' " *Southern Folklore Quarterly* 30 (1966) 313-22

McDonald, Arthur "Death Psychology of Historical Personages" *American Journal of Psychology* 33 (1921) 552-56

McGrady, Patrick *The Youth Doctors* New York: Ace Books 1969

McGrady, Patrick "The Youth Pill" *Ladies' Home Journal* 88 (7) (July 1971) 72-74, 128-29

McKay, L. *The Problem of Death in the Viennese School as Represented by Schnitzler, Rilke, and Hofmannsthal* PhD diss. Stanford 1940

McKenna, William *The Adventure of Death* New York: Putnam's Sons 1917

Mead, M. et al. "The Right to Die" *Nursing Outlook* 2 (1968) 102-13

Means, Marie "Fears of one thousand college women" *Journal of Abnormal and Social Psychology* 31 (1936) 291-311

Medawar, P. "Old Age and Natural Death" *Modern Quarterly* 1 (30) (1945)

Meiss, M. *Painting in Florence and Siena After the Black Death* Princeton 1951

Mencken, H. "Euphemisms" *The American Language* New York: Knopf 1919

Meninger, E. "Death from Psychic Causes" *Bulletin of the Meninger Clinic* 12 (1948) 31-36

Menninger, Karl *Man Against Himself* Harcourt 1948

Mental Hygiene 53 (July 1969) (entire issue devoted to death, dying, suicide)

Merhof, Austin "Jackson's Nine Areas of Concern" *Death and Bereavement* A. Kutscher pp. 166-67

546

Merkeley, Donald *The Investigation of Death* Illinois: Thomas 1957

Mervyn, Frances "The Plight of Dying Patients in Hospitals" *American Journal of Nursing* 71 (10) (1971) 1989-1990

Metchnikoff, Elie *The Nature of Man, Studies in Optimistic Philosophy* P. Mitchell, ed. New York: Putnam's Sons 1905

Metchnikoff, Elie *The Prolongation of Life* New York: Putnam's Sons 1908

Metzger, Arnold "Freedom and Death" *Human Context* 4 (1972) 215-243

Metzger, Arnold "Perception, Recollection and Death" *Review of Metaphysics* 4 (1) (1950) 13-30

Metzger, Arnold "The Socratic Longing for Death" *Review of Metaphysics* 2 (2) (1948) 13-39

Meyer, Pamela and A. "Life and Death in Tana Toradja" *National Geographic* 141 (6) (1972) 793-815

Meyer-Baer, Kathi *Music of the Spheres and the Dance of Death: Studies in Music Iconology* New Jersey: Princeton U. Press 1970

Mid-Continent Mortician (Journal)

Milici, Pompeo "The involutional death reaction" *Psychiatric Quarterly* 24 (4) (1950) 775-781

Miller, Paul "Provenience of the Death Symbolism in Van Gogh's Cornscapes" *Psychoanalytic Review* 52 (1965) 60-66

Mills, Liston "Pastoral Care of the Dying and the Bereaved" *Perspectives on Death*

Mills, Liston *Perspectives on Death* Nashville, Tenn.: Abingdon 1969

Minot, Charles "The Problem of Aging, Growth and Death" *Popular Science Monthly* 71 (1907) 97-120, 193-216, 359-377, 455-473, 509-523

Mitchell, Marjorie *The Child's Attitude to Death* New York: Schocken Books 1967

Mitford, Jessica *The American Way of Death* New York: Fawcett 1963

Mitford, Jessica "Fashions in Funerals" *Confrontations of Death* F. Scott and R. Brewer, eds. pp. 124-129

Mitford, Jessica "Have the Undertakers Reformed?" *Atlantic Monthly* 215 (June 1965) 69-73

Mitford, Jessica (See Toynbee 1972)

"Jessica Mitford Doesn't Like 'The American Way of Death'" *American Funeral Director* (Sept. 1963) p. 44

Mitra, D. "Mourning Customs and Modern Life in Bengal" *American Journal of Sociology* 52 (1947) 309-11

Moellenhoff, F. "Ideas of Children About Death" *Bulletin of the Menninger Clinic* 3 (1939) 148-156

Mogride, George *The Churchyard Lyrist* London 1832

Moloney, James "Death as a Culture Mechanism" *The Magic Cloak* Wakefield, Mass.: Montrose Press 1949

Monsour, Karem "Asthma and the Fear of Death" *Psychoanalytic Quarterly* 29 (1960) 56-71

Montague, William *The Chances of Surviving Death* Harvard U. Press 1934

Montaigne, Michel de "To Philosophize Is to Learn How to Die" *Complete Essays* D. Frame, trans. Stanford U. Press 1958 Chapt. 20

Moore, George *Judaism* Cambridge: Harvard U. Press 1946

Moore, Virginia *Ho for Heaven! Man's Changing Attitude Toward Dying* New York: Dutton 1956

Moore, W. "Time – the Ultimate Scarcity" *American Behavioral Scientist* 6 (1963) 58-60

Moore, Wilbert and M. Tumin "Some social functions of ignorance" *American Sociological Review* 14 (Dec. 1949) 787-795

Morduch, A. *No Screen for the Dying* London: Regina Press 1964

More, Sir Thomas *The Four Last Things* D. O'Conner, ed. London 1935 (ca. 1522)

Moreno, J. "The Social Atom and Death" *Sociometry* 10 (1947) 80-84

Morgan, Ernest "The Bier Barons" *Sociological Symposium* 1 (1968) 28-35

Morgan, Ernest "A Humanist Approach to the Problems of Death" *Humanist* 26 (2) (1966) 52-54

Morgan, Ernest *A Manual of Simple Burial* Burnsville, North Carolina: Celo Press 1971

Morgan, R. "Note on the psychopathology of senility: senescent defense against threat of death." *Psychological Reports* 16 (Feb. 1965) 305-306

Morgenstern, Julian *Rites of Birth, Death, Marriage and Kindred Occasions Among the*

Semites Chicago: Quadrangle Books 1966

Morgenthau, H. "Death in the Nuclear Age" *Commentary* 32 (1961) 231-234

Morin, Edgar *L'Homme et la mort dans l'histoire* Paris: Correa 1951

Morison, Robert "Death: Process or Event" *Science* 173 (1971) 694-698

Moritz, A. and N. Zamcheck "Sudden and Unexpected Death of Young Soldiers" *Arch. Path.* 42 (1946) 479-94

Morris, Ramona *Men and Snakes* New York: McGraw-Hill 1965

"Mortality Statistics — Suicides" *World Health Statist. Report* World Health Organization 21 (1968) 365-445

Morticians of the Southwest (Journal)

Mortuary Management (Journal)

Mosley, Glenn "Acceptance" *Death and Bereavement* A. Kutscher, ed. pp. 234-235

Mosley, Glenn "Guilt" *Death and Bereavement* A. Kutscher, ed. pp. 210-211

Moss, L. and D. Hamilton "The Psychotherapy of the Suicidal Patient" *American Journal of Psychiatry* 112 (1956) 814-820

Mothersill, Mary "Death" *Moral Problems* James Rachels, ed. New York: Harper Row 1971

Munk, William *Euthanasia, or Mental Treatment in Aid of Easy Death* London: Longmans, Green and Co. 1887

Murgoci, A. "Customs Connected with Death and Burial Among the Rumanians" *Folk-Lore* 30 (1919) 89-102

Murphy, G. "Some part of me will cheat the goddess of death" *Nursing Times* 61 (May 1965) 720

Murphy, Gardner "Difficulties Confronting the Survival Hypothesis" *Journal of American Society for Psychical Research* 39 (2) (1945) 67-94

Murphy, Gardner "Discussion" *The Meaning of Death* H. Feifel, ed. 1959 pp. 317-341

Murphy, Gardner "Meaning of Death" *Time* 75 (Jan. 1960) 52-4

Murphy, Gardner "An Outline of Survival Evidence" *Journal of American Society for Psychical Research* 39 (1) (1945)

Murphy, Gardner "Scientific Approaches to the Study of Survival" *Death and Bereavement* A. Kutscher, ed. pp. 139-145

Murray, Malcolm "The Geography of Death in England and Wales" *Annals of the Association of American Geographers* 52 (1962) 130-147

Murray, Malcolm "The Geography of Death in the U.S. and the U.K." *Annals of the Association of American Geographers* 57 (1967) 301-314

Musgrave, W. *The Theme of Death in the Essays of Montaigne* PhD diss. U. of Pennsylvania 1938

Myers, F. *Human Personality and Its Survival of Bodily Death* 2 vols. London: Longmans, Green 1954

Myers, James "Cooperative Funeral Associations" Cooperative League of the U.S.A. 1946

Myler, B. *Depression and Death in the Aged* PhD diss. Boston U. 1967

Nagel, Thomas "Death" *Moral Problems* J. Rachels, ed. New York: Harper Row 1971 Also in *Nous* 4 (1970) 73-80

Nagy, Maria *The Child and Death* Budapest 1936

Nagy, Maria "The Child's Theories Concerning Death" *Journal of Genetics and Psychology* 73 (1948) 3-27

Nagy, Maria "The Child's View of Death" *The Meaning of Death* H. Feifel, ed. pp. 79-98

Natanson, Maurice "Death and Situation" *American Imago* 4 (1959) 447-457

Natanson, Maurice "Humanism and Death" *Moral Problems in Contemporary Society* P. Kurtz, ed. Prentice Hall 1968

Nathanson, Sidney and W. Debald "References to Life and Death, Tribute and Money" *Death and Bereavement* A. Kutscher, ed. pp. 146-152

National Funeral Director and Embalmer (Official Publication of the National [Negro] Funeral Directors and Morticians Association)

National Funeral Service Journal

Natterson, Joseph and A. Knudson "Observations Concerning Fear of Death in Fatally Ill Children and Their Mothers" *Death and Identity* R. Fulton, ed. pp. 226-239

Needleman, Jacob "Death and the Plowman" *Death and Bereavement* A. Kutscher, ed. pp. 99-128

Needleman, Jacob "Imagining Absence, Non-Existence, and Death" *Review of*

Existential Psychol. Psychiatry 6 (3) (1966) 230-236

Needleman, Jacob "The Moment of Grief" *Confrontations of Death* F. Scott and R. Brewer, eds. 1971 pp. 47-52. Also *Death and Bereavement* A. Kutscher, ed. pp. 129-138

Nelson, Robert *We Froze the First Man* New York: Dell Pub. Co. 1968

Nettler, Gwynn "Review Essay: On Death and Dying" *Social Problems* 14 (1967) 335-44

Neugarten, Bernice *Middle Age and Aging* Chicago: U. of Chicago 1968

Newton, Berry "A Preface to the Death Fantasy. A Sequence of 'Judgement Day' " *Tri-Quarterly* 2 (1964) 124-138

Nielsen, Kai "Wittgenstein's Fideism" *Philosophy* 42 (1967) 191-210

Nietzsche, F. "On Free Death," "Twilight of the Idols" *The Portable Nietzsche* W. Kaufmann, ed. New York: Viking 1954

Nighswonger, Carl "Religious Faith and Death Implications in Work With the Dying Patient and Family" Center for Death Education and Research Minneapolis, Minn. 1971 (tape cassette 32 min)

Nohl, Johannes *The Black Death* C. Clarke, trans. London: Allen and Unwin 1926

Noon, J. "A Preliminary Examination of the Death Concepts of the Ibo" *American Anthropologist* 44 (1942) 638-54

Nora, Fred "Memorial Associations" Cooperative League of the U.S.A. 1962

Northeast Funeral Director (Journal)

Norton, Janice "Treatment of a Dying Patient" *Death: Interpretations* H. Ruitenbeek, ed. pp. 19-38

Nossen, Robert "A Critical Study of the *Holy Dying* of Jeremy Taylor" PhD diss. Evanston 1951

Oatfield, Harold *Literature of the Chemical Periphery — Embalming* American Chemical Society, number 16 1956

Obridki, Antonin "Gallows Humor — A Sociological Phenomenon" *American Journal of Sociology* 47 (1942) 709-16

Ochs, Robert *The Death in Every Now* New York: Sheed and Ward 1969

O'Connell, Walter "Humor and Death" *Psychological Reports* 22 (2) (1968) 391-402

O'Connor, M. *The Art of Dying Well: the Development of the Ars Moriendi* PhD diss. Columbia U. 1943. Also New York: AMS Press 1966

Odessky, Marjory " 'Sooner or Later Delicate Death' " *Journal of Historical Studies* 1 (1968) 355-359

Ohara, K. and D. Reynolds "Love-Pact Suicide" *Omega* 1 (3) (1970) 159-166

"Older Persons Look at Death" *Geriatrics* 11 (1956) 127-130

Oldfield, Josiah *The Mystery of Death* New York: Rider 1951

Olney, James "Experience, Metaphor, and Meaning: *The Death of Ivan Ilych*" *Journal of Aesthetics and Art Criticism* 31 (1972) 101-113

Olson, Robert "Death" *Encyclopedia of Philosophy* vol. 2, pp. 307-309

O'Mahony, B. "Martin Heidegger's Existential of Death" *Philosophical Studies* (Ireland) 18 (1969) 58-75

Omega An International Journal for the Psychological Study of Dying, Death, Bereavement, Suicide and Other Lethal Behaviors

Opler, M. "The Lipan Apache Death Complex and Its Extensions" *Southwestern Journal of Anthropology* 1 (1945) 122-41

Opler, M. "Reactions to Death Among the Mescalero Apache" *Southwestern Journal of Anthropology* 2 (1946) 454-67

Opler, M. and W. Bittle "The Death Practices and Eschatology of the Kiowa Apache" *Southwestern Journal of Anthropology* 17 (1961) 383-94

Orlansky, Harold "Reactions to the Death of President Roosevelt" *Journal of Social Psychology* 26 (1947) 235-266

Osborne, Ernest "When You Lose a Loved One" *Public Affairs Pamphlet* (269) revised 1972

O'Shaughnessy, Thomas *Muhammad's Thoughts on Death* Leiden: E. Brill 1969

Osis, Karlis *Deathbed Observations by Doctors and Nurses* New York: Parapsychology Foundation Mono. No. 3 (1961) 113 pp.

Ostow, M. "The Death Instinct — A Contribution to the Study of Instincts" *International Journal of Psychoanalysis* 39 (1958) 5-16

Owsley, Ron "The Attitude toward Death in Shakespeare, Webster, and Dekker" PhD diss. New York 1920

Owst, G. *Preaching in Mediaeval England* Cambridge: 1926

Pandey, C. "The Need for the Psychological Study of Clinical Death" *Omega* 2 (1) (1971) 1-9

Panofsky, Erwin *Tomb Sculpture* New York: H. Abrams 1964

Papageorgis, D. "On the ambivalence of death: the care of the nursing harlequin" *Psychological Reports* 19 (Aug. 1966) 325-6

Park, R. "Thanatology: A Questionnaire and a Plea for a Neglected Study" *Journal of the American Medical Assoc.* 58 (1912) 1243-46

Parkes, A. "Preservation of Tissue *in vitro* for the Study of Aging" *General Aspects of Aging* G. Wolstenholme and C. O'Connor, eds. Ciba Foundation Colloquia on Aging I, Boston pp. 162-169

Parkes, C. *Bereavement, Studies in Grief in Adult Life* London: Tavistock 1972

Parsons, Robert *Christian Directory: guiding men to their eternal salvation* Cork 1805

Parsons, Talcott "Death in American Society A Brief Working Paper" *American Behavioral Scientist* 6 (May 1963) 61-65

Pastoral Care of the Dying and Bereaved New York: Health Sciences

Paton, Lewis *Spiritism and the Cult of the Dead in Antiquity* New York: Macmillan 1921

Pattison, E. "Help in the Dying Process" *Voices: The Art and Science of Psychotherapy* 5 (1) (Spring/Summer 1969)

Pattison, E. "The Experience of Dying" *American Journal of Psychotherapy* 21 (1967) 32-43

Paul, Norman "Psychiatry: Its Role in the Resolution of Grief" *Death and Bereavement* A. Kutscher, ed. pp. 174-195

Paz, Octavio "The Day of the Dead" *Labyrinth of Solitude: Life and Thought in Mexico* L. Kemp, trans. New York: Grove Press (1961) 47-64

Peale, Norman "Beyond Death There Is Life" *Reader's Digest* 71 (Apr. 1963) 103-106

Peale, Norman "There Is No Death" *Reader's Digest* 63 (Oct. 1953) 121-23

Pearl, Raymond *The Biology of Death* Philadelphia: Lippincott 1922

Pearson, Karl *The Chances of Death and Other Studies in Evolution* London: Arnold 1897

Pearson, Leonard "Selected Bibliography on Death and Dying" *Death and Dying* L. Pearson, ed. pp. 133-235

Pecheux, Mary *Aspects of the Treatment of Death in Middle English Poetry* Catholic U. of Amer. Press 1951

Peck, R. *The Development of the Concept of Death in Selected Male Children* PhD diss. (No. 66-9468) New York U. 1966

Perkins, William *Salve for a Sicke Man* London 1595

Perrin, George and I. Pierce "Psychosomatic aspects of cancer" *Psychosomatic Medicine* 21 (5) (1959) 397-421

Petrarch, Francesco *The Triumph of Death* (from Italian 1470)

Pfouts, Jane "Laughter as an element in the casework relationship" *Social Work* 6 (3) (1961) 43-50

Philip, A. "On the nature of death" *Royal Society of London Philosophical Transactions* 124 (1834) 167-198

Phillips, D. and V. Pine "The Cast of Dying: A Sociological Analysis of Funeral Expenditures" *Confrontations of Death* F. Scott and R. Brewer, eds. pp. 130-139

Phillips, D. *Death and Immortality* London: Macmillan 1970

Phillips, Robert "Death and Resurrection: Tradition in Thomas's 'After the Funeral' " *McNeese State College Review* 15 (1964) 3-10

"The Philosophical Aspects of Thanatology" Symposium May 1973. Foundation of Thanatology and Columbia U. College of Physicians and Surgeons

"Philosophical Problems of Death" (entire issue) *Monist* 59 (2) (April 1975)

Piaget, J. *The Child's Conception of the World* New York: Harcourt 1929

Pieper, Josef *Death and Immortality* New York: Herder and Herder 1969

Pine, V. "Comparative Funeral Practices" *Practical Anthropology* 16 (March-April 1969) 49-62

Pirandello, Luigi "The Man With A Flower in His Mouth" [one act play] *Pirandello's One Act Plays* W. Murray, trans. New York: Funk and Wagnalls 1964

Platonov, K. *The Word as a Physiological and Therapeutic Factor* Moscow: Foreign Lang. Pub. House 1959

Platt, Robert "Reflections of aging and death" *Lancet* 1 (Jan. 1963) 1-6

Playboy June 1960. Pictures and story of Mr. Eaton of Forest Lawn. Also see June 1964 article by Frederic Pohl

Playfair, Lyon "On the dread of death" *British Medical Journal* 1 (Mar. 1889) 489

Poe, Edgar *Collected Works* New York: Armstrong 1900 "The Masque of the Red Death" "The Narrative of A. Gordon Pym" etc.

Pohl, Frederic (See *Playboy*)

Polson, C. et al, eds. *The Disposal of the Dead* London: English U. Press 1962

Pomedli, Michael "Heidegger and Freud: The Power of Death" PhD diss. Duquesne U. 1972

Porter, W. "Some Sociological Notes on a Century of Change in the Funeral Business" *Sociological Symposium* 1 (1968) 36-46

Portz, A. "The Meaning of Death to Children" *Diss. Abstracts* 25, 7383-84

Portz, A. "The Psychological Meaning of Death: A Review of the Literature" California State College at Los Angeles. Mimeographed 1963

Portz, John "Allusions and Structure in Hemingway's 'A Natural History of the Dead'" *Tennessee Studies in Literature* 10 (1965) 27-41

Post, Emily *Etiquette* New York: Funk and Wagnalls (1923) 1948

Poteat, W. "I Will Die" *Religion and Understanding* D. Phillips, ed. Blackwell 1967

Potter, Van Rensselaer "Biocybernetics and Survival" *Zygon* 5 (3) (1970) 229-246

Pound, Louise "Euphemisms for Death and Dying" *American Speech* 11 (1936) 195-202

Powers, Thomas "Learning to Die" *Harpers* 240 (June 1970) 72-80

Pratt, J. "Epilegomena to the Study of Freudian Instinct Theory" *International Journal of Psychoanalysis* 39 (1958) 17-24

Prehoda, Robert *Extended Youth* New York: Putnam's 1968

Prichard, Elizabeth "The Social Service Worker Can Help" *Death and Bereavement* A. Kutscher, ed. pp. 249-256

Pringle-Pattison, Seth *The Idea of Immortality* New York: Oxford U. Press 1972

Professional Embalmer (Journal) (Published by Undertakers Supply Co.)

Pruit, Angela and P. Rice "On death" *Tomorrow's Nurse* 4 (Aug.-Sept. 1963) 17-18

Psychology Today 4 (3) (Aug. 1970) (Entire issue devoted to death and dying)

Puckle, B. *Funeral Customs* London: T. Laurie 1926

Quint, Jeanne *The Nurse and the Dying Patient* New York: Macmillan 1967

Raether, Howard "Comments on Ruth Mulvey Harmer's 'Funerals, Fantasy, and Flight'" *Omega* 2 (3) (1971) 154-158

Raether, Howard *Successful Funeral Service Practice* New Jersey: Prentice-Hall 1971

Rahner, Karl *On the Theology of Death* C. Henkey, trans. New York: Herder and Herder 1962 (2nd ed. 1965)

Ramsey, Paul (On Kübler-Ross paper) Paper read at AAAS, National Academy of Sciences Symposium on "Problems in the Meaning of Death" 1970

Ramsey, P. *Updating Life and Death* Boston: Beacon 1968

Randolph, Vance "Death and Burial" *Ozark Magic and Folklore* New York: Dover 1947

Rees, D. "Bereavement" *Death and Bereavement* A. Kutscher, ed. pp. 207-209

Reeves, Robert "To Tell or Not to Tell the Patient" *Death and Bereavement* A. Kutscher, ed. pp. 5-9

Reik, Theodor *Curiosities of the Self: Illusions We Have About Ourselves* New York: Farrar 1965

Reiss, Paul "Bereavement and the American Family" *Death and Bereavement* A. Kutscher, ed. pp. 219-224

Rezek, J. "Dying and Death" *Journal of Forensic Science* 8 (1963) 200-208

Rheingold, J. "The Mother Anxiety and Death: the Catastrophic Death Complex" Boston: Little, Brown 1967

Richardson, Bessie *Old Age Among the Ancient Greeks* Baltimore: Johns Hopkins Press 1933

Richmond, Velma *Laments for the Dead in Medieval Narrative* Pittsburgh: Duquesne U. Press 1966

Richter, Curt "On the Phenomenon of Sudden Death in Animals and Man" *Psychosomatic Medicine* 19 (1957) 191-198

Rilke, M. *The Notebooks of Malte Laurids Brigge* M. Herter, trans. New York: Norton 1949

Rioch, D., et al. "The Psychophysiology of Death" *The Physiology of Emotions* A. Simon, ed. Springfield, Ill.: Charles Thomas 1961 pp. 77-225

Rivers, W. "The Primitive Conception of Death" *Hibbert Journal* 10 (1911-1912) 393-407

Roberts, Donald "The Death Wish in John Donne" *PMLA* 62 (1947) 958-976

Robinson, William *God's Acre Beautiful* London: John Murray 1883

Robitscher, Jonas "The Right to Die" *Hastings Report* 2 (4) (1972) 11-14

Rosell, Alan "Lindemann's Pioneer Studies of Reactions to Grief" *Death and Bereavement* A. Kutscher, ed. pp. 163-165

Rosenfeld, H. *Der Mittelalterliche Totentanz* Münster-Köln: Bohlau 1954

Rosenthal, Hattie "The Fear of Death as an Indispensable Factor in Psychotherapy" *American Journal of Psychotherapy* 17 (1963) 619-630

Rosenthal, Hattie "Psychotherapy for the Dying" *American Journal of Psychotherapy* 2 (1957) 626-637

Ross, Roslyn "Separation Fear and the Fear of Death in Children" *Diss. Abstracts* 27, 8-B (1967) 2878-79

Rossi, Alice "Abortion Laws and Their Victims" *Trans-Action* 3 (1966) 7-12

Rothstein, D. *Aging Awareness and Personalization of Death in the Young and Middle Adult Years* PhD diss. U. of Chicago 1968

Rowlandson, Thomas *Rowlandson's Drawings for the English Dance of Death* (Illus.) San Marino, Calif.: Huntington Library 1966

Royce, Josiah *The Conception of Immortality* Boston: Houghton Mifflin 1900

Ruitenbeek, Hendrik *Death: Interpretations* New York: Dell 1969

Rush, Alfred *Death and Burial in Christian Antiquity* Wash. D.C.: The Catholic U. of America Press 1941

Russell, Bertrand *Why I Am Not A Christian* Paul Edwards, ed. New York: Simon and Schuster 1957

Russell, Bertrand "Your Child and the Fear of Death" *The Forum* 81 (1929) 174-178

Russell, D. *Children's Thinking* Boston: Ginn 1956

Ryle, J. "The Sense of Dying – a postscript" *Guy Hospital Reporter* 99 (1950) 204-9

Sabatier, Robert *Dictionnaire de la Mort* Paris: Editions Albin Michel 1967

Sachs, Hans "Beauty, Life and Death" *American Imago* I (1940) 81-133

Safier, G. "A Study in Relationships Between the Life and Death Concepts in Children" *Journal of Genetic Psychology* 105 (1964) 283-94

Sage, M. *Mrs. Piper and the Society for Psychical Research* New York: Scott-Thaw 1904

St. Johns, Adela *First Step Up Toward Heaven* New York: Prentice-Hall 1959

Salomone, Jerome "An Attitudinal Study of Funeral Customs in Calcasieu Parish, Louisiana: A Sociological Analysis" PhD diss. Louisiana State U. 1966

Salomone, Jerome "An Empirical Report on Some Controversial American Funeral Practices" *Sociological Symposium* 1 (Fall 1968) 47-56

Samuels, A. "Death as an Illumination of Life" *Voices: The Art and Science of Psychotherapy* 5 (1) (Spring/Summer 1969) 43-44

Sanchez-Camargo, Manuel *La Muerte y La Pintura Espanola* Madrid: Editora Nacional 1954

Santayana, George *Reason in Religion* New York: Macmillan 1962 esp. "A Future Life," "Ideal Immortality"

Sarbin, Theodore "Anxiety: Reification of a Metaphor" *Essays on Metaphor* W. Shibles, ed. Whitewater, Wisc.: Language Press 1972

Sartre, Jean-Paul "My Death" *Being and Nothingness* Hazel Barnes, trans. New York: Philosophical Library 1956 pp. 531-553

Sattler, Joseph *A Modern Dance of Death* Berlin: J. Stargardt 1894

Saul, L. "Reactions of a Man to Natural Death" *Psychoanalytic Quarterly* 28 (1959) 383-86

Saunders, Cicely "The Moment of Truth: Care of the Dying Person" *Confrontations of Death* F. Scott and R. Brewer, eds. pp. 111-122

Saurat, Denis *Death and the Dreamer* London: Westhouse 1946

Scheler, Max "Tod und Fortleben" (Death and Survival) *Schriften aus dem Nachlass* Berne: Franke V (1933) 397-413

Scher, Jordon "Death – The Giver of Life" *Death: Interpretations* H. Ruitenbeek, ed. pp. 96-105

Schiele, Burtrum "Management of Emotional Problems in Aging" *Diseases of the Nervous System* 28 (1967) 35-39

Schilder, Paul "The Attitude of Murderers Toward Death" *Journal of Abnormal and*

Social Psychology 31 (1936) 348-363

Schilder, Paul *Goals and Desires of Man* New York: Columbia U. Press 1942 esp. pp. 61-110

Schilder, Paul and D. Wechsler "The Attitudes of Children Towards Death" *Journal of Genetic Psychology* 45 (1934) 406-451

Schmale, A. "Relationship of Separation and Depression to Disease" *Psychosomatic Medicine* 20 (1958) 259 ff

Schneck, Jerome "Hypnoanalytic elucidation of hypnosis-death concept" *Psychiatric Quarterly* (Suppl.) 24 (1950) 286-89

Schneck, Jerome "Unconscious Relationship Between Hypnosis and Death" *Psychoanalytic Review* 38 (1951) 271-75

Schoenberg, Bernard, et al., eds. *Loss and Grief: Psychological Management in Medical Practice* New York: Columbia U. Press 1970

Schoenberg, Bernard "The Nurse's Education for Death" *Death and Bereavement* A. Kutscher, ed. pp. 55-74

Schopenhauer, Arthur "On Death and Its Relation to the Indestructibility of Our True Nature" *The World as Will and Representation* 2 vols E. Payne, trans. New York: Dover 1966

Schrank, J. "Death Guide to Books and Audio Visual Aids" *Media and Methods* 7 (Feb 1971) 32-54

Schreiber, W. *Der Todentanz* Leipzig 1900

Schrut, Samuel "Attitudes Toward Old Age and Death" *Death and Identity* R. Fulton, ed. pp. 161-169

Sherrell, Richard *Ecology* Virginia: John Knox Press 1971 (chapt. on death)

Schur, Max *Freud: Living and Dying* New York: International U. Press 1971

Schur, T. "What Man Has Told Children About Death" *Omega* 2 (2) (1971) 84-90

Schwartz, M. "Death: A Neuroscientific Analysis" *Omega* 2 (1) (1971) 30-35

Scott, Colin "Old Age and Death" *American Journal of Psychology* 8 (1896-7) 54-122

Scott, Frances and R. Brewer, eds. *Confrontations of Death* Corvallis, Oregon: Oregon St. U. Press 1971

Scott, Nathan, ed. *The Modern Vision of Death* Richmond, Va.: John Knox Press 1967

Scott, Walter *Complete Poetical Works* Boston: Houghton 1900 e.g. "The Dance of Death"

Searles, H. *The Nonhuman Environment* New York: International U. Press 1960

Searles, H. "Schizophrenia and the Inevitability of Death" *Psychiatric Quarterly* 35 (1961) 631-665

Segal, Hanna "Fear of Death" *Death: Interpretations* H. Ruitenbeek, ed. pp. 116-124

Sellin, Thorsten, ed. *Capital Punishment* New York: Harper 1967

Selye, Hans *Stress* Montreal: Acta Endocrinologica 1950

Selye, Hans *Stress of Life* New York: McGraw Hill 1956

Sendak, M. *Higglety, pigglety, pop! or There must be more to life* New York: Harper 1967

Severin, Henry *An Experimental Study on the Death-feigning of Belostoma flumineum* New York: Holt 1911

Shaffer, Thomas *Death, property and lawyers: A behavioral approach* New York: Dunellen 1970

Shakir, Evelyn "Books, Death, and Immortality: A Study of Book II of Prelude" *Studies in Romanticism* 8 (1969) 156-169

Shaler, N. *The Individual: A Study of Life and Death* New York: Appleton 1901

Shanon, Edgar "The History of a Poem: Tennyson's Ode On the Death of the Duke of Wellington" *Studies in Bibliography* 13 (1960) 149-177

Shapiro, G. *Death in the Shakespeare Comedies* PhD diss. Brandeis U. 1961

Shelley, Percy (Poetry and essays)

Shenkin, A. "Attitudes of Old People to Death" *Achievements in Geriatrics* W. Anderson, B. Isaacs, eds. London: Cassell 1964

Sherlock, William *A Practical Discourse Concerning Death* Albany: Pratt 1815 (17th ed. London 1689)

Sherrill, Lewis and H. "Interpreting Death to Children" *International Journal of Religious Education* 28 (1951) 4-6

Shibles, Warren *An Analysis of Metaphor* The Hague: Mouton 1971

Shibles, Warren "Death and Emotion" Paper presented at "Symposium: Philosophical Aspects of Thanatology" Foundation of Thanatology and Columbia University

College of Physicians and Surgeons, May 1973

Shibles, Warren *Essays on Metaphor* Whitewater, Wisconsin: Language Press 1972

Shibles, Warren *Metaphor: An Annotated Bibliography and History* Whitewater, Wisconsin: Language Press 1971

Shibles, Warren *Models of Ancient Greek Philosophy* London: Vision 1971

Shibles, Warren *Philosophical Pictures* 2nd edition, Dubuque, Iowa: Kendall-Hunt 1972

Shibles, Warren "Review of D. Z. Phillips *Death and Immortality*" *Southern Journal of Philosophy* 10 (3) (1972) 391-394

Shibles, Warren "Review of G. Vernon *Sociology of Death*" *Journal of Value Inquiry* (forthcoming)

Shibles, Warren "Wittgenstein on Death" Paper presented at "Symposium: Philosophical Aspects of Thanatology" Foundation of Thanatology and Columbia University College of Physicians and Surgeons, May 1973

Shibles, Warren *Wittgenstein, Language and Philosophy* Dubuque, Iowa: Kendall-Hunt 1970

Shinn, Roger "What I Believe About Life After Death" *Union Seminary Quarterly Review* 17 (May 1962) 311-314

Shneidman, Edwin *Death and the College Student* New York: Behavioral Publications 1972

Shneidman, Edwin "The Deaths of Herman Melville" *Melville and Hawthorne in the Berkshires* Vincent 1966

Shneidman, Edwin "Orientation Toward Cessation: A Reexamination of Current Modes of Death" *Journal of Forensic Sciences* 13 (1968) 33 ff.

Shneidman, Edwin "Orientations Toward Death: A Vital Aspect of the Study of Lives" *International Journal of Psychiatry* 2 (1966) 167 ff

Shneidman, Edwin "Suicide, Sleep and Death" *Journal of Consulting Psychology* 28 (1964) 95-106

Shneidman, Edwin "You and Death" *Psychology Today* 5 (1) (1971) 43-45, 74-80

Shneidman, Edwin and N. Farberow *Clues to Suicide* New York: McGraw 1957

Shneidman, Edwin, N. Farberow, R. Litman *The Psychology of Suicide* New York: Science House 1970

Shneidman, Edwin and N. Farberow "Suicide and Death" *The Meaning of Death* H. Feifel, ed. pp. 284-301

Shock, Nathan *A Classified Bibliography of Gerontology and Geriatrics* Stanford U. Press 1951

Shock, Nathan "Gerontology and Geriatrics" *Encyclopaedia Britannica* 10 (1968) 363-365

Shock, Nathan "The Physiology of Aging" *Scientific American* 206 (1) (1962) 100-110

Shoor, Merwyn and M. Speed "Death Delinquency and the Mourning Process" *Psychiatric Quarterly* 37 (1963) 540-558

Shor, R. "A Survey of Representative Literature on Freud's Death-Instinct Hypothesis" *Journal of Humanistic Psychology* 1 (1961) 73-83

Shrut, S. "Attitudes Toward Old Age and Death" *Mental Hygiene* 42 (1958) 259-266

Shrut, S. *Old Age and Death Attitudes* PhD diss. New York U. 1956

Shuler, Nathaniel *The Individual: A Study of Life and Death* New York: Appleton 1901

Siggins, Lorraine "Mourning: A Critical Survey of the Literature" *International Journal of Psychiatry* 3 (5) (1967) 418-38

Silberman, Lou "Death in the Hebrew Bible and Apocalyptic Literature" *Perspectives on Death* L. Mills, ed. pp. 13-32

Silverman, Phyllis *Widow-to-Widow Program* New York: Health Sciences 1973

Simko, Annamarie "Death and the Hereafter: The Structuring of Immaterial Reality" *Omega* 1 (2) (1970) 121-135

Simmel, E. "Self-Preservation and the Death Instinct" *Psychoanalytic Quarterly* 13 (1944) 160-185

Simpson, H. "The Emotional Dimensions of the Concept of Death" Unpublished paper. Vanderbilt University 1971

Sisk, Glenn "Funeral Customs in the Alabama Black Belt, 1870-1910" *Southern Folklore Quarterly* 23 (4) (1959) 169-171

Slochower, Harry "Eros and the Trauma of Death" *Death: Interpretations* H.

Ruitenbeek, ed. pp. 183-194

Smith, A. *Biological Effects of Freezing and Supercooling* Baltimore: Williams 1961

Smith, Alson *Immortality: The Scientific Evidence* New York: New American Library 1967

Smith, Charles *Historical and Literary Curiosities* London 1840

Smith, H. *Care of the Dying Patient: A Comparison of Instructional Plans* EdD diss. Bloomington, Ind.: Indiana U. Press 1965

Snow, John "Fear of Death and the Need to Accumulate" *Ecology* R. Sherrell, ed. Virginia: John Knox Press 1971 pp. 45-58

Sociological Symposium 1 (Fall 1968) entire issue on death

Southern Funeral Director (Journal)

Spamer, A. "Krankheit und Tod als Metapher" *Niederdeutsche Zeitschrift für Volkskunde* 20 (1942) 1-17

Spark, Muriel *Memento mori* New York: Avon Books 1959

Spencer, Theodore *Death and Elizabethan Tragedy* Harvard U. Press 1936

Spilka, Daily "Religion, American Values and Death Perspectives" *Sociological Symposium* 1 (1968) 57-66

Spriggs, A. *Champion Textbook on Embalming* 1944

Spurgeon, Caroline *Shakespeare's Imagery* Cambridge: Univ. Press 1935 (section on death imagery)

Staff, Clement "Death Is No Outsider" *Psychoanalysis* 2 (1953) 56-70

Stammler, Wolfgang *Der Todentanz* Munich: C. Hanser 1948

Standard, Samuel and H. Nathan, eds. *Should the Patient Know the Truth* New York: Springer 1955

Stare, Frederick "Nutrition During Bereavement" *Death and Bereavement* A. Kutscher, ed. pp. 297-298

"Statutory Problems of Defining Death" *U. of Penn. Law Review* Nov. 1972

Steele, Peter "Time Death and the Modern Poet" *Twentieth Century* 16 (1962) 5-16

Stegemeier, Henri "The Dance of Death in Folk-song" PhD diss. U. of Chicago 1939

Steiner, Jerome, et al. "Psychological Aspects of Depression" *Death and Bereavement* A. Kutscher, ed. pp. 287-294

Steinzer, Bernard "Death and the construction of reality" *Festschrift for Gardner Murphy* J. Peatman, E. Hartley, eds. New York: Harper (1960) 358-375

Stendahl, Krister, ed. *Immortality and Resurrection* New York: Macmillan 1965

Stephens, C. *Long Life* Norway Lake, Maine 1896

Stephens, C. *Natural Life* Norway Lake, Maine 1909

Stephens, C. *Natural Salvation* Norway Lake, Maine 1903

Sterba, Richard "On Halloween" *American Imago* 5 (1948) 213-224

Stern, Karl, et al. "Grief Reactions in Later Life" *Death and Identity* R. Fulton, ed. pp. 240-248

Stern, M. "Fear of death and neurosis" *Journal of the American Psychoanalytic Association* 16 (Jan 1968) 3-31

Stern, M. "Fear of death and trauma" *Progress in Neurology and Psychiatry* 22 (1967) 457-63

Still, Joseph "The Levels of Life and Semantic Confusion" *ETC* 28 (1) (1971) 9-20

Still, Joseph "Are organismal aging and aging death necessarily the result of death of vital cells in the organism?" *Medical Annals* District of Columbia 25 (1956)

Stonecipher, David "Old Age Need Not be Old" *New York Times Magazine* (Aug. 18, 1957)

Strauss, Anselm "Awareness of Dying" *Death and Dying* L. Pearson, ed. pp. 108-133

Strauss, Anselm "Sociopsychologic studies of the aging process. Problems of death and the dying patient" *Psychiatric Research Reports of the American Psychiatric Association* 23 (Feb. 1968) 198-206

Strauss, Anselm and B. Glaser "Dying on Time" *Confrontations of Death* F. Scott and R. Brewer, eds. pp. 104-108

Strauss, Anselm and B. Glaser *Time for Dying* Chicago: Aldine 1967

Strauss, Anselm, B. Glaser and J. Quint "The Nonaccountability of Terminal Care" *Sociological Symposium* 1 (1968) 67-73

Strauss, Richard "Death and Transfiguration, Opus 24" Musical tone poem

Street, J. "A genetic study of immortality" *Pedagogical Seminary and Journal of Psychology* 6 (1899) 267-313

Strehler, Bernard, ed. *The Biology of Aging* (Symposium, Tennessee 1957) Washington, D.C.: American Institute of Biological Science, Publication No. 6, 1960

Strehler, Bernard *Time, Cells and Aging* New York: Academic Press 1970

Strinberg, August (Plays) "The Dance of Death," "The Ghost Sonata." "A Dream Play," etc.

Stringfellow, W. *Instead of Death* New York: Seabury Press 1963

Strode, George *The Anatomie of Mortalite* London: W. Jones 1618

Strub, Clarence and L. Frederick *The Principles and Practices of Embalming* Dallas: L. Frederick 1959

Stuart, J. *The Year of My Rebirth* New York: McGraw 1950

Sudnow, David "The Logistics of Dying" *Esquire* (Aug 1967) 102-103, 130-133

Sudnow, David *Passing On: The Social Organization of Dying* New Jersey: Prentice 1967

Sulzberger, Cyrus *My Brother Death* New York: Harper 1960

Suso, Henry *Little Book of Eternal Wisdom* J. Clark, trans. New York: Harper 1953 (London 1910)

Sutton, Christopher *Disce mori; or, Learn to die* Reprinted from the first edition of 1600 London: I. Wolfe 1839

Swenson, Wendell "A Study of Death Attitudes in the Gerontic Population and Their Relationship to Certain Measurable Physical and Social Characteristics" *Diss. Abstracts* 19 (1958)

Swenson, Wendell "Attitudes Towards Death Among the Aged" *Death and Identity* R. Fulton, ed. pp. 105-111

Swift, Jonathan *Gulliver's Travels* London: Oxford U. Press (1926) 1960 Part 3 chapt. 10 on the immortal Struldbrugs

Talbot, Charles "The Fountain of Life: A Greek Version" *Bulletin History of Medicine* 31 (1957) 1-16

Tarrant, Dorothy "Metaphors of Death in the *Phaedo*" *Classical Review* 2 (June 1952) 64-6

Tate, Allen "The Point of Dying: Donne's 'Virtuous Men' " *Sewanee Review* 61 (Winter 1953) 76-81

Taylor, Jeremy *The Rule and Exercises of Holy Dying* London: Cleveland World 1857

Teicher, Joseph " 'Combat Fatigue' or Death Anxiety Neurosis" *Journal of Nervous and Mental Disorders* 117 (1953) 234-243

Templer, D. *The Construction and Validation of a Death Anxiety Scale* PhD diss. U. of Kentucky 1968

Templer, D. "Death Anxiety Scale" Proceedings of the 77th American Psychological Association Annual Convention, 1969, Division 20 "Maturity and Old Age" *Amer. Psychol. Assn.* (1969) 737-738

Thanatology Abstracts (Annual) Abstracts and reviews of multidisciplinary literature. Estab. 1972

Thayer, T. *Death and Immortality in the Works of Klopstock* PhD diss. Harvard U. 1967

Thielicke, Helmut *Death and Life* E. Schroeder, trans. Philadelphia: Fortress 1970

Thompson, Edward *A Historical and Philosophical Enquiry into the Hindu Rite of Widow Burning* London: Allen & Unwin 1928

Thurmond, Charles "Last Thoughts Before Drowning" *Journal of Abnormal and Social Psychology* 38 (1943) 165-184

Tillich, Paul "The Eternal Now" *The Meaning of Death* H. Feifel, ed. pp. 30-38

Tolsma, F. "Psychological disturbances after a pet dog's death" *Psychiatria, Neurologia, Neurochirurgia* (Amsterdam) 67 (Sept-Oct 1964) 394-405

Tolstoy, Leo *The Death of Ivan Ilych* New York: New American Library.Also see his *Confessions*

Tolstoy, Leo "Fear of Death" In *Sochinenya (Works)* Moscow, Kushnerev, 13 (1903) 533

Tolstoy, Leo "There Is No Death" *Independent* 69 (Dec. 22, 1910)

Toobert, Saul "The Simulation of Personal Death: A T-Group Experience" *Confrontations of Death* F. Scott & R. Brewer, eds. pp. 170-175

Toole, James "The Neurologist and the Concept of Brain Death" *Perspectives in Biology and Medicine* (Summer 1971) 599-607

Toynbee, Arnold *Man's Concern With Death* New York: McGraw-Hill 1969

556

Toynbee, Arnold; Jessica Mitford, Ray Bradbury, Kurt Vonnegut, Lyn Helton (A discussion of death) *Rotarian* 120 (5) (May 1972) 21-27

Toynbee, Jocelyn *Death and Burial in the Roman World* London: Thames & Hudson 1971

Travis, Paul "A Rational Approach to Death" *Rational Living* 3 (2) (1968) 1-8

Troisfontaines, Roger *I Do Not Die* F. Albert, trans. New York: Desclee 1963

Tromp, Nicholas *Primitive Conceptions of Death and the Nether World in the Old Testament* Rome: Pontifical Biblical Institute 1969

Tunley, Roul "Can You Afford to Die?" *Saturday Evening Post* 234 (June 1961) 24-28

Turner, James *The Chemical Feast* New York: Grossman 1970

Ulanov, Barry *Death – A Book of Preparation and Consolation* New York: Sheed 1959

Unamuno, Miguel de *Tragic Sense of Life* J. Crawford, trans. London: Macmillan 1921

Valdes, M. *Death in the Literature of Unamuno* Illinois U. Press 1964

Van Evra, James "On Death as a Limit" *Analysis* 31 (April 1971) 170-176

Vandenberg, Donald "Kneller, Heidegger, and Death" *Educational Theory* 15 (3) (1965); 17 (1967) 176-7 (rejoinder)

Vandenbergh, Richard "Let's talk about death" *American Journal of Nursing* 66 (1) (1966) 71-73

The Vault Merchandiser (Journal)

Veatch, Robert "Remarks on Dr. Henry Beecher's Paper 'The New Definitions of Death, Some Opposing Views' " Paper read at AAAS National Academy of Sciences Symposium on "Problems in the Meaning of Death" 1970

Vernick, Joel *Selected Bibliography on Death and Dying* Washington D.C.: U. S. Govt. Printing Office ca. 1968

Vernon, Glen *Sociology of Death* New York: Ronald Press 1970

Vernon, Glenn "Some Questions About the 'Inevitable – Death Orientation' " *Sociological Symposium* 1 (Fall 1968) 82-84

Vickers, R. and D. Kazzaz "Geriatric Staff Attitudes Toward Death" *Confrontations of Death* F. Scott and R. Brewer, eds. pp. 98-103

Voegelin, E. "Mortuary Customs of the Shawnee and Other Eastern Tribes" Indianapolis, Indiana: Indiana Historical Publ. 1944

Voices: The Art and Science of Psychotherapy 5 (1) (1969) Entire issue devoted to death and dying

Volkart, Edmund and S. Michael "Bereavement and Mental Health" *Explorations in Social Psychology* A. Leighton, ed. New York: Basic Books 1957 chapt. 9

Von Hug-Hellmuth, H. "The child's concept of death" *Psychoanalytic Quarterly* 34 (Oct 1965) 499-516

Von Lerchenthal, Erich "Death from Psychic Causes" *Bulletin of the Menninger Clinic* 12 (1948) 31-36

Vonnegut, Kurt (see Toynbee 1972)

Vrasdonk, William "Beyond Thanatology: Immortality" *Journal of Value Inquiry* 6 (4) (1972) 280-285

Vuillemin, Jules *Essai sur la Signification de la Mort* Paris: Presses Univ. de France 1948

Vulliamy, Colwyn *Immortal Man – A Study of Funeral Customs and of Beliefs in Regard to the Nature and Fate of the Soul* London: Methuen 1926

Wagner, August, ed. *What Happens When You Die: Twentieth Century Thought on Survival After Death* London: Abelard-Schuman 1968

Wagner, B. "Teaching students to work with the dying" *American Journal of Nursing* 64 (11) (1964) 128-31

Wahl, Charles "The Fear of Death" *Bulletin of the Menninger Clinic* 22 (1958) 214-223

Wahl, Charles "Games People Play When They're Dying" *Medical Economics* (Jan. 20, 1969) 106-120

Wahl, Charles "Suicide as a Magical Act" *Bulletin of the Menninger Clinic* 21 (1957) 91-98

Waldman, Milton *America Conquers Death* New York: Rudge 1928

Walkenstein, Eileen "The Death Experience in Insulin Coma Treatment" *American Journal of Psychiatry* 112 (1956) 985-990

Walker, J. "Attitudes to Death" *Gerontologia Clin.* 10 (1968) 304-308

Wallis, Charles *Stories on Stone* New York: Oxford U. Press 1954

Walshe, W. "Death and Disposal of the Dead: Chinese" *Hastings Encyclopedia of Religion and Ethics* 4 (1911) 450-454

Walters, M. "Psychic Death: Report of a Possible Case" *Archives of Neurology and Psychiatry* 52 (1944) 84-85

Ward, J. "The Coffin" *Omega* 1 (2) (1970) 143-144

Wargotz, Helen "Widowers With Teen-Age Children" *Death and Bereavement* Austin Kutscher, ed. pp. 257-269

Warner, W. *The Living and the Dead* New Haven: Yale U. Press

Warthin, A. "The Physician of the Dance of Death" *Ann. Medical History* 2 (1930) 351, 453, 697

Watson, M. "Death — a necessary concern for nurses" *Nursing Outlook* 16 (Oct 1968) 22-25

Waugh, Evelyn "Death in Hollywood" *Life* 23 (Sept 29, 1947) 73-74

Waugh, Evelyn *The Loved One* Boston: Little, Brown 1950

Weber, Frederick *Art and Epigram Regarding Science and Medicine in Relation to Death and Epigram and Art in Relation to the Excessive Fear of Death* 1914

Weber, Frederick *Aspects of Death Correlated with Aspects of Life in Art Epigram & Poetry* London: Unwin 1918 (4th ed. 1970 McGrath)

Weisman, Avery "Comment on Shneidman's 'Orientations Toward Death' " *Internat'l Journal of Psychiatry* 2 (1966) 190-193

Weisman, Avery *On Dying and Denying* New York: Behavioral Publ. 1972

Weisman, Avery *The Psychology of Autopsy* New York: Community Health Journal 1968

Weisman, Avery and T. Hackett "Predilection to Death" *Psychosomatic Medicine* 23 (1961) 232-256

Weismann, August *Essays Upon Heredity* E. Poulton and A. Shipley, eds. Oxford: Clarendon esp. Vol. I "The Duration of Life" and "Life and Death" 1892

Wells, Malcolm "Undertaking With a Green Thumb" *Environmental Quality* 3 (Aug 1972) 29-32

Wenkart, Antonia "Death in Life" *Journal of Existentialism* 8 (29) (1967) 75-90

Werdmueller, Otto *Treatise on Death* Myles Coverdale trans. 1579

Wertenbaker, Lael *Death of a Man* New York: Random House 1957

Westberg, Granger "Good Grief" *Practical Nursing* 12 (Mar 1962) 14-15

Westcott, R. "Death and Culture" *Voices* 5 (1) (1969) 15-21

Western Undertaker (Journal)

"What is Life? When is Death?" *Time* 87 (May 27, 1966) 78

White, Douglas "An Undergraduate Course in Death" *Omega* 1 (3) (1970) 167-174

Whitefoot, John *Death's Alarum* London: 1657

Whyte, F. *The Dance of Death in Spain and Catalonia* PhD diss. Bryn Mawr 1931

Whytforde, Rycharde *A Dayly Exercyse and Experyence of Dethe* London 1537

Wilde, Oscar *The Picture of Dorian Gray* New York: Modern Library 1957

Wiles, Peter "On Physical Immortality" *Survey* (London) vol. 56 pp. 125-143, vol. 57 (1965) 142-161

Williams, Mary "Changing Attitudes To Death: A Survey of Contributions in Psychological Abstracts Over a Thirty-Year Period" *Human Relations* 19 (4) (1966) 405-422

Williams, Mary "The Fear of Death" *Journal of Analytic Psychology* 3 (2) (1958) 157-165; 7 (1) (1962) 29-40

Wilson, Arnold and H. Levy *Burial Reforms and Funeral Costs* New York: Oxford U. Press 1938

Wilson, T. "Swift's Death-Masks" *Review of English Literature* (Leeds) 3 (3) (1962) 58-68

Wimberly, Lowry *Death and Burial Lore in the English and Scottish Popular Ballads* U. of Nebraska 1927

Wisdom, John "Eternal Life" *Talk of God* London: Macmillan 1967-1968, Vol. 2

Wittgenstein, G. "Fear of Dying and of Death as a Requirement of the Maturation Process in Man" *Hippocrates* 31 (1960) 765-769

Wittgenstein, Ludwig *Tractatus* D. Pears, B. McGuinness, trans. London: Routledge 1961

Wohlford, P. "Extension of personal time, affective states, and expectation of personal death" *Journal of Personality and Social Psychology* 3 (May 1966) 559-566

Wolf, Anna *Helping Your Child to Understand Death* New York: Child Study

Association of America 1958

Wolfenstein, Martha and G. Kliman eds. *Children and the Death of a President* New York: Doubleday 1965

Wolff, K. "Helping elderly patients face fear of death" *Hospital and Community Psychiatry* 18 (May 1967) 142-4

Wood, William and J. Wharton *Death-bed scenes* 3 vols. London: Rivington 1826

Woodward, Kenneth "How America Lives with Death" *Newsweek* (April 6, 1970) pp. 81-88

Woolnough, J. "A time to die: further reflections" *Medical Journal of Australia* 1 (Feb 22, 1969) 427

Worchester, Alfred "The Care of the Aged, the Dying and the Dead" Springfield, Ill.: C. Thomas 1950

Wyschogrod, Edith, ed. *The Phenomenon of Death* New York: Harper 1973

Yarrow, H. "A Further Contribution to the Study of the Mortuary Customs of the North American Indians" *First Annual Report, Bureau of American Ethnology* 1 (1879) 87-203

Young, F. "Graveyards and Social Structure" *Rural Sociology* 25 (Dec. 1960) 446-450

Young, William "Death of a Patient During Psychotherapy" *Psychiatry* 23 (1960) 103-108

Yudkin, S. "Children and Death" *Lancet* 1 (1967) 37-41

Yuncker, Barbara "Is Aging Necessary" *New York Post* (Nov. 18, 1963)

Zahl, Paul "Ruminations on Death" *The American Scholar* 18 (1949) ca. 185-187

Zandee, J. *Death as an Enemy According to Ancient Egyptian Conceptions* Leiden 1960

Zeligs, R. "Children's attitudes toward death" *Mental Hygiene* 51 (July 1967) 393-396

Zilboorg, G. "Considerations on suicide, with particular reference to that of the young" *American Journal of Orthopsychiatry* 7 (1937) 15-31

Zilboorg, G. "The sense of immortality" *Psychoanalytic Quarterly* 7 (1938) 171-199

Zilboorg, G. "Fear of Death" *Psychoanalytic Quarterly* 12 (1943) 465-475

Zim, Herbert and S. Bleeker *Life and Death* New York: Morrow 1970

Zinker, Joseph *Rosa Lee: Motivation and the Crisis of Dying* Painesville, Ohio: Lake Erie College Press 1966

Zinker, J. "The possibility for psychological growth in a dying person" *Journal of General Psychology* 74 (Apr 1966) 185-191

Zinsser, William "Time-Saver for Busy Mourners" *Life* May 10, 1968 p. 22 (Drive-in funeral parlors)